Contemporary Readings in Organizational Behavior

McGraw-Hill Series in Management

Keith Davis and Fred Luthans, *Consulting Editors*

Allen: Management and Organization
Allen: The Management Profession
Argyris: Management and Organizational Development: The Path from XA to YB
Beckett: Management Dynamics: The New Synthesis
Benton: Supervision and Management
Brown: Judgment in Administration
Buchele: The Management of Business and Public Organizations
Campbell, Dunnette, Lawler, and Weick: Managerial Behavior, Performance, and Effectiveness
Cleland and King: Management: A Systems Approach
Cleland and King: Systems Analysis and Project Management
Cleland and King: Systems, Organizations, Analysis, Management: A Book of Readings
Dale: Management: Theory and Practice
Dale: Readings in Management: Landmarks and New Frontiers
Davis: Human Behavior at Work: Organizational Behavior
Davis and Newstrom: Organizational Behavior: Readings and Exercises
Davis, Frederick, and Blomstrom: Business and Society: Concepts and Policy Issues
DeGreene: Systems Psychology
Dunn and Rachel: Wage and Salary Administration: Total Compensation Systems
Edmunds and Letey: Environmental Administration
Fiedler: A Theory of Leadership Effectiveness
Finch, Jones, and Litterer: Managing for Organizational Effectiveness: An Experiential Approach
Flippo: Personnel Management
Glueck: Business Policy and Strategic Management
Glueck: Readings in Business Policy from *Business Week*
Glueck: Strategic Management and Business Policy
Hampton: Contemporary Management
Hicks and Gullett: Management
Hicks and Gullett: Modern Business Management: A Systems and Environmental Approach
Hicks and Gullett: Organizations: Theory and Behavior
Johnson, Kast, and Rosenzweig: The Theory and Management of Systems
Kast and Rosenzweig: Experiential Exercises and Cases in Management
Kast and Rosenzweig: Organization and Management: A Systems and Contingency Approach
Knudson, Woodworth, and Bell: Management: An Experiential Approach
Koontz: Toward a Unified Theory of Management
Koontz and O'Donnell: Essentials of Management

Contemporary Readings in Organizational Behavior

Third Edition

Fred Luthans
University of Nebraska

Kenneth R. Thompson
University of Notre Dame

McGraw-Hill Book Company

New York   St. Louis   San Francisco   Auckland   Bogotá   Hamburg
London   Madrid   Mexico   Montreal   New Delhi
Panama   Paris   São Paulo   Singapore   Sydney   Tokyo   Toronto

This book was set in Times Roman by Black Dot, Inc. (ECU).
The editors were Kathi A. Benson and Peggy Rehberger;
the production supervisor was Leroy A. Young.
New drawings were done by Fine Line Illustrations, Inc.
The cover was designed by Anne Canevari Green.

CONTEMPORARY READINGS IN ORGANIZATIONAL BEHAVIOR

678910 HDHD 8987

Library of Congress Cataloging in Publication Data

Luthans, Fred, comp.
    Contemporary readings in organizational behavior.

    Includes bibliographical references.
    1. Organizational behavior—Addresses, essays,
lectures. I. Thompson, Kenneth R. II. Title.
HD58.7.L87 1981   658.4   80-21900
ISBN 0-07-039148-3

To our parents,

Carl and Leona Luthans
Glen and Margaret Thompson

Contents

1

AN INTRODUCTION TO ORGANIZATIONAL BEHAVIOR

2

MICRO ISSUES: MOTIVATION, GOAL SETTING, AND JOB DESIGN

3

MICRO ISSUES: LEARNING AND ORGANIZATIONAL BEHAVIOR MODIFICATION

4

ORGANIZATIONAL BEHAVIOR DYNAMICS: GROUPS, COMMUNICATION, AND CONFLICT

5

ORGANIZATIONAL BEHAVIOR DYNAMICS: POWER, POLITICS, AND LEADERSHIP

6

MACRO ISSUES: THE MANAGEMENT PROCESSES AND ORGANIZATION THEORY

7

HUMAN RESOURCE MANAGEMENT APPLICATIONS

Readings Correlated with Organizational Behavior Textbooks

Organizational Behavior Textbooks

Contents (reading numbers are in parentheses)	Bobbitt, Breinholt, Doktor, and McNaul, second edition	Gannon	Gibson, Ivancevich, and Donnelly, third edition	Hamner and Organ	Hellriegel and Slocum second edition	Hodgetts and Altman
			Chapter numbers			
One An Introduction to Organizational Behavior (1–5)	1,2	1,2	1,2	1,2	1,2	1,2
Two Micro Issues						
Motivation (6,7)	5	8	5	7	11	5,6
Goal Setting (8)		12	5,13	7	17	15
Job Design (9,10,11)		14	11	12	12	12
Three Micro Issues						
Learning and Organizational Behavior Modification (12–15)	6	6	5,14	3,4,11	6	4
Four Organizational Behavior Dynamics						
Groups (16,17)	8	10	6	13,14	9,10	7,8
Communication (18,19)		7	15		8	14
Conflict (20,21)		11	4,7	9,15	14	16
Five Organizational Behavior Dynamics						
Power, Politics (22,23)		11		16	9,10	
Leadership (24,25)	9	9	8,9	17	13	9
Six Macro Issues						
Management Processes (26,27)	13–16	5,12	11,16	16	3,4	13
Organization Theory (28,29)		3	10,12	16	4	10,11
Seven Human Resource Management Applications						
Selection and Appraisal (30,31)	10,11,12	12	13			15
Organization Development (32,33)		14	17,18	12	15,16,17	17
Self-Management and Career Development (34,35)	15,16,17	15,16,17	18		6	

Organizational Behavior Textbooks

Contents (reading numbers are in parentheses)	Chapter numbers				
	Kerr	Mitchell	Nadler, Hackman, and Lawler	Robbins	Szilagyi and Wallace second edition
One An Introduction to Organizational Behavior (1–5)	1	1	1,2	1,2	1,2
Two Micro Issues					
Motivation (6,7)	3	3,7	2	6	2,3,5
Goal Setting (8)		14	4		2
Job Design (9,10,11)	14	16	5		6
Three Micro Issues					
Learning and Organizational Behavior Modification (12–15)		3	4	7	4,14
Four Organizational Behavior Dynamics					
Groups (16,17)	5	8	6,7	8,9	7,8
Communication (18,19)	6	9		10	12
Conflict (20,21)	7	16	12	13	8
Five Organizational Behavior Dynamics					
Power, Politics (22,23)	8	12,17		12,18	8
Leadership (24,25)	9	13	9	11	9
Six Macro Issues:					
Management Processes (26,27)	4,12	11	9,11	14,15	12
Organization Theory (28,29)	11,12,13	2	8,10		10,11
Seven Human Resource Management Applications					
Selection and Appraisal (30,31)	10	14	3,4	16	13
Organization Development (32,33)	15,16	15	8,10	17	15,16
Self-Management and Career Development (34,35)					16

Preface

The field of organizational behavior is one of the most exciting and rapidly changing areas of management. Organizational behavior is very dynamic, and seems to be moving in a multitude of different directions. Both macro and micro perspectives are beginning to provide valuable insights into the complexities and dynamics of people at work. This is the third edition of contemporary readings on organizational behavior. Since the first edition in 1972, the field has grown and matured. Over the years, we have attempted to include in this book readings that are particularly indicative of the "state of the art"—those articles that reflect current thought in organizational behavior and at the same time are directed toward the application of this thought in as pragmatic and interesting a way as possible. With this purpose in mind, we have again attempted to present a few articles from each of the major areas of the field. Nearly three-fourths of the articles are new to this third edition. This is a reflection of the changes that are constantly occurring in organizational behavior. The prospects for the future are even better.

The organization of this edition reflects the new edition of the accompanying text, *Organizational Behavior,* McGraw-Hill, New York, 1981. Part 1 provides the reader with an introduction and background to organizational behavior. In this section, we have provided articles that examine the total discipline of organizational behavior. Parts 2 and 3 cover some of the major micro issues that are relevant to individual behavior in organizations. Part 2 includes articles that touch on the issues of motivation, goal setting, and job design, and Part 3 addresses the important aspects of learning theory and gives comprehensive treatment to the applied area of organizational behavior modification. Part 4 discusses the dynamics of placing individuals in organizational settings. Specifically, the section looks at the role of groups in affecting individual behavior, why an individual is attracted to groups, and the significance of communication, conflict, and stress. Part 5 continues this analysis by examining the dynamics of politics and power groups in organizations and the importance of leadership. Part 6 covers the macro perspective of organizational behavior. In particular, the managerial processes of decision making and control and organization theory and design are given attention. The final part of this book of readings is aimed at the application of organizational behavior principles to the actual practice of human resource management. The first part of this final section is directed toward selection and appraisal, the middle part toward organization development, and the final part toward behavioral self-management and career development.

Although this book of readings is aimed primarily at supplementing the accompanying textbook, it also can be effectively used to give depth and a modern behavioral input into organizational behavior, human relations, and industrial/organizational psychology and sociology courses that use other textbooks. A chapter-by-chapter correlation chart for some of the most widely used textbooks in these areas precedes this preface. It is also intended that this book will be used to add a modern behavioral dimension to more traditional courses in management and personnel and in public and educational administration. Practicing managers who are attempting to keep up to date with the new behavioral aspects of management should also find the book very helpful.

We would like to acknowledge and thank our colleagues at the University of Nebraska and the University of Notre Dame. They have all given us a great deal of support and encouragement. Finally, we would like to thank Margaret Thompson for typing the initial draft of this edition, and we extend special thanks to our parents, to whom we dedicate this book.

Fred Luthans
Kenneth R. Thompson

Contemporary Readings in Organizational Behavior

Part One

An Introduction to Organizational Behavior

As a widely recognized and respected field of study, *organizational behavior* has arrived. It has replaced the study of human relations as being most representative of the behavioral approach to management. There are many factors that account for the shift in emphasis from a human relations to an organizational behavior approach. Perhaps the major cause can be found in American society itself, which has undergone tremendous change, characterized by some as a social revolution. The existing institutions of society are being carefully scrutinized, resulting in a reordering of priorities and changes in deeply held convictions and values. Whereas, the past few decades have been described as a technological society, the eighties and beyond may be depicted better as a human-oriented society. These changing societal values are reflected in organization and management theory and practice. At face value, *human relations* would seem to be a more accurate descriptive term of the behavioral approach to management taken in a human-oriented society. In reality, this is not the case. Human relations in management was concerned with problem areas such as: "How to make workers happy," "How to decrease boredom on the job," and "How to reduce line-staff conflict." Human relations solutions included two-way oral communication, participation, delegation, job rotation, and democratic supervision. However, the concerns of modern behavioral analysis of organization and management have changed. The emphasis has shifted to problems such

1

as: "How can organizational participants obtain dignity and self-worth from their jobs?" and "How can conflict and change be managed successfully?" Attempts to use old human relations solutions on new organization and management problems proved to be limiting and often misleading. The human relations approach was often guilty of attempting to provide simple, practical solutions to complex human problems in organizations. Contemporary society has finally learned the lesson that complete understanding must precede the application of simple solutions to complex human problems. The people of the United States have found out, often the hard way, that there are no easy solutions for the improvement of race relations, the elimination of poverty, the way to peace, and the protection of the environment. Understanding of the variables affecting these problems and then the development of theories and models that are thoroughly tested by scientifically derived research should precede application. The goals of the organizational behavior approach are threefold: the understanding, prediction, and control of human behavior in organizations. In effect, an organizational behavior approach implies taking a step back and saying: "Let's have complete understanding with a theoretical base backed by good research that allows us some confidence in prediction and control before solution applications are attempted." This does not mean that application is not important. In the final analysis, of course, effective application is "where it's at." As an applied field, organizational behavior should always be aimed at application, but it is the orderly, logical development of theory and research that will allow for effective problem solution in the final analysis.

The five readings in this section provide an introduction and overview of the field of organizational behavior. The first article, by Professor Larry L. Cummings, analyzes and defines the current state of the field and provides some throughts as to its current dimensions and future evolution. The second and third articles trace the evolution of organizational behavior over the last fifty years. The second article reflects upon the significance of the famous Hawthorne experiments conducted at the Western Electric plant in Cicero, Illinois, from 1929 to 1932. These experiments are often considered to be the starting point of the behavioral approach to management. The plant is still in operation, and upon the fiftieth anniversary of the experiments, Western Electric sponsored a special symposium. The fifty years that have transpired since these pioneering experiments have witnessed considerable change in the way in which organizational behavior is viewed by researchers and practitioners alike. While much has been accomplished in the past fifty years, it is exciting to realize what discoveries are on the horizon and what these discoveries might mean to the betterment of the quality of work life for all employees. The third article is a classic in the field. Douglas McGregor, now deceased, discusses the famous Theory X and Theory Y which represent an important milepost in the evolution of organizational behavior. His article also summarizes another hallmark of the field, Maslow's Hierarchy of Needs.

The last two articles in this opening part set the stage for the more specialized sections that follow. The fourth article gives a comprehensive overview of organizational behavior, and the last article provides a new, social learning theoretical foundation for the field. The social learning approach recognizes the interactive nature of the environment (including macro, structural variables), the organizational participant (including internal cognitive processes), and the organizational behavior itself. This comprehensive theoretical framework can be used to better understand, predict, and control human behavior in organizations.

Reading 1

Towards Organizational Behavior

Larry L. Cummings

Attempting to describe a field as dynamic and as multifaceted, or even as confusing, as Organizational Behavior (OB) is not a task for the timid. It may be a task that only the foolish, yet concerned, would even tackle.

What motivates one toward accepting such an undertaking? Two forces are operating. First, there is a clear need to parcel out knowledge into more understandable and convenient packages. Students, managers, and colleagues in other departments request that we respond to straightforward, honest questions like: What is OB? How is OB different from management? How is it different from human relations? It is difficult for students to understand the philosophy or the systematic nature of a program or curriculum if they cannot define the parts. Our credibility with the managerial world is damaged when OB comes out in executive programs as "a little of everything," as "a combination of behavioral jargon and common sense," or as "touchy-feely" without content. The field's lack of confidence in articulating its structure is occasionally reflected in ambiguous and fuzzy suggestions for improvement in the world that managers face.

Second, identification or assertion of the themes and constructs underlying OB, or any other discipline, represents an important platform for expanding knowledge. Without assumptions about what is included, excluded, and on the boundary, duplication among disciplines results. The efficiency of knowledge generation and transmission is hampered. Until a field is defined in relation to its intellectual cousins, it may develop in redundant directions. This leads to the usual awakening that parallel, and perhaps even superior, developments already have occurred in adjacent fields about which we are ignorant. Repetition of such occurrences in a field lessens its intellectual credibility among scholars. All of this is not to deny the benefits to be gained from cross-fertilization and exchange across subfields once these are delineated and common concerns and interests are discovered.

These are the forces underlying the concern. What is said here represents an unfinished product—a thought in process—not a finished, static, intellectually frozen definition. In fact, the argument is made that stimulating, dynamic fields are defined *in process* and that the processes of emergence and evolution should never end.

Perspectives on Organizational Behavior

Several partitions have been used in attempting to distinguish OB from related disciplines. Tracing some of these provides perspective on our task and builds a critical platform for appraising where the field is today.

From the *Academy of Management Review*, vol. 1, 1978, pp. 90–98. Reprinted with permission from the author and the *Academy of Management Review*.

Probably the most common segmentation of subfields relating behavior and organization is based on *units of analysis* where the units are differentiated by level of aggregation. Typically, using this framework, OB is defined as the study of individuals and groups within organizations. The units of analysis are individual and micro (e.g., dyadic) interactions among individuals. Organizational characteristics (e.g., structure, process, climate) are seen either as "givens" which assume a constant state or as independent variables whose variations are assumed to covary with or cause variations in the relevant dependent variables. These relevant dependent variables are measures of individual or micro unit affective and/or behavioral reactions.

Organizational Theory (OT) is typically defined by its focus upon the *organization* as the *unit of analysis*. Organizational structure, process, goals, technology, and, more recently, climate are the relevant dependent variables, assumed to vary systematically with variations in environmental characteristics but not with characteristics embedded within systematically clustered individuals. A comparative, cross-organizational framework is essential for development of knowledge in OT. Studies of single organizations add little to understanding of organizations when the unit of analysis and variation is assumed to be the organization itself. This realization is increasingly reflected in the empirical literature of OT.[1]

Some have distinguished the field of inquiry based upon an attribution of *typical or modal methodologies* to the respective subfields. OB is defined as studies utilizing laboratory and, occasionally, field experimentation. OT is identified with the predominant use of survey and, occasionally, case designs. While the simplicity of this methodological distinction is attractive, it does not reflect the current diversity of designs underlying current research on people in organizations and on organizations per se.

The adjective pairs "normative-descriptive" and "empirical-theoretical" are attractive labels for describing *epistemological differences*. Certainly, the two predominant versions of classical OT have been characterized, and criticized, as excessively normative and not descriptive of behavioral and organizational realities. Both Taylor and Fayol on the one hand, and Weber on the other, have provided much of the focus for the normative critics. Some OB scholars view their field's mission as adding descriptive, empirically based facts to what they see as the essentially normative and theoretical biases of classical OT. With the advent of data among OT scholars and the infusion of organizational development (OD) into the OB tent, these distinctions are no longer descriptive of our domain. Descriptive, empirical, theoretical, and normative can each be used to characterize some work in both OB and OT. Complexity now overshadows the simple straw man of yesterday.

As OD began to emerge a few years ago, the theme of several corridor

---

[1]Hannan and Freeman [1] have argued quite convincingly that comparative analyses of organizational effectiveness are inappropriate for scientific purposes.

conversations was that OB *was becoming the applied cousin of OT*. After all, some claimed, OT deals with the theory of organizations by definition. For a moment the distinctions between OB and OD became blurred, and the opaqueness was attractive for some. Reading between the lines, OT was to become the reservoir of accepted and evolving constructs, and OB would emerge as the behavioral engineering function. For managers and consultants we would have OB; for scholars, OT. The largest obstacle to enacting such a distinction is that scholars and appliers do not generally read or listen to one another. The OB people must have their own constructs and theories. The OT people need their own applications, their own means of establishing credibility within the world of action. From this insulation, two OD camps have emerged with their own strategies for change. One focuses on change via the individual and micro unit within the organization and the other on change through structural and environmental manipulation. Alas, another simple, definitional distinction melts!

My preference among these alternative taxonomic bases is the first. The unit of analysis perspective seems cleanest. The most severe problem with this view is finding intellectual bridges to link the subfields. This linkage is crucial for understanding the way organizations function, the impacts they exert, and the opportunities they provide. Some bridges begin to emerge which are at least suggestive. For example, an organization's structure (i.e., number of levels, average span of supervision, degree of horizontal differentiation) can be viewed as a construct linking OT and OB. In OT, structure is typically positioned in a nomological network as a dependent variable. In OB, structure is typically positioned as an independent variable. This differential positioning of the same construct suggests a possible general role that several constructs might take in linking OT and OB. Structure, climate, task design, reward systems, and leader behavior can each be conceived of as intervening between causal forces in the environment of organizations and the behavior and attitudes of persons within organizations. Each is beginning to be modeled as a dependent variable in one context and an independent variable in another.

This differentiation of subfields by unit of analysis and their integration by intervening constructs is subject to limitations. The boundaries of aggregation between levels of analysis are arbitrary, with no fundamental laws underlying the distinctions. That is a limitation shared with the biological and physical sciences, where subfields have arisen as linking mechanisms (e.g., biophysics, biochemistry, psychopharmacology). The conception also lacks feedback loops with reversible intervening constructs. It is likely that such reciprocal causation reflects reality and that models that omit these loops will not provide a full understanding.

If we were to assume this posture of differentiation, what would be the result? Remembering that the distinctions are based primarily on levels of analysis with a slight nod toward the other distinctions, we can propose the definitions in Figure 1.

Figure 1   Distinctions among Organizational Behavior, Organizational Psychology, Organizational Theory, and Personnel and Human Resources.

Organizational Behavior– **Organizational Psychology (OP)**	Both fields focus upon explaining human behavior within organizations. Their difference centers on the fact that OP restricts its explanatory constructs to those at the psychological level. OB draws constructs from multiple disciplines. As the domain of OP continues to expand, the difference between OB and OP is diminishing, perhaps to the point of identity between the fields.
Organizational Behavior– **Organizational Theory (OT)**	The distinction is based on two differences: unit of analysis and focus of dependent variables. OB is defined as the study of individual and group behavior within organizations and the application of such knowledge. OT is the study of structure, processes, and outcomes of the organization per se. The distinction is neither that OB is atheoretical and concerned only with behavior nor that OT is unique or exclusive in its attention to theory. Alternatively, the distinction can be conceived as between micro and macro perspectives on OB. This removes the awkward differentiation of behavior and theory.
Organizational Behavior– **Personnel and Human Resources** **(P&HR)**	This distinction usually depicts OB as the more basic of the two and P&HR as more applied in emphasis. OB is seen as more concept oriented while P&HR is viewed as emphasizing techniques or technologies. The dependent variables, behavior and affective reactions within organizations, are frequently presented as similar. P&HR can be seen as standing at the interface between the organization and the individual, focusing on developing and implementing the system for attracting, maintaining, and motivating the individual within the organization.

A DIMENSIONAL CHARACTERIZATION OF ORGANIZATIONAL BEHAVIOR

I believe that OB is evolving toward the model presented in Figure 2. The field is being enacted, not defined in some a priori sense, by scholars and teachers in ways that imply the dimensional, thematic conception suggested in that figure.

Three dimensions define the conceptual domain of OB. Most disciplines and emerging fields of inquiry that stand at the interface between science and professional practice are describable in terms of these dimensions. The specific articulation of the dimensions depends significantly upon the underlying epistemological themes adopted by the discipline.

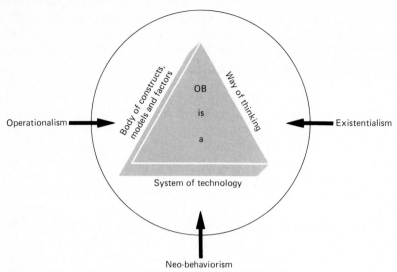

Figure 2 Dimensions and themes of organizational behavior.

A Way of Thinking

OB is a *way of thinking,* a manner of conceiving problems and articulating research and action solutions which can be characterized by five postures. First, problems and questions are typically formulated within an independent variable(s)–dependent variable(s) framework. Recently, OB has begun to incorporate personal and situational moderators into this framework. OB's assertion that behavior within organizations is subject to systematic study is based on conceptualization of the object of study as nonrandom, systematic, and generally purposive. This way of thinking is significantly influencing our methodologies. The field is engaged in a sometimes painful search for cause and effect within our models.

A second component of OB as a way of thinking is its orientation toward change as a desirable outcome for organizations and persons within organizations. Static phenomena possess diminishing prestige as topics of study. Conditions for stimulating change and models for evaluating change are an increasingly important part of the field.

Third, there is a distinctly humanistic tone within OB, reflected in concern for self-development, personal growth, and self-actualization. Although its influence on research and teaching seems to ebb and flow, and its reflection in scholarship and pedagogy varies by school, it is there, and its presence is causing both strain (given its positioning adjacent to scientism) and excitement, even relevance, within OB. The striving is toward humanism without softness. OB shares this dilemma with most of the person-oriented disciplines that attempt to combine basic, good science with a change orientation. Yet this tone of humanism is only one side of the current, slightly schizorphrenic posture of OB. The other side is reflected in a heavy emphasis on operant learning models and behavioral modification techniques, an orientation toward environmental determinism rather than self-actualization.

Fourth, OB is becoming increasingly performance oriented, with more studies including a performance-oriented dependent variable. The field is beginning to capture an important distinction between two types of dependent variables. One perspective focuses on description of a behavior, activity, or outcome, that is, the proper focus for scientific analysis and thinking. The other aims at application of a preference function to these behaviors, activities, or outcomes, resulting in a scaling of effectiveness or success. This is the proper focus for an engineering analysis—a managerial mind set.[2] We are beginning to hear the demands for relevance in our research and teaching. Unless OB can increase its performance payoffs, the field may be in danger of losing some of its hard battles for a niche in the curriculum or a moment in the board room.

Finally, OB uses the discipline imposed by the scientific method. The field is substantially influenced by norms of skepticism, caution, replication, and public exposure of knowledge based on facts. In many ways, this posture of "scientism" confuses some students and clients. It can be seen as the antithesis of several other postures that characterize OB thinking. Yet it is generally accepted as a crucial posture. It helps to keep the field straight, and it is the key ingredient in whatever longevity the field may possess. Scientific method, applied to OB, provides the mechanism for feedback and self-renewal.

A Body of Constructs, Models, and Facts

Even though OB is characterized by some definitional confusion, an implicit agreement is emerging about some of its components. Differences exist concerning the relative weighting of components and the emphasis given to basic science versus application in transmitting the field to others. But most treatments of the field now include coverage of constructs, models, and facts on: motivation, learning or socialization, group structure and process, leader behavior, task design, interpersonal communication, organizational structure, interpersonal change and conflict, and material on relevant dependent variables (e.g., satisfaction, other attitudes, participation measures, performance dimensions, and other behaviors).

This emergence of an identity for the field is evidenced by the second generation of OB textbooks, which are more similar in topical coverage than their ancestors. Some models sell and are thus influential in structuring the introductory level curricula underlying our field. Others stretch the field at its boundaries but do not become a part of the core. That core is gradually developing toward an identifiable body of components.

---

[2]My thinking here has been significantly influenced by Robert Kahn of the University of Michigan. His comments at the 1976 Carnegie-Mellon Workshop on Organizational Effectiveness have been particularly helpful.

A System of Technology

OB is also a system or a collection of technologies. These have evolved out of the primary areas of study identified as the independent variables of OB. Techniques now exist for: training leaders, designing tasks, designing organizations, evaluating performances, rewarding behaviors, and modeling behaviors.

The uncritical eye might be pleased with OB's tool kit. Superficially, it appears that the field is ready to move into the world of action with vigor and confidence. But our posture of scientism keeps the field honest. These technologies are largely exploratory, unvalidated and, in a few cases, under evaluation. The field has even spawned an occasional technology that has been adopted and later found damaging to an organization and its participants. In most cases, even when the technologies work, the field's theoretical models are not sufficiently developed to explain why they were effective. So, a system or collection of technologies? Yes. A behavioral engineering discipline? No.

THEMES INFLUENCING ORGANIZATIONAL BEHAVIOR

As depicted in Figure 2, three themes span the dimensions defining OB and influence the way each dimension is articulated. The relative emphasis given to each theme over time, by the various schools of thought within OB, determines our ways of thinking, constructs and facts, and development of technologies.

Existentialism

The emphasis here is upon the uncertain, contingent environment of people within organizations (and organizations). Existentialism emphasizes that in the face of this type of environment, persons must exercise self control in pursuit of their own objectives. The ultimate responsibility for designing productive and satisfying organizational environments rests with human beings. It is their responsibility to fashion themselves—to implement self control. This philosophical posture leaves a legacy of concepts within OB—goal, purpose, expectation, expectancy, instrumental, path, and contingency.

This theme is forcing OB to become a more complex discipline. It asserts that no meaning exists in absolutes. All meaning derives from comparison; meaning is always relative. Activities and outcomes within organizations are meaningful only within a context including implicit or explicit statements of purpose. This is at the core of one important, current development in conceptualizing the influence of most of the independent variables treated in OB—the concept of contingency.

With the realization that an independent variable's effects depend, the next logical question becomes: Depends upon what? When? etc. *Why* did *who* do *what* with *whom* with what *outcomes?* This seemingly simple question can be applied to most independent-dependent variable linkages currently of concern in OB. The *why* focuses on the causes, the reasons, the antecedents of variance in the dependent variable. The *who* focuses on the initiating party (individual, group, or organization). The *what* requires description of the behavior in question. The *whom* provides the interaction component, adding dimensionality to the search for meaningfulness. It provides a vertical, horizontal, or diagonal vector to the reality that OB attempts to understand. The *outcomes* provide the ultimate meaning to the field. Existentialism implies that the meaning in any act exists in its consequences, and OB seems to be moving toward this realization.

Operationalism

Operationalism is reflected in three ways. First, the field is searching for theories of the middle range in most of its subareas. The grand, general, abstract models of motivation, leadership, environment-structure interaction, and change are not yielding satisfying, systematic, cumulative data. Some models posit relations between environmental and organizational characteristics and individual attitudes and behaviors. Models are needed to describe the processes through which environment impacts structure and structure impacts attitudes and behavior.

Second, emphasis is being given to the operations or behaviors through which people within organizations function. Whether describing what managers do or analyzing the impact of leaders, the importance of formulating the issue in operational terms is being realized. The literature is beginning to be characterized by questions like:

1 Through what operations is structure actually designed?
2 Through what operations does a leader impact a subordinate?
3 Through what operations do rewards and punishments effect change?
4 Through what operations do groups actually make decisions?

In each case, the field is beginning to examine the physiology of behavior within organizations. The anatomy of OB is important, but its study has not led to understanding the processes through which persons and organizations interact.

Third, measurement issues are impacting the field. Questions of reliability and validity must be faced, and questions of scaling and measurement confronted. We are increasingly anxious about our inability to explain large amounts of variance in dependent variables. Three rather lengthy streams of research have reached the point where lack of early attention to how we operationalized constructs and validated measures has caused major problems for continued, meaningful work. Cases in point are research on: the two-factor model of motivation (with faulty measurement procedures); expectancy formulations of motivation (with testing of inappropriate models); and the impact of organizational design on attitudes and behaviors (with designs that confound independent variables). While not completely pessimistic, I believe that the field has been extremely inefficient and myopic in the research strategies applied in some areas.

Neo-Behavioralism

Finally, many causal assumptions and models in OB are moving toward a behavioristic orientation with a cognitive overtone. Motivation theory, under the influence of expectancy models, has moved in this direction. Leadership studies reflect the notion of instrumental, goal-oriented behavior with a significant emphasis on leader behavior being partially a function of the consequences which it produces. The concept of contingency plays a major role in several fields within OB, its general intellectual structure deriving directly from the behavioristic notion of structure and process evolving toward forms that are reinforcing to the organism. The behavioristic perspective also has surfaced in literature dealing with organizational design and organizational control and power. Distributions of influence and power are partially explained by environmental consequences of attempts at influence. The exercise of power generates consequences which, in turn, affect structural configurations of the organization.

Radical behaviorism is not the dominant theme, but rather a combination of general behavioral constructs *and* cognitions. It is not clear what functions are provided by the incorporation of cognitions within OB models. Little research has been addressed to the question of the variance explained in most OB models by cognitions beyond that explained by environmental determinants. Perhaps cognitive concepts do explain added variance, or perhaps they constitute a residual reservoir of unexplained variance to which we inappropriately attribute meaning.

CONCLUSIONS AND IMPLICATIONS

What are the implications of this perspective on the field? First, ultimately the definitions of the domains of OB, OT, OP, and OD are arbitrary. Definitions should be tested by their usefulness in specifying constructs and functional relations. Definitions are needed to guide the field toward middle range and operational theory. Movement toward definition by induction is needed. It may prove fruitful to aim toward definition through describing what is happening in the main streams of research within OB. Definitions established by assertion lead to debate without fruitful results.

Second, realities in organizations change so rapidly that our descriptions (ways of thinking, constructs and technologies) do not keep pace with the rate of change in the objects of our study.[3] I see two implications of this for OB. First, incredibly long periods of time are needed to assess organizations and to identify the fundamental, underlying nature of the field. Second, increasing energy will be devoted to collapsing the time intervals needed to develop relevant constructs and models and to testing these models. This implies that management, as a general field, will accelerate adoption of both simulation and experimental designs. These designs permit the modeling of time lags. Contrary to the usual

[3] I am indebted to Professor Lou Pondy for stimulating this notion.

evaluation of such designs, they will allow us to become more realistic in our modeling and measurement of OB.

Third, what might this line of reasoning mean for the Academy of Management and its members? The Academy is presently the only camp which attempts to house OB, OT, OD, and P&HR. For the moment, these fields have separate tents within the camp, but I believe that the traditional distinctions are beginning to melt. Several examples illustrate this permeability. The 1976 doctoral consortium conducted at the National Academy Convention included topics from both OT and OB. I suspect it is impossible to talk at an advanced level about one domain without the other. The P&HR division's program at the 1976 National Academy Convention consists of about 40 percent OB material. This reflects a healthy trend for both P&HR and OB. It is naive to deal with many of the important issues in P&HR without incorporating OB models and research. The *Academy of Management Journal,* the *Academy of Management Review, Organizational Behavior and Human Performance,* and *Administrative Science Quarterly* exhibit trends in submissions that reflect an increasing emphasis on *multiple* levels of analysis in both the independent and dependent variable domains.

I believe we are moving toward an enacted field, perhaps best labeled organizational analysis or organizational science (if we wish to emphasize the scientific lineage of our interests and our aspirations). Basically, we now have five divisions within the Academy, composing organizational analysis or science. These are Organizational Behavior, Organization and Mangement Theory, Personnel and Human Resources, Organization Development, and Organizational Communication. Such segmentation continues to provide important functions for the Academy and its members, but it remains an open question whether segmentation is the most efficient strategy to advance our common interest in behavior *in* and *of* organizations.

As Thurstone said:

> It is the faith of all science that an unlimited number of phenomena can be comprehended in terms of a limited number of concepts or ideal constructs. Without this faith no science could ever have any motivation. To deny this faith is to affirm the primary chaos of nature and the consequent futility of scientific effort. The constructs in terms of which natural phenomena are comprehended are man-made inventions. To discover a scientific law is merely to discover that a man-made scheme serves to unify, and thereby to simplify, comprehension of a certain class of natural phenomena. A scientific law is not to be thought of as having an independent existence which some scientist is fortunate to stumble upon. A scientific law is not a part of nature. It is only a way of comprehending nature.

REFERENCES

1   Hannan, M. T., and J. Freeman. "Obstacles for Comparative Studies," in P. S. Goodman and J. M. Pennings (Eds.), *New Perspectives in Organizational Effectiveness* (San Francisco: Jossey-Bass, 1977), pp. 106–131.

2 Thurstone, L. S. *Multiple-Factor Analysis* (Chicago: University of Chicago Press, 1947).

REVIEW AND DISCUSSION QUESTIONS

1 What are the differences between "organizational behavior" and "organizational theory"?
2 Compare and contrast "organizational development" and "organizational behavior."
3 What is the importance of the distinctions made in questions one and two?
4 Why is behavioral research important to the practitioner?
5 Is segmentation of organizational research an effective means to analyze the realm of organizations and organizational behavior?

Reading 2

Hawthorne Revisited: The Legend and the Legacy

The Western Electric Company and The Harvard Business School celebrated the 50th anniversary of the Hawthorne studies with a symposium addressed by a galaxy of behavioral science superstars, mainly social psychologists or professors with Ph.D.s in organizational behavior.

"Is Hawthorne worth revisiting?" was one of the main questions asked at the symposium. Answer: It's very much worth revisiting. After 50 years the Hawthorne experiments remain the most extensive, the most systematic, and the most exhaustive study of employees in an industrial work setting. Its influence is far from played out. Research is still being conducted that owes its inspiration to Hawthorne; programs are still being developed in response to some of the insights developed there.

One key reason for the persistent influence was noted in an address by Paul Lawrence: "We are told that it takes at least 15 to 20 years even today for a significant new finding in the physical sciences to find its way into everyday application. I am confident that it takes two or three times as long in the social sciences. . . . As we look at the 50 years that have elapsed since the start of the Hawthorne studies, it is therefore no cause for despair that many of the insights developed are still not widely applied. The studies are still a fruitful source of ideas for both research and practice."

Another key reason for the continuing influence of Hawthorne is the sheer complexity of the studies. As Ed Lawler remarked at the symposium, "They're so complex that there is something in them for almost everyone." In a real sense, each person's trip to Hawthorne is a very personal rediscovery. Different interpreters emphasize different facets of the study and different findings. For example, the now largely discredited school of human relations (or what Fritz Roethlisberger, one of the original Hawthorne researchers, in a moment of pique called "the ball of wax that came to be known as human relations") was based on an alleged Hawthorne finding. This purported discovery—which was in fact *not* demonstrated by the studies—was that relations between the supervisor and the worker depend on the supervisor's leadership skills and that these relationships, in turn, determine such key factors as job satisfaction, morale, and productivity.

But before we talk about the actual Hawthorne findings and the legitimate legatees, let's review briefly the studies themselves.

A QUICK WALK THROUGH HAWTHORNE

The parts of the overall study that have received the bulk of the critical attention are the two relay assembly test experiments and the bank wiring room project. In the relay assembly test room, as Roethlisberger wrote in *Management and Morale,* "the idea was very simple. A group of five girls were placed in a room where their condition of work (assembly of a telephone relay) could be carefully controlled, where their output could be measured, and where they could be closely observed. It was decided to produce at specified intervals different changes in working conditions and to see what effect these innovations had on output. Also, records were kept, such as the temperature and humidity of the room, the number of hours each girl slept at night, the kind and amount of food she ate for breakfast, lunch, and dinner." Over a two-and-one-half-year period, tons of material were collected and analyzed.

What did the data show? The key point was that with each variable—shorter rest periods, longer but fewer rest periods, the five-day week, introduction of group incentive pay, reversion to original working conditions—production increased period after period in an almost unbroken line. This confirmed the puzzling—to the researchers—results of an earlier illumination experiment in which either raising *or* lowering the light levels had consistently positive impact on productivity, except for one phase in which employees were compelled to work in semidarkness. Under some conditions the physical environment does count.

One reason for the continuing rise in productivity lay in the changing social environment. An ordinary group of workers, performing routine, low-status jobs with little or no recognition, had been transformed into important people. "Their physical health and well-being became matters of great concern. Their opinions, hopes, and fears were eagerly sought," observed Roethlisberger.

Nor was this all. They were questioned by investigators—frequently in the superintendent's office—sympathetically and at length about their reactions to working conditions. They traded an oppressive production-centered supervisor for a trained observer sympathetic to their needs. They could chat as they wished, and they set their own productivity quotas.

A change in morale occurred with the development of feelings of group responsibility. All labor turnover stopped and casual absences fell to a fraction of the rate in the department outside the test room. The "layout" girl, for example, who had been absent 85 times in the 32 months before the experiment, went for 16 months thereafter without an absence.

The bliss in the relay assembly test room was not unbroken. Of the six original women in the group, two reacted negatively to more latitude about work rules, more job scope, and so on. They were replaced, because of a "hostile and uncooperative attitude," by two women who welcomed the opportunity.

The second relay assembly experiment, which lasted for only 16 weeks, was set up solely in an effort to measure the effect of the group incentive payment on the productivity of the first group. Workers selected remained in their regular departments rather than being placed in a separate room. After working on the small-group incentive for nine weeks, they were put back on their previous departmental incentive and observed for a further seven weeks.

What happened? The group scored a 13 percent increase in productivity as compared with the 30 percent increase in the relay assembly test room— suggesting that the impact of the pure economic incentive could not be ignored. However, as Roethlisberger and Dickson caution in their close analysis in *Management and the Worker,* other factors were at work: (1) Some of the operators had started producing more well before the experiment. (2) There was a deliberate rivalry between the second group and the relay assembly test room.

The second principal part of the study, involving the bank wiring observation room, also viewed an informal work group, but one already in existence and hostile to change, especially management-initiated change. Close observation of 14 workers over a period of some seven months showed that they had developed an elaborate pattern of relationships among themselves, with their supervisor, and with aspects of their jobs. They had developed norms that covered areas such as what constituted a fair day's work, the appropriate mechanism for enforcing these standards—social ostracism for the deviants or banging them on the arm ("binging"), the standing of individuals within the group (the leaders were those who conformed most closely to the norms), how to spend their spare time, and so on.

The norm-setting process was a mysterious one. For example, take the production quota: In the bank wiring room, the workers had decided that 6,000 or 6,600 completed connections a day, depending on the type of equipment being wired, constituted a fair day's work. The quota was less than management felt the workers should do, but it was a quota management could live with. The quota was also highly inflexible. It was the same in the base period as it was during the observation period—remarkable when we recall that the observation period coincided with the onset of the Great Depression and the resulting imposition of a progressively shorter work week. George Homans, a close and astute student of the bank wiring room, wrote of it: "The behavior of employees could be described as an effort to protect themselves against such changes in routines and human associations: to give management the least possible opportunity of interfering with them. When they said that if they increased their output 'something' was likely to happen, a process of this sort was going on in their minds. But the process was not a conscious one. It is important to point out that the protective function of informal organization was not a product of deliberate planning. It was more in the nature of an automatic response."

INTERPRETATIONS AND DIRECTIONS

So much for the short guided tour of Hawthorne, into which we admit a certain amount of interpretation crept in. It's impossible to write more than a couple of consecutive sentences about Hawthorne and not succumb to the temptation to speculate what it might mean.

As an illustration of differences in interpretation, let's begin with Elton Mayo, who oversaw the project from Cambridge, and Roethlisberger, who was the chief onsite researcher. Mayo was a romantic conservative who saw the factory as a substitute for the broken social bonds of a lost traditional society. The principal reason for the formation of the bank wiring group was the group's spontaneous intuitive need to recreate a tribal society in miniature, or so Mayo thought. From what he found out about the form and function of work groups at Hawthorne and a few other places, he theorized that groups existed to secure "happiness and such sense of social security as may be found in subordination of an individual to a common purpose." We call Mayo conservative because if we take his views at their face value—as I think we're supposed to—all industrial conflict is symptomatic of social disease, and all cooperation symptomatic of social health. We call him romantic because the intensity of his vision led him to ignore so many facts—for example, that the solidarity of the bank writing room arose from the felt need to resist change.

Roethlisberger was a quite different type, and to him Hawthorne meant something different, a model of the clinical approach to studying people at work. To him, there was not substitute for the slow and laborious task of actually noting how workers behave on the scene; no generalization held water unless it had taken into account the work group as a social system; and for the investigator to query about the morale of the plant was about as sensible as for a visitor to ask about the health of the patients in the hospital.

Roethlisberger never, to our knowledge, used the term "contingency theory"—the dominant buzzword at the convocation. But he surely believed that the satisfactions and dissatisfactions of the individual employee were always relative to the demands he brought to the work situation and the demands the particular situation made on him. The important thing, in short, was the close study of the unique situation. People such as Paul Lawrence, Jay Lorsch, and John Morse are the natural legatees of that strain in Hawthorne that was best exemplified by the writings of Roethlisberger.

INDIVIDUAL DIFFERENCES REAFFIRMED

Lawrence, a key speaker at the conference, found in the Hawthorne experiment clues to what he calls the bimodal definition of the meaning of work, the distinction between the three women who appreciated the increased job scope and were productive and involved in their work and the two who were uncooperative and had to be replaced. To put it another way, it's the distinction between people who are turned on by job autonomy and challenge—the majority, says Lawrence—and those nurtured in urban subcultures "that have deeply conditioned them to see work as a simple exchange of time and minimal energy for fair pay and decent conditions. They do not expect to live on the job, only off the job."

To Lawrence, the applied behavioral scientist faces two major challenges: he must do a better job of matching individual differences, about which he already knows a great deal, with job characteristics, about which he needs to know a great deal more; second, he needs to help redesign jobs to close the gap in the underutilization of human resources. At present, there is a gross misalignment, not a reasonable match between the overall set of jobs that management has to offer employees and the characteristics of young people entering the job market. As Robert Ford of AT&T "work itself" fame put it: "Given that some 90 percent of our young people are graduating from high school, unless industry rapidly changes its job design practices, there will be a terrible rush for that other 10 percent."

Beyond this, Lawrence sees the need for a number of standard practices to change if management is to do a proper job of fitting a specific job to a specific individual. "We will need to carefully categorize the features of jobs in human terms to match our capacity for psychometrics." Current job descriptions contain little or nothing about the kind and complexity of the mental work required, little or nothing about the kind of interpersonal skills required, little or nothing about the emotional stress capacity, the required time horizon, and so on. To take full account of individual differences, we also need to make the applicant a partner in the fitting process and provide real trial periods for jobs.

Lawrence called on management to take more responsibility in making career paths available. True, few people want their careers chosen for them. But neither do they want to find jobs structured into dead ends such as currently face the nurse who decides that she would like to become a doctor.

Ed Schein of M.I.T., using a different tack to illustrate individual differences, employed the example of the bank wiring room to demonstrate that Theory Y is the dominant, although not the only, theory of motivation that most people carry around in their heads. Contrary to what most people think, Theory Y has to do with human motivation, not how to manage or run an organization. In what McGregor called a "cosmology" or world view, Theory Y states, in essence, that man is *capable* of integrating his own needs and goals with those of the organization, that he is not *inherently* lazy and indolent, that he is by nature *capable* of exercising self-control and self-direction.

At first glance it might seem difficult to find evidence to support Theory Y in the bank wiring room. After all, the employees (1) sabotaged the management control system by developing their own norms of "a fair day's work for a fair day's pay" and by vigorously enforcing these norms; (2) traded jobs in specific violation of company policy; (3) in general, expended a great deal of energy and creativity in thwarting some of management's goals and policies.

Schein has no problems reconciling the surface contradictions. Workers who expend great quantities of energy undermining management and its works are behaving consistently with Theory Y, he asserted. They are seeking self-actualization, but the organization or group that has involved them happens to be different from the group that employs them. If they failed to integrate their goals with management's, there were good and sufficient reasons. Perhaps there were people in the bank wiring room incapable of self-actualization, but the group cohesiveness that developed suggests that they were very much in the minority. Schein implied.

What the bank wiring room needed, he suggested, was a good Theory Y manager who would recognize the impact of past organizational history and develop bargaining strategies that would be integrative rather than exploitative. In fact, what any recalcitrant group—one that behaves in a counterorganization-al manner—needs is a Theory Y manager. Such groups behave the way they do, Schein believes, for one of two reasons: (1) Workers distrust management because of prior exploitation, or (2) workers are asked to perform, for reasons of technology, inherently meaningless tasks. In the latter case, the Theory Y manager "would acknowledge that the situation was inherently noninvolving and would undertake to assess the costs and benefits of changing that technology." If upon investigation he saw that the costs would be too high, he would level with the employees and be sympathetic to their demands for more pay or better benefits to compensate for the emptiness of the work. Schein concluded with a string of examples—Harwood and Weldon, some plants in Procter and Gamble, the Scanlon Plan team production experiences, and most recently Volvo—that show that it is possible for groups to work with and for the organization that employs them. It is *possible*, he argued, but it takes a combination of Theory Y managers and the kinds of production tasks and organizational conditions that make such group involvement productive.

YES, VIRGINIA, THERE IS A HAWTHORNE EFFECT

But the *real* Hawthorne effect may not be what most people have thought it was for 50 years: namely, to quote Herbert Simon and Andrew Stedry, "When special attention is paid to a given group of workers (say, by enlisting them in an experimental situation) production is likely to rise independently of changes in actual working conditions." Increased productivity in exchange for increased attention is the nub of the traditional Hawthorne effect.

To Robert L. Kahn, that is "stating the myth in its purest form." How would he reformulate the Hawthorne effect? "The significance of the finding has to do with participation. . . . The young women in the relay assembly test room increasingly took the opportunity to alter their work roles in content, duration, pace, rewards, and relationship to conventional authority. There was, in short, a genuine transfer of power, in specific degree and for no trivial period of time."

The Relay Assembly

The five women were all engaged in the same repetitive job—assembling, by hand, approximately 35 small parts in an "assembly figure" and securing them by four machine screws. The complete operation consumed no more than a minute. Each of the five women assembled approximately 500 relays per day. A sixth woman was the layout operator who assigned work and obtained parts. Each woman had a workbench with holes and chutes into which she would drop the completed relay.

In defense of his thesis, Kahn took two lines of attack: First, he questioned the validity of the traditional Hawthorne effect. Second, he marshalled evidence from *Management and the Worker* to demonstrate that there was a lot of participation from which the young women derived a lot of satisfaction. Under the first heading, he quoted an experiment conducted by Frederick Herzberg in which two groups of employees given the allegedly potent Hawthorne treatment behaved no differently from a group that received no attention. Unfortunately, Kahn knows of no other experiments that duplicate this design.

Under the second heading, he included substantial quotes from the participants and the observers that indicate both participation and satisfaction. For example, at one point the girls were offered the choice between starting one-half hour later than usual or stopping one-half hour earlier. They chose the latter and were very pleased with their choice. "Despite the fact that working time was 10 percent less than standard, the total production increased and hourly output increased sharply."

Kahn went on to point out that over 50 years the positive consequences of participation initially demonstrated with one small group have been replicated with dozens of groups, large and small, in the United States and with entire work systems in some organizations in foreign countries. Actually, he could have cited General Foods' dog food plant, Corning's Medfield operation, and several Procter and Gamble plants as examples of participative work systems in the United States.

He admitted caveats: Participation always increases employee satisfaction but not always group or unit effectiveness, for reasons that are not clear (to Kahn). And even the relationship between participation and satisfaction varies with the individual's personality. The most positive correlations occur in people with high needs for independence and low needs for authoritarianism. Furthermore, participation involves time and costs. The question, as Kahn defines it, is whether these costs are outweighed by the improvement in quality, the extra commitment to implementation, and the increase in satisfaction of human needs. A final caveat, said Kahn, is that many management practices that masquerade as participation fail to meet acceptable definitions. Either they restrict employee participation to peripheral issues ("picnics rather than pay") or they involve grand participative schemes that management never carries out. The first Kahn labeled "real participation around false issues," the second, "fake participation around real issues."

His overall conclusion was: "Real participation has real effects. When people take a significant and influential part in decisions that they value, the quality of decisions is likely to be improved and their implementation is almost certain to be improved." Last, he concluded, our failure to do much with the participative implications of the Hawthorne data tells much more about our industrial organizations than it does about the validity of the data.

DYNAMITE IN THE HAWTHORNE EFFECT

Ed Lawler's position is based partly on the evidence that the reward system meant something to girls in the relay assembly test room, that it contributed to their productivity, particularly because they had something to say about the conditions under which they were to be rewarded. There was an episode in which the investigators planned to institute a method of deferring part of the money earned above the usual rate; when the women objected, the investigators dropped their proposed alteration in the method of payment. But this seems a slender thread upon which to hang a theory.

Lawler did present some impressive evidence that employee participation in determining the method and even the quantity of rewards has impressive effects. In fact, he argued that any effort in organization development should begin by letting employees design their own pay system. He cited one plant in which, after designing their own pay system—a very delicate business requiring the fine honing of process skills—employees duplicated their success in redefining company policies in other areas such as terminations and layoffs. In short, Lawler suggested, pay may be a very effective change lever.

Participation, he claimed, has positive effects both in systems involving pay incentives and in those involving straight salary. He mentioned two similar pay-incentive plans; one worked and the other didn't. Participation appeared to make the difference. In one case the group had voted on the plan, whereas in the other the plan had been designed by management and imposed on the employees. But why does participation make such a difference? Lawler's answer: "It contributes to the amount of information employees have about what is occurring and to their feelings of control over and commitment to what is decided."

He also mentioned a small manufacturing plant in which employees set each other's salaries. Heresy, perhaps, but it worked. There was a small increase in the total salary tab—7 to 9 percent—and a significant realignment of salaries. More important, a survey six months after the system went into effect showed a significant increase in pay satisfaction and overall job satisfaction coupled with a significant decrease in turnover. Once more, why? As Lawler sees it, three things happened: (1) Employees felt better about their pay because they got a clearer, more accurate picture of how it compared with that of others. (2) Participation led them to feel they owned the plan; this in turn induced feelings that it was fair and trustworthy. (3) It was, in fact, fairer and more trustworthy because "what constitutes fair pay exists only in the cognition of the person who perceives the situation, and in this situation the plan allowed the people with the relevant feelings to control the plan directly." The decisions made then were better decisions because they were ones that led to increased satisfaction. The circle closed.

"FROM HAWTHORNE TO TOPEKA AND KALMAR"

As the title (above) of the paper by Richard Walton (author of the lead article in the same issue of *Organizational Dynamics* from which the present reading comes) suggests, he is concerned with comparing Hawthorne with two recent and radical experiments in work restructuring. In most cases the lines of influence are not direct. It is more the case that any restructuring of work must recognize the importance of supervision, informal groups, and payment systems, as well as the motivational effects of belonging to a unique and special project. With the last, the link between Topeka and Hawthorne is direct: "The Hawthorne effect," as it's usually defined, was recognized and consciously utilized by the designers of the Topeka system.

In general, reported Walton, Topeka and Kalmar built on and greatly extended trends that were present in Hawthorne. In the area of information and influence in the relay assembly room, workers were provided frequent, in fact daily, feedback on the effect of the changing situation on productivity, and their views sometimes influenced the nature and timing of the changes. With Topeka and Kalmar, information and participation have been carried to the point where the participants became the experimenters.

Hawthorne discovered the role of the informal work group in defining output norms—positive in the relay assembly test room, negative in the bank wiring room—and establishing a miniature social system. Topeka and Kalmar organized production around work teams, but recognized that they must provide tasks that were both whole and flexible if group norms were to support organizational goals.

The relay assembly test room hinted at the possibility that the group, under the proper conditions, could pretty much manage itself. The regular foreman adopted a hands-off attitude, while the observer, who was continually present, was perceived more as a counselor and friend than as a boss. The informal leadership that developed assumed the burden of maintaining cooperative attitudes toward a common goal. The implications of these insights were taken a few steps further and incorporated into the Topeka and Kalmar designs. The theory at Topeka, said Walton, was that "the self-management capabilities of the well-developed group make traditional supervisory roles redundant, provided there is an alignment between organizational and individual goals." Over time the reality has vindicated the theory. As the full-time team leaders helped the groups to become self-sufficient, their services became progressively less necessary, and eventually their jobs were eliminated.

Another suggestive parallel, Walton indicated, is between the initial processes of selection in the relay assembly test room and Topeka. In the former, two experienced operators, who were good friends, were asked to choose the remaining four members of the experimental group; in the latter, the Topeka manager chose as his immediate subordinates managers with whom he had worked previously and with whom he had developed a close rapport. In other words, the base for the future solidarity of the work group was built into the selection process. Another base for group solidarity from the start was, of course, the common feeling that they were an elite group engaged in a very special undertaking.

THE CONTINGENCY MODEL OF LEADERSHIP—I

The contingency approach to leadership evolved by Fred Fiedler on the basis of 23 years of empirical research argues that it is impossible to identify any individual as a good leader in all seasons and under all situations. It all depends on the nature of the situation. "We cannot really talk about a 'good' leader or a 'poor' leader but only about someone who performed well in one type of situation and poorly in another," he asserted. For example, take the relay assembly room, in which a highly cooperative group had made increased productivity—for whatever reasons—its key operative norm. This was obviously a very different situation from that in the bank wiring room, in which an equally cohesive group—but one hostile to management—had made fixed productivity its number one norm. These are different situations, obviously, and Fiedler's theory implies that they would call for different styles of leadership.

What kinds of leaders are most effective under what kinds of situations?

Fiedler's research has convinced him that there are two primary types of people—those who are relationship—motivated and those who are task-oriented. Furthermore, the research has demonstrated that task-motivated leaders tend to be most successful under conditions in which they exert a great deal of power and influence or under reverse conditions—where they have little power or influence. By contrast, relationship-motivated leaders tend to excel under conditions in which they have moderate influence and control.

Have we now solved the leadership problem? Is the answer to see to it that task-motivated leaders work in situations in which they possess very high or relatively low power, while the relationship-motivated leaders work in situations of moderate power and influence? The answer, Fiedler replied, is—alas—not that simple. Personality types persist, but the organizational variables that determine the degree to which the leadership situation fits the leader's personality and psychological needs are in continual flux.

Fiedler used numerous examples to illustrate this point—one of them being two hypothetical supervisors, the task-motivated Mr. Able and the relationship-motivated Mr. Baker. He went on to define the position in terms that gave the manager "a relatively high degree of power and influence after he gets to know his job well through experience or training." In the beginning, Fiedler predicted, the relationship-motivated Mr. Baker is likely to outperform the task-motivated Mr. Able, but the reverse will be true after the latter has gained sufficient experience or training. At the point at which Able is getting really involved in the job and his performance is improving, Baker's performance is likely to deteriorate—he will become "stale" or arrogant.

What is the answer to the problem? There's more than one answer, Fiedler maintained. If Able were the choice, then it would be highly desirable to start him with an intensive training course that would help to provide him with full control and influence as soon as possible. On the other hand, if Baker were the choice, an intensive training course would be a big mistake. And at some point, it would be good strategy to rotate Baker to another job in which he would have to learn new methods and work with new people. However, at the same point in time, it would be folly to rotate Able. He would just be hitting his stride and entering his period of maximum effectiveness.

By contrast, in a situation in which power and influence are moderate, such as the director of a research unit, the relationship-motivated Bakers would perform best after they were experienced or trained, while the task-minded Ables would perform better in the beginning. In general, Fiedler concluded, experience and training increase the leader's power and influence, while leadership rotation and changes in either subordinates or superiors decrease it. "The maintenance of an effective cadre of leaders," he maintained, "requires a sensitive and dynamic balance of organizational interventions and personnel strategies that keep the task-motivated leaders operating in situations of high or very low power and control and the relationship-motivated leaders in situations of moderate control and influence."

THE CONTINGENCY MODEL OF LEADERSHIP—II

Just before Fred Fiedler's paper, Victor Vroom advanced another contingency model of leadership that in key aspects conflicts with the Fiedler model. Fiedler divides all managers into two main categories, relationship-oriented leaders and task-oriented leaders, whose behaviors in a given situation are pretty consistent and predictable. In situations in which their power and influence are relatively high or low, task-oriented leaders will consistently outperform relationship-oriented leaders; the reverse is true in situations in which the leader possesses moderate power or influence. Fiedler also sees little chance that the leader's basic style can be modified by training or development. Leaders come cast in more-or-less immutable molds.

Vroom is just as situation-oriented as Fiedler, but he has a more flexible view of the leader's potential to vary his style to meet the requirements of the situation and a far more optimistic estimate of the leader's ability, through training and development, to enlarge the repetoire of his styles. In short, he feels that managers can learn to become more effective leaders.

Vroom's contingency model postulates five different types of management decision styles (see table). No one decision-making style, he contended, is best under all circumstances. The best style in the given situation depends on how the manager answers several questions:

- How important is quality in the decision?
- Do I possess sufficient information to make a high-quality decision?
- Is the problem structured?
- Is acceptance by my subordinates crucial to effective implementation?
- If I make the decision myself, is it reasonably certain that my subordinates will accept it?
- Do my subordinates share the organization goals to be attained in solving this problem?
- Is conflict over which is the best solution likely among my subordinates?

To take one simple example: If effective implementation depends on acceptance of the decision by subordinates and it its unlikely that these subordinates will accept an automatic decision, management styles A and B are both ruled out.

Sometimes after answering the seven questions, the manager will find that more than one style appears feasible. To choose between them, Vroom recommended that managers select either the style that would take the least time or the style that would maximize the development of his subordinates.

In subsequent research Vroom developed methods that allowed him to compare the model with how several thousand managers in fact had behaved or would behave in similar situations. Among his findings: "Differences in behavior between managers were small in comparison with differences *without* managers." On the hypothetical problems, no manager had indicated that he would use the same decision process on all problems or decisions, and most use all methods under some circumstances.

However, Vroom cautioned, it's necessary to dig into the details of the

---

Types of Management Decision Styles—Vroom

A —You solve the problem or make the decision yourself, using information available to you at that time.

B —You obtain necessary information from subordinate(s), then decide on the solution to the problem yourself. You may or may not tell subordinates what the problem is in getting the information from them. The role played by your subordinates in making the decision is clearly one of providing the necessary information to you rather than generating or evaluating alternative solutions.

C —You share the problem with relevant subordinates individually, getting their ideas and suggestions without bringing them together as a group. Then you make the decision, which may or may not reflect your subordinates' influence.

D —You share the problem with your subordinates as a group, collectively obtaining their ideas and suggestions. Then *you* make the decision, which may or may not reflect your subordinates' influence.

E —You share the problem with your subordinates as a group. Together you generate and evaluate alternatives and attempt to reach agreement (consensus) on a solution. Your role is much like that of a chairman. You do not try to influence the group to adopt "your" solution and are willing to accept and implement any solution that has the support of the entire group.

The Bank Wiring Job

The group consisted of nine wiremen, three solderers, and two inspectors. Each of these groups performed a specific task and collaborated with the other two in the completion of each unit of equipment. The task consisted of setting up the banks of terminals side-by-side on frames, wiring the corresponding terminals from bank to bank, soldering the connections, and inspecting with a test set for short circuits or breaks in the wire. One solderman serviced the work of three wiremen.

situation before the true significance of the decision style can be appreciated. Take, for example, two managers who on the surface appeared equally participative (or autocratic), but the situations in which they were respectively autocratic or participative were quite different. One might limit participation by his subordinates to decisions without much of a quality requirement, such as the time and place of the company picnic, while the other would limit participation by subordinates to decisions with a demonstrable impact on achieving important organizational goals. Same styles, but a crucial difference in where they were applied.

Vroom's typical manager said that he would use, or had used, exactly the same decision process as shown in the box in about 40 percent of the group problems. And in two-thirds of the situations, his behavior was consistent with the methods laid out in the model. Rules that protected the acceptance or commitment to a decision were violated much more frequently than rules that protected the quality or rationality of the decision. "These findings strongly suggest," concluded Vroom, "that decisions made by typical managers are more likely to prove ineffective due to deficiencies of acceptance by subordinates than due to deficiencies in decision quality."

Two very different contingency models of leadership—both supported by an impressive body of research data. Which is preferable—Fiedler's or Vroom's? We will let Vroom answer the question. "Fifty years from now, both contingency models will be found wanting in detail if not in substance. If either Professor Fiedler or I am remembered at that time, it will be for the same reason that we meet to commemorate the Hawthorne studies this week—the kinds of questions we posed rather than the specific answers we provided."

ILLUMINATIONS FROM HAWTHORNE

What are the lasting lessons of Hawthorne? And what light do they throw on the state of behavioral science in industry today?

The original lesson management derived from Hawthorne was the wrong lesson. From a superficial reading of the relay assembly test room results, the impression arose that a little attention and consideration on the supervisor's part would work wonders with employee morale and productivity. That approach has usually failed, for a couple of reasons: First, the revolutionary change in the attitudes of the girls toward their boss and their jobs—and it was just that—happened only as a consequence of a revolutionary change in their whole social system; second, the predominant form of industrial group is similar to what existed in the bank wiring room—a group with norms frozen in a pattern of resistance to change, especially managment-initiated change.

We also suspect, although we can't prove it, that the proliferation of small-group studies following Hawthorne, most of which replicated the bank wiring room findings, led many managements to conclude that the informal work group was the enemy. The answer to groups that restricted output, systematically misrepresented what they did produce, and generally undercut management policies was tighter and more sophisticated controls, accompanied by increased surveillance. This was also a strategy toward which most top managements were predisposed. If we go along with Chris Argyris, who has probably studied more chief executives more intensively than anyone else, most of them have a Theory X view of their employees' motivation: Employees are indolent, inherently hostile to the organization's goals, and incapable of self-control. On the surface, the bank wiring room and subsequent experiments confirmed this judgment and suggested the need for a Theory X strategy of management in coping with them. The temptation to opt for a Theory X strategy in dealing with industrial workers was aggravated because the heavy investments in the technology of Taylorism made it difficult and expensive to consider an alternative strategy that would at the very least raise the possibility of radical changes in the work situation.

The enduring message of Hawthorne is different and has only recently achieved prominence. It was the keynote of the convocation, best captured by Richard Hackman's remark that "The contingency theory of everything is the major theme of the conference." To put it more precisely, the contingency theory maintains that it takes different kinds of people and different kinds of organizations to perform different kinds of tasks. The function of the behavioral scientist in industry is to assist in the task of matching the person, the organization, and the task.

We think that's what Roethlisberger had in mind when he observed: "I wasn't preaching any model of the way an organization should be. The conceptual scheme of a social system was primarily an investigatory, diagnostic tool." Hawthorne preached no dogmas; held out no hope for panaceas; expounded no universal truths, except the universal that each work situation is different and that we can never assess the appropriateness of any one factor in the work situation except in relation to the totality.

Jay Lorsch, in summing up the convocation, commented on the babel in the behavioral sciences and the competition between paradigms or models, each one of which claimed to be the ultimate model of an organization. He cited the models developed by Likert, by Fiedler, and by March and Simon—and he could easily have extended his list. The problem, as Lorsch saw it, is the absence of any predominant model and the lack of sufficient evidence to prove decisively or to disprove the leading competitors. Until all the evidence is in, the wisest course for the practitioner, we suspect, is to stick with Hawthorne and the research-based contingency model that began developing more than 50 years ago. The oldest model can be the best.

NOTES AND REFERENCES

The book on Hawthorne is, of course, Fritz Roethlisberger's and W. J. Dickson's *Management and the Worker* (Harvard University Press, 1939). It still makes for absorbing, even occasionally exciting, reading. For a less compendious overview of much of the same material, also see Roethlisberger's *Management and Morale* (Harvard University Press, 1941). For what the Hawthorne studies meant to Roethlisberger six years or so after they ended, read Chapters XXIV and XXV of *Management and the Worker.* For a much longer time perspective, see "An Interview with Fritz J. Roethlisberger," *Organizational Dynamics,* Vol. I (Autumn 1972, pp. 31–45).

For Mayo's interpretations of Hawthorne and industrial society in general, see Elton Mayo's *The Human Problems of an Industrial Civilization* (The Macmillan Co., 1933) and *The Social Problems of an Industrial Civilization* (Graduate School of Business Administration, Harvard University, 1946). Both consistently stimulate and sometimes irritate.

George Homans' *The Human Group* (Harcourt, Brace, 1950) offers a by now classic explanation of the Mayo theory of groups. Henry Landsberger in his *Hawthorne Revisited* (Cornell University, 1958) presents a brief, objective, highly readable evaluation of both *Management and the Worker* and its critics—who have been legion.

Last, all the papers delivered at the Hawthorne symposium eventually will be incorporated in a book to be published by Van Nostrand Reinhold.

REVIEW AND DISCUSSION QUESTIONS

1 One of the major questions asked at the Western Electric/Harvard symposium was, "Is Hawthorne worth revisiting?" How would you answer this question? Why?
2 What is the *Hawthorne effect?* What are some traditional and more recent interpretations and implications of the Hawthorne effect?
3 How do the Hawthorne studies compare and contrast with recent experiments in work restructuring such as those conducted at Topeka and Kalmar?
4 How, if at all, do the Fiedler and Vroom leadership models relate to the Hawthorne studies?

Reading 3

The Human Side of Enterprise
Douglas M. McGregor

It has become trite to say that industry has the fundamental know-how to utilize physical science and technology for the material benefit of mankind, and that we must now learn how to utilize the social sciences to make our human organizations truly effective.

Reprinted by permission of the publisher from *Management Review,* November 1957, pp. 22–28; 88–92. © 1957 by the American Management Association, Inc. The article is based on McGregor's address before the Fifth Anniversary Convocation of the MIT School of Industrial Management.

To a degree, the social sciences today are in a position like that of the physical sciences with respect to atomic energy in the thirties. We know that past conceptions of the nature of man are inadequate and, in many ways, incorrect. We are becoming quite certain that, under proper conditions, unimagined resources of creative human energy could become available within the organizational setting.

We cannot tell industrial management how to apply this new knowledge in simple, economic ways. We know it will require years of exploration, much costly development research, and a substantial amount of creative imagination on the part of management to discover how to apply this growing knowledge to the organization of human effort in industry.

MANAGEMENT'S TASK: THE CONVENTIONAL VIEW

The conventional conception of management's task in harnessing human energy to organizational requirements can be stated broadly in terms of three propositions. In order to avoid the complications introduced by a label, let us call this set of propositions Theory X.

1 Management is responsible for organizing the elements of productive enterprise—money, materials, equipment, people—in the interest of economic ends.

2 With respect to people, this is a process of directing their efforts, motivating them, controlling their actions, modifying their behavior to fit the needs of the organization.

3 Without this active intervention by management, people would be passive—even resistant—to organizational needs. They must therefore be persuaded, rewarded, punished, controlled—their activities must be directed. This is management's task. We often sum it up by saying that management consists of getting things done through other people.

Behind this conventional theory there are several additional beliefs—less explicit, but widespread:

4 The average man is by nature indolent—he works as little as possible.

5 He lacks ambition, dislikes responsibility, prefers to be led.

6 He is inherently self-centered, indifferent to organizational needs.

7 He is by nature resistant to change.

8 He is gullible, not very bright, the ready dupe of the charlatan and the demagogue.

The human side of economic enterprise today is fashioned from propositions and beliefs such as these. Conventional organization structures and managerial policies, practices, and programs reflect these assumptions.

In accomplishing its task—with these assumptions as guides—management has conceived of a range of possibilities.

At one extreme, management can be "hard" or "strong." The methods for directing behavior involve coercion and threat (usually disguised), close supervision, tight controls over behavior. At the other extreme, management can be "soft" or "weak." The methods for directing behavior involve being permissive, satisfying people's demands, achieving harmony. Then they will be tractable, accept direction.

This range has been fairly completely explored during the past half century, and management has learned some things from the exploration. There are difficulties in the "hard" approach. Force breeds counter-forces: restriction of output, antagonism, militant unionism, subtle but effective sabotage of management objectives. This "hard" approach is especially difficult during times of full employment.

There are also difficulties in the "soft" approach. It leads frequently to the abdication of management—to harmony, perhaps, but to indifferent performance. People take advantage of the soft approach. They continually expect more, but they give less and less.

Currently, the popular theme is "firm but fair." This is an attempt to gain the advantages of both the hard and the soft approaches. It is reminiscent of Teddy Roosevelt's "Speak softly and carry a big stick."

IS THE CONVENTIONAL VIEW CORRECT?

The findings which are beginning to emerge from the social sciences challenge this whole set of beliefs about man and human nature and about the task of management. The evidence is far from conclusive, certainly, but it is suggestive. It comes from the laboratory, the clinic, the schoolroom, the home, and even to a limited extent from industry itself.

The social scientist does not deny that human behavior in industrial organization today is approximately what management perceives it to be. He has, in fact, observed it and studied it fairly extensively. But he is pretty sure that this behavior is *not* a consequence of man's inherent nature. It is a consequence rather of the nature of industrial organizations, of management philosophy, policy, and practice. The conventional approach of Theory X is based on mistaken notions of what is cause and what is effect.

Perhaps the best way to indicate why the conventional approach of management is inadequate is to consider the subject of motivation.

Physiological Needs

Man is a wanting animal—as soon as one of his needs is satisfied, another appears in its place. This process is unending. It continues from birth to death.

Man's needs are organized in a series of levels—a hierarchy of importance. At the lowest level, but preeminent in importance when they are thwarted, are his *physiological needs*. Man lives for bread alone when there is no bread. Unless the circumstances are unusual, his needs for love, for status, for recognition are inoperative when his stomach has been empty for a while. But when he eats regularly and adequately, hunger ceases to be an important motivation. The same is true of the other physiological needs of man—for rest, exercise, shelter, protection from the elements.

A satisfied need is not a motivator of behavior! This is a fact of profound significance that is regularly ignored in the conventional approach to the management of people. Consider your own need for air: Except as you are deprived of it, it has no appreciable motivating effect upon your behavior.

Safety Needs

When the physiological needs are reasonably satisfied, needs at the next higher level begin to dominate man's behavior—to motivate him. These are called *safety needs.* They are needs for protection against danger, threat, deprivation. Some people mistakenly refer to these as needs for security. However, unless man is in a dependent relationship where he fears arbitrary deprivation, he does not demand security. The need is for the "fairest possible break." When he is confident of this, he is more than willing to take risks. But when he feels threatened or dependent, his greatest need is for guarantees, for protection, for security.

The fact needs little emphasis that, since every industrial employee is in a dependent relationship, safety needs may assume considerable importance. Arbitrary management actions, behavior which arouses uncertainty with respect to continued employment or which reflects favoritism or discrimination, unpredictable administration of policy—these can be powerful motivators of the safety needs in the employment relationship *at every level,* from worker to vice president.

Social Needs

When man's physiological needs are satisfied and he is no longer fearful about his physical welfare, his *social needs* become important motivators of his behavior—needs for belonging, for association, for acceptance by his fellows, for giving and receiving friendship and love.

Management knows today of the existence of these needs, but it often assumes quite wrongly that they represent a threat to the organization. Many studies have demonstrated that the tightly knit, cohesive work group may, under proper conditions, be far more effective than an equal number of separate individuals in achieving organizational goals.

Yet management, fearing group hostility to its own objectives, often goes to considerable lengths to control and direct human efforts in ways that are inimical to the natural "groupiness" of human beings. When man's social needs—and perhaps his safety needs, too—are thus thwarted, he behaves in ways which tend to defeat organizational objectives: He becomes resistant, antagonistic, uncooperative. But his behavior is a consequence, not a cause.

Ego Needs

Above the social needs—in the sense that they do not become motivators until lower needs are reasonably satisfied—are the needs of greatest significance to management and to man himself. They are the *egoistic needs,* and they are of two kinds:

1 Those needs that relate to one's self-esteem—needs for self-confidence, for independence, for achievement, for competence, for knowledge.

2 Those needs that relate to one's reputation—needs for status, for recognition, for appreciation, for the deserved respect of one's fellows.

Unlike the lower needs, these are rarely satisfied; man seeks indefinitely for more satisfaction of these needs once they have become important to him. But they do not appear in any significant way until physiological, safety, and social needs are all reasonably satisfied.

The typical industrial organization offers few opportunities for the satisfaction of these egoistic needs to people at lower levels in the hierarchy. The conventional methods of organizing work, particularly in mass-production industries, give little heed to these aspects of human motivation. If the practices of scientific management were deliberately calculated to thwart these needs, they could hardly accomplish this purpose better than they do.

Self-Fulfillment Needs

Finally—a capstone, as it were, on the hierarchy of man's needs—there are what we may call the *needs for self-fulfillment.* These are the needs for realizing one's own potentialities, for continued self-development, for being creative in the broadest sense of that term.

It is clear that the conditions of modern life give only limited opportunity for these relatively weak needs to obtain expression. The deprivation most people experience with respect to other lower-level needs diverts their energies into the struggle to satisfy *those* needs, and the needs for self-fulfillment remain dormant.

MANAGEMENT AND MOTIVATION

We recognize readily enough that a man suffering from a severe dietary deficiency is sick. The deprivation of physiological needs has behavioral consequences. The same is true—although less well recognized—of deprivation of higher-level needs. The man whose needs for safety, association, independence, or status are thwarted is sick just as surely as the man who has rickets. And his sickness will have behavioral consequences. We will be mistaken if we attribute his resultant passivity, his hostility, his refusal to accept responsibility to his inherent "human nature." These forms of behavior are *symptoms* of illness—of deprivation of his social and egoistic needs.

The man whose lower-level needs are satisfied is not motivated to satisfy those needs any longer. For practical purposes they exist no longer. Management often asks, "Why aren't people more productive? We pay good wages, provide good working conditions, have excellent fringe benefits and steady employment. Yet people do not seem to be willing to put forth more than minimum effort."

The fact that management has provided for these physiological and safety needs has shifted the motivational emphasis to the social and perhaps to the egoistic needs. Unless there are opportunities *at work* to satisfy these higher-level needs, people will be deprived; and their behavior will reflect this deprivation. Under such conditions, if management continues to focus its attention on physiological needs, its efforts are bound to be ineffective.

People *will* make insistent demands for more money under these conditions. It becomes more important than ever to buy the material goods and services which can provide limited satisfaction of the thwarted needs. Although money has only limited value in satisfying many higher-level needs, it can become the focus of interest if it is the *only* means available.

The Carrot-and-Stick Approach

The carrot-and-stick theory of motivation (like Newtonian physical theory) works reasonably well under certain circumstances. The *means* for satisfying man's physiological and (within limits) his safety needs can be provided or withheld by management. Employment itself is such a means, and so are wages, working conditions, and benefits. By these means the individual can be controlled so long as he is struggling for subsistence.

But the carrot-and-stick theory does not work at all once man has reached an adequate subsistence level and is motivated primarily by higher needs. Management cannot provide a man with self-respect, or with the respect of his fellows, or with the satisfaction of needs of self-fulfillment. It can create such conditions that he is encouraged and enabled to seek such satisfactions for *himself,* or it can thwart him by failing to create those conditions.

But this creation of conditions is not "control." It is not a good device for directing behavior. And so management finds itself in an odd position. The high standard of living created by our modern technological know-how provides quite adequately for the satisfaction of physiological and safety needs. The only significant exception is where management practices have not created confidence in a "fair break"—and thus where safety needs are thwarted. But by making possible the satisfaction of low-level needs, management has deprived itself of the ability to use as motivators the devices on which conventional theory has taught it to rely—rewards, promises, incentives, or threats and other coercive devices.

The philosophy of management by direction and control—*regardless of whether it is hard or soft*—is inadequate to motivate because the human needs on which this approach relies are today unimportant motivators of behavior. Direction and control are essentially useless in motivating people whose important needs are social and egoistic. Both the hard and soft approach fail today because they are simply irrelevant to the situation.

People, deprived of opportunities to satisfy at work the needs which are now important to them, behave exactly as we might predict—with indolence, passivity, resistance to change, lack of responsibility, willingness to follow the demagogue, unreasonable demands for economic benefits. It would seem that we are caught in a web of our own weaving.

A NEW THEORY OF MANAGEMENT

For these and many other reasons, we require a different theory of the task of managing people based on more adequate assumptions about human nature and human motivation. I am going to be so bold as to suggest the broad dimensions of such a theory. Call it Theory Y, if you will.

1 Management is responsible for organizing the elements of productive enterprise—money, materials, equipment, people—in the interest of economic ends.

2 People are not by nature passive or resistant to organizational needs. They have become so as a result of experience in organizations.

3 The motivation, the potential for development, the capacity for assuming responsibility, the readiness to direct behavior toward organizational goals are all present in people. Management does not put them there. It is a responsibility of management to make it possible for people to recognize and develop these human characteristics for themselves.

4 The essential task of management is to arrange organizational conditions and methods of operation so that people can achieve their own goals *best* by directing *their own* efforts toward organizational objectives.

This is a process primarily of creating opportunities, releasing potential, removing obstacles, encouraging growth, providing guidance. It is what Peter Drucker has called "management by objectives" in contrast to "management by control." It does not involve the abdication of management, the absence of leadership, the lowering of standards, or the other characteristics usually associated with the "soft" approach under Theory X.

SOME DIFFICULTIES

It is no more possible to create an organization today which will be a full effective application of this theory than it was to build an atomic power plant in 1945. There are many formidable obstacles to overcome.

The conditions imposed by conventional organization theory and by the approach of scientific management for the past half century have tied men to limited jobs which do not utilize their capabilities, have discouraged the acceptance of responsibility, have encouraged passivity, have eliminated meaning from work. Man's habits, attitudes, expectations—his whole conception of membership in an industrial organization—have been conditioned by his experience under these circumstances.

People today are accustomed to being directed, manipulated, controlled in industrial organizations and to find satisfaction for their social, egoistic, and self-fulfillment needs away from the job. This is true of much of management as well as of workers. Genuine "industrial citizenship"—to borrow again a term from Drucker—is a remote and unrealistic idea, the meaning of which has not even been considered by most members of industrial organizations.

Another way of saying this is that Theory X places exclusive reliance upon external control of human behavior, while Theory Y relies heavily on self-control and self-direction. It is worth noting that this difference is the difference between treating people as children and treating them as mature adults. After generations of the former, we cannot expect to shift to the latter overnight.

STEPS IN THE RIGHT DIRECTION

Before we are overwhelmed by the obstacles, let us remember that the application of theory is always slow. Progress is usually achieved in small steps. Some innovative ideas which are entirely consistent with Theory Y are today being applied with some success.

Decentralization and Delegation   These are ways of freeing people from the too-close control of conventional organization, giving them a degree of freedom to direct their own activities, to assume responsibility, and, importantly, to satisfy their egoistic needs. In this connection, the flat organization of Sears, Roebuck and Company provides an interesting example. It forces "management by objectives," since it enlarges the number of people reporting to a manager until he cannot direct and control them in the conventional manner.

Job Enlargement   This concept, pioneered by I.B.M. and Detroit Edison, is quite consistent with Theory Y. It encourages the acceptance of responsibility at the bottom of the organization; it provides opportunities for satisfying social and egoistic needs. In fact, the reorganization of work at the factory level offers one of the more challenging opportunities for innovation consistent with Theory Y.

Participation and Consultative Management   Under proper conditions, participation and consultative management provide encouragement to people to direct their creative energies toward organizational objectives, give them some voice in decisions that affect them, provide significant opportunities for the satisfaction of social and egoistic needs. The Scanlon Plan is the outstanding embodiment of these ideas in practice.

Performance Appraisal   Even a cursory examination of conventional programs of performance appraisal within the ranks of management will reveal how completely consistent they are with Theory X. In fact, most such programs tend to treat the individual as though he were a product under inspection on the assembly line.

A few companies—among them General Mills, Ansul Chemical, and General Electric—have been experimenting with approaches which involve the individual in setting "targets" or objectives for *himself* and in a *self*-evaluation of performance semiannually or annually. Of course, the superior plays an important leadership role in this process—one, in fact, which demands substantially more competence than the conventional approach. The role is, however, considerably more congenial to many managers than the role of "judge" or "inspector" which is usually forced upon them. Above all, the individual is encouraged to take a greater responsibility for planning and appraising his own contribution to organizational objectives; and the accompanying effects on egoistic and self-fulfillment needs are substantial.

APPLYING THE IDEAS

The not infrequent failure of such ideas as these to work as well as expected is often attributable to the fact that a management has "bought the idea" but applied it within the framework of Theory X and its assumptions.

Delegation is not an effective way of exercising management by control. Participation becomes a farce when it is applied as a sales gimmick or a device for kidding people into thinking they are important. Only the management that has confidence in human capacities and is itself directed toward organizational objectives rather than toward the preservation of personal power can grasp the implications of this emerging theory. Such management will find and apply successfully other innovative ideas as we move slowly toward the full implementation of a theory like Y.

THE HUMAN SIDE OF ENTERPRISE

It is quite possible for us to realize substantial improvements in the effectiveness of industrial organizations during the next decade or two. The social sciences can contribute much to such developments; we are only beginning to grasp the implications of the growing body of knowledge in these fields. But if this conviction is to become a reality instead of a pious hope, we will need to view the process much as we view the process of releasing the energy of the atom for constructive humans ends—as a slow, costly, sometimes discouraging approach toward a goal which would seem to many to be quite unrealistic.

The ingenuity and the perseverance of industrial management in the pursuit of economic ends have changed many scientific and technological dreams into commonplace realities. It is now becoming clear that the application of these same talents to the human side of enterprise will not only enhance substantially these materialistic achievements, but will bring us one step closer to "the good society."

REVIEW AND DISCUSSION QUESTIONS

1 How many managers do you think still operate under Theory X assumptions? Can you cite some examples from your own experience?
2 We all know people who perfectly fit the assumptions of Theory X. How do you explain this? Is Theory Y wrong?
3 When, if ever, does the carrot-and-stick theory of motivation break down? Why?
4 Is Theory Y a "soft" approach to the management of people? Explain.
5 McGregor lists some organization and management concepts that are consistent with Theory Y assumptions. What are they? Are they still relevant in today's organizations? Why or why not?

Reading 4

Organizational Behavior: An Overview

George Strauss
Raymond E. Miles
Charles C. Snow
Arnold S. Tannenbaum

WHAT IS ORGANIZATIONAL BEHAVIOR?

Defining any academic field is difficult, but Organizational Behavior (OB) may be more difficult to define than most. As a new field, it has yet to stake out its jurisdiction definitively; further, as an applied field, it draws very heavily on more basic fields, making it difficult to distinguish between what is rightfully OB's and what belongs to the parent disciplines.

OB represents a combination of at least parts of two older fields in business schools. Human Relations and Management (the derivation of which will be discussed below), but, as just mentioned, it also includes liberal elements of other disciplines, especially of psychology and sociology. Political science, economics (at least those elements dealing with decision making and information economics), anthropology, and psychiatry have also had some (probably too little) influence on the development of OB. In addition, an increasingly substantial contribution is being made by a younger generation of scholars who have received their training in business schools under the rubric of Organization Behavior itself (or some related term).

As an academic discipline, most of what is called OB is taught in business schools and thus is focused primarily on profit-making organizations. But OB people are also interested in government, schools, hospitals, social agencies, and the like. In fact, much of the most interesting research has been done in these areas, and OB courses (though not necessarily under the title OB) are increasingly being taught in schools of education, public administration, public health, hospital administration, social work, and even forestry. It seems increasingly clear that OB principles apply (or do not apply) equally well in the nonprofit as well as in the profit sector, under socialism as well as capitalism. And—they most certainly apply to unions.

OB is an applied area, but some of the best OB research is not directly applicable. Seventeen years ago, in the Industrial Relations Research Association's last review of this subject, Wilensky [1956] argued that "not everything done by the social scientist can or should help the practitioner . . . the social scientist's job is basically different from the executive's job . . . much of what he comes up with is of only limited use to the practitioner" [pp. 27, 35]. Some

Reprinted with permission of the publisher from *Organizational Behavior; Research and Issues*, Industrial Relations Research Association, University of Wisconsin, Madison, 1974, pp. 1–3; 7–14.

progress has been made since 1957 in developing management applications; nevertheless Wilensky's warning still has much validity: in general, OB research is not designed to provide solutions for specific management problems.

True, much of what passes as OB "research" is mere description of management practices and sometimes consists of normative prescriptions not based on empirical data. However, the best research goes beyond this and is designed to develop theories or models which in turn can help scholars and practitioners understand behavior in organizations and therefore predict and even modify behavior.

Let us be a bit more specific as to OB's value to the practitioner. Untutored, the typical person draws inferences from his own immediate experience, and, on the basis of this experience, he develops "models" which consciously or unconsciously affect his perceptions of events and how he reacts to them. To take an example: if, on the basis of early experience (or folk wisdom picked up from others), a manager concludes that workers are generally lazy and seek to shun responsibility, he is likely to supervise his own subordinates closely, thereby to alienate many of them, and thus to induce them in fact to evade responsibilities. Under these circumstances, the manager's original hypothesis is confirmed.

For the practitioner who is a victim of this (and related) counterproductive cycles, OB may possibly offer three kinds of services:

1 Like any other science, OB is concerned with the relationships among organizational phenomena. On the basis of these observed relationships, theories (or models) can be developed and tested. Tested theories may, in turn, help the practitioner to understand the impact of his own current behaviors by telling him, "If you do X, there is considerable likelihood that Y will occur." As Kurt Lewin, one of the most influential of the early contributors to this field, was fond of saying, "There is nothing so practical as a good theory."

2 From the systematic study of behavior (in both real organizations and laboratory-based, simulated organizations), OB research can suggest a broader range of possible behaviors to the practitioner than he had previously considered—as well as the implications of each. Combined with good theory, an expanded repertoire of managerial behaviors can significantly extend the action alternatives most practitioners possess.

3 Finally, by expanding the practitioner's range of alternative behaviors and by placing these within frameworks which provide some basis for estimating the possible impact of each form of behavior, OB research may help the practitioner make informed evaluations of his future behaviors and their likely outcomes.

MORE RECENT APPROACHES

Human Resources By the late fifties, the term Human Relations had fallen into some disrepute, as did many of the oversimplified concepts accompanying it. To adopt a Hegelian analogy, if traditional management theories can be called the thesis, then Human Relations, the reaction against traditional theories, can be called the antithesis, and the new Organizational Behavior was the synthesis.

Organizational Behavior, a term which began to emerge in the early sixties, differed from Human Relations in two important respects. In the first place, it was concerned with both organization (the nature of tasks, structure, reporting relationships, and the like) *and* people. Secondly, at least some of its early advocates hypothesized that people wanted more from their work than merely financial rewards, job security, humane treatment, and a rich social life.

Those who placed primary emphasis on this second factor [e.g., Argyris, 1957; McGregor, 1960; Likert, 1961, 1967] might appropriately be called Human Resources theorists. Human Resources theorists argued that beyond physical and social needs, man has the desire to gain recognition and fulfillment from his job—to realize his potential through doing meaningful work. Managers, therefore, should consider not only how they supervise people but should also rethink how they use them—they should redesign jobs, decision processes, and control systems so as to provide greater opportunities for gaining a sense of accomplishment from work.

While participation and involvement in routine areas had been advocated by the Human Relationists to enhance feelings of importance and cooperation, Human Resources theorists advocated participative practices as a means of bringing more talent (and more commitment) to bear on important organizational decisions—and thus to make better use of the pool of human resources untapped by traditional organizational procedures. Such practices as job enrichment, management by objectives, self-controlled work teams, etc., have flowed out of this movement, as have some of the formal participative schemes. Most importantly, this concept of human needs restored performance as a legitimate concern of management—managers and their subordinates were expected to jointly set high performance goals and to exercise responsible self-control in their achievement.

Human Resources theorists resolved some of the outstanding dilemmas in the field of Organizational Behavior. They acknowledged that structure and responsibility were crucial but argued that these could be jointly achieved by superiors and subordinates working together, rather than unilaterally by superiors alone. Similarly, they acknowledged man's needs to belong and to feel important but argued that these could be designed into jobs and processes, rather than appended to them. Change, they argued, was important but should be introduced participatively by such processes as Organizational Development.

Although the Human Resources approach represented a considerable advance over simple Human Relations, for many scholars this was not enough. In the first place, early Human Resources seemed wedded to finding a "one best way" appropriate to all situations. Secondly, it appeared to focus primarily on the work team—the manager and his immediate subordinates; it did not directly address itself to the growing concern for coordination across departmental and hierarchical levels. In part to answer these two objectives, there arose two new lines of research, one of which has become known as the *contingency approach* and the other as *organizational sociology*.

The Contingency Approach   The Human Resources approach seemed to argue, at least in its most oversimplified versions, that all workers were desirous of self-actualization on the job and that participative management was uniformly appropriate in every organizational context. Surely, its critics argued, not all employees are equally responsive to enriched jobs or opportunities for joint goal setting, and certainly one cannot advocate the same degree of self-direction and self-control across all types of technological and structural characteristics. Furthermore, others argued, not all organizational objectives require the same level of commitment and utilization of human resources. Routine, repetitive work may still be best accomplished through well planned, directive procedures which require only that subordinates make a minimal emotional commitment to organizational objectives. Conversely, jobs whose nature is difficult to specify in advance may require a high degree of employee motivation and even radically new organizational structures.

As early as the mid-fifties, laboratory research with simulated organizations revealed "quite dramatically what type of organization is best suited for which kinds of environment. Specifically, for simple tasks under static conditions, an autocratic, centralized structure, such as has characterized most industrial organizations in the past, is quicker, neater, and more efficient. But for adaptability to changing conditions, for rapid acceptance of new ideas, for flexibility in dealing with novel problems, generally high morale and loyalty, the more equalitarian and decentralized type seems to work better" [Bennis and Slater, 1968, p. 5]. And there were other studies [e.g., Blauner, 1964; Whyte, *et al.*, 1955; Dubin, 1959] which suggested that workers differed greatly in their expectations about their jobs and that these expectations were in large part determined by variations in individual personality and cultural background.

Leading out of this early research, there has been a stream of studies which seek to specify which forms of motivation, supervisory practice, etc., work best with what sorts of people and with what sorts of jobs. As a consequence of this research, a host of complicated, multi-variate models of motivation [Porter and Lawler, 1968], job design [Hackman and Lawler, 1971], leadership [Fiedler, 1967], and departmentalization and coordination [Lawrence and Lorsch, 1967] have emerged within the last ten years, along with a massive body of theory and research which examines the linkages between environmental demands, technology, and organizational structure and processes.

Some impacts on managerial practice can be associated with this movement. New approaches to interdepartmental coordination and conflict resolution appear to be emerging in many organizations; NASA, for example, has experimented with a variety of novel organizational forms [Sayles and Chandler, 1971]. Perhaps most importantly, the recognition of variability among individuals and situations has helped (perhaps forced) managers to search for and consider a wider range of alternatives in solving their human and organizational problems.

Organizational Sociology   The Human Relations and the Human Resources approaches shared a common focus on the individual and his needs and motivations. Though the Human Resources approach led to important insights regarding leadership behavior and the design of reward systems, the emphasis was still on personal and interpersonal factors. Indeed, it can be argued that early Human Resources theorists viewed the ideal organization as a series of cohesive and committed interlocking work groups.

An increasing number of scholars [e.g., Selznick, 1953; Chandler, 1962; Woodward, 1965; Thompson, 1967] during the mid-sixties became concerned with questions relating to the structure of the organization as a whole and, in a sense, returned to issues of primary interest to traditional theorists. For the most part, these scholars were sociologists (as opposed to those in the Human Resources school, who tended to be psychologists), and their work is increasingly becoming known as *organizational sociology*. (Another name for this field is "complex organization," to distinguish it from the simple or face-to-face organization of primary interest to psychologists.)

Organizational sociology is concerned chiefly with what are sometimes called the formal aspects of organization—written rules, channels of communications, reporting relationships, control and reward systems, and the like. Included within its domain are such issues as staff-line relationships, centralization and decentralization, product vs. functional organization, and spans of control. And, the subject of greatest interest today relates to how the organization adjusts to the demands of its technology and external environment. The approach of organizational sociologists is heavily contingency oriented, but by contrast with some psychologists, the former focus on impersonal rather than personal determinants of structure.

A Systems Approach   As will be mentioned below, some OB scholars stress the individual orientation of the Human Resources approach more than the structural approach of the organizational sociologist, and vice versa. Similarly, there are some who look primarily for generalizations applicable to all organizations while others carry the contingency approaches to the point where they insist that no generalizations are possible. More and more, however, there has been argument on the need for systems models which take all of these factors into account—which explicitly acknowledge the great variability among people, tasks, and environments—and that these factors are constantly changing.

TENSIONS WITHIN OB

As a recognized academic field, OB is little more than ten years old (in 1958, Harold Leavitt had great difficulty finding a publisher for his now highly respected book, *Managerial Psychology;* most publishers felt that there would be no market in this area). OB is still "an orphan among fields. It has no professional society, no leading journal, no annual convention, and one of the most imperfect, disorganized labor markets in all academia" [Strauss, 1970, p.

146]. Nevertheless, the subject is taught in almost every major business school, and there is now surprising agreement among OB scholars as to the subject matter and limits of their field.

Despite this basic agreement as to domain, there are some important differences as to emphasis, research methodology, and values. To these we now turn.

People vs. Organizations   As mentioned above, OB represents something of a merger of the older fields of Management, with its emphasis on the impersonal factors of organization, and Human Relations, which stressed people problems. Though there has been a considerable resolution of the issues, the synthesis is far from complete, and the field is still marked by considerable disagreement in emphasis. For some, these differences are merely matters of research emphasis or training (psychology as against sociology), but for others they take on moral connotations. There is considerable agreement among OB scholars that organizational pressures sometimes inhibit the full development of the individual personality. Some see this as inevitable; others feel a strong ethical imperative to help make the organization more participative and thus expand the area of individual freedom.

Harmony vs. Conflict   A related question concerns the role of conflict between the individual and the organization, or among individuals or even subdivisions of the organization. On one side are those who see conflict as inevitable and even desirable, at least within limits. On the other side are those who believe that the ideal organization should enjoy substantial harmony. Likert [1961] suggests that in such an organization, "Every member of the organization would see the accomplishment of [organizational goals] as the best way to meet his own needs and personal goals" [p. 269]. Again, something of a contingency approach is developing which seeks to identify the situations under which conflict may be helpful and to channel it so that it does greatest good and least harm.

Research vs. Application   Probably more serious is the split between those who are research oriented and those who are practice oriented. The Traditional and Human Relations approaches were primarily prescriptive—they had a message for management. Their research methodology (if any) was fairly naive. It usually consisted of case methods and anecdotal material, and its meaning to management was obvious and direct. Over the years, both research and theory have become more complex. The simple case method has given way to survey research methodology, controlled laboratory experiments, and the like. Research results are frequently reported not as easy-to-understand stories but in terms of sophisticated conceptual and statistical analyses. Even when these findings are comprehensible to the practitioner (or the student), they seem to add up to "it all depends." No wonder there are many OB research-oriented professors who enjoy high status within academia but are virtually unknown among practitioners—and vice versa.

Other scholars have gone the applied route, and even among these there are some substantial differences in value orientation. There are those who see their role simply as helping to make the organization more efficient, but there are others who, as Bennis [1966] put it, are working "ambitiously to transform the basic value system of the enterprise so that humanistic and democratic values are infused and related to policy" [p. 192]. This second group insists that OB cannot and should not be value-free, and it sees its mission primarily as helping the individual operate more effectively and creatively in the organizational context—with the expectation that greater individual creativity will also redound to the benefit of both organizations and society generally.

Obviously, there is considerable overlap among these positions. At one end of a possible continuum, we find humanistically and application oriented scholars who tend to engage in research which focuses on individuals rather than the organization as a whole and who tend to value organizational harmony relatively highly. At the other pole are more sociologically oriented individuals who use sophisticated methodologies to study impersonal, structural organizational characteristics and who make few claims as to the applicability of their work to real life (often insisting that their work is value free). Between these two extremes lie the majority of the profession—individuals who mix research and practice, make use of a variety of research techniques, and hope eventually to arrive at the kind of systems approach previously discussed. (For an interesting statement of the issues, see Argyris's *The Applicability of Organizational Sociology*, 1972, and the various reviews discussing this book which appeared in the March 1973 issue of the *Administrative Science Quarterly*.)

OB OVERVIEW

Our discussion to this point has emphasized the development of OB and the divisions still existing within the field. And, yet, as mentioned earlier, there is substantial agreement among OB scholars as to the general area covered by the field. One way of illustrating this consensus is the chart below [adapted from Miles, 1975], which may also help us to understand the interrelationships among the chapters which follow.

Although, as noted earlier, OB scholars vary in their interests, all recognize the fact that organizations are made up of both organizational and people variables. Because no organization could perform effectively and still maintain a high level of job satisfaction among its members with these two sets of variables operating independently, it becomes management's task to successfully integrate people and organizational variables by manipulating the integrating mechanisms—that is, by designing jobs and organization structures in appropriate ways, by planning for the use of and controlling resources, by creating motivating reward systems, and so on.

In addition, as indicated by the arrows in the chart, there is a synergistic relationship among the people and organizational variables and the integrating

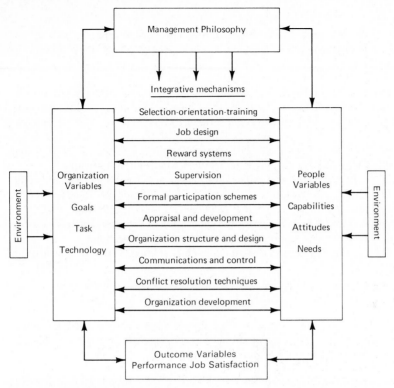

Figure 1 Organizational behavior.

mechanisms employed to bring them together. Managerial action taken in any one area is quite often likely to affect processes in another. Thus, a management which designs jobs so as to allow a great deal of employee discretion and responsibility is also likely to use participative leadership methods and nonpunitive approaches to control. The overriding factor here is management philosophy. For instance, managements which make the assumption that their employees are responsible and capable of self-control are likely to approach the use of the integrating mechanisms in a manner which is consistently different than that employed by managements which believe their employees are lazy and seek to avoid work.

Finally, the chart shows that the organization does not exist in a vacuum. Environmental factors affect both organization members and the task and structural characteristics of the organization. On the individual side, environmental factors such as societal and family practices have an impact on the beliefs and behaviors individuals bring to the organization. Conversely, the goals and tasks of the organization are influenced by environmental factors such as the nature of the product market, governmental pressures, changes in technology, and the like—and all of these may be changing rapidly.

BIBLIOGRAPHY

Argyris, Chris. 1957. *Personality and Organization*. New York: Harper.
———, 1972. *The Applicability of Organizational Sociology*. New York: Cambridge University Press.
Bennis, Warren G. 1966. *Changing Organizations*. New York: McGraw-Hill.
———, and Philip E. Slater, 1968. *The Temporary Society*. New York: Harper & Row.
Blauner, Robert. 1964. *Alienation and Freedom*. Chicago: University of Chicago Press.
Chandler, Alfred D., Jr. 1966. *Strategy and Structure*. Garden City, N.Y.: Doubleday Anchor.
Dubin, Robert. 1959. "Industrial Research and the Discipline of Sociology." *Proceedings of the Industrial Relations Research Association*. Madison, Wisconsin.
Fiedler, Fred E. 1967. *A Theory of Leadership Effectiveness*. New York: McGraw-Hill.
Hackman, J. Richard, and Edward E. Lawler, III. 1971. "Employee Reactions to Job Characteristics." *Journal of Applied Psychology*. 55 (June), 259–286.
Lawrence, Paul R. 1958. *The Changing of Organizational Behavior Patterns*. Boston: Harvard University. Graduate School of Business Administration.
Leavitt, Harold J. 1972. *Managerial Psychology*. Third edition. Chicago: University of Chicago Press.
Likert, Rensis. 1961. *New Patterns of Management*. New York: McGraw-Hill.
———, 1967. *The Human Organization: Its Management and Value*. New York: McGraw-Hill.
McGregor, Douglas. 1960. *The Human Side of Enterprise*. New York: McGraw-Hill.
Miles, Raymond E. 1975. *Theories of Management: Implications for Organizational Behavior and Development*. New York: McGraw-Hill.
Porter, Lyman, and Edward E. Lawler, III. 1968. *Managerial Attitudes and Performance*. Homewood, Ill.: Irwin.
Sayles, Leonard, and Margaret K. Chandler. 1971. *Managing Large Systems*. New York: Harper & Row.
Selznick, Philip. 1949. *TVA and the Grass Roots*. Berkeley and Los Angeles: University of California Press.
Strauss, George. 1970. "Organization Behavior and Personnel Relations." In Woodrow L. Ginsburg, et al., *A Review of Industrial Relations Research*. Madison, Wisc.: Industrial Relations Research Association.
Thompson, James D. 1967. *Organizations in Action*. New York: McGraw-Hill.
Whyte, William F. 1955. *Money and Motivation*. New York: Harper.
Wilensky, Harold L. 1957. "Human Relations in the Workplace: An Appraisal of Some Recent Research." In C. M. Arensberg, et. al., editors, *Research in Industrial Human Relations*. New York: Harper.
Woodward, Joan. 1965. *Industrial Organization: Theory and Practice*. London: Oxford University Press.

REVIEW AND DISCUSSION QUESTIONS

1 What is *organizational behavior?*
2 What kind of services can organizational behavior offer the practitioner?
3 Briefly describe some of the recent approaches to organizational behavior.
4 Take a position and defend it on the people versus organizations and research versus applications controversies in organizational behavior.

Reading 5

A Social Learning Approach to Organizational Behavior

Tim R. V. Davis
Fred Luthans

Just as the management field in general has been depicted as a theory jungle [Koontz, 1961, 1980; Luthans, 1973], the emerging field of organizational behavior has seemed to reach the same point. There is today a jungle of theories that attempt to explain human behavior in organizations. Unfortunately, many of the theoretical explanations have seemed to stray from behavior as the unit of analysis in organizational *behavior*. There is a widespread tendency for both scholars and practitioners to treat such hypothetical constructs as motivation, satisfaction, and leadership as ends in themselves. We think it is time to re-emphasize the point that *behaviors* are the empirical reality, not the labels attached to the attempted explanations of the behaviors.

If behavior is given its rightful place as the focus of attention in the theoretical development of organizational behavior, three major approaches can be readily identified. Briefly summarized, they are:

1 $B=f(P)$ According to this theoretical position, behavior is explained as a function of the person. In particular, internal psychological constructs such as motivation, perception, attitudes, expectancies, and personality characteristics are used to explain why people behave the way they do. Most of the motivational theories [e.g., Maslow, 1954; Vroom, 1964; Adams, 1965; Locke, 1968] that are popular in the field of organizational behavior today are closely associated with this theoretical base.

2 $B=f(E)$ According to this theoretical position, behavior is explained as a function of the environment. Most closely associated with Skinner's [1953] operant conditioning, this position is externally oriented and, in particular, is concerned with the role that reinforcing contingencies play in maintaining and changing behavior. The recent attention given to an operant [Nord, 1969] and a general learning approach [Luthans & Ottemann, 1973] to organizational behavior and, more specifically, to organizational behavior modification [Luthans & Kreitner, 1975] and behavioral management [Miller, 1978] is representative of this theoretical position.

3 $B=f(P,E)$ The third major theoretical base that has been widely adopted by the organizational behavior field is a compromise position that says organizational behavior is a function of the person *and* the environment. Usually attributed to the work of Kurt Lewin, this theoretical framework recognizes that both the person (internal constructs) and the environment (external contingencies) must be taken into account in order to explain behavior. The traditional

From the *Academy of Management Review*, vol. 2, 1980, pp. 281–290. Reprinted with permission from the authors and the *Academy of Management Review*.

definition of organizational behavior (i.e., the study of human behavior in organizations) recognizes this theoretical position. The vast majority of organizational behavior scholars today stress the importance of both the person and the environment. For example, the widely recognized Porter and Lawler [1968] model contains both internal cognitive variables and external environmental variables.

Our purpose in this paper is to point out still another, often overlooked, theoretical base for organizational behavior. This fourth alternative base for organizational behavior is best embodied in the term *social learning theory*. Although traditionally there have been implicit assumptions of the interactive nature between the participant and the organizational environment, the behavior itself, as an interacting variable, has been ignored. In addition, there have been some recent applications of modeling to employee training [Burnaska, 1976; Kraut, 1976; Latham & Saari, 1979], but a social learning approach— which is becoming an increasingly important theoretical base for psychology— has been largely ignored by organizational behavior researchers. In fact, to our knowledge there has been no direct attempt to include social learning in the conceptual framework of organizational behavior.

Fortunately, a social learning theory base for organizational behavior is complementary rather than competitive with previous approaches. We contend that the existing theoretical bases [i.e., $B=f(P)$, $B=f(E)$, and $B=f(P,E)$] are not wrong, but instead are too limiting and, at best, provide only a partial explanation of the complexities of organizational behavior. What seems to be needed is a comprehensive theory that is able to incorporate the *interactive* nature of *all* the variables of organizational behavior—the behavior itself, the environment (especially other organizational participants and the organization), and the organizational participant (including internal cognitions). Social learning theory seems to best fill in some of the existing deficiencies.

WHAT IS MEANT BY SOCIAL LEARNING THEORY?

From the outset it should be recognized that social learning theory is a behavioral theory. It utilizes the principles of classical and operant conditioning. But it deviates from a strict, Skinnerian approach to behavior. Over the years, the failure to account for the development of complex social behavior through S-R bonds or selective reinforcement of each discrete response (R-S) has gradually led to a less restricted theory that recognizes the role of social learning and imitation. Recent expositions of this social learning approach have been provided by Mischel [1973, 1976], Mahoney [1974], Meichenbaum [1974, 1977], Staats [1975], and Bandura [1968, 1976, 1977b]. The various interpretations of social learning theory are complex and difficult to integrate. However, the work of Albert Bandura provides a complete, yet parsimonious, interpretation of social learning.

Bandura [1977b] takes the position that the best explanation of behavior is in terms of a continuous, reciprocal interaction between cognitive, behavioral, and environmental determinants. In a unidirectional conception of interaction [e.g., the Lewin formula that B=f(P,E)], the person and the environment are considered to be independent entities that somehow combine to determine behavior. Social learning posits that the person and the environment do not function as independent units but instead determine each other in a reciprocal manner. In other words, under social learning theory the conception that B=f(P,E) is rejected as being too limiting and not accounting for the interactive effect between the person, the environment, and the behavior itself.

The same is true of more one-sided cognitive views of behavior [i.e., B=f(P)] which suggest that internal cognitions be considered as causal determinants irrespective of their behaviors and the environment. The social learning theory approach would explain that it is largely through their actions that people produce the environmental conditions that affect their behavior in a reciprocal fashion. The experiences generated by behavior also partly determine what a person becomes and can do which, in turn, affects subsequent behavior [Bandura, 1977b, p. 9].

Even those organizational behavior theorists who argue that they are taking a bi-directional or reciprocal approach (either in an exchange sense between superior and subordinate or between organizational participant and situation) still retain a unidirectional view toward the behavior itself. The causal input into the organizational participant's behavior is the result of the interdependent exchange between the person and the environment (including other persons), but the behavior itself is ignored as an interacting determinant. In other words, under social learning theory the conception that B=f (P⇌E) is also rejected.

In summary, a social learning theory of organizational behavior can best be depicted by the model in Figure 1 [adapted from Bandura, 1977b]. It can be seen that in a social learning theory approach, organizational behavior is in reciprocal interaction with cognitive processes and the environment. Organizational behavior is viewed as affecting and being affected by the participant's cognitions, the environment, and the person-situation interactions.

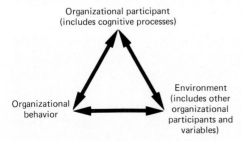

Organizational participant
(includes cognitive processes)

Organizational
behavior

Environment
(includes other
organizational
participants and
variables)

Figure 1   Model of social learning theory of organizational behavior.

HOW DOES SOCIAL LEARNING THEORY DIFFER FROM OPERANT THEORY?

So far the discussion has emphasized that a social learning approach considers the person-behavior-environment interaction as a theoretical base for organizational behavior. There may be lingering doubts or confusion as to how this really differs from an operant learning approach. Like operant learning, social learning is viewed as deriving from the consequences of behavior. In other words, the person learns from the effects that a particular behavior has on the environment. How, then, does social learning differ from operant learning? According to Bandura [1969, 1977b], the major differences between the two revolve around three major factors: (1) the role of vicarious processes (i.e., modeling), (2) the effects of covert cognitive processes, and (3) the part played by self-control processes. A brief review of each of these will give us a better understanding of social learning theory and of how these factors can be applied to the study of organizational behavior.

The Role of Vicarious Processes

Social learning theory derives its name from the emphasis it places on learning from other people—that is, *social* learning. While social learning theory agrees with the operant view that learning takes place as a result of directly experienced response consequences, it also emphasizes that learning can take place vicariously through observing the effects on the social environment of other people's behavior. The operant view is therefore considered as incomplete rather than incorrect. According to social learning theory, vicarious observational learning accounts for the acquisition of complex patterns of social behavior more readily than does the isolated reinforcement of discrete behavioral responses:

> Although behavior can be shaped into new patterns to some extent by rewarding and punishing consequences, learning would be exceedingly laborious and hazardous if it proceeded solely on this basis . . . it is difficult to imagine a socialization process in which the language, mores, vocational activities, familial customs, and the educational, religious, and political practices of a culture are taught to each new member by selective reinforcement of fortuitous behaviors, without benefit of models who exemplify the cultural patterns in their own behavior. Most of the behaviors that people display are learned either deliberately or inadvertently, through the influence of example [Bandura, 1976, p. 5].

Considerable research has demonstrated how people quickly reproduce the actions, attitudes, and emotional responses exhibited by models [Bandura & Walters, 1963; Bandura, 1969; Flanders, 1968]. Vicarious, imitative learning seems to better explain the rapid transference of behavior than does the tedious selective reinforcement of each discriminable response. The operant and social learning views do converge in treating the maintenance of behavior as being ultimately dependent on the reinforcing effects of the environment. However, social learning theory extends this view by showing that learning also takes place through observing or modeling the reinforcing or punishing outcomes of other people's behavior.

According to Bandura [1969, 1976, 1977b], modeling is regulated by interrelated subprocesses such as attention, retention, motoric reproduction, and reinforcement. These processes account for the acquisition and maintenance of observational learning or modeling. On the other hand, the operant learning approach accounts for the *acquisition* of behavior by a process of natural selection and reinforcement. Similarly, reinforcement and the notion of the organism "operating" on the environment are used to explain the *maintenance* of behavior. Social learning theory posits a fuller explanation of the process affecting both the acquisition and maintenance of new behavior.

Vicarious learning has important implications for training [Sorcher & Goldstein, 1972] and the development of general behavior patterns at work [Imitating models, 1978]. According to the social learning theory view, organizational participants learn how to behave from observing those around them. The dictum "Do as I say, not as I do" seems unlikely to be followed. Job descriptions, rules, and policies are more likely to be interpreted from watching what others do than following written directives. The example by behavior that managers provide for their people may be more important than the instructions they provide.

The Effects of Cognitive Processes

A second major difference between social and operant learning theory concerns the mediating effects of covert cognitive processes. Virtually all aspects of social learning are considered to be affected by cognitive processes. Staats [1968], Bandura [1969], and Kanfer [1970] were among the first behaviorists to demonstrate the importance of covert cognitions (feelings, images, and symbolic processes) in the regulation of human behavior. Before their work, the majority of behavioral psychologists [starting with Watson (1913) and continuing with Skinner (1953)] had dismissed cognitive processes as being largely metaphysical and having no rightful place in the scientific study of behavior.

An ever-increasing research literature reports on the important role that cognitive processes play in human behavior [Bandura, 1968, 1969, 1977a; Jacobs & Sachs, 1971; McGuigan & Schoonhover, 1973; Meichenbaum, 1974, 1977]. Bandura holds that:

> [If] human behavior could be fully explained in terms of antecedent inducements and response consequences, there would be no need to postulate any additional regulatory mechanisms. However, most external influences affect behavior through intermediary cognitive processes. Cognitive factors partly determine which external events will be observed, how they will be perceived, whether they leave any lasting effects, what valence and efficacy they have, and how the information they convey will be organized for future use [1977b, p. 160].

An implicit assumption of the operant approach is that all behavior is controlled by the immediate environmental consequences. The ability to re-evoke situations in the imagination and represent them verbally in symbolic form liberates human action from the stimulus effects of the immediate situation. This self-reflective capability is responsible for self-regulatory activity and sustained goal-oriented behavior.

Skinnerian behaviorism has often been criticized on the grounds of strict environmental determinism. This view of one-way causality has been a major reason why cognitive theorists have rejected the operant model. The operant approach depicts the organism as "operating" on the environment but both the acquisition and maintenance of behavior are considered to be controlled by the environmental consequences. Social learning theorists [Bandura, 1977b, 1978; Mahoney, 1977; Thoresen & Mahoney, 1974], with their recognition of cognitive processes, view the person, environment, and behavior as operating in an interactive state of reciprocal determinism (as depicted in Figure 1). From an individual learning perspective, Mahoney describes this relationship as follows:

> Our actions—and particularly their consequences—help to shape our cognitive representations. . . . Cognitions influence behaviors, which influence environments which influence cognitions . . . and so on. The circularity here is not one of logical tautology, however. It is a causal circularity that is far more comprehensive and defensible than traditional unilateral views [1977, p. 8].

Mahoney points out that in the social learning view each person responds not only to the environment per se but also to a cognitive representation of the environment. This means that the same physical environment can take on vastly different meaning for those who share it.

At this point we should emphasize that there are some major differences between the social learning approach to explaining and studying cognitive processes and the more traditional [i.e., B=f(P)] cognitive theories. Social learning theory examines both behavioral and cognitive processes in the environmental context in which they take place [Mash & Terdal, 1976]. In other words, in a social learning approach, reliance solely on indirect questionnaire methods of measuring behavior is inadequate. In addition, the behavior and its interactive elements should be directly observed in specific situations.

A social learning approach requires an analysis technique that allows for both overt and covert variables. Although usually accused otherwise, Skinner [1953] does give recognition to the place of cognitive processes in his discussion of covert operants, but his suggested technique for the scientific study of behavior that he called functional analysis is not designed to account for the role of cognitive processes. The recognition of covert processes is not included in the operant functional analysis of antecedent-behavior-consequence, or A-B-C [Skinner, 1969]. Social learning theorists stress that the variables in this three-term contingency—i.e., the antecedent stimulus conditions, the behavior, and the consequences—may be overt or covert. As Mahoney [1974, p. 77] points out, this gives rise to eight possible combinations. Thus, there is a possibility that the three-term contingency may be completely covert and thus unobservable and undetectable to anyone but the affected party. Meichenbaum [1974], for example, has drawn attention to situational antecedents, behaviors, and consequences created entirely in the imagination of the person. It is this capability that allows a person to think through the possibilities of alternative courses of action without having to experience them directly. However, from a philosophy of science perspective that stresses operationalism, the study of behavior must focus as closely as possible on observable, verifiable behavioral events. Thus, the main focus of social learning theory is to investigate the mediating effects that covert cognitive processes may have on an otherwise observable sequence of events.

To account for cognitive mediating processes and covert variables in a social learning approach to organizational behavior, we employ an expanded four-term contingency framework. This framework can be used to analyze the functional relationships. We use S-O-B-C to represent the four interacting variables. It is intended to portray the interactive, reciprocal nature of environmental events [both antecedent discriminative stimuli (S) and consequences (C)], intrapersonal, cognitive processes (O), and behavioral (B) variables. Figure 2 shows the S-O-B-C model. Note that there are implicit interactions and feedback loops between the environmental (S and C), cognitive (O), and behavioral (B) variables.

One could argue what letters to use in representing the variables, but we chose these based on their use in our earlier writings [Luthans, 1977, 1979; Luthans & Davis, 1979; Davis & Luthans, 1979], in which we tried to combine the established, widely recognized cognitively based S-O-R model (stimulus-organism-response) and the operant-based A-B-C model (antecedent-behavior-consequence). In other words, the S-O-B-C framework permits functional analysis of environmental-cognitive-behavioral events (both antecedent and consequent environment). It represents a departure from the operant A-B-C functional analysis by inserting the O to recognize the role of cognitive mediating processes and also to recognize that both environmental events (both S and C) and the behavior itself can be covert as well as overt. Just as the A-B-C model serves as a technique for functional analysis in the operant approach to

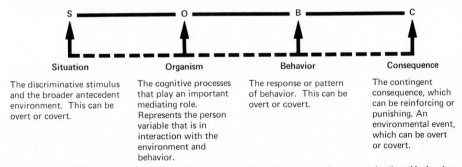

Figure 2 Functional analysis framework for a social learning approach to organizational behavior.

organizational behavior [Luthans & Kreitner, 1975; Luthans, 1980], so does the S-O-B-C model serve as a technique for functional analysis in the social learning approach to organizational behavior. This S-O-B-C framework is especially important to the explanation and application of the third major factor in social learning theory—self-control processes.

Self-Control Processes

Although Skinner [1953] should probably be credited with laying the foundations of a behavioral approach to self-control, the operant approach, with its almost total emphasis on the controlling role of the environment, may be considered inimical to theories of "self" regulation. Thus, the emphasis given to self-control processes in social learning theory marks a significant departure from operant theory. A fuller understanding of the processes of behavioral self-control has important implications for organizational behavior and managerial effectiveness [Luthans & Davis, 1979].

The recognition given to the mediating role that cognitive processes play in the individual's relationship with the environment establishes the important influence that self-regulatory functions can have on the control of behavior. Research by social learning theorists [Bandura, 1968, 1977a; Kanfer & Karoly, 1972; Mahoney & Thoresen, 1974] reveals that a given action typically produces two outcomes—an external environmental consequence and an internal self-evaluative consequence. In other words, people are affected not only by the external consequences of their behavior but also by the consequences they create for themselves. Bandura explains this interpretation as follows:

> The notion that behavior is controlled by its consequence is unfortunately interpreted by most people to mean that actions are at the mercy of situational influences. In fact, behavior can, and is, extensively self-regulated by self-produced consequences for one's own actions. In writing a term paper or preparing a manuscript for publication, for example, authors do not require someone sitting at their sides differentially reinforcing each written statement until a satisfactory version is produced. Rather, authors possess a standard of what constitutes an acceptable work and they engage in repeated self-editing of their own writing performance until they are satisfied with what they have written. . . . Because of their great representational and self-reactive capacities, humans are less dependent upon immediate external supports for their behavior. The inclusion of self-reinforcement phenomena in learning theory thus greatly increases the explanatory power of reinforcement principles as applied to human functioning [1976, p. 28].

Self-evaluative reactions to self-created consequences may be considered the underlying self-controlling processes. This suggests that people learn to modify their behavior when their own self-created consequences or standards are not fulfilled. The self-reinforcement consequence is particularly important to virtually all sustained goal-oriented behavior and explains how behavior persists despite the lack of immediately compelling external support.

Kanfer and Karoly [1974, p. 209] note that self-controlling responses come into being when a choice point is reached, or an external event interrupts and refocuses attention, or if the activation level suddenly changes. In effect, behavioral control switches from automated, environmental control (habitual responding) to a state of cognitive awareness in which a self-evaluative judgment is made about the appropriateness of behavior. This does not mean that a clearcut distinction can be made between environmental control and self-control. Kanfer and Karoly view self-control as the introduction by the individual of *supplementary* cognitive contingencies that are overlaid on the existing environmental contingencies and allow the person to analyze and alter the external regulatory relationship. Cognitive awareness alone, however, is not enough to allow self-controlling behavior to take place. In Kanfer and Karoly's words, "The degree to which internal stimulation and self-generated reinforcing events take on importance depends on the magnitude and specificity of these variables, and on the richness and complexity of the person's available covert behaviors as they moderate and interact with the effects and directions of external controlling events" [p. 208]. Thus, in this view, the cognitively based contingencies regulating behavior must be accurately identified if they are to play an instrumental role in the systematic control of behavior.

SOCIAL LEARNING THEORY IN PERSPECTIVE

So far we have seen that social learning extends operant theory by recognizing the role of vicarious, cognitive, and self-control processes. Obviously, there is more to social learning theory than these three dimensions. In a social learning approach to organizational behavior, there is a shift away from metaphoric constructs such as motivation and leadership. The unit of analysis becomes behavior patterns studied in relation to antecedent and consequent environmental situations and cognitively mediated processes. As Mischel [1973, p. 265] points out, in the social learning approach the focus shifts (1) from attempting to compare and generalize about what different individuals "are like" to an assessment of what they *do* behaviorally and cognitively—in relation to the psychological conditions in which they do it; and (2) from describing situation-free people with broad trait adjectives to analyzing the specific interactions between conditions and the cognitions and behaviors of interest.

Mischel's last point is at the very heart of a social learning approach to organizational behavior. We must begin to study an organizational participant's behavior in *specific interaction* with particular *in situ* organization conditions. In other words, as posited in a social learning approach, we must begin to study and analyze the dynamics of organization member-behavior-environment interaction. For too long we have tended to concentrate only on the organization member (e.g., what motivates him or her) or only on the organization environment (e.g., what is the appropriate structure) or, in a few cases, the organization member/environment interaction (e.g., contingency models of leadership or task design). What the social learning approach calls for is an ecological analysis of the interaction between the organization member, behavior, and environment [i.e., the study of real people in real situations; see Gibbs (1979)].

A SOCIAL LEARNING APPLICATION: BEHAVIORAL SELF-MANAGEMENT

One way of demonstrating how social learning theory can be specifically applied to organizational behavioral analysis, especially an ecologically oriented analysis, is through a behavioral self-management strategy in real-world organizations. Because the field of organizational behavior is eventually grounded in the actual practice of management, such a demonstration seems appropriate. As mentioned before, a modeling approach to employee training (which, of course, is grounded in social learning theory) is already well established. Just beginning, but what we feel has considerable potential for managerial effectiveness, is behavioral self-management.

To implement a self-management approach, awareness of the contingencies regulating behavior is acquired mainly through self-observation and self-monitoring. This requires that the person not only attend to a particular target behavior but also carefully record its occurrence. Generally, 4″ x 5″ cards, wrist counters, behavioral diaries, and wall charts are used for this purpose. Self-monitoring provides information on the frequency of the behavior and helps define the contingencies [antecedent cues (A), cognitions (O), response consequences (C)] when they take place. Self-monitoring also provides an objective basis for evaluating behavior and designing an intervention strategy. Generally, the goal is to establish a new behavior, increase or maintain an existing behavior, or reduce or eliminate a behavior [Mahoney & Thoresen, 1974; Watson & Tharp, 1977].

Following the lead of Mahoney and Thoreson, we can identify two major strategies for behavioral self-management: (1) stimulus management and (2) consequence management. *Stimulus management* refers to methods of overt or covert stimulus control such as antecedent stimulus modification, self-regulated stimulus exposure, preprogramming of response consequences, or the use of self-instructions. The individual plans and implements changes in these relevant situational factors before emitting the target behavior. For instance, a manager who is trying to cut down on her paperwork may have her secretary keep all incoming mail (antecedent stimulus modification); permit handling correspondence only during certain times of the day (self-regulated stimulus exposure); ask others to stop sending her correspondence (preprogramming of response consequences); and continually re-evoke certain self-instructions—"I must cut down on my paperwork; I want a clean desk when I go home every evening!" A number of studies in clinical and educational psychology [Upper & Meredith, 1971; Bernard & Efram, 1972; Stunkard, 1972; Beneke & Harris, 1972] have shown how managing the stimulus conditions can aid in successful self-modification programs. In some of our preliminary research with managers in real organizations, we have been able to demonstrate that stimulus management can lead to increased effectiveness [Luthans & Davis, 1979].

The *consequence management* method of self-management administers the consequences that follow a given behavior. This includes the act of self-monitoring as well as the use of self-administered rewards and punishments. After engaging in a behavior, certain cognitive self-evaluations occur. The act of self-monitoring provides the individual with performance feedback that may serve to increase or decrease future behavioral responses, depending on whether the individual's own self-created consequences or standards are fulfilled. Alternatively, the individual may introduce an added consequence—a reward or punishment—contingent on satisfactory or unsatisfactory performance of a target response. For instance, the manager may give himself an extra coffee break for having a clean desk the preceding day or stay after work for a half hour for each day that the paperwork is not taken care of. A number of studies in educational and clinical psychology have clearly demonstrated the effectiveness of self-recording, self-reward, and self-punishment [Bucher & Fabricatore, 1970; Broden, Hall, & Mitts, 1971; Johnson & White, 1971; Bolstad & Johnson, 1972; Flannery, 1972; Sobell & Sobell, 1973; Axelrod, Hall, Weiss, & Rohrer, 1974], and our own work has shown that it works in a managerial setting [Luthans & Davis, 1979].

The stimulus and consequence management strategies of self-management involve manipulating the stimulus conditions or response consequences that regulate behavior. These methods may be used separately or in combination to bring about a desired behavior change. To date, research on this approach to behavioral change has dealt with a relatively narrow range of behavior problems (e.g., obesity, smoking, alcoholism, psychiatric disorders, study habits, or marital difficulties). The number of studies using a variety of measures (not just self-reports), employing adequate controls, and focusing on issues of accuracy and reliability, is very small. Most of the studies have been carried out in limited (clinical, laboratory, and classroom) settings. Thus, to date, the majority of the support for self-control techniques stems from clinical evidence from behavior therapy. Our own preliminary research on self-management in organizational settings indicates the potential value that this approach may have for managerial effectiveness. However, before any generalizations can be made, more research needs to be done.

SUMMARY AND CONCLUSIONS

Social learning is proposed as a theoretical base for organizational behavior. If researchers in this field concentrate on the behavior part of organizational behavior, then the prevailing theoretical explanations (i.e., that behavior is a function of the person, behavior is a function of the environment, or behavior is a function of the environment and the person) will be seen to be too limiting. Social learning theory suggests that organizational behavior can be best understood in terms of an interacting, reciprocal determinism between the behavior itself, the organizational participant, and the environment. Even though many organizational behavior theorists would claim that they have always given attention to the person-organizational environment interface, its interactive, reciprocal deterministic nature has not been stressed, and the role that the behavior itself plays has been almost completely ignored. We believe it is time to recognize that all three interacting components play a vital role in organizational behavior. Perhaps even more important is the *interactive* tenant of a social learning approach. It must be recognized that organizational behavior does not occur in isolation or in the response sets of researchers' questionnaires. Instead, organizational behavior occurs in interactive, unique, real-world situations. There is a definite need to study organizational behavior *in situ* or from an ecological perspective and get away from reliance on indirect question-naire measures of behavior, which are too limiting and fail to analyze the organization member-behavior-situation interaction.

One way to a better understanding of social learning theory is to dif-ferentiate it from the more established operant theory. In particular, the key social learning processes of modeling, cognition, and self-control emerge as important factors that can contribute to a better understanding of organizational behavior. Both the operant and social learning theories treat behavior as a function of its response consequences. The major difference between the two concerns the role of cognitive processes. Research by social learning theorists has clearly shown that both vicarious learning and self-control processes are influenced by cognitive processes. The operant approach provides a more parsimonious interpretation of organizational behavior and certainly has pragmatic advantages for diagnosing, predicting, and controlling employee behaviors in the workplace [Luthans, 1980], but the notion of the organism "operating" on the environment provides too limited an *explanation* of how behavior is actively acquired and maintained. The lack of attention given to covert cognitive processes by the operant approach implicitly suggests that individual reasoning and other cognitions play no important role in organization-al behavior. The social learning theory concepts of modeling, cognitive processes, and self-control provide a more comprehensive view of organizational behavior. They help explain that an organizational participant's behavior may be grounded in the environment but is also partly socially derived and partly a product of conscious self-regulation and choice.

The ultimate usefulness of social learning theory depends on whether it can be effectively applied. The modeling process has already proved its worth as a training application, and we suggest that the self-control process has potentially significant implications for overall managerial effectiveness. In the final analysis, however, ecologically based research that carefully examines the interaction of the person-behavior-environment dynamic is needed to establish social learning as a viable theoretical base for studying organizational behavior.

REFERENCES

Adams, J. S. Inequity in social exchange. In L. Berkowitz (Ed.), *Advances in ex-perimental social psychology* (Vol. 2). New York: Academic Press, 1965, pp. 267–299.

Axelrod, S.; Hall, R. V.; Weiss, L.; & Rohrer, S. Use of self-imposed contingencies to reduce the frequency of smoking behavior. In M. J. Mahoney & C. E. Thoresen (Eds.), 1974, pp. 77–85.

Bandura, A. A social learning interpretation of psychological dysfunctions. In P. London & D. Rosenham (Eds.), *Foundations of abnormal psychology.* New York: Holt, Rinehart & Winston, 1968, pp. 293–344.

Bandura, A. *Principles of behavior modification.* New York: Holt, Rinehart & Winston, 1969.

Bandura, A. Social learning theory. In J. T. Spence, R. C. Carson, & J. W. Thibaut (Eds.), *Behavioral approaches to therapy.* Morristown, N.J.: General Learning Press, 1976, pp. 1–46.

Bandura, A. Self-efficacy: Toward a unifying theory of behavior change. *Psychological Review,* 1977, *84,* 191–215. (a)

Bandura, A. *Social learning theory.* Englewood Cliffs, N.J.: Prentice-Hall, 1977. (b)

Bandura, A. The self-system in reciprocal determinism. *American Psychologist,* 1978, *33,* 344–358.

Bandura, A.; & Walters, R. H. *Social learning and personality development.* New York: Holt, Rinehart & Winston, 1963.

Beneke, W. M.; & Harris, M. B. Teaching self-control of study behavior. *Behavior Research & Therapy,* 1972, *10,* 35–41.

Bernard, H. S.: & Efram, J. S. Eliminating versus reducing smoking using pocket timers. *Behavior Research & Therapy,* 1972, *10,* 399–401.

Bolstad, O. D.; & Johnson, S. M. Self-regulation in the modification of disruptive classroom behavior. *Journal of Applied Behavior Analysis,* 1972, *5,* 443–454.

Broden, M.; & Hall, R. V.; & Mitts, B. The effects of self-recording on the classroom behavior of two eighth-grade students. *Journal of Applied Behavior Analysis,* 1971, *4,* 191–199.

Bucher, B.; & Fabricatore, J. Use of patient-administered shock to suppress hallucinations. *Behavior Therapy,* 1970, *1,* 382–385.

Burnaska, R. F. The effects of behavior modeling training upon managers' behavior and employees' perceptions. *Personnel Psychology,* 1976, *29,* 329–335.

Davis, T. R. V.; & Luthans, F. Leadership re-examined: A behavioral approach. *Academy of Management Review,* 1979, *4,* 237–248.

Flanders, J. P. A review of research on imitative behavior. *Psychological Bulletin,* 1968, *69,* 316–337.

Flannery, R. B. Use of covert conditioning in the behavioral treatment of a drug-dependent college dropout. *Journal of Counseling Psychology,* 1972, *19,* 547–550.

Gibbs, J. C. The meaning of ecologically oriented inquiry in contemporary psychology. *American Psychologist,* 1979, *34,* 127–140.

Imitating models: A new management tool. *Business Week,* May 8, 1978, pp. 119–120.

Jacobs, A.; & Sachs, L. B. (Eds.). *The psychology of private events: Perspectives on covert response systems.* New York: Academic Press, 1971.

Johnson, S. M.; & White, G. Self-observation as an agent of behavior change. *Behavior Therapy,* 1971, *2,* 488–497.

Kanfer, F. H. Self-monitoring: Methodological limitations and clinical applications. *Journal of Consulting & Clinical Psychology,* 1970, *35,* 148–152.

Kanfer, F. H.; & Karoly, P. Some additional conceptualizations. In R. C. Johnson, P. R. Dokecki, & O. H. Mowrer (Eds.), *Conscience, contract, and social reality.* New York: Holt, Rinehart & Winston, 1972, pp. 428–437.

Kanfer, F. H.; & Karoly, P. Self-control: A behavioristic excursion into the lion's den. In
    M. J. Mahoney & C. E. Thoresen (Eds.), 1974, pp. 200–217.

Koontz, H. The management theory jungle. *Academy of Management Journal*, 1961, *4*,
    174–188.

Koontz, H. The management theory jungle revisited. *Academy of Management Review*,
    1980, *5*, 175–187.

Kraut, A. I. Developing managerial skills via modelling techniques: Some positive
    research findings—A symposium. *Personnel Psychology*, 1976, *29*, 325–369.

Latham, G. P.; & Saari, L. M. Application of social-learning theory to training
    supervisors through behavior modeling. *Journal of Applied Psychology*, 1979, *64*,
    239–246.

Locke, E. A. Toward a theory of task motivation and incentives. *Organizational Behavior
    & Human Performance*, 1968, *3*, 157–189.

Luthans, F. Contingency theory of management: A path out of the jungle. *Business
    Horizons*, 1973, *16*, 67–72.

Luthans, F. *Organizational behavior* (2nd ed.). New York: McGraw-Hill, 1977.

Luthans, F. Leadership: A proposal for a social learning theory base and observational
    and functional analysis techniques to measure leadership behavior. In J. G. Hunt &
    L. L. Larson (Eds.), *Crosscurrents in leadership*. Carbondale: Southern Illinois
    University Press, 1979, pp. 201–208.

Luthans, F. Functional analysis is the best technique for diagnostic evaluation of
    organizational behavior. In B. Karmel (Ed.), *Point and counterpoint in organiza-
    tional behavior*. Hinsdale, Ill.: Dryden, 1980, pp. 48–90.

Luthans, F.; & Davis, T. R. V. Behavioral self-management: The missing link in
    managerial effectiveness. *Organizational Dynamics*, Summer 1979, *8*,(1), 42–60.

Luthans, F.; & Kreitner, R. *Organizational behavior modification*. Glenview, Ill.:
    Scott-Foresman, 1975.

Luthans, F.; & Ottemann, R. Motivation vs. learning approaches to organizational
    behavior. *Business Horizons*, 1973, *16*, 55–62.

Maslow, A. H. *Motivation and personality*. New York: Harper, 1954.

McGuigan, F. J.; & Schoonhover, R. A. *The psychophysiology of thinking*. New York:
    Academic Press, 1973.

Mahoney, M. J. Reflections on the cogntive-learning trend in psychotherapy. *American
    Psychologist*, 1977, *32*, 5–13.

Mahoney, M. J.; & Thoresen, C. E. (Eds.). *Self-control: Power to the person*. Monterey,
    Calif.: Brooks/Cole, 1974.

Mash, E. J.; & Terdal, L. G. (Eds.). *Behavior therapy assessment: Diagnosis, design, and
    evaluation*. New York: Springer, 1976.

Meichenbaum, D. *Cognitive behavior modification*. Morristown, N. J.: General Learning
    Press, 1974.

Meichenbaum, D. *Cognitive behavior modification: An integrative approach*. New York:
    Plenum, 1977.

Miller, L. M. *Behavior management*. New York: Wiley, 1978.

Mischel, W. Toward a cognitive reconceptualization of personality. *Psychological
    Review*, 1973, *80*, 284–302.

Mischel, W. *Introduction to personality* (2nd ed.). New York: Holt, Rinehart & Winston,
    1976.

Nord, W. Beyond the teaching machine: The neglected area of operant conditioning in the theory and practice of management. *Organizational Behavior & Human Performance*, 1969, *4*, 375–401.

Porter, L. W.; & Lawler, E. E. *Managerial attitudes and performance*. Homewood, Ill.: Irwin, 1968.

Skinner, B. F. *Science and human behavior*. New York: Free Press, 1953.

Skinner, B. F. *Contingencies of reinforcement*. New York: Appleton-Century-Crofts, 1969.

Sobell, L. C.; & Sobell, M. B. A self-feedback technique to monitor drinking behavior in alcoholics. *Behavior Research & Therapy*, 1973, *11*, 223–238.

Sorcher, M.; & Goldstein, A. P. A behavior modeling approach in training. *Personnel Administration*, 1972, *35*, 35–41.

Staats, A. W. *Learning language and cognition*. New York: Holt. Rinehart & Winston, 1968.

Staats, A. W. *Social behaviorism*. Homewood, Ill.: Dorsey Press, 1975.

Stunkard, A. New therapies for the eating disorders: Behavior modification of obesity and anorexia nervosa. *Archives of General Psychiatry*, 1972, *26*, 391–398.

Thoresen, C. E.; & Mahoney, M. J. *Behavioral self-control*. New York: Holt, Rinehart & Winston, 1974.

Upper, D.; & Meredith, L. A. *A times-interval procedure for modifying cigarette-smoking behavior*. Unpublished manuscript, Brockton Veteran's Administration Hospital, Brockton, Mass., 1971.

Vroom, V. H. *Work and motivation*. New York: Wiley, 1964.

Watson, D. L.; & Tharp, R. G. *Self-directed behavior: Self-modification for personal adjustment* (2nd ed.). Monterey, Calif.: Brooks/Cole, 1977.

Watson, J. B. Psychology as the behaviorist views it. *Psychological Review*, 1913, *20*, 158–177.

REVIEW AND DISCUSSION QUESTIONS

1 What are the major dimensions of social learning theory?
2 In what ways can social learning theory aid in the understanding of organizational behavior?
3 Compare and contrast social learning theory and the operant theory. Explain these differences.
4 What are some possible limitations of analyzing organizational behavior through the cognitive approach?
5 How do Davis and Luthans suggest that a social learning approach can be applied? Give a realistic example of this application.

Part Two

Micro Issues: Motivation, Goal Setting, and Job Design

The micro perspective of organizational behavior focuses upon very narrow individually oriented units of analysis. In this part, the issues surrounding the micro variables of motivation, goal setting, and job design are examined.

Over the past fifty years there have been numerous motivation theories that attempt to explain human behavior at work. Two directions to motivation research have emerged in recent years. On the one hand researchers are attempting to develop comprehensive models of motivation. The second approach takes a relatively limited, precise experimental orientation that attempts to define and relate variables that are important to motivation. These directions imply that in the future motivation models will be based more on empirical research that tests the relationship between the identifiable variables. For the time being there are some difficulties that are being faced in motivation research. It is apparent that the degree of motivation that an individual has in a particular situation is a function of many variables. It is proving difficult to isolate or operationally measure the relevant variables. Another limitation is that current statistical methods make it difficult to effectively measure a multitude of variables at any one time. The measurement problem is compounded when interactions between variables are considered. With these limitations, there are some definite inhibiting factors in the development of a meaningful and useful model of work motivation.

Besides the overall issues surrounding work motivation per se, it is becoming increasingly clear that some techniques can have a definite impact on motivation and performance of employees. In particular, it has been found that goal setting is an important aspect in the resultant motivation and performance of employees. The research of Professor Edwin Locke and his colleagues indicates that performance will improve under the following conditions. First, employee performance will improve by the establishment of specific goals instead of vague "do your best" type of goals. Second, hard to achieve goals improve performance more than easier to reach goals, at least to a point. For example, it has been found that once people feel a goal is totally out of reach, they may either give up or set their own goals that are lower than the established ones. In essence, this implies that there is a curvilinear relationship between performance and goal setting. In addition, there seem to be several moderating factors that can influence the degree of performance improvement attributable to goal setting. Examples of moderators would be individual attributes, the amount and nature of feedback, and, to some degree, the consequences for goal attainment. Reaching the objective, in itself, can be intrinsically satisfying, but it has also been shown that the application of an extrinsic reward can lead to performance improvement.

Another micro area of organizational behavior that has received a lot of recent research attention has been the motivation and performance resulting from a job design change. Studies over the last several years have indicated that job redesign can have a definite impact on employee motivation and can lead to performance improvement over the long run. These findings led to the popular movement of job enrichment. With the increasing maturation and sophistication of the research in job design, some new dimensions are being given attention. For example, it is now generally recognized that job enrichment is not an effective change process for all individuals. There are also some specific job characteristics that seem vital to the successful implementation of a job enrichment program. Without consideration of these characteristics, a job enrichment program may not lead to the degree of success anticipated. It is now recognized that job restructuring, by itself, is not the key ingredient to increases in job performance. The job design changes should precipitate a change in the work environment so that the job characteristics provide more motivating potential for the individual. For example, a job redesign program may lead to an increase in an employee's autonomy over the work. This autonomy characteristic is considered to be an important motivational input for the employee. Hence, the job itself will become more motivating for the individual. In a similar manner, a job design change can lead to an increase in the degree of opportunity for participation in decision making, the frequency of social interaction, and the degree of wholeness in the completed process. In the latter case, the employee has the opportunity to become involved in a greater share of the total operations so that the final outcome can be more readily attributed to the individual's efforts.

The articles in this part reflect the micro analysis of organizational behavior from the perspective of motivation, goal setting, and job design. The first two articles are concerned with motivation. The first article, by Professor David Terpstra, is an attempt to combine the best of several motivation theories into some positive action steps that a practitioner may apply. The article is a comprehensive overview of several motivation theories and offers some questions as to the practicability of the approach that the author is suggesting. The second article, by Professor Larry Pate, compares the cognitive approach to motivation with the behavioral approach. The author's contention is that more time should be spent on finding the commonality of each approach and using the knowledge gained from each to improve the "state of the art" knowledge of motivation. The third article of this section is concerned with goal setting. The article is written by two of the most active researchers in the field and provides a very comprehensive review of research on goal setting. The last three articles in this part are concerned with job design. The first one outlines the new approach used in job enrichment programs. The following article then recaps some of the job enrichment programs in the United States over the past decade. Finally, the last article compares the German environment with that in the United States and tells how this cultural difference can impact upon the attempts of labor unions to change job design and upon joint management/labor cooperative change programs.

Reading 6

Theories of Motivation—Borrowing the Best

David E. Terpstra

Motivation remains one of the most fascinating and perplexing areas of managerial concern. The question, "How can I motivate my people?" has been philosophically and practically posed in many eras and many tongues.

It is not that the question is unanswerable; rather, too many answers exist. A multitude of methods for motivating employees have been proposed, each bearing some degree of validity and utility for the practicing manager.

It is not this author's intent to push one popular or preferred theory of motivation, but rather to borrow the best from each of a number of current theories of motivation.

MASLOW'S NEED HIERARCHY

Abraham H. Maslow, on the basis of his clinical studies, observed that individuals appear to be motivated to satisfy the following basic types of needs: 1) physiological, 2) safety, 3) belongingness, 4) esteem and 5) self-actualization. Furthermore, Maslow posited that those needs are related in the form of a hierarchy and that the needs emerge sequentially. For example, the physiological needs of an individual would have to be largely satisfied or fulfilled before the next level of needs (safety) could motivate behavior. According to Maslow, a need that is relatively satisfied loses its importance as a motivator, causing the next higher level need to come into play and motivate the individual.[1]

The idea of an individual climbing the hypothetical ladder of need fulfillment being motivated by the next highest "rung" is an intuitively appealing one; however, very little evidence exists to support this notion of hierarchical progression. Nor have factor-analytic studies been able to reproduce those five specific factors or types of needs thought by Maslow to motivate behavior.[2]

The value of Maslow's theory lies in its emphasis on motivating employees by appealing to their individual needs. The implications are obvious. To motivate employees, the manager must accurately identify and gauge their most important needs and utilize those needs by linking their satisfaction to effort or performance. For example, if a need for security has been identified, perhaps the manager could communicate and stress the relationship between high effort and job tenure. If a need for recognition has been identified, opportunities for satisfying that need should be provided for and made contingent on increased effort. Again, the primary value of Maslow's need hierarchy theory appears to be its focus on the recognition and identification of individual needs for the purposes of motivating behavior.

HERZBERG'S DUAL-FACTOR THEORY

A second need-based theory of motivation is the dual-factor or motivation-hygiene theory suggested by Frederick Herzberg and his associates. On the basis of data collected from 200 engineers and accountants, Herzberg concluded that there were two basic sets of factors with which employees were concerned: hygienes and motivators. Hygiene factors were those associated with the type of supervision, company policies, pay, working conditions, interpersonal relations, status, security and personal life. According to Herzberg, proper attention to these factors is important in preventing employees from becoming dissatisfied in their work. However, Herzberg asserts that those factors do not play an important role in satisfying or motivating employees, as only the motivator factors can do this. The motivator factors include achievement, recognition, responsibility, advancement, growth and the work itself. To the extent that the motivator factors are present on the job, Herzberg contends, motivation will occur.[3]

Herzberg's theory has generated proportionally more heat than light, and the primary debate stems from Herzberg's contention that hygiene factors can prevent dissatisfaction, but cannot satisfy or motivate workers. The research evidence does not, in general, support this contention.[4,5] Furthermore, it would seem logical that hygiene factors such as pay or supervision could indeed influence an employee's level of motivation or satisfaction.

While Herzberg's theory may be somewhat flawed, the recommendations flowing from the theory would seem to merit the manager's attention. He recommends enriching jobs by making the work more meaningful and interesting and by providing more opportunities for achievement, recognition, responsibility, advancement and growth on the job.[6] For certain types of employees, job enrichment might positively influence worker motivation. But again, it is important to consider the nature of the employees and their needs, as some classes of workers simply do not respond to or enjoy "enriched" tasks.[7]

GOAL SETTING

Edwin A. Locke has proposed a partial model of task motivation, the basic premise of which is that an individual's conscious intentions or goals are the primary determinants of task motivation. Furthermore, his theory posits that hard goals result in greater effort than easy goals and that specific goals result in higher effort than no goals or more generalized goals.[8]

A great deal of research has been carried out in organizations to test Locke's propositions, and one of the better reviews of the research is provided by Latham and Yukl. On the basis of their review, they concluded that the data clearly supported the effectiveness of setting specific goals for employees, as improved performance generally resulted. Additionally, the proposition that hard goals lead to increased effort was generally supported by the available data, as long as those difficult goals were "accepted" by the employees. For example, if the goal was so difficult as to seem unreasonable, it would not be accepted, and increased effort would not result.[9] One additional aspect of goal setting that has received considerable attention has to do with the effects of subordinate participation in goal setting. Several studies have compared the performance levels of groups with assigned goals to groups which participated in setting their goals.[10,11] With regard to this issue, the research data are mixed and inconclusive. A number of variables seem to moderate the effectiveness of varying degrees of subordinate participation in goal setting.

Based on the available literature, motivational recommendations to managers would include the provision of clear, specific goals for employees. Furthermore, the goals should be of sufficient difficulty to be perceived as challenging, yet not so difficult as to seem impossible. It is quite possible that an unrealistically difficult goal could be worse than no goal whatsoever.

EXPECTANCY/VALENCE THEORY

Expectancy/valence theory also known as an instrumentality theory, valence-instrumentality-expectancy—VIE—theory, or simply expectancy theory) draws heavily on the formulations of Victor Vroom.[12] However, the more widely known version presented here is that of Campbell and associates.[13] Basically, this theory assumes that motivation or effort is a function (multiplicative) of three components: 1) an effort → performance (E → P) expectancy, 2) a performance → outcome (P → O) expectancy and 3) valence. The E → P expectancy refers to the individual's perception of the chances that increased effort will lead to good job performance. The P → O expectancy refers to the individual's perception of the chances that good performance will lead to certain outcomes or rewards. Valence refers to the value or attractiveness of a given outcome or reward to the individual. Thus, for an individual to be motivated, he or she must believe that additional effort will result in higher performance (as defined and measured by the organization). The employee must also believe that higher performance will be associated with greater rewards or outcomes. Furthermore, those rewards or outcomes must be valent, or valued by the individual.

Expectancy/valence theory provides one of the better general frameworks for viewing and understanding the process of motivation. A number of recommendations for managers concerned with motivating employees derive from this theory. If an employee's level of motivation is deemed inadequate, each of the three basic components of the motivational model could be focused on in an attempt to locate the causal factor(s). Perhaps the E → P component could be the culprit. The employee may not believe that effort is related to organizationally defined performance. If performance is influenced by factors not under the control of the employee, this belief would be justified. In this case, the manager's attention would turn to the development of more relevant performance criteria. An alternative explanation for some motivational deficit involving the E → P component might be the case where an employee may simply lack self-confidence and thus believe that no amount of effort would result in the desired performance. In such a situation, the manager might take steps to increase the employee's level of self-confidence or self-esteem. A lack of ability or proper training might also explain one's low E → P expectancy.

If the P → O component was considered the crucial cause for inadequate motivation, the manager's attention would turn toward efforts aimed at improving the perceived link between performance and outcomes/rewards. A salesperson would not be expected to set his or her sights on increased sales (performance) if it wouldn't result in increased pay (outcome). One recommendation for improving the perceived P → O link might involve tying outcomes more directly to performance through the use of incentive plans, commissions, merit raises or merit-based promotions.

In focusing on the third component (valence), it is evident that for outcomes or rewards to motivate effort, those outcomes must be valued by the individual. The manager's task is to identify employees' relevant and valued outcomes, whether those outcomes take the form of pay, promotions, job security, recognition or other potentially valent outcomes.

REINFORCEMENT

While not a theory of motivation per se, reinforcement theory has much to offer the manager concerned with increasing employees' levels of effort. Based largely on the research efforts of Burrhus Frederick Skinner, the general idea behind reinforcement theory is that an individual's behavior or "motivation" is a function of the consequences of that behavior.[14] Behavior that is reinforced tends to be repeated, whereas behavior that is not reinforced is less likely to recur.

A major strategy or "contingency" of reinforcement includes *positive reinforcement*, which attempts to increase the strength or frequency of some desired behavior by making the presentation of positive reinforcers or outcomes contingent on the occurrence of that behavior. *Negative reinforcement*, on the other hand, tries to increase the strength or frequency of some desired response by making avoidance of a negative stimulus contingent on the occurrence of the desired response (e.g., an employee may work harder to avoid being "chewed out" by the supervisor). *Punishment* focuses on decreasing some specific behavior by making the application of some noxious stimulus or punishment contingent on the occurrence of the unwanted behavior, while *extinction* attempts to decrease some undesired behavior by withholding reinforcement when the behavior occurs.[15]

Many of the criticisms aimed at reinforcement theory center on the ethical concerns associated with the approach. Indeed, the terms "reinforcement theory" and "behavior modification" frequently conjure up visions of worker control and manipulation. However, regardless of one's view on the issue, the fact remains that the principles and strategies of reinforcement can be of potential use to managers in influencing employee behavior and effort. With respect to the least objectionable strategy (positive reinforcement), the manager—by simply making positive reinforcers such as praise, recognition, pay or promotions contingent on the desired behavior (increased effort or perhaps goal attainment)—can usually increase recurrence of that behavior. It should be noted that care should be taken in selecting the outcomes to be used as reinforcers, as individual differences again enter into the motivation equation.

RELATIONSHIPS AND RECOMMENDATIONS

In light of the preceding review, some general recommendations for motivating employees suggest themselves. It is apparent that any motivational attempt must begin by focusing on the individual and his or her needs. Having identified those needs, one can, to the extent realistically possible, structure the work experience to best accommodate the fulfillment of those needs. Also, care should be taken in the selection and use of work rewards and outcomes. The individual's needs dictate which outcomes will be considered highly "valent" and "reinforcing."

Additionally, an emphasis on goal setting would seem to be motivationally advisable. While the nature of the goals should depend somewhat on the individual and his or her needs and abilities, an attempt should be made to provide clear, specific and somewhat challenging goals. To the extent that goals are clear-cut and unambiguous, employees will be able to more clearly visualize the link between effort and performance ($E \rightarrow P$ expectancy), and increased motivation should result. Furthermore, the factors related to goal attainment should be under the employees' control to positively influence the $E \rightarrow P$ expectancy component.

Finally, goal attainment and goal-directed behavior should be consistently and positively reinforced by the contingent application of valent outcomes. The link between performance and outcomes ($P \rightarrow O$ expectancy) will thus become stronger, serving to further increase motivation.

In recognition of the fact that no one theory of motivation has all of the answers, an attempt has been made to borrow the best motivational bits and pieces from each of a number of theories. By selectively choosing from several sources, a more complete understanding of the process and problems of motivating individuals can be achieved.

REFERENCES

1   A. H. Maslow, "A Theory of Human Motivation," *Psychological Review,* 1943, pp. 370–396.
2   M. Wahba and L. G. Bridwell, "Maslow Reconsidered: A Review of Research on the Need Hierarchy Theory," *Organizational Behavior and Human Performance,* 15 (1976): 217–240.
3   F. Herzberg, B. Mausner and B. Snyderman, *The Motivation to Work* (New York: John Wiley & Sons, Inc., 1959).
4   R. J. House and L. A. Wigdor, "Herzberg's Dual-Factor Theory of Job Satisfaction and Motivation: A Review of the Evidence and a Criticism," *Personnel Psychology,* 20 (1967): 369–389.
5   E. A. Locke, "The Nature and Causes of Job Satisfaction" in M. Dunnette (ed.) *Handbook of Industrial and Organizational Psychology* (Chicago: Rand McNally, 1976).

6 F. Herzberg, "One More Time: How Do You Motivate Employees?" *Harvard Business Review,* Vol. 46, No. 1 (1968): 53–62.

7 C. L. Hulin and M. R. Blood, "Job Enlargement, Individual Differences, and Worker Responses," *Psychological Bulletin,* 69 (1968): 41–55.

8 E. A. Locke, "Toward a Theory of Task Motivation and Incentives," *Organizational Behavior and Human Performance,* 3 (1968): 157–189.

9 G. P. Latham and G. A. Yukl, "A Review of Research on the Application of Goal-Setting in Organizations," *Academy of Management Journal,* 18 (1975): 824–845.

10 G. P. Latham and G. A. Yukl, "Assigned Versus Participative Goal-Setting With Educated and Uneducated Wood Workers," *Journal of Applied Psychology,* 60 (1975): 299–302.

11 R. M. Steers, "Task-Goal Attributes, Need For Achievement, and Supervisory Performance," *Organizational Behavior and Human Performance,* 13 (1975): 392–403.

12 V. Vroom, *Work and Motivation* (New York: John Wiley & Sons, Inc., 1964).

13 J. P. Campbell, M. D. Dunnette, E. E. Lawler and K. E. Weick, *Managerial Behavior, Performance, and Effectiveness* (New York: McGraw-Hill Book Co., 1970).

14 B. F. Skinner, *Science and Human Behavior* (New York: Free Press, 1953).

15 B. F. Skinner, *Contingencies of Reinforcement* (New York: Appleton-Century-Crofts, 1969).

REVIEW AND DISCUSSION QUESTIONS

1 Explain Herzberg's Dual Factor Theory of Motivation.
2 How can a manager apply a motivation theory like the dual factor theory?
3 What can be gained by "borrowing the best" from several motivation theories? Does this approach make sense? What are some of the problems associated with this approach?
4 How can goal setting and reinforcement improve performance?

Reading 7

Cognitive versus Reinforcement Views of Intrinsic Motivation[1]

Larry E. Pate

A central thrust of managerial psychology has been to determine the motivating forces that energize, direct, and sustain individual work behavior [59]. Lewin's [37] conceptualization that behavior is the result of interactions between

From the *Academy of Management Review,* 1978, p. 505–514. Reprinted with permission from the author and the *Academy of Management Review.*

[1]I am indebted to Rick Mowday, Barry Staw and two anonymous reviewers for their helpful comments on a preliminary draft of this article.

individual and environmental factors is still widely accepted; but this approach is too global from a research standpoint, and there is disagreement on the composition of these factors. A major controversy historically surrounds the relative importance of each factor as a determinant of behavior and the extent to which other concepts (such as needs and drives) are innate or learned. Cognitive theorists argue that the individual's cognitive processes play an important role in determining behavior, while reinforcement theorists retort that it is unnecessary, if not impossible, to examine such thought processes, and therefore our central concern should be the behavior itself. Each theoretical position specifies alternative mixes and categories of variables.

This article makes no attempt to resolve such debate, but rather explicates the positions of mechanistic-reinforcement theorists (such as Scott) and organismic-cognitive theorists (like Deci), specifically as they relate to the current controversy regarding intrinsic motivation. Briefly, this controversy centers on Deci's research, a departure from the central thrust of the cognitive school and one which has provided a convenient target for reinforcement theorists like Scott. First the theoretical roots of each group of theorists will be traced, and then specific points of disagreement on the measurement of intrinsic motivation and on potential areas of application in organizations will be highlighted.

REINFORCEMENT THEORY BACKGROUND

The work of Watson [65] and his commitment to the concept of learning is said to mark the formal beginning of behaviorism [38, 66]. Watson's emphasis on stimulus-response (S-R) mechanisms extended the earlier classical-conditioning work of Russian psychologists, notably Pavlov. Behavioral learning theorists traditionally draw a distinction between *respondent* (unlearned: controlled or elicited by prior stimulation) and *operant* (learned: influenced by events which follow) behavior [see 24, 30, 54, 55, for detailed reviews of reinforcement theory and research].

The earliest reinforcement theory of learning, Thorndike's [61] "law of effect," states that satisfying consequences serve to reinforce S-R connections. In essence, reinforcement theories are an extension of Watson's S-R paradigm and posit that external or internal stimuli (goads) determine behavior through mechanistic S-R bonds and reinforcement histories. All behavior is said to be learned and solely a function of its consequences, so that behavior toward an object will persist only when the individual performing the behavior is adequately reinforced; in the absence or removal of either continuous or intermittment reinforcement, extinction of the behavior is said to occur.

These and other theories, such as Hull's [29] drive-reduction theory and Spence's [56] refinements of it, influenced the work of current reinforcement theorists, notably Skinner [54, 55]. Skinner first made the important distinction between operant and respondent behavior and focused upon the conditioning aspects of operant behavior [38]. Table 1 compares neobehaviorist and

Table 1 Summary of Mechanistic Theories

Theory classification	Theory structure	Description
Behaviorist	S-R	Behavior explained in terms of stimulus-response connections. Intervening hypothetical constructs are not employed in the analysis of action. Proponents include Skinner, Watson, other associationists, and behaviorists.
Neobehaviorist	S-Construct-R	Behavior explained in terms of stimulus-response connections. Intervening constructs also are employed in the analysis of action, such as drive, incentive, etc. Proponents include Spence, Hull, Miller, Brown, and other neobehaviorists.

Adapted from B. Weiner, *Theories of Motivation: From Mechanisms to Cognition* (Chicago: Rand McNally, 1972).

behaviorist classes of mechanistic-reinforcement-theories that explain behavior with and without the use of intervening (but non-cognitive) constructs.

Behavior modification, a scientifically derived set of behavioristic principles and techniques, represents a major attempt to apply operant and respondent conditioning techniques for the purpose of achieving effective behavior change and control. While the use of behavior modification principles has largely been neglected in the management and organizational behavior (OB) literature [cf. 44], there have been several recent attempts to test these principles in natural and organizational settings [2, 34, 38, 43, 46, 47, 52, 60].

COGNITIVE THEORY BACKGROUND

Following Weiner, "there are types of reinforcement theories, types of cognitive theories, and all shades of grey in between" [66, p. 7]. The cognitive versus reinforcement dichotomy is artificial. Weiner refers to the theories of Lewin and Atkinson as only quasi-cognitive, for reinforcement concepts seem to have had a greater influence on these theorists than cognitive constructs. The common element shared by cognitive theorists is the belief that it is necessary to examine a particular class of intervening variables when explaining behavior; cognitive theories posit that an antecedent stimuli is separated from the final behavioral response by a mediating cognitive event. These theories differ on what constitutes the cognitive act as well as on how the cognition influences behavior. The intervening cognition may be a perceived path to the goal [37], expectancy [64], or subjective probability of success [3].

The theoretical foundation of a cognitive approach is traceable to the writings of Kant [31] and to phenomenological thinking; Lewin, for example, was greatly influenced by Cassirer, a prominent neo-Kantian [66]. Van de Geer and Jaspers [63] note that cognitive theory ranges from neobehavioristic mediation to phenomenological interpretation. Baldwin defines the approach as follows:

A cognitive theory of behavior assumes that the first stage in the chain of events initiated by the stimulus situation and resulting in the behavioral act is the construction of a congitive representation of the distal environment. The later events in the chain are instigated, modified and guided by this cognitive representation. The cognitive representation thus acts as the effective environment which arouses motives and emotions, and guides overt behavior toward its target or goal [4, p. 321].

One type of cognitive theory, expectancy theory, limits the range of cognitive constructs by focusing on anticipatory end states or goals. The theories of Lewin [37], Rotter [50], Tolman [62], Edwards [19], Atkinson [3], Vroom [64], and Porter and Lawler [48] fall within this category. Expectancy models have been thoroughly reviewed and criticized elsewhere [27, 28, 41, 42, 57] and will not be discussed here.

A second class of cognitive theories, referred to here as extraexpectancy, examines cognitive concepts, such as causal attributions and social comparisons, in addition to anticipatory end states. The theories of Freud [21], Festinger [20], Heider [26], Adams [1], and Deci [12] are included in this category. Table 2 compares these two classes of cognitive theories. Other distinctions, such as the humanistic approaches typified by Maslow, McGregor, and Rogers, could also be made.

In terms of the motivation construct, the writing of deCharms [8] is often cited as a more recent point of departure of cognitive theory. He distinguishes between behavior that is intrinsically motivated and behavior that is extrinsically motivated and argues that intrinsic and extrinsic motivation may interact rather than summate, counter to other cognitive theorists [e.g., 48, 64]. Further, deCharms predicts an interaction between intrinsic and extrinsic dimensions if rewards are withheld. Although the meaning of *intrinsic motivation* remains obscure [cf. 17, 53], it generally refers to the pleasure or value associated with the content of the task itself, while *extrinsic motivation* refers to the value an individual derives from the environment surrounding the context of the work.

Table 2 Summary of Cognitive Theories

Theory classification	Theory structure	Description
Expectancy	S-Cognition-R	Thoughts intervene between incoming information and the final behavioral response. The main cognitive determinant of action is an "expectancy." Proponents include Atkinson, Lewin, Porter, Rotter, Tolman, and Vroom.
Extraexpectancy	S-Cognition-R	Thoughts intervene between incoming information and the final behavioral response. Many cognitive processes determine action, such as information seeking, causal attributions, etc. Proponents include Adams, Deci, Festinger, Heider, Kelley, and Lazarus.

Regardless of what intrinsic motivation actually is, the crucial issues are whether individuals distinguish between intrinsic and extrinsic causes [57] and how to determine the consequences of such distinctions[7].

Research stimulated by deCharms' theorizing, particularly that conducted by Deci and associates [5, 9, 10, 11, 12, 13, 14, 15, 16], raises important questions regarding the effects of extrinsic rewards, such as pay, on intrinsic motivation and on subsequent behavioral acts. With this brief background, let us now turn to Deci's cognitive framework, which makes predictions counter to reinforcement and other cognitive theorists.

RESEARCH ON INTRINSIC MOTIVATION

Essentially, Deci's argument is that individuals who are paid to perform an interesting task will attribute their behavior to external forces and thus reduce their intrinsic interest in the task itself. Deci conducted a series of laboratory studies (and a tangentially related field study with an N = 4) in which subjects, under varying degrees of contingent and noncontingent reward conditions, engaged in a presumably interesting task (such as completing the Soma puzzle), after which behavioral measures of the subject's intrinsic motivation were obtained. Subjects in most of these studies were students who participated in the experiment to satisfy requirements for an introductory course in psychology. The dependent measure of intrinsic motivation was the amount of time subjects continued to engage in the puzzle-completion task during a free-choice period following the experimental time period; Deci's assumption was that subjects' intrinsic motivation could be aroused during the experiment and that the presence of contingent versus noncontingent rewards would systematically alter these internal motivation states. Deci also hypothesized that verbal reinforcement would increase intrinsic motivation [9, 10], but that noncontingent monetary rewards would not affect intrinsic motivation [11].

Although slight variations exist in each study, Deci found consistent differences between experimental and control groups on the dependent measures when rewards were given contingent upon desired behavior [12, 14]. He interpreted these findings as support for deCharms' hypothesis that extrinsic rewards can decrease intrinsic motivation. Similar findings have been reported in studies conducted by other investigators [18, 22, 23, 32, 35, 36, 49], lending some support to this position. To account for such findings, and perhaps even in anticipation of the charge that he has not contributed to theoretical development of the intrinsic motivation construct [53], Deci has proposed a cognitive evaluation theory [12, 13, 14] which equates intrinsic motivation with Heider's [26] concept of perceived locus of causality (see Figure 1).

Deci's research has been criticized in a number of recent papers [6, 25, 39, 45, 51, 53, 57]. Salancik [51] discusses two procedural limitations to Deci's work: (a) his failure to report performance data as an indication of the difficulty of the task, and (b) his reliance on task persistence as the sole dependent measure. In an attempt to control for these limitations, Salancik tested the interaction effects

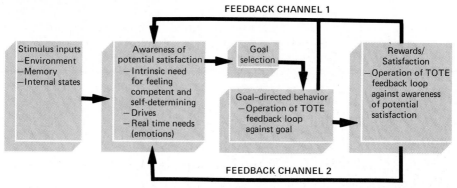

Figure 1 A schematic representation of a cognitive system of intrinsically and extrinsically motivated behavior.

of pay and level of performance of an interesting task by using an innovative road racing task; his results contradicted Deci's and suggested that subjects are less intrinsically motivated when the task is perceived as easy relative to their ability.

Further methodological problems exist with the magnitude and timing of Deci's rewards and the question of whether or not these rewards were expected by subjects [6]. Research by Lepper, Greene, and Nisbett [36] suggests that intrinsic motivation may decrease only when extrinsic rewards are expected, yet there is no mention of subjects' expectations in Deci's research. Calder and Staw [6] point out that Deci's conclusions regarding the effects of noncontingent rewards on intrinsic motivation are not justified by his data, since Deci has essentially affirmed the null hypothesis.

Perhaps the strongest attack on Deci's work is that of Scott [53], who effectively argues that uncontrolled and differential conditioning was taking place and that even Deci's statistical procedures were inappropriate. Deci used difference scores between experimental and free-time periods minus the time spent on the puzzle by control group subjects, rather than simply the average numbers of seconds for all subjects in the experimental session, as Scott suggests. But Scott's attack centers on the conditioning aspects of Deci's experiments:

> Not only were the reinforcing events different in the third study, but more importantly, they were also contingent upon persisting at the task rather than upon successful solutions of the task as in the first study. Deci concluded that social approval does not seem to impair intrinsic motivation as does money. However, we cannot be certain that the differences between the experimental group and the control group in any of the sessions were not due to differences in conditioning treatments prior to the observations [53, p. 123].

Scott also notes Deci's failure to provide sufficient information on the nature of these different conditioning treatments.

Scott's position is that suitably scheduled reinforcers increase the rate of responding, although such behavior-maintaining reinforcers are not easily discerned. He suggests that since "an additional reinforcer may not produce behavior incompatible with operants maintained by other reinforcers" then "*other* conditions may produce a significant increment in the probability or rate of operant responding" [53, p. 127]. Thus, even discarding the methodological limitations surrounding Deci's data, the logic of his interpretations is still open to serious question. Essentially, Scott maintains there is a more logical (better tested) theory which is not consistent with Deci's interpretations:

> It is possible that the addition of contingent reinforcers would produce a rather intricate interaction effect. On the one hand, the additional reinforcer might retard habituation to the response-produced sensory stimuli and might even enhance their reinforcing effectiveness by virtue of their being classically paired with the added reinforcing event. However, should the additional reinforcer be administered on an effective interval or ratio schedule, the consequent increase in rate of responding may result in a reduction in the reinforcing effectiveness of response-produced sensory reinforcers if they, in turn, occurred more frequently. The performance effects under these circumstances would be difficult to predict, and it may be that Deci's contribution was in alerting us to this particular complexity and its potential significance [53, p. 127].

Similar criticism and discussion of alternative reinforcement explanations of Deci's findings are forwarded by Luthans, Martinko, and Kess [39]—notably the impact of satiation, stimulus control, reinforcement contrast, and punishing consequences.

In response, Deci [13] argues that the essential disagreement between himself and others centers on their discrepant philosophical orientations regarding the causes of behavior—namely, the reinforcement-cognitive split. Deci also argues that Scott confuses intrinsic motivation with behavior, presumably a result of Scott's reinforcement position. In his cognitive evaluation theory (see Figure 1), Deci maintains that extrinsic rewards have two aspects—a controlling aspect and an informational aspect. Implicit in Deci's response to Scott is the notion that reinforcement theorists have focused narrowly on the controlling aspect and have neglected the informational aspect. Conversely, the cognitive framework allows for the situation where extrinsic rewards, such as pay, serve as feedback about how past behavior has been received, rather than as reinforcement per se. Deci [13] also provides performance data previously omitted from his published reports; these data show no significant differences between paid and unpaid subjects during the manipulation phase of his earlier [9, 10] experiments.

A problem with Deci's remarks is that alternative cognitive explanations for his findings exist and have been discussed in other critiques. Luthans, et al. [39], for example, offer both expectancy and locus of control explanations. An expectancy theory explanation is that paid subjects did not expect to receive payments beyond the third experimental period, thereby decreasing the amount of time they engaged in the free-time task. The combined effects of these criticisms cast serious doubt on the accuracy of Deci's research and theorizing.

IMPLICATIONS AND POTENTIAL AREAS OF APPLICATION

Perhaps the major areas of disagreement are with respect to the controlling aspects of organizational reward systems and the design of jobs themselves. Some kinds of organizational rewards, such as pay and promotion, are intentionally based on performance. There must be evidence that the worker is deserving of the reward before it is supplied. The merits of such a practice generally have been espoused by both cognitive and reinforcement theorists [33], although for different reasons.

But Deci argues that such contingent reward practices may run counter to the interests and intentions of the organizations using them. People may begin to like their work less when their organizational rewards are made contingent upon it. The rationale for Deci's position lies in his theory, which states that when extrinsic rewards are interpreted as a form of control, intrinsic motivation may suffer; when interpreted as a form of feedback that also informs the worker that she or he is competent and self-determining, then intrinsic motivation may increase. Such reasoning is not completely counter to existing studies of pay in organizational settings [33], but determining how such rewards are interpreted is a key issue Deci neglects.

The issue for reinforcement theorists is whether or not the reward is a reinforcer of desired behaviors. To the extent that pay is such a reinforcer, reinforcement theorists would argue that job behaviors should be made contingent upon it. But they would also argue that rewards are a form of environmental stimuli which can reinforce undesired behaviors. To be truly effective, immediate reinforcement should be provided for desired behaviors; withdrawal of such reinforcers is punishing to the individual. Several research efforts in non-organizational settings support this contention [54, 55], but there is insufficient evidence to indicate that principles of reinforcement can be applied effectively in complex organizational settings, although a few notable exceptions exist [2, 34, 38, 43, 46, 47, 52].

Meyer [40] argues that some of the more important rewards, specifically those associated with intrinsic motivation, are not under the control of management and thus cannot be administered according to reinforcement schedules. One could argue that a central goal of leaders is to manage the renforcement contingencies of their workers and that such control can be obtained through task and job design efforts. Since the reinforcing properties of a given reinforcer may vary across individuals, perhaps a cafeteria-style reward system, as suggested long ago by Lawler, is appropriate. These considerations should probably be included in any organizational analysis prior to committing resources to reinforcement practices in work settings.

Deci suggests that organizations should supply rewards on a noncontingent basis or expect possible negative effects [14]. To attempt to counter these effects, he suggests that jobs be designed to offer the potential for intrinsic motivation. In a sense, such sentiment parallels the job enrichment movement and argues that jobs can be made intrinsically motivating. The implicit assumption in some of the literature is that cognitive processes are important in intrinsic motivation but not in extrinsic (i.e., extrinsic motivation is the sole province of reinforcement theorists). Vroom, Porter, Lawler, and other recognized cognitive theorists probably would disagree.

The issue here is not to resolve such debate, for debate can be a healthy exercise for any science. For example, Herzberg's motivation-hygiene theory has received much criticism, yet in the process it has stimulated thought and research on the motivation constructs [59]. More research on the effects of extrinsic rewards on intrinsic motivation, as advocated by both Deci and Scott, needs to be conducted before knowing with any precision the outcomes, for the individual or the organization. The effects Deci describes may exist, but this has not yet been demonstrated unambiguously.

In spite of the methodological limitations of Deci's studies, one clear prescription can be offered to researchers and practitioners. Provision must be made for interpretation of findings, consequences, and causation from *both* cognitive and reinforcement positions. Given the state of the art, the researcher who hastily opts for a single interpretation and excludes consideration of the other does science a disservice. The practitioner who relies on prescriptions solely from one position may commit major organizational errors. These views provide a firm basis for true theory-testing research, an unusual occurrence in the behavioral sciences.

Future efforts should attempt to overcome the methodological limitations noted in Deci's research and focus on the multidimensional tasks one might find in actual organizational settings [25]. Further work also is needed to determine the conditions under which the effects of extrinsic rewards on intrinsic motivation are limited in scope (e.g., to voluntary or intentionally motivated behaviors). For example, Calder and Staw [7] showed that the effect is limited to interesting tasks; more recently, Staw, Calder, and Hess [58] showed that payment must be counter to situational norms. The issue at present is to answer the question: when is a reward a genuine reward or a cue that one is attempting to control another or to obtain compliance? The answer may lie in the situational cues present or in subtle cues given off by the allocator of rewards, and so on. This is potentially a difficult question, but certainly not an either-or proposition as presented in past studies.

REFERENCES

1 Adams, J. S. "Inequity in Social Exchange," in L. Berkowitz (Ed.), *Advances in Experimental Social Psychology,* Vol. 2 (New York: Academic Press, 1965).
2 "At Emery Air Freight: Positive Reinforcement Boosts Performance," *Organizational Dynamics* (Winter 1973).
3 Atkinson, J. W. *An Introduction to Motivation* (Princeton, N.J.: Van Nostrand, 1964).

4 Baldwin, A. L. "A Cognitive Theory of Socialization," in D. Goslin (Ed.), *Handbook of Socialization Theory and Research* (Chicago: Rand McNally, 1969).

5 Benware, C., and E. L. Deci. "Attitude Change as a Function of the Inducement for Espousing a Pro-Attitudinal Communication," *Journal of Experimental Social Psychology,* Vol. 11 (1975), 271–278.

6 Calder, B. J., and B. M. Staw. "Interaction of Intrinsic and Extrinsic Motivation: Some Methodological Notes," *Journal of Personality and Social Psychology,* Vol. 31 (1975), 76–80.

7 Calder, B. J., and B. M. Staw. "Self-perception of Intrinsic and Extrinsic Motivation," *Journal of Personality and Social Psychology*, Vol. 31 (1975), 599–605.

8 DeCharms, R. *Personal Causation: The Internal Affective Determinants of Behavior* (New York: Academic Press, 1968).

9 Deci, E. L. "Effects of Externally Mediated Rewards on Intrinsic Motivation," *Journal of Personality and Social Psychology,* Vol. 18 (1971), 105–115.

10 Deci, E. L. "Intrinsic Motivation, Extrinsic Reinforcement, and Inequity," *Journal of Personality and Social Psychology,* Vol. 22 (1972), 113–120.

11 Deci, E. L. "The Effects of Contingent and Non-Contingent Rewards and Controls on Intrinsic Motivation," *Organizational Behavior and Human Performance,* Vol. 8 (1972), 217–229.

12 Deci, E. L. *Intrinsic Motivation* (New York: Plenum, 1975).

13 Deci, E. L. "Notes on the Theory and Metatheory of Intrinsic Motivation," *Organizational Behavior and Human Performance,* Vol. 15 (1975), 130–145.

14 Deci, E. L. "The Hidden Costs of Rewards," *Organizational Dynamics,* Vol. 4, No. 3 (1976), 61–72.

15 Deci, E. L., and W. F. Cascio. "Changes in Intrinsic Motivation as a Function of Negative Feedback and Threats." Paper presented at the 43rd Annual Meeting of the Eastern Psychological Association, Boston, 1972.

16 Deci, E. L., W. F. Cascio, and J. Krusell. "Cognitive Evaluation Theory and Some Comments on the Calder, Staw Critique," *Journal of Personality and Social Psychology,* Vol. 31 (1975), 81–85.

17 Dyer, L., and D. R. Parker. "Classifying Outcomes in Work Motivation Research: An Examination of the Intrinsic-Extrinsic Dichotomy," *Journal of Applied Psychology*, Vol. 60 (1975), 455–458.

18 Eden, D. "Intrinsic and Extrinsic Rewards Both Have Motivating and Demotivating Effects," *Journal of Applied Social Psychology,* in press.

19 Edwards, W. "The Prediction of Decision among Bets," *Journal of Experimental Psychology,* Vol. 50 (1955), 201–214.

20 Festinger, L. *A Theory of Cognitive Dissonance* (Stanford, Calif.: Stanford University Press, 1957).

21 Freud, S. *Collected Papers* (London: Hogarth Press, 1948).

22 Greene, D. *Immediate and Subsequent Effects of Differential Reward Systems on Intrinsic Motivation in Public School Classrooms* (Ph.D. dissertation, Stanford University, 1974).

23 Greene, D., and M. R. Lepper. "Effects of Extrinsic Rewards on Children's Subsequent Intrinsic Interest," *Child Development,* Vol. 45 (1974), 1141–1145.

24 Hamner, W. C. "Reinforcement Theory and Contingency Management in Organizational Settings," in H. L. Tosi and W. C. Hamner (Eds.), *Organizational Behavior and Management: A Contingency Approach* (Chicago, St. Clair Press, 1974), pp. 86–112.

25 Hamner, W. C., and L. W. Foster. "Are Intrinsic and Extrinsic Rewards Additive: A Test of Deci's Cognitive Evaluation Theory of Task Motivation," *Organizational Behavior and Human Performance,* Vol. 14 (1975), 398–415.

26 Heider, F. *The Psychology of Interpersonal Relations* (New York: Wiley, 1958).

27 Heneman, H. G., III, and D. P. Schwab. "Expectancy Theory Predictions of Employee Performance: A Review of the Theory and Evidence," *Psychological Bulletin,* Vol. 78 (1972), 1–9.

28 House, R. J., H. J. Shapiro, and M. A. Wahba. "Expectancy Theory as a Predictor of Work Behavior and Attitude: A Reevaluation of Empirical Evidence," *Decision Sciences,* Vol. 5 (1974), 481–506.

29 Hull, C. L. *Principles of Behavior* (New York: Appleton-Century-Crofts, 1943).

30 Jablonsky, S. F., and D. L. DeVries. "Operant Conditioning Principles Extrapolated to the Theory of Management," *Organizational Behavior and Human Performance,* Vol. 7 (1972), 340–358.

31 Kant, I. "The Critique of Pure Reason" (1781), in R. M. Hutchins (Ed.), *Great Books of the Western World,* Vol. 42 (Chicago: Encyclopedia Britannica, 1952).

32 Kruglanski, A. W., S. Alon, and T. Lewis. "Retrospective Mis-Attribution and Task Enjoyment," *Journal of Experimental Social Psychology,* Vol. 8 (1972), 493–501.

33 Lawler, E. E. *Pay and Organizational Effectiveness* (New York: McGraw-Hill, 1971).

34 Lawler, E. E., and J. R. Hackman. "Impact of Employee Participation in the Development of Pay Incentive Plans: A Field Experiment," *Journal of Applied Psychology,* Vol. 53 (1969), 467–471.

35 Lepper, M. R., and D. Greene. "Turning Play Into Work: Effects of Adult Surveillance and Extrinsic Rewards on Children's Intrinsic Motivation," *Journal of Personality and Social Psychology,* Vol. 31 (1975), 479–486.

36 Lepper, M. R., D. Greene, and R. E. Nisbett. "Undermining Children's Intrinsic Interest with Extrinsic Rewards: A Test of the Overjustification Hypothesis," *Journal of Personality and Social Psychology,* Vol. 28 (1973), 129–137.

37 Lewin, K. *The Conceptual Representation and the Measurement of Psychological Forces* (Durham, N.C.: Duke University Press, 1938).

38 Luthans, F., and R. Kreitner. *Organizational Behavior Modification* (Glenview, Ill.: Scott Foresman, 1975).

39 Luthans, F., M. Martinko, and T. Kess. "An Analysis of the Impact of Contingent Monetary Rewards on Intrinsic Motivation," *Proceedings of the 19th Annual Meeting of the Midwest Academy of Management,* 1976, pp. 209–221.

40 Meyer, H. H. "The Pay for Performance Dilemma," *Organizational Dynamics* (Winter 1973), 39–50.

41 Mitchell, T. R. "Expectancy Models of Job Satisfaction, Occupational Preference and Effort: A Theoretical, Methodological and Empirical Appraisal," *Psychological Bulletin,* Vol. 81 (1974), 1096–1112.

42 Mitchell, T. R., and A. Biglan. "Instrumentality Theories: Current Uses in Psychology," *Psychological Bulletin,* Vol. 76 (1971), 432–454.

43 "New Tool: Reinforcement for Good Work," *Psychology Today* (April 1972), 68–69.

44 Nord, W. R. "Beyond the Teaching Machine: Operant Conditioning in Management," *Organizational Behavior and Human Performance,* Vol. 4 (1969), 375–401.

45 Notz, W. W. "Work Motivation and the Negative Effects of Extrinsic Rewards: A Review with Implications for Theory and Practice," *American Psychologist,* Vol. 30 (1975), 884–891.

46 Ottemann, R., and F. Luthans. "An Experimental Analysis of the Effectiveness of an Organizational Behavior Modification Program in Industry," *Proceedings of the 35th Annual Meeting of the Academy of Management,* 1975, pp. 140–142.

47 Pedalino, E., and V. U. Gamboa. "Behavior Modification and Absenteeism: Intervention in One Industrial Setting," *Journal of Applied Psychology,* Vol. 59 (1974), 694–698.

48 Porter, L. W., and E. E. Lawler. *Managerial Attitudes and Performance* (Homewood, Ill.: Irwin-Dorsey, 1968).

49 Ross, M. "Salience of Reward and Intrinsic Motivation," *Journal of Personality and Social Psychology,* Vol. 32 (1975), 245–254.

50 Rotter, J. B. *Social Learning and Clinical Psychology* (Englewood Cliffs, N.J.: Prentice-Hall, 1954).

51 Salancik, G. R. "Interaction Effects of Performance and Money on Self-Perception of Intrinsic Motivation," *Organizational Behavior and Human Performance,* Vol. 13 (1975), 339–351.

52 Scheflen, K. C., E. E. Lawler, and J. R. Hackman. "Long Term Impact of Employee Participation in the Development of Pay Incentive Plans: A Field Experiment Revisited," *Journal of Applied Psychology,* Vol. 55 (1971), 182–186.

53 Scott, W. E. "The Effects of Extrinsic Rewards on Intrinsic Motivation," *Organizational Behavior and Human Performance,* Vol. 15 (1975), 117–129.

54 Skinner, B. F. *Contingencies of Reinforcement* (New York: Appleton-Century-Crofts, 1969).

55 Skinner, B. F. "The Steep and Thorny Way to a Science of Behavior," *American Psychologist,* Vol. 30 (1975), 42–49.

56 Spence, K. W. *Behavior Theory and Conditioning* (New Haven, Conn.: Yale University Press, 1956).

57 Staw, B. M. *Intrinsic and Extrinsic Motivation* (Morristown, N.J.: General Learning Press, 1976).

58 Staw, B. M., B. J. Calder, and R. K. Hess. "Intrinsic Motivation and Norms About Payment." Unpublished paper, Northwestern University, 1976.

59 Steers, R. M., and L. W. Porter. *Motivation and Work Behavior* (New York: McGraw-Hill, 1975).

60 Tharp, R. G., and R. J. Wetzel. *Behavior Modification in the Natural Environment* (New York: Academic Press, 1969).

60 Thorndike, E. L. *Animal Intelligence* (New York: Macmillan, 1911).

62 Tolman, E. C. "Principles of Performance," *Psychological Review,* Vol. 62 (1955), 315–326.

63 Van de Geer, J. P., and J. M. F. Jaspers. "Cognitive Functions," *Annual Review of Psychology,* Vol. 17 (1966), 145–176.

64 Vroom, V. H. *Work and Motivation* (New York: Wiley, 1964).

65 Watson, J. B. "Psychology as the Behaviorist Views It," *Psychological Review,* Vol. 20 (1913), 158–177.

66 Weiner, B. *Theories of Motivation: From Mechanism to Cognition* (Chicago: Rand McNally, 1972).

REVIEW AND DISCUSSION QUESTIONS

1 Compare and contrast the cognitive and reinforcement views of motivation.
2 What are some of the shortcomings of Deci's experiments?

3 Can the cognitive and reinforcement viewpoints be reconciled? What are some of the best points of each? How does a combination of both aid in understanding motivation.?
4 What is the role of rewards in each approach?
5 Cite a situation in which a manager may use intrinsic rewards to motivate a subordinate. External rewards. Both intrinsic and extrinsic.
6 Can an extrinsic reward become an intrinsic reward? Explain.

Reading 8

A Review of Research on the Application of Goal Setting in Organizations[1]

Gary P. Latham
Gary A. Yukl

Locke's [36] theory of goal setting deals with the relationship between conscious goals or intentions and task performance. The basic premise of the theory is that an individual's conscious intentions regulate his actions. A goal is defined simply as what the individual is consciously trying to do. According to the theory, hard goals result in a higher level of performance than do easy goals, and specific hard goals result in a higher level of performance than do no goals or a generalized goal of "do your best." In addition, the theory states that a person's goals mediate how performance is affected by monetary incentives, time limits, knowledge of results (i.e., performance feedback), participation in decision making, and competition. Goals that are assigned to a person (e.g., by a supervisor) have an effect on behavior only to the degree that they are consciously accepted by the person. Thus, Locke states, "It is not enough to know that an order or request was made; one has to know whether or not the individual heard it and understood it, how he appraised it, and what he decided to do about it before its effects on his behavior can be predicted and explained" [36, p. 174].

Locke's theory is based primarily on a series of well-controlled laboratory experiments with college students who performed relatively simple tasks (e.g., adding numbers) for short periods of time. Some psychologists legitimately have questioned whether something so deceptively simple as setting specific hard goals can increase the performance of employees in real organizational settings, where experimental "demand effects" are absent and acceptance of goals cannot be obtained so easily [5, 15]. Although Locke [36] cites a large number of

From the *Academy of Management Journal*, Vol. 4, 1975, p. 824–845. Reprinted with permission from the authors and the *Academy of Management Journal*.
[1]The authors wish to thank E. A. Locke and T. R. Mitchell for their many helpful suggestions in preparing this review.

laboratory studies in support of his theory, only four field studies are discussed in his article. Most of the field research on goal setting has been conducted since Locke's 1968 theoretical article was published.

The purpose of the present article is to review research on the application of goal setting in organizations, particularly in industry. The article is concerned with evaluating the practical feasibility of goal setting as well as with evaluating Locke's theory. The review includes 27 published and unpublished reports of field research. The major characteristics of these studies are summarized in Table 1.

A few laboratory studies conducted since 1968 also are discussed when the research appears to be particularly relevant for evaluating the theory. The review is divided into sections corresponding to the following aspects of Locke's theory: (a) the effects of specific goals versus generalized goals or no goals; (b) the effects of goal difficulty on performance; and (c) goals as mediators of performance feedback, monetary incentives, and time limits. Some research on goal setting within the context of a management by objectives (MBO) program also is examined. Finally, studies on the relative effectiveness of assigned versus participative goal setting are reviewed. The article concludes with a general evaluation of the theory and a discussion of desirable directions for future research on goal setting.

SPECIFIC VERSUS GENERALIZED GOALS OR NO GOALS

One of the earliest field studies providing information on the effects of goal setting was conducted by Lawrence and Smith [33]. The objective of the study was to investigate the effects of employee participation in decision making and goal setting, rather than to determine the effects of setting specific goals. However, since the researchers compared a participative goal setting condition with a condition in which work problems and company policy were discussed without any explicit goal setting, the study can appropriately be interpreted as an assessment of the effects of goal setting. Lawrence and Smith found that employees were equally satisfied in both conditions, but production (quantity) increased significantly more in the goal setting condition than in the no-goal condition.

Sorcher [53] conducted a study to evaluate the effects of a program consisting of employee participation in goal setting together with "role training" (i.e., an explanation of the importance of each employee's job). This program resulted in substantial improvement in the quality of production, as well as in some increases in quantity of production. A possible limitation of both this and the preceding study is the difficulty in determining the extent to which the improvements were due to the goal setting rather than to other features of the experimental treatment, such as the role training.

A study by Burke and Wilcox [4] assessed the effects of goal setting during the appraisal interview. Data were obtained by means of a questionnaire survey of a sample of nonmanagerial female employees. Burke and Wilcox found that

Table 1   Summary of Goal Setting Field Studies

Investigators	Type of study*	Sample	Criterion	Goal measure or manipulation
Blumenfield and Leidy [2]	C	55 vending machine servicemen	Supervisor report of typical output quantity	Supervisor report of assigned goal level or absence of goals
Burke and Wilcox [4]	C	323 female telephone operators	Self-rated performance improvement	Employee perception that specific goals were set and perceived participation
Carroll and Tosi [6, 7, 8, 9]	C	150 managers	Self-reported goal attainment and effort increase	Self-reported goal difficulty, participation, and feedback
Dachler and Mobley [14]	C	596 production employees	Output quantity†	Employees' stated goals
Duttagupta [16]	C	18 R&D managers	Self-reported motivation	Self-reported participation and feedback
French, Kay, and Meyer [17]	E	92 managers	Self-rated goal acceptance, self and superior-rated goal attainment	Assigned vs. participative goal setting in MBO and perceived participation
Ivancevich [22]	QE	166 managers	Change in self-rated need satisfaction	Goal setting in MBO programs
Ivancevich [23]	QE	181 groups of salesmen and production workers	Sales; output quantity and quality†	MBO with and without reinforcement vs. comparison group
Ivancevich, Donnelly, and Lyon [24]	QE	166 managers	Change in self-rated need satisfaction	Goal setting in MBO programs
Kolb and Boyatzis [26]	C	111 management students in T-groups	Self- and trainer-rated behavior change	Self-reported goal for behavior change
Kolb, Winters, and Berlew [27]	E-C	79 management students in T-groups	Self- and trainer-rated behavior change	Self-reported goal for behavior change
Latham and Baldes [29]	QE	36 truck drivers	Net weight of truck loads†	Assigned individual goals vs. prior no-goal condition
Latham and Kinne [30]	E	20 logging crews	Quantity of output†	Assigned group goals vs. no-goal control condition
Latham and Yukl [32]	E	48 logging crews	Quantity of output†	Assigned group goals, participative group goals, and no-goal control condition
Latham and Locke [31]	QE	379 logging crews	Quantity of output†	Time limitations on output disposal

Table 1 *(Continued)*

Investigators	Type of study*	Sample	Criterion	Goal measure or manipulation
Lawrence and Smith [33]	E	22 office and garment factory workers	Improvement in output quantity†	Participative group goal setting vs. discussion without goal setting
Mendleson [42]	C	25 superior-subordinate pairs in 8 companies	Superior ratings of subordinate performance	Superior-subordinate reported degree of goal setting
Raia [48]	QE	112 managers and supervisors	Output quantity†	MBO participative goal setting vs. prior no-goal condition
Raia [49]	QE	74 managers and supervisors	Output quantity†	(See above)
Ronan, Latham, and Kinne [50]	C	1184 logging crews	Quantity of output†	Supervisor reported goal specificity
Shetty and Carlisle [52]	C	109 professors in a public university	Perceived improvement in performance and commitment	Goal setting in MBO
Sorcher [53]	QE	14 assembly work groups	Improvement in output quality†	Participative goal setting vs. prior no-goal condition
Stedry and Kay [54]	E-C	19 manufacturing work groups	Productivity and rework costs†	Assigned goals for two performance criteria
Steers [55]	C	133 female first-line supervisors	Superior ratings of performance	Perceived goal specificity, goal difficulty, and participation
Wexley and Nemeroff [58]	E	27 managers and 125 subordinates	Absenteeism,† LBDQ, and JDI	Assigned goals vs. no goals
Zander, Forward, and Albert [63]	C	255 members of 64 United Fund campaigns	Dollars collected†	Official annual goal set by each local committee
Zander and Newcomb [62]	C	149 United Fund campaign	Dollars collected†	Official annual goal set by each local committee

*E = experiment, C = correlational study, QE = quasi-experimental study.
†Denotes "hard" objective criterion.

employee perception of the extent to which an employee and her supervisor set mutual goals was correlated with the employee's self-reported desire to improve her performance ($r = .45$) and her self-ratings of actual performance improvement ($r = .29$).

In another correlational study, Blumenfeld and Leidy [2] found that soft drink salesmen and servicemen checked more vending machines when specific hard goals were assigned than when no goals were assigned. However, assignment of easy goals did not result in better performance than no goals.

In a factor analysis of data obtained from 292 independent pulpwood producers, Ronan, Latham, and Kinne [50] found that the effects of goal setting depended on the extent to which logging crews were closely supervised. Goal setting was correlated with high performance only when it was accompanied by close supervision. Goal setting without supervision correlated with labor turnover but not with performance. Supervision that did not include goal setting was not correlated with any performance criterion. In a follow-up study by the same authors, an analysis of variance was performed on the man-day production of 892 producers. These producers were classified on the basis of the three factor patterns cited above: (a) producers who supervise their men and set production goals; (b) "absentee" producers who set production goals only; and (c) producers who supervise their men but do not set production goals. The results indicated that producers who supervise their employees and set production goals have higher productivity than do producers who supervise their men but do not set production goals. The difference between "absentee producers" who set production goals only, and producers who set production goals and supervise their men was in the expected direction. In summarizing the results of these two studies, Ronan, Latham, and Kinne [50] interpreted their findings as supporting the conclusion that setting a specific task goal does not affect performance in an industrial setting unless a supervisor is present to encourage goal acceptance.

A limitation of the studies on pulpwood producers is that they were correlational in nature, and inferences about causality could not be made with confidence. In order to overcome this limitation, Latham and Kinne [30] matched and randomly assigned 20 pulpwood producers and their crews to either a one day training program in goal setting or to a control condition. Data on cords per man-hour production, turnover, absenteeism, and injuries then were collected for 12 consecutive weeks. Analyses of variance revealed that those individuals who received training in goal setting had a significant increase in production and a decrease in absenteeism compared to workers in the control condition. No significant trend effects over time were found. There were no significant differences between conditions with respect to injuries or turnover, which were very low in both conditions.

Latham and Baldes [29] conducted a quasi-experimental study of a goal setting program with unionized truck drivers. The goal setting program was designed to increase the net weight of truckloads of logs, which previously had been considerably below the legal limit. A specific hard goal of 94 percent of the legal maximum was assigned to the drivers, which resulted in an immediate increase in average net weight from approximately 60 percent of the legal maximum to approximately 94 percent. Performance remained relatively stable at this improved level over the nine month study period, resulting in a cost savings of over a quarter of a million dollars for the company. Although the performance improvement was attributed primarily to goal specificity, anecdotal information suggested that goal setting also led to informal competition among drivers, and this competition probably helped to maintain goal commitment over the nine month period.

Latham and Yukl [32] conducted an experiment in which two methods of goal setting were compared to a control condition in which no specific goals were set. Goal setting resulted in higher performance of logging crews in only one of the four goal setting conditions. Some problems in the implementation of the goal setting program, such as a lack of support by local management, were cited as the likely reason for the failure of goal setting in the other three conditions. This study is discussed in more detail in the section "Assigned versus Participative Goal Setting."

Mendleson [42] conducted a questionnaire survey of goal setting in eight companies and analyzed the responses of 25 pairs of superior-subordinate managers. The extent of goal setting, as perceived by both the superior and the subordinate was positively correlated with superior ratings of subordinate promotability, but not with superior ratings of subordinate performance. Due to the lack of consistency in these results, and the low reliability of the goal setting measure developed by Mendleson for use in this study, it is difficult to draw firm conclusions.

In a study differing in several respects from those preceding, Kolb and Bayatzis [26] examined the effect of goal setting on behavior change and attainment of personal development goals, rather than on performance and task goal attainment. In a management course requiring extensive T-Group participation, each student established a personal development goal relevant to his behavior in groups and formulated a method for measuring goal attainment. At the end of each T-group session, the students filled out a form recording relevant feedback received from other group members during the session. Behavior change after the 30 hours of T-group sessions was reported by each student and was rated by the group trainers. Positive behavior change was greater for behavior dimensions related to the students' goals than for behavior dimensions not related to the goals.

Wexley and Nemeroff [58] evaluated the effects of goal setting and feedback when used in conjunction with role playing exercises in a two day supervisory training program. In two variations of the experimental treatment, hospital supervisors were assigned goals for behavior improvement, and they received coaching and feedback regarding their performance as leaders in the role playing exercises. The supervisors also were assigned specific behavioral goals after the first and third weeks back on the job, and additional feedback and coaching were provided. A control group of supervisors participated in the role playing, but were not assigned goals or given feedback either during or after the training. Wexley and Nemeroff found that supervisors in the experimental conditions had less subordinate absenteeism and more positive improvement in leadership behavior than did supervisors in the control group.

In summary, eleven studies in organizations have examined the effects of setting specific goals. In ten of these studies, evidence in support of the effectiveness of setting specific goals was obtained, although some possible limiting conditions also were discovered. Only one study [42] failed to find any support for the goal specificity proposition of Locke's theory, and the measure of goal setting in this study was of dubious validity.

EFFECTS OF SPECIFIC GOALS IN MBO PROGRAMS

Indirect evidence on the effectiveness of setting specific goals is provided by studies of MBO programs in organizations. Management by objectives is an approach to planning and performance appraisal that attempts to clarify employee role requirements, relate employee performance to organization goals, improve manager-subordinate communication, facilitate objective evaluation of employee performance, and stimulate employee motivation. An essential feature of the MBO approach is the setting of specific performance goals and, in many cases, goals for personal development of the employee. Employees are expected to be more committed to goals as a result of participation in setting them and involvement in the development or criteria for assessing goal attainment. Most of the published literature on MBO consists of anecdotal reports about employee reactions and the problems encountered in implementing an MBO program in a particular organization, or of discussions about the best procedures for implementing MBO [e.g., 3, 18, 19, 20, 25, 28, 46, 59]. Only eight studies were found in which the effects of specific goals versus generalized goals or no goals were assessed with an acceptable degree of scientific rigor.

The first of these studies was conducted by Raia [48] in 15 plants of the Purex Corporation. The MBO program resulted in an increase in productivity over a 10-month period, even though the goals had to be revised downward several times during the fiscal year. Some improvements in absenteeism, accidents, grievances, turnover, and customer service also were noted in the plants that set goals for these criteria. The percentage of plants reporting an improvement for these criteria ranged from 33 percent for absenteeism to 80 percent for accident reduction.

Raia [49] obtained an additional 12 months of data from a follow-up study in the same company. These data indicated a stabilization of productivity at the higher level attained during the earlier period, and the attainment of budgetary goals continued to improve. The major weakness of Raia's research is that, with neither a control group nor an immediate large improvement in the performance curve following implementation of the MBO program, it is impossible to determine if the improvement was due to MBO. The gradual improvements in performance could have been due to extraneous conditions unrelated to the MBO program.

French, Kay, and Meyer [17] conducted an experiment on goal setting within an MBO program at General Electric Company. The sample consisted of 92 low-level managers who either participated in goal setting with their boss or were assigned goals during an appraisal interview. Regardless of how the goals were set, when criticisms of the subordinate manager were translated into specific goals, both the subordinate and the boss reported that twice as much improvement in performance occurred than when criticisms were made without being formulated as specific goals. No objective criterion measures were obtained in this study, however.

Shetty and Carlisle [52] evaluated an MBO program in a public university by means of a questionnaire survey of faculty opinions. There was no indication that the MBO program resulted in any substantial improvement in performance or commitment to the university. However, it should be noted that the criterion measures were entirely subjective and of questionable validity, and no measure of the extent of goal setting was obtained.

Ivancevich, Donnelly, and Lyon [24] did a comparative study of two companies with an MBO program. Managers in both companies were asked to complete a Porter-type job satisfaction questionnaire before the MBO programs were initiated and again after the programs were in effect for a year. Need satisfaction improved in one company but not in the other. Interviews with the managers to obtain their reactions to the program revealed that MBO was used primarily at the top management level in the second company. The MBO program was never effectively implemented with lower level managers, due in part to a lack of top management involvement in setting up the program. Some problems also were found in the first company, despite the improvement in need deficiency scores. The most frequent complaints were an excess of paperwork and the difficulty of stating quantitative goals for all aspects of the job. These same problems have been noted in some of the case study and discussion articles on MBO; they also were found by Raia [49].

In what was essentially a follow-up study, Ivancevich [22] measured need satisfaction again in the two companies 18 to 20 months after the MBO program had been initiated. He found that any improvements in need satisfaction were short-lived and had disappeared by the time of his final measurement. This extinction phenomenon was attributed to a lack of sustained top management commitment to the program and the absence of any additional training or reinforcement after the program was initiated. Although this research by Ivancevich and his associates suggests some conditions which may prevent an MBO program from being implemented and maintained, the absence of a performance criterion makes it impossible to determine whether MBO ever really had an effect on the behavior and performance of the managers in these companies.

In a more recent study, Ivancevich [23] used objective measures of employee performance to evaluate an MBO program in a manufacturing company. The performance of production departments in three plants was compared. One plant had an MBO program for supervisors which included encouragement and support from top management in the form of letters, memos, telephone conversations, and meetings. The second plant had an MBO program that was not given encouragement and support by top management. The third plant did not have an MBO program and served as a control condition. Only the production department in the first plant had a sustained improvement in quantity and quality of performance over the course of the three year study.

In addition, there was a significant decrease in absenteeism and grievances in this one plant.

Ivancevich also compared the performance of marketing departments in the three plants. Unlike the production workers, salesmen in the two plants with an MBO program were involved in the goal setting process along with their supervisors. The results indicated that sales performance improved in both MBO programs, but there was no improvement in the plant without an MBO program.

In the final MBO study, by Steers [55], questionnaire data on task-goal perceptions and need strength were obtained from 133 female first-line supervisors in a company with an ongoing MBO program. In addition, ratings of goal effort and performance for the supervisors were obtained from each supervisor's boss. Steers found that a supervisor's perception of goal specificity was significantly correlated with goal effort but not with the rating of overall performance. Steers also found that these relationships were moderated by the supervisor's need for achievement. Goal specificity was significantly correlated with goal effort and overall performance only for those supervisors with a high need for achievement.

In summary, the eight studies on MBO appear to provide a diverse set of findings. However, if we disregard the studies which had no measure of performance or goal attainment, the results are more consistent. French et al. [17], Ivancevich [23], Steers [55], and Raia [48, 49] all found some support for the proposition that setting specific goals can result in improved performance although some limiting conditions were present. The major problem with this MBO research as a means of evaluating goal setting is that MBO programs typically involve other changes besides the introduction of goal setting. Therefore, it is difficult to determine the extent to which performance improvements in these studies were due to goal setting rather than to other changes.

THE EFFECTS OF GOAL DIFFICULTY ON PERFORMANCE

Locke [36] proposed that, as long as goals are accepted, the more difficult the goals the higher the level of performance. This proposition is supported by results from a number of laboratory studies reported by Locke [36], including correlations between stated goals and subsequent performance and experiments with different levels of assigned goals. Seven field studies also have attempted to determine the effects of goal difficulty.

In the first study, by Stedry and Kay [54], goal difficulty was manipulated for two different performance criteria: productivity and rework cost. Performance goals were set either at the average level of performance attained during the previous six months (easy goal) or at a level substantially higher than average previous performance (difficult goal). The 19 foremen were assigned in a nonrandom manner to one of the following four experimental conditions: (a) easy productivity goal and difficult rework goal; (b) difficult productivity goal and easy rework goal; (c) both goals easy; (d) both goals difficult. In addition to the experimental manipulation, Stedry and Kay measured the extent to which the foremen actually perceived the assigned goals to be easy, challenging, or impossible, and these perceptions corresponded closely to actual difficulty. Performance improvement was defined as the difference between average performance during the 13 weeks after the manipulation and the 13 weeks before the manipulation. The data were analyzed first for each criterion separately. Performance improved more for the goals perceived to be easy or challenging than for the goals perceived to be impossible; and for the impossible goals, performance actually decreased. This finding is consistent with Locke's theory if it can be assumed that impossible goals are not accepted. Performance improvement was not significantly related to the difficulty of the productivity goal or the difficulty of the rework goal when analyzed separately. However, the theory may be tested more appropriately by an analysis of the combined difficulty of both goals since they are independent and a person must decide how to allocate his effort between them. Stedry and Kay conducted a regression analysis and found that total perceived difficulty for both goals was significantly related to a composite criterion of performance improvement ($R^2 = .59$), which is clearly in support of Locke's theory.

Zander and Newcomb [62] examined the effects of goals set in United Fund campaigns in 149 communities. They found a significant relationship between the difficulty of the goal, in terms of how far it was above the previous year's performance, and subsequent performance improvement. When the sample was subdivided according to the frequency of goal attainment success in the previous four years, prior success was found to be a moderator of the effects of goal difficulty. Goal difficulty was significantly correlated with subsequent perform-ance improvement for communities with more prior successes than failures ($r = .76$) and for communities with an equal number of successes and failures ($r = .73$). However, for communities with more prior failures than successes in goal attainment, goal difficulty was not significantly correlated with performance improvement.

One explanation for these results is provided in a follow-up study by Zander, Forward, and Albert [63]. They compared consistently successful and consistently unsuccessful United Funds and found that the successful Funds set higher absolute goals and attained a higher absolute level of performance. However, expressed as a percentage of the prior year's performance, the goals of successful Funds were more reasonable than were those of unsuccessful Funds. Furthermore, members of the successful Funds attributed more importance to attainment of the goal than did members of failing Funds. The unreasonableness of the goal and the lack of importance attributed to it by the members of consistently failing Funds suggest that there was little goal acceptance and commitment in these Funds. Therefore, it is not surprising that goal difficulty was unrelated to performance for the unsuccessful Funds.

Blumenfeld and Leidy [2] evaluated the effect of goal difficulty in an incentive program designed to motivate salesmen and servicemen to check and adjust soft drink vending machines to an optimal temperature. Employees who were assigned hard goals checked more vending machines than did employees who were assigned easy goals.

Steers [55] surveyed female first-line supervisors in a company with an MBO program and analyzed the relationship between perceived goal difficulty and performance ratings made by each supervisor's boss. No significant correlation was obtained, even when the sample was subdivided according to measures of supervisor needs.

In another survey of managers in an MBO program, Carroll and Tosi [6, 7] found that perceived goal difficulty was positively correlated with the self-rated effort of managers who were high in self-assurance ($r = .26$) and maturity ($r = .31$) and who perceived rewards to be contingent upon performance ($r = .26$). For managers with low scores on self-assurance and maturity or who did not perceive a strong contingency between rewards and performance, goal difficulty was negatively correlated ($r = -.25, -.26, -.19$) with self-rated effort. For the combined sample of managers, there was no significant correlation between goal difficulty and self-rated effort. Although Carroll and Tosi used a different criterion measure from that used by Steers [55], these results suggest that Steers also might have found significant correlations if he had used similar moderator variables.

Dachler and Mobley [14] examined the relationship between stated performance goals and objective performance of production workers in two organizations. Performance was measured in terms of piece rate earnings in the first organization and work rate as a percentage of standard in the second organization. A significant positive correlation ($r = .46$) between an employee's stated current goal and his performance was found in the first organization. This relationship was moderated by employee tenure. The correlation was significant ($r = .44$) for employees who had been on the job for more than two years but not for employees who had been on the job for less than two years ($r = .13$). This difference was consistent with the additional finding that long tenure employees perceived desirable outcomes to be contingent upon performance, whereas short tenure employees did not, presumably because of their limited experience in their current job situation.

The current performance goal stated by an employee also was significantly correlated with performance in the second organization. However, the correlation was very low ($r = .16$), and the relationship was not moderated by job tenure. The difference in magnitude of relationships between goal level and performance for the two organizations may have been due to differences in criterion measures, but more likely it is due to the lower perceived contingency of desirable outcomes on performance in the second organization, in which jobs were less structured and where there was no incentive system. This interpretation is consistent with the tenure results found in the first organization and with the findings of Carroll and Tosi [6, 7] summarized earlier.

In summary, seven studies have examined the relationship between goal difficulty and performance. With one exception [55], support was found in each study for Locke's [36] proposition that hard goals lead to greater performance than do easy goals, as long as the goals are accepted. The major limitation of this research is that, except for the study by Stedry and Kay [54], the effects of goal difficulty were assessed by means of a correlational design rather than by manipulation of goal difficulty. Some of the correlational studies attempted to deal with the problem of determining causality when there is likely to be an influence of prior performance on goals by measuring both difficulty and performance in relation to prior performance. Since the results from these studies, most other correlational studies, the experiment by Stedry and Kay [54], and a large number of laboratory experiments are generally consistent, it can be concluded that there is strong support for Locke's goal difficulty proposition.

Because goal acceptance is a necessary condition of this proposition, it is important to identify the factors that determine whether employees will accept hard goals. Some of the studies reviewed in this section provide insights into the nature of these determinants. The variables found to moderate the effects of goal difficulty probably also influence goal acceptance. These variables include the employee's perception that the goal is reasonable, and the perceived contingency between goal attainment and desirable outcomes. Hard goals are more likely to be perceived as challenging rather than impossible if the employee has a high degree of self-assurance and has previously had more successes in goal attainment than failures. The perceived instrumentality of goal attainment depends largely upon the type of incentive systems and the objectivity of performance appraisal in the organization.

GOALS AS MEDIATORS OF PERFORMANCE FEEDBACK, MONETARY INCENTIVES, AND TIME LIMITS

Locke's [36] theory proposes that the effects of performance feedback, monetary incentives, and time limits are mediated by goal setting and conscious intentions. Performance feedback or "knowledge of results" can lead to an increase in effort and performance for at least four different reasons: (a) feedback may induce a person who previously did not have specific goals to set a goal to improve performance by a certain amount; (b) feedback may induce a person to raise his goal level after attaining a previous goal; (c) feedback that informs a person that his current level of effort is insufficient to attain his goal may result in greater effort; and (d) feedback may inform a person of ways in which to improve his methods of performing the task. Locke's theory is concerned primarily with the first three "motivational" aspects of feedback and not with the final "cueing" aspect. Locke also proposed that the form or quality of feedback partly determines what effect the feedback will have. These feedback propositions are supported by a substantial number of laboratory studies that are reviewed in the article by Locke, Cartledge, and Koeppel [38]. Some recent laboratory studies have provided additional support and insight [e.g., 13, 37, 60].

Field studies in which goal setting and performance feedback are independently manipulated, or feedback is manipulated and the effects of goals are controlled, would provide evidence as to the validity of Locke's feedback propositions in real organizations. Unfortunately, no studies of this type were found. In fact, only a few field studies have investigated the effects of performance feedback on subsequent performance. Since use of feedback alone may be viewed by some persons as an alternative approach to goal setting, it is worthwhile to briefly review studies on the effects of feedback in comparison to no feedback. In addition, since the amount and frequency of feedback necessary for an effective goal setting program have not been established, it also is useful to examine studies on the effects of feedback in combination with goal setting.

Three studies investigated the effects of feedback on performance in the absence of explicit goal setting. Hundal [21] found that feedback resulted in increased productivity of industrial workers with a repetitive task; productivity also was higher than was that of a no-feedback control group. However, Chapanis [11] failed to find any effect of feedback on the performance of students hired to work an hour per day for 24 days on a repetitive job. Miller [44] found that feedback regarding errors resulted in only a temporary improvement in performance quality for manufacturing employees, unless used in conjunction with incentives or the threat of negative consequences for failure to improve. The improvement that occurred with feedback plus incentives may well have been due to employees setting goals to reduce errors. However, since the subjects in these studies were not asked if they set private goals, no firm conclusions can be drawn in relation to Locke's theory. With so few studies and the inconsistent results, it also would be premature to reach any conclusions about the effectiveness of feedback as a motivational technique when used without explicit goal setting. Of course, the importance of feedback for learning, as opposed to motivation, has been well established in the literature on training research.

A study on the effects of feedback in conjunction with goal setting was conducted by Kolb, Winters, and Berlew [27]. Explicit goals for behavior change were set by students in a management course with extensive T-group participation. In T-groups instructed to provide relevant feedback, more positive change (self-rated and trainer-rated) occurred than in T-groups instructed not to discuss the behavior change projects of their members. The results also supported the importance of feedback quality (e.g., timing, relevance, and manner of presentation) for goal attainment. In a study of managers in a company with an MBO program, Carroll and Tosi [8] found that the amount and frequency of perceived feedback were positively correlated with self-rated goal attainment, but not with an increase in self-rated effort level. Duttagupta [16] found that frequency and amount of feedback were associated with greater self-reported motivation and a better perceived understanding of job requirements by the R&D managers in a company with an MBO program. Finally, Steers [55] found that the amount of perceived feedback in a company with an MBO program was positively correlated with goal effort and overall performance ratings for supervisors with high achievement motivation, but not for supervisors with low achievement motivation. Although these results tend to support the conclusion that frequent, relevant feedback is needed for a successful goal setting program, the evidence is limited, and further research clearly is warranted.

In contrast to performance feedback, monetary incentives are more likely to increase goal acceptance and commitment than to induce a person to set a harder goal. "Offering an individual money for output may motivate him to set his goals higher than he would otherwise, but this will depend on how much money he wishes to make and how much effort he wishes to expend to make it" [36, p. 185]. Locke's propositions about goals as mediators of monetary incentives are based on a series of five laboratory studies in which he found that, when goal level was controlled or partialled out, incentives did not affect performance. Also, a particular goal level resulted in the same performance, regardless of whether monetary incentives were provided. A similar type of field study would provide evidence regarding the generalizability of these findings to real organizations. Unfortunately, no studies of this type have been conducted in an organizational setting. However, a recent laboratory study by Prichard and Curtis [47] appears to be relevant to evaluating Locke's proposition. Prichard and Curtis point out that Locke used small incentives with little potential for motivating his subjects. In a study designed to overcome this potential limitation, the effects of assigned goals were compared for three levels of incentive (large, small, and no incentive). Prichard and Curtis found, as did Locke, that small incentives did not increase performance in comparison to no incentive when goal level was held constant. However, contrary to Locke, large incentives resulted in higher performance than did small or no incentives when goal level was held constant. Moreover, the self-reported commitment of subjects to the goal was not greater in the large incentive condition than in the small and no-incentive conditions. In other words, Prichard and Curtis found that incentives can affect performance independently of goal level and goal commitment.

Latham and Locke [31] conducted a study which provided evidence in support of Locke's theory that time limits affect performance only to the degree that they lead to goal setting. The authors found that when pulp and paper mills limited their buying of wood to one or two days per week, they implicitly urged a higher production goal (per man-hour) on independent harvesting crews. To minimize income loss, the crews tried to harvest as much wood in one or two days as they normally harvested in five days. Thus logging crews with limitations on the number of days they could sell timber had higher productivity than crews without such restrictions. These findings are in basic agreement with the results of the early British studies [51] which found that a reduction in the work week led to a higher hourly rate of production.

In summary, there is little relevant data for evaluating Locke's proposition that goals mediate the effects of performance feedback. The few field studies on the effects of feedback alone or in combination with goal setting are not directly relevant for testing the mediation hypothesis. The three studies on the consequences of feedback without explicit goal setting do not yield consistent results. The four studies on feedback in combination with goal setting tend to support the importance of frequent, relevant feedback for goal setting effectiveness. No field studies have been conducted to provide a direct test of Locke's mediation proposition concerning monetary incentives, but one laboratory study provides evidence contrary to the proposition and raises doubts about the external validity of the earlier supporting results found by Locke and associates. One field study provides indirect support for the hypothesis that goals mediate the effects of time limits on performance.

ASSIGNED VERSUS PARTICIPATIVE GOAL SETTING

Locke's [36] theory specifies that goals mediate the effects of employee participation in decision making. The theory is not directly concerned with the manner in which goals are set. However, the most appropriate manner of setting goals is an important practical question. The consequences of subordinate participation in decision making have been the subject of considerable speculation in the leadership and management literature. According to the classical management theories [40], it is the leader's responsibility to assign goals and ensure that they are attained. Humanistic organization theories [35, 41] favor substantial subordinate participation in decision making, and such participation is believed to increase acceptance of the decision and commitment to implement it. More recently, various contingency theories [39, 45, 56, 57, 61] have proposed that participation is effective in some situations but not in others. Leadership research on the effects of employee participation in decision making tends to support the contingency approach.

Several studies have attempted to assess the effects of different amounts of subordinate participation in goal setting. In the first of these studies, French, Kay, and Meyer [17] compared assigned and participative goal setting during performance appraisal interviews with lower-level managers. In addition to the experimental manipulation of participation, the perceived participation of the managers and observer judgments of the amount of participation during the appraisal interview also were measured, as well as the managers' perception of the usual amount of participation they previously had been allowed. Perception of the usual amount of participation, which was measured prior to the appraisal interview, was positively related to acceptance of job goals. However, goal acceptance and goal attainment were not significantly related to the other participation measures and were not affected by the experimental manipulation. A number of limitations of this study make it difficult to reach any clear conclusions. The participation manipulation was not always successful, the participation treatment was somewhat confounded with the usual level of participation that occurred between the supervisor and his subordinates, and no objective performance measures were obtained. Despite these problems and the scarcity of significant differences, the authors reach the following conclusions in another report of this research [43]: (a) subordinates who received a high participation level in the performance interview in most cases achieved a greater percentage of their improvement goals; (b) men who usually worked under high participation levels performed best on goals they set for themselves, and men who usually worked under low participation levels performed best on goals that their boss set for them.

Carroll and Tosi [6, 7] included a measure of perceived influence in establishing goals in their questionnaire survey of managers in an MBO program. The results indicate that participation in goal setting was not significantly correlated with the amount of goal attainment or effort increase. However, there was some indication that a manager's self-assurance moderated the effects of participation. Participation in goal setting tended to be positively correlated ($r = .33$) with effort increase for managers with high self-assurance but not for managers with low self-assurance ($r = .08$).

In a study by Duttagupta [16] R&D managers in an MBO program were interviewed and answered a short questionnaire. No relationship was found between self-reported motivation and perceived influence in the goal setting process.

In a questionnaire survey of first-line supervisors, Steers [55] found that perceived participation was significantly correlated with goal effort and overall performance ratings for supervisors with low need for achievement ($r = .41$), but was not significantly correlated for supervisors with a high need for achievement. For the overall sample, there was only a low correlation ($r = .20$). The major limitation of this study and the study by Carroll and Tosi is the subjective nature of the participation in goal setting measures. The leadership literature suggests that subordinate judgments about their influence in decision making are of questionable accuracy. Furthermore, since the conclusions reached in these studies are based on a large number of correlations and correlational comparisions, there also is a strong possibility that some significant findings occurred by chance. Therefore, the results should be regarded as tentative until they are replicated.

Latham and Yukl [32] conducted a field experiment on the effects of assigned and participative goal setting. Specifically, they attempted to determine which method of goal setting was most effective for independent logging crews with different levels of education. Twenty-four "educated" crews were randomly assigned to a participative goal setting condition, an assigned goal setting condition, or a "do your best" condition. Twenty-four educationally disadvantaged crews in another geographical location were randomly assigned to the same three conditions. In the sample of educationally disadvantaged crews, the participative goal setting condition yielded higher performance and more frequent goal attainment during the eight week period of the study than did the assigned goal setting condition. The average goal level was significantly higher for the participative condition than for the assigned goal condition, which suggests that the performance difference was due in part to greater goal difficulty in the participative condition. The fact that goal attainment was higher in the participative condition than in the assigned condition, despite more difficult goals, suggests that goal acceptance was increased by participation in the goal setting process.

In the sample of educated crews, performance, goal attainment, and average goal level were not significantly different for the participative and assigned conditions. Due to the unavoidable confounding of education level with geographical region and other factors in this study, it is not clear whether the failure to find a significant difference in the educated sample was due to education level or to other factors. Anecdotal evidence suggested that the goal setting program was not effectively implemented for this sample due to the lack of support by local management.

In summary, five studies in organizations provide data on the effects of participation in goal setting, but each of these studies has major limitations or problems. None of the studies provides an adequate test of Locke's mediation proposition regarding the effects of participation. With respect to the more applied question of whether participative goal setting results in higher perform- ance than assigned goals, the results are not consistent. Although most of the studies found some evidence supporting the superiority of participative goal setting, a significant difference is found only under certain conditions or with certain types of employees. The most satisfactory way of explaining these discrepancies probably is in terms of a contingency model, but further research is needed to clarify the nature of the limiting conditions and the manner in which the moderating variables operate.

DISCUSSION AND CONCLUSIONS

The organizational research reviewed in this article provides strong support for Locke's [36] propositions that specific goals increase performance and that difficult goals, if accepted, result in better performance than do easy goals. The field studies do not provide relevant evidence concerning Locke's propositions that goal setting mediates the effects of participation, monetary incentives, and performance feedback. With respect to monetary incentives, the results from a laboratory experiment by Prichard and Curtis [47] are contrary to the mediation proposition. Field research designed to test the mediation propositions and to investigate the possiblity that participation, monetary incentives, and feedback affect performance independently of goal setting, or interact with goal setting, is clearly desirable.

Perhaps the greatest deficiency of Locke's theory is the failure to specify the determinants of goal acceptance and goal commitment. In recent research, investigators have used expectancy theory concepts to aid in explaining how goal acceptance is determined. In field studies by Dachler and Mobley [14] and Steers [55] and in a laboratory study by Cartledge [10], goal acceptance and performance appeared to be predictable from measures of a person's expectancy that effort will lead to goal attainment, his expectancy that goal attainment will lead to various outcomes, and the subjective values (valence) assigned to those outcomes. These studies and the accompanying efforts to develop a model integrating goal theory with expectancy theory appear to be the most promising direction for further elaboration of goal theory.

Another important gap in theory development and research is the manner in which goal acceptance, goal difficulty, and other aspects of goal setting combine to determine a person's task effort. This subject takes on added complexity as a history of successes or failures in goal attainment is accumulated. For example, if pressures exist to set excessively hard goals or to prevent a downward revision of goals that have proved to be unreasonable, a series of failures in goal attainment is likely, and this in turn will greatly reduce the likelihood of subsequent goal acceptance by subordinates. There clearly is a need for more longitudinal research on the complex interactions that determine if goal setting will be effective. An understanding of *why* goal setting affects employee performance has only begun.

Another promising approach for elaboration of Locke's theory is the inclusion of propositions concerning the cueing function of goals. The usefulness of goal setting for clarifying role requirements and the effects of goals on the employee's allocation of effort to different aspects of his job have been emphasized in the MBO literature. The effects of goals and feedback on learning as well as motivation, specifically the development of better job procedures by employees, also have been noted in some of the goal setting studies. As yet, these processes have not been incorporated into Locke's goal setting theory in any systematic fashion.

As for the practical feasibility of goal setting as a means of improving employee performance, the research shows goal setting programs to be effective over an extended time period in a variety of organizations, at both the managerial and nonmanagerial levels. Substantial increases in performance were obtained in some of the studies without any special prizes or incentives for goal attainment, although in other studies reward contingencies were an important consideration. Assigned goal setting and participative goal setting each was effective in several studies. In the few studies where the relative effectiveness of these two goal setting methods could be compared, the results were not conclusive. Further research on the consequences or subordinate participation in goal setting and on variables moderating these effects is highly desirable.

Although goal setting was found to be effective in many situations, some limiting conditions and moderating variables also were identified. One determinant of goal setting feasibility may be the complexity of the job and the availability of reasonably accurate performance measures. Goal setting for simple jobs with only one or two important performance dimensions may be much easier and more effective than goal setting for jobs with many performance dimensions, especially when some of these dimensions cannot be measured quantitatively. Since managerial jobs usually are of this complex nature, it is not surprising that goal setting programs with managers have encountered more problems and have been less successful than goal setting with nonmanagerial employees. One problem found by Levinson [34] is the tendency to neglect aspects of the job that are not easily quantified, such as customer service. The way in which multiple goals direct behavior and effort allocation is an important applied question that has received little attention except for the initial exploration of this subject by Charnes and Stedry [12] and Stedry and Kay [54].

Additional research is needed to determine what goal setting procedures are most effective for very complex jobs, and to determine if there are some jobs for which goal setting may be impractical or even dysfunctional.

Another type of limiting condition found in several studies is the degree of managerial attention and support received by a goal setting program. In some of the studies in which goal setting was unsuccessful, the failure was attributed to a lack of strong support by key managerial personnel. The importance of management support and involvement in all types of organizational interventions has been emphasized in the organization development literature as well as the MBO literature.

The interrelationships among jobs in an organization are another possible limiting condition for effective goal setting. There first is the problem of evaluating individual performance and goal attainment by employees with highly interdependent jobs. As Levinson has pointed out, "The more a man's effectiveness depends upon what other people do, the less he himself can be held responsible for the outcome of his efforts" [34, p. 127]. Group goals can be used instead of individual goals for some types of interdependent jobs, but this remedy would not be applicable to many types of jobs. An additional problem with setting specific goals for interdependent jobs was found by Baumler [1]. He conducted a laboratory study of simulated organizations with either independent or interdependent jobs and compared the effects of defined criteria (i.e., specific goals) and no defined criteria in both types of organizations. Specific goals facilitated performance when jobs were independent but inhibited performance when jobs were interdependent. The inhibiting effects in the latter case were attributed to coordination difficulties and a preoccupation with individual goals at the expense of overall organizational effectiveness. The possibility that individual goal setting can be dysfunctional for interdependent jobs is important enough to warrant further investigation in actual as opposed to simulated organizations.

Even when goal setting is feasible for a job, it may not be effective for all types of employees who hold that job. Individual traits were found to be moderators of goal setting effectiveness in several studies. Needs, attitudes, personality, and perhaps education and cultural background may determine whether an employee will respond favorably to goal setting, and such traits also may moderate the effects of goal difficulty and participation in goal setting. However, the research to date on this subject should be regarded as exploratory rather than definitive, and additional studies on employee traits as moderators of goal setting effectiveness are clearly needed.

In conclusion, the laboratory and field research on goal setting has provided impressive support for portions of Locke's theory and has demonstrated the practical feasiblity of goal setting programs as a means of improving employee performance. Nevertheless, much still remains to be learned, and several lines of research are essential for further validation and elaboration of the theory. Such research is likely to result eventually in the formulation of a contingency model of goal setting effectiveness.

REFERENCES

1 Baumler, J. V. "Defined Criteria of Performance in Organizational Control," *Administrative Science Quarterly,* Vol. 16 (1971), 340–350.
2 Blumenfeld, W. E., and T. E. Leidy. "Effectiveness of Goal Setting as a Management Device: Research Note," *Psychological Reports*, Vol. 24 (1969), 24.
3 Brady, R. H. "MBO Goes to Work in the Public Sector," *Harvard Business Review,* Vol. 51 (1973), 65–74.
4 Burke, R. J., and D. S. Wilcox. "Characteristics of Effective Employee Performance Reviews and Developmental Interviews," *Personnel Psychology,* Vol. 22 (1969), 291–305.
5 Campbell, J. P., M. D. Dunnette, E. E. Lawler, and K. E. Weick, Jr. *Managerial Behavior, Performance and Effectiveness* (New York: McGraw-Hill, 1970).
6 Carroll, S. J., and H. L. Tosi. "Relationship of Goal Setting Characteristics as Moderated by Personality and Situational Factors to the Success of the Management by Objectives Approach," *Proceedings of the 77th Annual Convention,* American Psychological Association, 1969.
7 Carroll, S. J., and H. L. Tosi. "Goal Characteristics and Personality Factors in a Management by Objectives Program," *Administrative Science Quarterly,* Vol. 15 (1970), 295–305.
8 Carroll, S. J., and H. L. Tosi. "Relationship of Characteristics of the Review Process to the Success of the MBO Approach," *Journal of Business,* Vol. 44 (1971), 299–305.
9 Carroll, S. J., and H. L. Tosi. *Management by Objectives: Applications and Research* (New York: Macmillan, 1973).
10 Cartledge, N. D. *An Experimental Study of the Relationship Between Expectancies, Goal Utility, Goals, and Task Performance* (Ph.D. dissertation, University of Maryland, 1973).
11 Chapanis, A. "Knowledge of Performance as an Incentive in Repetitive, Monotonous Tasks," *Journal of Applied Psychology,* Vol. 48 (1964), 263–267.
12 Charnes, A., and A. C. Stedry. "Exploratory Models in the Theory of Budgetary Control," in W. W. Cooper, H. J. Leavitt, and M. W. Shelly (Eds.), *New Perspectives in Organizational Research* (New York: Wiley, 1964).
13 Cummings, L. L., D. P. Schwab, and M. Rosen. "Performance and Knowledge of Results as Predeterminants of Goal Setting," *Journal of Applied Psychology,* Vol. 55 (1971), 526–530.
14 Dachler, H. P., and W. H. Mobley. "Construct Validation of an Instrumentality-Expectancy-Task-Goal Model of Work Motivation," *Journal of Applied Psychology,* Vol. 58 (1973), 397–418.
15 Dobmeyer, T. W. "A Critique of Edwin Locke's Theory of Task Motivation and Incentives," in H. L. Tosi, R. J. House, and M. D. Dunnette (Eds.), *Managerial Motivation and Compensation* (East Lansing, Mich.: MSU Business Studies, 1971), pp. 244–259.
16 Duttagupta, D. *An Empirical Evaluation of Management by Objectives* (Master's thesis, Baruch College, 1975).
17 French, J. R. P., E. Kay, and H. H. Meyer. "Participation and the Appraisal System," *Human Relations,* Vol. 19 (1966), 3–19.
18 Gell, T., and C. F. Molander. "Beyond Management by Objectives," *Personnel Management,* Vol. 2 (1970), 18–20.

19 Howell, R. A. "A Fresh Look at Management by Objectives," *Business Horizons,* Vol. 10 (1967), 51–58.

20 Howell, R. A. "Managing by Objectives—A Three Stage System," *Business Horizons Vol.* 13, (1970), 41–45.

21 Hundal, P. S. "Knowledge of Performance as an Incentive in Repetitive Industrial Work," *Journal of Applied Psychology,* Vol. 53 (1969), 244–226.

22 Ivancevich, J. M. "A Longitudinal Assessment of Management by Objectives," *Administrative Science Quarterly,* Vol. 17 (1972), 126–138.

23 Ivancevich, J. M. "Changes in Performance in a Management by Objectives Program," *Administrative Science Quarterly,* Vol. 19 (1974), 563–574.

24 Ivancevich, J. M., J. H. Donnelly, and H. L. Lyon. "A Study of the Impact of Management by Objectives on Perceived Need Satisfaction," *Personnel Psychology,* Vol. 23 (1970), 139–151.

25 Kirchoff, B. A. "Using Objectives: The Critical Variable in Effective MBO," *Michigan Business Review,* Vol. 26 (1974), 17–21.

26 Kolb, D. A., and R. E. Boyatzis. "Goal Setting and Self-Directed Behavior Change," in D. A. Kolb, I. M. Rubin, and J. M. McIntyre (Eds.), *Organizational Psychology: A Book of Readings* (Englewood Cliffs, N.J.: Prentice-Hall, 1971), pp. 317–337.

27 Kolb, D. A., S. Winters, and D. Berlew. "Self-Directed Change: Two Studies," *Journal of Applied Behavioral Science,* Vol. 4 (1968), 453–473.

28 Lasagna, J. B. "Make Your MBO Pragmatic," *Harvard Business Review,* Vol. 49 (1971), 64–69.

29 Latham, G. P., and J. J. Baldes. "The Practical Significance of Locke's Theory of Goal Setting," *Journal of Applied Pscyhology,* Vol. 60 (1975), 122–124.

30 Latham, G. P., and S. B. Kinne, III. "Improving Job Performance Through Training in Goal Setting," *Journal of Applied Psychology,* Vol. 59 (1974), 187–191.

31 Latham, G. P., and E. A. Locke. "Increasing Productivity with Decreasing Time Limits: A Field Replication of Parkinson's Law," *Journal of Applied Psychology,* Vol. 60 (1975), 524–526.

32 Latham, G. P., and G. A. Yukl. "Assigned Versus Participative Goal Setting with Educated and Uneducated Woods Workers," *Journal of Applied Psychology,* Vol. 60 (1975), 299–302.

33 Lawrence, L. C., and P. C. Smith. "Group Decision and Employee Participation," *Journal of Applied Psychology,* Vol. 39 (1955), 334–337.

34 Levinson, H. "Management By Whose Objectives?" *Harvard Business Review,* Vol. 48, No. 4 (1970), 125–134.

35 Likert, R. *The Human Organization* (New York: McGraw-Hill, 1967).

36 Locke, E. A. "Toward a Theory of Task Motivation and Incentives," *Organizational Behavior and Human Performance,* Vol. 3 (1968), 157–189.

37 Locke, E. A., N. Cartledge, and C. S. Knerr. "Studies of the Relationship Between Satisfaction, Goal Setting and Performance," *Organizational Behavior and Human Performance,* Vol. 5 (1970), 135–158.

38 Locke, E. A., N. Cartledge, and J. Koeppel. "Motivational Effects of Knowledge of Results: A Goal Setting Phenomenon," *Psychological Bulletin,* Vol. 70 (1968), 474–485.

39 Lowin, A. "Participative Decision-Making: A Model, Literature Critique and Prescription for Research," *Organizational Behavior and Human Performance,* Vol. 3 (1968), 68–106.

40   Massie, J. L. "Management Theory," in J. G. March (Ed.), *Handbook of Organizations* (Chicago: Rand McNally, 1965), pp. 387–422.

41   McGregor, D. *The Human Side of Enterprise* (New York: McGraw-Hill, 1960).

42   Mendleson, J. L. *Managerial Goal Setting: An Exploration into Meaning and Measurement* (Ph.D. dissertation, Michigan State University, 1967).

43   Meyer, H. H., E. Kay, and J. R. P. French. "Split Roles in Performance Appraisal," *Harvard Business Review,* Vol. 43 (1965), 123–129.

44   Miller, L. *The Use of Knowledge of Results in Improving the Performance of Hourly Operators* (Crotonville, N.Y.: General Electric Company, Behavioral Research Service, 1965).

45   Morse, J. H., and J. W. Lorsch. "Beyond Theory Y," *Harvard Business Review,* Vol. 48 (1970), 61–68.

46   Murray, R. K. "Behavioral Management Objectives," *Personnel Journal,* Vol. 52 (1973), 304–306.

47   Prichard, R. D., and M. I. Curtis. "The Influence of Goal Setting and Financial Incentives on Task Performance," *Organizational Behavior and Human Performance,* Vol. 10 (1973), 175–183.

48   Raia, A. P. "Goal Setting and Self-Control: An Empirical Study," *Journal of Management Studies,* Vol. 2 (1965), 32–53.

49   Raia, A. P. "A Second Look at Management by Goals and Controls," *California Management Review,* Vol. 8 (1966), 49–58.

50   Ronan, W. W., G. P. Latham, and S. B. Kinne. "Effects of Goal Setting and Supervision on Worker Behavior in an Industrial Situation," *Journal of Applied Psychology,* Vol. 58 (1973), 302–307.

51   Ryan, T. A. *Work and Effort* (New York: Ronald, 1947).

52   Shetty, Y. K., and H. M. Carlisle. "Organizational Correlates of a Management by Objectives Program," *Academy of Management Journal*, Vol. 17 (1974), 155–159.

53   Sorcher, M. *Motivating the Hourly Employee* (Crotonville, N.Y.: General Electric Company, Behavioral Research Service, 1967).

54   Stedry, A. C., and E. Kay. "The Effects of Goal Difficulty on Performance," *Behavioral Science,* Vol. 11 (1966), 459–470.

55   Steers, R. M. "Task-Goal Attributes, n-Achievement, and Supervisory Performance," *Organizational Behavior and Human Performance,* Vol. 13 (1975), 392–403.

56   Tannenbaum, R., and W. Schmidt. "How to Choose a Leadership Pattern," *Harvard Business Review,* Vol. 36 (1958), 95–101.

57   Vroom, V. H., and P. Yetton. *Leadership and Decision-Making* (Pittsburgh, Pa.: University of Pittsburgh Press, 1973).

58   Wexley, K. N., and W. F. Nemeroff. "Effects of Positive Reinforcement and Goal Setting as Methods of Management Development," *Journal of Applied Psychology,* Vol. 60 (1975), 446–450.

59   Wickens, J. D. "Management by Objectives: An Appraisal," *Journal of Management Studies,* Vol. 5 (1968), 365–379.

60   Wilsted, W. D., and H. H. Hand. "Determinants of Aspiration Levels in a Simulated Goal Setting Environment of the Firm," *Academy of Management Journal,* Vol. 6 (1971), 414–440.

61   Yukl, G. A. "Toward a Behavioral Theory of Leadership," *Organizational Behavior and Human Performance,* Vol. 6 (1971), 414–440.

62   Zander, A., and T. T. Newcomb, Jr. "Group Levels of Aspiration in United Fund Campaigns," *Journal of Personality and Social Psychology,* Vol. 6 (1967), 157–162.

63 Zander, A., J. Forward, and R. Albert. "Adaptation of Board Members to Repeated Failure or Success by the Organization," *Organizational Behavior and Human Performance,* Vol. 4 (1969), 56–76.

REVIEW AND DISCUSSION QUESTIONS

1 Is goal setting a way to improve performance?
2 What is the role of feedback in performance? Under what conditions is feedback most effective?
3 Under what conditions is participation an effective way to increase individual performance?
4 Is management by objectives an effective change strategy?
5 How do monetary incentives seem to affect performance?

Reading 9

A New Strategy for Job Enrichment

J. Richard Hackman
Greg Oldham
Robert Janson
Kenneth Purdy

Practitioners of job enrichment have been living through a time of excitement, even euphoria. Their craft has moved from the psychology and management journals to the front page and the Sunday supplement. Job enrichment, which began with the pioneering work of Herzberg and his associates, originally was intended as a means to increase the motivation and satisfaction of people at work—and to improve productivity in the bargain.[1-5] Now it is being acclaimed in the popular press as a cure for problems ranging from inflation to drug abuse.

Much current writing about job enrichment is enthusiastic, sometimes even messianic, about what it can accomplish. But the hard questions of exactly what should be done to improve jobs, and how, tend to be glossed over. Lately, because the harder questions have not been dealt with adequately, critical winds have begun to blow. Job enrichment has been described as yet another "management fad," as "nothing new," even as a fraud. And reports of job-enrichment failures are beginning to appear in management and psychology journals.

This article attempts to redress the excesses that have characterized some of the recent writings about job enrichment. As the technique increases in popularity as a management tool, top managers inevitably will find themselves making decisions about its use. The intent of this paper is to help both managers and behavioral scientists become better able to make those decisions on a solid basis of fact and data.

Succinctly stated, we present here a new strategy for going about the redesign of work. The strategy is based on three years of collaborative work and cross-fertilization among the authors—two of whom are academic researchers and two of whom are active practitioners in job enrichment. Our approach is new, but it has been tested in many organizations. It draws on the contributions of both management practice and psychological theory, but it is firmly in the middle ground between them. It builds on and complements previous work by Herzberg and others, but provides for the first time a set of tools for *diagnosing* existing jobs—and a map for translating the diagnostic results into specific action steps for change.

What we have, then, is the following:

1 A theory that specifies when people will get personally "turned on" to their work. The theory shows what kinds of jobs are most likely to generate excitement and commitment about work, and what kinds of employees it works best for.

2 A set of action steps for job enrichment based on the theory, which prescribe in concrete terms what to do to make jobs more motivating for the people who do them.

3 Evidence that the theory holds water and that it can be used to bring about measurable—and sometimes dramatic—improvements in employee work behavior, in job satisfaction, and in the financial performance of the organizational unit involved.

THE THEORY BEHIND THE STRATEGY

What Makes People Get Turned On to Their Work?

For workers who are really prospering in their jobs, work is likely to be a lot like play. Consider, for example, a golfer at a driving range, practicing to get rid of a hook. His activity is *meaningful* to him; he has chosen to do it because he gets a "kick" from testing his skills by playing the game. He knows that he alone is *responsible* for what happens when he hits the ball. And he has *knowledge of the results* within a few seconds.

Behavioral scientists have found that the three "psychological states" experienced by the golfer in the above example also are critical in determining a person's motivation and satisfaction on the job.

Experienced Meaningfulness The individual must perceive his work as worthwhile or important by some system of values he accepts.

Experienced Responsibility He must believe that he personally is accountable for the outcome of his efforts.

Knowledge of Results   He must be able to determine, on some fairly regular basis, whether or not the outcomes of his work are satisfactory.

When these three conditions are present, a person tends to feel very good about himself when he performs well. And those good feelings will prompt him to try to continue to do well—so he can continue to earn the positive feelings in the future. That is what is meant by "internal motivation"—being turned on to one's work because of the positive internal feelings that are generated by doing well, rather than being dependent on external factors (such as incentive pay or compliments from the boss) for the motivation to work effectively.

What if one of the three psychological states is missing? Motivation drops markedly. Suppose, for example, that our golfer has settled in at the driving range to practice for a couple of hours. Suddenly a fog drifts in over the range. He can no longer see if the ball starts to tail off to the left a hundred yards out. The satisfaction he got from hitting straight down the middle—and the motivation to try to correct something whenever he didn't—are both gone. If the fog stays, it's likely that he soon will be packing up his clubs.

The relationship between the three psychological states and on-the-job outcomes is illustrated in Figure 1. When all three are high, then internal work motivation, job satisfaction, and work quality are high, and absenteeism and turnover are low.

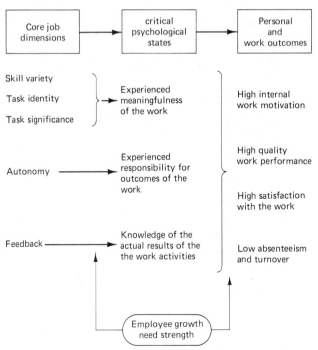

Figure 1   Relationships among core job dimensions, critical psychological states, and on-the-job outcomes.

What Job Characteristics Make It Happen?

Recent research has identified five "core" characteristics of jobs that elicit the psychological states described above.[6-8] These five core job dimensions provide the key to objectively measuring jobs and to changing them so that they have high potential for motivating people who do them.

Toward Meaningful Work Three of the five core dimensions contribute to a job's meaningfulness for the worker:

1 Skill Variety—the degree to which a job requires the worker to perform activities that challenge his skills and abilities. When even a single skill is involved, there is at least a seed of potential meaningfulness. When several are involved, the job has the potential of appealing to more of the whole person, and also of avoiding the monotony of performing the same task repeatedly, no matter how much skill it may require.

2 Task Identity—the degree to which the job requires completion of a "whole" and identifiable piece of work—doing a job from beginning to end with a visible outcome. For example, it is clearly more meaningful to an employee to build complete toasters than to attach electrical cord after electrical cord, especially if he never sees a completed toaster. (Note that the whole job, in this example, probably would involve greater skill variety as well as task identity.)

3 Task Significance—the degree to which the job has a substantial and perceivable impact on the lives of other people, whether in the immediate organization or the world at large. The worker who tightens nuts on aircraft brake assemblies is more likely to perceive his work as significant than the worker who fills small boxes with paper clips—even though the skill levels involved may be comparable.

Each of these three job dimensions represents an important route to experienced meaningfulness. If the job is high in all three, the worker is quite likely to experience his job as very meaningful. It is not necessary, however, for a job to be very high in all three dimensions. If the job is low in any one of them, there will be a drop in overall experienced meaningfulness. But even when two dimensions are low the worker may find the job meaningful if the third is high enough.

Toward Personal Responsibility A fourth core dimension leads a worker to experience increased responsibility in his job. This is *autonomy*, the degree to which the job gives the worker freedom, independence, and discretion in scheduling work and determining how he will carry it out. People in highly autonomous jobs know that they are personally responsible for successes and failures. To the extent that their autonomy is high, then, how the work goes will be felt to depend more on the individual's own efforts and initiatives—rather than on detailed instructions from the boss or from a manual of job procedures.

Toward Knowledge of Results The fifth and last core dimension is *feedback*. This is the degree to which a worker, in carrying out the work activities required by the job, gets information about the effectiveness of his efforts. Feedback is most powerful when it comes directly from the work itself—for example, when a worker has the responsibility for gauging and otherwise checking a component he has just finished, and learns in the process that he has lowered his reject rate by meeting specifications more consistently.

The Overall "Motivating Potential" of a Job Figure 1 shows how the five core dimensions combine to affect the psychological states that are critical in determining whether or not an employee will be internally motivated to work effectively. Indeed, when using an instrument to be described later, it is possible to compute a "motivating potential score" (MPS) for any job. The MPS provides a single summary index of the degree to which the objective characteristics of the job will prompt high internal work motivation. Following the theory outlined above, a job high in motivating potential must be high in at least one (and hopefully more) of the three dimensions that lead to experienced meaningfulness and high in both autonomy and feedback as well. The MPS provides a quantitative index of the degree to which this is in fact the case (see Appendix for detailed formula). As will be seen later, the MPS can be very useful in diagnosing jobs and in assessing the effectiveness of job-enrichment activities.

Does the Theory Work for Everybody?

Unfortunately not. Not everyone is able to become internally motivated in his work, even when the motivating potential of a job is very high indeed.

Research has shown that the *psychological needs* of people are very important in determining who can (and who cannot) become internally motivated at work. Some people have strong needs for personal accomplishment, for learning and developing themselves beyond where they are now, for being stimulated and challenged, and so on. These people are high in "growth-need strength."

Figure 2 shows diagrammatically the proposition that individual growth needs have the power to moderate the relationship between the characteristics

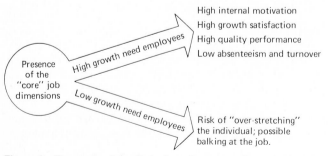

Figure 2   The moderating effect of employee growth-need strength.

of jobs and work outcomes. Many workers with high growth needs will turn on eagerly when they have jobs that are high in the core dimensions. Workers whose growth needs are not so strong may respond less eagerly—or, at first, even balk at being "pushed" or "stretched" too far.

Psychologists who emphasize human potential argue that everyone has within him at least a spark of the need to grow and develop personally. Steadily accumulating evidence shows, however, that unless that spark is pretty strong, chances are it will get snuffed out by one's experiences in typical organizations. So, a person who has worked for twenty years in stultifying jobs may find it difficult or impossible to become internally motivated overnight when given the opportunity.

We should be cautious, however, about creating rigid categories of people based on their measured growth-need strength at any particular time. It is true that we can predict from these measures who is likely to become internally motivated on a job and who will be less willing or able to do so. But what we do not know yet is whether or not the growth-need "spark" can be rekindled for those individuals who have had their growth needs dampened by years of growth-depressing experience in their organizations.

Since it is often the organization that is responsible for currently low levels of growth desires, we believe that the organization also should provide the individual with the chance to reverse that trend whenever possible, even if that means putting a person in a job where he may be "stretched" more than he wants to be. He can always move back later to the old job—and in the meantime the embers of his growth needs just might burst back into flame, to his surprise and pleasure, and for the good of the organization.

FROM THEORY TO PRACTICE:
A TECHNOLOGY FOR JOB ENRICHMENT

When job enrichment fails, it often fails because of inadequate *diagnosis* of the target job and employees' reactions to it. Often, for example, job enrichment is assumed by management to be a solution to "people problems" on the job and is implemented even though there has been no diagnostic activity to indicate that the root of the problem is in fact how the work is designed. At other times, some diagnosis is made—but it provides no concrete guidance about what specific aspects of the job require change. In either case, the success of job enrichment may wind up depending more on the quality of the intuition of the change agent—or his luck—than on a solid base of data about the people and the work.

In the paragraphs to follow, we outline a new technology for use in job enrichment which explicitly addresses the diagnostic as well as the action components of the change process. The technology has two parts: (1) a set of diagnostic tools that are useful in evaluating jobs and people's reactions to them prior to change—and in pinpointing exactly what aspects of specific jobs are most critical to a successful change attempt; and (2) a set of "implementing concepts" that provide concrete guidance for action steps in job enrichment.

The implementing concepts are tied directly to the diagnostic tools; the output of the diagnostic activity specifies which action steps are likely to have the most impact in a particular situation.

The Diagnostic Tools

Central to the diagnostic procedure we propose is a package of instruments to be used by employees, supervisors, and outside observers in assessing the target job and employees' reactions to it.[9] These instruments gauge the following:

1   The objective characteristics of the jobs themselves, including both an overall indication of the "motivating potential" of the job as it exists (that is, the MPS score) and the score of the job on each of the five core dimensions described previously. Because knowing the strengths and weaknesses of the job is critical to any work-redesign effort, assessments of the job are made by supervisors and outside observers as well as the employees themselves—and the final assessment of a job uses data from all three sources.

2   The current levels of motivation, satisfaction, and work performance of employees on the job. In addition to satisfaction with the work itself, measures are taken of how people feel about other aspects of the work setting, such as pay, supervision, and relationships with co-workers.

3   The level of growth-need strength of the employees. As indicated earlier, employees who have strong growth needs are more likely to be more responsive to job enrichment than employees with weak growth needs. Therefore, it is important to know at the outset just what kinds of satisfactions the people who do the job are (and are not) motivated to obtain from their work. This will make it possible to identify which persons are best to start changes with, and which may need help in adapting to the newly enriched job.

What, then, might be the actual steps one would take in carrying out a job diagnosis using these tools? Although the approach to any particular diagnosis depends upon the specifics of the particular work situation involved, the sequence of questions listed below is fairly typical.

Step 1. Are Motivation and Satisfaction Central to the Problem? Sometimes organizations undertake job enrichment to improve the work motivation and satisfaction of employees when in fact the real problem with work performance lies elsewhere—for example, in a poorly designed production system, in an error-prone computer, and so on. The first step is to examine the scores of employees on the motivation and satisfaction portions of the diagnostic instrument. (The questionnaire taken by employees is called the Job Diagnostic Survey and will be referred to hereafter as the JDS.) If motivation and satisfaction are problematic, the change agent would continue to Step 2; if not, he would look to other aspects of the work situation to identify the real problem.

Step 2. Is the Job Low in Motivating Potential? To answer this question, one would examine the motivating potential score of the target job and compare it to the MPS's of other jobs to determine whether or not *the job itself* is a probable cause of the motivational problems documented in Step 1. If the job turns out to be low on the MPS, one would continue to Step 3; if it scores high, attention should be given to other possible reasons for the motivational difficulties (such as the pay system, the nature of supervision, and so on).

Step 3. What Specific Aspects of the Job are Causing the Difficulty? This step involves examining the job on each of the five core dimensions to pinpoint the specific strengths and weaknesses of the job as it is currently structured. It is useful at this stage to construct a "profile" of the target job, to make visually apparent where improvements need to be made. An illustrative profile for two jobs (one "good" job and one job needing improvement) is shown in Figure 3.

Job A is an engineering maintenance job and is high on all of the core dimensions; the MPS of this job is a very high 260. (MPS scores can range from 1 to about 350; an "average" score would be about 125.) Job enrichment would not be recommended for this job; if employees working on the job were unproductive and unhappy, the reasons are likely to have little to do with the nature or design of the work itself.

Job B, on the other hand, has many problems. This job involves the routine and repetitive processing of checks in the "back room" of a bank. The MPS is 30, which is quite low—and indeed, would be even lower if it were not for the moderately high task significance of the job. (Task significance is moderately high because the people are handling large amounts of other people's money, and therefore the quality of their efforts potentially has important consequences for their unseen clients.) The job provides the individuals with very little direct

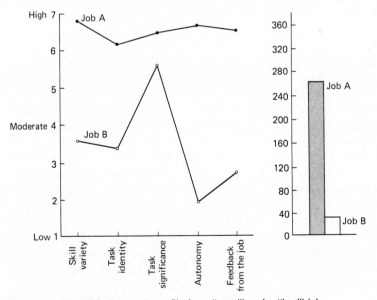

Figure 3   The JDS diagnostic profile for a "good" and a "bad" job.

feedback about how effectively they are doing it; the employees have little autonomy in how they go about the job; and the job is moderately low in both skill variety and task identity.

For Job B, then, there is plenty of room for improvement—and many avenues to examine in planning job changes. For still other jobs, the avenues for change often turn out to be considerably more specific: for example, feedback and autonomy may be reasonably high, but one or more of the core dimensions that contribute to the experienced meaningfulness of the job (skill variety, task identity, and task significance) may be low. In such a case, attention would turn to ways to increase the standing of the job on these latter three dimensions.

Step 4. How "Ready" Are the Employees for Change?　Once it has been documented that there is need for improvement in the job—and the particularly troublesome aspects of the job have been identified—then it is time to begin to think about the specific action steps which will be taken to enrich the job. An important factor in such planning is the level of growth needs of the employees, since employees high on growth needs usually respond more readily to job enrichment than do employees with little need for growth. The JDS provides a direct measure of the growth-need strength of the employees. This measure can be very helpful in planning how to introduce the changes to the people (for instance, cautiously versus dramatically), and in deciding who should be among the first group of employees to have their jobs changed.

In actual use of the diagnostic package, additional information is generated which supplements and expands the basic diagnostic questions outlined above. The point of the above discussion is merely to indicate the kinds of questions which we believe to be most important in diagnosing a job prior to changing it. We now turn to how the diagnostic conclusions are translated into specific job changes.

The Implementing Concepts

Five "implementing concepts" for job enrichment are identified and discussed below.[10] Each one is a specific action step aimed at improving both the quality of the working experience for the individual and his work productivity. They are: (1) forming natural work units; (2) combining tasks; (3) establishing client relationships; (4) vertical loading; (5) opening feedback channels.

The links between the implementing concepts and the core dimensions are shown in Figure 4, which illustrates our theory of job enrichment, ranging from the concrete action steps through the core dimensions and the psychological states to the actual personal and work outcomes.

After completing the diagnosis of a job, a change agent would know which of the core dimensions were most in need of remedial attention. He could then turn to Figure 4 and select those implementing concepts that specifically deal with the most troublesome parts of the existing job. How this would take place in practice will be seen below.

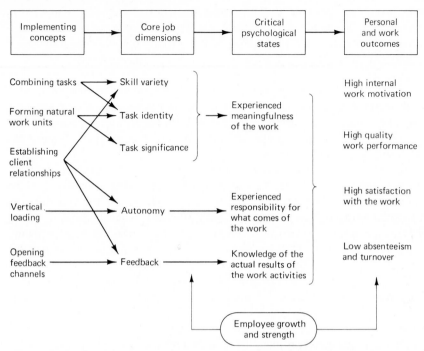

Figure 4   The full model: How use of the implementing concepts can lead to positive outcomes.

Forming Natural Work Units   The notion of distributing work in some logical way may seem to be an obvious part of the design of any job. In many cases, however, the logic is one imposed by just about any consideration except jobholder satisfaction and motivation. Such considerations include technological dictates, level of worker training or experience, "efficiency" as defined by industrial engineering, and current workload. In many cases the cluster of tasks a worker faces during a typical day or week is natural to anyone *but* the worker.

For example, suppose that a typing pool (consisting of one supervisor and ten typists) handles all work for one division of a company. Jobs are delivered in rough draft or dictated form to the supervisor, who distributes them as evenly as possible among the typists. In such circumstances the individual letters, reports, and other tasks performed by a given typist in one day or week are randomly assigned. There is no basis for identifying with the work or the person or department for whom it is performed, or for placing any personal value upon it.

The principle underlying natural units of work, by contrast, is "ownership"—a worker's sense of continuing responsibility for an identifiable body of work. Two steps are involved in creating natural work units. The first is to identify the basic work items. In the typing pool, for example, the items might be "pages to be typed." The second step is to group the items in natural categories. For example, each typist might be assigned continuing responsibility for all jobs requested by one of several specific departments. The assignments should be made, of course, in such a way that workloads are about equal in the long run. (For example, one typist might end up with all the work from one busy department, while another handles jobs from several smaller units.)

At this point we can begin to see specifically how the job-design principles relate to the core dimensions (cf. Figure 4). The ownership fostered by natural units of work can make the difference between a feeling that work is meaningful and rewarding and the feeling that it is irrelevant and boring. As the diagram shows, natural units of work are directly related to two of the core dimensions: task identity and task significance.

A typist whose work is assigned naturally rather than randomly—say, by departments—has a much greater chance of performing a whole job to completion. Instead of typing one section of a large report, the individual is likely to type the whole thing, with knowledge of exactly what the product of the work is (task identity). Furthermore, over time the typist will develop a growing sense of how the work affects co-workers in the department serviced (task significance).

Combining Tasks   The very existence of a pool made up entirely of persons whose sole function is typing reflects a fractionalization of jobs that has been a basic precept of "scientific management." Most obvious in assembly-line work, fractionalization has been applied to non-manufacturing jobs as well. It is typically justified by efficiency, which is usually defined in terms of either low costs or some time-and-motion type of criteria.

It is hard to find fault with measuring efficiency ultimately in terms of cost-effectiveness. In doing so, however, a manager should be sure to consider *all* the costs involved. It is possible, for example, for highly fractionalized jobs to meet all the time-and-motion criteria of efficiency, but if the resulting job is so unrewarding that performing it day after day leads to high turnover, absentee-ism, drugs and alcohol, and strikes, then productivity is really lower (and costs higher) than data on efficiency might indicate.

The principle of combining tasks, then, suggests that whenever possible existing and fractionalized tasks should be put together to form new and larger modules of work. At the Medfield, Massachusetts plant of Corning Glass Works the assembly of a laboratory hot plate has been redesigned along the lines suggested here. Each hot plate now is assembled from start to finish by one operator, instead of going through several separate operations that are performed by different people.

Some tasks, if combined into a meaningfully large module of work, would be more than an individual could do by himself. In such cases, it is often useful to consider assigning the new, larger task to a small *team* of workers—who are given great autonomy for its completion. At the Racine, Wisconsin plant of Emerson Electric, the assembly process for trash disposal appliances was restructured this way. Instead of a sequence of moving the appliance from station to station, the assembly now is done from start to finish by one team.

Such teams include both men and women to permit switching off the heavier and more delicate aspects of the work. The team responsible is identified on the appliance. In case of customer complaints, the team often drafts the reply.

As a job-design principle, task combination, like natural units of work, expands the task identity of the job. For example, the hot-plate assembler can see and identify with a finished product ready for shipment, rather than a nearly invisible junction of solder. Moreover, the more tasks that are combined into a single worker's job, the greater the variety of skills he must call on in performing the job. So task combination also leads directly to greater skill variety—the third core dimension that contributes to the overall experienced meaningfulness of the work.

Establishing Client Relationships   One consequence of fractionalization is that the typical worker has little or no contact with (or even awareness of) the ultimate user of his product or service. By encouraging and enabling employees to establish direct relationships with the clients of their work, improvements often can be realized simultaneously on three of the core dimensions. Feedback increases, because of additional opportunities for the individual to receive praise or criticism of his work outputs directly. Skill variety often increases, because of the necessity to develop and exercise one's interpersonal skills in maintaining the client relationship. And autonomy can increase because the individual often is given personal responsibility for deciding how to manage his relationships with the clients of his work.

Creating client relationships is a three-step process. First, the client must be identified. Second, the most direct contact possible must be established. Third, criteria must be set up by which the client can judge the quality of the product or service he receives. And whenever possible, the client should have a means of relaying his judgments directly back to the worker.

The contact between worker and client should be as great as possible and as frequent as necessary. Face-to-face contact is highly desirable, at least occasionally. Where that is impossible or impractical, telephone and mail can suffice. In any case, it is important that the performance criteria by which the worker will be rated by the client must be mutually understood and agreed upon.

Vertical Loading   Typically the split between the "doing" of a job and the "planning" and "controlling" of the work has evolved along with horizontal fractionalization. Its rationale, once again, has been "efficiency through specialization." And once again, the excess of specialization that has emerged has resulted in unexpected but significant costs in motivation, morale, and work quality. In vertical loading, the intent is to partially close the gap between the doing and the controlling parts of the job—and thereby reap some important motivational advantages.

Of all the job-design principles, vertical loading may be the single most crucial one. In some cases, where it has been impossible to implement any other changes, vertical loading alone has had significant motivational effects.

When a job is vertically loaded, responsibilities and controls that formerly were reserved for higher levels of management are added to the job. There are many ways to accomplish this:

- Return to the job holder greater discretion in setting schedules, deciding on work methods, checking on quality, and advising or helping to train less experienced workers.
- Grant additional authority. The objective should be to advance workers from a position of no authority or highly restricted authority to positions of reviewed, and eventually, near-total authority for his own work.
- Time management. The job holder should have the greatest possible freedom to decide when to start and stop work, when to break, and how to assign priorities.
- Troubleshooting and crisis decisions. Workers should be encouraged to seek problem solutions on their own, rather than calling immediately for the supervisor.
- Financial controls. Some degree of knowledge and control over budgets and other financial aspects of a job can often be highly motivating. However, access to this information frequently tends to be restricted. Workers can benefit from knowing something about the costs of their jobs, the potential effect upon profit, and various financial and budgetary alternatives.

When a job is vertically loaded it will inevitably increase in *autonomy*. And as shown in Figure 4, this increase in objective personal control over the work will also lead to an increased feeling of personal responsibility for the work, and ultimately to higher internal work motivation.

Opening Feedback Channels   In virtually all jobs there are ways to open channels of feedback to individuals or teams to help them learn whether their performance is improving, deteriorating, or remaining at a constant level. While there are numerous channels through which information about performance can be provided, it generally is better for a worker to learn about his performance *directly as he does his job*—rather than from management on an occasional basis.

Job-provided feedback usually is more immediate and private than supervisor-supplied feedback, and it increases the worker's feelings of personal control over his work in the bargain. Moreover, it avoids many of the potentially disruptive interpersonal problems that can develop when the only way a worker has to find out how he is doing is through direct messages or subtle cues from the boss.

Exactly what should be done to open channels for job-provided feedback will vary from job to job and organization to organization. Yet in many cases the changes involve simply removing existing blocks that isolate the worker from naturally occurring data about performance—rather than generating entirely new feedback mechanisms. For example:

- Quality-control efforts in many organizations often eliminate a natural source of feedback. The quality check on a product or service is done by persons other than those responsible for the work. Feedback to the workers—if there is any—is belated and diluted. It often fosters a tendency to think of quality as "someone else's concern." By placing quality control close to the worker (perhaps even in his own hands), the quantity and quality of data about performance available to him can dramatically increase.

• Tradition and established procedure in many organizations dictate that records about performance be kept by a supervisor and transmitted up (not down) in the organizational hierarchy. Sometimes supervisors even check the work and correct any errors themselves. The worker who made the error never knows it occurred—and is denied the very information that could enhance both his internal work motivation and the technical adequacy of his performance. In many cases it is possible to provide standard summaries of performance records directly to the worker (as well as to his superior), thereby giving him personally and regularly the data he needs to improve his performance.

• Computers and other automated operations sometimes can be used to provide the individual with data now blocked from him. Many clerical operations, for example, are now performed on computer consoles. These consoles often can be programmed to provide the clerk with immediate feedback in the form of a CRT display or a printout indicating that an error has been made. Some systems even have been programmed to provide the operator with a positive feedback message when a period of error-free performance has been sustained.

Many organizations simply have not recognized the importance of feedback as a motivator. Data on quality and other aspects of performance are viewed as being of interest only to management. Worse still, the *standards* for acceptable performance often are kept from workers as well. As a result, workers who would be interested in following the daily or weekly ups and downs of their performance, and in trying accordingly to improve, are deprived of the very guidelines they need to do so. They are like the golfer we mentioned earlier, whose efforts to correct his hook are stopped dead by fog over the driving range.

THE STRATEGY IN ACTION: HOW WELL DOES IT WORK?

So far we have examined a basic theory of how people get turned on to their work; a set of core dimensions of jobs that create the conditions for such internal work motivation to develop on the job; and a set of five implementing concepts that are the action steps recommended to boost a job on the core dimensions and thereby increase employee motivation, satisfaction, and productivity.

The remaining question is straightforward and important: *Does it work?* In reality, that question is twofold. First, does the theory itself hold water, or are we barking up the wrong conceptual tree? And second, does the change strategy really lead to measurable differences when it is applied in an actual organizational setting?

This section summarizes the findings we have generated to date on these questions.

Is the Job-Enrichment Theory Correct?

In general, the answer seems to be yes. The JDS instrument has been taken by more than 1,000 employees working on about 100 diverse jobs in more than a dozen organizations over the last two years. These data have been analyzed to test the basic motivational theory—and especially the impact of the core job dimensions on worker motivation, satisfaction, and behavior on the job. An illustrative overview of some of the findings is given below.[8]

   1 People who work on jobs high on the core dimensions are more motivated and satisfied than are people who work on jobs that score low on the dimensions. Employees with jobs high on the core dimensions (MPS scores greater than 240) were compared to those who held unmotivating jobs (MPS scores less than 40). As shown in Figure 5, employees with high MPS jobs were higher on (a) the three psychological states, (b) internal work motivation, (c) general satisfaction, and (d) "growth" satisfaction.
   2 Figure 6 shows that the same is true for measures of actual behavior at work—absenteeism and performance effectiveness—although less strongly so for the performance measure.
   3 Responses to jobs high in motivating potential are more positive for people who have strong growth needs than for people with weak needs for growth. In Figure 7 the linear relationship between the motivating potential of a job and employees' level of internal work motivation is shown, separately for people with high versus low growth needs as measured by the JDS. While both groups of employees show increases in internal motivation as MPS increases, the *rate* of increase is significantly greater for the group of employees who have strong needs for growth.

How Does the Change Strategy Work in Practice?

The results summarized above suggest that both the theory and the diagnostic instrument work when used with real people in real organizations. In this

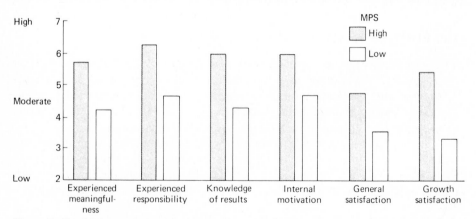

Figure 5   Employee reactions to jobs high and low in motivating potential for two banks and a steel firm.

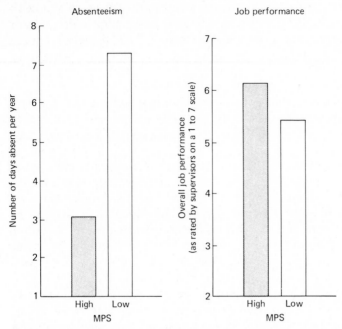

Figure 6 Absenteeism and job performance for employees with jobs high and low in motivating potential.

section, we summarize a job-enrichment project conducted at The Travelers Insurance Companies, which illustrates how the change procedures themselves work in practice.

The Travelers project was designed with two purposes in mind. One was to achieve improvements in morale, productivity, and other indicators of employee well-being. The other was to test the general effectiveness of the strategy for job enrichment we have summarized in this article.

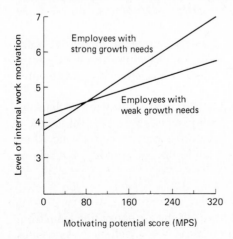

Figure 7 Relationship between the motivating potential of a job and the internal work motivation of employees. (Shown separately for employees with strong versus weak growth-need strength.)

The work group chosen was a keypunching operation. The group's function was to transfer information from printed or written documents onto punched cards for computer input. The work group consisted of ninety-eight keypunch operators and verifiers (both in the same job classification), plus seven assignment clerks. All reported to a supervisor who, in turn, reported to the assistant manager and manager of the data-input division.

The size of individual punching orders varied considerably, from a few cards to as many as 2,500. Some work came to the work group with a specified delivery date, while other orders were to be given routine service on a predetermined schedule.

Assignment clerks received the jobs from the user departments. After reviewing the work for obvious errors, omissions, and legibility problems, the assignment clerk parceled out the work in batches expected to take about one hour. If the clerk found the work not suitable for punching it went to the supervisor, who either returned the work to the user department or cleared up problems by phone. When work went to operators for punching, it was with the instruction, "Punch only what you see. Don't correct errors, no matter how obvious they look."

Because of the high cost of computer time, key-punched work was 100 percent verified—a task that consumed nearly as many man-hours as the punching itself. Then the cards went to the supervisor, who screened the jobs for due dates before sending them to the computer. Errors detected in verification were assigned to various operators at random to be corrected.

The computer output form the cards was sent to the originating department, accompanied by a printout of errors. Eventually the printout went back to the supervisor for final correction.

A great many phenomena indicated that the problems being experienced in the work group might be the result of poor motivation. As the only person performing supervisory functions of any kind, the supervisor spent most of his time responding to crisis situations, which recurred continually. He also had to deal almost daily with employees' salary grievances or other complaints. Employees frequently showed apathy or outright hostility toward their jobs.

Rates of work output, by accepted work-measurement standards, were inadequate. Error rates were high. Due dates and schedules frequently were missed. Absenteeism was higher than average, especially before and after weekends and holidays.

The single, rather unusual exception was turnover. It was lower than the companywide average for similar jobs. The company has attributed this fact to a poor job market in the base period just before the project began, and to an older, relatively more settled work force—made up, incidentally, entirely of women.

The Diagnosis

Using some of the tools and techniques we have outlined, a consulting team from the Management Services Department and from Roy W. Walters & Associates concluded that the keypunch-operator's job exhibited the following serious weaknesses in terms of the core dimensions.[9]

- Skill variety: there was none. Only a single skill was involved—the ability to punch adequately the data on the batch of documents.
- Task identity: virtually nonexistent. Batches were assembled to provide an even workload, but not whole identifiable jobs.
- Task significance: not apparent. The keypunching operation was a necessary step in providing service to the company's customers. The individual operator was isolated by an assignment clerk and a supervisor from any knowledge of what the operation meant to the using department, let alone its meaning to the ultimate customer.
- Autonomy: none. The operators had no freedom to arrange their daily tasks to meet schedules, to resolve problems with the using department, or even to correct, in punching, information that was obviously wrong.
- Feedback: none. Once a batch was out of the operator's hands, she had no assured chance of seeing evidence of its quality or inadequacy.

Design of the Experimental Trial

Since the diagnosis indicated that the motivating potential of the job was extremely low, it was decided to attempt to improve the motivation and productivity of the work group through job enrichment.[10] Moreover, it was possible to design an experimental test of the effects of the changes to be introduced: the results of changes made in the target work group were to be compared with trends in a control work group of similar size and demographic make-up. Since the control group was located more than a mile away, there appeared to be little risk of communication between members of the two groups.

A base period was defined before the start of the experimental trial period, and appropriate data were gathered on the productivity, absenteeism, and work attitudes of members of both groups. Data also were available on turnover; but since turnover was already below average in the target group, prospective changes in this measure were deemed insignificant.

An educational session was conducted with supervisors, at which they were given the theory and implementing concepts and actually helped to design the job changes themselves. Out of this session came an active plan consisting of about twenty-five change items that would significantly affect the design of the target jobs.

The Implementing Concepts and the Changes

Because the job as it existed was rather uniformly low on the core job dimensions, all five of the implementing concepts were used in enriching it.

- Natural units of work. The random batch assignment of work was replaced by assigning to each operator continuing responsibility for certain accounts—either particular departments or particular recurring jobs. Any work for those accounts now always goes to the same operator.

- Task combination. Some planning and controlling functions were combined with the central task of keypunching. In this case, however, these additions can be more suitably discussed under the remaining three implementing concepts.
- Client relationships. Each operator was given several channels of direct contact with clients. The operators, not their assignment clerks, now inspect their documents for correctness and legibility. When problems arise, the operator, not the supervisor, takes them up with the client.
- Feedback. In addition to feedback from client contact, the operators were provided with a number of additional sources of data about their performance. The computer department now returns incorrect cards to the operators who punched them, and operators correct their own errors. Each operator also keeps her own file of copies of her errors. These can be reviewed to determine trends in error frequency and types of errors. Each operator receives weekly a computer printout of her errors and productivity, which is sent to her directly, rather than given to her by the supervisor.
- Vertical loading. Besides consulting directly with clients about work questions, operators now have the authority to correct obvious coding errors on their own. Operators may set their own schedules and plan their daily work, as long as they meet schedules. Some competent operators have been given the option of not verifying their work and making their own program changes.

Results of the Trial

The results were dramatic. The number of operators declined from ninety-eight to sixty. This occurred partly through attrition and partly through transfer to other departments. Some of the operators were promoted to higher-paying jobs in departments whose cards they had been handling—something that had never occurred before. Some details of the results are given below.

- Quantity of work. The control group, with no job changes made, showed an increase in productivity of 8.1 percent during the trial period. The experimental group showed an increase of 39.6 percent.
- Error rates. To assess work quality, error rates were recorded for about forty operators in the experimental group. All were experienced, and all had been in their jobs before the job-enrichment program began. For two months before the study, these operators had a collective error rate of 1.53 percent. For two months toward the end of the study, the collective error rate was 0.99 percent. By the end of the study the number of operators with poor performance had dropped from 11.1 percent to 5.5 percent.
- Absenteeism. The experimental group registered a 24.1 percent decline in absences. The control group, by contrast, showed a 29 percent *increase*.
- Attitudes toward the job. An attitude survey given at the start of the project showed that the two groups scored about average, and nearly identically, in nine different areas of work satisfaction. At the end of the project the survey was repeated. The control group showed an insignificant 0.5 percent improvement, while the experimental group's overall satisfaction score rose 16.5 percent.
- Selective elimination of controls. Demonstrated improvements in

operator proficiency permitted them to work with fewer controls. Travelers estimates that the reduction of controls had the same effect as adding seven operators—a saving even beyond the effects of improved productivity and lowered absenteeism.

• Role of the supervisor. One of the most significant findings in the Travelers experiment was the effect of the changes on the supervisor's job, and thus on the rest of the organization. The operators took on many responsibilities that had been reserved at least to the unit leaders and sometimes to the supervisor. The unit leaders, in turn, assumed some of the day-to-day supervisory functions that had plagued the supervisor. Instead of spending his days supervising the behavior of subordinates and dealing with crises, he was able to devote time to developing feedback systems, setting up work modules and spearheading the enrichment effort—in other words, managing. It should be noted, however, that helping supervisors change their own work activities when their subordinates' jobs have been enriched is itself a challenging task. And if appropriate attention and help are not given to supervisors in such cases, they rapidly can become disaffected—and a job-enrichment "backlash" can result.[11]

Summary

By applying work-measurement standards to the changes wrought by job enrichment—attitude and quality, absenteeism, and selective administration of controls—Travelers was able to estimate the total dollar impact of the project. Actual savings in salaries and machine rental charges during the first year totaled $64,305. Potential savings by further application of the changes were put at $91,937 annually. Thus, by almost any measure used—from the work attitudes of individual employees to dollar savings for the company as a whole—the Travelers test of the job-enrichment strategy proved a success.

CONCLUSIONS

In this article we have presented a new strategy for the redesign of work in general and for job enrichment in particular. The approach has four main characteristics:

1 It is grounded in a basic psychological theory of what motivates people in their work.

2 It emphasizes that planning for job changes should be done on the basis of *data* about the jobs and the people who do them—and a set of diagnostic instruments is provided to collect such data.

3 It provides a set of specific implementing concepts to guide actual job changes, as well as a set of theory-based rules for selecting *which* action steps are likely to be most beneficial in a given situation.

4 The strategy is buttressed by a set of findings showing that the theory holds water, that the diagnostic procedures are practical and informative, and that the implementing concepts can lead to changes that are beneficial both to organizations and to the people who work in them.

We believe that job enrichment is moving beyond the stage where it can be considered "yet another management fad." Instead, it represents a potentially powerful strategy for change that can help organizations achieve their goals for higher quality work—and at the same time further the equally legitimate needs of contemporary employees for a more meaningful work experience. Yet there are pressing questions about job enrichment and its use that remain to be answered.

Prominent among these is the question of employee participation in planning and implementing work redesign. The diagnostic tools and implementing concepts we have presented are neither designed nor intended for use only by management. Rather, our belief is that the effectiveness of job enrichment is likely to be enhanced when the tasks of diagnosing and changing jobs are undertaken *collaboratively* by management and by the employees whose work will be affected.

Moreover, the effects of work redesign on the broader organization remain generally uncharted. Evidence now is accumulating that when jobs are changed, turbulence can appear in the surrounding organization—for example, in supervisory-subordinate relationships, in pay and benefit plans, and so on. Such turbulence can be viewed by management either as a problem with job enrichment, or as an opportunity for further and broader organizational development by teams of managers and employees. To the degree that management takes the latter view, we believe, the oft-espoused goal of achieving basic organizational change through the redesign of work may come increasingly within reach.

The diagnostic tools and implementing concepts we have presented are useful in deciding on and designing basic changes in the jobs themselves. They do not address the broader issues of who plans the changes, how they are carried out, and how they are followed up. The way these broader questions are dealt with, we believe, may determine whether job enrichment will grow up—or whether it will die an early and unfortunate death, like so many other fledgling behavioral-science approaches to organizational change.

Appendix

For the algebraically inclined, the Motivating Potential Score is computed as follows:

$$\text{MPS} = \frac{\text{skill variety} + \text{task identity} + \text{task significance}}{3} \times \text{Autonomy} \times \text{Feedback}$$

It should be noted that in some cases the MPS score can be *too* high for positive job satisfaction and effective performance—in effect overstimulating the person who holds the job. This paper focuses on jobs which are toward the low end of the scale—and which potentially can be improved through job enrichment.

Acknowledgements: The authors acknowledge with great appreciation the editorial assistance of John Hickey in the preparation of this paper, and the help of Kenneth Brousseau, Daniel Feldman, and Linda Frank in collecting the data that are summarized here. The research activities reported were supported in part by the Organizational Effectiveness Research Program of the Office of Naval Research, and the Manpower Administration of the U.S. Department of Labor, both through contracts to Yale University.

REFERENCES

1 F. Herzberg, B. Mausner and B. Snyderman, *The Motivation to Work* (New York: John Wiley & Sons, 1959).
2 F. Herzberg, *Work and the Nature of Man* (Cleveland: World, 1966).
3 F. Herzberg, "One More Time: How Do You Motivate Employees?" *Harvard Business Review* (1968), pp. 53–62.
4 W. J. Paul, Jr., K. B. Robertson and F. Herzberg, "Job Enrichment Pays Off," *Harvard Business Review* (1969), pp. 61–78.
5 R. N. Ford, *Motivation Through the Work Itself* (New York: American Management Association, 1969).
6 A. N. Turner and P. R. Lawrence, *Industrial Jobs and the Worker* (Cambridge, Mass.: Harvard Graduate School of Business Administration, 1965).
7 J. R. Hackman and E. E. Lawler, "Employee Reactions to Job Characteristics," *Journal of Applied Psychology Monograph* (1971), pp. 259–286.
8 J. R. Hackman and G. R. Oldham, *Motivation Through the Design of Work: Test of a Theory,* Technical Report No. 6, Department of Administrative Sciences, Yale University, 1974.
9 J. R. Hackman and G. R. Oldham, "Development of the Job Diagnostic Survey," *Journal of Applied Psychology* (1975), pp. 159–170.
10 R. W. Walters and Associates, *Job Enrichment for Results* (Cambridge, Mass.: Addison-Wesley, 1975).
11 E. E. Lawler III, J. R. Hackman, and S. Kaufman, "Effects of Job Redesign: A Field Experiment," *Journal of Applied Social Psychology* (1973), pp. 49–62.

REVIEW AND DISCUSSION QUESTIONS

1 Briefly summarize the "new strategy for going about the redesign of work" proposed by the authors.
2 What are the core job dimensions? The critical psychological states?
3 What is the *motivating potential score* (MPS)?
4 What are some of the "implementing concepts" for job enrichment?
5 How well does the strategy for the redesign of work described in the reading actually work in practice?

Reading 10

Work Innovations in the United States

Richard E. Walton

Americans tend to do things by trial and error, and in dealing with changes in the way they work, they are no different. Whereas changes in European workplaces tend to be guided by government intervention and ideological rationalizations and involve an explicit transfer of authority, innovations in American work-places are voluntary and pragmatic and involve no such transfer.[1] Despite its random nature, however, much change that has been planned has occurred in American workplaces during the past ten years.

Observers differ about whether work improvement is a fad or a long-term transformation in the nature of work organizations. Scientists differ in their theoretical explanations of why it works or when the conditions are right for it. Managers invariably wonder whether it has application in their organizations, and some union officials are concerned about its implications for the union as an institution. These concerns imply varying conceptions of work innovation and hence indicate the amount of confusion that exists about what work improvement is.

In this article, I want to look at what has actually changed in workplaces, find out what we can learn from these work improvement activities, and derive some principles from what is reflected in the most successful ones. First, though, let us clarify what "work improvement" means and how I will be using it in the remainder of this article.

WHAT WORK IMPROVEMENT IS

The planned changes called "work improvements" have appeared in workplaces in many guises—as "quality of work life," "humanization of work," "work reform," "work restructuring," "work design," and "sociotechnical systems."

Although some of these terms have special connotations for the profession-als who employ them, in method and goals the actual activities pursued under the various labels are not very different. I find it useful to distinguish three separate aspects of a work improvement effort.

1 Design Techniques

The element of work improvement activities that is most apparent is the specific changes in the way work is organized and managed. For instance, the content of

Reprinted from the *Harvard Business Review,* July–August, 1979, pp. 88–98. Copyright © 1979 by the President and Fellows of Harvard College, all rights reserved.

Author's note: I wish to express my special thanks to Leonard Schlesinger, who has reviewed this manuscript at different stages of its development and made helpful suggestions for improving it.

[1]See Ted Mills, "Europe's Industrial Democracy: An American Response," HBR November–December 1978, p. 143.

tasks changes when jobs are enriched, work teams affect the way tasks are organized and how they relate to each other, and consultative management gives workers the opportunity to influence decisions that affect them. The techniques may also affect the information provided workers as well as their compensation, security, physical environment, and access to due process.

The techniques employed and their possible combinations are many. For example, in changing assembly methods, auto plants have assigned related tasks to work teams, allowed them to decide how to allocate the work among themselves (provided they meet quality and quantity requirements), and created buffer inventories between adjacent work teams to increase latitude in the rhythm of their work. Also, management and unions in competitive manufacturing situations have designed plantwide schemes to share productivity increases and have structured mechanisms to ensure that workers' ideas for improvement are considered.

2 Intended Results

Another aspect of work improvement is the results it is intended to produce. They can be either economic (for the benefit of the organization) or human (for the benefit of employees). The business benefits can take many forms—quality, delivery, materials usage, machine capacity utilization, and labor efficiency. The human benefits can take form as real income, security, challenge, variety, advancement opportunity, dignity, equity, and sense of community. The relative importance of these depends on the needs and aspirations of the employees in question.

Most of the work improvement labels focus narrowly on either techniques or results. For example, "job enrichment" directs attention to the techniques level and only to one technique. The connotation of "job design" is only slightly broader. "Quality of work life" has the same limitations. It refers directly to an objective that can be served in innumerable ways. Moreover, as labels, "quality of work life" and its first cousin, "humanization of work," have serious drawbacks; they refer only to human gains, which in today's business environment need to be closely coupled with improved competitive performance.

In my experience, I have found that organizations can improve business results in a humane way and improve the quality of the human experience in a businesslike manner by identifying the work cultures that promote both improvements simultaneously. Such work cultures are the links between technique and results in my three-level conception of work improvements.

3 Work Culture: The Intermediate Effects

The combination of attitudes, relationships, developed capabilities, habits, and other behavioral patterns that characterize the dynamics of an organization is a work culture.

Some changes in the culture, such as high-cost consciousness, responsiveness to authority, and high activity norms, may promote performance but do little or nothing for people. Conversely, under some circumstances, high sensitivity to feelings and concern for the personal growth of the individual are cultural attributes that may be appreciated by the people affected but may not by themselves contribute to business performance.

In the most successful work improvement efforts, the culture simultaneously enhances business performance and the quality of human experience. In one food plant, for instance, management sought to promote employee identification with goals. Such positive identification increases not only workers' motivation to work but also their sense of belonging in the workplace and their pride in the plant's achievement. Similarly, a behavior pattern that influences both employee self-esteem and the soundness of business decisions is another desirable cultural attribute.

Identification and mutual influence are ideals common to many work improvement projects, but no single culture is ideal for all businesses or all people. What particular set of attitudes, capabilities, and relationships a company should emphasize will depend on its industry's strategic performance indexes and its employees' work life values. Whatever the work culture sought, it cannot be mandated by anyone. It can only be shaped over time by a combination of things—including the techniques by which work is organized and managed.

Let us review how these three aspects of work improvement activities relate to each other.

Techniques are the elements of the work organization that people can alter directly; intended results are the fundamental business and human criteria by which to judge effectiveness; and the work culture mediates the impact of the former on the latter. The techniques create the culture, which strongly influences business performance and the human experience at work.

According to this conception, one's choice of techniques is guided by continuously referring to the type of work culture that they promote, and in turn to projected business and human outcomes. For example, in a paper manufacturing plant, the business ends required that the manpower be flexible, and employees wanted the opportunity to acquire new skills. The plant adopted a design in which teams are responsible for a cluster of tasks and members are rewarded for acquiring the skills to perform all the team tasks. Such a design promotes both flexibility and opportunity. (The three-level conception of work improvement is shown in the *Exhibit;* the arrows indicate influence.)

The exhibit illustrates how important it is to specify the proper business and work life outcome for a particular company.

Applying this concept, one is also guided in the quality of choice one should make at each level. As one moves backward in the exhibit from intended results through work culture to design techniques one's stance should become increasingly pragmatic. If the desired outcomes are clear and one's commitment to both business and human values is firm, then one can evaluate cultural attributes and in turn design techniques in terms of their efficacy in achieving the desired results.

The ruled insert on page 137 outlines some principles that arise out of the three-level conception of work innovation.

Exhibit   Three-Level Conception of Work Improvement

Level I Design techniques	Level II Work culture ideals	Level III Intended results
Job design	High skill levels and flexibility in using them	*For business:* Low cost
Pay		Quick delivery
Supervisor's role	Identification with product, process, and total business viewpoint	High-quality product
Training		Low turnover
Performance feedback		Low absenteeism
Goal setting	Problem solving instead of finger pointing	Equipment utilization
Communication		*For quality of work life:*
Employment stability policies	Influence by information and expertise instead of by position	Self-esteem
Status symbols		Economic well-being
Leadership patterns	Mutual influence	Security
	Openness	
	Responsiveness	
	Trust	
	Egalitarian climate	
	Equity	

Note: The design techniques, cultural ideals, and intended results listed above are presented as illustrative, not as comprehensive or even universally applicable. Also, the items in the three columns are not horizontally lined up to relate to each other. The arrows indicate influence.

INTEREST IN WORK INNOVATION

Over the past decade, media attention has gradually shifted from focusing on the symptoms of disaffection with work to possible solutions. The amount of work improvement activity in plants and offices throughout the United States has grown steadily, appearing to be on the path of a classical S growth curve, in which growth climbs slowly at first, accelerates, and then slows again. Today, the rate of growth in these experiments continues to increase annually, suggesting that we are approaching the steeper portion of the curve.

Extrapolating from available information, I estimate that an important minority of the *Fortune "500"* companies are attempting some significant work improvement projects. And, not surprisingly, the companies that have greater commitment to the experience with such projects are among the leaders in their respective industries: General Motors, Procter & Gamble, Exxon, General Foods, TRW, and Cummins Engine. Less prominent but similarly well-managed manufacturing companies such as Butler Manufacturing and Mars, Inc. have also become increasingly active in this area. Citibank is one company with major work improvement efforts in the office environment.[2] Prudential Insurance is another.

All of the manufacturing companies I have listed have regarded new plant start-ups as opportunities to introduce major new work structures. In recent years, major projects have begun in organizations of various sizes (from 100 to

[2]See Richard J. Matteis, "The New Back Office Focuses on Customer Service," HBR March–April 1979, p. 146.

over 3,000), with varying technologies (from simple hand assembly to sophisticated continuous flow processes) and in different geographical locations from
upstate New York to the deep South and the West). As these companies extend
their innovative work systems to other new plant sites, managers learn from the
experience of the pioneers, and the systems cease to be regarded as experimental. Although the diffusion generally occurs slowly, the principles that underlie
these new designs usually spread to companies' established plants as well. Let us
look at some of these work innovations in detail.

Individual Projects

HBR readers have been exposed to a number of accounts of individual efforts
(e.g., the Topeka Pet Food Plant) and to the distinctive approaches of several
U.S. companies (e.g., Donnelly Mirrors and Eaton Corporation).[3] Although not
fully representative of the diverse practices that one can observe, these
experiments do illustrate the growing work improvement activity in the United
States.

To my knowledge, the activity of General Motors is the most extensive of
any company in the United States and may be more extensive than that of Volvo,
whose pioneering efforts have been well publicized internationally. GM's dozens
of projects take a variety of forms. One long-term effort at GM began in the
early 1970s in an assembly plant in Tarrytown, New York. What began as a
"What-have-we-got-to-lose?" experiment in which workers and the union were
involved in redesigning the hard- and soft-trim departments' facilities has
blossomed into a plantwide quality of work life program involving over 3,500
people.

A different type of project at GM began in 1974 at a new battery plant in
Fitzgerald, Georgia, where the pay system was set up to reward knowledge and
skills acquisition. After four years, almost all workers there have become
familiar with a wide range of jobs and have detailed knowledge of the
production process. Initially, inspectors evaluated the workers' performance,
but eventually the production teams themselves acquired the responsibility to
ensure high-quality performance. Since 1977, work teams have prepared their
own departmental budgets for materials and supplies. Managers provide
workers with information such as cost data, which is traditionally not shown to
them. The sparse and functional offices reveal the prevailing attitude about
status symbols.

The pay system, self-supervision, and other design techniques have been
combined at the Fitzgerald plant to create a work culture characterized by
flexibility, mutual trust, informality, equality, and commitment. Reportedly, the
Fitzgerald plant's performance has been very favorable, compared both with
other plants and with its own plan. Those familiar with the plant attribute much

---

[3]See my article, "How to Counter Alienation in the Plant," HBR November–December 1972,
p. 70; "Participative Management at Work," An Interview with John F. Donnelly, HBR
January–February 1977, p. 117; and Donald N. Scobel, "Doing Away with the Factory Blues," HBR
November–December 1975, p. 132.

of its superior performance to the work structure and to the fact that workers take pride in establishing new levels of output and quality.

Another innovator in this field is as much a leader in nondurable consumer goods as GM is in durable goods but shuns publicity of any of its work improvements. It regards the knowledge it has developed about implementing innovative work systems as proprietary, similar to other types of know-how that give it a competitive edge.

In the late 1960s in one plant of a major division, this company introduced a new work system designed around the idea that workers would be paid according to their skill levels. Under this system, the company does not impose quotas to limit the number who could advance to higher levels. The work system promotes the development of relatively self-supervising work teams. The basic features of this system have been adapted to the six new plants built subsequently as well as to departments in the preexisting, unionized plants of the division.

Because successful work improvement approaches have not always spread to other plants within the same company, it is worth noting why transfer did occur in this case. The acceptance of change in the existing plants has been fueled by their need to remain competitive with the newer plants, which employ more productive work structures. The change has been facilitated by transferring managers with experience from the innovative plants to the established ones. Also, whenever a new technology or project has been launched or major physical renovations planned, work innovations have been introduced in the old plants.

I have observed many of the plants in this company. Without a doubt, their innovative work systems have contributed significantly to the impressive performance of these plants and to the fact that by a wide margin the plants are usually regarded as the best places to work in their respective communities.

Although GM and the manufacturer of nondurable goods are leaders in the field of work improvements, they are not typical. Most companies, such as Butler Manufacturing, have only a few projects. In 1976, Butler introduced innovative work structures similar to the one at GM's Fitzgerald plant in two new plants. In one plant, the program is working exceptionally well; participants are enthusiastic about the work system and think it contributes strongly to their performance. According to pertinent internal criteria, this plant is 20% more productive and 35% more profitable than comparable plants in the same company.

The other new plant has experienced difficulties, and it is less clear that it has benefited from the work innovations.

The experience of a large paper company is also typical. With encouragement and support from the company's chairman, management launched two major facilitywide projects at the time of the plants' start-ups. When I last heard, the paper mill project was regarded as successful, but the other, in a converting plant, was not. Extenuating circumstances in the marketplace have contributed to the lack of profitability of the converting plant. Also, misjudgments in design reportedly have not been remedied, and optimism is declining.

Most companies experience both success and failure. One large company with four major plantwide projects has experienced almost the full spectrum. A plant that started up with a bold and imaginative work structure three and a half years ago has been very disappointing in terms of economic performance and the work system itself. Local management and union officials judge a second plant to be only somewhat more effective than it would have been without the innovations. A third is solidly effective, and a fourth is a big success according to both human and economic criteria.

The examples I have discussed so far are plant projects, but comparably conceived work improvement efforts have been occurring in office settings as well. In 1972, the clerical work in the Group Policyholders' Service Department of the Guardian Life Insurance Company was fragmented. To process a case file required several steps, each performed by a different person at a different desk in assembly line fashion. Files were hard to find, and responses to client inquiries were delayed. No one person performed or had responsibility for a whole job. Consequently, there was little basis for meaningful recognition of achievement, and morale was low.

The work improvement effort created natural units of work by combining policyholder services and accounting functions for a particular geographic area. The new "account analyst" became identified with a limited and stable set of clients with whom he or she provided a number of services previously assigned to different desks. Control over individual aspects of the work was removed, and individual accountability for overall results was increased.

Although the new work system at Guardian required people to go through complex training, with the result that 6 out of 120 employees could not meet the demands of the redesigned jobs, management reports that the system was effective in producing cumulative increases in productivity of about 33% in four years.

Top Management Interest

Part of the evidence supporting my projection of a continued acceleration of the growth rate of new projects goes beyond concrete activities; it is found in the trend toward increased top management attention to work innovation. Whereas five years ago it was plant or division level managers who invariably sought educational or consultative assistance for potential projects, today it is equally likely that inquiries will come from top corporate managers who are interested in advancing their own understanding of the field, formulating appropriate policies, and promoting constructive corporate activity.

Also, whereas before managers would invite professors to meet with them and report on developments in the field, today it is equally likely that managers with direct experience in promoting work innovations will address these management groups. For example, the chairman of the board of a major packaging company recently assembled his top corporate and divisional executives to learn about the work innovations of a major automobile company by a firsthand report of the auto company's vice chairman.

A particularly striking example of the trend toward top management interest in work innovations and toward more manager-to-manager consultation on the subject is provided by a November 1977 conference sponsored by the American Center for the Quality of Working Life. Convened for the purpose of exchanging experiences and examining from the "practical viewpoint of operating executives the principles underlying quality of work life efforts and their efficacy in society," the conference was attended by 40 senior executives from Xerox, General Motors, Nabisco, and Weyerhaeuser.

The "blue collar blues" may promote the adoption and diffusion of innovative work designs in a wide range of industries, from blue collar manufacturing work to white collar and service work and in both the private and the public sector, but a major reason companies are trying work improvement projects is competition. Another is the changing expectations of workers, whose consciousness of quality of work life issues continues to rise. Another is the implicit threat of legislation that might set new, more embracing quality of work environment standards or that might require workers to participate in the governance of private industry.

ASKING THE RIGHT QUESTIONS

Despite the many good reasons for attempting work improvement systems, their future depends on how managers approach some fundamental issues and whether they reject the myths surrounding these efforts. Some misconceptions yield easily to more valid assumptions; others appear to need more direct challenge.

Have Work Improvements Been Effective?

There has been a tendency for people to assume that work innovation projects are either spectacular successes or abject failures. At the expense of some widely held myths, however, people active in the field have become increasingly realistic, recognizing that, in fact, projects can and do fall at every point along a broad spectrum of effectiveness.

I have been deeply involved in 4 major projects and am familiar with aspects of another 30 or so. In terms of their effectiveness in achieving excellence in business and quality of work life outcomes, my impression is that these three dozen projects represent roughly a normal distribution around the mean, just as the effectiveness of more conventionally organized plants would be expected to form a normal distribution.

I believe that the average effectiveness of these innovative work systems is higher than the average of more conventionally organized but otherwise comparable plants. Certainly, however, the poorly managed innovative plants are less effective than the better managed conventional ones. I cannot offer proof that these assumptions are valid, but the mixed experiences of the companies I have discussed illustrate my observations.

Despite the evidence, the myths persist. I have visited a few innovative plants that were advertised as significantly successful, only to discover that they were at best marginally more effective than they would have been without the work innovations. And I have read reports of the "failures" of previously publicized projects, which, on investigation, I found were faulty. People had blown some difficulties encountered in the design or implementation of the projects way out of proportion.

Why these exaggerations? First, people view such efforts with emotion—some being deeply committed to work improvement activities, others being basically hostile to them. Second, when they are involved, the media deem dramatic successes and failures to be newsworthy. Third, because their expectations are high, people readily see any shortfall as a failure.

Even assuming that work innovations have merit, managers and researchers need to have the realistic expectation that their effectiveness will conform to some normal distribution.

What Are the Sponsors' Motives?

Myths have surrounded the motives of those promoting or undertaking work improvement activities. People see sponsors as narrowly interested in either productivity or the human condition, each at the expense of the other. During the early 1970s, when much interest in work improvement was stimulated by one of the two objectives, these beliefs had some basis in reality, but the situation has gradually changed.

In the successful innovations, managers behave as if both economic and human values count. I am familiar with several major innovative work systems that have taken a long time to become effective (and in one plant remain not very effective today) because management's choices were too heavily influenced by quality of work life considerations in the beginning.

In one case, for example, while stability of assignments and mastery of jobs was necessary to get the plant's new technology under control, employees were permitted to move among jobs and learn multiple skills that would advance their pay. Management later recognized that it had erred in not continuously keeping economic as well as human considerations in mind.

Conversely, I am aware of some abortive job redesign efforts in which management strictly viewed worker satisfaction either as a means to improve productivity or as an incidental by-product. Not surprisingly, management's orientation affected not only what changes were made but also workers' attitudes toward the changes. Many union officials believe it unwise to be publicly committed to productivity as well as to quality of work life goals lest the former be identified with speedups and other activities that achieve productivity at the workers' expense. Nevertheless, union officials often implicitly acknowledge the legitimacy of improved business results.

A commitment to dual outcomes is congruent with the values increasingly held by knowledgeable people, but also it has proved to be the most practical approach to making significant advances toward either end. Consider the point negatively. When changes in the work structure do not improve the work

Principles Reflected in the
Three-Level Conception of Work
Innovation

Most effective work improvement efforts have reflected the following principles. I have induced them largely from experience rather than deduced them from social science theory.

1   In designing work structures, it is imperative to be absolutely committed to the results one chooses (shown on the far right of the *Exhibit*). One should become pragmatic in the choice of techniques to achieve these ends (shown on the far left of the *Exhibit*).

2   Recognize that no universally applicable set of human preferences and priorities regarding quality of work life exists. Hypotheses about what would enhance human experience at work may be useful, provided that they are tested with the people in question and are revised or discarded and replaced on the basis of that experience. The same points apply to the determination of the business results that the work culture should promote.

3   Accept that most techniques affect business and human results indirectly, altering first the culture of the organization. Even if in their designs planners ignore cultural considerations, the latter will nevertheless surface as the most important elements of the operation. Participants and visiting observers are quick to appreciate the motivation, cooperation, problem solving, openness, and candor that often mark a successful effort in practice.

4   Imagine the attitudes, relationships, and capabilities that would promote both business achievement and quality of work life in a particular setting, and then use these cultural attributes as proximate criteria for guiding the design of the work structure. In many cases, duality of goals is absent, or the step of idealizing a work culture is omitted, or both. An elaborate methodology is not required, but a certain type of thinking is advantageous.

5   Be sure that at the technique level the many different elements of design and management practice—reward scheme, division of labor, performance reporting scheme, status symbols, and leadership style—are consistent with each other, each reinforcing or complementing the other. When these elements of the work structure serve common or compatible signals, the culture will be internally consistent; if they send "mixed signals," people will feel ambivalent. Also, the more comprehensive the planned work structure and the more the design elements are aligned with each other, the more powerful the structure will be in shaping a distinctive work culture.

environment from a human perspective, they will not increase employees' contribution to the business; likewise, changes in work structure that require managers to relate differently to workers but do not also benefit the business are not as likely to be sustained by those managers over time.

One should not confuse a dedication to achieving both results with the assumption that meeting one will guarantee the other; morale and productivity are not necessarily linked. Morale can be enhanced in any number of ways. Rather, a commitment to dual objectives sets in motion a search for the limited set of changes that will promote both human and economic ends.

Some issues will inevitably not yield to dual orientation. Planners and managers will have to make trade-off decisions in areas where achieving human goals can occur only at the expense of the business, and vice versa. Nevertheless, it is more important for those involved in work improvement to recognize that in most work structures there is an abundance of opportunities to make changes that will advance both objectives.

What Do Workers Really Want from Work?

Individuals and groups will always express broad differences in the types of work structure they prefer. Therefore, as the multiple-level framework indicates, the ideal culture and the design features of the work structure need to be responsive to the employee population at a given location. Even though researchers and managers are learning which questions about employees' needs and preferences will provide good guidelines to practice, they continue to ask a few either-or questions, which are more confusing than helpful.

Observers often ask variations of the following question: "Are people motivated more by intrinsic factors, such as tasks that use and develop their skills, or by extrinsic factors, such as variable pay for performance and the prospect of advancement?" Both kinds of factor are important, albeit one may be more important to any one group at any one time. The most significant question is how to integrate both extrinsic and intrinsic factors in a practical way.

My observation is that workers in innovative systems have not had to choose between more interesting work and more pay; and that where intrinsic satisfaction has increased, the pay has been improved, reflecting the workers' greater contribution. As Irving Bluestone of the UAW has said of the American worker, "While his rate of pay may dominate his relationship to his job, he can be responsive to the opportunity for playing an innovative, creative, and imaginative role in the production process."[4]

A related question people often ask is: "Are people more interested in finding meaning in the workplace or in minimizing the time spent there?" While the answer to this question may add to our understanding of the sociology of work today, it is not a productive question for improving current practice. It is better to assume that the work force as a whole would like both in some measure.

But, even if some workers care more about time off than a meaningful work life, it may still pay to heed the lower priority issue because improving the meaning of the workplace may be much more feasible than reducing the workweek. Speculating about workers' desires also leads to the related myths about regional differences and the need for selective hiring. Each myth is built on the assumption that a relatively small subset of the work force has attitudes and talents compatible with work restructuring. I have heard managers assert, "It may work in a plant located in a small town in the Midwest, but workers in the South (or the Northeast, California, big cities, and so on) are different."

If an innovative plant is located in an abundant labor market where supervisors screen, say, six times as many applicants as they actually hire, then their myth may be: "Only one in six is a high achiever who will be receptive to

[4]See Irving Bluestone, "The Next Step Toward Industrial Democracy" (Detroit: UAW Paper 1972), p. 4.

the new work structure. It is okay to redesign work if you can be selective but not if you are in a tight labor market."

Fortunately, since projects are launched in all regions of the country, in both rural and urban areas, in both tight and abundant labor markets, and appear to have a degree of effectiveness not determined by these factors, belief in these myths is weakening.

What Economic Benefits Can One Expect?

Managers frequently ask: "How much productivity gain can one expect from work redesign?" Unfortunately, some advocates answer: "One should be able to achieve 15% to 20% improvement in productivity." The question itself is emphatically misdirected, and the response just cited is meaningless without knowing what index of productivity the questioner has in mind and whether it is appropriate. For example, the number of output units per man-hour may not be an important index when labor is a low fraction of total costs. Moreover, prior to analysis of the operations in question, one cannot assume a basis for the estimates.

An inquiry and response should focus on methods by which managers can answer the question for themselves. The form of potential gains will vary significantly according to the technology used. The magnitude of possible gains will depend on how well the unit is already performing and on whether the aspects of performance that can be improved are strongly influenced by employees' attitudes and skills. Finally, whether potential gains ever materialize depends on the quality of redesign ideas and their implementation.

The following examples illustrate how productivity indexes can take different forms:

- A facility that warehouses and supplies engine parts to dealers and dealer chains could gain new accounts by speeding up its delivery response; it could add very profitable business if it could promise certain large national chains 48 hours versus 72 hours for delivery.
- In a capital-intensive plant that machines casted parts, management determined that it was technically feasible to increase by 15% the maximum throughput of a $10 million segment of the technology manned by 10 employees. This rate has, however, been achieved only for brief periods of time because of the limitations of operating personnel. Running speeds and machine downtime play a similarly important role in other parts of this plant and strongly affect its competitiveness.
- In a relatively high labor-intensive business, management was experiencing a high rate of turnover. The particular tasks, mostly assembly line jobs, did not require great skill, but learning the idiosyncracies of the company's many different products took a lot of time. While the new employees were learning to deal with these peculiarities, their higher scrap rates and lower labor efficiency significantly affected unit costs. As a result, the turnover costs were significant.

To assess the potential of work improvements in the foregoing operations, one should ask: "How much difference would it make if workers cared more and knew more about this work?" Let us examine the first example in light of this question to show how one can begin to analyze the situation.

First, one needs some facts: the replacement engine parts center employs about 100 hourly workers; the pay is good for this type of work in the area; turnover is relatively low; and labor relations are amicable. While workers do not especially identify with management and many are known to goof off whenever possible, they are not antagonistic.

After a preliminary analysis of the various ways in which performance is sensitive to employee motivation and knowledge, the management of the center estimated that:

1 Employees could reasonably handle a 10% additional volume, even allowing for increased time to be devoted to training and regular meetings. But the 10% savings would not create a net economic benefit because the wage increases reflecting greater job scope and skills would offset them.

2 The cost of errors (orders lost, wrong parts pulled, overages, underages, or damages in shipment due to carelessness) could be reduced by $100,000 per year.

3 The work system could reliably handle up to 25% of the facility's volume within a 48-hour response time, enabling the management to win over some additional accounts and increase the margins on some existing ones and thereby to add an estimated $200,000 more profit per year.

4 The potential benefits of $300,000 assumes a work force that cares more and knows more and that is amenable to flexibility in work assignments based on the needs of the business, the latter point being especially critical to reducing the center's response time.

The foregoing analysis illustrates good practice.

First, management identified particular points in the system where poor labor utilization, errors, and limitations in response time occurred. It did not rely on global hunches.

Second, by converting potential gains to annual dollar amounts, management could see the relative importance of error reduction and improved response time. Moreover, management could relate the benefits to other factors; for example, $300,000 would be a savings equal to 25% of the annual payroll.

Third, management understood these were potential benefits and not certain gains that would automatically flow from the adoption of some set of design techniques. Its ability to achieve any of these benefits depended on its ingenuity and skill. It always ran the risk that it would not be able to modify the work culture as intended.

Fourth, management knew that for any changes to be effective from a business standpoint, it would also have to improve the work from the workers' point of view.

Managers in the machining operation and assembly unit followed procedures similar to the one just outlined. However, their estimate of benefits took a different form. Because they could spread the large fixed interest and depreciated expenses, managers in the capital-intensive machining operation figured that increasing the output rate of finished parts by 15% would result in lower unit costs. The estimated annual savings represented 150% of the $140,000 payroll for the unit—that is, $210,000.

In the assembly line unit, the managers concluded that it was not feasible to reduce turnover significantly, that only modest improvements in scrap and labor efficiency were possible, and that costs associated with any changes contemplated would largely offset the estimated gains.

In cases such as those just described, management's analyses are limited by the same difficulties encountered in estimating the costs and benefits of untried technologies or management systems—that is, the estimates can prove to be incomplete, too optimistic, too conservative, and so on. Nevertheless, the analytic approach presented here illustrates the systematic and realistic efforts managers should make to assess the potential performance gains.

Which procedures a manager actually uses and the level of detail of the analysis is not the point. The important point is that planners have some systematic approach for assessing potential benefits that might accrue if the cultural ideals are actually realized. The methodology need not be elaborate.

SOME LESSONS FROM EXPERIENCE

For those who consider undertaking new initiatives and promoting the spread of successful innovations to other units in the organization, I offer the following guidelines. Though not comprehensive, they are nonetheless derived from observations of the contrasts between relatively effective work improvement efforts and less effective ones.

1 Attempt work improvement because of its intrinsic positive values, not because it might be a way to avoid unionization. Apart from the fact that I believe in the institution of collective bargaining, trying to avoid unionization has several drawbacks. One is that unions are more likely to join in efforts to adapt innovations to existing facilities if work patterns are not being used as an antiunion device in the new plants. Another is that, although most projects in the United States have been in nonunionized offices and plants, the amount of joint union-management cooperation is increasing. Such projects as Harman Industries, Weyerhaeuser, Tennessee Valley Authority, the Rushton Coal Mines, and Rockwell International attest to the benefit of cooperation.

As I stated earlier, GM and UAW have a very active program of work improvement. The approach contractually agreed on by the parties is oriented to quality of work life, but as the Tarrytown experience illustrates, management, union officials, and workers are all genuinely interested in the business results. Irving Bluestone, international vice president of the UAW, describes the joint GM-UAW program as follows:

"The objective of our quality of work life program is to create a more participative and satisfying work environment. If, as a result of increased participation, unit costs are improved because turnover rates go down and product quality goes up, that is fine.

"But if a plant manager is thinking of a quality of work life project as a means for increasing productivity, we don't proceed. There are certain other constraints—people must not be compelled to work harder, changes must not result in workers getting laid off, and the local and national agreements remain inviolate. The projects must be from the ground up and participation voluntary on the part of workers. The first phase of all projects is to improve the climate of mutual respect between union and management; if this doesn't succeed, there is no basis to proceed on. Plant management and the local union must both be committed."[5]

During the past half dozen years, as work improvement activities have been growing in number, diversity, and visibility, both labor and management have encountered doubt within their own ranks. UAW officials have not found it easy to convince union members that the program is not a management gimmick to increase productivity and perhaps weaken the union.

At GM, managers at certain levels express concern that the program will result in a loss of authority and prestige. These fears are diminishing gradually but can flare up at any event that seems to support them. Still, the commitment at the top of both organizations has been extraordinary and is bolstered by a growing constituency of local managers and union officials who have had positive experiences.

According to Bluestone, very few projects have actually failed, but more time must pass before the majority of projects currently under way can be declared successes.

2 Recognize the basic difference between opportunities in new facilities and opportunities in existing ones. Once, most people assumed that the major innovations introduced in new plant start-ups could serve as inspirational and instructive examples for managements and union officials of established plants. I have concluded that providing examples of what was done in a new organization is not helpful in enabling managers of established units to visualize alternative futures for their units and is not an effective stimulus for developing a program for transforming them.

The reasons are severalfold and go beyond the fact that a particular work structure that is successful in a new plant may be inappropriate in an old one. More fundamentally, the processes of innovation (diagnosing, planning, inventing, and implementing) are significantly different for new and existing units. In established facilities, the level of aspiration for change and the time frame allotted for achieving it must be much more modest than in new facilities.

In selecting aspects of work structure that can be changed, planners need to be opportunistic—doing what they can when they can. Also, the main job of planners in old facilities is defrosting the old work culture and creating a sense of

---

[5]Irving Bluestone, in personal conversation with the author.

the potential for change. To do this, they need to give careful attention to the participative processes for deciding the direction and method of the change.

Fortunately, the literature is providing us with a growing number of instructive examples of productive change in established organizations. The Tarrytown plant is one such example.

3 Avoid either-or conceptions of work organization.   An example of this faulty thinking relates to the sources and types of controls: "Traditional systems rely on hierarchical controls. The innovative system is the opposite; therefore, it must rely on individual or team self-management." Another example of this thinking is: "If we need to rely on self-discipline and peer group pressure to minimize counterproductive behavior, then there is no place for management-administered discipline."

Indeed, as managers in these work systems have sooner or later discovered, a selective emphasis and sensible mixture of management techniques are called for. A number of organizations have had to go through a period of permissiveness before management discovered the need to set and enforce certain boundaries on the behavior of members of the company.

Managers make a related mistake when they assume that an organization at start-up can be at an idealized, advanced state of development. Some plans for new plant organization neglect the important distinction between conceiving of the steady state design and designing the initial organization. These plants start up with workers and supervisors having roles and responsibilities that reflect the planners' idealized view of the mature organization. Workers lack the technical and human skills as well as the problem-solving capacities to perform effectively. Supervisors cannot merely "facilitate"—they must provide directive supervision.

Delegation is the cornerstone of new plant development. Such delegation must be rooted in careful diagnosis of the existing base of skills and capabilities in the work force and a realistic view of their ability to develop over time.

4 Do not advocate one answer; spread a way of looking for answers. Managers and planners need to inculcate their people with a way of thinking about the diagnosis and designing of innovative work structures, not the work structures themselves. This is a major implication of any three-level conception of work improvement activity. It is less appropriate (and sometimes counterproductive) to promote the spread of particular techniques—for example, enriched jobs, team concepts, productivity gain sharing—than it is to promote the diffusion of a diagnostic and innovative planning process.

REVIEW AND DISCUSSION QUESTIONS

1 Give five examples of work innovations.
2 Describe General Motors' job change program.
3 In terms of goal setting, feedback, and participation research, would you expect GM changes to increase performance?

4 Is job enrichment acceptable to all employees? What might be some of the shortcomings of the GM job changes?

Reading 11

Is Codetermination a Workable Idea for U.S. Labor-Management Relations?

Kenneth A. Kovach
Ben F. Sands, Jr.
William W. Brooks

Participation by employees in decision making at the upper levels in private industry has been the exception rather than the rule in the United States, but there are indications this situation will change. Such diverse individuals as United Auto Workers Vice President Irving Bluestone, Undersecretary of Commerce Sidney Harman, and Federal Mediation Service Commissioner Samuel Sackman have spoken of the increasing need for worker involvement in decision making. In addition, experiments with employee participation in such firms as Harman International Industries and Carborundum Co., and the current Chrysler–U.A.W. agreement allowing union president Douglas Fraser a seat on the company's board of directors, are evidence that rhetoric is being replaced, at least in some instances, by action.

To evaluate the potential for this idea in the United States, it is necessary to define several terms. It would also be helpful to trace the history of one of the more highly developed, legally mandated systems of labor participation in an industrialized nation.

The degree of integration of all members of an organization into the decision-making process ranges from zero (all decisions made by one person) to 100 percent (anarchy). The types of decisions (working conditions, societal responsibilities, production, financial matters, marketing approach, and so forth) form subsets within the overall system of decision.

Originally, the major decisions affecting workers were made by religious leaders or the nobility. With the coming of industrialization, decisions were made by the owners of capital, who regarded workers as one of the means of production. For various reasons—increasing wealth of the workers, higher levels of education in the labor force, greater complexity of the technological means of production, organization among the workers, and so forth—it was deemed necessary and desirable to introduce a degree of industrial democracy, involving

From *MSU Business Topics,* Winter, 1980, p. 49–55. Reprinted with permission of the publisher, Division of Research, Graduate School of Business Administration, Michigan State University.

the labor force in the decisions affecting conditions of work, methods of production, and, ultimately, financial and investment decisions.

Research into the evolution of this development reveals many descriptive terms. Among the more popular are *participative management, industrial democracy, autogestion* (French for *self-management*), and *Mitbestimmung* (German for *codetermination*). It is interesting to note that one of the major indices used in the United States usually lumps these terms under *participative management,* although they mean entirely different things insofar as management, labor, and society are concerned.[1] While it may be true that they are parts of a spectrum along which worker participation may be measured, the results of each can differ greatly, and the workability of each may be dependent upon exogenous factors such as culture, economic development, and other environmental conditions.

Labor leaders, industrialists, and society should be aware of the distinctions and differences among the various levels of organizational democracy, if for no other reason than that the subject cannot be discussed rationally unless our terms are well defined.

Henry Mintzberg points out that many movements (degrees of participation in our terms) have hardly touched the United States.

> What has received considerable attention there [in the United States] instead is "participative management." In discussing this concept, two of its propositions should be clearly distinguished. One, of a factual—that is, testable—nature, is that participation leads to increased productivity: Involve your employees and they will produce more, management is told [e.g., Likert, 1961]. The other, a value proposition and so not subject to verification, is that participation is a value worthy in and of itself: "In a 'democratic' society workers have the right to participate in the organizations that employ them." The American debate over participative management has focused almost exclusively on the first, factual proposition (although the proponents seem really to be committed to the second, value position).[2]

The latter concept, the right of workers to participate in decision making, is the one that forms the ideological base for the actions of many European unions. It also is the one that causes major concern among U.S. managers and, it may be added parenthetically, many U.S. unions. James Furlong says that "the theme of extending to economic life the principles of political democracy—the right of all citizens to help choose their leaders and to express their opinions freely on the choice and fulfillment of group goals— is the *red thread* that runs through all defenses of Mitbestimmung [codetermination]."[3]

CODETERMINATION IN WEST GERMANY

One West German experiment is of particular interest. A combination of historical developments—a perception of common interests among industrialists and labor in dealing with an occupying army, and general cultural and social factors—has resulted in legislation that requires the participation of many West German workers in decision making at all levels. Since July 1976, West German law has given workers near parity with stockholders in controlling the management of approximately 625 major companies, employing about five million workers.[4]

In March 1979, West Germany's high court dismissed a suit brought by twenty-nine employers' associations and nine companies asserting that the 1976 law undermined property rights and blurred the line between companies and unions in collective bargaining.[5]

The 1976 law, Mitbestimmung in der Bundes Republic Deutschland (Codetermination in the Federal Republic of Germany) is the latest in a long series of legislative acts establishing and defining the rights of workers in German industry.

As early as 1848, political representatives of German labor demanded the establishment of factory committees which were to include workers. Although no legislation resulted from this first parliamentary discussion, worker committees were established in some companies on a voluntary basis. These were consulted primarily on social matters.[6] In 1905, mining companies with more than 100 employees were required to establish worker committees under the provisions of the Prussian Mining Law.[7] This law and subsequent regulations in 1916 and 1920 established worker committees with full rights of participation in decisions concerning working conditions and limited rights in financial and personnel matters, although final decisions were made by management alone.

The Nazi regime dissolved all trade unions. Union headquarters were occupied by the military and their funds confiscated. Most of the leading trade unionists were arrested, and workers and employers were placed in the German work front.

Following World War II, German industrialists, in an attempt to prevent the decartelization of the steel industry, made common cause with German trade unions in dealing with the occupation authorities. Works councils were established along the lines of the Works Councils Act of 1920. The 1946 Allied Control Council Law No. 22 provided the basis for these councils. Finally, in 1951 the Act on the Codetermination of Workers in the Supervisory and Management Boards of Undertakings in the Mining Industry was passed. This was, according to Furlong, the "high-water point in the Mitbestimmung movement."[8]

Current German law requires a works council (Betriebsrat) in any firm employing more than five workers. The council must represent both blue-collar and white-collar workers in proportion to their numbers in the company. Nationwide elections to the councils are held triennially. Ballots are secret, and only workers are allowed to vote. The number of representatives elected ranges from one (five to twenty employees) to thirty-one (7,001 to 9,000 employees). In companies with more than 9,000 employees, two additional works council members are required for every additional 3,000 employees or part thereof.

Companies with several plants or divisions must establish a central council for the firm. Normally, each works council furnishes two representatives to the central council. In conglomerates, a group works council may be established at the option of the separate councils.

Certain works council members must be released to devote all their time to council matters. The number released ranges from one (in units with more than 300 employees) to twelve (in units with more than 10,000 employees). All members are entitled to four weeks of paid vacation during the first year to attend training courses and other educational functions related to the activities of the council. The firm must provide facilities, information, and assistance to the council.

The works council does not bargain for wages and working conditions normally negotiated by the unions on a regional or national basis, but it has a right to codetermination—an equal say with management in deciding such issues as

- Job evaluation, piece rates, and wage structures;
- Working hours, overtime arrangements, breaks, and holiday schedules;
- Staffing policies, including guidelines for recruiting, assigning, and dismissing workers;
- Social plans, that is, measures to mitigate the effect of layoffs on workers in the event of redundancy;
- Training, occupational safety, and welfare schemes;
- Allocation of company housing; and
- Workers' conduct on the shop floor.[9]

Hiring, discharge, work allocation, promotion, and demotion decisions require the consent of the council. Unilateral action by the employer in these areas is not allowed.

In companies with more than 100 employees, an economic council *(Wirtschaftausschuss)* of four to eight members is appointed by the works council. The economic council has limited powers but has the right to information on important issues such as manufacturing methods, automation, production programs, and data concerning the financial condition of the firm. Analysis of this information is the responsibility of the economic council, while final approval of proposed actions of the firm rests with the works council.

Codetermination also functions at the management level. In German joint stock or incorporated public firms, a supervisory board *(Aufsichtsrat)* is elected by the shareholders and is generally comparable to the board of directors in U.S. firms. A management board *(Vorstand)* conducts the day-to-day business of the firm. No member of either board may serve on the other. Private limited liability firms (the most popular form of organization in Germany) are not required to have a supervisory board unless they have more than 500 employees. Smaller private firms with unlimited liability (partnerships, and so forth) are outside the limits of the Codetermination Act.

The power of the supervisory board to appoint and supervise the management board and to make major decisions concerning the goals and objectives of the firm makes membership on the board extremely important to the worker.

Current law requires three general levels of worker representation on the supervisory boards:

1 Parity with shareholders in coal, iron, and steel producing industries employing more than 1,000 workers;

2 One-third representation in joint stock companies employing up to 2,000 workers and in other limited liability companies employing between 500 and 2,000 workers; and

3 Equal representation (with a bias in favor of the shareholders) in firms with a work force of more than 2,000.[10]

The management board constitutes the lower half of the two-tier board system. In the steel industry, the workers choose the labor director *(Arbeitsdirektor),* although this power is not inherent in current law. The labor director (personnel director in U.S. terms) has specific competencies in staff and social matters.

Experience has shown that, to fulfill the purpose and objectives of the Codetermination Act and in the interest of the undertaking, concerned persons appointed as labor directors should have the special confidence of the employees.[11] Furlong says that "whether the unions in fact control the post will be left to capital and labor to thrash out."[12]

We are beginning to hear discussion of the desirability and practicality of implementing a codetermination system in the United States. It is important, then, to address the issue from the relative perspectives of U.S. management and labor organizations, since the latter most likely will be the structure through which employee involvement is channeled.

THE UNION PERSPECTIVE

Since most codetermination schemes which have been implemented in the United States include the particular labor organization representing the workers on the governing board instead of, or in addition to, unspecified employee representatives, it becomes imperative to discuss codetermination from a labor perspective.[13]

Before doing so, it is important to reemphasize the differences between U.S. unions and their West German counterparts which have embraced the concept of codetermination. As noted earlier, the works councils in West Germany have two main roles. They are responsible for plant bargaining over issues—such as job evaluation, working hours, training, and so forth—not dealt with in collective agreements at regional or national levels. Many of these issues are also of primary interest to national unions in the United States. In addition, the works council is considered the first and fundamental forum for codetermination.

The wildcat strikes at the plant level that plague so many European industries are virtually unknown in Germany. Strikes can be called only at the regional or national level. If the works council and the employer are unable to agree on an issue, either may apply for arbitration by a committee of an equal number of worker and employee representatives and one neutral member.

Unlike members of shop steward committees in the United States, German works council members (with the exception of two or three members, depending on the size of the company) are not required to be union members. Any employee aged 18 or older may vote for council members; candidates must have been with the firm for at least six months.[14]

Much of the real power in unions in West Germany rests in small local units rather than at the national level. Unions thus structured will be more receptive to ideas such as codetermination than will national unions, as in the U.S. system, which are legally guaranteed formal interaction with employers to discuss conditions of employment.

Many alleged experts, while acknowledging the success of codetermination or similar schemes in West Germany, Sweden, Israel, and so forth, contend that similar systems will not work in this country due to the different role of labor organizations in the United States. The ultimate goal of organized labor in many countries in which the industrial democracy experiments are working has been to achieve an unspecified equal footing with management in the operation of the business. Thus, ideas such as codetermination have fit nicely into their long-range objectives. Government legislation of such schemes, as in West Germany, is viewed by labor as welcome assistance from an unexpected source. In the United States, however, organized labor has sought to fill a different role. Most U.S. unions think of themselves as the protectors of employees, as the intervening variable between workers and management, serving as a safeguard against exploitive management action. The fact that, after "economic gain," the reason given most frequently by new union members for joining is "protection against arbitrary management action" is evidence of popular perception of the degree to which unions fulfill this role.[15]

This being the case, many U.S. unions question the desirability of sitting with management on codetermination boards. They certainly must work with management, and they may wish their members to see them as interacting with management on an equal footing, but a checks-and-balances relationship still may be the most advantageous from organized labor's standpoint. As Albert Zack, AFL-CIO director of public relations, has said, it is preferable for U.S. unions to meet company representatives across the bargaining table rather than try to get involved in traditional management functions.[16] The feeling of many union officials—that under the present collective bargaining arrangement labor probably bargains on as many, if not more, issues than the number they might have any effect on as members of a board of directors—adds to the conviction that the present way is the best. In addition, many in the labor movement feel that, unlike most European unions, they finally have won equality at the bargaining table, and they are reluctant to throw it away for the promise of equality in the boardroom.

Nevertheless, some unions in the public sector would welcome the introduction of codetermination. Richard Calistri of the American Federation of Government Employees has said that his organization would be delighted to have codetermination introduced, provided management genuinely cooperates and does not just look out for its own interests.[17] Part of the reason public sector unions are more positive about codetermination may be that they have not been afforded the opportunity to bargain collectively on a range of issues, as have their private sector counterparts. Thus, for them, the prospect of sitting on a corporate board of directors may hold the promise of affecting an increased number of issues, a promise not as easily envisioned by private sector unions.

Another union perspective is represented by the International Brotherhood of Teamsters, Warehousemen, and Helpers of America, who regard the question of codetermination in U.S. industry as moot. While agreeing that it might benefit organized labor, the Teamsters contend that implementation in this country would be both impractical (the membership is not seen as favoring it) and counter to the free enterprise system.[18]

The only major private sector union to endorse the idea wholeheartedly appears to be the United Automobile Workers. As mentioned earlier, U.A.W. Vice-President Irving Bluestone and Undersecretary of Commerce Sidney Harman have worked together to bring codetermination closer to implementation in the United States through experiments with its introduction in such places as Bolivar, Tennessee (Harman), and Jamestown, New York (Carborundum). In both instances, the experiment has been reasonably successful.[19] Results of the current experiment at Chrysler will be closely followed to see if the results are equally satisfactory.

It is ironic that while many in the management sector of the federal government, such as Sidney Harman and Commissioner Sackman, have spoken favorably of codetermination, it is the increased involvement of such individuals in labor-management relations, necessitated by the new system, that may well be the major negative aspect of the plan in the eyes of labor leaders. Based on experience in other countries, there is no doubt that the introduction of codetermination would, at least initially, mean increased government involvement in labor-management relations. It is generally accepted that more laws will be needed to govern the composition of these boards as well as their jurisdiction over traditional collective bargaining subjects and their relationship to stockholders, and so forth. The imposition of the federal government to this extent in private sector labor-management relations is outside the traditions and interests of the American labor movement. Most labor leaders would much prefer to bargain with private employers than to wrestle with government bureaucrats.

THE MANAGEMENT PERSPECTIVE

From the perspective of American business owners and managers, industrial democracy represents both threat and promise. The perceived threat to managerial aims has been evidenced by more than a century of active struggle against organized labor—from resistance to early railroad strikes in the Midwest to present-day textile industry boycotts and legal battles in the South. While steady inroads have been made into formerly management-determined conditions of employment such as employee benefits, health, and safety, resistance to workers' sharing in decisions on planning and operations has remained strong and effective. Decision making in the American workplace is still viewed as management property.

Notwithstanding the threatening aspect of industrial democracy, its promise has received increasing emphasis as concern about worker productivity has risen in the 1970s. Several recent studies have indicated that worker participation programs often have been successful in raising productivity.[20] Such venerable strategies of worker participation as the Scanlon Plan and the incentive plans at Kaiser Steel and Lincoln Electric Company have been outdone in popularity by latter-day formulas for job enrichment, team projects, management by objectives, and other participative schemes. These attempts to involve American workers in the operation of business do not envision participation in direction of the firm. The traditional role of management as paternalistic initiator has been altered very little.

In fact, many strategies of industrial democracy have been motivated by management's desire to deny union representation or at least to limit its influence. Industrial democracy and worker participation programs have been used as planned, preemptive tactics by such management representative organizations as the National Association of Manufacturers.[21]

Codetermination, which represents the extreme form of industrial democracy—granting labor a formal voice in company decision making—is, of course, anathema to tradition conscious American employers. It has been acknowledged as a threat in publications of the NAM.[22]

SUMMARY

The fact that U.S. unions have not generally endorsed codetermination as an aim of the labor movement seems to preclude its receiving significant support in the political arena at present. Since the red thread referred to by Furlong is a specter that alarms union leaders as well as managers, it appears political capital could not be made by backing codetermination. That fact probably accounts for the evident lack of enthusiasm on the U.S. legislative scene. There is no pending legislation in either house of Congress addressed to the topic.[23]

In view of the reservations about worker participation in company decision making which are expressed by American managers and labor representatives, it appears unlikely that any sweeping movement to include worker representatives in the management process is in prospect. No evidence of such a movement has surfaced in recent national political campaigns.

Since neither the legislative nor the electoral arena offers encouragement for proponents of codetermination in the United States, it would seem that the traditional political path to such a change is barred. Thus, any near-term adoption of a codetermination strategy for worker participation in American firms will take place in individually negotiated cases. Single organizations may agree with their labor representatives on incorporating some features of the *Mitbestimmung* model. Even as such beachheads are established, there is little likelihood that codetermination will become a major force furthering employee participation in U.S. management.

REFERENCES

1 Jane Bettie, *Business Periodicals Index,* 3rd ed. (New York: The H. W. Wilson Co., January 1958, annual).
2 Henry Mintzberg, *The Structure of Organizations* (Englewood Cliffs, N.J.: Prentice-Hall, 1979), pp. 203–204.
3 James Furlong, *Labor in the Boardroom* (Princeton, N.J.: Dow Jones Books, 1977), p. 28 (emphasis added).
4 Ibid., p. 5.
5 James Furlong, "Workers in the Boardroom," *Wall Street Journal,* 12 March 1979, p. 18.
6 "Codetermination in the Federal Republic of Germany," translation, International Labor Organization, Geneva (Bonn: Refererat Presse und Offentlichkeitsarbeit, 1976), p. 18.
7 Ibid.
8 Furlong, *Labor in the Boardroom,* p. 19.
9 *Co-Determination: Worker Participation in German Industry* (New York: German Information Center, 1977), p. 13.
10 Ibid., p. 18.
11 "Codetermination in the Federal Republic of Germany," p. 18.
12 Furlong, *Labor in the Boardroom,* p. 74.
13 Meade Paper Co., Eaton Corp., Carborundum Co., and Harman International Industries are a few companies with such schemes.
14 *Labor News and Social Policy,* no. 3, June–July 1978 (periodical pamphlet issued by the Embassy of the Federal Republic of Germany, 4645 Reservoir Road N.W., Washington, D.C.).
15 Joel Seidman, Jack London, and Bernard Karsh, "Why Workers Join Unions," *Annals of the American Academy of Political and Social Science* 274 (January 1979): 84.
16 Statement by Albert Zack, AFL-CIO director of public relations, 18 April 1979 (emphasis added).
17 Statement by Richard Calistri, director of public relations, American Federation of Government Employees, 16 April 1979.
18 Statement by Bernard Henderson, director of public relations, International Brotherhood of Teamsters, Warehousemen, and Helpers of America, 14 April 1979.
19 U.S. Department of Labor, Bureau of International Labor Affairs, *Industrial Democracy in 12 Nations,* Monograph No. 2, January 1979, p. 4.
20 Bruce Stokes, "Answered Prayers," *MBA* 12 (December 1978–January 1979): 22.
21 *Industrial Democracy in 12 Nations,* p. 2.
22 National Association of Manufacturers, *Codetermination: Labor's Voice in Corporate Management* (Washington, D.C.: 1975).

23 Telephone interview with Jeffrey E. Friedman, office of the Subcommittee on Labor-Management Relations, U.S. House of Representatives, 8 June 1979.

REVIEW AND DISCUSSION QUESTIONS

1 Compare the United States' and Germany's histories of worker participation.
2 Is the role of the union different in Germany than in the United States?
3 Is codetermination an effective approach to improve worker satisfaction? Performance?
4 Why have the unions in the United States been reluctant to include codetermination as an issue in contract negotiations?

Part Three

Micro Issues: Learning and Organizational Behavior Modification

The human relations movement of thirty or forty years ago was based upon some general notions of how managers should treat employees. Often this approach was based more on humanistic feelings rather than on concrete empirical tests of relationships between variables. The emerging discipline of organizational behavior found the human relations movement, although incomplete and insufficiently proven, to still be a helpful guide for the practitioner. Yet, the research of the behavioral specialists has led to the formation of many more explanations of human behavior in organizations than were supplied by the relatively simplistic solutions offered by human relations. The bulk of the research in the sixties and into the seventies was directed toward an explanation of the cognitive aspects of motivation. In essence, motivation was explained by a series of internal cognitive processes that led to a high or low degree of effort within the individual. While the theories presented under the cognitive approach did provide some intuitive consonance, there still was difficulty in testing the various components of the theories. The major premises of the cognitive theories rest with the measurement of the internal states of the individual. It is difficult, and some would say impossible, to identify and validly measure these internal states. This reliance upon internal states made it hard to develop a model that could accurately predict, and be used for, the effective change of individual behavior. Also, there was, and still is, some frustration from practitioners that find the cognitive approach of limited value for their own application because of its inability to predict and control human behavior. These shortcomings have led some researchers to look for an alternative approach that would be more capable of predicting and controlling human behavior and be especially valuable to the practitioner of human resource management.

A dominant movement in psychology is concerned with the manner in which one learns. It may be that an individual can learn in several ways. For example, direct learning via reinforcing consequences can lead to an acquisition of a skill. However, imitative or vicarious learning may also be an effective means for an individual to acquire a skill. In vicarious learning, an individual learns through the observation of another's action and the consequence of that action. In essence, the other individual becomes the model for the observing individual. In both direct and vicarious learning theories, the person learns through the consequences of specific behaviors. The consequence of a behavior can reinforce, or not reinforce, that behavior. This notion of behavior being explained by its consequences is a fundamental principle of the learning approach to organizational behavior.

Organizational behavior modification (or, more simply, O.B. Mod.) represents an applied learning approach and is analogous to the role that goal setting and job design play in the motivational approach. O.B. Mod. only deals in specific, observable behaviors. Measurement is also important, and the approach is based on the operant learning principle of behavior being a function of its consequences. Thus, in order to predict and change behavior, attention must be devoted to contingent consequences.

The readings in this section are related to learning theory and organizational behavior modification. The first article traces the history of learning theory from its beginnings to the currently popular theories. The second article provides an example of the application of O.B. Mod. to total organizational performance. Specific steps of application and the results are presented. In the third article, an overall review of the applications of behavior modification in organizational settings is made. An analysis of the approach and of the methodology of the research is presented. The final article in this part provides arguments against the behavior modification approach. Professor Edwin Locke is one of the most vocal critics of behavior modification. He maintains that the most effective way of viewing behaviors is through the use of a cognitive model. He feels that an O.B. Mod. approach is too simplistic a way of explaining the motivational patterns of individuals. He maintains that internal goal setting is a key determinant in the motivational process.

Reading 12
Learning Theory
Fred Luthans
Robert Kreitner

An important variant of the question "What makes people behave?" is the question "How do people learn?" Probably everyone, in varying degrees of sophistication, has their own personal learning theory. Then again, some of us may simply admit to knowing some things and not knowing others without any real idea of how we learned the things we know.

Numerous learning theories have been proposed by behavioral scientists and philosophers as well. There is little agreement among them; there is no single, universally accepted theory of learning. However, one common thread running through the behavioral science definitions of learning is the observation that a change in behavior takes place. After concurring on behavioral change, agreeing upon other aspects of learning becomes more difficult.

DEFINITION OF LEARNING

One of the most heated controversies about learning stems from the internal versus external approaches. The internal approach or *cognitive* learning theories explain the acquisition of knowledge, but not necessarily behavior, through perception, thinking, judgment, and reason. The external approach or *behavioral* learning theories deal only with behavioral change, not cognitive, unobservable knowledge acquisition.

The behavioral learning theorists or behaviorists first make a careful distinction between *respondent* (reflexive, unlearned) behavior and *operant* (voluntary, learned) behavior. By definition, operant behavior is of major concern in learning. After giving examples of respondent behavior such as the shedding of tears while peeling onions, Keller [1954] offers a profound statement of what is meant by learned (operant) behavior:

> Operant (voluntary) behavior includes an even greater amount of human activity—from the wrigglings and squirmings and crowings of an infant in its crib to the highest perfection and complication of adult skills and reasoning power. It takes in all those movements of an organism that may at some time be said to *have an effect upon* or *do something to* his outside world. Operant behavior *operates* on this world, so to speak, either directly or indirectly [p. 2].

This behavior which operates on and changes the environment is what learning is all about. Thus, learning is defined and used in this book as *any change in behavior that results in a change in the environment.*

From *Organizational Behavior Modification,* Scott, Foresman and Company, Glenview, Ill., pp. 18–29. Used with permission.

As Keller [1945] notes; it isn't always easy to determine just how the environment is changed by the operant behavior. "Only when you look into the history of such behavior will you find that, at some time or other, some form of the response in question really did make things happen" [p. 2].

Because learned behavior is defined as having some effect on the environment, behaviorists deal primarily with objective or observable behavior. The cry of a child, the depressing of typewriter keys by a secretary, and the pushing of a turret lathe start button by a machinist are all objective, observable behaviors which have an effect on the environment. On the other hand, the child's need for attention, the secretary's attitude toward work, and the machinist's drive for self-actualization are subjective and unobservable. However, a broad interpretation of learning could deal with learned needs, attitudes, and drives because they can also affect the environment.

WATSONIAN BEHAVIORISM

In 1913, an outspoken young American psychologist, John B. Watson, opened up a whole new area of thought in the study of human behavior in this country. His article, entitled "Psychology as the Behaviorist Views It," became known as "The Behaviorist Manifesto." He picked up the conditioned reflex or stimulus-response (S-R) approach to behavior where the Russian physiologists, Sechenov and, more notably, Ivan Pavlov, left off. Although the article started a revolution in American psychology, it was not entirely original [Razran, 1965]. Watsonian behaviorism and Russian physiology had some features in common, such as using objective behavior as a dependent variable and conditioned reflexes as the explanatory mechanism of the objective behavior.

The Classic Stimulus-Response Mechanism

The Watsonian doctrine held that consciousness (e.g., thoughts or feelings) belonged in the realm of fantasy; human behavior could best be understood by studying observable, objective, and practical facts. In other words, Watson wanted to approach the study of behavior from the perspective of science rather than conscious experience and introspection. The latter approach had dominated psychology up to that time, but the European structuralists and American philosophers who espoused that approach were now being challenged by Watson to be more scientific.

Watson believed that all learned behavior consisted of responses elicited by prior stimuli. The stimuli supposedly came from within the organism as well as from the outside environment and continually bombarded the organism. In Watson's words [1924], "Now the organism does something when it is assailed by stimuli. It responds. It moves. The response may be so slight that it can be observed only by the use of instruments" [p. 13]. Typical human responses ranged from gross motor activity to minute changes in respiration or blood pressure, and each response could be observed under the proper conditions.

Since Watson felt that most human behavior was learned, he abandoned the concept of instinct (inborn tendencies to behave in certain ways), the then popular explanation for behavior. He substituted habit for instinct. A habit was simply a learned response which eventually became paired with stimuli capable of evoking it. Hence, a trained behaviorist, according to Watson, was capable of predicting and controlling behavior by identifying the appropriate stimulus-response (S-R) pairings. Watson's intentions were clear when he stated: "The interest of the behaviorist in man's doings is more than the interest of the spectator—he wants to control man's reactions as physical scientists want to control and manipulate other natural phenomena" [Watson, 1924, p. 11].

Classic Stimulus-Response Experiments

A frequently cited experiment by watson and Rayner [1920] probably best illustrates Watsonian behaviorism. The object of the classic experiment was to produce a conditioned emotional response in an eleven-month-old subject named Albert. In proper Watsonian fashion, the subject's behavior was carefully and systematically observed prior to the experiment. Albert was seen as sluggish but healthy. He responded with no fear to successive presentations of unfamiliar neutral stimuli such as a monkey, a dog, a white rat, a rabbit, cotton, wool, masks with and without hair, and burning newspapers. This alone tended to refute or at least question some of the popularly held notions about instinctive fear. However, the experimenters did discover an unconditioned aversive stimulus when they struck an iron bar with a hammer above and behind the subject's head. The usually quiet Albert broke into a crying fit after three such stimulations.

With this background, Watson and Rayner [1920] asked the hypothetical question: "Can we condition fear of an animal, e.g., a white rat, by visually presenting it and simultaneously striking a steel bar?" The experimenters proceeded to present the subject with the paired stimuli, one naturally aversive and one neutral. After several pairings, Albert cried at the sight of the white rat alone. He had learned to associate the white rat with the naturally fearful noise of the hammer hitting the iron bar. In Watsonian terminology, an emotional response of fear had been conditioned through the systematic manipulation of environmental stimuli. Moreover, his conditioned fear of the white rat generalized to other furry things such as a rabbit, a dog, and a hairy Santa Claus mask.

In terms of a conditioning or learning paradigm (an ideal model), Watson and Rayner conditioned an emotional response in Albert in much the same manner that Pavlov [1927] had conditioned dogs to salivate at the sight of a luminous circle on a screen. Initially, Albert's crying in the presence of the white rat was as unnatural as a dog salivating at the sight of a lighted circle. But through the systematic presentation of paired stimuli, the child learned to associate the rat with a fearful noise and Pavlov's dogs learned to associate the sight of a luminous circle with food. Figure 1 outlines the conditioning paradigm which was operative during Watson's and Rayner's experiment with Albert.

Following the Pavlovian tradition, Figure 1 shows that a neutral stimulus (N.S.), the white rat, was paired with an unconditioned aversive stimulus

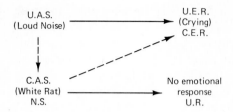

Figure 1 The reflex or classical conditioning paradigm.

(U.A.S.), which was the sound of a hammer hitting an iron bar. After a number of stimulus pairings, the previously neutral stimulus (white rat), when presented alone, elicited a conditioned emotional response (C.E.R.), which was crying. The conditioning (indicated by broken lines in Figure 1) gave a previously neutral stimulus aversive properties. As hypothesized, the experimenters were able to condition a fear response in Albert.

Watson's Contributions

In spite of the legitimate criticism of Watson's somewhat thoughtless choice of subjects, his relatively crude research designs, and his overzealous generalizations, there can be little argument that he made some valuable contributions to the study of human behavior. As Watson's work became known, many American psychologists jumped on the Watsonian bandwagon. The popularity was a result of the confident and forceful simplicity with which Watson presented the behavioral constructs. Watson's approach especially appealed to those who had become disenchanted with the structural and functional approaches which were preoccupied with the study of the mind. As is often stated with tongue in cheek, Watson caused psychology to lose its mind.

In retrospect, Watsonian behaviorism became almost a fad and, like all fads, went out of style about as fast as it came in. According to Hilgard [1962]:

> As enthusiastic supporters of such systems tend to do, they [the behaviorists] went to extremes, but gradually the excitement about behaviorism has subsided. There are still a few ardent behaviorists, but most contemporary psychologists are not extreme about it [p. 17].

In spite of the fact that modern psychologists are generally not Watsonian behaviorists, the field of psychology has been greatly influenced by his work. Probably the single greatest impact comes from his recognition of the scientific value of studying observable behavior. Instead of taking hypothetical trips into the mind, Watson offered a viable, scientific alternative. He challenged the field of psychology to be scientific in the following words:

> Why don't we make what we can observe the real field of psychology? Let us limit ourselves to things that can be observed, and formulate laws concerning only the observed things. Now what can we observe? Well, we can observe *behavior—what the organism does or says* [Watson and MacDougall, 1929, p. 18].

His challenge to deal only with observable behavior has been heeded by many modern psychologists. On the other hand, his preoccupation with S-R connections has been questioned. Contemporary behaviorists do not go along with Watson's S-R explanation for all learned behavior. Today, more attention is focused on the effect of subsequent stimuli on objective behavior than on causal prior stimuli. The reinforcement learning theorists are largely responsible for this shift in focus.

REINFORCEMENT LEARNING THEORIES

Like Watsonian behaviorism, the reinforcement theories deal with objective behavior rather than consciousness or cognitive processes. However, with the exception of Edwin R. Guthrie, who, like Watson, believed that learning resulted from the pairing of stimuli and responses. Watson's behaviorist successors placed increasing emphasis on the use of *reinforcement* or rewards in learning. This marked a significant departure from Watson's S-R paradigm in which prior stimuli evoked or elicited a response.

Generally interpreted, reinforcement can only have an effect if the response comes first. This has meant a reversal of the traditional S-R paradigm. Since a reinforcing event in the environment could be interpreted as a stimulus, an R-S pairing actually replaced S-R as the dominant theme of behaviorism. Among the learning theorists most often associated with this R-S orientation are Edward L. Thorndike, Clark Hull, Neal Miller, and most notably B. F. Skinner.

The reinforcement theorists were convinced that Watsonian behaviorism was not an adequate explanation of complex behavior. They saw learned behavior as strengthened or reinforced by rewards. The effect of reinforcement on behavior was initially proposed in the concept of hedonism. However, the reinforcement learning theorists went beyond simple hedonism.

Law of Effect

The first comprehensive reinforcement theory of learning can be found in Edward L. Thorndike's law of effect. Through years of scientific animal research he discovered the impact of behavioral consequences. Rather than depending exclusively upon prior eliciting stimuli as the causal factor in learned behavior, as Watson had done, Thorndike turned to consequences for explaining behavior. The resulting law of effect is described by Thorndike [1913] as follows:

> When a modifiable connection between a situation and a response is made and is accompanied or followed by a satisfying state of affairs, that connection's strength is increased: when made and accompanied or followed by an annoying state of affairs, its strength is decreased [p. 4].

Stimulus-response connections, according to Thorndike's interpretation, are reinforced or strengthened by satisfying consequences. His law has had a lasting impact on the understanding, prediction, and control of behavior. For example, Millenson [1967] claims that the law of effect ". . . survives today as a fundamental principle in the analysis and control of adaptive behavior" [p. 10] and Vroom [1964], after reviewing the motivation literature, concluded:

> Without a doubt the law of effect or principle of reinforcement must be included among the most substantiated findings of experimental psychology and is at the same time among the most useful findings for an applied psychology concerned with the control of human behavior [p. 13].

Drive-Reduction Theory

Another pioneering reinforcement theorist was Clark L. Hull. A Yale psychologist with an engineering background, Hull formulated a complex scientific theory of psychology, complete with mathematical postulates, logic, and theorems. Hill [1963] notes that "Hull did not regard his theory as a final statement about the nature of learning. Rather, it was intended as a tentative formulation, always subject to revision to bring it in line with new data or new ideas" [p. 132].

Hull proposed a drive-reduction theory characterizing behavior as caused by the independent variables of deprivation, painful stimulation, magnitude of reward, and number of previously reinforced training trials. He felt that these four independent variables led to three intervening variables: drive, resulting from deprivation and pain; incentive motivation, tied to the magnitude of reward; and habit strength, derived from the number of previously reinforced training trials. Finally, a combination of drive, incentive motivation, and habit strength generate an excitatory potential, i.e., a tendency to respond in a given manner in the presence of an appropriate stimulus.

Despite the fact that it was more sophisticated than Watson's mechanistic interpretation, Hull's theory largely followed Watson's lead by contending that all behavior involves stimulus-response connections. Hull simply considered the effect of reinforcement while Watson did not. It is the habit-strength variable, based upon the number of previously reinforced training trials, that qualifies Hull as a reinforcement learning theorist. Otherwise, he could be considered a motivation theorist.

Neal Miller, another Yale psychologist, extended Hull's theory. Miller divided learning into four basic elements: drive, cue, response, and reward. Like Thorndike and Hull, Miller considered the effects of both prior and subsequent stimuli on behavior. According to Miller, subsequent stimuli in the form of rewarding events have the capacity to strengthen behavior. For example, a small boy may learn to run to his father when he comes home from a trip. Broken down into Miller's elements, the boy likes candy (drive), so when he hears the garage door slam (cue), he runs (response) to his dad to get some candy (reward). If the boy in fact does receive the candy, this will strengthen the probability of running to his father in the future. Miller believed that all learned behavior could be broken down this way.

SKINNERIAN BEHAVIORISM

Like the others discussed above, the Harvard psychologist B. F. Skinner could also be considered a reinforcement theorist. But in terms of empirical research, written literature, conceptual formulations, or controversy, Skinner certainly deserves special attention. He is so important that a few years ago the American Psychological Association voted him the most influential living psychologist. In an articulate and logical fashion, Skinner has merged his predecessors' and his own work into a practical technology of learned behavior [see: Skinner, 1969; Skinner, 1971].

Watson and Thorndike laid the primary historical foundation for Skinner's work. Conceptually, Skinner's approach can be traced to Watson's preoccupation with objective, observable behavior and Thorndike's emphasis on the effect of the consequences of behavior. Over forty years of exacting laboratory and field research by Skinner, his students, and conceptual adherents have produced an impressive theoretical and empirical base for a comprehensive behavioral learning theory.

At the very heart of Skinnerian behaviorism is a single contention. *Behavior is a function of its consequences.* The Skinnerian explanation is based on the external approach; it emphasizes the effect of environmental consequences on objective, observable behavior. In Skinner's words [1953]:

> The practice of looking inside the organism for an explanation of behavior has tended to obscure the variables which are immediately available for a scientific analysis. These variables lie outside the organism, in its immediate environment and in its environmental history [p. 31].

The collective influence of both Watson and Thorndike are apparent in this statement. Before discussing the more technical aspects of Skinnerian behaviorism, however, it may be interesting to analyze why Skinner and his works are so controversial.

The Controversy Surrounding Skinner

Find a dozen people who have heard of B. F. Skinner and quite probably a surprising number of them will be critical of him and his work. If the matter is pursued and the critics are asked exactly how familiar they are with Skinner's work, typically the answer will be that they have read excerpts from *Beyond Freedom and Dignity* [1971], Skinner's most recent and controversial work. When one considers the logical sequence of a scientist's career (basic research, formulation, application, publication, and extrapolation), it appears that critics who are familiar with Skinner's work only through a quick reading or a second-hand account of *Beyond Freedom and Dignity* have overlooked the other crucial steps of Skinner's extensive career [see: Skinner, 1938; Skinner, 1953; Skinner, 1969].

Too often, the criticisms of Skinner and his works are based upon misinformation and misunderstanding. The general public and particularly many management scholars and practitioners have not been exposed to Skinner's basic premises and the many valuable contributions he has made to the study of human behavior. Instead, most people are familiar only with the extrapolation stage of Skinner's career. All they know of him is that he suggested behavioral control and manipulation of people as ways to change our culture. This, of course, collides with the cherished American concepts of freedom, dignity, and democracy. The desirability or lack of desirability of Skinner's extrapolation should not be allowed to depreciate the quality, importance, or relevance of his other work. It is his basic research findings and theoretical formulations that are of particular interest to the development of O. B. Mod.

Management scholars or practitioners who take the time to carefully study Skinner's fundamental concepts of behavior control should see the potential application to managing people. Many of Skinner's concepts and principles have been empirically validated both in the laboratory and in field settings. Even his most ardent critics admit that his behavior principles work. The position taken here is that the behavioral approach to management should study Skinnerian behaviorism and apply its techniques as the situation warrants. Skinnerian behaviorism certainly does not represent the final answer to the behavioral approach to management, but it does represent a badly neglected area that needs study and application.

The Essence of Skinnerian Behaviorism

In 1938, B. F. Skinner, then an assistant professor of psychology at the University of Minnesota, wrote a book, entitled *The Behavior of Organisms,* which permanently altered the course of twentieth-century behaviorism and the entire field of psychology. While citing the significance of this book, Skinner [1938] noted: "One outstanding aspect of the present book, which can hardly be overlooked, is the shift in emphasis from respondent to operant behavior" [p. 438]. With the publication of this book, Skinner made a break with his behaviorist predecessors by relegating stimulus-response connections to a comparatively minor role in the explanation of behavior.

While Pavlov, Watson, Thorndike, Hull, and Miller each to a greater or lesser degree characterized all behavior as chains of S-R connections, Skinner looked beyond reflexes to environmental consequences as the controlling mechanisms of learned behavior. He attached the label *operant* to learned behavior because it operates on the environment to produce a consequence. He called unlearned or reflexive behavior *respondent* behavior.

Skinner was the first to make the important distinction between operant and respondent behavior. Had he not done so, behaviorists might have spent years developing patchwork formulations intended to explain all behavior in terms of S-R connections. The respondent/operant distinction has permitted learning theorists to accurately portray the environment as a source of both prior and consequent stimuli relative to objective behavior. The traditional S-R paradigm has been found acceptable for explaining respondent behavior but unacceptable for explaining operant behavior. Operant behavior, as initially conceived by Skinner, is seen as that behavior which is shaped, strengthened, maintained, or weakened by its consequences.

Respondent and Operant Behavior

Respondent behavior is that behavior which is *elicited* by a prior stimulus. It most commonly occurs in the form of reflexes. To the extent that reflexive behavior comes naturally, it is unlearned. Healthy human beings do not have to learn to jerk their knee in response to a doctor's tap with a hammer or learn to shed tears while peeling onions. Respondent behavior is a function of our genetic history or endowment. It was this type of S-R scheme that the early behaviorists generalized to all behavior. Operant behavior, on the other hand, is *emitted* by the organism rather than elicited by a definite prior stimulus; operant behavior must be learned. Most complex human behavior falls into this operant category.

Operant behavior, although it may become paired with prior stimuli, is not caused by the prior stimuli in the sense that the doctor's tap causes the knee-jerk response. For example, if an individual emits behavior appropriate to the successful driving of an automobile only when sitting behind the steering wheel, the steering wheel cannot be called a stimulus which elicits or causes the driving behavior. The driving responses are said to be emitted because of the effects they will produce in the environment, namely, getting quickly and safely from one location to another.

The fundamental difference between respondent and operant behavior may be further illustrated by the functional relationship between a response and the environment. With respondent behavior the environment acts on the organism in the form of a stimulus-response connection. The reverse functional relationship is true in operant behavior. The organism must act on the environment to produce a consequence. The doctor must tap the knee in respondent behavior but the individual must drive the automobile in operant behavior. This difference is very important in understanding learned behavior.

Operant Conditioning

With the distinction between respondent and operant behavior clarified, it is now possible to examine a procedure Skinner called *operant conditioning*. Skinner [1953] makes the distinction between operant conditioning and respondent or classical conditioning as follows:

> Pavlov . . . called all events which strengthened behavior 'reinforcement' and all the resulting changes 'conditioning.' In the Pavlovian experiment, however, a reinforcer is paired with a *stimulus;* whereas in operant behavior it is contingent upon a response. Operant reinforcement is therefore a separate process and requires a separate analysis [p. 65].

The influence of Thorndike's law of effect on operant conditioning is obvious. Essentially, an operant, once emitted by an organism, may be effectively controlled or conditioned (strengthened, maintained, or eliminated) through the systematic management of the consequences of that behavior. It is important to emphasize that this can only occur with operant or learned behavior.

Recent experiments indicate there is more accurately a gray rather than a black and white distinction between respondent and operant behavior. Further experimentation will eventually make this important distinction more operational. However, relative to the use of operant conditioning in management, there is no question that virtually all organizational behavior falls into the operant category. Organizational behavior is largely learned. It follows that the mechanism of learning brought out by Skinner may be managed and applied to organizational behavior.

The Concept of Contingency

The final Skinnerian contribution to be discussed is the concept of contingency. Contingencies are specific formulations of the interaction between an organism's operant behavior and its environment [Skinner, 1969, p. 7]. A contingent relationship could be simply thought of as an if-then relationship. Learned behavior operates on the environment to produce a change in the environment. Therefore, if the behavior causes the environmental change, then the environmental change can be said to be contingent upon the behavior. In other words, the specific environmental change only comes when the behavior has been emitted. For example, getting coffee from the office coffee machine is contingent upon inserting the proper coinage in the slot. *If* the proper coin is inserted; *then* coffee will come out. In this particular contingency we see an obvious behavior (putting in the coin) and an equally obvious consequence (coffee).

Technically, prior environmental conditions or cues also play an important role in contingencies. The Skinnerian concept of contingency involves three major elements: (1) a prior environmental state or cue; (2) a behavior; and (3) a consequence. The process of reducing complex behavior into these three elements of the contingency is termed *functional analysis*. Functional analysis attempts to systematically determine what cues are present when a specific response is emitted and, more importantly, what consequences are supporting that response.

Skinner [1969] contrasted the contingency concept (cue-behavior-consequence) with the more traditional S-R scheme in the following way:

> The relationships are much more complex than those between a stimulus and a response, and they are much more productive in both theoretical and experimental analyses. The behavior generated by a given set of contingencies can be accounted for without appealing to hypothetical inner states or processes. If a conspicuous stimulus does not have an effect, it is not because the organism has not attended to it or because some central gatekeeper has screened it out, but because the stimulus plays no important role in the prevailing contingencies [pp. 7–8].

By viewing all learned behavior in the context of contingencies, Skinnerian behaviorists have been able to study how behavior is learned by systematically managing the contingencies of animals in highly controlled experimental settings and studying humans in less controlled environments. The result of this research has been a reliable technology of learned behavior.

REFERENCES

Hilgard, E. R. *Introduction to Psychology* (3rd ed.). Harcourt Brace Jovanovich, 1962.

Hill, W. F. *Learning: A Survey of Psychological Interpretations.* Chandler Publishing Company, 1963.

Keller, F. S. *Learning: Reinforcement Theory.* Random House, 1954.

Millenson, J. R. *Principles of Behavioral Analysis.* Macmillan, 1967.

Pavlov, I. P. *Conditioned Reflexes: An Investigation of the Physiological Activity of the Cerebral Cortex.* Translated and edited by G. V. Anrep. Oxford University Press, 1972.

Razran, G. "Russian Physiologists' Psychology and American Experimental Psychology: A Historical and a Systematic Collation and a Look into the Future." *Psychological Bulletin,* 63 (1965): 42–64.

Skinner, B. F. *The Behavior of Organisms.* Appleton-Century-Crofts, 1938.

Skinner, B. F. *Science and Human Behavior.* The Free Press, 1953.

Skinner, B. F. *Contingencies of Reinforcement.* Appleton-Century-Crofts, 1969.

Skinner, B. F. *Beyond Freedom and Dignity.* Bantam Books, 1971.

Thorndike, E. L. *Educational Psychology: The Psychology of Learning,* Vol. II. Columbia University, Teachers College, 1913.

Vroom, V. H. *Work and Motivation.* Wiley, 1964.

Watson, J. B. "Psychology as the Behaviorist Views It." *Psychological Review,* 20 (1913): 158–77.

Watson, J. B. *Behaviorism.* W. W. Norton, 1924.

Watson, J. B., and W. MacDougall. *The Battle of Behaviorism.* W. W. Norton, 1929.

Watson, J. B., and R. Rayner. "Conditioning Emotional Reactions," *Journal of Experimental Psychology,* 3 (February 1920): 1–14.

REVIEW AND DISCUSSION QUESTIONS

1 Define *learning.* What is the difference between respondent and operant behavior?
2 How does Watsonian behaviorism differ from Skinnerian behaviorism? What is the major contribution of each?
3 What is the *law of effect?* What are the implications for the prediction and control of human behavior?
4 What are the three major elements of the Skinnerian concept of contingency? Give an example.

Reading 13

How Behavior Modification Techniques Can Improve Total Organizational Performance

Fred Luthans
Jason Schweizer

Organization behavior modification (or simply O.B. Mod.) has become an increasingly popular human resource management technique. Both systematic research and practical experience have clearly demonstrated that O.B. Mod. can change individual and in some cases group behaviors.

But what about the use of O.B. Mod. as a total organizational performance improvement strategy? Organizational development (O.D.) techniques (for example, team building or process consultation), which concentrate on changing attitudes rather than behaviors, have traditionally claimed the sole right of being able to handle a total organizational improvement effort. O.B. Mod. has been relegated to solving individual behavior problems or, at most, group problems such as absenteeism or turnover.

Through our own O.B. Mod. projects in industrial and public service organizations, we became convinced that the approach could be successfully applied as a total organization strategy. We persuaded the owner/manager of a waterbed factory to try this approach to performance improvement.

The company, which makes two types of waterbed liners, has grown over the last decade from a five-man "back of a building operation" to a 50-employee national supplier to wholesale and retail outlets. The managerial hierarchy comprises the owner/manager, his four immediate subordinates in charge of the various functions (production, shipping, quality control, and specials) and their eight team leaders, who act as coordinators/supervisors. The management team members were unusually concerned about the well-being of their employees (who were mostly in their early twenties) and were very willing to try innovative techniques.

Since this was a total organizational effort, all managerial employees were involved in the O.B. Mod. intervention, and "bottom line" quality and quantity were measured for results. The intervention developed in three phases.

Phase One   We began by training all managerial personnel in the O.B. Mod. approach. The three levels of management successively received four one-hour training sessions over a two-week period. The training consisted of theoretical background (for example: operant conditioning, law of effect, positive/negative reinforcement, punishment/extinction, contingency analysis, shaping, and modeling) and the specific steps of O.B. Mod. (identify, measure,

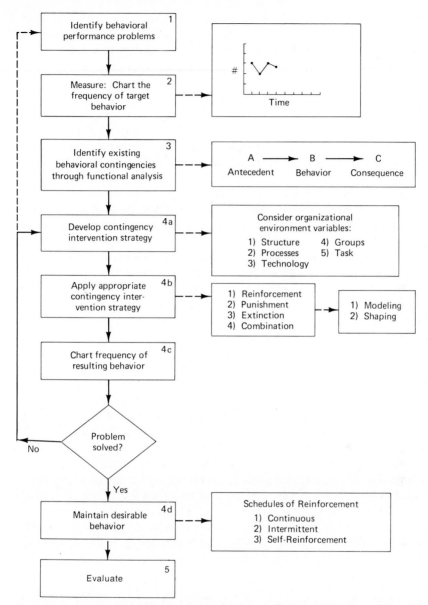

Figure 1 O.B. Mod. problem-solving model. (Source: Fred Luthans and Robert Kreitner, "The Management of Behavioral Contingencies," *Personnel,* July–August, 1974.)

analyze, intervene, and evaluate). Figure 1 illustrates the basic steps followed in the training and the subsequent application. All managerial personnel were required to attend the training sessions, and a give-and-take discussion format was used.

Phase Two   The second phase focused on practice, using a simulation/ experiential approach. To avoid potential problems caused by turning the managers loose too quickly to apply the newly learned O.B. Mod., it was decided that they should begin slowly with two experiential exercises.

The trainer provided two short cases for the participants to read and analyze, after which they were told to develop a program for changing behavior according to the O.B. Mod. model. These exercises were brought back to additional training sessions and discussed in light of the information provided in phase one. As was made clear from the beginning, this program would be "self-perpetuating," and we sought maximum input by the trainees themselves, as opposed to simply dominating discussion with our own views on possible solutions. These exercises proved useful in getting the participants to begin thinking in terms of O.B. Mod. and also provided for improved interaction between members of the groups concerning possible uses and misuses of the approach.

Following completion of the simulation exercises, the trainees were directed to select an actual behavior in their work environment that they would like to change and to structure it around the steps of the O.B. Mod. model. Once this assignment was completed and analyzed by both the trainer and the group, the participants were allowed to implement their programs, thus providing an opportunity to practice on a small scale the O.B. Mod. approach that they would later employ on a total organizational basis.

After identifying the critical behavior (step 1), participants were required to chart the frequencies (step 2), functionally analyze what kinds of things preceded the behavior and what the consequences were (step 3), develop and implement a behavioral change strategy that would accelerate desired behaviors and decelerate undesired behaviors (step 4), and evaluate their effectiveness (step 5). At this point, however, little attempt was made to be precise or accurate in terms of measurement. For example, the charts kept were minimal in terms of both duration and elaborateness. No real effort was made to assess the effectiveness of the supervisors as they implemented their individual O.B. Mod. programs. Although many of the programs showed improvement in the targeted behaviors, some were terminated because of loss of subject (quitting his/her job, for example), correction of the problem upon telling the subject, or other miscellaneous causes. Each trainee, however, got actual practice with O.B. Mod.

Phase Three   In this final phase the managers implemented an actual O.B. Mod. approach designed to lead to the improvement of "bottom line" productivity and quality measures for the firm as a whole. The managers were told which performance measures were to be emphasized, and the feedback system was jointly developed; however, the day-to-day application was left up to the individual managers. It was in this final phase that the feedback system was installed as the major intervention, and the managers at each level applied reinforcement techniques on a contingent basis to improve overall performance.

THE FEEDBACK INTERVENTION

A performance feedback system is vital to a successful O.B. Mod. application. Without accurate and timely feedback, it is impossible to reinforce or punish the appropriate or inappropriate performance behaviors. Objective information must be fed back to employees so that they know how they are performing and so that their supervisors know when to reinforce performance.

Prior to establishment of the feedback system, performance information in this company was readily available to employees if they sought it out. For example, each knew approximately how many errors he or she had made because they caught some themselves, but unless they specifically asked, they would not know how many had been caught by quality control. The only performance feedback came from (1) vague evaluation forms made up monthly, (2) the weekly paycheck, which reflected error penalties in the form of deductions (25 cents for each error caught by the employee and 50 cents for each caught by quality control), and incentive bonuses for exceeding quota. The paycheck amount could be analyzed to determine the number of errors—if the employee was willing to take the time and effort to find out. It was difficult to check out, however, because the deduction-incentive system was not easily understood and little effort was made to explain its complexities.

In terms of the criteria for an effective performance feedback system, the existing process thus fell way short. For example, one of the requirements for effective feedback is that it be objective and accurate. Questioning of the employees revealed that few had any idea how many beds were made or how many errors were committed over the course of the week.

Subjective evaluations via supervisors or team leaders were equally vague. There was no direct system for delivering feedback to the individual employee. In addition, the few employees who did attempt to determine from their paychecks their error or productivity rate were still not operating under an effective type of feedback system.

It is widely recognized that feedback is most effective when it comes immediately after the relevant behavior. At this plant, the employees who determined their rates received that information a week or more after they performed. Not only was it difficult for the employee to see the relationship (the contingency) between performance and pay, but there was also the problem of comparison. Although the employee might know how he/she had performed that week, seldom was information available on how that performance compared to previous performance.

Another problem stemmed from the manner in which negative results were provided. Prior to the new feedback system, if quality control spotted a consistent problem, Q.C. would take that problem to the person(s) responsible. They would show the offender the kind of mistake he/she was making and urge him/her to correct the problem. Thus the production employee interacted with the quality control person only after a number of mistakes.

The problem with this procedure can readily be seen from a reinforcement/

punishment perspective. The quality control person never reinforced the operator when he/she was doing a good job, but only visited him/her when there was some problem; thus quality control was a generalized punisher. The essence of this situation was summed up by one employee who remarked, "Oh, hell. Here comes quality control. What have I done wrong now?"

Another facet of this problem was that quality control was a department separate from the production department. Although the Q.C. people would tell production workers of errors, they had no authority to direct compliance. Accordingly, production people paid little attention to quality control unless the latter's corrections were backed up by the production supervisor. Although quality control personnel could provoke unpleasant consequences by noting operator errors, they did not have the power to reward or punish. No wonder, then, that quality control became the "bad guys," whose feedback was often disregarded as being "unimportant" or something to put up with but do nothing about.

The solution was to devise a new system under which employees would receive accurate feedback from their immediate supervisor on both quantity and quality of performance. Under the new feedback system, quality control personnel no longer went directly to the person responsible for an error; instead they sent that information to the appropriate production supervisor. He in turn provided feedback to his team leaders on their performance and that of their subordinates. Initially, the feedback was scheduled on a daily basis, but it soon became apparent that a weekly basis was more feasible.

Although a daily feedback system was possible, it became clear after a week of trial and error that there were logistical problems. Having supervisors and team leaders collect and disseminate the information every day produced too much paperwork and consumed too much time, nor were there sufficient data on a daily basis. Supervisors and production workers alike decided it was pointless to gather and disseminate the information every day, but the weekly feedback system was well received.

OTHER REINFORCERS

Whereas the feedback system was jointly developed by managers and workers, other reinforcements, methods, and techniques used to improve quality and quantity were largely determined by the managers themselves. They suggested general social reinforcers such as praise, attention, and recognition, and administered them on the basis of behaviors that they determined led to improved performance. For example, if there was an improvement over the previous week, the supervisor would give attention and/or praise, but if there was no improvement or there was a decline, he would say nothing. This objective feedback by an authoritative source was also coupled with social reinforcement when there was improvement.

In addition to the social reinforcers, such things as time available to spend with other members of the group or organization, special duties of a favorable nature, and contingent time off were suggested. The time-off benefit was particularly popular. Top-level management decided to allow employees time off when their productivity goals had been met for the week. Thus, if an employee completed his/her quota prior to Friday, he/she was allowed to take Friday off with pay.

THE "BOTTOM LINE" RESULTS

The effects of O.B. Mod. on both quantity and quality performance were systematically analyzed. Productivity is measured by the number of beds made per week divided by the total number of hours worked by all hourly employees. As shown in the productivity chart (Figure 2), two intervention periods follow the baseline measurement. The first period, which extended from January 3 to March 4, is the baseline period (no intervention); the second period shows the effect of the intervention of contingent time off (the first intervention), and the third period represents the new feedback system coupled with social reinforcement (second intervention).

It is evident that a substantial increase in the productivity rate occurred following the first intervention. During the week of March 4–11 (the first week of contingent time off for hitting quota), the productivity rate rose from 1.6 to 2.3. The following weeks reveal equally high productivity rates during this first intervention. Productivity fluctuated somewhat during this time but, overall, during the period of March 4 to April 7, it averaged 2.13—.56 higher than during the baseline period. This translates into a 36 percent improvement in productivity for that period of time.

The second intervention—the feedback system and social reinforcers—began April 10 and continued for the duration of the analysis (the contingent time-off program also continued during this period). Little average improvement occurred between period 2 and period 3—the average productivity rate during period 3 was 2.19 compared to a productivity rate of 2.13 in period 2. On the

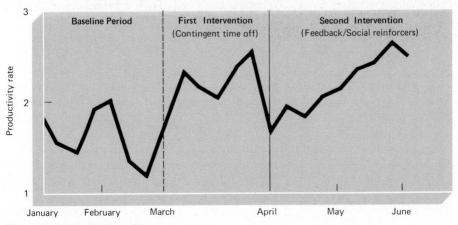

Figure 2   Productivity results.

other hand, an obvious qualitative difference occurred in the slope and variability of the productivity data. Performance following the feedback and social reinforcement by supervisors took on a steady characteristic from week to week during period 3 and the wide fluctuations that characterized productivity during periods 1 and 2 changed to a constant level of improvement.

Performance during period 3 rose from a low point of 1.6 just before the second intervention to an organization record high of 2.6 the week before completion of the study. Performance not only reached the highest point in organizational history, but did so in an ever-increasing consistent pattern. Top-level managers noted that the O.B. Mod. approach not only greatly improved the total productivity of employees but also facilitated other aspects of the operation such as planning, scheduling, and inventory control—reflecting the predictability of productivity rates from week to week.

Comparisons were also made between period 1 and periods 2 and 3 combined to establish quantitative differences between baseline and intervention periods. The combined productivity rate for periods 2 and 3 was an average of 2.16, compared with a rate of 1.57 prior to any intervention. The .59 difference translated to a 38 percent improvement in productivity. Thus the management team was reinforced by both an overall increase in productivity and a more predictable productivity rate from week to week. A more sophisticated time-series statistical analysis also verified the significance of the O.B. Mod. intervention on productivity improvement.

QUALITY IMPROVEMENT

An analysis of quality revealed equally dramatic improvements stemming from the O.B. Mod. intervention. Two measures of quality were used. One was the total error expressed as a percentage of the total number of beds made during a corresponding time period. The second was the number of "cutdowns" and "seconds." "Cutdowns" are beds that, because of nonrepairable errors, must be produced in smaller sizes. "Seconds" are beds with obvious blemishes or problems that must be sold at a reduced price.

Figure 3 reveals the impact that the O.B. Mod. intervention had on both measures of quality. Whereas both the contingent time off and feedback/social reinforcer interventions were applied to boost productivity, only the feedback/social reinforcer intervention was applied to quality. Management previously had made no concerted effort to improve quality other than use of the standard posters extolling the virtues of quality, the periodic "pep" talks on the importance of quality, and the reductions in pay made for errors.

The baseline period of the quality analysis included the period from January 1 to March 24. The O.B. Mod. approach to quality improvement began March 27 and continued to the end of the study on June 2. Visual inspection of the quality data in Figure 3 shows the definite impact that the intervention had on quality improvement.

The error rate appears to fluctuate widely prior to the intervention. For

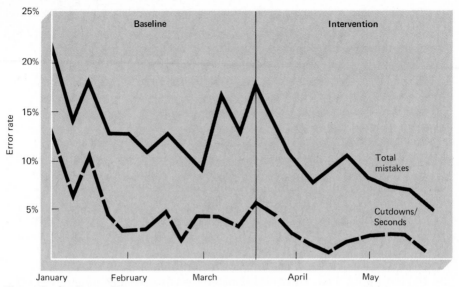

Figure 3 Quality results.

example, before the intervention the total error rate ranged between 10 percent and more than 20 percent. The actual average rate of errors was 15.42 percent for the entire baseline period.

After the intervention not only was there a reduction in variability in the week-to-week quality rate (again improving the prediction of costs, scheduling, and inventories), but there was also a dramatic reduction in total average error rate. From the 15.42 percent rate of total errors prior to the O.B. Mod. intervention of feedback/social reinforcers, there was a 5.53 point drop in rate to 9.89 percent. Most of the quality improvement occurred in the first few weeks following the introduction of the feedback system coupled with social reinforcers from supervisors. These figures represent a 36 percent reduction in total error rate that, because of the quality-product emphasis of the firm, was obviously good news.

Even more exciting to the managers, however, were the data on the more expensive errors—cutdowns and seconds. Again, as shown in Figure 3, the error rate of cutdowns and seconds varied widely during the baseline period. Error rate ranged between a low of 3 percent to a high of 14 percent during this baseline period. The average rate of cutdowns and seconds was 6.46 percent. Despite efforts to lower this rate (the pep talks, threats, and the "incentive system" under which money was not subtracted if no errors were made), none had met with more than minimal and temporary improvement.

Figure 3 indicates that not only did the introduction of the feedback system and social reinforcers improve quality (it reduced the cutdowns and seconds) but, as with productivity and total mistakes, there was a marked reduction in variability. The highs and lows were not nearly as pronounced from one week to the next. Quality performance during the intervention phase showed a reduction in the cutdowns and seconds error rate from 6.46 percent prior to intervention to only 3.09 percent following the intervention. This reduction resulted in 52 percent fewer beds having to be made into smaller beds or sold at lower prices because of visible mistakes. On the basis of this performance, the total error rate fell by 36 percent.

VALIDITY OF THE RESULTS

One of the major problems with either behavioral or OD techniques is that causality is seldom proved. For example, a widely publicized behavioral management program at Emery Air Freight supposedly saved the company $2 million over a three-year period. But what has not been answered in the Emery case or similar programs that have been reported is whether the impressive results were due to the behavioral intervention or to some other factor such as the economy or technological change. We designed our analysis to overcome some of these problems and can confidently conclude that our results were valid and the O.B. Mod. intervention did indeed cause the change in performance.

We used a multiple baseline design to provide as much support as possible for internal and external validity. The multiple baseline is a technique that uses staggered interventions over time—that is, baseline measures are taken on two or more dependent variables, and then an intervention is made on one of the variables while baseline measures are continued on the others. This measurement continues until all the dependent variables are brought under the intervention. Figure 4 depicts the multiple baseline design used in this study (note the staggered interventions over time). The widely recognized criteria for internal validity were met by our design in the following ways:

1   **History**   The problem with history concerns the changes in the setting other than the intervention that is introduced. In this case, no intentional changes were made by the managers other than the interventions affecting quality and productivity. Nevertheless, unintentional changes still could have occurred to affect the performance measures. The data depicted in Figure 4, however, suggest that this possibility was very remote. It is highly unlikely that changes in the environment would exactly coincide with each intervention phase. In order to get the changes in performance indicated in Figure 4, it would be necessary for those unintentional, random changes to parallel exactly the interventions made by the managers. Since this is unlikely, there seems little doubt that the introduction of the O.B. Mod. techniques caused the changes in performance.

2   **Selection and Maturation**   Two other variables to consider in assessing validity are those of selection and maturation. Since there is only one group (and it is used throughout the program), there is no problem of control versus experimental group comparability. Maturation problems are also eliminated

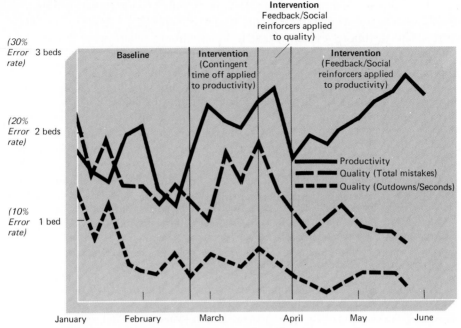

Figure 4   Multiple baseline to demonstrate intervention effects.

because behavior changes rapidly each time an O.B. Mod. intervention is introduced. Not only does maturation usually occur more evenly over time, but again, it is unlikely that changes in maturation would happen to coincide with the interventions.

3 Mortality and regression   Two other internal validity concerns are those of experimental mortality and statistical regression. Both of these are easily eliminated in our study because there was only one group. Thus differential loss from one group was not a concern of experimental mortality. The fact that there was one experimental group and no control group also negated statistical regression as a possible confounding influence on the results. Since statistical regression operates when *groups* have been selected on their extreme scores, this too can be eliminated as a reason for the changes in performance.

4 Testing and instrumentation   These factors represent the final two widely recognized criteria for analyzing internal validity. Since the organization had been measured on the same basis for many years, there was no "new" testing that would affect a "second" testing. For the same reason, changes in the calibration of a measuring instrument or changes in the *observers* (instrumentation) would not apply. In both cases, company records were continued as they had been collected in the past, and there were no changes in what constituted an error, or in this case a finished waterbed.

The reported results are objectively measured by observation or organizational reports. Subjective, indirect questionnaire methods, "perceived performance," and testimony evidence that is so commonly relied upon in most OD studies were not used. The major conclusions resulting from this analysis are based on objective measurement of behaviors and performance. The use of "bottom line" performance measures for measuring the impact of O.B. Mod. leaves little doubt as to the "actual" changes in performance.

In summary, we were able to obtain considerable total organizational performance improvement by an O.B. Mod. approach to human resource management. We certainly cannot generalize our conclusions at this point to all sizes or types of organizations. But we strongly urge human resource managers to try this approach for performance improvement. It definitely worked in this waterbed factory, and if implemented properly we think it will work for you.

REVIEW AND DISCUSSION QUESTIONS

1 What are the independent and dependent variables in this O.B. Mod. study?
2 Can this O.B. Mod. application be tried in other settings? Set up a hypothetical experiment using O.B. Mod. in another organizational setting.
3 What is meant by functional analysis?
4 Why is the charting of behavior frequencies considered important to the O.B. Mod. approach?
5 How, if at all, are goal setting and O.B. Mod. related?

Reading 14

Organizational Behavior Modification in Business Settings: A Methodological and Content Review

Frank Andrasik

In recent years, applied behavioral analysis principles have been increasingly utilized in business settings. Although articles urging the use of behavior modification techniques first appeared several years ago [e.g., Aldis, 1961], it was not until the late sixties and early seventies that the management literature began to reveal a steady, increasing interest in the use of applied behavior analysis as a management technique in business settings. Investigations during

From the *Journal of Organizational Behavior Management*, vol. 2, 1979, pp. 85–102. © 1979 by Behavioral Systems, Inc., reprinted with permission.

An abridged version of this review was presented at the meeting of the Midwestern Association of Behavior Analysis, Chicago, May, 1978. The author wishes to express appreciation to Theresa Abell for her assistance with the data analysis.

this time period that appear to have been most influential in the growth of applied behavior analysis in business settings are those prepared by Nord [1969], the management team of Luthans and Kreitner [Kreitner, 1975, Luthans, 1973; Luthans & Kreitner, 1973, 1974, 1975; Luthans & Martinko, 1976; Luthans & Otteman, 1973], and the reports of successful applications in various "live" settings [see Hamner & Hamner, 1976, for a discussion of application in 10 such settings].

Applied behavior analysis in business is more than just a fad and appears likely to continue in popularity. The label "Organizational Behavior Modification" (O.B.Mod.) has been coined to represent this approach in the more general sense [Luthans & Kreitner, 1975]. The *Journal of Organizational Behavior Management* has been created to "advance the knowledge of applied behavior analysis in work and organizational settings" [*Journal of Organizational Behavior Management*, 1977, cover page]. Last, but certainly not least, O.B.Mod. "Interest Groups" have recently been established within some professional organizations (for example, within the Association for Advancement of Behavior Therapy and the Association for Behavior Analysis). The above illustrate the support thus far received for the O.B.Mod. approach. A critical question, it is felt, needs to be addressed at this time. To what extent do the reports of applications contribute to our knowledge of O.B.Mod. and, more importantly, to what extent do these reports justify the acclaim already received. Stated in another way, to what extent have the reports of "successful" applications of O.B.Mod. demonstrated that the imposed treatments have in fact been responsible for the observed effects.

In an attempt to answer these questions, a critical examination of the design integrity and obtained results of recent O.B.Mod. applications in business settings was performed. Applications selected for review in the present paper were those containing sufficient information and data to evaluate critically. Further details of the procedure can be found in the next section.

METHODS

Recent issues of seven major journals *(Academy of Management Journal, Behavior Therapy, Journal of Applied Behavior Analysis, Journal of Applied Psychology, Journal of Organizational Behavior Management, Organizational Behavior and Human Performance,* and *Personnel Psychology)* were comprehensively searched to identify applications of O.B.Mod. in business settings. Pertinent applications referenced in these journal accounts were also reviewed. Nineteen articles, presenting 20 such applications, were identified. These applications were then subjected to methodological analysis, each application was evaluated for the presence of certain design variables to determine whether the application would permit cause-and-effect conclusions. Four design criteria were selected for the present review: (1) Reliability of Measurement, (2) Baseline, (3) Systematic Intervention, and (4) Follow-up. It is not the intent of the present article to comprehensively discuss each of these design criteria. This has been done adequately elsewhere [e.g., Campbell & Stanley, 1972; Goldstein, Heller, & Sechrest, 1966; MacDonough & McNamara, 1973; Paul, 1969; Sidman, 1960]. However, brief discussion and description of these criteria are necessary and follow below.

Design Criteria Analysis

Reliability of Measurement   To meet this criterion, data collection had to be performed, on at least some occasions, by two or more independent observers. A quantification of the measure of agreement or correspondence also had to be presented.

Baseline   To satisfy this criterion, data collection had to have begun prior to intervention. No attempt was made to evaluate the adequacy of the baseline period, only the occurrence or non-occurrence of it.

Systematic Intervention   Here the concern was with whether the intervention had been introduced in a manner that would permit cause-and-effect statements, irrespective of the reliability of the data. This criterion was satisfied by the use of withdrawal, reversal, multiple baseline, changing criteria, or multiple schedule designs, as described by Hersen and Barlow [1976], Kazdin [1975], and Komaki [1977], or by the use of an untreated control/comparison group. This category was divided into two subcategories—Single Systematic and Multiple Systematic Interventions. To satisfy the Single Systematic Intervention criterion the application had to employ one of the designs discussed above and report the introduction of no more than one intervention at a time. In applied settings it is often not possible to gain this degree of control over the intervention. Applications, in which multiple interventions occur simultaneously, can also be sufficiently well-controlled to allow cause-and-effect interpretations. The Multiple Systematic Intervention criterion was satisfied when an application, which involved two or more simultaneous interventions, employed one of the designs discussed above. In these cases, while it can be established that the interventive "package" produced the resultant effects, the relative contributions of the interventive components cannot be determined.

Follow-up   To satisfy this criterion, data collection had to be performed after a time lapse during which no data were obtained. Thus, a distinction was made between post data collection, which here is referred to as data collection immediately following the intervention, and follow-up data collection. No minimum time lapse was established for this criterion. Again, no attempt was made to evaluate the adequacy of any follow-up reported, only the occurrence of such a follow-up.

Content Analysis

To give the reader an understanding of the nature of the applications critiqued in this article, a summary of key content dimensions is also provided. For each application the following were recorded: subject population, basic design, specific treatments/interventions employed, and the dependent measures analyzed. Other content dimensions are discussed when relevant.

Procedure

Each of the 20 applications, contained in the 19 articles located during the journal search, was rated by the author and an undergraduate research assistant for the presence of each of the 4 above design criteria. Ratings of content were prepared by the author alone.

RESULTS AND DISCUSSION

Table 1 lists the 20 applications and the degree in which each intervention satisfied the 4 design criteria. The ratings presented in Table 1 are those assigned

Table 1   Classification of Design Variables

| | Design Criteria | | | | |
| | | | Systematic Intervention | | |
Study	Reliability	Baseline	Single	Multiple	Follow-up
Adam (1975)	no	yes	no	yes	yes
Bourdon (1977)	no	yes	no	no	no
Chandler (1977)	no	yes	no	no	no
Emmert (1978)	no	yes	no	no	no
Gupton & LeBow (1971)	no	yes	yes		no
Hermann, de Montes, Dominguez, Montes, & Hopkins (1973)	yes	yes	yes		no
Kempen & Hall (1977)	yes	yes	no	yes	no
Komaki, Waddell, & Pearce (1977)					
Experiment 1	yes	yes	no	yes	yes
Experiment 2	yes	yes	no	yes	no
Lamal & Benfield (1978)	yes	yes	no	yes	yes
Latham & Dossett (1978)	no	yes	no	no	no
McCarthy (1978)	no	yes	no	yes	no
Marholin & Gray (1976)	yes	yes	yes		no
Miller (1977)	no	yes	no	no	no
Orpen (1974)	no	yes	no	no	no
Orpen (1978)	no	yes	yes		no
Pedalino & Gamboa (1974)	no	yes	no	yes	no
Runnion, Johnson, & McWhorter (1978)	no	yes	no	no	yes
Yukl & Latham (1975)	no	yes	yes		no
Yukl, Latham, & Pursell (1976)	no	yes	no	no	no

by the author. Interventions meeting the Single Systematic Intervention sub-criterion were not rated for the Multiple Systematic Intervention sub-criterion. Collapsing across the two subcategories of the Systematic Intervention criterion, a total of 80 ratings were made (20 applications × 4 design criteria). The extent of inter-rater agreement was determined as follows: (number of agreements divided by 80) × 100%. Applying this formula, 83% agreement between the 2 raters was obtained.

Key content dimensions are presented in Table 2. In categorizing the designs and the treatment/interventive features, the following notations were used. When standard comparison group procedures were employed, the letter E was used to represent the experimental group and the letter C was used to represent the control group. In the case of multiple experimental groups, these were denoted by placing numbers behind the identifying letters (e.g., E1, E2, E3, etc.). In the case of within subject designs, the letter A represented baseline, and the letters B, C, D, etc. represented the differing treatment interventions. When subtle differences were made (the intervention remained basically the same) in subsequent phases, these were indicated by placing numbers behind the identifying letters, as illustrated for the comparison group procedure. Intervention periods or phases are separated by slashes.

Design Analysis

Only 6 of the 20 (30%) applications met the Reliability of Measurement criterion. Given the dependent measures employed, this may not be a serious shortcoming. However, even with variables such as tardiness, absences, sales volume, etc. there is still the possibility of recording error (e.g., employees punching in for each other, pre- and post-dating of records, etc.). An example from one of the studies will further illustrate this point. Marholin and Gray [1976] performed reliability checks but, as they point out, this did not ensure that the target behavior under investigation changed as desired. The dependent measure in this application was cash shortages. The authors originally speculated that cash shortages were occurring because of employee theft. Following the initiation of group response cost, cash shortages decreased significantly. However, as the authors themselves point out, a topographic change may have actually accounted for the obtained results; i.e., underringing of a bill and pocketing of the difference, shortchanging the customer, etc. Although Reliability of Measurement is not judged to be a serious problem at this point, this needs more attention in the future.

One hundred percent of the applications incorporated Baseline measurement procedures. The baseline periods varied from a single data point, insufficient to rule out trends in the data, to multiple data points, demonstrating that stability had occurred prior to intervention.

Twelve of the 20 (60%) applications met the Systematic Intervention criterion. Five applications (25%) were sufficiently well-controlled to allow confident cause-and-effect statements about single interventions; 7 applications (35%) were sufficiently well-controlled to permit cause-and-effect statements about multiple interventions. Given the nature of the applications and the settings in which they were performed, this finding is viewed positively. However, given that only one-fourth of the investigations met the Single Systematic Intervention criterion, further attention needs to be directed at partialing out the independent effects of the various "package" components employed. When this is begun, it may be found that many of the components do not in fact contribute significantly to the resultant effects, as has been demonstrated in various areas of clinical research.

Some of the investigators may have been able to eliminate or reduce these additional package components without significantly compromising their interventions. For example, Lamal and Benfield [1978] were interested in the effects of self-monitoring of behavior on various work performance measures. However, the draftsman performing the self-monitoring was informed that his supervisors would be inspecting his data as well. With the introduction of this second component, it is no longer possible to determine the effects due to self-monitoring alone. Responsible work behavior may have, in part, been produced in response to expected punishment, etc. Another point needs to be mentioned in this context. At a recent regional conference several participants attending an O.B.Mod. Interest Group meeting [Frederiksen & Bourdon, Note 1] stressed the importance and desirability of consequation by social reinforcement. However, none of the presently reviewed studies employing social reinforcement was sufficiently well-controlled to document its effectiveness. Of the seven applications that reported the use of social reinforcement, all consisted of multiple interventions. And of these seven, only three were sufficiently well-controlled to satisfy the Multiple Systematic Intervention criterion. The effectiveness of social reinforcement has yet to be documented.

Only 4 of the 20 investigations (20%) reported the collection of follow-up data. These follow-up data collections occurred after 5 weeks, 11 weeks, 6 months, and approximately 3½ years. All reported maintenance of initial findings. Lack of follow-up data is viewed as the most serious design shortcoming. This lack of follow-up is not surprising (and somewhat to be expected) given the newness of the field and recency of the applications. The longterm effectiveness of O.B.Mod. needs further documentation.

Content Analysis

As can be seen in Table 2, the O.B.Mod. approach has been successfully applied to varying numbers of target individuals (from case studies to literally thousands), by varying interventions, for varying types of target problems. The reported results are uniformly promising. The scope of some of the projects is commendable. For example, Boudon's [1977] intervention consisted basically of a company-wide token economy. Readers who have struggled with instituting similar procedures on smaller scales will especially appreciate this endeavor. A few additional content dimensions, not summarized in Table 2, are worthy of mention.

One consideration meriting discussion is the cost-benefit ratio that results

Table 2 Classification of Content

Study	Subject population	Design	Treatment/intervention	Dependent measures
Adam (1975)	Factory workers: E = 3 diecasting shifts (28-39); C = 1 production shift (23-28)	Comparison group procedure: 1 experimental group & 1 control group	E: Individual feedback + group feedback + attitude change procedures (newsletter, banners, wall graphs, & check inserts) + praise or admonishment	(1) Job Description Index (job satisfaction) (2) Percent scrap (quality measure) (3) Percent Performance (quantity measure)
Bourdon (1977)	Textile manufacturing employees at 2 different plants (approximately 1,500)	A/B	B: Points (backup reinforcement = catalog purchase + food during work + after work dinners + praise + recognition & pictures on bulletin board + reinforcing memos) + feedback reports + behavior management training + goal setting (with shaping) + individual management behavior change projects	(1) Attendance (2) Efficiency (3) Quality (4) + Others
Chandler (1977)	1 male shift supervisor in fabric finishing plant	A/B	B: Informed would be monitoring negative comments + informal reminders + performance feedback for number of loads dyed + feedback on number of negative comments at one point + reinforcement	(1) Negative comments by supervisor (2) Number of loads of fabric dyed
Emmert (1978)	4 fiber glass factory work crews (32 hourly employees)	A/B/BC	B: Group feedback + praise BC: Group feedback + praise + individual performance reviews with foremen	(1) Number of splices made + number of spliced metered bobbins
Gupton & LeBow (1971)	2 male part-time telephone solicitors	A/B/A	B: Warranty sales contingent upon renewal sales	(1) Renewal contracts sold (2) Purchase of new warranties
Hermann, et al. (1973)	6 industrial workers with control group (6 industrial workers)	A/B/A/B/A/B with a control group	B: Monetary bonus	(1) Tardiness

Author (Year)	Subjects	Design	Treatment	Dependent measures
Kempen & Hall (1977)	Hourly-rated manufacturing workers (approximately 7,500 in 2 factories) with control group (salaried employees at 2 plants + hourly employees at 11 plants)	Multiple baseline across 2 plants with multiple comparison groups	B: Attendance management system = absence control plan (progressive disciplinary procedure) & attendance reinforcement plan (freedom from punching time clock + earned time off + temporary immunity from discipline + reduction in position on disciplinary ladder + bonus free day)	(1) Absenteeism
Komaki, et al. (1977) Experiment 1	2 neighborhood grocery store clerks	Multiple baseline across behaviors	B: Time off with pay + feedback + self-recording + praise + modeling & role playing as needed + goal clarification	(1) Presence in store (2) Customer assistance (3) Shelf restocking
Experiment 2	1 game room attendant	A/B/A/B	B: Goal clarification + contingent pay + performance reviews with manager on random basis	(1) Engaging in work behavior (room presence + "making good" machine malfunction + cleaning up)
Lamal & Benfield (1978)	1 adult draftsman	Multiple baseline across behaviors	B: Self-monitoring (of hours at work for 1st behavior & of time spent working and not working for 2nd behavior) + data inspection by supervisor	(1) Arrival time (2) Percent time working
Latham & Dossett (1978)	Male mountain beaver trappers (E1 = 7, E2 = 7)	Comparison group procedure: 2 experimental groups with no control group	E1: Hourly rate pay + $1/beaver trapped; E2: Hourly rate pay + $4/every 4th beaver trapped	(1) Number of beavers trapped
McCarthy (1978)	Textile doffers on 4 different shifts	A/B1/A/B2	B1: Group feedback + reinforcement (public commendation from plant manager to department manager) + goal setting; B2: B1 in absence of goal setting	(1) Incidence of high bobbins
Marholin & Gray (1976)	6 full-time and part-time restaurant cashiers	A/B/A/B	B: Group response cost	(1) Cash shortages
Miller (1977)	17 chemical salesmen	A/B	B: Monthly objective setting with district manager + monthly performance feedback + point system (backup = annual bonus)	(1) Sales volume (2) New business created (3) Forecast accuracy (4) Reporting responses (5) + Others

Table 2 *(Continued)*

Study	Subject population	Design	Treatment/intervention	Dependent measures
Orpen (1974	South African factory workers (E1 = 75; E2 = 75; E3 = 75)	Comparison group procedure: 3 experimental groups with no control group	E1: High contingent reward E2: Low contingent reward E3: Noncontingent reward	(1) Number of error-free batches passed (2) Job satisfaction
Orpen (1978)	46 female garment factory workers	A/B/A/B with control group	B: Monetary bonus	(1) Absenteeism
Pedalino & Gamboa (1974)	Employees at manufacturing distributing company (215) with control group (508) groups	A/B/A with 4 comparison groups	B: Weekly lottery incentive system (poker game format) + group feedback (weekly & bi-weekly)	(1) Absenteeism
Runnion, *et al.* (1978)	Truck drivers at 58 textile plants (92–199)	A/B1/B2/B3	B1: Weekly performance feedback to plant managers + letter prompts to drivers + group reinforcement (certificates, photographs, & plaques) + individual reinforcement (posted memos, letters, & praise) + behavior management program with supervisory personnel B2: B1 with two-week performance feedback B3: B1 with four-week performance feedback	(1) Truck turnaround time
Yukl & Latham (1975)	Seedling planting crews: E = 3 crews; C = 1 crew	Comparison group procedure: 3 experimental groups & 1 control group	E1: Hourly pay + $2/each seedling planted E2: Hourly pay + $4/every 2 planted (VR2) E3: Hourly pay + $8/every 4 planted (VR4)	(1) Number of seedlings planted
Yukl, *et al.* (1976)	Seedling planters	A/B/C/B/D	B: Hourly pay + $2/each seedling planted C: Hourly pay + $8/every 4 planted (VR4) D: Hourly pay + $4/every 2 planted (VR2)	(1) Number of seedlings planted

from the intervention. The costs (staff, time, additional expenditures, etc.) involved in the implementation of some of the projects were presumably quite high. Six of the studies reported cost-benefit data; all reported benefits outweighing implementation costs. Two of the six reported that cost-savings were realized but gave no actual figures [Runnion et al., 1978; Yukl & Lathan, 1975]. The four remaining studies reported a 23% reduction in costs [Lathan & Dossett, 1978], an estimated annual savings of $25,000 [Emmert, 1978], an estimated annual savings of $76,000 [Adam, 1975], and a cost/payback ratio of approximately 1/200 [Bourdon, 1977]. These results are most encouraging. However, one set of authors, reporting favorable cost-benefit returns, also reported the early discontinuance of another project because of the "inordinate amount of data analysis and recording necessary" [Runnion et al., 1978].

Two remaining points, given limited coverage in the above reviewed articles, also deserve mention. While reliability of measurement was a source of concern in many of the articles, reliability of program intervention was virtually ignored. Persons responsible for program implementation recognize that often programs are not implemented as originally designed. Only one study [Adam, 1975] reported the presence of monitoring to ensure that the intervention was being carried out as intended. However, data regarding this were not presented. This needs further investigation. While some of the interventions reviewed did compare various applied behavior analysis techniques, none of the studies consisted of comparisons with alternative, non-behavioral approaches. It may be argued that this was in fact accomplished because the baseline periods were actually times during which other management procedures were in effect. However, none of the interventions adequately described the management systems previously in effect. Comparisons with alternative approaches deserve attention and should be investigated in future studies.

By and large, the interventions reviewed have been reported as being well-received. This appears in large part due to the approaches employed by the researchers. For example, a number of the interventions were preceded by thorough training and comprehensive negotiations with personnel at various levels. Most notable in this respect are the interventions reported by Bourdon [1977], Kempen and Hall [1977], and Miller [1977]. Also, many of the interventions were undertaken under the direction of full-time "live-in" consultants or full-time permanent staff. These two procedures have most probably minimized resistance to the interventions. However, the investigations have not been without resistance. The problems encountered in mental health settings have been well documented [e.g., Atthowe, 1972; Hall & Baker, 1973; Kazdin & Bootzin, 1972; Reppucci, 1977; Reppucci & Saunder, 1974]. A few of the present investigations have met with similar problems. For example, Gupton and LeBow [1971] reported that management did not permit them to re-institute their intervention after a planned return to baseline. Yukl and Latham [1975] used the flipping of a coin to effect variable ratio schedules. Negative reactions occurred from some employees who likened this to gambling. Yukl, et al. [1976] report compromising their design because of intense reactions to one of the variable ratio schedules employed. However, Latham and Dossett [1978], employing designs similar to Yukl and Latham [1975] and Yukl, *et al.* [1976], report their intervention as being well received by union and labor officials. Lastly, Pedalino and Gamboa [1974] report their intervention was prematurely terminated because the company did not want to include their lottery system in the new contract that was up for approval.

The present review indicates that certain individual and multicomponent applications of applied behavior analysis impact favorably upon worker performance. The results are encouraging, given the relative youth of the O.B.Mod. approach. The present review suggests a number of issues/points in need of further investigation and consideration. From both a design and content standpoint, the following should be given further attention: (1) assessing reliability of the dependent measures employed and of the treatment execution, (2) determining the relative contributions of single (independent) treatment interventions (such as social reinforcement), (3) documenting cost effectiveness, (4) determining the differential effectiveness of the O.B.Mod. approach versus alternative, non-behavioral approaches, and (5) assessing the long-term maintenance of the applications.

REFERENCE NOTE

1   Frederiksen, L., and Bourdon, R. (Moderators). *Special interest group: organizational behavior management.* Presented at the meeting of the Midwestern Association of Behavior Analysis, Chicago, May, 1978.

REFERENCES

Adam, E.E., Jr. Behavior modification in quality control. *Academy of Management Journal,* 1975, *18,* 662–679.

Aldis, O. Of pigeons and men. *Harvard Business Review,* 1961, *39,* 59–63.

Atthowe, J.M. Behavior innovation and persistence. *American Psychologist,* 1973, *28,* 34–41.

Bourdon, R. D. A token economy application to management performance improvement. *Journal of Organizational Behavior Management,* 1977, *1,* 23–37.

Campbell, D. T., and Stanley, J. C. *Experimental and quasi-experimental designs for research.* Chicago: Rand McNally, 1973.

Chandler, A. B. Decreasing negative comments and increasing performance of a shift supervisor. *Journal of Organizational Behavior Management,* 1977, *1,* 99–103.

Emmert, G. D. Measuring the impact of group performance feedback versus individual performance feedback in an industrial setting. *Journal of Organizational Behavior Management,* 1978, *1,* 134–141.

Goldstein, A. P., Heller, K., and Sechrest, L. B. *Psychotherapy and the psychology of behavior change.* New York: Wiley, 1966.

Gupton, T., and LeBow, M. D. Behavior management in a large industrial firm. *Behavior Therapy,* 1971, *2,* 78–82.

Hall, J., and Baker, R. Token economy systems: breakdown and control. *Behavior Research and Therapy,* 1973, *11,* 253–263.

Hamner, W. C., and Hamner, E. P. Behavior modification on the bottom line. *Organizational Dynamics*, 1976, *3*, 3–21.

Hermann. J. A., deMontes, A. I., Dominguez, B., Montes, F., and Hopkins, B. L. Effects of bonuses for punctuality on the tardiness of industrial workers. *Journal of Applied Behavior Analysis*, 1973, *6*, 563–570.

Hersen, M., and Barlow, D. H. *Single case experimental designs: strategies for studying behavior change.* Elmsford, New York: Pergamon Press, 1976.

Kazdin, A. E. *Behavior modification in applied settings.* Homewood, Illinois: Dorsey Press, 1975.

Kazdin, A. E., and Bootzin, R. R. The token economy: an evaluative review. *Journal of Applied Behavior Analysis*, 1972, *5*, 343–372.

Kempen, R. W., and Hall, R. V. Reduction of industrial absenteeism: results of a behavioral approach. *Journal of Organizational Behavior Management*, 1977, *1*, 1–21.

Komaki, J. Alternative evaluation strategies in work settings: reversal and multiple-baseline designs. *Journal of Organizational Behavior Management*, 1977, *1*, 53–77.

Komaki, J., Wadell, W. M., and Pearce, M. G. The applied behavior analysis approach and individual employees: improving performance in two small businesses. *Organizational Behavior and Human Performance*, 1977, *19*, 337–352.

Kreitner, R. PM–A new method of behavior change. *Business Horizons*, 1975, *18*, 79–86.

Lamal, P. A., and Benfield, A. The effect of self-monitoring on job tardiness and percentage of time spent working. *Journal of Organizational Behavior Management*, 1978, *1*, 142–149.

Latham, G. P., and Dossett, D. L. Designing incentive plans for unionized employees: A comparison of continuous and variable ratio reinforcement schedules. *Personnel Psychology*, 1978, *31*, 47–61.

Luthans, F. The contingency theory of management: a path of the jungle. *Business Horizons*, 1973, *16*, 67–72.

Luthans, F., and Kreitner, R. *Organizational behavior modification.* Glenview, Illinois: Scott, Foresman and Co., 1975.

Luthans, F., and Kreitner, R. The management of behavioral contingencies. *Personnel*, 1974, *51*, 7–16.

Luthans, F., and Kreitner, R. The role of punishment in organizational behavior modification (O.B.Mod.). *Public Personnel Management*, 1973, *2*, 156–161.

Luthans, F., and Martinko, M. An organizational behavior modification analysis of absenteeism. *Human Resource Management*, 1976, *15*, 11–18.

Luthans, F., and Otteman, R. Motivation vs. learning approaches to organizational behavior. *Business Horizons*, 1973, *16*, 55–62.

MacDonough, T. S., and McNamara, J. R. Design-criteria relationships in behavior therapy research with children. *Journal of Child Psychology and Psychiatry*, 1973, *14*, 271–282.

Marholin, D., and Gray, D. Effects of group response-cost procedures on cash shortages in a small business. *Journal of Applied Behavior Analysis*, 1976, *9*, 25–30.

McCarthy, M. Decreasing the incidence of "high bobbins" in a textile spinning department through a group feedback procedure. *Journal of Organizational Behavior Management*, 1978, *1*, 150–154.

Miller, L. M. Improving roles and forecast accuracy in a nationwide sales organization. *Journal of Organizational Behavior Management*, 1977, *1*, 39–51.

Nord, W. R. Beyond the teaching machine: the neglected area of operant conditioning in the theory and practice of management. *Organizational Behavior and Human Performance,* 1969, *4,* 375–401.

Orpen, C. The effect of reward contingencies on the job satisfaction-task performance relationship: an industrial experiment. *Psychology,* 1974, 9–14.

Orpen, C. Effects of bonuses for attendance on the absenteeism of industrial workers. *Journal of Organizational Behavior Management,* 1978, *1,* 118–124.

Paul, G. L. Behavior modification research: design and tactics. In C. M. Franks (Ed.), *Behavior Therapy: appraisal and status.* New York: McGraw-Hill, 1969.

Pedalino, E., and Gamboa, J. Behavior modification and absenteeism: intervention in one industrial setting. *Journal of Applied Psychology,* 1974, *58,* 694–698.

Reppucci, N. D. Implementation issues for the behavior modifier as institutional change agent. *Behavior Therapy,* 1977, *8,* 594–605.

Reppucci, N. D., and Saunders, J. T. Social psychology of behavior modification: problems of implementation in natural settings. *American Psychologist,* 1974, *29,* 649–660.

Runnion, A., Johnson, T., and McWhorter, J. The effects of feedback and reinforcement on truck turn-around time in materials transportation. *Journal of Organizational Behavior Management,* 1978, *1,* 110–117.

Sidman, M. *Tactics of scientific research.* New York: Basic Books, 1960.

Yukl, G. A., and Latham, G. P. Consequences of reinforcement schedules and incentive magnitudes for employee performance: problems encountered in an industrial setting. *Journal of Applied Psychology,* 1975, *60,* 294–298.

Yukl, G. A., Latham, G. P., and Pursell, E. D. The effectiveness of performance incentives under continuous and variable ratio schedules of reinforcement. *Personnel Psychology,* 1976, *29,* 221–231.

REVIEW AND DISCUSSION QUESTIONS

1   On balance, do you feel that O.B. Mod. is an effective means to improve performance?

2   Select three of the experiments discussed in this article. Are the dependent variables indicated observable and measurable? What if they are not?

3   Choose one of the experiments reviewed in this article. How would you apply a different intervention strategy to get better results? Explain why you feel your approach would be better.

Reading 15

The Myths of Behavior Mod in Organizations[1]

Edwin A. Locke

Behavior modification, the application of behavioristic conditioning principles to practical problems, has proliferated in the last decade. While the earliest applications were to such fields as education, clinical psychology (psychotherapy), and behavior management in institutions (e.g., mental hospitals, homes for delinquents), recent attempts have been made to apply these ideas to management of employees in work organizations [13, 16, 28, 29, 30, 43, 52]. One article claims: "The long range potential for behavior modification seems limitless" [31, p. 46].

Behaviorism asserts that human behavior can be understood without reference to states or actions of consciousness [54, 55]. Its basics premises are:

1 Determinism: With respect to their choices, beliefs, and actions individuals are ruled by forces beyond their control (according to behaviorism, these forces are environmental). Individuals are totally devoid of volition.

2 Epiphenomenalism: People's minds have no causal efficacy; their thoughts are mere by-products of environmental conditioning and affect neither their other thoughts nor their observable actions.

3 Rejection of introspection as a scientific method. It is unscientific, and its results (the identification of people's mental contents and processes) are irrelevant to understanding their actions [23].

The major theoretical concept in Skinner's [54] version of behaviorism, the one most often applied to industry, is that of reinforcement. Behavior, Skinner argues, is controlled by its consequences. A reinforcer is some consequence which follows a response and makes similar responses more likely in the future. To change the probability of a given response, one merely modifies either the contingency between the response and the reinforcer or the reinforcer itself. The concept of reinforcement is, by design, devoid of any theoretical base, e.g., the experiences of pleasure and pain. The term is defined by its effects on behavior and only by these effects. Reinforcements modify responses automatically, independent of the organism's values, beliefs or mental processes, i.e., independent of consciousness.

While this theory of behavior may be appealing in its simplicity, the facts of human behavior do not correspond to it. All behavior is not controlled by

From the *Academy of Management Review,* vol. 4, 1977, p. 543–553. Reprinted with permission from the authors and the *Academy of Management Review.*

[1]A shorter version of this paper was delivered at the Academy of Management meetings, New Orleans, August, 1975. The author is indebted to Professor Harry Binswanger of Hunter College for his helpful comments and suggestions.

reinforcements given to an acting organism. People can learn a new response by seeing other people get reinforced for that response; this is called "vicarious reinforcement" [17]. People sometimes learn by imitating others who are not reinforced for their actions: this is called "vicarious learning" [33]. Some behaviorists now acknowledge that people can control their own thoughts and actions by "talking to themselves," i.e., thinking. This is called "self-reinforcement" [18] or "self-instruction." These last two concepts flatly contradict the assumption of determinism.

Recent experiments and reviews of the learning literature have further undermined the behaviorist position. Not only do an individual's values, knowledge and intentions have a profound effect on behavior [9, 22], but even the simplest forms of learning may not occur in the absence of conscious awareness on the part of the learner [8].

Studies of actual practices of behavior modifiers show that their techniques implicitly contradict all the main premises of behaviorism. For example, the procedures employed by behavioral psychotherapists assume that: (a) patients are conscious; (b) they can understand the meaning of words and can think; (c) they can introspect; and (d) they can control the actions of their own minds and bodies [6, 23, 32].

In view of conclusions drawn about behavior modification in other areas, will the same hold true when behavior modification principles are applied to industrial-organizational settings? One thesis to be explored here is that "behavior mod" applications to industry do not actually rest on behaviorist premises—they do not ignore the employee's consciousness and/or assume it to be irrelevant to the employer's behavior.

If true, this thesis would mean that, since organizational changes do not automatically condition the employee's response, attention must be paid to what the employee *thinks* about such changes. Are they wanted? Are they understood? What are they expected to lead to, etc.?

A second issue concerns the originality of the techniques used by behavior mod practitioners in industry. Because the concept of reinforcement is defined solely by its consequences, if an alleged reinforcer does not reinforce, it is not a reinforcer. If it does, it is. Since the concept of reinforcement itself has no content (no defining characteristics independent of its effects on behavior), how are behavior modifiers to know what to use as reinforcers? In practice, behaviorists must use rewards and incentives which they observe people already acting to gain and/or keep; they must cash in on what they already know or believe people value or need. Thus when it comes to the choice of reinforcers, behavior mod can offer nothing new [4]. A second thesis is that the actual techniques used by behavior modifiers in industry to "reinforce" behavior are no different from the rewards and incentives already used by non-behaviorist practitioners in this field or related fields.

If this thesis is true, then the claims of originality by behavior mod practitioners are spurious and the attention of researchers would be focused best on further development of existing approaches to motivating employees (e.g., human relations, job enrichment, incentives).

Behavior mod advocates might reply that even if the particular reinforcers they use are not new, they do have something original to offer the practicing manager, namely, the idea of contingency. While the contingency idea is emphasized strongly in behaviorism, it is certainly not new. It has been used, if inconsistently, for centuries by animal trainers, parents, diplomats, and employers. Furthermore, the principle does not work unless the individual is aware of the contingency [8]. Finally, the principle is of limited usefulness in real life work situations where the manager cannot control everything that happens to subordinates [4].

Supporters of behavior mod might also argue that an original aspect of the behavior mod approach to management is its exclusive emphasis on the use of positive rewards and the avoidance of punishment. Such an argument would be misleading, since behaviorists are by no means averse to the use of punishment. Electric shock is often used to change the habits of unruly, disturbed children and to "cure" homosexuals. Furthermore, there is an element of arbitrariness in the behaviorist definition of this and related terms. Punishment is defined as an aversive stimulus which decreases the frequency of a response when it follows the response. Withholding a positive reinforcer, such as food, is not called punishment but extinction. A starving schizophrenic who is told, "No work, no food" might see the withholding of food as very punishing, despite the benign label "extinction" which the behaviorists attach to the process. Similarly, "negative reinforcement," the removal of an aversive stimulus when the organism does what you want, may be viewed justifiably as very punishing and coercive.

Most industrial-organizational practices claiming to represent the application of behavior modification principles fall into one of four categories: programmed instruction; modeling; performance standards with feedback; and monetary incentives, including lotteries. Each of these will be considered in turn from the standpoint of two issues: Are the techniques actually behavioristic? Are they original to behavior mod?

PROGRAMMED INSTRUCTION

The concept of programmed instruction (PI) was first popularized by Skinner [53]. The four crucial elements of PI are: small units, presented in a logical, hierarchical sequence; active involvement (overt response); immediate confirmation (knowledge of results); and reinforcement (reward), although this is not usually distinguished from confirmation.

These individual elements of PI are certainly not new. Task analysis, including breaking down tasks into smaller units for training purposes, was a mainstay of Scientific Management [10], has been used for decades in military training [11], and has been recognized for centuries as a basic principle of all training. Similarly, knowledge of results and reward have long been recognized as facilitators of learning [2, 58]. Overt responding is similar in meaning to the concept of practice which has always been acknowledged as essential to skill development.

In fairness to the developers of PI, the particular combination of elements which comprise the essence of PI were relatively original, although Pressey had laid the groundwork for this development over two decades previously.

The most startling result of recent research on the effectiveness of PI is the finding that none of its particular elements seem to be necessary for learning to occur. The most recent review of the PI literature concludes:

1 Knowledge of results [of the type used in PI] is not necessary for learning.
2 Delayed knowledge of results may be more effective than immediate knowledge of results.
3 [Extrinsic] rewards seem not always to function to improve learning. . . .
4 Learning by a sequence of small steps may be less effective than learning by larger jumps [35, p. 186].

Gagné [11] concludes that standard principles of laboratory learning are largely irrelevant to successful training in applied settings. He does favor breaking the task down into its elements, providing the elements are then re-integrated, a procedure which is omitted in typical PI programs. Pressey [49] and Locke [25] emphasize the importance of mental integrations in learning. Such integrations, Pressey claims, are actually retarded by the use of small, discrete frames characteristic of PI.

Gagné [11] and Annett [3] argue that knowledge of results, while helpful, does not automatically facilitate learning. Locke, Cartledge and Koeppel [27] show that certain types of knowledge of results do not produce improved performance unless they lead to the setting of explicit improvement or performance goals.

A number of studies show that making an overt response in a PI program is no better than making a "covert" response, i.e., practicing the answer mentally [45, 59].

Bolles [7] asserts that what is learned when a response is allegedly "reinforced" is not a stimulus-response connection but rather an expectancy. Expectancy is a concept referring to a conscious state of anticipation. A comprehensive review of the academic learning literature by Brewer [8] concludes that there is no such thing as automatic conditioning through reinforcement. The evidence shows that human learning requires the operation of consciousness.

To the degree that PI does encourage learning, it is probably the element of "forced" rehearsal or practice, including the mental integrations which accompany it, which is most responsible. Of course, rehearsal can also occur at the option of the learner in the absence of a PI format, and can occur "covertly," in the mind, as well as overtly.

Recent research throws increasing doubt on the claim that the PI format is superior to other methods of presenting didactic material. A thorough review of PI studies in applied settings by Nash, Muczyk and Vettori [41] concludes that PI is not practically superior to other forms of instruction, especially with respect to retention. They also found that the more carefully designed the study, the less favorable the results are to the PI method. For example, although PI takes about one third less time than the conventional methods with which it is usually compared, typical comparisons are biased by the fact that PI and non-PI programs nearly always differ with respect to content. When content is controlled, so that PI can be compared with other *methods* of instruction, this superiority not only vanishes but is reversed. Jabara [15] found that material presented in the form of a text was completed two to three times faster than the *identical material* presented in a PI format and was no less effective in terms of learning.

MODELING

The term modeling is similar in meaning to imitation, although its proponents claim that it is something more. Meichenbaum writes:

> The exposure to a modeling display permits the discrimination and organized memory of relatively complex and integrated behavior chains which may then be retrieved to satisfy environmental demands. . . . The information which observers gain from models is converted to covert perceptual-cognitive images and covert mediating rehearsal responses that are retained by the observer and later used by him as symbolic cues to overt behaviors [36].

Stripped of their behavioristic jargon, these statements assert that modeling involves the learning (mental integration) of complex actions which are stored in memory and called out on order based on the individual's perception of what is appropriate to the situation.

The main industrial application of modeling has been to training supervisors [12, 29, 39, 40, 56]. Supervisory trainees are shown video-taped illustrations of models coping successfully with simulated real-life problems involving subordinates. This is often followed by role playing sessions in which the trainees attempt to apply the same principles and are given feedback by the trainer and/or by video-tape. Application then proceeds to the trainee's actual job situation. This may be accompanied by discussions of one's experience with other trainees during periodic follow-up meetings.

The formal use of modeling for supervisory training is certainly new, although it has long been used in motor skill training and sports. De facto modeling has probably always existed in hierarchical organizations. The content of the model's actions in formal supervisory training emphasizes principles derived from the "Human Relations" school of thought—"elicit[ing] the employee's ideas for improving the situation" [39, p. 5].

Whatever the status of modeling with respect to originality, by no stretch of the imagination can it be called behavioristic. Modeling, even according to its proponents, requires perception, imagination, memory, mental rehearsal ["reviewing in one's own mind the enactment of the displayed behaviors," 12, p. 30], and thinking. All these are actions of consciousness which ultimately are presumed to regulate the individual's overt behavior.

Despite some behaviorists' implicit admission that modeling assumes the existence of conscious, thinking trainees, its proponents do not seem to fully understand what modeling is. This writer believes that modeling is a technique for translating abstractions into concretes, for learning the application of general principles to specific situations. Since such applications require that the individual correctly perceive the situation, clearly understand which principle or principles apply to it, and know how to translate these principles into action, learning such applications can be extremely difficult. Modeling, in effect, shows trainees how it is done, and thus helps them to translate abstract knowledge into actions appropriate to specific situations. It provides a useful bridge between theoretical understanding and actual practice.

There is insufficient evidence to evaluate the usefulness of modeling as a training technique. One issue that is not clear from descriptions of this process is the degree to which principles of effective supervision are explicitly given to the trainees—as opposed to requiring them to discover the principles through induction. Since many people have neither the capacity nor the inclination to perform complex inductions, the former procedure should be more effective than the latter. For example, an emphasis on making the principles explicit should facilitate transfer from the observed (modeled) situations to the greater variety of situations the trainees will encounter in their own experience.

PERFORMANCE STANDARDS WITH FEEDBACK

Perhaps the most well known applications of behavior mod to industry are Feeney's quasi-experiments at Emery Air Freight [5, 42, 48, 60, 61]. Related ideas are presented by Hersey and Blanchard [14] and Morasky [38]. Feeney's basic procedure is to:

1 Specify the desired level or standard of performance, preferably in quantitative terms. The concept of "performance standard" in this context is clearly a behavioristic euphemism for "goal."

2 Provide immediate, quantitative feedback informing employees of their level of performance in relation to the standard (preferably this feedback will come directly to the employees such as through performance records which they keep themselves).

3 Provide positive reinforcement in cases where the feedback indicates that performance meets the standard, and encouragement in cases where it does

not meet the standard. Praise is recommended as the most practical positive reinforcer.

The evidence indicates that praise is not essential to achieve output gains. When the frequency of praise is decreased, no performance decrement results; but when feedback is eliminated, performance immediately drops to its previous level. According to Feeney, "feedback is the critical variable in explaining the success of the program" [5, p. 45]. Another writer offers a feedback explanation to explain the productivity increases observed in the Hawthorne studies [46].

Both writers favor a behavioristic interpretation of the effects of feedback. They argue that feedback automatically reinforces the behavior which precedes it, and that the existence of the feedback explains the results of the foregoing studies.

Taken literally, this claim is absurd. If feedback *as such* automatically reinforced previous behavior, people should never change since the feedback would reinforce whatever they did previously. (Feeney's methods actually violate good behaviorist technique since the feedback is not contingent on high performance.)

Parson's [46] hypothesis about the Hawthorne studies is refuted by findings obtained in one of those very studies. In the Bank-Wiring Observation Room individual output was recorded daily; "each man seemed to know just where he stood at any time [during the day]" [51, p. 428]. In spite of this, output among these workers did not go up; it remained at a fairly constant level because the employees were deliberately restricting their output.

There are additional facts that do not coincide with the behavioristic interpretation of the effects of feedback. In Feeney's studies [5], performance in the customer service offices improved "rapidly"—in one case from 30 percent to 95 percent of standard in a single day! In the container departments, container use jumped from 45 percent to 95 percent, and in 70 percent of the cases this improvement also occurred within a day [42]. Since genuine conditioning is asserted to be a gradual process, the very speed of these improvements militates against a conditioning explanation of the results. More likely what occurred was a conscious *redefinition* of the job resulting from the new standards and the more accurate feedback regarding performance in relation to those standards.

Further support for this interpretation comes from the extensive research on feedback and knowledge of results which do *not* automatically lead to performance improvement [3, 26, 27]. The effects of feedback on subsequent performance depend upon such factors as: (a) amount and usefulness of information (knowledge) provided by the feedback; (b) degree to which the information source is trusted; and (c) utilization of the feedback to set goals and/or to regulate one's performance in relation to these goals.

The results obtained by Feeney are more logically explained by the joint operation of explicit goal-setting and feedback regarding performance in relation to the goals, i.e., by the employee's conscious, self-regulation of action, than by the concept of automatic conditioning through reinforcement.

Another study claiming to illustrate the positive effects of behavior mod in improving employee performance can be interpreted similarly. Adam [1] instructed the line supervisors of a die-casting department to meet with each operator weekly and to provide him or her with feedback concerning perform- ance quantity and quality, either on an absolute basis or in relation to set standards, as well as in relation to the shift and department averages. Operators with average or below average quality scores were asked explicitly to improve, although the supervisors evidently stressed quantity more than quality during their daily interactions with the operators. The use of goal-setting led to a significant increase in work quantity but no change in quality.

The concepts of goal and feedback or knowledge of results are in no sense behavioristic concepts. The term goal, as used in industrial contexts, refers to the *consciously* held aim of an action, e.g., a work norm or an output standard. The concept of knowledge refers to the *awareness* of some fact of reality. Both concepts refer to states or actions of consciousness.

Furthermore, the concepts of goal and feedback are not new, not even as applied to industry. There is little difference between Feeney's ideas and some key elements of Scientific Management presented more than 60 years ago by Taylor [57]. Taylor's central concept, the task, which consisted of an assigned work goal (with the work methods also specified), is virtually identical in meaning to Feeney's concept of a "performance standard," a term which also was used by advocates of Scientific Management. Similarly, Taylor argued that work should be measured continually and the results fed back to employees so that they could correct errors and improve or maintain their quantity of output. Taylor favored a monetary bonus as a reward for increased productivity while Feeney's results indicate that this may not be necessary.

Latham and his colleagues also obtained dramatic results in industry by the use of goals and feedback without monetary incentives [19, 20, 21]. Their work was based on the results of laboratory studies of goal setting which had an explicit non-behavioristic base [22].

Two additional concepts occasionally used by Feeney are praise and participation. Both are taken directly from the Human Relations school of management.

MONETARY INCENTIVES

The effectiveness of monetary incentives in improving work performance has long been recognized in industry. The use of large bonus payments for reaching assigned tasks or work goals was a cornerstone of Scientific Management [57], although the use of piece-rate payment systems was common even before the turn of the century.

Payment programs designed explicitly around behavior mod principles and employing behavior mod terminology have been rare in industrial settings. Yukl and Latham [62] compared the effect of continuous and variable ratio piece-rate bonuses among tree planters. Contrary to predictions, the continuous schedule yielded the highest level of performance. One reason for less effectiveness of the variable ratio schedules was that some members of work groups receiving those schedules were consciously opposed to the program, some on the grounds that "gambling" was immoral, and some due to general distrust. Clearly the effect of the so-called reinforcers was far from automatic.

Other studies have used monetary reinforcers or their equivalent (e.g., valued prizes such as appliances) to reduce absenteeism [44, 47]. Either payments were made to all individuals showing perfect attendance for a given time period, or rewards were based on lottery drawings with only those with perfect attendance being eligible.

Nord [44] observed that such systems may become progressively less effective with time, although no explanation was offered for this finding. Presumably the reinforcers are no longer as reinforcing, but this does not explain anything [24].

A striking finding of the Pedalino and Gamboa [47] study was that employees in the experimental, lottery group showed a significant reduction in absenteeism during the very first week of the program, *before anyone in the group had been, or could have been, reinforced* [34].

The concept of conditioning through reinforcement cannot account for these results since the behavior change *preceded* the reinforcement. Obviously the employees' expectations of and desire for the reward caused their change in behavior. Expectation and desire are not behavioristic concepts since they refer to states and actions of consciousness. Furthermore, these expectations were not, according to any evidence presented, generated by past reinforcements (lottery experiences) but by the explanation of the proposed incentive system to the employees.

CONCLUSION

The conclusion is inescapable that behavior mod in industry is neither new nor behavioristic. The specific techniques employed by behavior mod advocates have long been used in industry and other fields. What the behaviorists call reinforcers do not condition behavior automatically, but affect action through and in conjunction with the individual's mental contents and processes (integrations, goals, expectancies, etc.). While operant conditioning principles avoid the necessity of dealing with phenomena which are not directly observable, such as the minds of others, for this very reason they lack the capacity to explain human action [24].

The typical behaviorist response to arguments like the foregoing is, in effect, "Who cares why the procedures work, so long as they work?" [60]. This is the kind of pragmatic answer one might expect from primitive witch doctors who are challenged to explain their "cures." One has the right to expect more from a modern day scientist.

Unless one knows why and how something "works," one does not know *when* it will work or even *that* it will work in a given circumstance. Many things which behaviorists do to change behavior, do, in fact, change it. But many of them do not, and most behaviorists do not have the slightest idea what accounts for these inconsistencies. Post-hoc speculations about past conditioning or improper scheduling of the reinforcements do not solve this problem.

Skinner has long argued that resorting to mentalistic concepts tends to prematurely cut off the search for the real causes of behavior [55]. While this may be true if the mentalistic concepts involved are pseudo-scientific, semi-mystical constructs like Freud's "id," the opposite is the case if the mentalistic concepts are clearly definable and verifiable through introspection. It is empty behavioristic concepts like "reinforcement" which delude investigators into thinking they understand the organism's behavior, and thus cut off the search for the real causes, i.e., those characteristics of the organism, including its mental contents and processes, which explain why it reacted as it did in response to, or in the absence of, the so-called reinforcements [24].

As Argyris [4] and Mitchell [37] have pointed out, there are numerous contextual assumptions which are untrue, non-universal or inappropriate in most applied settings, which behaviorists make when applying their techniques. Examples are the assumptions that individuals are basically passive responders to external stimulation; and that when subjects are being exposed to reinforcers, they will not think about what is happening, talk to anyone else about it, focus on the long term implications or consider their own goals.

There is a common element in the above assumptions, a premise which underlies and unites all of the behaviorist theories of human behavior and of management. It is the premise that *humans do not possess a conceptual faculty.* The frequently made distinction between metaphysical and methodological behaviorism does not contradict this characterization of behaviorism since, in practice, both versions amount to the same thing. While Skinner does not openly deny that people have minds, he does assert that the environment is the ultimate cause of all thinking and action [54, 55]. *But if mind is an epiphenomenon, then, for all practical purposes, it does not exist.*

Only if humans were by nature limited to the perceptual level of functioning, like dogs or cats, could one reasonably argue that they were passive responders to outside influences and that they would do nothing that they were not conditioned to do.[2] To quote Ayn Rand, a critic of behaviorism, on the issue of human nature:

> Man's sense organs function automatically; man's brain integrates his sense data into percepts automatically; but the process of integrating percepts into concepts—the process of abstraction and of concept-formation—is *not* automatic.
>   The process of concept-formation does not consist merely of grasping a few

---

[2]Even the assertion that animals are passive organisms is misleading. While animals lack free will (i.e., they cannot choose to think), they are still motivated by internal states (e.g., needs, wants, experiences of pleasure and pain). They are only passive by comparison to humans in that they cannot (through thinking) choose their wants nor means of achieving them. Nor can they reflect on the significance of what they are doing. Thus through arranging suitable external conditions, much of their behavior can be controlled.

simple abstractions, such as "chair," "table," "hot," "cold," and of learning to speak. It consists of a method of using one's consciousness, best designated by the term "conceptualizing." It is not a passive state of registering random impressions. It is an actively sustained process of identifying one's impressions in conceptual terms, of integrating every event and every observation into a conceptual context, of grasping relationships, differences, similarities in one's perceptual material and of abstracting them into new concepts, of drawing inferences, of making deductions, of reaching conclusions, of asking new questions and discovering new answers and expanding one's knowledge into an ever-growing sum. The faculty that directs this process, the faculty that works by means of concepts, is: *reason*. The process is *thinking.*

Reason is the faculty that perceives, identifies, and integrates the material provided by man's senses. It is a faculty that man has to exercise *by choice.* Thinking is not an automatic function. In any hour and issue of his life, man is free to think or to evade that effort. Thinking requires a state of full, focused awareness. The act of focusing one's consciousness is volitional. Man can focus his mind to a full, active, purposefully directed awareness of reality—or he can unfocus it and let himself drift in a semi-conscious daze, merely reacting to any chance stimulus of the immediate moment, at the mercy of his undirected sensory-perceptual mechanism and of any random, associational connections it might happen to make [50, pp. 20–21].

Since people can choose to think (a fact which can be validated by introspection), the behaviorist view of human nature is false. Thus the claim that behaviorism, taken literally, can serve as a valid guide to understanding and modifying human behavior in organizations is a myth.

REFERENCES

1 Adam, E. E. "Behavior Modification in Quality Control," *Academy of Management Journal,* Vol. 18 (1975), 662–679.

2 Ammons, R. B. "Effects of Knowledge of Performance: A Survey and Tentative Theoretical Formulation," *Journal of General Psychology,* Vol. 54 (1956), 279–299.

3 Annett, J. *Feedback and Human Behaviour* (Baltimore: Penguin, 1969).

4 Argyris, C. "Beyond Freedom and Dignity by B. F. Skinner (An Essay Review)," *Harvard Educational Review,* Vol. 41, No. 4 (1971), 550–567.

5 "At Emery Air Freight: Positive Reinforcement Boosts Performance," *Organizational Dynamics,* Vol. 1, No. 3 (1973), 41–50.

6 Bergin, A. E., and R. M. Suinn. "Individual Psychotherapy and Behavior Therapy," *Annual Review of Psychology,* Vol. 26 (1975), 509–556.

7 Bolles, R. C. "Reinforcement, Expectancy, and Learning," *Psychological Review,* Vol. 79 (1972), 394–409.

8 Brewer, W. F. "There is No Convincing Evidence for Operant or Classical Conditioning in Adult Humans," in W. B. Weimer and D. S. Palermo (Eds.), *Cognition and the Symbolic Processes* (Hillsdale, N.J.: L. Erlbaum, 1974), pp. 1–42.

9 Dulany, D. E. "Awareness, Rules and Propositional Control: A Confrontation with S-R Behavior Theory," in T. R. Dixon and D. L. Horton (Eds.), *Verbal Behavior and General Behavior Theory* (Englewood Cliffs, N.J.: Prentice-Hall, 1968), pp. 340–387.

10 Fry, F. L. "Operant Conditioning in Organizational Settings: Of Mice or Men?" *Personnel* (July–August 1974), 17–24.

11 Gagné, R. M. "Military Training and Principles of Learning," *American Psychologist,* Vol. 17 (1962), 83–91.

12 Goldstein, A. P., and M. Sorcher. *Changing Supervisory Behavior* (Elmsford, N.Y.: Pergamon Press, 1974).

13 Hamner, W. C. "Reinforcement Theory and Contingency Management in Organizational Settings," in R. M. Steers and L. W. Porter (Eds.), *Motivation and Work Behavior* (New York: McGraw-Hill, 1975), pp. 477–504.

14 Hersey, P., and K. H. Blanchard. "The Management of Change," *Training and Development Journal,* Vol. 29, No. 2 (1972), 20–24.

15 Jabara, R. F. *A Comparison of Programmed Instruction and Text Methods of Presentation, With Time Controlled* (Master's Thesis, University of Maryland, College Park, 1970).

16 Jablonsky, S. F., and D. L. DeVries. "Operant Conditioning Principles Extrapolated to the Theory of Management," *Organizational Behavior and Human Performance,* Vol. 7 (1972), 340–358.

17 Kanfer, F. H. "Vicarious Human Reinforcement: A Glimpse into the Black Box," in L. Krasner and L. P. Ullman (Eds.), *Research in Behavior Modification* (New York: Holt, Rinehart and Winston, 1965), pp. 244–267.

18 Kanfer, F. H., and P. Karoly. "Self-Control: A Behavioristic Excursion into the Lion's Den," *Behavior Therapy,* Vol. 3 (1972), 398–416.

19 Latham, G. P., and J. J. Baldes. "The 'Practical Significance' of Locke's Theory of Goal-Setting," *Journal of Applied Psychology,* Vol. 60 (1975), 122–124.

20 Latham, G. P., and S. B. Kinne. "Improving Job Performance Through Training in Goal-Setting," *Journal of Applied Psychology,* Vol. 59 (1974), 187–191.

21 Latham, G. P., and G. A. Yukl. "Assigned Versus Participative Goal Setting with Educated and Uneducated Woods Workers," *Journal of Applied Psychology,* Vol. 60 (1975), 299–302.

22 Locke, E. A. "Toward a Theory of Task Motivation and Incentives," *Organizational Behavior and Human Performance,* Vol. 3 (1968), 157–189.

23 Locke, E. A. "Is 'Behavior Therapy' Behavioristic? (An Analysis of Wople's Psychotherapeutic Methods)," *Psychological Bulletin,* Vol. 76 (1971), 318–327.

24 Locke, E. A. "Critical Analysis of the Concept of Causality in Behavioristic Psychology," *Psychological Reports,* Vol. 31 (1972), 175–197.

25 Locke, E. A. *A Guide to Effective Study* (New York: Springer, 1975).

26 Locke, E. A., and J. F. Bryan. "The Directing Function of Goals in Task Performance," *Organizational Behavior and Human Performance,* Vol. 4 (1969), 35–42.

27 Locke, E. A., N. Cartledge, and J. Koeppel. "Motivational Effects of Knowledge of Results: A Goal-Setting Phenomenon?" *Psychological Bulletin,* Vol. 70 (1968), 474–485.

28 Luthans, F. "An Organizational Behavior Modification (O. B. Mod) Approach to O. D." Paper presented at the National Academy of Management, Seattle, 1974.

29 Luthans, F., and R. Kreitner. "The Management of Behavioral Contingencies," *Personnel* (July–August 1974), 7–16.

30 Luthans, F., and R. Kreitner. *Organizational Behavior Modification* (Glenview, Ill.: Scott Foresman, 1975).

31 Luthans, F., and D. D. White. "Behavior Modification: Application to Manpower Management," *Personnel Administration,* Vol. 34, No. 4 (1971), 41–47.

32 Mahoney, M. J. *Cognition and Behavior Modification* (Cambridge, Mass.: Ballinger, 1974).

33 Marlatt, G. A. "A Comparison of Vicarious and Direct Reinforcement Control of Verbal Behavior in an Interview Setting," *Journal of Personality and Social Psychology,* Vol. 16 (1970), 695–703.

34 Mawhinney, T. C. "Operant Terms and Concepts in the Description of Individual Work Behavior: Some Problems of Interpretation, Application, and Evaluation," *Journal of Applied Psychology,* Vol. 60 (1975), 704–712.

35 McKeachie, W. J. "Instructional Psychology," *Annual Review of Psychology,* Vol. 25 (1974), 161–193.

36 Meichenbaum, D. "Self-Instructional Methods," in F. H. Kanfer and A. P. Goldstein (Eds.), *Helping People Change* (Elmsford, N.Y.: Pergamon, 1974).

37 Mitchell, T. R. "Cognitions and Skinner: Some Questions about Behavioral Determinism." Paper presented at the National Academy of Management, Seattle, 1974.

38 Morasky, R. L. "Self-Shaping Training Systems and Flexible-Model Behavior, i.e., Sales Interviewing," *Educational Technology,* Vol. 11, No. 5 (1971), 57–59.

39 Moses, J. E. "A Behavioral Method of Evaluating Training or: A Light at the End of the Tunnel." Paper presented at National Society for Performance and Instruction, New York, 1974.

40 Moses, J., and D. Ritchie. "Assessment Center Used to Evaluate an Interaction Modeling Program," *Assessment and Development,* Vol. 2, No. 2 (1975), 1–2.

41 Nash, A. N., J. P. Muczyk, and F. L. Vettori. "The Relative Practical Effectiveness of Programmed Instruction," *Personnel Psychology,* Vol. 24 (1971), 397–418.

42 "New Tool: 'Reinforcement' for Good Work." *Business Week,* December 18, 1971, 76–77.

43 Nord, W. R. "Beyond the Teaching Machine: The Neglected Areas of Operant Conditioning in the Theory and Practice of Management," *Organizational Behavior and Human Performance,* Vol. 4 (1969), 375–401.

44 Nord, W. R. "Improving Attendance Through Rewards," *Personnel Administration,* Vol. 33, No. 6 (1970), 37–41.

45 O'Day, E. F., R. W. Kulhavy, W. Anderson, and R. J. Malczynski. *Programmed Instruction, Techniques and Trends* (New York: Appleton-Century-Crofts, 1971).

46 Parsons, H. M. "What Happened at Hawthorne?" *Science,* Vol. 183 (1974), 922–932.

47 Pedalino, E., and V. U. Gamboa. "Behavior Modification and Absenteeism: Intervention in One Industrial Setting," *Journal of Applied Psychology,* Vol. 59 (1974), 694–698.

48 "Performance Audit Feedback, and Positive Reinforcement," *Training and Development Journal,* Vol. 29, No. 11 (1972), 8–13.

49 Pressey, S. L. "Teaching Machine (and Learning Theory) Crisis," *Journal of Applied Psychology,* Vol. 47 (1963), 1–6.

50 Rand, A. "The Objectivist Ethics," in A. Rand, *The Virtue of Selfishness* (New York: New American Library, 1964), pp. 13–35.

51 Roethlisberger, F. J., and W. J. Dickson. *Management and the Worker* (Cambridge, Mass.: Harvard, 1956).

52 Schneier, C. E. "Behavior Modification in Management: A Review and Critique," *Academy of Management Journal,* Vol. 17 (1974), 528–548.

53 Skinner, B. F. "Teaching Machines," *Science,* Vol. 128 (1958), 969–977.

54 Skinner, B. F. *Beyond Freedom and Dignity* (New York: Alfred A. Knopf, 1971).

55 Skinner, B. F. "The Steep and Thorny Way to a Science of Behavior," *American Psychologist,* Vol. 30 (1975), 42–49.

56 Sorcher, M., and A. P. Goldstein. "A Behavior Modeling Approach to Training," *Personnel Administration,* Vol. 35, No. 2 (1972), 35–41.

57 Taylor, F. W. *The Principles of Scientific Management,* 1911 (New York: Norton, 1967).

58 Thorndike, E. H. *Human Learning,* 1931 (Cambridge, Mass.: M.I.T. Press, 1966).

59 Welsh, P., J. A. Antoinetti, and P. W. Thayer. "An Industrywide Study of Programmed Instruction," *Journal of Applied Psychology,* Vol. 49 (1965), 61–73.

60 "Where Skinner's Theories Work," *Business Week,* Dec. 2, 1972, 64–65.

61 Wiard, H. "Why Manage Behavior? A Case for Positive Reinforcement," *Human Resource Management,* Vol. 11, No. 2 (1972), 15–20.

62 Yukl, G. A., and G. P. Latham. "Consequences of Reinforcement Schedules and Incentive Magnitudes for Employee Performance: Problems Encountered in an Industrial Setting," *Journal of Applied Psychology,* Vol. 60 (1975), 294–298.

REVIEW AND DISCUSSION QUESTIONS

1 What are some of the major arguments against O.B. Mod. according to Locke?
2 Given the results of the O.B. Mod. research in the previous articles, how would you counter Locke's arguments?
3 How, if at all, might we empirically analyze Locke's postulates?
4 In general, do you agree or disagree with this article? Why?

Part Four

Organizational Behavior Dynamics: Groups, Communication, and Conflict

There are several important dynamics of organizational behavior. The two major components of organizational behavior are the individual employee and the organization. There is a synergistic effect when the individual is placed into the organizational setting. The individual has many psychological attributes and much previous knowledge that he or she brings into the organization. Every individual is different from every other individual. These individual differences can lead to a wide variety of actions and reactions when the person is placed into an organizational setting. Like individuals, organizations are also unique entities. For example, the structure of organizations do much to set the parameters of the participants' behaviors. The organizational policies, technology, and even the physical surroundings can do much to affect an individual's behavior. The resulting dynamics of the person-organization interaction is vital to the study and understanding of organizational behavior.

The formation of informal work groups is one prime example of the dynamics of organizational behavior. One of the considerations of this approach to the dynamics of organizational behavior is the formation and resulting behavior of such groups. While informal groups were condemned by early management theorists, such as the scientific management pioneer Frederick W.

Taylor, there is increasing evidence that the informal group can provide many benefits to the organization. Much of what goes on in organizations is often facilitatcd by informal group dynamics. For example, much of the training that is done in organizations is more a function of the individual attention that the new employee receives from more seasoned employees in the work group than by the formal training programs that attempt to teach the basic skills to the employee. Informal groups can also facilitate communication.

Communication, whether in groups or interpersonally, is an important dynamic in organizational behavior. The communication process is very pervasive and involves many of the management and organizational functions. For example, leadership involves communication, so does decision making, planning, controlling, and organizing. In fact, effective communication seems to underlie almost all organizational behavior. In Part Two, goal setting and feedback were discussed. In essence, one of the key ingredients in the successful use of goal setting is to be able to communicate the degree of expectations that the person has with respect to performance. The establishment of goals requires communication. In terms of feedback or knowledge of results, it is generally acknowledged that for goal setting to be effective, such feedback communication must be available to the individuals performing their tasks. Good communication, therefore, provides the initial framework for performance and provides an effective means for the assessment of the individual's performance.

Besides groups and communication, conflict and stress in organizations are other important dynamics in the person-organization interface. It is now generally recognized that conflict can be good for the organization. For example, change and growth can come from the exchanging of views and experiencing some dissatisfaction over the current situation. The main objective, therefore, is not to eradicate conflict, but to attempt to manage it so that it can work for the organization and not against it. Stress and conflict are natural parts of most jobs. How the individual copes with stress and manages conflict can be the deciding factor in the effectiveness of today's organizations.

The first reading in this section provides some of the major theories of organizational and interpersonal attraction. It is this attraction that provides the basis for group formation in organizations. The second article traces the major studies of group dynamics over the past forty years. Some logical conclusions and extensions are provided. Professor Zander also discusses some directions for future work in the area of informal groups in his article. The next two articles provide a framework for discussions of the important dynamics of communication in organizations. Professor Jablin discusses communications primarily in a hierarchical sense, while Professor Schuler directs his attention to what a manager can do, via communication, to reduce stress in an organization. The final two articles discuss the prevalence of conflict and stress in organizations and how they may be managed to increase an organization's effectiveness.

Reading 16

Theories of Interpersonal Attraction

Paul F. Secord
Carl W. Backman

Although much early sociometric research was not guided by systematic theory, in more recent years the accumulation of empirical findings has led to the development of several theories of interpersonal attraction. No attempt will be made to include them all; only a few representative theories will be discussed. The theories are of two general kinds: those that focus on the characteristics of individuals, and those that focus on the rewards and costs experienced in the interactional process.

Theories of friendship which explain attraction in terms of the characteristics of the dyad go back to antiquity.[1] The basic question has been whether persons who are similar or those who are different are attracted to each other. Today it is known that this question greatly oversimplifies the matter.

NEWCOMB'S THEORY OF INTERPERSONAL ATTRACTION

Newcomb[2] [1961], following Heider[3] [1958], has developed and tested a theory that persons with similar orientations (attitudes) are attracted to each other. Through long experience, an individual becomes dependent upon other persons for information about the environment. He uses this information to confirm and extend the impressions of his senses. Thus the individual is conceived to need support from others for his attitudes and beliefs. When he encounters a person with attitudes contrary to his own, a state of strain arises, particularly if he likes the person. This strain is uncomfortable, and the individual seeks to resolve it by finding agreement with other persons. This basic motivation has been called the need for *consensual validation* [Sullivan, 1947], which means that people attempt to validate their attitudes through seeking agreement with others.[4]

The greater the importance and common relevance of the attitude object to the persons in a dyad, the stronger the attraction. By *importance* is meant the strength of the feeling, cognition, or behaviors toward the object in question. These may be positive or negative. By *common relevance* is meant the degree to which the object is perceived as having common consequences for the persons in question. The term *object* refers to any focus of perception, including physical objects, symbols, other persons, or one's own self. For example, for most married couples it is more important that they agree on whether or not they like children than on whether or not they like a particular make of automobile. Agreement on the former will lead to more attraction to each other than will agreement on the latter.

Newcomb's theory is couched in system terms. Each variable—attraction, orientation, perception of the orientation of the other person—is in part a consequent of and in part a determinant of each other variable. Not only is the attraction of A toward B affected by the similarity between A's attitude toward X and his perception of B's attitude toward X but his own attitude and his perception of B's attitude are influenced by the degree to which he is attracted to B. For example, assume that A, who is attracted to B, discovers a discrepancy between his attitude and B's attitude toward an object of common relevance, such as another person, X. A likes person X; i.e., has a variety of affective and cognitive components of a positive or favorable nature with respect to X. He discovers, however, that B dislikes X and views many of X's attributes unfavorably. Given the attraction of A toward B, this discrepancy between A's attitude and his perception of B's attitude would give rise to strain and to a postulated force toward change in the realtions between these three system components.

A change returning the system to a state of balance could take a number of forms. First, a shift could occur in A's perception of B's attitude: A might decide that he was mistaken in attributing to B a negative attitude toward X. Assuming that B actually has a negative attitude, this form of resolution would be labeled *misperception*. Second, A might change his own attitude in the direction of B's and develop a similarly negative attitude toward X. Third, A might attempt to convince B that he is mistaken about X. If B were attracted to A and experienced a similar strain, he might be amenable to such a persuasive attempt. Fourth, A might simply restore the system to balance by reducing his attraction toward B.[5]

This illustration suggests that, depending on the system variable focused upon, Newcomb's theory of strain toward symmetry can be viewed not only as a theory of interpersonal attraction, but also as a theory of social perception and social influence. Since our main concern here is with explanations of interpersonal attraction, the theory will be considered mainly from that point of view.

From his theory Newcomb predicted that, as strangers in a new group begin to interact and thus to gain information concerning each other's attitudes, the bonds of attraction making up the affect or sociometric structure of the group form most strongly between those who hold similar attitudes toward objects of importance and common relevance. These predictions were tested in a study of two groups. Both were composed of male college students who were initially strangers and who lived together in a house provided by the experimenter. Their orientations toward a variety of objects, including each other, and the patterns of attraction that developed were measured at various points during a sixteen-week period.

The observations and the changes that occurred over the period observed were in accord with the theory. Preacquaintance similarities, measured by the experimenter from the students' responses to questionnaires on a variety of specific topics and from their rankings of certain values, led to the development of patterns of attraction between persons at a late stage in the sixteen-week period, but not at an early stage. Since these attitudinal values did *not* change to any extent over the period studied, it would appear that as persons became acquainted with each other's values, attraction formed between those who were similar. When two persons held relevant and similar orientations toward themselves and toward other house occupants, they were especially likely to be attracted to each other. As acquaintance increased, consensus between members of a pair in attitudes toward other house members increased, and there was a parallel increase in their attraction to each other.

If the assumption is made that persons positively value themselves, the theory would predict that a close association would be found between liking oneself and believing that other persons like one. Such was the case: A person liked others who had the same feeling toward him as he had toward himself. The association between attraction to a person and perceiving him as having similar attitudes was true for cognitive elements as well. Each subject described himself by checking a series of adjectives and then used the same adjective checklist to describe himself as he thought each of the others in the group would. A close association was found between attraction and agreement on such a self-description. This appeared to hold for unfavorable as well as favorable items: and individual was attracted to persons whom he perceived as seeing him the way he saw himself, in terms of both faults and virtues. These findings with regard to the self as an object have been confirmed by others [Tagiuri, 1958; Backman and Secord, 1959, 1962; Broxton, 1963].[6] Also, a study conducted in another theoretical context to be described below showed that attraction was affected not only by perceived similarity but by actual similarity as well [Backman and Secord, 1962].[7]

Finally, another study, while not concerned with attraction as the dependent variable, provides experimental evidence for strain toward symmetry. Using a confederate, Sampson and Insko [1964] created two balanced and two imbalanced conditions in a perceptual task situation.[8] In one, subjects were led to like their partner and to perceive him as making judgments similar to their own. In the other, they were led to dislike their partner and to perceive his judgments as different from theirs. The two imbalanced situations were manipulated so that a disliked partner was seen as making similar judgments, and a liked partner, as making dissimilar judgments. The prediction that subjects would change their judgment more frequently in the *imbalanced* situations was confirmed. In another similar experimental situation, however, where judgments of the outcome of jury trials were made, the prediction that subjects would respond so as to be different from a disliked partner and similar to a liked partner received less conclusive support.

In summary, Newcomb's theory of strain toward symmetry postulates that individuals strive to achieve a state of balance. Balance is present when persons *A* and *B* are attracted to each other and hold similar attitudes toward objects of common relevance to them. When imbalance occurs, one or more of the component parts are changed to restore balance. These various components of the system are not independent, but have mutual effects upon each other.

Attitudes toward the self and other group members are of particular significance for the determination of strain or balance. Studies of living groups[9] by Newcomb and by others are generally consistent with his theory.

THEORY OF COMPLEMENTARY NEEDS

Perhaps the most widely known theory that stresses differences rather than similarities as a basis of attraction is the theory of complementary needs, proposed by Winch[10] [1958]. This theory, developed and tested largely in the context of mate selection, has been offered as a general principle of dyad formation, of which mate selection is a special case. While not denying that persons who fall in love and marry are similar in a number of respects such as social-background characteristics, Winch proposed that the need structure of persons attracted to each other is different or complementary rather than similar.

Winch suggested two general reasons why persons who differ in need structure are attracted to each other. First, each member of the dyad finds interaction mutually or reciprocally rewarding because his needs are expressed in behavior that is rewarding to the other member. For example, a person with strong nurturance needs behaves in a protective, nurturant manner toward another person who has strong needs to be dependent. In this way, each individual satisfies his needs and is in turn satisfied. Second, persons are attracted to others who have characteristics they once aspired to but were prevented by circumstances from developing. Instead, they have modeled themselves after the image of a person with the opposite traits. But they still retain a wistful admiration for individuals who possess the once-coveted traits. To illustrate [Winch, 1958]:

> To tie these ideas together, let us dream up a little boy, Herbert, whose mother demanded "model" behavior and gave him to understand that neither she nor anyone else would ever have anything to do with him unless he did as she said. Let us imagine that little Herbert was frightened and conformed but realized that occasionally he had impulses to be "bad." Let us assume that he was worried about those impulses and subsequently became a very "good" and "controlled" boy—a bit of a sissy and not very popular. One of his ego-models—taken up, cherished, and abandoned—would probably be a swashbuckling exemplar of derring-do, mobilized at all times to run his sword through anyone who might cross his path. And as Herbert became an adult, we might expect that he would be attracted to expressive people, to people who talk back and don't take nonsense from others. This is something we might feel sure that he would wish he could do—just feel some aggression well up in his veins. We might expect him to draw vicarious gratification from seeing other people "blow their tops." We might even expect that he would marry a girl who would blow her top regularly.[11]

Need complementarity may take either of two forms. Persons *A* and *B* may be regarded as complementary in needs because *A* is high and *B* is low on the *same* needs, or because *A* is high on one or more needs and *B* is high or low on certain *different* needs. To illustrate the former, which is called Type I complementarity, a person who is very high in the need to dominate others and a person who is very low in this need would be mutually attracted. Type II complementarity is illustrated by the previous description of a nurturant and a dependent person attracted to each other.

Evidence for this theory is far from conclusive. Winch and his associates studied the need structure of twenty-five married couples and concluded that the bulk of the evidence supported his general hypothesis of complementarity. Since his initial investigations, a number of others have tested these ideas. Several studies[12] failed to confirm Winch's conclusions, but another recent investigation has supported them [Kerchkoff and Davis, 1962].[13] Since the investigations differed from each other in the populations studied, the manner in which the needs were assessed, and a number of other respects, it is difficult to pinpoint the reasons for such disparity in findings. Yet, the preponderance of evidence casts doubt on the plausibility of this hypothesis, at least as originally formulated. Further refinements, however, may still result in specifying those conditions under which complementarity does in fact produce attraction.

Elsewhere, the present writers have outlined a theory of stability and change in behavior that has implications for interpersonal attraction [1961].[14] It has certain implications for need complementarity. It proposed that persons will like others whose characteristics, behavioral and otherwise, aid them in maintaining *congruency.* Such a perceptual-cognitive state is achieved by an individual in a relation with another person when the other's characteristics or behavior contain implications congruent with elements of his own behavior and self-concept. The present writers have made the following suggestions.

> Implications for self-definitions may take three forms: *S* may perceive *O*'s behavior as directly confirming a component of self, *O*'s behavior may enable *S* to behave in ways that would confirm a component of self, *O*'s behavior may (by comparison) lead other *O*'s to confirm a component of *S*'s self-concept. Examples of each form are:
>
> An *S* who regards himself as mature and responsible perceives that *O*'s respect him for these characteristics.
>
> An *S* who regards himself as a nurturant encounters an *O* in need of help; this allows him to behave toward *O* in a manner which supports his nurturant aspect of self.
>
> A girl who regards herself as popular and well-liked keeps company with an unpopular girl; *O*'s are viewed by her as judging her favorably by contrast.[15]

Depending on the implications for congruency, this theory predicts that attraction between two persons is a function of *similarity* in certain traits and further, that certain combinations of dissimilar traits in a dyad result in attraction. Some predictions from this theory are the same as those of Winch, but others are opposite to his. To illustrate attraction through similarity, a person who regards himself as friendly and outgoing is expected to be attracted to others who are similar in this respect, since their behavior would allow him to behave in a manner congruent with this particular facet of his self-conception. Attraction between a nurturant and a dependent person illustrates attraction based on dissimilar needs and is consistent with the notion of congruency.

In summary, Winch's theory of need complementarity proposes two forms of interpersonal attraction based upon the need structures of individuals in a dyad. In one, persons A and B are complementary in need structure because A is high and B is low in the same need. In the other, A is high on a need, and B is low on a different need. Both situations are believed to be complementary because each member finds the behavior of his partner rewarding. Empirical evidence is at present preponderantly negative.

In interpersonal congruency theory, the extent to which the other person is perceived as behaving in a manner congruent with the self-concept is taken as a basis for need complementarity. This theory appears to provide a somewhat clearer rationale for need complementarity, but empirical findings in support of it must be regarded as tentative.

EXCHANGE THEORIES OF ATTRACTION

The theories of attraction examined so far have emphasized personality characteristics. Those which will be briefly reviewed here emphasize factors in the history of the interaction between persons. Recently Thibaut and Kelley[16] [1959] and Homans[17] [1961] have independently arrived at general theoretical formulations which are remarkably similar and which are consistent with the findings presented here. Both theories attempt to explain social behavior in terms of the rewards exchanged and the costs incurred in interaction. As such, both include a theory of interpersonal attraction. The following four concepts are basic to exchange theory: reward, cost, outcome, and comparison level.

The term *reward* is a familiar one. The review of other theories has taken note of rather important rewards that are achieved in interaction. For example, consensual validation about the world as well as about oneself is a kind of reward that theories such as Newcomb's suggest people exchange in interaction. Any activity on the part of one person that contributes to the gratification of another person's needs can be considered a reward from the standpoint of the latter person. The term *cost* is similarly a very broad concept. The costs of engaging in any activity not only include "punishment" incurred in carrying out that activity, such as fatigue or anxiety, but also, as Homans argues, include the value of rewards foregone by engaging in this activity rather than alternative activities. The term *outcome* refers to rewards less costs. If the outcome of an interaction is positive, it may be said to yield a *profit*; if it is a negative, a *loss*. Because a person profits from an interaction with another, however, does not necessarily mean that he likes that person. For attraction to occur, the outcome must be above some minimum level of expectation or desserts, called the *comparison* level. This level is influenced by his past experiences in this relation, his past experiences in comparable relations, his judgment of what outcomes others like himself are receiving, and his perceptions of outcomes available to him in alternative relations.

This way of looking at interpersonal attraction has two advantages. First, it provides a general rationale for explaining why persons with certain characteristics receive more than their share of choices as well as why persons with one characteristic choose others with certain different characteristics. Second, it permits an examination from a process standpoint of the changes in attraction that occur among members of a group.

NOTES AND REFERENCES

1 For excellent reviews of these theories, see V. W. Grant, *The Psychology of Sexual Emotion: The Basis of Selective Attraction,* New York: Longmans, Green, 1951; and C. B. Broderick, *Predicting Friendship Behavior: A Study of the Determinants of Friendship Selection and Maintenance in a College Population,* unpublished doctoral dissertation, Cornell University, 1956.
2 T. M. Newcomb, *The Acquaintance Process,* New York: Holt, 1961.
3 F. Heider, *The Psychology of Interpersonal Relations,* New York: Wiley, 1958.
4 H. S. Sullivan, *Conceptions of Modern Psychiatry,* Washington: The William Alanson White Psychiatric Foundation, 1947.
5 In order not to complicate this illustration further, two other changes have been omitted. Since the degree of strain is in part a function of the importance and perceived common relevance of person X to A, changes might be made with regard to those two variables in order to reduce strain.
6 See R. Tagiuri, "Social Preference and Its Perception," in R. Tagiuri and L. Petrullo, eds., *Person Perception and Interpersonal Behavior,* Stanford, California: Stanford University Press, 1958, pp. 316–336; C. W. Backman and P. F. Secord, "The Effect of Perceived Liking on Interpersonal Attraction," *Human Relations,* vol. 12, 1959, pp. 379–384; C. W. Backman and P. F. Secord, "Liking, Selective Interaction, and Misperception in Congruent Interpersonal Relations," *Sociometry,* vol. 25, 1962, pp. 321–335; and June Broxton, "A Text of Interpersonal Attraction Predictions Derived from Balance Theory," *Journal of Abnormal and Social Psychology,* vol. 66, 1963, pp. 394–397.
7 Backman and Secord, op. cit., 1962.
8 E. E. Sampson and C. A. Insko, "Cognitive Consistency and Performance in the Autokinetic Situation," *Journal of Abnormal and Social Psychology,* vol. 68, 1964, pp. 184–192.
9 The term *living group* refers to a group of persons who share a common domicile, such as occupants of a dormitory, members of a sorority living in the sorority house, etc.
10 R. F. Winch, *Mate-Selection: A Study of Complementary Needs,* New York: Harper, 1958.
11 Ibid., p. 87.
12 C. Bowerman and B. Day, "A Test of the Theory of Complementary Needs as Applied to Couples During Courtship," *American Sociological Review,* vol. 21, 1956, pp. 602–605; J. A. Schellenberg and I. S. Bee, "A Re-Examination of the

Theory of Complementary Needs in Mate Selection," *Marriage and Family Living,* vol. 22, 1960, pp. 227–232; B. L. Murstein, "The Complementary Need Hypothesis in Newlyweds and Middle-Aged Married Couples," *Journal of Abnormal and Social Psychology,* vol. 63, 1961, pp. 194–197; and C. W. Hobart and Lauralee Lindholm, "The Theory of Complementary Needs: A Reexamination," *Pacific Sociological Review,* vol. 6, 1963, pp. 73–79.

13 A. Kerchkoff and K. A. Davis, "Value Consensus and Need Complementarity in Mate Selection," *American Sociological Review,* vol. 27, pp. 295–303.

14 P. F. Secord and C. W. Backman, "Personality Theory and the Problem of Stability and Change in Individual Behavior: An Interpersonal Approach," *Psychological Review,* vol. 68, 1961, pp. 21–32.

15 Ibid.

16 J. W. Thibaut and H. H. Kelley, *The Social Psychology of Groups,* New York: Wiley, 1959.

17 G. C. Homans, *Social Behavior: Its Elementary Forms,* New York: Harcourt, Brace & World, 1961.

REVIEW AND DISCUSSION QUESTIONS

1 Briefly summarize Newcomb's theory of interpersonal attraction. How can the systems concept be incorporated into this theory?

2 What are some reasons why persons who differ in need structure are attracted to each other? Can you relate these reasons to your own observation and/or experience?

3 Two common "folk hypotheses" for explaining interpersonal attraction are "birds of a feather flock together" and "opposites attract." Relate these to the theories presented by Secord and Backman. Which do you think is a more plausible explanation for interpersonal attraction?

Reading 17

The Study of Group Behavior During Four Decades

Alvin Zander

Without much warning, about 40 years ago, students of human behavior developed an interest in how groups conduct their activities. This rise of attention among scholars was evident in the number and content of their publications, the creation of a communications network, and a zealous desire of some individuals in this network to improve ineffective groups before anyone knew how such improving could be done. Citizens were attracted to research on groups and some stated (extravagantly enough) that the products of this research

Reprinted from the *Journal of Applied Behavioral Science,* vol. 3, 1978, pp. 272–282, with permission of the publisher.

would at last provide answers to tough problems in government and social relations.

During subsequent decades the quick growth of those early years settled down to a more measured pace and to a deeper perusal of particular topics, while scholars interested in training members of groups drew away, for the most part, from college campuses, or at least from researchers, and nurtured groups in natural settings and training laboratories. In this article we briefly review some of the main features in the history of research into group behavior, commenting on training activities only where these had an impact on empirical investigations.

PRIOR TO 1940

Before 1935 there had been little scientific effort to understand processes in groups. Research had been done on laughter in audiences and on the personality traits of designated leaders, but the only work close to current studies in group life were studies comparing how groups and individuals go about solving problems, a topic that remains of interest today. The dearth of earlier inquiries into group activities is not surprising when we recall that psychologists in the 30s devoted most of their attention to the study of physiology, motor skills, and cognitive processes of the individual. Social psychologists had hardly discovered their identity, and sociologists, for their part, were not yet collecting empirical data on groups.

In the last half of the 30s the time had come for attempts to explain events within organizations; several notable developments in research signalled this fact. Work on group structure and attraction between individual members [Moreno, 1934], the influence of group norms on members [Sherif, 1936], the impact of shared beliefs on the political attitudes of college students [Newcomb, 1943], and the effect that membership in a workgroup had upon the sentiments of factory workers [Roethlisberger & Dickson, 1939], revealed that aspects of collective behavior, previously of interest to social philosophers, could usefully be brought under scientific investigation.

The most influential research by far in the emerging study of group behavior was that of Lewin, Lippitt, and White [1939]. Their investigations of group climate, intergroup conflict, and styles of leadership (autocratic, democratic, and laissez-faire) made use, with important modifications, of the available techniques in experimental psychology, controlled observations of behavior, and methods of social group work. Their purpose was to expose some of the ways in which the behavior of leaders may differ and to discover how methods of leadership influence the properties of groups and the behavior of members. We should note that these investigations were not intended to make a contribution to the technology of group management per se. Rather, they sought to provide insight into the underlying dynamics of groups. The methods and results of the studies suggested that it might be feasible to construct a coherent body of knowledge about the nature of group life and eventually a general theory of groups. These studies had an originality and significance which produced a marked impact on the social sciences and professions. Almost immediately, associates of Lewin, and others, began research projects, most of them laboratory experiments, designed to contribute information relevant to a theory of group dynamics. The results of this work formed the core of a "critical mass" which eventually made this speciality distinctive and accepted.

Lewin's assumptions about the causes of human behavior were particularly suited to the study of group life, as he held that most of the variables determining behavior at a given time and place are extant in that setting. Past events and future ones were to be interpreted in terms of their current psychological representation. Lewin's emphasis on the forces and constraints arising in situations led to a concentration on the here-and-now in both research and training about group life. Because such notions were especially appropriate in the developing of theory, prediction, and experimentation, they helped to generate a special style of investigation.

DURING THE 1940s

As these investigations were getting under way, the United States entered World War II and little research on groups was accomplished for 5 years or so. In 1946, Lewin, and a set of his former students, founded the Research Center for Group Dynamics at the Massachusetts Institute of Technology, and in 1948 the Center moved to The University of Michigan after the untimely death of Lewin.

Through research done at this center, at half a dozen other centers with similar purposes in several countries, and at a number of campuses and government laboratories, knowledge about the social psychology of groups entered a period of active growth. Some of the topics studied most often in the 40s were: social pressures members place on one another within a group [Festinger, 1950], the direction and amount of communication among members [Bavelas, 1950], contrasts in the behavior of members in cooperative and competitive groups [Deutsch, 1949], the consequences of training community leaders [Lippitt, 1949], and the effects of social power among children [Lippitt, Polansky, Redl & Rosen, 1952].

The concepts and methods in this research were radical for their time and discipline. Thus, the scientists immersed in these efforts found it helpful to organize themselves informally to work toward a common end. Researchers distant from one another created a loose network, exchanged drafts of papers, and talked about their investigations in small meetings, conferences, and visits. The formation of this "invisible college" among students of groups was not unlike the voluntary associations, described by Griffith and Mullins [1972], that arise throughout the history of science whenever a strikingly new topic is taken up by members of a given discipline. Many of the early group scholars firmly believed that the output of their research would have a wide impact toward improving democratic methods, and the researchers consciously worked toward such ends. After World War II, it was more acceptable than it is now to claim that research in human behavior would have practical value for society.

Ordinary citizens gave considerable attention to this research, and the study of group processes received as much interest in the media of those days as have recombinant DNA, toxic chemicals, tranquilizers, or the effects of computers, in more recent years. The reasons for the wide appeal of this research at that time merits detailed study someday. One can guess, however, that the attractiveness of the work arose in part because everyone was worried then about the fate of this country in World War II and about the future of democracy as a form of government. They were inclined, therefore, to welcome work by scientists who might increase our understanding of the dynamics of governing and might suggest ways of improving its procedures. Also, there was a widespread fear, during the 40s, that dictatorships had developed irresistible methods for manipulating the minds of men. Perhaps we could learn how to oppose such pressures through research by students of groups. Not least was the wide interest, even delight, in the methods and results of experiments on small societies in the laboratory where it was shown that contrasting behavior of group members, under contrasting circumstances, could be predicted and explained. Citizens highly approved of scientists in physics and engineering during the 40s and 50s because these latter had helped in the winning of World War II. Perhaps social scientists could be as useful in problems of group life if they were given proper encouragement and support. Accordingly, late in the decade, the Office of Naval Research created a unit to provide funds for research on group behavior regardless of the work's relevance to military conditions.

One other development in the 1940s is notable. In 1947 the National Training Laboratory for Group Development was organized by the Adult Education Division of the National Education Association, in cooperation with the Research Center for Group Dynamics. This was a three-week workshop attended by professional persons from various walks of life who wished to improve their knowledge of groups and their abilities as members and managers. Because there was a limited supply of knowledge available for participants in this kind of laboratory, the teachers relied on having students learn from their experiences in small discussion groups. This procedure encouraged talk about the matters that excited them most and these turned out to be personal feelings, relations among members, differences in perceptions, and explanations for these differences. Such person-centered interaction, as we shall see, reduced regard for the study of groups. An account of these developments is offered in the book *Beyond Words* by Kurt Back [1972].

From the beginning, the founders of the National Training Laboratory had different ideas among them as to the purposes of the unit. Some of these objectives were: to teach group dynamics, to teach consultants how to facilitate change within an organization, to teach members "basic skills" of membership, to train participants in the teaching methods being employed at the laboratory, and to conduct research on behavior in groups. Because of these unlike views, the meetings of staff members when planning each laboratory were lively and stimulating, to say the least. There was no initial interest, we should emphasize, in encouraging personal growth, mental health, or sensitivity in interpersonal relations.

DURING THE 1950s

In the decade of the 50s, research in the social psychology of groups was highly innovative and the rate of publication more than doubled, according to Hare [1976]. Authors of chapters on group research in the *Annual Review of Psychology* published in 1951, 1953, 1954, and 1958 remarked that study of groups was the most lively and creative work in social psychology and provided a focus for the entire field.

The topics for investigation were those already mentioned, plus: the flow of communication in groups when members have different degrees of connectedness among them, interpersonal power to influence, the sources of coalitions, and the nature and consequences of balanced relations within groups. Bales [1950] developed a method for observing and coding comments made by participants in small problem-solving groups. His treatment of these data, called interaction process analysis, revealed the kind of remarks (questions, suggestions, agreements, etc.) that were more likely to appear at each phase in a group's problem-solving effort. This work formed the basis of what sociologists came to call the study of small groups [Hare, Borgata & Bales, 1955]. It concentrated, however, on the acts and roles of individuals, and paid little attention to the group as a unit.

The properties of groups, their origins and consequences, provided, by this time, a framework for the study of group dynamics; many of the findings of research concerned one or more of these properties, such as cohesiveness, goals, or leadership. A book summarizing results of research in group dynamics, arranged according to such headings, was published by Cartwright and Zander in 1953.

Even though one could now identify a coherent body of knowledge from the results of group research, there were "islands" of findings that did not fit together well and these separated results were not included in summaries of the field. The topics given most study, moreover, were not noticed most often by readers. Nelson and Kannenberg [1976] report a correlation of only $r = .12$ between the popularity of a topic among researchers in the 1950s and the interest accorded to it in subsequent articles. Additional government agencies began to provide financial aid for research on groups: the United States Public Health Service, the National Institute for Mental Health, parts of the Department of Defense, and (later on) the National Science Foundation. In addition, grants were not hard to obtain, for promising projects, from private foundations and industrial firms. It was a lively but not a well organized time to be involved in the study of groups.

By the middle of this decade the National Training Laboratory in Group Development, which no longer had a formal relationship with the Research Center for Group Dynamics, dropped the words: "in Group Development" from its title, and moved toward independence from the National Education Association. The NTL now encouraged laboratories in several parts of the country. Most prominent among these branches was one at the University of Los

Angeles, run by students of personality theory, not social psychology. These teachers fostered an emphasis on personal growth and interpersonal relations, using the group as a setting for their teaching, not as a subject of instruction in itself. They placed more emphasis on personal feelings and problems than on cognitions or information—thus the term "sensitivity training" was an appropriate designation for their style of teaching.

Comparable developments were occurring at the original laboratory as the training began to emphasize self-awareness and personal improvement rather than understanding of group properties. Critics arose, especially among psychologists and professionals in mental health. They believed activities at training laboratories engendered stress for participants and that there was little evidence the activities had favorable effects on those who experienced them. Supporters of the training defended their programs by asserting that they were doing research and teaching about group behavior, not providing counseling for individuals. It had become evident, however, that a training laboratory was not a satisfactory place for conducting basic research, as the collecting of data often interfered with teaching activities and adequate experimental controls could seldom be developed in a training group.

DURING THE 1960s

By the 60s, the study of group behavior had become an accepted sub-discipline in departments of psychology, and in places for the study of sociology, speech, social work, public health, education, and business. Technical articles in this specialty appeared somewhat less often than they did in the previous decade. The number of research publications dropped from perhaps 150 a year to 120, but I know of no accurate count of this frequency. In contrast, essays on the use of groups in education, therapy, and management increased in numbers. Many who had earlier been doing research on the social psychology of groups moved to other interests unrelated to group life, and all of the centers established for research on groups, except the one at Michigan, were gone by the middle of the decade. Sherif [1977] and Steiner [1974] assert that many social psychologists turned from the study of groups and other collective phenomena to the study of individuals during the 60s.

If this reduction of interest in groups occurred in fact, why did it happen? Several reasons may have played a part.

1 Research on groups is more difficult than research on individuals: When groups (compared to individuals) are the units of study, many more subjects are needed, they are harder to assemble in the required number at the proper time, the costs are higher, and the design, measurement, and analyses are more complicated and tricky.
2 Concepts about group life are often too clumsy to use, too austere to attract much interest, or too intricate to test with confidence.
3 Results of research on groups can be weak and unconvincing because it

is hard to rule out noise and artifacts when measuring the varied behaviors in a group. Thus, many group researchers obtain small satisfaction from their efforts.

4   A researcher can get more help from current literature when studying individuals than when studying groups.

5   Funds for the support of social research began to be scarce late in the 60s and the study of groups did not compete well for these funds.

The fans of group dynamics dwindled in number during the 60s as their interests also moved, along with changes in social issues of the time, to topics where the study of groups was no longer as crucial. Some of the problems of group life during both the 60s and the 70s were not the kind, moreover, that stimulated theorizing about how groups effectively conduct their business. Unlike the 40s, much interesting group action was now intended to change conditions outside the group through demonstrations, disruptions, and other forms of confronting and militancy, rather than through the use of the democratic process. One cannot easily observe efforts to create social change, and thus research on such topics was done after the fact. As a result, sound theories have not been developed on these matters. "Group watchers" may have noticed, furthermore, that results from research in group behavior had not lived up to the grand expectations held for them after World War II—the world had not been changed. Also, many of the best known results of group research emphasized the bad effects of groups on their members—a one-sided view that did not arouse enthusiasm for the study of group behavior. Accompanying this shift of interest among nonscientists was a gradual dissolution of the network that had been formed among like-minded scholars. The reduction of activist fervor within this network, however, was not a characteristic of this field alone. Griffith and Mullins [1972] observed that the most successful of informal associations among scientists lasted no longer than 10 to 15 years, usually because of low scientific vitality or low distinctiveness of the members' work, and because fashions changed among supporters of research. These authors believed that a network must develop a coherent theory in order to last, and a coherence had not yet developed in the explanations of behavior in groups.

The fashionable topics for research on groups during these 10 years were conformity to group pressures, interpersonal relations between pairs of persons with mixed motives (e.g., the prisoner's dilemma), the "risky shift," and social facilitation. In 1967, Gerard and Miller remarked in the *Annual Review of Psychology* that most of the recent work on groups supported already familiar conclusions. In part, this was true.

DURING THE 1970s

In the 70s, the prime research topics were still familiar ones. Evidence for this can be seen in an account of group investigations during 1975, 1976, and 1977 that I prepared for the *Annual Review of Psychology* [1979]. The most frequently studied topics during the 3 years were: social pressures in groups, the sources (not the consequences) of group cohesiveness, and cooperating versus competing groups. Less popular, but not less familiar, were: leadership, group structure, and problem solving in groups. Polarization of beliefs among members, and other cognitive processes in groups, newly attracted interest from researchers, as did research on group size, crowding, and patterns of physical distance between participants. A good degree of activity, therefore, occurred in research, even though the number of agencies, and the dollars to support the work, had declined in the 70s to much less than in the early 60s. Social psychologists began to worry about the nature and direction of their field and subfields, including group behavior [Ring, 1967; Steiner, 1974; Elms, 1975; Silverman, 1977]. Finally, the use of groups for helping the "personal growth" of individuals became big business during the 70s, providing a fast service for anxious people who hoped to purchase comfort for themselves without investing in therapy.

SOME GENERAL OBSERVATIONS

Over the years, ever since research on groups came into its own, several features have typified its methods. Most investigations have been controlled experiments and a good proportion of these have used an instrument, experimental design, or procedure invented by someone else. Part of the reason for this dependence on established methods is that many graduate students, and their teachers too, cannot obtain funds for a program of studies, so they conduct isolated experiments that have a high probability of success.

Despite the preference for the experimental method, there have been surprisingly few full-blown theories in group dynamics. This says something about the difficult in explaining collective events. No doubt many theories have been discarded because the results of research obstinately would not provide support for hypotheses developed in the theories; and revisions in these ideas to fit the actual findings fared no better in later tests. In other sciences and in other branches of psychology, scholars may refresh and adjust their supply of ideas outside the laboratory by observing phenomena that interest them. But group researchers seldom have collectives available for such observations and show little interest in them when they are available. Indeed, the phenomena they study may not resemble anything they can notice in a natural group. As a result, theories about groups are too often long on logic and short on researchability.

As is true in many other fields, earlier concepts in the social psychology of group life are gradually replaced by newer ideas, and these latter are stated a bit more precisely than the parent notions. To illustrate: Work on the impact of group decisions led to studies of social pressures in groups; demonstrations of leadership style moved into research on social power; research on the risky shift became work on the origin of polarized ideas in discussion; and, investigations of intragroup competition developed into ways of resolving intergroup conflicts. Although we can easily find examples like those just cited, in which there has been movement toward greater specificity in concepts, research in group behavior still suffers from an absence of useful and well-stated primary notions. Examples of vaguely understood terms used in research are: role, group goal, group structure, status, de-individuation, leadership, socialization, and social environment. In the absence of adequate precision, ideas like these cannot be manipulated in a consistent fashion in the laboratory or measured validly in the conference room. Perhaps students of groups would benefit from a return to the days when scholars worried about how to construct useful concepts; but that idea is not yet ready for resurrection, I fear.

It seems likely that the soundness of knowledge increases as key ideas in a field are more neatly defined. When concepts become more valid and more commonly accepted, new results of research will more easily be integrated into a (growing) body of wisdom. As things now stand, researchers in group life are remarkably inventive in creating new terms for phenomena that already have a perfectly useful name, thus creating more semantic confusion than need be. A number of synonyms exist, for example, to denote each of: a member's desire to remain in a group, the functions of leadership, the ends toward which groups strive, and the dimensions of group structure. Different terms, furthermore, are often used for the same definition, and a given scholar may ignore research done under a label unlike one he or she prefers even though the results of that research are quite relevant to his or her own interests. What may be worse is illustrated in a recent book where interpersonal power to influence is a primary theme. The author provides a definition of social power that is nowhere near the definition used in the studies of power she thoroughly summarizes. Thus, she brings data together to support a view that the studies do not support at all. Clearly, the slipperiness of concepts in group behavior can lead to a lack of precision in specifying them.

A relatively limited number of topics have been explored out of the number available for investigation. Some examples of questions that have had little study, considering their importance in the life of an organization, are: Why is it so difficult to expel a member from a group? Why do groups recruit certain persons rather than others? What are the reasons for secrecy as a routine practice in organizations? Why is a modern manager met by abrasive behavior from subordinates? Why do groups set difficult goals? How can members improve the efficiency of meetings? How do organizations respond to regulations that limit their actions? One can easily think of other subjects that warrant study: changes in the properties of groups over time, why members participate in a group, the sources of conflict between groups, the contrasting effects of centralization and decentralization in a group, the origins of a group's goals, the causes of productivity in a group, or the effects of the social environment on a group. In a recent volume I have discussed a number of these issues with a view toward stimulating research into them [Zander, 1977].

Why are ripe topics not picked for study? One reason, already implied, is that investigators are busy planning and conducting experiments on more familiar issues; in fact, a researcher seldom moves to matters that are vastly different from his or her former areas of interest. Another reason is that a problem may be widely recognized as a candidate for research but it is not an acceptable topic in the eyes of potential investigators, those who advise researchers, those who edit journals, or those who provide funds for research. The problem may be well known but set aside because there are no basic data on the matter, reliable measures cannot be made of the phenomena involved, the theoretical issues are not clearly stated, or the project is too costly in time, energy, and number of human subjects needed. Such obstacles turn researchers away from matters worthy of attention.

As is often said, it is true that nothing is so practical as a well-stated theory. Such a theory can explain the causes and effects of a given event in different settings. Through results of research, people discern how best to help themselves because they identify what conditions lead to what consequences, and why. The innovativeness of research in group dynamics has been on a plateau for a few years. It will not stay on that level long when new needs and means stimulate new developments among students of group behavior.

REFERENCES

Back, K. *Beyond words.* New York: Russell Sage Foundation, 1972.

Bales, R. F. *Interaction process analysis.* Cambridge, Mass.: Addison-Wesley Press, 1950.

Bavelas, A. Communication patterns in task-oriented groups. *Journal of Acoustical Society of America,* 1950, 22, 725–730.

Cartwright, D., & Zander, A. *Group dynamics, research and theory.* Evanston, Ill.: Row Peterson, 1953.

Deutsch, M. The effect of cooperation and competition upon group process. *Human Relations,* 1949, 2, 129–152 and 199–231.

Elms, A. C. The crisis of confidence in social psychology. *American Psychologist,* 1975, 30, 967–976.

Festinger, L. Informal social communication. *Psychological Review,* 1950, 57, 271–282.

Gerard, H., & Miller, N. Group dynamics. *Annual Review of Psychology,* 1967, 18, 287–332.

Griffith, B. C., & Mullins, N. C. Coherent social groups in scientific change. *Science,* 1972, 177, 959–964.

Hare, A. P., Borgatta, E. F., & Bales, R. F. *Small groups, studies in social interaction.* New York: Knopf, 1955.

Hare, A. P. *Handbook of small group research.* New York: The Free Press, 1976.

Lewin, K., Lippitt, R., & White, R. Patterns of aggressive behavior in experimentally created "social climates." *Journal of Social Psychology,* 1939, 10, 271–299.

Lippitt, R. *Training in community relations.* New York: Harper & Bros., 1949.

Lippitt, R., Polansky, N., Redl, F., & Rosen, S. The dynamics of power. *Human Relations,* 1952, 5, 37–64.

Moreno, J. L. *Who shall survive.* Washington, D.C.: Nervous and Mental Diseases Publishing Company, 1934.

Nelson, C., & Kannenberg, P. Social psychology in a crisis. *Personality and Social Psychology Bulletin,* 1976, 2, 14–21.

Newcomb, T. *Personality and social change.* New York: Dryden, 1943.

Ring, K. Experimental social psychology: Some sober questions about some frivolous values. *Journal of Experimental Social Psychology,* 1967, 3, 113–123.

Roethlisberger, F. J., & Dickson, W. J. *Management and the worker.* Cambridge, Mass.: Harvard University Press, 1939.

Sherif, M. *The psychology of social norms.* New York: Harper, 1936.

Sherif, M. Crisis in social psychology: Some remarks towards breaking through the crisis. *Personality and Social Behavior Bulletin,* 1977, 3, 368–382.

Silverman, I. Why social psychology fails. *Canadian Psychological Review,* 1977, 18, 353–358.

Steiner, I. Whatever happened to the group in social psychology? *Journal of Experimental Social Psychology,* 1974, 10, 93–108.

Zander, A. *Groups at work.* San Francisco: Jossey-Bass, 1977.

Zander, A. The psychology of group processes. *Annual Review of Psychology,* 1979, 30, 417–451.

REVIEW AND DISCUSSION QUESTIONS

1 Briefly trace the evolution of group research over the years.
2 What is the current "state of the art" concept of group theory?
3 Why are there so few comprehensive models of group dynamics?
4 How can one determine causality when studying group behavior? How can one isolate variables when studying group dynamics? Consider both in terms of research design and in the measurement of results.

Reading 18

Superior–Subordinate Communication: The State of the Art

Fredric M. Jablin

Status hierarchy is inherent in the nature of purposeful organizations. As Redding [1972] observes, within organizations "there are 'superiors' and 'subordinates'—even though these terms may not be expressly used, and even though there may exist fluid arrangements whereby superior and subordinate roles may be reversible" [p. 18]. How superiors and subordinates interact and communicate to achieve both personal and organizational goals has been an object of investigation by social scientists for most of the 20th century. Empirical research examining superior–subordinate communication is diverse, is strewn across a multitude of disciplines, lacks coherent organization and classification, and in general, has not received sufficient review and interpretation as a body of literature. The present article attempts to alleviate this confusion by reviewing,

From *Psychological Bulletin,* vol. 6, 1979, pp. 1201–1222. Copyright © 1979 by the American Psychological Association. Reprinted with permission.

classifying, interpreting, and providing directions for future research in the area of organizational communication that is loosely termed *superior–subordinate communication.*

This article focuses on empirical research solely in the domain of organizational communication. To avoid generalizations from communication research outside of the organizational environment, I do not review investigations exploring small group and interpersonal communication extraneous of purposeful organizations (with occasional exception). Since organizational communication is different, in a variety of ways, from communication in other settings [e.g., Redding, 1972, Rogers & Rogers, 1976] and given the difficulty of generalizing from social science research, regardless of area, limiting the setting (or scope) certainly adds to the validity of any knowledge claims. For example, it is difficult to generalize from small group communication research, which is external to organizational environments, to group communication within organizations, in which groups of groups are tied together in networks of networks. Hence, this review focuses on studies conducted within organizations or simulations of organizations.

In addition, this collection and critique of superior–subordinate communication research has excluded studies related to interviewing, despite the fact that they may have involved superior–subordinate interaction. [See Daly, Note 1, for a complete review of this literature.] Moreover, the nucleus of this review is the examination of interpersonal dyadic interactions between superiors and subordinates. Specifically, an attempt was made to avoid examination of research concerned with the use of impersonal, media-related (e.g., house organ, bulletin board, suggestion box) superior–subordinate communication. However, both written and oral face-to-face communication transactions, when of an interpersonal dyadic nature, were reviewed.

The article is organized into three sections; the first presents a basic definition of superior–subordinate communication. The second section reviews and organizes empirical research related to superior–subordinate communication into nine topical categories. The final section provides a discussion of the review and directions for future research.

SUPERIOR–SUBORDINATE COMMUNICATION DEFINED

The expressions superior and subordinate are derived from Latin roots, which when joined suggest that within an interpersonal relationship one individual is of subrank or is situated below another. In purposeful organizations, both formal and informal superior–subordinate relations usually exist. Moreover, most research evidence indicates that informal (i.e., not prescribed by organizational directives) superior–subordinate affiliations may be as important as formal veritable relations in determining communicative behavior. However, for the purposes of the present review, the definition of superior–subordinate communication is limited to those exchanges of information and influence between organizational members, at least one of whom has formal (as defined by official organizational sources) authority to direct and evaluate the activities of other organizational members.

Katz and Kahn [1966] provide probably the most parsimonious yet complete description of the types of communication that are typically exchanged in superior–subordinate interactions. These theorists suggest that downward communications from superior to subordinate are of five basic types: (a) job instructions, (b) job rationale, (c) organizational procedures and practices, (d) feedback about subordinate performance, and (e) indoctrination of goals [pp. 239–241]. On the other hand, communication upward from subordinate to superior is reported to take four primary forms: (a) information about the subordinate himself/herself, (b) information about co-workers and their problems, (c) information about organizational practices and policies, and (d) information about what needs to be done and how it can be done [p. 245]. More specific and detailed taxonomies of messages exchanged in superior–subordinate communication are available in the literature [e.g., Eilon, 1968; Melcher & Beller, 1967; Yoder, 1970].

REVIEW OF LITERATURE

The empirical literature on superior–subordinate communication has been divided into nine topical categories.[1] Each of these categories represents a series of investigations that appear to be researching similar constructs from analogous theoretical foundations.[2] Many of the studies reviewed share more than one category but were classified into conceptually distinguishable groupings for purposes of clarification and parsimony.

Interaction Patterns and Related Attitudes

Researchers have investigated a variety of issues related to interaction patterns between superiors and subordinates. For example, numerous studies report that between one third and two thirds of a supervisor's time is spent in communicating with subordinates and that face-to-face discussion is the dominant mode of interaction [e.g., Berkowitz & Bennis, 1961; Brenner & Sigband, 1973; Dubin & Spray, 1964; Hinrichs, 1964; Kelly, 1964; Lawler, Porter, & Tenenbaum, 1968; Penfield, 1974]. Moreover, results from a number of investigations indicate that the majority of superior–subordinate interaction concerns task issues [e.g., Baird, 1974; Richetto, 1969; Zima, 1969; Walton, Note 2] and that superiors and

---

[1]The reader will note that this review contains no single category of research related to downward communication in superior-subordinate interaction. Since Redding [1972, see especially pp. 388–404] provides an extensive review of this literature prior to 1970 and given that less research has been pursued in this area subsequent to 1970, the present review has not directly focused attention on this area. Rather, research related to downward communication is discussed within the confines of the other categories.

[2]The reader will also note that this review does not consider research that could be classified as relating to participative decision making. Since exhaustive reviews of this literature already exist [e.g., Redding, 1972, pp. 154–250; Vroom, 1970, pp. 227–240; Vroom, 1976, pp. 1538–1546] further critique would be redundant.

subordinates talk more about impersonal (focus of topics external to self) than about personal (directly related to self) topics [Baird, 1974]. Further, research suggests that superiors are more likely to initiate interactions with subordinates than the other way around [e.g., Berkowitz & Bennis, 1961; Dubin & Spray, 1964]. Yet, it is of interest to observe that superiors are less positive toward and less satisfied with interactions with their subordinates than they are with contacts with their bosses [e.g., Clement, 1974; Lawler et al., 1968; Tenenbaum, 1971]. This finding is even more ironic when considered in light of Baird and Diebolt's [1976] discovery that a subordinate's job satisfaction is positively correlated with estimates of communication contact with superiors.

Several other studies present findings relevant to interaction patterns between superiors and subordinates. The results of these investigations suggest the following conclusions: (a) Superiors perceive that they communicate more with subordinates than subordinates perceive, whereas subordinates feel they send more messages to their superiors than the latter perceive [Webber, 1970]; (b) superiors who lack self-confidence in their leadership abilities are less willing to hold face-to-face discussions with their subordinates than are superiors who are confident in their leadership abilities [Kipnis & Lane, 1962]; (c) role conflict and role ambiguity are strongly correlated with "leader behavior indicative of direct as opposed to indirect interactions with subordinates" [Rizzo, House, & Lirtzmann, 1970, p. 162]; (d) when a subordinate needs informal help in the work setting, he/she is more likely to seek assistance from his/her superior than peers or subordinates (as reported by helpees) [Burke, Weir, & Duncan, 1976]; and (e) supervisors are more likely to serve as "production" communication liaisons than as "maintenance" or "innovation" liaisons [MacDonald, 1976].

In summary, studies that explored interaction patterns between superiors and subordinates suggest frequent task-oriented communication within the dyad but differential attitudes and perceptions of those interactions. Moreover, personal characteristics and needs of the interactants seem to mediate their desire for and perceptions of superior–subordinate communication.

Openness in Communication

Two basic dimensions of openness in superior–subordinate communication can be distinguished: openness in message sending and openness in message receiving. Redding [1972] describes openness in message sending as the "candid disclosure of feelings, or 'bad news,' and important company facts" [p. 330], whereas openness in message receiving involves "encouraging, or at least permitting, the frank expression of views divergent from one's own; the willingness to listen to 'bad news' or discomforting information" [p. 330]. Baird [1974] adds that it is essential that researchers clearly specify whether they are referring to task-relevant openness or non-task-relevant openness when investigating each of the above dimensions.

Much of the impetus for studying openness in superior–subordinate communication has been provided by management theorists who have suggested that openness is an essential element for an effective organizational climate [e.g., Haney, 1967; Likert, 1967]. Support for this proposition is furnished in studies by Burke and Wilcox [1969], Baird [1974], and Jablin [1978a], who have found that employees are more satisfied with their jobs when openness of communication exists between subordinate and superior. Furthermore, several inquiries report that openness of communication is directly correlated with organizational performance [e.g., Indik, Georgopoulos, & Seashore, 1961; Willits, 1967]. However, it should be noted that the results of one investigation suggest that managerial effectiveness is unrelated to openness of communication between superior and subordinate [Rubin & Goldman, 1968].

A series of doctoral dissertations completed at Purdue University have attempted to explore in detail the communication characteristics of openness in superior–subordinate relationships. The first of these researches [Baird, 1974] examined subordinates' "upward communication freedom" with superiors. Results of the study revealed that willingness of superiors and subordinates to talk as well as actual talk about a topic are a function of each interactant's perception of the other's willingness to listen. Extrapolating on Baird's study, Stull [1975] investigated superior and subordinate attitudes toward various types of supervisory responses to task-relevant and non-task-relevant open messages sent by subordinates. Analyses disclosed that for task and nontask topics, subordinates and superiors preferred supervisory responses that were accepting (encouraging) or reciprocating ("owning-up" to one's feelings, ideas, etc.) rather than neutral-negative (unfeeling, cold, or nonaccepting). Finally Jablin [1978a, 1978b], attempting to determine the types of communicative responses that characterize open and closed relationships between superiors and subordinates, experimentally studied the attitudes of subordinates toward five basic types of message responses occurring in a dyad: confirmation (a response that provides a speaker with positive content and positive relational feedback), disagreement (a response that provides a speaker with negative content feedback but positive relational feedback), accedence (a response that provides a speaker with positive content feedback but negative relational feedback), repudiation (a response that provides a speaker with both negative content and negative relational feedback), and disconfirmation (a response that provides a speaker with irrelevant content and equally irrelevant relational feedback). Results from the investigation indicated (a) that disconfirming responses are not acceptable in superior–subordinate communication; (b) that subordinates prefer message responses from superiors that provide positive relational feedback; (c) that regardless of perceived openness or closedness of the communication relationship with their superior, subordinates expected the same types of responses from a superior but evaluated the appropriateness of these responses differently; (d) that a substantial degree of reciprocity exists for confirming messages, regardless of the openness or closedness of the superior–subordinate relationship; and (e) that subordinates who perceive a closed relationship with their superior are prepared to respond to a superiors' message, which contains negative relational feedback toward the subordinate, with a response transmitting negative relational feedback toward the superior; however, this is not true for subordinates who perceive an open relationship with their superior.

In summary, these studies suggest that in an open communication relationship between superior and subordinate, both parties perceive the other interactant as a willing and receptive listener and refrain from responses that might be perceived as providing negative relational or disconfirming feedback. Moreover, these inquiries suggest that what distinguishes an open from a closed superior–subordinate relationship may not be the types of messages exchanged but how the interactants evaluate the appropriateness of these communications. Finally, these studies provide strong evidence for the proposition that employees are more satisfied with their jobs when openness of communication exists between superior and subordinate than when the relationship is closed.

Upward Distortion

Closely related to research examining openness in superior–subordinate relationships are a group of investigations exploring message distortion in subordinate upward communication to superiors. Mellinger [1956], who collected questionnaire data from 330 scientists in a medical laboratory, is generally credited with the initiation of this research tradition. [For a discussion of related research antecedent to Mellinger's investigation, see Guetzkow, 1965, pp. 553–555.] Results of this early inquiry into message distortion revealed that when Individual A does not trust Individual B, Individual A will conceal his/her feelings when communicating to B about a particular issue. Moreover, concealment of Individual A's true feelings was found to be often associated with evasive, compliant, or aggressive communicative behavior on his/her part and with under- or overestimation of agreement on the issue by Individual B. Cohen's [1958] replication and clarification of Kelly's [1951] investigation of upward communication in experimentally created hierarchies also inspired a tradition of research in the area of upward communication distortion. Results of this study suggested that within a hierarchy, if an individual has power over the advancement of persons of lower rank, those of lower rank will omit critical comments in their communication with the person of higher rank. Thus with these seminal studies, Mellinger [1956] and Cohen [1958] initiated a sphere of research that examined the moderating effects of trust and mobility aspirations on upward communication distortion.

Building on the previously described research, Read and his associates [Maier, Hoffman, & Read, 1963; Read, 1962] explored the relationships among upward mobility aspirations, trust, and the accuracy with which managers communicate information upward in organizational hierarchies. Data analyses supported the earlier findings of Mellinger and Cohen, which indicated that mobility aspirations (i.e., desire for advancement and status seeking proclivity) and low trust in one's superior are negatively related to accuracy of upward communication. Moreover, results suggested that even when a subordinate trusts his/her superior, high mobility aspriations "strongly militate against accurate communication of potentially threatening information" [Read, 1962, p. 13]. In addition, it was discovered that "subordinates feel less free to communicate with superiors who previously have held their position than with those who have not" [Maier et al., 1963, p. 9].

More recently, research by Roberts and O'Reilly [1974] and O'Reilly and Roberts [1974] has supported the notion that a subordinate's trust in his/her superior is a facilitator of distortion-free upward communication. However, these researchers did not find strong correlations between subject's mobility aspirations and propensity towards upward communication distortion. Finally Sussman [1974], investigating upward communication distortion from the perspective of the superior (i.e., the recipient of distorted messages), failed to find that superiors perceive greater accuracy in messages from subordinates who are perceived as trusting the superior than in messages from subordinates perceived as nontrusting.

In contrast to these studies, several researchers have investigated the origins and concomitants of upward communication distortion from slightly different perspectives. Athanassiades [1973, 1974] argues that ascendency and security needs, risk-taking propensity, and organizational climate, when perceived as instrumental to a subordinate's goals, will produce upward communication distortion. Results of his research indicate that for both male and female subordinates, upward distortion is need motivated, with distortion being positively related to achievement needs and negatively related to level of security. Furthermore, Athanassiades's findings suggest that distortion of upward communication is negatively related to an autonomous organizational climate and positively related to a heteronomous climate. It is of interest to observe that his findings [1974] also show that "women in managerial positions feel more suppressed—less autonomous, less independent—than men do in similar positions" [p. 208].

A recent study by Young [1978] supports Athanassiades's finding that organizational climate is related to distortion of upward communication. Specifically, results suggest that in organic as compared with mechanistic organizational environments, subordinates perceive greater appropriateness, expect fewer harmful consequences, and evidence greater willingness to disclose important yet personally threatening information to superiors. However, his data also disclose that the upward communication behavior of female subordinates follows more closely the behavior of subordinates in an organic work setting than does the upward communication of male subordinates.

Extrapolating on Athanassiades's research, Level and Johnson [1978] have recently found that upward distortion is most likely to be associated with messages in which information about the following personality factors is communicated: ascendency, responsibility, emotional stability, cautiousness, and original thinking. Their data also suggest that in certain areas subordinate tendencies to distort upward communication can be reduced by increasing the superior's "consideration" leadership style, or increasing the accuracy with which the superior transmits downward information. In addition, Krivonos [1976] examined the role of motivation theory in upward communication distortion and found that superiors perceive that intrinsically motivated subordinates distort messages less than do extrinsically motivated subordinates.

Research that investigates types of messages that tend to be distorted in upward communication indicates that subordinates will be less reluctant to communicate information that is positive-favorable than negative-unfavorable [O'Reilly & Roberts, 1974; Rosen & Tesser, 1970] and that superiors view messages that are favorable to subordinates as less accurate than messages that are unfavorable to subordinates [Sussman, 1974]. Moreover, O'Reilly and Roberts [1974] report that when information is both favorable and important, subordinates do not hesitate to communicate it upward to their superiors. In addition, Housel and Davis [1977] have discovered that subordinate satisfaction with upward communication tends to vary as a function of the channel used; face-to-face channels are most satisfactory, followed by telephone and written channels. Finally, a recent study of Rosen and Adams [1974],which examined the severity of discipline administered to subordinates who distorted upward communication, reveals that "recommended disciplinary measures were relatively mild when the subordinate's motives were altruistic and when his superior was dependent on him for expertise" [p. 382].

In summary, research that explored upward distortion in superior–subordinate communication has examined numerous variables that may moderate the occurrence of upward distortion. These variables include trust, mobility aspirations, ascendency and security needs, organizational climate, sex differences, motivation, message characteristics, and a variety of upward communication channels. Although the effects of subordinate trust in superior, surordinate mobility aspirations/ascendency needs, and the contingent role of organizational climate on upward distortion seem best supported, evaluation of the research in total suggests that probably no one variable can sufficiently explain the phenomena and that additional multivariate research is required before we can place confidence in any one of these explanations.

Upward Influence

Influence processes are a central feature of superior–subordinate communication. And, as Walter [1966] notes,

> . . . to study influence, one must first study communication, for influence without communication is as wildly implausible as action at a distance. Influence is always accompanied by some form of communication, blunt or subtle, overt or tacit: Advertising, lobbying, arguing a case before a jury or on a suitor's knee. [p. 190]

In studies of superior–subordinate communication, researchers have focused attention on two basic dimensions of influence: (a) the effects a superior's influence in the organizational hierarchy has on his/her relationships with subordinates and (b) the transmission of influence by subordinates to superiors. Research in this latter category is diffused and varied, and since it is represented in other sections of this article (e.g., upward distortion, feedback), it is not directly discussed here.

Due to its effects on superior–subordinate relations, the upward influence of a subordinate's superior with his/her boss has received considerable attention in the research literature. Probably best known is the so-called "Pelz effect." In his seminal study Pelz [1952], who collected data from over 8,000 supervisory and nonsupervisory personnel in the Detroit Edison Company, discovered that a superior's upward influence in an organization moderates his/her social closeness with subordinates. Specifically, he found that "employee-centered supervisors are associated with higher levels of employee satisfaction *only when the supervisor apparently exercises influence 'upward' with his own superiors*" [Redding, 1972, p. 438]. More recently Wager [1965], who explored leadership behaviors and influence in one organization, reported findings similar to those of Pelz but also observed that the magnitude of the moderating effect of influence varied positively with the organizational status of the respondent. At this point it is important to note that Pelz's and Wager's influence measures were concerned only with supervisory influence with respect to personnel management of subordinates and did not assess influence in such areas as resource allocation, organizational changes, policy formation, or objective setting [Wager, 1965]. Moreover, this typifies most of the research in this area.

In recent years investigators have once again begun to explore the relationship between superior's upward influence and communication with subordinates. For example, House, Filley, and Gujarati [1971] report that the interaction between superior's hierarchical influence and consideration behavior with subordinates varies from company to company (i.e., it is situational). Perhaps of even greater importance is their finding that when a superior is too high in upward influence, dysfunctional consequences may emerge in relation to subordinate willingness to openly communicate with the superior. They argue that

> . . . where supervisors are seen to have such high influence, it is likely that there will be greater status separation between them and their subordinates, and that such status differentiation will result in a restriction of upward information flow, less willingness on the part of subordinates to approach superiors, and less satisfaction with the social climate of the work unit. [p. 429]

In a related study, Roberts and O'Reilly [1974] report that subordinates who perceive their superior as having high upward influence also have a high desire for interaction with the superior, high trust in the superior, and a high estimation of accuracy of information received from the superior. Similarly, Jones, James, and Bruni [1975] have found that subordinate confidence and trust in a superior is positively related to the superior's success in interactions with higher levels of management. Finally, O'Reilly and Roberts [1974] and Roberts and O'Reilly [1974], who examined the association between superior upward influence and subordinate upward communication distortion, have discovered only weak correlations between these variables.

In summary, results from studies that explored the relationship between superior's upward influence and communication with subordinates suggest the following conclusion: Subordinates who perceive their superior as having substantial but not excessive upward influence with their bosses will be more satisfied with their superior and will interact and trust him/her more than will subordinates who perceive their superior as low in upward influence. However, since several of the previously described investigations indicate that this conclusion may be situation bound and may be contingent on factors other than those already studied, the conclusion warrants only tentative acceptance.

Semantic-Information Distance

Originally coined by Tompkins [1962], the term *semantic-information distance* describes the gap in information and understanding that exists between superiors and subordinates (or other groups within an organization) on specified issues. This concept is analogous to the concept of "disparity" advanced by Browne and Neitzel [1952], to Weaver's [1958] construct of "semantic barrier," to "categorical and syndectic similarity" as proposed by Triandis [1959a, 1959b, 1959c, 1960], to "semantic agreement" as discussed in Maier, Hoffman, Hooven, and Read [1961] and Maier et al. [1963], and to "congruence" as explored in research by Minter [1969]. Studies that examined the nature and definitional qualities of semantic-information distance through 1970 are discussed in detail in Redding's [1972] review of organizational communication literature.

The basic conclusions that can be drawn from the early research on semantic-information distance can be briefly described as follows: (a) The larger the semantic distance between superior and subordinate, the lower will be the subordinate's morale [Browne & Neitzel, 1952]; (b) superiors tend to overestimate the amount of knowledge subordinate's possess on given topics [Odiorne, 1954]; (c) management personnel tend to describe themselves by traits that are different from those that subordinates use to describe themselves [Porter, 1958]; (d) managers and workers differ in the criteria that they use in making judgments about people [Triandis, 1959a, 1959b, 1959c, 1960]; (e) significant gaps in semantic distance exist between union and management [Schwartz, Stark, & Schiffman, 1970; Weaver, 1958] and between union leadership and their members [Tompkins, 1962]; (f) superiors and subordinates have difficulty agreeing on the basic job duties and demands facing subordinates [Maier et al., 1961; Rosen, 1961]; (g) whether a superior has previously held his/her subordinate's job has little affect on reducing the semantic-information distance between them [Maier et al., 1963]; (h) superior's perceptions of the attitudes of subordinates toward him/her is often unrelated to their actual attitudes [Bowers, 1963; White, 1976]; (i) serious semantic differences between superior and subordinate are frequent [e.g., Minter, 1969, reports that they occur over 60% of the time]; and (j) there is some evidence that indicates that superiors "find it easier to communicate with subordinate managers whose attitudes are similar [rather than dissimilar] to their own" [Miles, 1964, p. 324].

In general, most research related to semantic-information distance conducted since 1970 is supportive of the aforementioned studies. Greene [1972] has found that the more accurately a subordinate complies with his/her superior's expectations of subordinate behavior, the higher the subordinate's job satisfaction and the better his/her performance evaluation by the superior. Supportive of the results of Greene's research is a study by Pfeffer and Salancik [1975] that suggests that the behavior of subordinates and superiors is constrained by the expectations of other members of the role set. Several recent investigations contribute to the list of areas in which significant superior–subordinate semantic-information distance exists. Examining superior–subordinate dyads, Boyd and Jensen [1972] found that first-line managers and their superiors experience difficulty in agreeing on the authority of the first-line manager, whereas Moore [1974] reports that a new manager's superior and his/her subordinates tend to disagree on how long it will take the manager to learn the new position. Assuming that empathic ability is negatively correlated to semantic-information distance, Northouse's [1977] study would strongly indicate that one means of reducing semantic distance is by increasing trust between superior and subordinate. Finally, a study by Baird and Diebolt [1976] found no relationships between superior–subordinate role congruence and several communication variables; however, limitations within the study restrict the generalizability of its findings.

In summary, results of empirical research in the area of superior–subordinate semantic-information distance probably provide some of the most consistent conclusions of any topic of study in organizational communication. Incessantly, we find the existence of semantic-information distance in superior–subordinate relations, often at levels that would appear to seriously obstruct organizational effectiveness. The catalogue of topical areas in which semantic differences between superiors and subordinates tend to occur is expanding and would strongly suggest that future research should pursue the development of valid and reliable techniques to reduce this semantic gap.

Effective versus Ineffective Superiors

Interest in identifying the communicative behaviors of effective leaders probably has existed since the earliest days of civilization, when humankind became proficient at organizing for battlefield warfare and thus required an expendable supply of effective leaders. Hence, over the years the identification of effective as compared to ineffective communication behaviors of superiors has received more investigation than any other area of organizational communication.

From the period of 1950 to the mid-1960s, a series of doctoral dissertations completed at Purdue University attempted to determine the communication correlates of "good" supervisors [Funk, 1956; Kelly, 1963; Minter, 1969; Miraglia, 1964; Pyron, 1964; Richetto, 1969; Simons, 1962; Sincoff, 1970; Smith, 1968; Zima, 1969]. For the majority of these studies, good supervision as compared to poor supervision was determined by higher management evaluation of supervisors. Redding [1972, pp. 436–446] succinctly summarizes the results of these researchers and suggests the following general conclusions:

> **1** The better supervisors tend to be more "communication-minded"; e.g., they enjoy talking and speaking up in meetings; they are able to explain instructions

and policies; they enjoy conversing with subordinates. [See especially Funk, 1956; Pyron, 1964.]

   2   The better supervisors tend to be willing, empathic listeners; they respond understandingly to so-called "silly" questions from employees; they are approachable; they will listen to suggestions and complaints, with an attitude of fair consideration and willingness to take appropriate action. [See especially Funk, 1956; Simons, 1962; Kelly, 1963; Zima, 1969.]

   3   The better supervisors tend (with some notable exceptions) to "ask" or "persuade," in preference to "telling" or "demanding." [See especially Simons, 1962; Pyron, 1964.]

   4   The better supervisors tend to be sensitive to the feelings and ego-defense needs of their subordinates; e.g., they are careful to reprimand in private rather than in public. [See, e.g., Simons, 1962.]

   5   The better supervisors tend to be more open in their passing along of information; they are in favor of giving advance notice of impending changes, and of explaining the "reasons why" behind policies and regulations. [See especially Funk, 1956; Simons, 1962.] [Redding, 1972, p. 443]

Other research on superior–subordinate communication contemporary to that of the Purdue group generally supports the thrust of the above conclusions [Brown, 1964; Jain, 1971; Ponder, 1959; Sadler, 1970; Tacey, 1959, Walker, Turner, & Guest, 1956].

   For example, Ponder [1959] reports that effective as compared to ineffective foremen tend to be better communicators: They spend more time with employees carrying out the job, providing general supervision, and handling personnel matters. Moreover, more recent research provides additional testimony to the validity of the claims of these investigators [Duffy, 1975; Heizer, 1972; Sank, 1974; White, 1972] or has attempted to further elucidate the communication behaviors associated with various managerial interaction styles [e.g., Bradley & Baird, 1977].

   Despite the strong evidence that characterizes the communication profile of effective superiors, other research suggests that effective supervisory communication behaviors are situational and contingent on a variety of factors [e.g., Downs & Pickett, 1977]. As Redding [1972] notes in his own review of the Purdue studies, "The precise combination of behaviors or attitudes which 'works' in one company is likely to be different from what 'works' in another company or organization" [p. 445]. The importance of viewing effective as compared to ineffective superior communication behavior from a contingency perspective is demonstrated by developments in three areas of leadership research: (a) the traditional study of leadership that employs the "consideration-initiating structure" framework [e.g., Fleishman & Harris, 1962], (b) Fiedler's contingency approach to leadership [e.g., Fiedler, 1967], and (c) a more recent view of leadership that uses a dyadic linkage–role-making model [e.g., Dansereau, Graen, & Haga, 1975].

   As a result of extensive leadership research conducted at Ohio State University during the 1950s and early 1960s, two basic dimensions of leadership behavior were identified: (a) "consideration" and (b) "initiating structure." [See Stogdill, 1974, pp. 128–141, for a complete review of these studies.] Leader consideration was found to be typified by friendship and warmth, mutual trust, rapport and tolerance, and two-way communication between a leader and his/her work group [Fleishman, Harris, & Burtt, 1955]. Initiating structure includes "behaviors in which the supervisor organizes and redefines group activities and his relation to the group. . . . This dimension seems to emphasize overt attempts to achieve organizational goals" [Fleishman & Harris, 1962, p. 43]. These two basic dimensions of leader behavior are analogous to those denoted as "employee orientation" and "production orientation" in the University of Michigan Institute for Social Research leadership studies [e.g., Katz, Maccoby, & Morse, 1950]. The importance of the above investigations to the identification of the effective communication behaviors of supervisors rests on the similarity between the constructs of consideration and employee orientation, and communication. For example, Miraglia [1964], who studied the parallels between consideration and communication ability, discovered that consideration "is largely a matter of *communication* behavior" [Redding, 1972, p. 148]. This conclusion has been supported in research by Jain [1973] and more recently in a study by Dennis [1974].

The general conclusion drawn from the early consideration and initiating structure research was that superiors are "rated as more effective when they score high in both consideration and leadership structure" [Stogdill, 1974, p. 140]. Perhaps of even greater significance for communication researchers is the general finding that leaders high in consideration (good communicators) can increase structure within their work groups and still be rated as effective leaders [e.g., Fleishman & Harris, 1962]. However, current inquiries suggest that numerous situational variables impinge on the validity and reliability of consideration-initiating structure (C-IS) to predict leader effectiveness. Reviewing this literature through 1973, Kerr, Schriesheim, Murphy, and Stogdill [1974] identify the following as situational variables that moderate the C-IS ability to predict leader behavior and performance:

> . . . subordinate need for information, job level, subordinate expectations of leader behavior, perceived organizational independence, leader's similarity of attitudes and behavior to managerial style of management, leader upward influence; and characteristics of the task, including pressure and provision of intrinsic satisfaction. [p. 62]

More recent investigations also suggest that the following situational variables may moderate the C-IS predictive capability: sex [Day & Stogdill, 1972], task type [Hill & Hughs, 1974], length of employment and organizational climate [Kavanagh, 1975], and work-unit size [Schriesheim & Murphy, 1976].

Fiedler's work on leadership likewise indicates that researchers should be examining the communication attributes of effective superiors from a contingency perspective [e.g., Fiedler, 1964, 1967, 1970, 1971a, 1971b, 1972a, 1972b].

Emphasizing the role of leader personality and style of interaction on work-group performance, Fiedler argues that three dimensions of task *situations* primarily determine leader effectiveness: leader–member relations (which obviously are dominated by communication behavior), task structure and leader-position power. In essence, this research suggests that supervisors have predominant styles of interacting with subordinates and that their effectiveness will vary, depending on whether the situation (as previously defined) is best suited to that style.

Finally, recent research that views leadership from a dyadic linkage–role-making perspective shows that supervisors do not develop the same kinds of relationships with all subordinates and superiors, and thus the communicative behavior that may be effective in one type of relationship may not be effective in another [Cashman, Dansereau, Graen, & Haga, 1976; Dansereau, Cashman, & Graen, 1973; Dansereau et al., 1975; Graen, Cashman, Ginsburgh, & Schiemann, 1977; Haga, Graen, & Dansereau, 1974]. Specifically, results of this research indicate that supervisors tend to develop one of two types of exchange patterns with subordinates, that is, either a pattern of leadership exchange (characterized by "influence over a member without resort to authority" [Cashman, 1976, p. 281]) or supervision exchange (in which "influence over a member is based primarily upon authority" [Cashman et al., 1976, p. 281]). Moreover, it has been found that supervisors in turn develop either leadership exchanges or supervision exchanges with their bosses. In addition, findings suggest that

> . . . subordinate members of the upper dyad who develop leadership exchanges with their bosses have greater influence with their bosses and receive more latitude, support and attention from their bosses than their colleagues who fail to develop leadership exchanges. [Graen et al., 1977, p. 502]

In summary, investigations that explored a dyadic linkage–role-making model of leadership suggest that superior–subordinate communication patterns are not stable across all superior–subordinate interactions and may vary as a function of organizational understructure.

As noted in the opening of this section, we are rich in research studies that have attempted to identify the effective and ineffective communication correlates of supervision. Clear evidence has been presented that suggests a certain profile that characterizes the communication behaviors of effective supervisors. On the other hand, several other research traditions were reviewed which indicate that the qualities of effective leadership vary from situation to situation and are contingent on numerous factors. Which set of findings and conclusions are we to believe? The answer would appear to be both. Data that comprise the Purdue and other related effectiveness studies have been collected from a myriad of organizations and supervision situations—the pattern of results is too consistent to reject without further research. It may be that for 60% of the superior-subordinate communication situations, these findings are applicable, yet they may only apply to 10% of the cases. Obviously, the only way we will be able to resolve this question is by research that investigates the effects situational variables have on superior–subordinate communication.

Personal Characteristics

In the process of studying superior–subordinate communication, researchers have attempted to discover the personal characteristics of members of that dyad that mediate their communication behavior. Since the variables examined in these investigations are extremely diverse and at present lack coherent organization, this section endeavors to provide such structure.

Several investigators have explored the effects interactant tendencies for internal as compared to external locus of control have on superior–subordinate interaction [Durand & Nord, 1976; Mitchell, Smyser, & Weed, 1975]. Findings from these studies suggest (a) that internal subordinates see their supervisors as more considerate than do externals; (b) that internals are most satisfied with participative superiors, whereas externals are most satisfied with directive superiors; and (c) that internal superiors tend to use persuasion to obtain subordinate cooperation, whereas externals rely more on coercive power. In addition, research related to the study of locus of control indicates that subordinates and superiors with passive personalities tend to exaggerate the volume of their interaction with others, whereas active persons tend to underestimate their interaction [Webber, 1970].

Studies that examined the characteristics of supervisors and their communication-related behavior with subordinates suggest the following interesting conclusions: (a) High-least-preferred-co-worker (LPC) leaders under conditions of threat tend to engage in considerate behavior, whereas low-LPC leaders tend to increase initiating structure [Green, Nebeker, & Boni, 1976]; (b) lower level supervisors tend to be more dogmatic than upper-middle and top-level managers [Close, 1975]; (c) young managers (20–29 years) tend to be more autocratic and low in human relations skills than are middle-aged (30–40 years) or late middle-aged (40–55 years) managers [Pinder & Pinto, 1974]; and (d) superiors tend to rate subordinates as competent when they have values similar to those of the superior [Senger, 1971].

On the other hand, studies exploring subordinates' perceptions of superior's communication behavior and personality indicate (a) that superiors who are apprehensive communicators are not particularly liked by subordinates [Daly, McCroskey, & Falcione, Note 3]; (b) that subordinate's satisfaction with superiors can be predicted from several dimensions of homophily–heterophily [Daly, McCroskey, & Falcione, Note 4]; (c) that authoritarian subordinates are most satisfied when they work for directive superiors [Bass, Valenzi, Farrow, & Solomon, 1975; Tosi, 1973]; (d) that subordinate satisfaction with immediate supervision is related to subordinate perception of superior's credibility [Falcione, 1974]; (e) that confirmation of subordinate's needs for affection and dominance results in greater perceived frequency of interaction between superior and subordinate [Hawkins, 1976]; (f) that subordinates in small work groups, who require high interaction with co-workers and superiors and high interdependence, have negative attitudes toward authoritarian supervisors, whereas subordinates in large work groups, with restricted interaction and highly independent work, have more positive attitudes toward authoritarian supervision [Vroom & Mann, 1960]; and (g) that subordinates, regardless of their personality, tend to be most satisfied with superiors high in human relations orientation [Weed, Mitchell, & Moffitt, 1976]. In addition, it should be noted that Hall [1974, 1975] has conducted a series of investigations that examine, in part, personality correlates of organizational members that affect superior–subordinate communication, the results of which are too voluminous to report here.

An area of superior–subordinate research that has received considerable attention of late is concerned with differences between male and female supervisory behaviors. The general results of these inquiries indicate that subordinates do not describe the behaviors of male and female leaders differently [e.g., Bartol & Wortman, 1975; Day & Stogdill, 1972] but do agree on the existence of leader sex role stereotypes [e.g., Rosen & Jerdee, 1973; Schein, 1973, 1975]. Specifically, there is strong evidence which suggests that subordinates of both sexes are more satisfied with consideration behavior from a female superior than a male and are more satisfied with exhibition of initiating structure by male superiors than with similar behaviors from female superiors [Bartol & Butterfield, 1976; Petty & Lee, 1975; Petty & Miles, 1976]. Moreover, Sussman, Pickett, Berzinski, and Pearce (in press) report that the sexual composition of superior–subordinate dyads does impose "norms and restrictions" on upward communication in the dyad.

In summary, studies that examined the effects of personal characteristics on superior–subordinate communication have tended to focus on three basic areas: (a) single characteristics of superiors or subordinates that affect their communication behavior, (b) characteristics of superiors and subordinates, taken together, and their effect on superior–subordinate communication, and (c) differences in superior–subordinate communication as a function of the sex of the interactants. Although the findings of most of this research are interesting and important, on the whole they tend to be isolated and to lack theoretical foundations. Future investigations should endeavor to remedy this situation by relating such studies to the larger scope of organizational communication theory.

Feedback

Probably one of the most common complaints aired by superiors and subordinates about their communication relationship is that one of the interactants does not provide the other with sufficient and relevant feedback. Both upward and downward feedback appear to be essential for effective superior–subordinate relations, since such feedback provides information that denotes the success of failure of policies and objectives, that suggests the need for corrective actions and controlling mechanisms, and that provides the members of the dyad with

knowledge of the other party's sentiments about formal and informal organizational activities. In his collection of theory and research in organizational
communication, Redding [1972] provides an extensive review of empirical
inquiries that explore feedback in superior–subordinate communication through
about 1970 (see especially pp. 39–62). Now classic studies such as Leavitt and
Mueller [1951], Smith and Kight [1959], Gibb [1961], Zajonc [1962], Bowman
[1963], Haney [1964], Meyer, Kay, and French [1965], Cook [1968], and Minter
[1969] are summarized in Redding's anthology. Hence, the following review
examines only empirical research conducted in the area of feedback in
superior–subordinate communication after 1970.

Studies that examined feedback in superior–subordinate communication
since 1970 can be grouped into one of two categories: (a) investigations that
explored the effects of subordinate's feedback to superiors on superior's
behavior and (b) research analyzing the effects of superior's feedback to
subordinates on subordinate's behavior. Investigations in the former category
report a number of interesting findings. Brenner and Sigband [1973], who
surveyed over 700 managers in a major aerospace firm have found that
subordinate's feedback to superiors is greater when

> . . . (a) subordinates were told what was to be done with completed assignments,
> (b) the superior formerly held the subordinate's position, (c) the superior made the
> largest proportion of assignments to the subordinate, and (d) the subordinate felt
> that he could secure clarification of assignments from his immediate superior. [p.
> 325]

Attempting to determine if a leader's verbal behavior could be altered by
manipulating feedback to him/her, Butler and Jaffee [1974] report that positive
feedback to a leader made him/her more task oriented, whereas negative
feedback increased negative social-emotional behavior (as classified by Bales's
Interaction Process Analysis category system). These researchers argue that
their results

> . . . indicate that in a production-oriented organization, positive feedback is to be
> preferred to negative feedback, and negative feedback might have very little to offer
> if no specific suggestions for changing one's behavior are given. [p. 335]

In a related study, Fodor [1974] explored the effects of a subordinate's
disparagement of a superior's competence on the superior's distributions of
rewards to subordinates. Results indicated that the superior tended to favor a
compliant subordinate who was not an ingratiator. Finally, several studies have
also attempted to determine whether the subordinate's feedback to superiors
elicits changes in the superior's behavior and, concomitantly, changes in the
subordinate's attitudes toward the superior. For example, Hegarty [1974], who
used survey feedback methods, found that supervisory performance improved
subsequent to subordinate feedback, whereas Burnaska [1976] relates findings

which suggest that feedback and subsequent training can quickly change a supervisor's behavior but that worker perceptions of the superior change only with time.

A number of investigations have examined the effects of a superior's feedback to subordinates on the behavior of those subordinates. Harvey and Boettger [1971], in an experiment designed to improve communication in a managerial work group, reported a norm among subordinates against asking superiors for clarification of memos that are unclear or contain double messages. In a preliminary investigation that explored sources of feedback, Greller and Herold [1975] suggest that intrinsic (i.e., psychologically close to the individual) sources of information are seen by workers as providing more feedback than sources that are seen as external (i.e., psychologically distant). Moreover, in a related study, Kim and Hamner [1976] provide evidence that evaluative supervisory feedback to subordinate performance (i.e., extrinsic feedback) and nonevaluative feedback (i.e., subordinate self-generated or intrinsic feedback), when combined with a goal-setting production program, increase subordinate performance significantly beyond that of groups involved in just goal setting. Recent research also suggests (a) that superiors' feedback to a subordinate, which shows a lack of trust in the subordinate, results in subordinate dissatisfaction and aggressive feelings [Brenenstuhl, 1976]; (b) that superiors perceived as expressive (high in human relations) are more likely to provide subordinates with social approval than those superiors perceived as instrumental (a Weberian orientation) [Marcus & House, 1973]; (c) that in conflict situations supervisory responses that relate acceptance and encouragement of subordinate disagreement are associated with high subordinate satisfaction [Burke, 1970; Renwick, 1975]; and (d) that under low surveillance (infrequent need to report to superior) positive feedback from superior to subordinate leads to greater subordinate compliance than when the subordinate receives no direct feedback, whereas under high surveillance conditions subordinates who receive positive feedback from their superiors comply less than when they receive no direct feedback from their superiors [Organ, 1974].

In addition, a variety of research has explored the effects of superior reward or reinforcement behavior on subordinate performance and satisfaction. These studies suggest the following conclusions: (a) Leader positive reward behaviors (e.g., recognition of subordinate performance) are generally associated with subordinate satisfaction, but the relationship between leader punitive rewards (e.g., corrective actions) and subordinate satisfaction varies as a function of the nature of the task performed by each work group [Sims & Szilagyi, 1975]; (b) superiors who frequently criticize their subordinates for poor work are generally rated as less effective than those who criticize less frequently [Oldham, 1976]; and (c) a superior tends to positively reinforce a subordinate when he/she is positively reinforced by the subordinate's performance and to negatively reinforce a subordinate when he/she is negatively reinforced as a result of the subordinate's performance [Barrow, 1976; Greene, 1975; Hinton & Barrow, 1975; Lowin & Craig, 1968].

It should also be noted that research discussed earlier by Stull [1975] and Jablin [1978a] indicates that both superiors and subordinates prefer message responses from one another that provide positive relational feedback to the source of the message. In addition, Hill's [1973] findings suggest a significant tendency for subordinates to perceive their bosses as using one style of response to "handle interpersonal problems and another, different style to tackle technical problems" [p. 45].

In summary, results of investigations since 1970 that inquired into the nature of superior–subordinate feedback processes are generally consistent with conclusions from earlier research. Feedback from superiors to subordinates appears to be related to subordinate performance and satisfaction. However, at the same time, findings suggest that the subordinate's performance to a large extent controls the nature of his/her superior's feedback. Thus, present evidence indicates that future research should continue to explore the reciprocal character of feedback in superior–subordinate relationships, with particular emphasis on specific influence mechanisms.

Systemic Variables

Researchers have long been concerned with the effects that systemic organizational variables (e.g., technology, control structure, hierarchy, environment) have on the quality and nature of superior–subordinate communication. However, without doubt, less empirical as compared to theoretical research has been conducted in this area.

The exact role of technology in determining communication in organizations has puzzled researchers for at least two decades. For example, in the late 1950s Simpson [1959] found what he believed was the critical variable mediating the flow of vertical and horizontal communication in organizations: the degree of "mechanization" of work processes. Trist and Bamforth [1951], Gouldner [1954], Woodward [1958, 1965, 1970], Lawrence and Lorsch [1967], Perrow [1967], Pugh, Hickson, Hinings, and Turner [1969], and Peterson [1975], among others, all report findings which suggest that organizational members' perceptions of organizational and communication climate are linked to technological processes within organizations. Of even greater significance is Dubin's [1965] discovery that what is considered effective supervision may, in part, be a function of an organization's or work group's technology. Moreover, a recent doctoral study by Derry [1973] directly examined the effects technology and hierarchical position have on supervisory style, "communication responsiveness," and social interaction startegy. Results from two technologically diverse units within a manufacturing company (i.e., a manufacturing group and a research and development unit) indicated different patterns of superior–subordinate communication, depending on the interaction between technology and hierarchy.

Several investigations have also examined the relationship between organizational structure and participant communication behavior [e.g., Bass, 1976; Blankenship & Miles, 1968; Ghiselli & Siegel, 1972; Porter & Lawler, 1964].

Findings from these studies suggest the following conclusions that are relevant to superior–subordinate communication: (a) Upper level managers tend to involve their subordinates more in decision making than do lower level managers, whereas lower level managers tend to have decisions initiated for them by their superiors [Blankenship & Miles, 1968; Jago & Vroom, 1977]; (b) "As compared with firms which have tall organizational structures, those which have flat structures reward with more rapid advancement those managers who favor sharing information and objectives with subordinates" [Ghiselli & Siegel, 1972, p. 622]; and (c) in situations that are "regular, clear and structured," authoritative managerial direction is frequent, but subordinates often perceive such direction "to be more effective under reverse conditions" [Bass, 1976, p. 215].

In summary, empirical research that has examined the relationship between systemic organizational variables and communication between superiors and subordinates has tended to focus on one of two areas: (a) technology or (b) organizational structure. However, the major portion of this research has often been simplistic and/or of limited generalizability. Future research in this area is sorely needed, for if we are to ever understand the micro system of superior–subordinate communication, we must first explicate its relationship with variables in the organization's macro system.

DISCUSSION

This literature review has attempted to organize into nine topical categories empirical research on superior–subordinate communication. A close examination of this research suggests a number of conclusions. First, inspection of the variables explored within each category indicates that several basic constructs appear in more than one grouping. Specifically, we find at least three items that are consistently being studied: (a) the effects of power and status on superior–subordinate communication, (b) trust as a moderator of superior–subordinate communication, and (c) semantic-information distance as a source of misunderstanding in superior–subordinate communication. Moreover, these three variables tend to be explored concurrent to one another rather than in isolation of each other. Power and status differentials are an inevitable result of organizational development and in part serve as the impetus for the semantic-information distance between superiors and subordinates. However, the relationship of interpersonal trust to these variables is not perfectly clear, since in some situations it facilitates openness and understanding between superior and subordinates, whereas in other circumstances it appears to have no effect whatsoever. Moreover, there is some empirical and theoretical evidence [e.g., Sussman, 1975] which suggests that superior–subordinate semantic-information distance is a valuable and important feature of organization and that too large an attenuation of this gap may have dysfunctional consequences for organizational effectiveness. In short, the relationship between superior–subordinate semantic-information distance and organizational effectiveness may be a curvilinear association and may be one that is differentially moderated in various situations by interpersonal trust and perceived power and status differentials between the interactants. Obviously, additional multivariate research is required before we can fully understand the relationships between interpersonal trust, power and status, semantic-information distance, and superior–subordinate communication.

The second major conclusion to be drawn from the preceding review of literature is that a contingency/situational approach to the study of superior–subordinate communication is necessary. Repeatedly, we find that situational variables moderate the type and quality of communication exchanged between superiors and subordinates. Furthermore, if future research confirms the above proposition, much of the existing literature relating to superior–subordinate communication will become suspect and will require replication and clarification within and between organizations. In addition, it is essential that researchers start to explore the effects systemic organizational variables have on superior–subordinate communication, for as Graham and Roberts [1972] observe,

> We will only increase our understanding of organizational behavior as more researchers simultaneously investigate individual, group and organizational variables within organizations, and between organizations and the effects of environmental factors on those components. [p. 130]

Moreover, it is likely that such an approach will be more conducive to theory building in the area of superior–subordinate communication and organizational communication in general.

Finally, this review and interpretation of the literature identifies a need for some changes in the research questions we are asking about superior–subordinate communication and in the methods that are employed to answer those questions. At present, the majority of investigations exploring superior–subordinate communication have focused on describing the various problematic states of superior–subordinate relations. For example, we can describe with a fair degree of confidence an open and closed superior–subordinate relationship, the communication qualities and characteristics of effective supervisors (for at least a limited number of situations), and the types of messages that tend to be distorted in upward communication. However, a much smaller amount of research has been directed towards discovering the antecedents to these conditions. For instance, we need to start asking questions such as How do open and closed superior–subordinate communication relationships develop? How do initial attributions and expectations of new superior–subordinate relations affect subsequent communication behavior? What stages of growth are characteristic of superior–subordinate communication relationships? How do superior–subordinate communication patterns change over time, and what causes these changes? And, of course, while these questions are being explored, a contingency orientation within our research investigations should be maintained. As Redding [1972] has observed, "the *contingency* nature of most generalizations about organizational phenomena should be kept in mind when interpreting the findings of studies dealing with supervisory communication" [p. 439].

The approach that Graen and his associates have employed to study dyadic linkages in superior–subordinate leadership exchanges provides an excellent model for the general study of superior–subordinate communicattion. Specifically, these researchers have attempted to trace the development of superior–subordinate relations from their initiation through the emergence of stable interaction patterns. In other words, they have used a developmental and longitudinal research design in exploring leadership behavior. Such an approach also appears to be ideal for the study of superior–subordinate communication, since it can provide descriptive, analytical, and often quasi-experimental data about superior–subordinate relationships. It should also be noted that a growing body of research is emerging that explores the relationships between applicant job expectations and employee attitudes, satisfaction, and so forth subsequent to employment in an organization [e.g., Ilgen & Seely, 1974; Katzell, 1968; Wanous, 1973]. Information from these studies that relates to potential characteristics of superior–subordinate communication can serve as the initial point to begin our inquiries into the development of superior–subordinate communication patterns. In summary, combining our current knowledge of superior–subordinate communication with future studies that examine the dyad from a developmental, longitudinal perspective appears to provide the most promise for increased understanding of the phenomena we call superior–subordinate communication.

REFERENCE NOTES

1 Daly, J. A. *Communication and the personnel selection process: The state of the art.* Paper presented at the meeting of the International Communication Association, Chicago, April 1978.

2 Walton, E. *A magnetic theory of organizational communication* (Report No. 111). China Lake, Calif.: U.S. Naval Ordinance Test Station, January 1962.

3 Daly, J. A., McCroskey, J. C., & Falcione, R. L. *Communication apprehension, supervisor communication receptivity and satisfaction with superiors.* Paper presented at the meeting of the Eastern Communication Association, Philadelphia, Pa., April 1976.

4 Daly, J. A., McCroskey, J. C., & Falcione, R. L. *Homophily-heterophily and the prediction of supervisor satisfaction.* Paper presented at the meeting of the International Communication Association, Portland, Ore., April 1976.

REFERENCES

Athanassiades, J. C. The distortion of upward communication in hierarchical organizations. *Academy of Management Journal*, 1973, *16*, 207–226.

Athanassiades, J. C. An investigation of some communication patterns of female subordinates in hierarchical organizations. *Human Relations*, 1974, *27*, 195–209.

Baird, J. W. An analytical field study of "open communication" as perceived by supervisors, subordinates, and peers (Doctoral dissertation, Purdue University, 1973). *Dissertation Abstracts International,* 1974, *35,* 562B. (University Microfilms No. 74–15, 116)

Baird, J. E., & Diebolt, J. C. Role congruence, communication, superior-subordinate relations and employee satisfaction in organizational hierarchies. *Western Speech Communication,* 1976, *40,* 260–267.

Barrow, J. C. Worker performance and task complexity as causal determinants of leader behavior. *Journal of Applied Psychology,* 1976, *61,* 433–440.

Bartol, K. M., & Butterfield, D. A. Sex effects in evaluating leaders. *Journal of Applied Psychology,* 1976, *61,* 446–454.

Bartol, K. M., & Wortman, M. S. Male versus female leaders: Effect on perceived leader behavior and satisfaction in a hospital. *Personnel Psychology,* 1975, *28,* 533–547.

Bass, B. M. A systems survey research feedback for management and organizational development. *Journal of Applied Behavioral Science,* 1976, *12,* 215–229.

Bass, B. M., Valenzi, E. R., Farrow, D. L., & Solomon, R. J. Management styles associated with organizational, task, personal, and interpersonal contingencies. *Journal of Applied Psychology,* 1975, *60,* 720–729.

Berkowitz, N. H., & Bennis, W. G. Interaction patterns in formal service-oriented organizations. *Administrative Science Quarterly,* 1961, *6,* 25–50.

Blankenship, V., & Miles, R. E. Organizational structure and managerial decision behavior. *Administrative Science Quarterly,* 1968, *13,* 106–120.

Bowers, D. G. Self-esteem and the diffusion of leadership style. *Journal of Applied Psychology,* 1963, *47,* 135–140.

Bowman, E. H. Consistency and optimality in managerial decision making. *Management Science,* 1963, *9,* 310–321.

Boyd, B. B., & Jensen, J. M. Perceptions of the first-line supervisor's authority: A study of superior-subordinate communication. *Academy of Management Journal,* 1972, *15,* 331–342.

Bradley, P. H., & Baird, J. E. Management and communicator style: A correlational analysis. *Central States Speech Journal,* 1977, *28,* 194–203.

Brenenstuhl, D. C. An empirical investigation of the leadership function as affected by leader style, interpersonal trust and commitment to future interaction (Doctoral dissertation, Indiana University, 1975). *Dissertation Abstracts International,* 1976, *36,* 6183A. (University Microfilms No. DAH 76–06, 027)

Brenner, M. H., & Sigband, N. B. Organizational communication—An analysis based on empirical data. *Academy of Management Journal,* 1973, *16,* 323–325.

Brown, D. S. Subordinate's views of ineffective executive behaviors. *Academy of Management Journal,* 1964, *7,* 288–299.

Browne, G. G., & Neitzel, B. J. Communication, supervision and morale. *Journal of Applied Psychology,* 1952, *36,* 86–91.

Burke, R. J. Methods of resolving superior-subordinate conflict: The constructive use of subordinate differences and disagreements. *Organizational Behavior and Human Performance,* 1970, *5,* 393–411.

Burke, R. J., & Wilcox, D. S. Effects of different patterns and degrees of openness in superior-subordinate communication on subordinate job satisfaction. *Academy of Management Journal,* 1969, *12,* 319–326.

Burke, R. J., Weir, T., & Duncan, G. Informal helping relationships in work organizations. *Academy of Management Journal,* 1976, *19,* 370–377.

Burnaska, R. F. The effects of behavior modeling training upon managers' behaviors and employees' perceptions. *Personnel Psychology,* 1976, *29,* 329–335.

Butler, R. P., & Jaffee, C. L. Effects of incentive, feedback, and manner of presenting the feedback on leader behavior. *Journal of Applied Psychology,* 1974, *59,* 332–336.

Cashman, J., Dansereau, F., Graen, G., & Haga, W. J. Organizational understructure and leadership: A longitudinal investigation of the managerial role-making process. *Organizational Behavior and Human Performance,* 1976, *15,* 278–296.

Clement, S. D. An analytical field study of selected message and feedback variables in the officer hierarchy of the U.S. Army (Doctoral dissertation, Purdue University, 1973). *Dissertation Abstracts International,* 1974, *35,* 609A. (University Microfilms No. 74–15, 144)

Close, J. M. Dogmatism and managerial achievement. *Journal of Applied Psychology,* 1975, *60,* 395–396.

Cohen, A. R. Upward communication in experimentally created hierarchies. *Human Relations,* 1958, *11,* 41–53.

Cook, D. M. The impact on managers of frequency of feedback. *Academy of Management Journal,* 1968, *11,* 263–278.

Dansereau, F., Cashman, J., & Graen, G. Instrumentality theory and equity theory as complementary approaches in predicting the relationship of leadership and turnover among managers. *Organizational Behavior and Human Performance,* 1973, *10,* 184–200.

Dansereau, F., Graen, G., & Haga, W. J. A vertical dyad linkage approach to leadership within formal organizations. *Organizational Behavior and Human Performance,* 1975, *13,* 46–78.

Day, D. R., & Stogdill, R. M. Leader behavior of male and female supervisors: A comparative study. *Personnel Psychology,* 1972, *25,* 353–360.

Dennis, H. S. *A theoretical and empirical study of managerial communication climate in complex organizations.* Unpublished doctoral dissertation, Purdue University, 1974.

Derry, J. D. A correlational and factor-analytic study of attitudes and communication networks in industry (Doctoral dissertation, Purdue University, 1972). *Dissertation Abstracts International,* 1973, *34,* 442A. (University Microfilms No. 73–15, 797)

Downs, C. W., & Pickett, T. An analysis of the effects of nine leadership-group compatability contingencies upon productivity and member satisfaction. *Communication Monographs,* 1977, *44,* 220–230.

Dubin, R. Supervision and productivity: Empirical findings and theoretical considerations. In R. Dubin (Ed.), *Leadership and productivity.* San Francisco: Chandler, 1965.

Dubin, R., & Spray, S. L. Executive behavior and interaction. *Industrial Relations,* 1964, *3,* 99–108.

Duffy, P. D. *Perceptions of satisfactory and unsatisfactory leadership styles of the junior high school principal.* Unpublished doctoral dissertation, University of Southern California, 1975.

Durand, D. E., & Nord, W. R. Perceived leader behavior as a function of personality characteristics of supervisors and subordinates. *Academy of Management Journal,* 1976, *19,* 427–438.

Eilon, E. Taxonomy of communication. *Administrative Science Quarterly,* 1968, *13,* 266–288.

Falcione, R. L. Credibility: Qualifier of subordinate participation. *Journal of Business Communication,* 1974, *11,* 43–54.

Fiedler, F. E. A contingency model of leadership effectiveness. In L. Berkowitz (Ed.), *Advances in experimental social psychology* (Vol. 1). New York: Academic Press, 1964.

Fiedler, F. E. *A theory of leadership effectiveness.* New York: McGraw-Hill, 1967.

Fiedler, F. E. Leadership experience and leadership performance: Another hypothesis shot to hell. *Organizational Behavior and Human Performance,* 1970, *5,* 1–14.

Fiedler, F. E. *Leadership.* New York: General Learning Press, 1971. (a)

Fiedler, F. E. Validation and extension of the contingency model of leadership effectiveness: A review of empirical findings. *Psychological Bulletin,* 1971, *76,* 128–148. (b)

Fiedler, F. E. The effects of leadership training and experience: A contingency model interpretation. *Administrative Science Quarterly,* 1972, *17,* 453–470. (a)

Fiedler, F. E. Predicting the effects of leadership training and experience from the contingency model. *Journal of Applied Psychology,* 1972, *56,* 114–119. (b)

Fleishman, E. A., & Harris, E. F. Patterns of leadership behavior related to employee grievances and turnover. *Personnel Psychology,* 1962, *15,* 43–56.

Fleishman, E. A., Harris, E. F., & Burtt, H. E. *Leadership and supervision in industry.* Columbus, Ohio: Ohio State University, Bureau of Educational Research, 1955.

Fodor, E. M. Disparagement by a subordinate as an influence on the use of power. *Journal of Applied Psychology,* 1974, *59,* 652–655.

Funk, F. E. Communication attitudes of industrial foremen as related to their rated productivity (Doctoral dissertation, Purdue University, 1956). *Dissertation Abstracts,* 1956, *16,* 1015. (University Microfilms No. 00–16, 464)

Ghiselli, E. E., & Siegel, J. P. Leadership and managerial success in tall and flat organization structures. *Personnel Psychology,* 1972, *25,* 617–624.

Gibb, J. R. Defensive communication. *Journal of Communication,* 1961, *11,* 141–148.

Gouldner, A. W. *Patterns of industrial bureaucracy.* New York: Free Press, 1954.

Graen, G., Cashman, J. F., Ginsburgh, S. G., & Schiemann, W. Effects of linking-pin quality on the quality of working life of lower participants. *Administrative Science Quarterly,* 1977, *22,* 491–504.

Graham, W. K., & Roberts, K. H. (Eds.), *Comparative studies in organizational behavior.* New York: Holt, Rinehart, & Winston, 1972.

Green, S. G., Nebeker, D. M., & Boni, A. M. Personality and situational effects on leader behavior. *Academy of Management Journal,* 1976, *19,* 184–194.

Greene, C. N. Relationships among role accuracy, compliance, performance evaluation and satisfaction within managerial dyads. *Academy of Management Journal,* 1972, *15,* 205–216.

Greene, C. N. The reciprocal nature of influence between leader and subordinate. *Journal of Applied Psychology,* 1975, *60,* 187–193.

Greller, M. M., & Herold, D. M. Sources of feedback: A preliminary investigation. *Organizational Behavior and Human Performance,* 1975, *13,* 244–256.

Guetzkow, H. Communication in organizations. In J. G. March (Ed.), *Handbook of organizations.* Chicago: Rand McNally, 1965.

Haga, W. G., Graen, G., & Dansereau, F. Professionalism and role making in a service organization: A longitudinal investigation. *Administrative Science Quarterly,* 1974, *39,* 122–133.

Hall, J. Interpersonal style and the communication dilemma: I. Managerial implications of the Johari Awareness Model. *Human Relations,* 1974, *27,* 381–399.

Hall, J. Interpersonal style and the communication dilemma: II. Utility of the Johari Awareness Model for genotypic diagnosis. *Human Relations,* 1975, *28,* 715–736.

Haney, W. V. A comparative study of unilateral and bilateral communication. *Academy of Management Journal,* 1964, *7,* 128–136.

Haney, W. V. *Communication and organizational behavior—Text and cases* (2nd ed.). Homewood, Ill.: Irwin, 1967.

Harvey, J. B., & Boettger, C. R. Improving communication within a managerial workgroup. *Journal of Applied Behavioral Science,* 1971, *7,* 164–179.

Hawkins, B. L. Superior-subordinate communication as related to interpersonal need confirmation (Doctoral dissertation, Purdue University, 1975). *Dissertation Abstracts International,* 1976, *36,* 6366A. (University Microfilms No. DAH–76–07, 074)

Hegarty, H. W. Using subordinate ratings to elicit behavioral changes in supervisors. *Journal of Applied Psychology,* 1974, *59,* 764–766.

Heizer, J. H. Manager action. *Personnel Psychology,* 1972, *25,* 511–521.

Hill, W. A. Leadership style: Rigid or flexible. *Organizational Behavior and Human Performance,* 1973, *9,* 35–47.

Hill, W. A., & Hughes, D. Variations in leader behavior as a function of task type. *Organizational Behavior and Human Performance,* 1974, *11,* 83–96.

Hinrichs, J. R. Communications activity of industrial research personnel. *Personnel Psychology,* 1964, *17,* 193–204.

Hinton, B. L., & Barrow, J. C. The superior's reinforcing behavior as a function of reinforcements received. *Organizational Behavior and Human Performance,* 1975, *14,* 123–143.

House, R. L., Filley, A. C., & Gujarati, D. W. Leadership style, hierarchical influence, and the satisfaction of subordinate role expectations: A test of Likert's influence proposition. *Journal of Applied Psychology,* 1971, *55,* 422–432.

Housel, T. J., & Davis, W. E. The reduction of upward communication distortion. *Journal of Business Communication,* 1977, *14,* 49–65.

Ilgen, D. R., & Seely, W. Realistic expectations as an aid in reducing voluntary resignations. *Journal of Applied Psychology,* 1974, *59,* 452–455.

Indik, B. P., Georgopoulos, B. S., & Seashore, S. E. Superior-subordinate relationships and performance. *Personnel Psychology,* 1961, *14,* 357–374.

Jablin, F. M. An experimental study of message-response in superior-subordinate communication (Doctoral dissertation, Purdue University, 1977). *Dissertation Abstracts International,* 1978, *38,* 5796A. (University Microfilms No. 78–03, 241) (a)

Jablin, F. M. Message-response and "openness" in superior-subordinate communication. In B. D. Ruben (Ed.), *Communication yearbook II.* New Brunswick, N.J.: Transaction Books, 1978. (b)

Jago, A. G., & Vroom, V. H. Hierarchical level and leadership style. *Organizational Behavior and Human Performance,* 1977, *18,* 131–145.

Jain, H. C. Internal communications and supervisory effectiveness in two urban hospitals (Doctoral dissertation, University of Wisconsin—Madison, 1970). *Dissertation Abstracts International,* 1971, *31,* 5594A. (University Microfilms No. 71–03, 133)

Jain, H. C. Supervisory communication and performance in urban hospitals. *Journal of Communication,* 1973, *23,* 103–117.

Jones, A. P., James, L. R., & Bruni, J. R. Perceived leadership behavior and employee confidence in the leader as moderated by job involvement. *Journal of Applied Psychology,* 1975, *60,* 146–149.

Katz, D., & Kahn, R. *The social psychology of organizations.* New York: Wiley, 1966.

Katz, D., Maccoby, N., & Morse, N. C. *Productivity, supervision, and morale in an office situation.* Ann Arbor, Mich.: University of Michigan, Institute for Social Research, 1950.

Katzell, M. E. Expectations and dropouts in the schools of nursing. *Journal of Applied Psychology*, 1968, *52*, 154–158.

Kavanagh, M. J. Expected supervisory behavior, interpersonal trust and environmental preferences. *Organizational Behavior and Human Performance*, 1975, *13*, 17–30.

Kelly, C. M. "Actual listening behavior" of industrial supervisors, as related to "listening ability," general mental ability, selected personality factors and supervisory effectiveness (Doctoral dissertation, Purdue University, 1962). *Dissertation Abstracts*, 1963, *23*, 4019. (University Microfilms No. 63–02, 103)

Kelly, H. H. Communication in experimentally created hierarchies. *Human Relations*, 1951, *4*, 39–56.

Kelly, J. The study of executive behavior by activity sampling. *Human Relations*, 1964, *17*, 277–287.

Kerr, S., Schriesheim, C. A., Murphy, C. J., & Stogdill, R. M. Toward a contingency theory of leadership based upon the consideration and initiating structure literature. *Organizational Behavior and Human Performance*, 1974, *12*, 62–82.

Kim, J. S., & Hamner, C. W. Effects of performance feedback and goal setting on productivity and satisfaction in an organizational setting. *Journal of Applied Psychology*, 1976, *61*, 48–57.

Kipnis, D., & Lane, W. D. Self-confidence and leadership. *Journal of Applied Psychology*, 1962, *46*, 291–295.

Krivonos, P. D. Superior-subordinate communication as related to intrinsic and extrinsic motivation: An experimental field study (Doctoral dissertation, Purdue University, 1975). *Dissertation Abstracts International*, 1976, *36*, 4108A. (University Microfilms No. DAH 76–00, 552)

Lawler, E. E., Porter, L. W., & Tenenbaum, A. Managers' attitudes toward interaction episodes. *Journal of Applied Psychology*, 1968, *52*, 432–439.

Lawrence, P. R., & Lorsch, J. W. *Organization and environment: Managing differentiation and integration.* Boston, Mass.: Harvard University, Graduate School of Business Administration, Division of Research, 1967.

Leavitt, H. J., & Mueller, R. Some effects of feedback on communication. *Human Relations*, 1951, *4*, 401–410.

Level, D. A., & Johnson, L. Accuracy of information flows within the superior/ subordinate relationship. *Journal of Business Communication*, 1978, *15*, 13–22.

Likert, R. *The human organization.* New York: McGraw-Hill, 1967.

Lowin, A., & Craig, J. R. The influence of level of performance on managerial style: An experimental object-lesson in the ambiguity of correlational data. *Organizational Behavior and Human Performance*, 1968, *3*, 440–458.

MacDonald, D. Communication roles and communication networks in a formal organization. *Human Communication Research*, 1976, *2*, 365–375.

Maier, N. R. F., Hoffman, R. L., & Read, W. H. Superior-subordinate communication: The relative effectiveness of managers who held their subordinate's positions. *Personnel Psychology*, 1963, *16*, 1–11.

Maier, N. R. F., Hoffman, R. L., Hooven, J. L., & Read, W. H. Superior-subordinate communication: A statistical research project. *American Management Research Studies*, 1961, *52*, 9–30.

Marcus, P. M., & House, J. S. Exchange between superiors and subordinates in large organizations. *Administrative Science Quarterly*, 1973, *18*, 209–222.

Melcher, A. J., & Beller, R. Toward a theory of organizational communication: Consideration in channel selection. *Academy of Management Journal*, 1967, *10*, 39–52.

Mellinger, G. D. Interpersonal trust as a factor in communication. *Journal of Abnormal Social Psychology*, 1956, *52*, 304–309.

Meyer, H. H., Kay, E., & French, J. R. P. Split roles in performance appraisal. *Harvard Business Review*, 1965, *43*, 123–129.

Miles, R. E. Attitudes toward management theory as a factor in managers' relationships with their superiors. *Academy of Management Journal*, 1964, *7*, 308–314.

Minter, R. L. A comparative analysis of managerial communication in two divisions of a large manufacturing company (Doctoral dissertation, Purdue University, 1969). *Dissertation Abstracts International*, 1969, *30*, 2653A. (University Microfilms No. 69–17, 221)

Miraglia, J. F. An experimental study of the effects of communication training upon perceived job performance of nursing supervisors in two urban hospitals (Doctoral dissertation, Purdue University, 1963). *Dissertation Abstracts*, 1964, *24*, 5611. (University Microfilms No. 64–05, 749)

Mitchell, T. R., Smyser, C. M., & Weed, S. E. Locus of control: Supervision and work satisfaction. *Academy of Management Journal*, 1975, *18*, 623–631.

Moore, M. L. Superior, self, and subordinate differences in perceptions of managerial learning times. *Personnel Psychology*, 1974, *27*, 297–305.

Northouse, P. G. Predictors of empathic ability in an organizational setting: A research note. *Human Communication Research*, 1977, *3*, 176–178.

Odiorne, G. S. An application of the communication audit. *Personnel Psychology*, 1954, *7*, 235–243.

Oldham, G. R. The motivational strategies used by superiors: Relationships to effectiveness indicators. *Organizational Behavior and Human Performance*, 1976, *15*, 66–86.

O'Reilly, C. A., & Roberts, K. H. Information filtration in organizations: Three experiments. *Organizational Behavior and Human Performance*, 1974, *11*, 253–265.

Organ, D. W. Social exchange and psychological reactance in a simulated superior-subordinate relationship. *Organizational Behavior and Human Performance*, 1974, *12*, 132–142.

Pelz, D. C. Influence: A key to effective leadership in the first-line supervisor. *Personnel*, 1952, *29*, 3–11.

Penfield, R. V. Time allocation patterns and effectiveness of managers. *Personnel Psychology*, 1974, *27*, 245–255.

Perrow, C. A framework for the comparative analysis of organizations. *Administrative Science Quarterly*, 1967, *32*, 194–208.

Peterson, R. B. The interaction of technological process and perceived organizational climate in Norwegian firms. *Academy of Management Journal*, 1975, *18*, 288–299.

Petty, M. M., & Lee, G. L. Moderating effects of sex of supervisor and subordinate on relationships between supervisory behavior and subordinate satisfaction. *Journal of Applied Psychology*, 1975, *60*, 624–628.

Petty, M. M., & Miles, R. H. Leader sex-role stereotyping in a female dominated work culture. *Personnel Psychology*, 1976, *29*, 393–404.

Pfeffer, J., & Salancik, G. R. Determinants of supervisory behavior: A role set analysis. *Human Relations*, 1975, *28*, 139–154.

Pinder, C. C., & Pinto, P. R. Demographic correlates of managerial style. *Personnel Psychology*, 1974, *27*, 257–270.

Ponder, Q. D. Supervisory practices of effective and ineffective foremen (Doctoral dissertation, Columbia University, 1958). *Dissertation Abstracts*, 1959, *20*, 3983. (University Microfilms No. 59–01, 497)

Porter, L. W. Differential self-perceptions of management personnel and line workers. *Journal of Applied Psychology*, 1958, *42*, 105–108.

Porter, L. W., & Lawler, E. E. The effects of "tall" versus "flat" organization structures on managerial job satisfaction. *Personnel Psychology*, 1964, *17*, 135–148.

Pugh, D. S., Hickson, D. J., Hinings, C. R., & Turner, C. The content of organization structures. *Administrative Science Quarterly*, 1969, *14*, 91–114.

Pyron, H. C. The construction and validation of a forced-choice scale for measuring oral communication attitudes of industrial foremen (Doctoral dissertation, Purdue University, 1964). *Dissertation Abstracts*, 1964, *25*, 1413. (University Microfilms No. 64–08, 702)

Read, W. H. Upward communication in industrial hierarchies. *Human Relations*, 1962, *15*, 3–15.

Redding, W. C. *Communication within the organization: An interpretive review of theory and research.* New York: Industrial Communication Council, 1972.

Renwick, P. A. Perception and management of superior-subordinate conflict. *Organizational Behavior and Human Performance*, 1975, *13*, 444–456.

Richetto, G. M. Source credibility and personal influence in three contexts: A study of dyadic communication in a complex aerospace organization (Doctoral dissertation, Purdue University, 1969). *Dissertation Abstracts International*, 1969, *30*, 1668A. (University Microfilms No. 69–17, 245)

Rizzo, J. R., House, R. J., & Lirtzmann, S. I. Role conflict and ambiguity in complex organizations. *Administrative Science Quarterly*, 1970, *15*, 150–163.

Roberts, K. H., & O'Reilly, C. A. Failures in upward communication: Three possible culprits. *Academy of Management Journal*, 1974, *17*, 205–215.

Rogers, E. M., & Rogers, R. A. *Communication in organizations.* New York: Free Press, 1976.

Rosen, B., & Adams, J. S. Organizational coverups: Factors influencing the discipline of information gatekeepers. *Journal of Applied Social Psychology*, 1974, *4*, 375–384.

Rosen, B., & Jerdee, T. H. The influence of sex role stereotypes on evaluations of male and female supervisory behavior. *Journal of Applied Psychology*, 1973, *57*, 44–48.

Rosen, H. Managerial role interaction: A study of three managerial levels. *Journal of Applied Psychology*, 1961, *45*, 30–34.

Rosen, S., & Tesser, A. On reluctance to communicate undesirable information: The MUM effect. *Sociometry*, 1970, *33*, 253–263.

Rubin, I. M., & Goldman, M. An open system model of leadership performance. *Organizational Behavior and Human Performance*, 1968, *3*, 143–156.

Sadler, D. J. Leadership style, confidence in management and job satisfaction. *Journal of Applied Behavioral Science*, 1970, *6*, 3–19.

Sank, L. I. Effective and ineffective managerial traits obtained as naturalistic descriptions from executive members of a super corporation. *Personnel Psychology*, 1974, *27*, 423–434.

Schein, V. E. The relationship between sex role stereotypes and requisite management characteristics. *Journal of Applied Psychology*, 1973, *57*, 95–100.

Schein, V. E. Relationships between sex role stereotypes and requisite management characteristics among female managers. *Journal of Applied Psychology*, 1975, *60*, 340–344.

Schriesheim, C. A., & Murphy, C. J. Relationships between leader behavior and subordinate satisfaction and performance: A test of some situational moderators. *Journal of Applied Psychology*, 1976, *61*, 634–641.

Schwartz, M. M., Stark, H. F., & Schiffman, H. R. Responses of union and management leaders to emotionally toned industrial relations terms. *Personnel Psychology,* 1970, *23,* 361–367.

Senger, J. Managers' perceptions of subordinates' competence as a function of personal value orientations. *Academy of Management Journal,* 1971, *14,* 415–423.

Simons, H. W. A comparison of communication attributes and rated job performance of supervisors in a large commercial enterprise (Doctoral dissertation, Purdue University, 1961). *Dissertation Abstracts,* 1962, *22,* 3778. (University Microfilms No. 62–00, 887)

Simpson, R. L. Vertical and horizontal communication in formal organizations. *Administrative Science Quarterly,* 1959, *4,* 188–196.

Sims, H. P., & Szilagyi, A. D. Leader reward behavior and subordinate satisfaction and performance. *Organizational Behavior and Human Performance,* 1975, *14,* 426–438.

Sincoff, M. Z. An experimental study of the effects of three "interview styles" upon judgments of the interviewees and observer-judges (Doctoral dissertation, Purdue University, 1969). *Dissertation Abstracts International,* 1970, *30,* 5100A. (University Microfilms No. 70–08, 972)

Smith, C. G., & Kight, S. S. Effects of feedback on insight and problem solving efficiency in training groups. *Journal of Applied Psychology,* 1959, *43,* 209–211.

Smith, R. L. Communication correlates of interpersonal sensitivity among industrial supervisors (Doctoral dissertation, Purdue University, 1967). *Dissertation Abstracts,* 1968, *28,* 4743A. (University Microfilms No. 68–06, 361)

Stogdill, R. M. *Handbook of leadership.* New York: Free Press, 1974.

Stull, J. B. "Openness" in superior-subordinate communication: A quasi-experimental field study (Doctoral dissertation, Purdue University, 1974). *Dissertation Abstracts International,* 1975, *36,* 603A. (University Microfilms No. 75–17, 285)

Sussman, L. Upward communication in the organizational hierarchy: An experimental field study of perceived message distortion (Doctoral dissertation, Purdue University, 1973). *Dissertation Abstracts International,* 1974, *34,* 5366A. (University Microfilms No. 74–05, 055)

Sussman, L. Communication in organizational hierarchies: The fallacy of perceptual congruence. *Western Speech Communication,* 1975, *39,* 191–199.

Sussman, L., Pickett, T. A., Berzinski, I. A., & Pearce, F. W. Sex and sycophancy: Communication strategies for ascendance in same sex and mixed sex superior-subordinate dyads. *Sex Roles,* in press.

Tacey, W. S. *Critical requirements for the oral communication of industrial foremen.* Pittsburgh, Pa.: Author, 1959.

Tenenbaum, A. Dyadic communications in industry (Doctoral dissertation, University of California, Berkeley, 1970). *Dissertation Abstracts International,* 1971, *31,* 7662B. (University Microfilms No. 71–15, 902)

Tompkins, P. K. *An analysis of communication between headquarters and selected units of a national labor union.* Unpublished doctoral dissertation, Purdue University, 1962.

Tosi, H. L. The effect of the interaction of leader behavior and subordinate authoritarianism. *Personnel Psychology,* 1973, *26,* 339–350.

Triandis, H. C. Categories of thought of managers, clerks and workers about jobs and people in an industry. *Journal of Applied Psychology,* 1959, *43,* 338–344. (a)

Triandis, H. C. Cognitive similarity and interpersonal communication in industry. *Journal of Applied Psychology,* 1959, *43,* 321–326. (b)

Triandis, H. C. Differential perceptions of certain jobs and people by managers, clerks and workers in industry. *Journal of Applied Psychology,* 1959, *43,* 221–225. (c)

Triandis, H. C. Cognitive similarity and communication in a dyad. *Human Relations,* 1960, *13,* 175–183.

Trist, E. L., & Bamforth, K. W. Some social and psychological consequences of the longwall method of coal-getting. *Human Relations,* 1951, *4,* 3–38.

Vroom, V. H. Industrial social psychology, In G. Lindzey & E. Aronson (Eds.), *Handbook of social psychology* (Vol. 5). Reading, Mass.: Addison-Wesley, 1970.

Vroom, V. H. Leadership. In M. C. Dunnette (Ed.), *Handbook of industrial and organizational psychology.* Chicago: Rand McNally, 1976.

Vroom, V. H. & Mann, F. C. Leader authoritarianism and employee attitudes. *Personnel Psychology,* 1960, *13,* 125–140.

Wager, L. W. Leadership style, influence, and supervisory role obligations. *Administrative Science Quarterly,* 1965, *9,* 391–420.

Walker, C. R., Turner, A. N., & Guest, R. H. *The foreman on the assembly line.* Cambridge, Mass.: Harvard University Press, 1956.

Walter, B. Internal control relations in administrative hierarchies. *Administrative Science Quarterly,* 1966, *11,* 179–206.

Wanous, J. P. Effects of a realistic job preview on job acceptance, job attitudes, and job survival. *Journal of Applied Psychology,* 1973, *58,* 327–332.

Weaver, C. H. The quantification of the frame of reference in labor-management communication. *Journal of Applied Psychology,* 1958, *42,* 1–9.

Webber, R. A. Perceptions of interactions between superiors and subordinates. *Human Relations,* 1970, *23,* 235–248.

Weed, S. E., Mitchell, T. R., & Moffitt, W. Leadership style, subordinate personality, and task type as predictors of performance and satisfaction with supervision. *Journal of Applied Psychology,* 1976, *61,* 58–66.

White, B. Y. Superordinate and subordinate perceptions of managerial styles of selected male and female college administrators (Doctoral dissertation, Brigham Young University, 1976). *Dissertation Abstracts International,* 1976, *37,* 841A. (University Microfilms No. DAH76-18, 355).

White, H. C. Perceptions of leadership by managers in a federal agency. *Personnel Administration/Public Personnel Review,* 1972, *1,* 51–56.

Willits, R. D. Company performance and interpersonal relations. *Industrial Management Review,* 1967, *7,* 91–107.

Woodward, J. *Management and technology.* London. Her Majesty's Stationery Office, 1958.

Woodward, J. *Industrial organization: Theory and practice.* London: Oxford University Press, 1965.

Woodward, J. *Industrial organization: Behaviour and control.* London: Oxford University Press, 1970.

Yoder, D. *Personnel management and industrial relations* (6th ed.). Englewood Cliffs, N.J.: Prentice-Hall, 1970.

Young, J. W. The subordinate's exposure of organizational vulnerability to the superior: Sex and organizational effects. *Academy of Management Journal,* 1978, *21,* 113–122.

Zajonc, R. B. The effects of feedback and probability of group success on individual and group performance. *Human Relations,* 1962, *15,* 149–161.

Zima, J. P. The counseling-communication of supervisors in a large manufacturing company (Doctoral dissertation, Prudue University, 1968). *Dissertation Abstracts,* 1969, *29,* 3956B. (University Microfilms No. 69-07, 518).

REVIEW AND DISCUSSION QUESTIONS

1 How does the power relationship of the supervisor affect communication between the supervisor and the subordinate?
2 How can trust in the supervisor aid supervisor–subordinate communication?
3 What are some of the major limitations of the current research on communication?
4 Establish a hypothetical experiment to measure the effectiveness of supervisor–subordinate communication. What are the independent and dependent variables? How would you measure the effectiveness of the communication?

Reading 19

Effective Use of Communication to Minimize Employee Stress

Randall S. Schuler

Stress results from many activities, events and behaviors which we experience in our daily lives, especially in the organizations where we spend so much of our time. The effects of stress, unfortunately, are usually as unfavorable for us as for the companies or organizations in which we work. Stress can come from the pressures of deadlines, from too many things to do, or from the last minute customer. Generally stress arises from not knowing what to do or when to do it, from our values or just the number of hours in a day we work. Stress also arises when we feel we don't have the ability to do the job. It also comes from not knowing how well we are doing. The phrase "management by exception" is really a stress-including principle. It suggests that we won't be informed of how "well" we are doing, but just how "unwell" we are doing. In other words, we need to do something bad to get information or feedback about how we're doing. Thus stress often results from a lack of communication or lack of the right type of communication at the right time. The right type of communication at the right time may, therefore, be an important way to reduce stress.

The unfavorable effects of stress—high blood pressure, tension, alcoholism, absenteeism, low job involvement, to name just a few—are difficult to remove. Most of us really can't act much differently in response to stressful situations. We can, however, help remove *sources* of stress for our employees, especially if we are in supervisory or managerial positions. But just what can a supervisor, i.e., a leader, really do to reduce stressful situations for others? Of course, a supervisor can always provide more resources, such as hiring more employees or not enforcing the rules or deadlines. These things may reduce some sources of stress, but they do so at the cost of reducing performance or efficiency levels of the employees and the organization. However, a supervisor can get both lower stress levels and higher employee performance or at least a greater willingness to perform. These results can be obtained by just knowing about and engaging in the appropriate leader communication behaviors. Thus, although the appropriate use of communications may not be the only way to handle stress, it may be the most effective way supervisors or managers can deal with it in relation to their employees. Most supervisors are aware of some of these communication behaviors, but find such behaviors difficult to practice because they're not sure when it's best to use them or why they work.

Let's take a look at some important leader communication behaviors which can reduce stress and describe *how* and *why* these behaviors work. Research suggests that if you practice the following behaviors appropriately, you'll be a better supervisor and have employees who are much more involved in their work, more satisfied with both you and their jobs and who are more likely to perform better quality work because their stress levels are lower.

There are many categories of leader communication behaviors, but there are seven which are important here because of their stress effects on employees. All of these behaviors can be practiced by supervisors or managers; it's just a matter of being aware of these behaviors and the situation of the employee.

LEADER COMMUNICATION BEHAVIOR

Achievement communication behavior by the supervisor conveys statements of goals, challenge, confidence and high expectations to the employee. Such a statement may be "You know, Sam, that I really feel ygu can do this job, even though it is especially complex and difficult." Achievement communication behavior builds the self-worth of the employee and gives him or her confidence that (s)he has the *ability* to do the job. Knowing one has the ability to do the job can reduce or eliminate a potentially stressful situation.

This communication behavior is especially important to new employees, to employees whose jobs generally exceed their abilities, or to employees facing new or unpredictable job situations. The specific effect of this behavior is the employee's increased perception of his or her ability to do a job well if (s)he really exerts effort to do so. A *non-verbal* communication of achievement would be allowing the employee freedom to do the job the way (s)he thinks best, not the way the supervisor thinks best.

Ego deflation communication behavior is the reverse of achievement communication behavior. As suggested by the title, this leader behavior reduces the employee's feeling of self-worth, reduces the employee's self-confidence and makes the employee feel incapable of doing anything. Ego deflation communication is captured in this statement of a supervisor to an employee: "You know, I can never trust you to do it right!" A *non-verbal* communication of ego deflation would be closely watching or checking-up on the employee. The phrase "he's always on my back" is a classic description of ego deflation communication by a supervisor.

Ego deflation communication reduces the employee's concept of his or her ability to do the job. Stress is induced because the employee perceives an

inability to do what is expected. Both ego deflation and achievement communication behavior tend to be self-fulfilling. If the supervisor expects and acts as
though the employee can perform, the employee usually does; but if the
supervisor doesn't expect and act as if the employee can succeed, even the *same*
employee doesn't. It happens all the time!

Contingent approval communication behavior aids the employee in knowing
what is expected and how well (s)he is doing. The supervisor communicates a
contingent approval by praising or otherwise rewarding the employee when
performance is good. The approval or reward given by the supervisor is
contingent or dependent upon the employee's performance. The phrase "That's
really a good job, Mary" is an example of contingent approval communication.
That phrase lets Mary know how well she is doing and also that she is performing
as expected. This communication behavior tends, however, to be historically-
oriented, not future-oriented. If jobs are constantly changing, the employee who
receives only contingent approval may be in a state of uncertainty about future
expectations, since past behaviors and rewards may not continue.

However, contingent approval communication generally acts to increase the
employee's perceptions of what's expected (especially in situations that don't
change much) and perceptions of what's rewarded. These perceptions, in turn,
will help reduce stressful situations. It's also helpful if the employee knows
what's not rewarded.

Contingent disapproval communication behavior lets the employee know
what is *not* rewarded or, more specifically, what results in punishment or
disapproval. A supervisor engaging in this communication behavior may tell an
employee "You really loused up that job" or "I could have done *that* better
myself." The employee suffers from negative or embarrassing information or
feedback from the supervisor because the performance level wasn't up to par. In
order to get the most benefit from this communication behavior, the supervisor
should specify the *exact* behavior or performance of the employee which was
below par. Frequently, because the supervisor wasn't specific enough, the
employee doesn't know why (s)he was reprimanded. In addition to being related
to specific behavior, the contingent disapproval should be aimed only at the
behavior or *performance* of the employee, not at the employee—such as "You're
really a crummy worker."

Contingent disapproval communication and contingent approval communication require the supervisor to be aware to decide how to do the job, but the
supervisor should appraise the final results so that (s)he can provide rewards or
punishments. Effective use of contingent communications also requires that
performance indicators exist and are known by both the supervisor and the
employee. Taking time to develop performance standards and to observe or be
aware of employee performance results is well worth while. These communication behaviors minimize stress levels of the employee.

Participative communication behavior of the supervisor can be helpful in
establishing future goals for the employee and/or deciding how best to do a job.
This communication behavior usually refers to decisions that should be made

and can refer to how and when to do things and to what can and should be done. This behavior is especially useful when the employee is faced with a difficult job and/or when the job changes without new performance levels and goals being established. Used in these conditions, participative communication behavior can clarify what is expected and what is rewarded and can even reduce some conflicts because the supervisor and employee discuss and iron out inconsistencies or conflicts. Participation could be extended to include more than two supervisors of an employee and is then perhaps the most useful tool in reducing conflict.

Participation, used in situations where it clarifies what is expected, or rewarded and/or where it reduces conflict, is functional or legitimate. Participation also reduces conflict by determining values of the employee and which things or jobs may be objectionable, so that the supervisor may consider these in job assignments. Participation in situations that are not changing and/or are relatively simple may not be legitimate, but rather a "con job" by the supervisor.

There are occasions, however, when an employee, regardless of the situation, would prefer just to be told what to do. Low or no participative communication may then be in order. A supervisor, therefore, needs to diagnose both the situation and the employee before utilizing participative communication. However, when the situation warrants participation, the supervisor benefits as much as the employee, because of insights and skills that the employee provides to the decisions to be made. When the employee wants to be told what to do, then directive or instrumental communication behavior is appropriate.

Directive communication behavior is especially appropriate when the employee wants directions and guidance and/or when circumstances warrant it. Such circumstances occur when the employee is just joining the organization, when changes are being made by others and need to be communicated to the employee and when time may preclude participation. Directive communications may also prove appropriate when the employee is not performing well because (s)he doesn't really know the desired performance. When directive communication is used with contingent disapproval, the combination is sometimes called scolding and instructing communication behavior. This behavior is used frequently by coaches to get the best performances from their players in a short period of time.

Directive communication behavior sounds like "Here's what I want you to do today." Directive behavior may refer to both what to do and what the goals are, as well as how to get to them. For example, "Here's what I want you to do today (goals) and here's how I want you to do it (how to)." If the employee doesn't want or have the information to determine what to do or how to do something, directive communication behavior is appropriate. The end result is an employee who better knows what is expected and how to do it. Directive communication can also help reduce conflict when directions take the form of ordering and specifying the importance of goals and/or providing the time and resources to do what is expected.

For many of the leader communication behaviors to work, to clarify expectations and ultimately to reduce stress, the communications have to be *accepted* by the employee. If the employee doesn't accept the communication, the effect on stress is lost. The employee's trust of the supervisor is necessary for acceptance. But what fosters trust? Considerate or supportive communication behavior does.

Supportive communication behavior indicates concern for the employee as a person, not as an instrument of production. This quality helps increase the trust level between the supervisor and the employee. Supportive communication is necessary for the preceding six leader communication behaviors to be effective. For a supervisor it's necessary to be good, to be supportive. A supportive supervisor may say to an employee: "Good morning, Ruth. How are you feeling today?" *Non-verbal* supportive communication includes keeping commitments, being on time and removing some barriers of distinction between supervisor and employee.

Supportive communication has nothing *directly* to do with an employee knowing what is expected, how to do something, or what is rewarded. Its impact on employee stress is indirect through increasing trust between supervisor and employee to facilitate other leader communication behaviors, which do directly influence employee stress.

Seven leader communication behaviors have been discussed independently of each other, as though a supervisor could choose any one of the behaviors and not the others. Although this might be possible, in reality most supervisors engage in several communication behaviors. It should be emphasized that effective supervisors are distinguished from ineffective or less effective supervisors by practicing appropriate leader communication behavior—and a sufficiently high level of that behavior—so that stressful conditions are reduced. For example, the *more* the employee wants participation and the *more* complex and/or changing are the job conditions, the more appropriate is *more* participative leader communication behavior. Similarly, all other leader communication behaviors have a range or a number of levels. It's usually not just a matter of behaviors being there or not being there, but how much is there.

It was indicated that all supervisors could practice or engage in leader communication behaviors. This highlights the fact that any supervisor can be effective. However, some supervisors may have more difficulties in practicing some behaviors primarily because of style of interaction and/or personal values and preferences. Some supervisors may posses an interaction style that tends to make them be quiet, or avoid confrontation or problem-solving. They may avoid participation that causes conflict or may need to justify uncomfortable actions. It is necessary that each supervisor be aware of his or her style of interaction. Most supervisors have values or preferences on how to be supervisors—ranging from directive and autocratic to *laissez-faire*. These preferences could be based on culture, upbringing, assumptions about people, or experience. Each supervisor should know his or her preferences and examine how they relate to the seven communication behaviors. A supervisor may have a set of values or preferences which conflict with some leader communication behaviors. In the short run, the supervisor can engage in the appropriate leader communication behavior regardless of values, but, over the long run, continued conflict would be too stressful. The supervisor should seek a situation and/or type of employee where the appropriate leader communication behavior is consistent with personal values.

On a more general level, each supervisor, to successfully utilize any of the leader communication behaviors, should have the *basic skills of good listening, good communicating, receiving and giving specific task-related feedback, nonverbal communicating* and *diagnosing a situation.* Good communication skills embody several characteristics:

1   Seeking to clarify your ideas before communicating;
2   Examining the true purpose of each communication;
3   Considering the total physical and human setting whenever you communicate;
4   Consulting with others, when appropriate, in planning communications;
5   Being mindful, while you communicate, of the overtones as well as the basic content of your message;
6   Taking the opportunity, when it arises, to convey something of help or value to the employee;
7   Following up your communication;
8   Communicating for tomorrow as well as today;
9   Being sure your actions support your communications;
10 Seeking not only to be understood but to be understanding—being a good listener.

Efficient and effective listening skills are:

1   Action listening;
2   Listening for total meaning;
3   Listening to feelings;
4   Avoiding the stumbling blocks to listening which include:

- Pre-judging,
- Jumping to conclusions,
- Assuming that others think as you do,
- The wandering mind,
- The closed mind,
- Wishful hearing,
- Plural meanings,
- Excessive talking,
- Absence of humility,
- Fear and
- Absence of good feedback.

The characteristics of good feedback are its being:

1 Specific rather than general;
2 Focused on the behavior, not the person;
3 Considerate of the needs of receiver;
4 Directed at behavior which the receiver can do something about;
5 Solicited rather than imposed;
6 Involved with sharing of information rather than giving advice;
7 Well-timed;
8 Involved with the amount of communication the receiver can use;
9 Concerned with what is said or done, not why; and
10 Checked to ensure clear communication.

Finally, the ability to diagnose a situation by determining the employee's perception of the clarity of what is expected, the level of conflict and the behaviors rewarded and punished is crucial. The supervisor can both ask the employee and give a questionnaire to the employee to determine these perceptions. Regardless of the method of gathering information, the supervisor must do it fairly frequently—especially if there are many changes in the employees, the situation and structure of the organization, or the tasks of the employees. Good, effective supervision is not merely practicing appropriate leader communication behaviors, good listening skills, good communicating skills and good feedback skills, but is also *continuous* practicing of these behaviors and skills.

REVIEW AND DISCUSSION QUESTIONS

1 What are some of the causes of employee stress?
2 How can the communication process help reduce stress?
3 Why is listening important to communication?
4 What are some specific actions that you personally could take to communicate more effectively?

Reading 20

Organizational Stress: A Call for Management Action

Manfred F. R. Kets de Vries

There is a story about a wily bandit who was finally captured by the king's troopers. The king, a man fond of games and riddles, made the bandit a proposition. He told him that he could make one statement. If the truth was told in that statement he would be shot; in case of a lie, hanged. After a short period of deliberation, the bandit said, "I am going to be hanged."

From the *Sloan Management Review,* Fall 1979, pp. 3–14. Reprinted with permission.

The position in which the king suddenly found himself is very similar to that of the manager. Double-bind situations seem to be the rule rather than the exception in organizations; the management of paradoxes, an inevitability. The manager, for all appearances sake in pursuit of rational action, is continually confronted with irrational behavior, ambiguity, and stress. Added to these pressures are societal changes, such as the knowledge revolution and accelerated technological developments, as well as changes in social structure, occupations, and organizations—factors which make for an increasingly complex living environment.

In this changing environment, participation, interaction, transaction, planning, and regulation become key issues, each with its own frustrations attached. In addition, modern industrial society is characterized by the temporary organization, one of the implications of which is the necessity to create collaborative entities able to function on short-term notice. In these evolving organizations, greater emphasis will be placed on the process of adaptation and organizational renewal. Obviously, the implication of these developments is that learning to live with one another is becoming increasingly important. At the same time, however, this rise in interpersonal activity increases the potential for conflict and stress.

It can be argued that, historically, organizations have far too often shown greater concern about the technology of work than social inputs and human assets. The emphasis usually has tended to be on production, technology, and markets within a framework of an acceptable physical work environment. Restructuring an organization to meet the psychological needs of its members frequently has been a relatively low priority item. Top management has been more interested in fitting the man to the job than fitting the job to the man.

But times are changing. Questions are raised about the need to change priorities in view of the greater demands placed on human adaptability. Presently, there is an increased awareness of the limits to adaptability. The futurologist Alvin Toffler recognized these limits when he stated that:

> When we alter our life style, when we make and break relationships with things, places or people, when we move restlessly through the organizational geography of society, when we learn new information and ideas, we adapt; we live. Yet there are finite boundaries, we are not infinitely resilient. Each orientation response, each adaptive reaction exacts a price, wearing down the body's machinery bit by minute bit, until perceptible tissue damage results.
>
> Thus man remains in the end what he started as in the beginning: a bio-system with a limited capacity for change. When this capacity is overwhelmed, the consequence is future shock.[1]

What Toffler calls future shock, or exceeding the adaptive range of the human organism, is symptomized by stress reactions. What seems to be occuring is that chronic diseases have replaced the contagious diseases as major contributors to mortality. Coronary disease has become the new scourge of mankind, estimated to account for more than 50 percent of all deaths in most developed societies. This increase in wear-and-tear diseases is not without its impact on organizations. Obvious consequences are work below capacity, inefficiencies on the job, output problems, excessive absenteeism, morale problems, and labor unrest. The costs to the organization of premature death of highly trained executives can only be estimated, but are probably phenomenal. Contemporary concern about quality of working life, human resource accounting, and the corporate social audit can be taken as reflections of increasing awareness of the effects of stress symptoms on organizational processes.[2] The common theme found among these new concerns is the need to create and maintain an attractive social-psychological work environment to enhance organizational functioning.

One way of arriving at a more realistic view of organizational functioning and creating more effective organizational structures and patterns of decision making is to use stress symptoms as social indicators of organizational well-being. A stress audit, complementary to the more traditional financial and strategic measurement tools, will give a more realistic view of the organization by providing the manager with an overall diagnostic picture reflecting the impact of the organization on its participants. This type of information will create a more discriminating base from which to start making individual and organizational adjustments. A stress audit can be used to create a better fit between individual and organization by finding compatible stress levels.

THE MEANING OF STRESS

In introducing the notion of a stress audit as a possible input in managerial decision making, a few words are in order about the definition of stress. Stress was originally an engineering term introduced into the social sciences by Hans Selye in 1936. Selye views stress as the "non-specifically induced changes within a biological system"[3]—non-specific, because it implies that any adaptation to a problem faced by the body, irrespective of the nature of the problem, is included. According to Selye, an individual's reaction to stress occurs in three major stages, a process which he summarizes as the General Adaptation Syndrome. The first stage of this process, the alarm reaction, includes an initial shock phase during which resistance is lowered, and a counter-shock phase, during which the body's defenses are mobilized. This phase is followed by the resistance state, during which the bodily signs of alarm reaction disappear and maximum adaptation occurs. If the stressors persist or the defenses prove to be inadequate, adaptation energy will be depleted and the stage of exhaustion will be reached. The signs of the alarm reaction reappear, but in this instance irreversibly, since the adaptive mechanisms have collapsed. Death will be the eventual result. In this context, adaptation energy can be compared to a bank account with one peculiarity; it allows withdrawals but does not permit any new deposits. When the supply of adaptation energy is exausted, the organism will die. The speed of the aging process will depend on the rate of wear and tear, on the prudence of the individual in making withdrawals from this symbolic bank account. It explains the often observed contrast between the physiological and chronological age. Intensity of life style will determine which age predominates.

In spite of Selye's conceptualizations, lack of clarity about the definition of stress remains. One of the reasons is the confusion among stress situations, stress stimuli or stressors, and stress responses. Some researchers have resolved this dilemma by viewing stress as a transactional process between individual and environment, a definition which would include stimulus, response, and intervening variables.[4] Stress is then viewed as a imbalance between the demands of the enviornment and the ability of the indiviual to adapt. However, for the sake of simplicity, many researchers have focused on stress reactions, these being less diverse and more measurable denominators of stress.

MODEL OF SYMPTOM RESPONSE

Stress research in organizations is still in its infancy. But, notwithstanding the paucity of research, a number of researchers can be found who have looked at the effects of organizational variables on stress.[5] Unfortunately, in many instances, research boundaries have been narrowly defined. Frequently, studies have focused exclusively on the work situation, substituting the notion of stress reactions (with is associations with illness and psychiatry) for more neutral indicators less fraught with emotionally charged connotations, such as job satisfaction, organizational climate measures, alienation, and morale. Usually, the fact that an individual will be subjected to more influences than the organizational enviornment alone has been ignored. These omissions have been particularly evident in job satisfaction studies. The staleness, with often vague and contradictory findings, and lack of promise of these studies can be explained in part by these overly narrow research designs.

The few examples of research on stress in a broader context, without its replacement by job satisfaction or other job attitude indicators, have been epidemiological studies of a social-psychiatric nature.[6] In these studies, the importance of personality factors, cultural variables, genetic predispositions, and nonwork environment was recognized. A concept of mental health (with all its definitional problems) was usually taken to explain the complex interrelationships among the various forces acting upon an individual.[7] Although these social-psychiatric studies were of a broader nature, the organizational environment was in turn de-emphasized, making the conclusions also less than satisfactory.

What these studies seem to indicate is that a more balanced approach is needed to explain the interface of personality and organization. Job variables in isolation appear to be insufficient to explain reactions of individuals to organizational life. Individuals can express their dissatisfaction and frustration with organizations in many other ways apart from responding to various measurement scales of satisfaction, alienation, career aspiration, or the like. It is suggested that a better and more accurate way of measuring organizational well-being and effectiveness in using human resources would be through measuring stress reactions. Stress reactions are composite indicators reflecting that many other factors besides organizational variables can be responsible for feelings of dissatisfaction on the job, and are thus of a less abstract, more realistic nature. Studies of a psychoneurotic or psychosomatic nature which have included selected job variables point in this direction.[8]

Research on stress reactions in organizations, and the use of a stress audit as an imput in organizational design and decision making, can have a great potential, but only if a balance is reached in research procedures among socio-cultural variables (i.e., ethnicity, religion, social class); personality variables (i.e., life history, personality dimensions, traits); nonwork environmental variables (i.e., critcial events in an individual's contemporary life); and organizational variables. (See Figure 1 for a model of symptom response.)

The reasoning behind the suggested model is the very simple proposition that the development of stress reactions or symptoms in an individual is a reaction to both internal needs and external conditions, whereby the latter are defined in their broadest sense and include the organizational environment. The nature of these interrelationships will determine the prevalence, causes, and consequences of stress reactions.

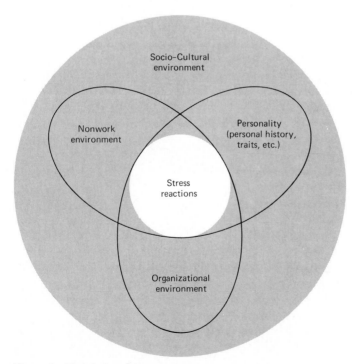

Figure 1   Model of symptom response.

A POSSIBLE RESEARCH STRATEGY

In setting up a stress audit in an organization, a distinction can be made among three categories of variables: causal stress variables (the stressors), mediating variables (the effects of personality, culture, and contemporary nonwork environment), and end-result variables (the stress reations). (Figure 2 gives an overview of stressors, mediating variables, and stress reaction patterns.)

The causal organizational variables are independent variables which can be affected by the organization and its management. We can summarize these stressors under the headings of organizational design variables, interpersonal variables, and career variables.[9] The mediating variables represent the effects of personality, the nonwork environment, and the specific culture on the general etiology of stress reactions in the organization. The end-result variables reflect the outcome of the combined effect of stressors and mediating variables on organization and individual. We are referring to both individual stress reactions (i.e., psychosomatic and psychoneurotic symptoms) and dysfunctional organizational patterns, such as absenteeism, strikes, and labor turnover.

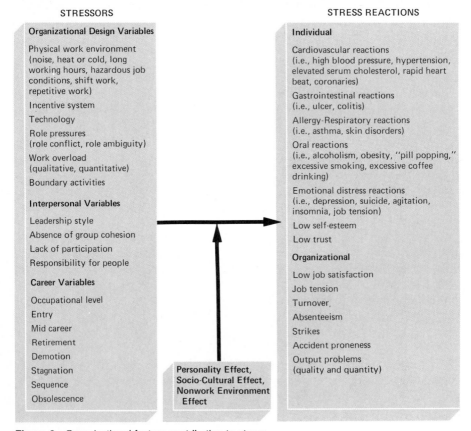

Figure 2   Organizational factors contributing to stress.

The data needed for the stress audit can be collected with the aid of questionnaires, clinical-diagnostic interviews, and, if possible, physical examinations. A typical questionnaire includes a stress symptom survey, an organizational survey (including questions about job demands, task characteristics, role demands, organizational characteristics, career variables, performance variables, and the characteristics of the organization's environment), and questions pertaining to extraorganizational variables (i.e., psychological characteristics and questions about life style).[10] In the latter case questionnaires, such as the social readjustment rating scale[11] and the type A personality scale,[12] are possible inclusions.

Through factor analysis and multiple regression, stress reaction patterns can be identified and relationships established among causal, mediating, and end-result variables. Occupational, departmental, divisional, and locational differences will be highlighted. Stress peaks warranting special attention in the organization will be located. Moreover, if the stress audit becomes a more accepted procedure in organizations, a data bank will be established allowing comparisons between different types of organizations and different industries.

In identifying these stressors and measuring the existing stress level in the organization, it must be noted, however, that a certain amount of stress in organizations is desirable. Each individual needs a moderate amount of stress to be alert and capable of functioning. An organization completely without stress might make for complacency among its participants, may neglect environmental danger signs, and may soon be out of business. On the other hand, an excess of stress can also become dysfunctional since it will detract from the organization's goals. Naturally, the threshold of stress varies for each individual. It could very well be that specific types of people flock to particular occupations with the most compatible stress levels. Misfits may drop out and find more agreeable types of jobs. If they persist in what are for them stressful occupations, they may in some cases suffer from serious stress reactions (such as coronary heart disease), and may die prematurely. Because of these personality differences, "stress engineering" becomes a complex endeavor.

ORGANIZATIONAL FACTORS CONTRIBUTING TO STRESS

The Effect of Organizational Design

Traditionally, concern has centered on the physical conditions of the work environment which can contribute to stress. Many physiological experiments and observations of work under adverse conditions have supported the existence of such a relationship. Factors, such as noise, heat and cold, long working hours, shift work, repetitive work, and hazardous work, can be stressful. The way incentive systems are designed can have a stress-producing impact. Piece-rate remuneration has its incumbent strain. Rapidly changing technology in the work setting has its own stress-inducing effect.

The infra- and supra-structures of organizations, which involve such relationships as hierarchy of authority, departmentalization, organizational goals, control and information systems, work flow, technology, and degree of differentiation or integration, can be great sources of stress. Attention must be given to these design variables to create organizations with satisficing stress levels. The designs of the infra- and supra-structures will determine the degree of conflict and ambiguity experienced by the individual working in an organization. This relationship to stress has been noted by, among others, Kahn and his associates, who introduced the concepts of role conflict and role ambiguity in a study of stress reactions in organizations.[13]

Ambiguity in organizations is related to the adequacy of information to do a job properly. It refers to both role definition and accuracy of feedback. When this information is missing, ambiguity and helplessness are experienced. The greater the task uncertainty, the greater the amount of information that must be processed. Clarity in role definition is necessary to mitigate ambiguity. Feedback is another crucial variable in the management of ambiguity. Depending on the amount of accurate feedback available, ambiguity will intensify or decrease, and so may stress symptoms. The validity of this latter relationship has found support in many physiological experiments done with animals.[14] Many of these findings seem to be applicable to human situations as well.[15]

Work overload is another factor which can be stress-producing. This experience can be divided into quantitative overload (the sum total of all the work which has to be done) and qualitative overload (what the job requires in skills, ability, and knowledge beyond the person's capacity). In both cases the extremes on the continua of too much work–too little work, and too easy work–too difficult work, can have a stress-inducing impact.

Individuals occupying positions at the organization's boundaries are potentially susceptible to a considerably higher degree of conflict and ambiguity. This applies to both external boundaries (the dividing line between organization and environment) and intraorganizational boundaries. A typical example is a project manager in a matrix organization. The nature of his job requires that he continually cross the boundaries of such departments as research and development, engineering, production, marketing, and sales, in addition to coordinating activities with people from outside the organization. Another example is the systems analyst. These boundary-spanning activities (as these two examples of "integrators" indicate) can be stressful, particularly given the exposure to such a high degree of ambiguity. It seems that the potential for conflict is related to the degree of organizational differentiation. The likely increase in role conflict and role ambiguity in these situations may be partially responsible. Obviously, the increasing presence of the temporary organization adds to the likelihood of organizational conflict.

Interpersonal Processes

The importance of interpersonal relations, group processes, and leadership style as variables influencing motivation, attitudes, satisfaction, and productivity has to be emphasized. Studies dealing with these topics suggest an association between interpersonal relations and stress reactions. A dominant, rather obvious theme in many of these studies has been the realization that members of cohesive groups are more capable of dealing with stressful conditions than members of loosely structured groups.[16]

Signs of stress in organizations originating from difficulties in interpersonal processes can be manifold. Sudden increases in vertical and lateral interpersonal communication are often symptomatic of interpersonal problems, as is complete withdrawal from interaction. A change in the content and type of interaction can be another indication.

Apart from the supportive group interaction that may occur as a buffer against the development of stress symptoms, relationships between stress and leadership style can be found. A common, again rather obvious finding seems to be that considerate leadership style has a stress-reducing effect.[17]

French and Caplan argued that increased "participation is an efficient way of reducing many other stresses which also lead to psychological strain."[18] These researchers emphasized the importance of participation in decision making. This seems to be true, but only if the participants are dealing with substantive issues, as opposed to ritualistic, nonessential forms of decision making. It is apparent that participation increases a sense of control over one's destiny and mastery of uncertainty, and may be in some way stress-reducing. Participation, however, can also contribute to stress. Some individuals may be frustrated by the delays often associated with shared decision making. These managers may not only find it hard to deal with participation but, in addition, may view shared decision making and delegation of responsibility as threats to the traditional rights of management. Depending on the intensity of this experience, stress may be the consequence. Moreover, participation can lead to new forms of confrontation, which again may be stress-inducing.

Research findings also indicate that responsibility for people can be stress-inducing. For example, in a study done at NASA, a strong relationship was found between the degree of responsibility for others, and intensity of cigarette smoking and high diastolic blood pressure.[19] It appeared that, if an individual's responsibility was directed more toward "things" than people, diastolic blood pressure declined. It was also observed that, in situations where a person had more or less responsibility for the work of others than desired, serum cholesterol level tended to be higher than when desired responsibility matched given responsibility. Apparently, the nature of responsibility, as well as the match between desired and given responsibility, are in some way related to stress reactions.

Studies dealing with specific occupational groups point in a similar direction. Stress symptoms are unusually high among foremen (sometimes called the ulcer prone personality) and air traffic controllers; both occupations involve a high level of responsibility for people.[20]

The Effect of Career

Career plays a critical role in a person's life. Studies of career and occupations suggest that a relationship exists between occupational level and nature and intensity of stress. Another finding is that certain times and events in the career life cycle can be more stressful than others.

A consistent pattern among various studies dealing with occupational levels is that a higher incidence of stress reactions seems to occur among the lower-level occupations.[21] The reasons for these differences are manifold. Variations in dietary practices according to social strata, unhealthy and unsafe working conditions, less careful diagnosis of stress reactions, a drift downward in occupational status because of illness, or the experience of helplessness in controlling the events of the organizational environment can be viewed as contributing factors.

Three points in the career life cycle seem to be particularly stressful: entry, mid career, and retirement.[22] Apparently, many individuals experience career entry with a sense of reality shock. A conflict may arise between aspirations and frustrating on-the-job experiences. The reason is frequently that the new recruit is exposed to very little challenge and the predictable outcome is dissatisfaction and boredom with his job. Stress reactions may result. A poor "fit" between individual and job can also be a result of either a wrong occupational choice or a job which is beyond the capability of the individual, again with predictable strains attached.

Mid-career stress can be considered as one aspect of what is sometimes described as the mid-life crisis. For many, it is a time when one becomes more aware of physical aging and the increasing proximity of death. With this realization comes an assessment of one's accomplishments in meeting previously set career goals. Many managers will be left with feelings of disappointment and frustration. In many cases, a plateau has been reached in their career. The executive's place on the social clock of time accentuates the notion of being "early" or "late" on the "career clock" (given Western society's emphasis on career progression) and emphasizes this sense of frustration. Another contributing factor is that competition for a limited number of positions within the organizational pyramid is inevitable. Such competition may be stressful for the majority of managers, who will be disappointed in their career goals. Management by ambiguity, not only to avoid confrontation and face reality, but also to prevent short-term morale problems, becomes the rule and may contribute to the incidence of stress symptoms.[23] Mid career is also the period when job obsolescence becomes noticeable. Low job satisfaction and morale, absenteeism, and decreased productivity will be side effects. For some it will mean that their role in the organization has become untenable, which can be an extremely stressful experience.

With approaching retirement come other forms of stress. Given society's emphasis on career for personal identity, retirement can be traumatic. It evokes an image of uselessness and disrupts the rhythm of life. It is also a time when the manager reviews his past career. For some managers this is an experience of despair—when the feeling prevails that one's one-and-only life has been a failure and a waste.

Demotion or dismissal is often associated with stress reactions.[24] Such incidents raise questions about self-worth and identity. Depending on the individual's threshold to stress, these events may be the last ones in a string of incidents pushing the person to illness. A similar statement can be made about the anticipation of demotion or losing a job, which can be as stressful, or even more so, than the actual event itself.[25] Apparently, accurate information will mitigate anticipatory fear and the "work of worrying." More accurate expectations will develop, which subsequently will cushion the dramatic impact of hostility, depression, and other stress symptoms.

Career change can be extremely stressful. Often, a major reorientation in life style will be needed. It may involve a geographical move, bringing many uncertainties. Retraining can also be stressful, since it usually will bring the individual into unknown domains, creating a sense of helplessness. Job rotation can have the same effect.

Control Is Therapeutic

In this brief discussion of major organizational factors contributing to the etiology of stress reactions, the intervening role of the effects of personality, culture, and nonwork environment has to be emphasized. Simple causal relationships between organizational variables and stress do not exist. Only a contributing quality can be cited. An important organizational variable which influences individual threshold to stress, however, does stand out—the degree of control the person has over his work environment. For example, this relationship was noticed in a coronary disease study at Bell Telephone System, where it was shown that upwardly mobile managers—despite the uprooting connected with mobility—did not have a higher risk of coronary heart disease.[26] Career progression, by increasing perceived control over one's destiny, seemed to have a buffering effect against stress. In contrast, if the individual experiences a sense of powerlessness in affecting organizational life, susceptibility to stress seems to increase.[27]

One possible explanation for this phenomenon is that successful managers, as opposed to "plateauees," staff members, and lower-level operational people, have a considerable amount of control and influence over their environment; they are the ones with the greatest opportunity to decrease the dissonance between aspirations and achievement. These differences in stress reactions suggest that uncertainty reduction through control over information may be a countervailing force to feelings of helplessness, is supportive to self-esteem, and appears to have considerable therapeutic value by limiting stress reactions.

WAYS OF COPING WITH STRESS

The findings of the stress audit can be dealt with in a variety of ways. Actually, either an individual or an organizational approach can be used. However, we have to keep in mind that many of the strategies for coping with stress are still in their infancy. More empirical work is needed before we can arrive at general recommendations of which strategy is most applicable in a specific situation.[28]

Many strategies for stress reduction are of an individual nature, and vary from symptom suppression through psychopharmacological interventions (the prescription of medicines) to other change strategies ranging from psychotherapy to various relaxation techniques (i.e., transcendental meditation, zen meditation, autogenic training, and biofeedback). The main purpose of psychotherapy may be the restructuring of personality to either reduce stress or make it more tolerable. What the various relaxation techniques have in common is a basic relaxation of habitual thought and behavior patterns. A disruption of ordinary routines occurs, which might lead to greater self-exploration and self-understanding, making for both acceptance of limitations and a more realistic assessment of alternatives.

It is important for the manager to be aware of these individual ways of dealing with stress. These ways of coping are usually outside the organizational context. The user of the stress audit, however, will be particularly interested in how this information can be used in an organizational setting. But the user should realize, when selecting organizational change strategies, that the impact of changes in organizational variables is more of an evolutionary nature. The information obtained from the stress audit can be effectively used only if its limitations are recognized. Many variables (particularly personality factors) are largely outside the control of organizations and necessitate individual action. In addition, organizations operate under their own sets of constraints. The stress audit is only one of the inputs in corporate planning. Profitability, technology, idiosyncrasies of leadership, strategy-making patterns, dynamism, heterogeneity, and turbulence in the environment will determine the corporate planner's zone of indifference in selecting and implementing organizational change strategies.

One area in which organizations can have important positive effects is career development. This area, in particular, is one where preventive steps can be taken. Selection and placement become especially important in view of what we know now about individual variability in ways of handling stress. Therefore, the "social contract" between individual and organization should be clearly spelled out to limit confusion and prevent the existence of unrealistic expectations. Much care should be taken to achieve compatibility between organizational task and individual interest, capacity, and stress tolerance.

Continuous career monitoring is essential if the danger of job obsolescence, demotion, or dismissal is to be reduced. Job rotation and training programs are other examples of preventive steps. Specific consideration should be given to critical points in the career life cycle, such as entry, mid career, and retirement. Specialized forms of counseling may have to be set up.

The importance of power and the experience of helplessness in the etiology of organizational stress must be remembered. Role conflict, role ambiguity, work overload, and the existing feedback mechanisms play important roles. Many of these stress-inducing conditions evolve from the particular design of infra- and supra-structure.

The manager, however, needs to realize that a certain amount of uncertainty about organizational processes will always remain; only the degree of uncertainty can be modified. Satisficing uncertainty reduction is needed. To combat the harmful effects of these structural arrangements, a reallocation of work load compatible with capability, the restructuring of organizational units, and a clarification of tasks and responsibilities may be necessary. An attitude of openness and trust in organizations becomes a priority. A free flow of information will be uncertainty-reducing and can thus have a stress-reducing impact. The avoidance of realistic feedback (because of fear of confrontation and demotivation) will in the long run have a far more stressful impact than the cost of doing some unpleasant "housecleaning" work immediately. In addition, criteria for evaluation and promotion must be spelled out clearly. But, at the same time, the strength of the counterforces fostering organizational ambiguity should not be underestimated.

More traditional elements of organizations, such as the physical design of work environments, compensation standards, work flow, and technology, may need modification. Responsiveness to complaints is another important issue. Changes in patterns of decision making and leadership style are in some instances advisable, particularly if leadership is perceived as unpredictable. Clear decision-making parameters are necessary. A redistribution of power and authority, and participation in decision making, can be beneficial in view of what we know about the consequences of the effects of powerlessness. This change can be difficult, however, given man's tendency to become addicted to power.

CONCLUSION

Many factors seem to be responsible in the etiology of stress reactions. Organizational life is only one element, but a very important one. Monitoring the level of stress reactions in organizations will be more useful in determining an organization's health than the traditional, more financially oriented measurement instruments. Certainly, the use of the stress audit is only in its infancy. Further research is needed to make the stress audit more useful in the design of organizations' infra- and supra-structures and management and career development. Only then will organizational variables, such as information, control, and incentive systems, hierarchy, technology, work flow, span of control, and patterns of decision making, fall into place and become truly operational, making for more effective and efficient functioning of the organization. By taking stress reactions as the focal point in a model of organizational functioning and design, strategy formulation and implementation are moved from idealistic mechanical descriptions (how managers would like organizations to be) to a greater degree of realism (how organizations actually can function given available management talent). By measuring stress reactions among occupational groups in their specific task environments and identifying stress patterns, possible areas of conflict will be identified. This will in turn enable organizational leadership to set up problem-solving systems capable of coping with both the requirements of the different organizational task environments and the unique characteristics of the individuals who work in these organizations.

REFERENCES

1 See A. Toffler, *Future Shock* (New York: Bantam Books, 1971), p. 342.
2 For example, treatment of quality of working life is given by: N. Q. Herrick and M. Maccoby, "Humanizing Work: A Priority Goal of the 1970's," in *The Quality of Working Life,* vol. 1, ed. L. E. Davis and A. B. Cherns (New York: The Free Press, 1975); R. E. Walton, "Criteria for the Quality of Working Life," in *The Quality of Working Life,* vol. 1, ed. L. E. Davis and A. B. Cherns (New York: The Free Press, 1975). Human resource accounting is commented on by: R. Likert and D. G. Bowers, "Organizational Theory and Human Resource Accounting," *American Psychologist* 24 (1969): 585–592; T. Mills, "Human Resources—Why the New Concern?" *Harvard Business Review,* March-April 1975. Attention to the corporate social audit is given by: G. A. Steiner, "Should Business Adopt the Social Audit?" *The Conference Board,* May 1972; R. A. Bauer and D. H. Fenn, Jr., "What Is a Corporate Social Audit?" *Harvard Business Review,* January-February 1973, pp. 37–48.
3 See: H. Selye, *The Stress of Life* (New York: McGraw-Hill, 1956), p. 311; H. Selye, *Stress without Distress* (Philadelphia: Lippincott, 1974).
4 See for example: R. S. Lazarus, *Psychological Stress and the Coping Process* (New York: McGraw-Hill, 1966); M. H. Appley and R. Trumbull, eds., *Psychological Stress* (New York: Meredith Publishing, 1967).
5 See for example: R. Kahn et al., *Organizational Stress* (New York: John Wiley & Sons, 1964); A. Kornhauser, *Mental Health of the Industrial Worker: A Detroit Study* (New York: John Wiley & Sons, 1965); J. R. P. French and R. D. Caplan, "Organizational Stress and Individual Strain," in *The Failure of Success,* ed. A. J. Marrow (New York: AMACOM, 1972).
6 See: L. Srole et al., *Mental Health in the Metropolis: The Mid-town Study,* vol. 1 (New York: McGraw-Hill, 1962); T. S. Langner and S. T. Michael, *Life Stress and Mental Health,* vol. 2 (London: The Free Press of Glencoe, 1963); A. H. Leighton, *My Name Is Legion: Foundations for a Theory of Man in Relation to Culture,* vol. 1 (New York: Basic Books, 1959); A. H. Leighton et al., *People of Cove and Woodlot: Communities from the Viewpoint of Social Psychiatry,* vol. 2 (New York: Basic Books, 1960); A. H. Leighton et al., *The Character of Danger: Psychiatric Symptoms in Selected Communities,* vol. 3 (New York: Basic Books, 1963).
7 See J. R. P. French and R. L. Kahn, "A Programmatic Approach to Studying Industrial Environment and Mental Health," *Journal of Social Issues* 43 (1962). This article takes the mental health point of view that may result in definitional problems about mental health as opposed to taking a stress symptoms approach.
8 See for example: G. L. Engel, "Studies of Ulcerative Colitis, III: The Nature of the Psychologic Processes," *American Journal of Medicine* 19 (1955): 232–233; S. Wolf, "Disease as a Way of Life: Neural Integration in Systemic Pathology," *Perspectives in Biological Medicine* 4 (1961); P. Castelnuovo-Tedesco, "Emotional Antecedents of Perforation of Ulcers of the Stomach and Duodenum," *Psychosomatic Medicine* 24 (1962): 398–416; R. H. Rosenman, "A Predictive Study of Coronary Heart

275

Disease: The Western Collaborative Group Study," *Journal of the American Medical Association* 189 (1964): 15–22; R. H. Rahe, "Life Change Measurement as a Prediction of Illness," *Proceedings of the Royal Society of Medicine* 62 (1968): 44–46; C. D. Jenkins, "Psychological and Social Precursors of Coronary Disease," part 2, *The New England Journal of Medicine* 284 (1971); T. Tores and R. H. Rahe, "Behavior and Life Satisfaction: Characteristics of Swedish Subjects with Myocardial Infarction," *Journal of Chronic Diseases* 25 (1972): 139–147.

9 For example, see: French and Caplan (1972); C. L. Cooper and J. Marshall, "Occupational Sources of Stress: A Review of the Literature Relating to Coronary Heart Disease and Mental Ill Health," *Journal of Occupational Psychology* 49 (1976): 11–18; A. Zaleznik, M. F. R. Kets de Vries, and J. Howard, "Stress Reactions in Organizations: Symptoms, Causes and Consequences," *Behavioral Science* 22 (1977): 151–162.

10 For an example of a completed stress audit and specific instruments used, see: M. F. R. Kets de Vries, A. Zaleznik, and J. Howard, "Stress Reactions and Organizations: The Minotaur Revisited" (McGill University, Faculty of Management Working Paper, 1976); Zaleznik, Kets de Vries, and Howard (1977). For another excellent checklist of factors to consider in a stress audit, see T. A. Beehr and J. E. Newman, "Job Stress, Employee Health, and Organizational Effectiveness: A Facet Analysis, Model, and Literature Review," *Personnel Psychology* 31 (1978).

11 See T. H. Holmes and R. H. Rahe, "The Social Readjustment Rating Scale," *Journal of Psychosomatic Research* 11 (1967): 213–218.

12 See M. Freedman and R. H. Rosenman, *Type A Behavior and Your Heart* (New York: Alfred A. Knopf, 1974).

13 See Kahn et al. (1964).

14 For example, see J. M. Weiss, "Psychological Factors in Stress and Disease," *Scientific American,* June 1972.

15 See: R. A. Champion, "Studies of Experimentally Induced Disturbance," *Australian Journal of Psychology* 2 (1950): 90–99; J. G. Geer, G. C. Davidson, and R. I. Gatchel, "Reduction of Stress in Humans through Nonveridical Perceived Control of Aversive Stimulation," *Journal of Personality and Social Psychology* 16 (1970): 731–738.

16 See for example: I. L. Janis, *Psychological Stress* (New York: John Wiley & Sons, 1958); R. T. Golembiewski, "Small Groups and Large Organizations," in *Handbook of Organizations,* ed. J. G. March (Chicago: Rand McNally, 1965).

17 See for example: H. Oaklander and E. A. Fleishman, "Patterns of Leadership in Hospital Settings," *Administrative Science Quarterly* 8 (1964): 520–532; D. T. Hall and E. E. Lawler III, "Job Characteristics and Pressures and the Organizational Integration of Professionals," *Administrative Science Quarterly* 15 (1970): 271–281; L. L. Cummings and T. A. Decotiis, "Organizational Correlates of Perceived Stress in a Professional Organization," *Public Personnel Management,* July-August 1973, pp. 275–282; J. R. P. French, "Person Role Fit," *Occupational Mental Health* 3 (1973): 15–20.

18 See French and Caplan (1972), p. 51.

19 See R. D. Caplan, "Organizational Stress and Individual Strain: A Socio-Psychological Study of Risk Factors in Coronary Heart Disease among Administrators, Engineers, and Scientists" (Ph.D. diss., University of Michigan, Ann Arbor, 1971).

20 For example, see: P. G. Vertin, *Bedrijfsgeneeskundige Aspecten van het Ulcus Pepticum* (Groningen: Thesis, 1954); J. P. Dunn and S. Cobb, "Frequency of Peptic Ulcer among Executives, Craftsmen, and Foremen," *Journal of Occupational Medicine* 4 (1962): 343–348; S. Cobb, "Role Responsibility: The Differentiation of a Concept," *Occupational Mental Health* 3 (1973): 10–14.

21 A brief review can be found in M. F. R. Kets de Vries and A. Zaleznik, "A Socio-Psychological Inquiry into the Nature and Significance of Stress Reactions in Organizations," *INSEAD Research Paper Series,* No. 88, November 1972.

22 For example, see: D. T. Hall, *Careers in Organizations* (Pacific Palisades: Goodyear Publishing, 1976); M. F. R. Kets de Vries, "The Mid-Career Conundrum," *Organizational Dynamics,* Fall 1978; M. F. R. Kets de Vries, "Is There Life at Retirement?" *California Management Review,* in press.

23 See M. F. R. Kets de Vries, "The Management of Organizational Ambiguity," in *Organizational Paradoxes: Clinical Approaches to Management* (London: Tavistock Publications, forthcoming).

24 For example, see S. V. Kasl, S. Gore, and S. Cobb, "The Experience of Losing a Job: Reported Changes in Health Symptoms and Illness Behavior," *Psychosomatic Medicine* 37 (1975): 106–122.

25 See: S. V. Kasl and S. Cobb, "Blood Pressure Changes in Men Undergoing Job Loss: A Preliminary Report," *Psychosomatic Medicine* 32 (1970): 19–38; Kasl, Gore, and Cobb (1975).

26 See L. E. Hinkle, Jr., L. H. Whitney, and E. W. Lehman, "Occupation, Education, and Coronary Heart Disease," *Science* 161 (1968): 238–246.

27 See: Zaleznik, Kets de Vries, and Howard (1977); Kets de Vries (forthcoming).

28 For an excellent critical review of personal and organizational strategies of handling job stress, see J. E. Newman and T. A. Beehr, "Personal and Organizational Strategies for Handling Job Stress: A Review of Research and Opinion," *Personnel Psychology* 32 (1979).

REVIEW AND DISCUSSION QUESTIONS

1 What is a stress audit?
2 How can an organization contribute to stress?
3 Do individuals react to stress in the same way? Explain.
4 How can you personally improve your effectiveness in dealing with stress?

Reading 21

Organizational Conflict: Concepts and Models[1]

Louis R. Pondy

There is a large and growing body of literature on the subject of organizational conflict. The concept of conflict has been treated as a general social phenomenon, with implications for the understanding of conflict within and between organizations.[2] It has also assumed various roles of some importance in attempts at general theories of management and organizational behavior.[3] Finally, conflict has recently been the focus of numerous empirical studies of organization.[4]

Slowly crystallizing out of this research are three conceptual models designed to deal with the major classes of conflict phenomena in organizations.[5]

Reprinted from *Administrative Science Quarterly,* September 1967, pp. 296–320 with permission of the author and the publisher.

[1]The author wishes to thank H. Jerome Zoffer, Jacob G. Birnberg, James A. Wilson, and Victor H. Vroom for helpful comments on a draft of this paper.

[2]Jessie Bernard, T. H. Pear, Raymond Aron, and Robert C. Angell, *The Nature of Conflict* (Paris: UNESCO, 1957); Kenneth Boulding, *Conflict and Defense* (New York: Harper, 1962); Lewis Coser, *The Functions of Social Conflict* (Glencoe, Ill.: Free Press, 1956); Kurt Lewin, *Resolving Social Conflict* (New York: Harper, 1948); Anatol Rapaport, *Fights, Games, and Debates* (Ann Arbor: University of Michigan, 1960); Thomas C. Schelling, *The Strategy of Conflict* (Cambridge, Mass.: Harvard Univ., 1961); Muzafer Sherif and Carolyn Sherif, *Groups in Harmony and Tension* (Norman, Okla.: University of Oklahoma, 1953); Georg Simmel, *Conflict,* trans. Kurt H. Wolff (Glencoe, Ill.: Free Press, 1955).

[3]Bernard M. Bass, *Organizational Psychology* (Boston, Mass.: Allyn and Bacon, 1965); Theodore Caplow, *Principles of Organization* (New York: Harcourt Brace, and World, 1964); Eliot D. Chapple and Leonard F. Sayles, *The Measure of Management* (New York: Macmillan, 1961); Michael Crozier, *The Bureaucratic Phenomenon* (Glencoe, Ill.: Free Press, 1964); Richard M. Cyert and James G. March, *A Behavioral Theory of the Firm* (Englewood Cliffs, N. J.: Prentice-Hall, 1963); Alvin W. Gouldner, *Patterns of Industrial Bureaucracy* (Glencoe, Ill.: Free Press, 1954); Harold J. Leavitt, *Managerial Psychology* (Chicago: University of Chicago, 1964); James G. March and Herbert A. Simon, *Organizations* (New York: Wiley, 1958); Philip Selznick, *TVA and the Grass Roots* (Berkeley: University of California, 1959); Victor Thompson, *Modern Organization* (New York: Knopf, 1961).

[4]Joseph L. Bower, The Role of Conflict in Economic Decision-making Groups, *Quarterly Journal of Economics,* 79 (May 1965), 253–257; Melville Dalton, *Men Who Manage* (New York: Wiley, 1959); J. M. Dutton and R. E. Walton, "Interdepartmental Conflict and Cooperation: A Study of Two Contrasting Cases," dittoed, Purdue University, October 1964; William Evan, Superior-Subordinate Conflict in Research Organizations, *Administrative Science Quarterly,* 10 (June 1965), 52–64; Robert L. Kahn, *et al., Studies in Organizational Stress* (New York: Wiley, 1964); I. R. Pondy, Budgeting and Inter-Group Conflict in Organizations, *Pittsburgh Business Review,* 34 (April 1964), 1–3; R. E. Walton, J. M. Dutton, and H. G. Fitch, *A Study of Conflict in the Process, Structure, and Attitudes of Lateral Relationships* (Institute Paper No. 93; Lafayette, Ind.: Purdue University, November 1964); Harrison White, Management Conflict and Sociometric Structure, *American Journal of Sociology,* 67 (September 1961), 185–199; Mayer N. Zald, Power Balance and Staff Conflict in Correctional Institutions, *Administrative Science Quarterly,* 7 (June 1962), 22–49.

[5]The following conceptualization draws heavily on a paper by Lawrence R. Ephron, Group Conflict in Organizations: A Critical Appraisal of Recent Theories, *Berkeley Journal of Sociology,* 6 (Spring 1961), 53–72.

1 *Bargaining model.* This is designed to deal with conflict among interest groups in competition for scarce resources. This model is particularly appropriate for the analysis of labor-management relations, budgeting processes, and staff-line conflicts.

2 *Bureaucratic model.* This is applicable to the analysis of superior-subordinate conflicts or, in general, conflicts along the vertical dimension of a hierarchy. This model is primarily concerned with the problems caused by institutional attempts to control behavior and the organization's reaction to such control.

3 *Systems model.* This is directed at lateral conflict, or conflict among the parties of a functional relationship. Analysis of the problems of coordination is the special province of this model.

Running as common threads through each of these models are several implicit orientations. The most important of these orientations follow:

1 Each conflict relationship is made up of a sequence of interlocking conflict episodes; each episode exhibits a sequence or pattern of development, and the conflict relationship can be characterized by stable patterns that appear across the sequence of episodes. This orientation forms the basis for a working definition of conflict.

2 Conflict may be functional as well as dysfunctional for the individual and the organization; it may have its roots either within the individual or in the organizational context; therefore, the desirability of conflict resolution needs to be approached with caution.

3 Conflict is intimately tied up with the stability of the organization, not merely in the usual sense that conflict is a threat to stability, but in a much more complex fashion; that is, conflict is a key variable in the feedback loops that characterize organizational behavior. These orientations are discussed before the conceptual models are elaborated.

A WORKING DEFINITION OF CONFLICT

The term "conflict" has been used at one time or another in the literature to describe: *(1) antecedent conditions* (for example, scarcity of resources, policy differences) of conflictful behavior, *(2) affective states* (e.g., stress, tension, hostility, anxiety, etc.) of the individuals involved, *(3) cognitive states* of individuals, i.e., their perception or awareness of conflictful situations, and *(4) conflictful behavior,* ranging from passive resistance to overt aggression. Attempts to decide which of these classes—conditions, attitude, cognition, or behavior—is really conflict is likely to result in an empty controversy. The problem is not to choose among these alternative conceptual definitions, since each may be a relevant stage in the development of a conflict episode, but to try to clarify their relationship.

Conflict can be more readily understood if it is considered a dynamic process. A conflict relationship between two or more individuals in an organization can be analyzed as a sequence of conflict episodes. Each conflict episode begins with conditions characterized by certain conflict potentials. The parties to the relationship may not become aware of any basis of conflict and they may not develop hostile affections for one another. Depending on a number of factors, their behavior may show a variety of conflictful traits. Each episode or encounter leaves an aftermath that affects the course of succeeding episodes. The entire relationship can then be characterized by certain stable aspects of conditions, affect, perception, and behavior. It can also be characterized by trends in any of these characteristics.

This is roughly analogous to defining a "decision" to include activities preliminary to and following choice, as well as the choice itself. In the same sense that a decision can be thought of as a process of gradual commitment to a course of action, a conflict episode can be thought of as a gradual escalation to a state of disorder. If choice is the climax of a decision, then by analogy, open war or aggression is the climax of a conflict episode.

This does not mean that every conflict episode necessarily passes through every stage to open aggression. A potential conflict may never be perceived by the parties to the conflict, or if perceived, the conflict may be resolved before hostilities break out. Several other alternative courses of development are possible. Both Coleman and Aubert make these points clearly in their treatments of the dynamics of conflict.[6]

Just as some decisions become programmed or routinized, conflict management in an organization also becomes programmed or institutionalized sometimes. In fact, the institutionalization of means for dealing with recurrent conflict is one of the important aspects in any treatment of the topic. An organization's success hinges to a great extent on its ability to set up and operate appropriate mechanisms for dealing with a variety of conflict phenomena.

Five stages of a conflict episode are identified: *(1)* latent conflict (conditions), *(2)* perceived conflict (cognition), *(3)* felt conflict (affect), *(4)* manifest conflict (behavior), and *(5)* conflict aftermath (conditions). The elaboration of each of these stages of a conflict episode will provide the substance for a working definition. Which specific reactions take place at each stage of a conflict episode, and why, are the central questions to be answered in a theory of conflict. Only the framework within which those questions can be systematically investigated is developed here.

Latent Conflict

A search of the literature has produced a long list of underlying sources of organizational conflict. These are condensed into three basic types of latent conflict: *(1)* competition for scarce resources, *(2)* drives for autonomy, and *(3)* divergence of subunit goals. Later in the paper each of these fundamental types of latent conflict is paired with one of the three conceptual models. Briefly,

---

[6]James S. Coleman, *Community Conflict* (Glencoe, Ill.: Free Press, 1957); Vilhelm Aubert, Competition and Dissensus: Two Types of Conflict and Conflict Resolution, *Journal of Conflict Resolution,* 7 (March 1963), 26–42.

competition forms the basis for conflict when the aggregated demands of participants for resources exceed the resources available to the organization; autonomy needs form the basis of conflict when one party either seeks to exercise control over some activity that another party regards as his own province or seeks to insulate itself from such control; goal divergence is the source of conflict when two parties who must cooperate on some joint activity are unable to reach a consensus on concerted action. Two or more types of latent conflict may, of course, be present simultaneously.

An important form of latent conflict, which appears to be omitted from this list, is role conflict. The role conflict model treats the organization as a collection of role sets, each composed of the focal person and his role senders. Conflict is said to occur when the focal person receives incompatible role demands or expectations from the persons in his role set.[7] This model has the drawback that it treats the focal person as merely a passive receiver rather than as an active participant in the relationship. It is argued here, that the role conflict model does not postulate a distinct type of latent conflict. Instead, it defines a conceptual relationship, the role set, which may be useful for the analysis of all three forms of latent conflict described.

Perceived Conflict

Conflict may sometimes be perceived when no conditions of latent conflict exist, and latent conflict conditions may be present in a relationship without any of the participants perceiving the conflict.

The case in which conflict is perceived when no latent conflict exists can be handled by the so-called "semantic model" of conflict.[8] According to this explanation, conflict is said to result from the parties' misunderstanding of each others' true position. It is argued that such conflict can be resolved by improving communications between the parties. This model has been the basis of a wide variety of management techniques aimed at improving interpersonal relations. Of course, if the parties' true positions are in opposition, then more open communication may only exacerbate the conflict.

The more important case, that some latent conflicts fail to reach the level of awareness also requires explanation. Two important mechanisms that limit perception of conflict are the suppression mechanism and the attention-focus mechanism.[9] Individuals tend to block conflicts that are only mildly threatening out of awareness.[10] Conflicts become strong threats, and therefore must be acknowledged, when the conflicts relate to values central to the individual's personality. The suppression mechanism is applicable more to conflicts related to personal than to organizational values. The attention-focus mechanism, however, is related more to organizational behavior than to personal values.

---

[7]Kahn, *et al.*, *op. cit.*, pp. 11–35.

[8]Bernard, Pear, Aron, and Angell, *op. cit.*

[9]These two mechanisms are instances of what Cyert and March, *op. cit.*, pp. 117–119, call the "quasi-resolution" of conflict.

[10]Leavitt, *op. cit.*, pp. 53–72.

Organizations are characteristically faced with more conflicts than can be dealt with, given available time and capacities. The normal reaction is to focus attention on only a few of these, and these tend to be the conflicts for which short-run, routine solutions are available. For organizations successfully to confront the less programmed conflicts, it is frequently necessary to set up separate subunits specifically to deal with such conflicts.

Felt Conflict

There is an important distinction between perceiving conflict and feeling conflict. *A* may be aware that *B* and *A* are in serious disagreement over some policy, but it may not make *A* tense or anxious, and it may have no effect whatsoever on *A*'s affection towards *B*. The personalization of conflict is the mechanism which causes most students of organization to be concerned with the dysfunctions of conflict. There are two common explanations for the personalization of conflict.

One explanation is that the inconsistent demands of efficient organization and individual growth create anxieties within the individual.[11] Anxieties may also result from identity crises or from extra-organizational pressures. Individuals need to vent these anxieties in order to maintain internal equilibrium. Organizational conflicts of the three latent types described earlier provide defensible excuses for displacing these anxieties against suitable targets. This is essentially the so-called "tension-model."[12]

A second explanation is that conflict becomes personalized when the whole personality of the individual is involved in the relationship. Hostile feelings are most common in the intimate relations that characterize total institutions, such as monasteries, residential colleges, and families.[13] In order to dissipate accumulated hostilities, total institutions require certain safety-valve institutions such as athletic activities or norms that legitimize solitude and withdrawal, such as the noncommunication norms prevalent in religious orders.

Thus, felt conflict may arise from sources independent of the three types of latent conflict, but latent conflicts may provide appropriate targets (perhaps symbolic ones) for undirected tensions.

Manifest Conflict

By manifest conflict is meant any of several varieties of conflictful behavior. The most obvious of these is open aggression, but such physical and verbal violence is usually strongly proscribed by organizational norms. Except for prison riots, political revolutions, and extreme labor unrest, violence as a form of manifest

[11]Chris Argyris, *Personality and Organization: The Conflict Between the System and the Individual* (New York: Harper, 1957).

[12]Bernard, Pear, Aron, and Angell, *op. cit.*

[13]It should be emphasized that members of total institutions characteristically experience both strong positive *and* negative feelings for one another and toward the institution. It may be argued that this ambivalence of feeling is a primary cause of anxiety. See Coser, *op. cit.*, pp. 61–65; and Amitai Etzioni and W. R. Taber, Scope, Pervasiveness, and Tension Management in Complex Organizations, *Social Research,* 30 (Summer 1963), 220–238.

conflict in organizations is rare. The motivations toward violence may remain, but they tend to be expressed in less violent form. Dalton has documented the covert attempts to sabotage or block an opponent's plans through aggressive and defensive coalitions.[14] Mechanic has described the tactics of conflict used by lower-level participants, such as apathy or rigid adherence to the rules, to resist mistreatment by the upper levels of the hierarchy.[15]

How can one decide when a certain behavior or pattern of behavior is conflictful? One important factor is that the behavior must be interpreted in the context in which it takes place. If A does not interact with B, it may be either because A and B are not related in any organizational sense, or because A has withdrawn from a too stressful relationship, or because A is deliberately frustrating B by withdrawing support, or simply because A is drawn away from the relationship by other competing demands upon his time. In other words, knowledge of the organizational requirements and of the expectations and motives of the participants appears to be necessary to characterize the behavior as conflictful. This suggests that behavior should be defined to be conflictful if, and only if, some or all of the participants perceive it to be conflictful.

Should the term manifest conflict be reserved for behavior which, in the eyes of the actor, is deliberately and consciously designed to frustrate another in the pursuit of his (the other's) overt or covert goals? But what of behavior which is not *intended* to frustrate, but does? Should not that behavior also be called conflictful? The most useful definition of manifest conflict seems to be that behavior which, in the mind of the actor, frustrates the goals of at least some of the other participants. In other words, a member of the organization is said to engage in conflictful behavior if he consciously, but not necessarily deliberately, blocks another member's goal achievement. He may engage in such behavior *deliberately* to frustrate another, or he may do so in spite of the fact that he frustrates another. To define manifest conflict in this way is to say that the following question is important: "Under what conditions will a party to a relationship *knowingly* frustrate another party to the relationship?" Suppose A unknowingly blocks B's goals. This is not conflictful behavior. But suppose B informs A that he perceives A's behavior to be conflictful; if then A acknowledges the message and *persists* in the behavior, it is an instance of manifest conflict.

The interface between perceived conflict and manifest conflict and the interface between felt conflict and manifest conflict are the pressure points where most conflict resolution programs are applied. The object of such programs is to prevent conflicts which have reached the level of awareness or the level of affect from erupting into noncooperative behavior. The availability of appropriate and effective administrative devices is a major factor in determining whether conflict becomes manifest. The collective bargaining apparatus of labor-management disputes and budgeting systems for internal resource alloca-

[14]Dalton, *op. cit.*

[15]David Mechanic, "Sources of Power of Lower Participants in Complex Organizations," in W. W. Cooper, H. J. Leavitt, and M. W. Shelly (eds.), *New Perspectives in Organization Research* (New York: Wiley, 1964), pp. 136–149.

tion are administrative devices for the resolution of interest-group conflicts. Evan and Scott have described due process or appeal systems for resolving superior-subordinate conflicts.[16] Mechanisms for resolving lateral conflicts among the parties to a functional relationship are relatively undeveloped. Transfer-pricing systems constitute one of the few exceptions. Much more common are organizational arrangements designed to *prevent* lateral conflicts, e.g., plans, schedules, and job descriptions, which define and delimit subunit responsibilities. Another alternative is to reduce the interdependence between conflicting subunits by introducing buffers, such as inventories, which reduce the need for sales and production departments in a business firm to act in perfect accord.

The mere availability of such administrative devices is not sufficient to prevent conflict from becoming manifest. If the parties to a relationship do not value the relationship, or if conflict is strategic in the pursuit of subunit goals, then conflictful behavior is likely. Furthermore, once conflict breaks out on some specific issue, then the conflict frequently widens and the initial specific conflict precipitates more general and more personal conflicts which had been suppressed in the interest of preserving the stability of the relationship.[17]

Conflict Aftermath

Each conflict episode is but one of a sequence of such episodes that constitute the relationships among organization participants.[18] If the conflict is genuinely resolved to the satisfaction of all participants, the basis for a more cooperative relationship may be laid; or the participants, in their drive for a more ordered relationship may focus on latent conflicts not previously perceived and dealt with. On the other hand, if the conflict is merely suppressed but not resolved, the latent conditions of conflict may be aggravated and explode in more serious form until they are rectified or until the relationship dissolves. This legacy of a conflict episode is here called "conflict aftermath."[19]

However, the organization is not a closed system. The environment in which it is imbedded may become more benevolent and alleviate the conditions of latent conflict, for example, by making more resources available to the organization. But a more malevolent environment may precipitate new crises. The development of each conflict episode is determined by a complex combina-

---

[16]Evan, *op. cit.;* William G. Scott, *The Management of Conflict: Appeals Systems in Organizations* (Homewood, Ill.: Irwin, 1965). It is useful to interpret recent developments in leadership and supervision (e.g., participative management, Theory Y, linking-pin functions) as devices for preventing superior-subordinate conflicts from arising, thus hopefully, avoiding the problem of developing appeals systems in the first place.

[17]See Coleman, *op. cit.,* pp. 9–11, for an excellent analysis of this mechanism. A chemical analogue of this situation is the supersaturated solution, from which a large amount of chemical salts can be precipitated by the introduction of a single crystal.

[18]The sequential dependence of conflict episodes also plays a major role in the analysis of role conflicts by Kahn, *et al., op. cit.,* pp. 11–35. Pondy, *op. cit.,* has used the concept of "budget residues" to explain how precedents set in budgetary bargains guide and constrain succeeding budget proceedings.

[19]Aubert, *op. cit.*

tion of the effects of preceding episodes and the environmental milieu. The main ideas of this view of the dynamics of conflict are summarized in Figure 1.

FUNCTIONS AND DYSFUNCTIONS OF CONFLICT

Few students of social and organizational behavior have treated conflict as a neutral phenomenon to be studied primarily because of scientific curiosity about its nature and form, its causes, and its effects. Most frequently the study of conflict has been motivated by a desire to resolve it and to minimize its deleterious effects on the psychological health of organizational participants and the efficiency of organization performance. Although Kahn and others pay lip service to the opinion that, "one might well make a case for interpreting some conflict as essential for the continued development of mature and competent human beings," the overriding bias of their report is with the "personal costs of excessive emotional strain," and, they state, "the fact that common reactions to conflict and its associated tensions are often dysfunctional for the organization as an on-going social system and self-defeating for the person in the long run."[20] Boulding recognizes that some optimum level of conflict and associated personal stress and tension are necessary for progress and productivity, but he portrays conflict primarily as a personal and social cost.[21] Baritz argues that Elton Mayo

[20]Kahn *et al., op. cit.,* p. 65.
[21]Boulding, *op. cit.,* pp. 305–307.

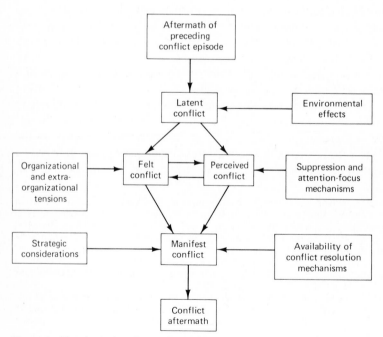

Figure 1 The dynamics of a conflict episode.

has treated conflict as "an evil, a symptom of the lack of social skills," and its alleged opposite, cooperation, as "symptomatic of health."[22] Even as dispassionate a theory of organization as that of March and Simon defines conflict conceptually as a "*breakdown* in the standard mechanism of decision making"; i.e., as a malfunction of the system.[23]

It has become fashionable to say that conflict may be either functional or dysfunctional and is not necessarily either one. What this palliative leaves implicit is that the effects of conflict must be evaluated relative to some set of values. The argument with those who seek uniformly to abolish conflict is not so much with their *a priori* assertion that conflict is undesirable, as it is with their failure to make explicit the value system on which their assertion rests.

For the purposes of this research, the effects of organizational conflict on individual welfare are not of concern. Conflict may threaten the emotional well-being of individual persons; it may also be a positive factor in personal character development; but this research is not addressed to these questions. Intra-individual conflict is of concern only in so far as it has implications for organizational performance. With respect to organizational values, *productivity,* measured in both quantitative and qualitative terms, is valued; other things being equal, an organization is "better" if it produces more, if it is more innovative, and if its output meets higher standards of quality than other organizations. *Stability* is also valued. An organization improves if it can increase its cohesiveness and solvency, other things being equal. Finally *adaptability* is valued. Other things being equal, organizations that can learn and improve performance and that can adapt to changing internal and environmental pressures are preferred to thost that cannot. In this view, therefore, to say that conflict is functional or dysfunctional is to say that it facilitates or inhibits the organization's productivity, stability, or adaptability.

Clearly, these values are not entirely compatible. An organization may have to sacrifice quality of output for quantity of output; if it pursues policies and actions that guarantee stability, it may inhibit its adaptive abilities. It is argued here that a given conflict episode or relationship may have beneficial or deleterious effects on productivity, stability, and adaptability. Since these values are incompatible, conflict may be simultaneously functional and dysfunctional for the organization.

A detailed examination of the functional and dysfunctional effects of conflict is more effectively made in the context of the three conceptual models. Underlying that analysis is the notion that conflict disturbs the "equilibrium" of the organization, and that the reaction of the organization to disequilibrium is the mechanism by which conflict affects productivity, stability, and adaptability.

---

[22]Loren Baritz, *The Servants of Power* (Middletown, Conn.: Wesleyan University, 1960), p. 203.

[23]March and Simon, *op. cit.,* p. 112, italics mine. At least one author, however, argues that a "harmony bias" permeates the entire March-Simon volume. It is argued that what March and Simon call conflicts are mere "frictions" and "differences that are not within a community of interests are ignored." See Sherman Krupp, *Patterns in Organization Analysis* (New York: Holt, Rinehart and Winston, 1961), pp. 140–167.

CONFLICT AND EQUILIBRIUM

One way of viewing an organization is to think of each participant as making contributions, such as work, capital, and raw materials, in return for certain inducements, such as salary, interest, and finished goods. The organization is said to be in "equilibrium," if inducements exceed contributions (subjectively valued) for every participant, and in "disequilibrium" if contributions exceed inducements for some or all of the participants. Participants will be motivated to restore equilibrium either by leaving the organization for greener pastures, when the disequilibrium is said to be "unstable," or by attempting to achieve a favorable balance between inducements and contributions within the organization, when it is considered "stable." Since changing organizational affiliation frequently involves sizable costs, disequilibria tend to be stable.

If we assume conflict to be a cost of participation, this inducements-contributions balance theory may help in understanding organizational reactions to conflict. It suggests that the perception of conflict by the participants will motivate them to reduce conflict either by withdrawing from the relationship, or by resolving the conflict within the context of the relationship, or by securing increased inducements to compensate for the conflict.

The assumption that conflict creates a disequilibrium is implicit in nearly all studies of organizational conflict. For example, March and Simon assume that "where conflict is perceived, motivation to reduce conflict is generated," and conscious efforts to resolve conflict are made.[24] Not all treatments of the subject make this assumption, however. Harrison White attacks the March-Simon assumption of the disequilibrium of conflict as "naive."[25] He bases his assertion on his observation of chronic, continuous, high-level conflict in administrative settings. This, of course, raises the question, "Under what conditions *does* conflict represent a disequilibrium?"

To say that (perceived) conflict represents a state of disequilibrium and generates pressures for conflict resolution, is to say three things: *(1)* that perceived conflict is a *cost* of participation; *(2)* that the conflict disturbs the inducements-contributions balance; and *(3)* that organization members react to perceptions of conflict by attempting to resolve the conflict, *in preference to* (although this is not made explicit in the March-Simon treatment) other reactions such as withdrawing from the relationship or attempting to gain added inducements to compensate for the conflict.

1. *Conflict as a cost.* Conflict is not necessarily a cost for the individual. Some participants may actually enjoy the "heat of battle." As Hans Hoffman argues, "The unique function of man is to live in close creative touch with chaos and thereby experience the birth of order."[26]

Conflict may also be instrumental in the achievement of other goals. One of the tactics of successful executives in the modern business enterprise is to create

[24]March and Simon, *op. cit.,* pp. 115, 129.
[25]Harrison White, *op. cit.*
[26]Quoted in H. J. Leavitt and L. R. Pondy, *Readings in Managerial Psychology* (Chicago: University of Chicago, 1964), p. 58.

confusion as a cover for the expansion of their particular empire,[27] or, as Sorensen observes, deliberately to create dissent and competition among one's subordinates in order to ensure that he will be brought into the relationship as an arbiter at critical times, as Franklin D. Roosevelt did.[28] Or, conflict with an out-group may be desirable to maintain stability within the in-group.

In general, however, conflict can be expected to be negatively valued; particularly if conflict becomes manifest, and subunit goals and actions are blocked and frustrated. Latency or perception of conflict should be treated as a cost, only if harmony and uniformity are highly valued. Tolerance of divergence is not generally a value widely shared in contemporary organizations, and under these conditions latent and perceived conflict are also likely to be treated as costly.

2. *Conflict as a source of disequilibrium.* White's observation of *chronic* conflict creates doubt as to whether conflict represents a disequilibrium.[29] He argues that if conflict *were* an unstable state for the system, then only transient conflict or conflict over shifting foci would be observable. Even if organizational participants treat conflict as a cost, they may still endure intense, chronic conflict, if there are compensating inducements from the organization in the form of high salary, opportunities for advancement and others. To say that a participant will endure chronic conflict is not to deny that he will be motivated to reduce it; it is merely to say that if the organization member is unsuccessful in reducing conflict, he may still continue to participate if the inducements offered to him exceed the contributions he makes in return. Although conflict may be one of several sources of disequilibrium, it is neither a necessary nor a sufficient condition of disequilibrium. But, as will be shown, equilibrium nevertheless plays an important role in organizational reactions to conflict.[30]

3. *Resolution pressures a necessary consequence of conflict.* If conflicts are relatively small, and the inducements and contributions remain in equilibrium, then the participants are likely to try to resolve the conflict within the context of the existing relationship.[31] On the other hand, when contributions exceed inducements, or when conflict is intense enough to destroy the inducements-

---

[27]Dalton, *op. cit.*

[28]Theodore Sorensen, *Decision Making in the White House* (New York: Columbia University, 1963), p. 15. This latter tactic, of course, is predicated on the fact that, *for the subordinates,* conflict is indeed a cost!

[29]Harrison White, *op. cit.*

[30]Conflict may actually be a source of equilibrium and stability, as Coser, *op. cit.,* p. 159, points out. A multiplicity of conflicts internal to a group, Coser argues, may breed solidarity, provided that the conditions do not divide the group along the same axis, because the multiplicity of coalitions and associations provide a web of affiliation for the exchange of dissenting viewpoints. The essence of his argument is that some conflict is inevitable, and that it is better to foster frequent minor conflicts of interest, and thereby gradually adjust the system, and so forestall the accumulation of latent antagonisms which might eventually disrupt the organization. Frequent minor conflicts also serve to keep the antagonists accurately informed of each other's relative strength, thereby preventing a serious miscalculation of the chances of a successful major conflagration and promoting the continual and gradual readjustment of structure to coincide with true relative power.

[31]For example, labor unions, while they wish to win the economic conflict with management, have no interest in seeing the relationship destroyed altogether. They may, however, choose to threaten such disruptive conflict as a matter of strategy.

contributions balance and there is no prospect for the re-establishment of equilibrium, then conflict is likely to be reduced by dissolving the relationship. Temporary imbalances, of course, may be tolerated; i.e., the relationship will not dissolve if the participants perceive the conflicts to be resolvable in the near future.

What is the effect of conflict on the interaction rate among participants? It depends on the stability of the relationship. If the participants receive inducements in sufficient amounts to balance contributions, then perception of conflict is likely to generate pressures for *increased* interaction, and the content of the interaction is likely to deal with resolution procedures. On the other hand, if conflict represents a cost to the participant and this cost is not compensated by added inducements, then conflict is likely to lead to *decreased* interaction or withdrawal from the relationship.

To summarize, conflict is frequently, but not always, negatively valued by organization members. To the extent that conflict *is* valued negatively, minor conflicts generate pressures towards resolution without altering the relationship; and major conflicts generate pressures to alter the form of the relationship or to dissolve it altogether. If inducements for participation are sufficiently high, there is the possibility of chronic conflict in the context of a stable relationship.

THREE CONCEPTUAL MODELS OF ORGANIZATIONAL CONFLICT

As Ephron points out, only a very abstract model is likely to be applicable to the study of all organizational conflict phenomena.[32] To be useful in the analysis of real situations, a general theoretical framework must at least fit several broad classes of conflict, some or all of which may occur within the same organization. This suggests that different ways of abstracting or conceptualizing a given organization are required, depending on what phenomena are to be studied. The three models of organization described at the beginning of this paper are the basis of the general theory of conflict presented here.

Bargaining Model

A reasonable measure of the potential conflict among a set of interest groups is the discrepancy between aggregated demands of the competing parties and the available resources. Attempts at conflict resolution usually center around attempting either to increase the pool of available resources or to decrease the demands of the parties to the conflict. Because market mechanisms or elaborate administrative mechanisms have usually evolved to guarantee orderly allocation of scarce resources, bargaining conflicts rarely escalate to the manifest level, except as strategic maneuvers.[33] Walton and and McKersie describe such conflicts as complex relationships which involve both integrative (cooperative)

---

[32]Ephron, *op. cit.*, p. 55.

[33]However, the Negro demonstrations of the 1960's and the labor riots of the early twentieth century testify to the futility of managing interest-group conflicts when mechanisms for resolutions are not available or when the parties in power refuse to create such mechanisms.

and distributive (competitive) subprocesses.[34] Each party to the conflict has an interest in making the total resources as large as possible, but also in securing as large a share of them as possible for itself. The integrative subprocess is largely concerned with joint problem solving, and the distributive subprocess with strategic bargaining. A major element of strategy in strategic bargaining is that of attitudinal structuring, whereby each party attempts to secure the moral backing of relevant third parties (for example, the public or the government).

An important characteristic of interest-group conflicts is that negotiation is frequently done by representatives who face the dual problems of *(1)* securing consensus for the negotiated solution among respective group members, and *(2)* compromising between the demands for flexibility by his opposite number and the demands for rigidity by his own group.[35] The level of perceived conflict will increase as the deadline for a solution approaches: and interest-group conflicts are invariably characterized by deadline pressures.

Most of Walton and McKersie's framework has been developed and applied within the context of labor-management relations. But the interest-group model is not limited to this sphere of activity. Pondy has described the process of capital budgeting as a process of conflict resolution among departments competing for investment funds.[36] Wildavsky has described government budgeting as a political process involving the paraphernalia of bargaining among legislative and executive interest groups.[37] Just as past labor agreements set precedents for current labor agreements, budgeting is an incremental process that builds on the residues of previous budgetary conflicts. But, whereas the visible procedures of bargaining are an accepted part of labor-management relations, there are strong pressures in budgeting (particularly *business* budgeting) to conceal the bargaining that goes on and to attempt to cloak all decisions in the guise of rationality.[38]

Bureaucratic Model

The bureaucratic model (roughly equivalent to Ephron's "political" model) is appropriate for the analysis of conflicts among the *vertical* dimension of a hierarchy, that is, conflicts among the parties to an authority relation. Vertical conflicts in an organization usually arise because superiors attempt to control the behavior of subordinates, and subordinates resist such control. The authority relation is defined by the set of subordinate activities over which the subordinate has surrendered to a superior the legitimacy to exercise discretion.[39] The potential for conflict is thus present when the superior and subordinate have different expectations about the zone of indifference. The subordinate is likely to

[34]R. E. Walton and R. B. McKersie, *A Behavioral Theory of Labor Negotiations* (New York: McGraw-Hill, 1965).

[35]These two negotiator problems are termed "factional conflict" and "boundary conflict" by Walton and McKersie, *op. cit.,* p. 283 ff.

[36]Pondy, *op. cit.*

[37]Aaron Wildavsky, *The Politics of the Budgetary Process* (Boston: Little, Brown 1964).

[38]March and Simon, *op. cit.,* p. 131.

[39]This set of activities is usually called the "zone of indifference" or "zone of acceptance." See Chester Barnard, *The Functions of the Executive* (Cambridge, Mass.: Harvard University, 1960), pp. 168–170, and Herbert A. Simon, *Administrative Behavior* (New York: Macmillan, 1960), pp. 11–13.

perceive conflict when his attempts at control are thwarted. Superiors are likely to interpret subordinate resistance as due to resentment of the exercise of *personal* power. A typical bureaucratic reaction to subordinate resistance is therefore the substitution of impersonal rules for personal control. As numerous students of bureaucracy are quick to point out, however, the unanticipated reaction to rules is more conflict, not less. The usual reasoning goes as follows: The imposition of rules defines the authority relation more clearly and robs the subordinate of the autonomy provided by ambiguity. Replacing supervision with control by rules invariably narrows the subordinate's freedom of action, makes his behavior more predictable to others, and thus weakens his power position in the organization. Control over the conditions of one's own existence, if not over others', is highly valued in organizations, particularly in large organizations. The subordinate therefore perceives himself to be threatened by and in conflict with his superiors, who are attempting to decrease his autonomy.

But why should autonomy be so important? What is the drawback to being subject to a benevolent autocrat? The answer, of course, is that autocrats seldom are or seldom remain benevolent. There is no assurance that the superior's (the organization's) goals, interests, or needs will be compatible with those of the subordinate, especially when: *(1)* organizations are so large that the leaders cannot identify personally with the rank and file; *(2)* responsibilities are delegated to organizational subunits, and subunit goals, values, etc. become differentiated from those of the hierarchy; and *(3)* procedures are formalized, and the organization leaders tend to treat rank and file members as mere instrumentalities or executors of the procedures.

In short, numerous factors influence goals and values along the vertical dimension of an organization; therefore, because subordinates to an authority relation can not rely on superiors to identify with their goals, autonomy becomes important. This leads to resistance by subordinates to attempts by superiors to control them, which in turn generates pressures toward routinization of activities and the institution of impersonal rules. This may lead to relatively predictable, conflict-free behavior, but behavior which is rigid and largely immune to personal persuasion. It is ironic that these very factors provide the potential for conflict when the organization must adapt to a changing environment. Rigidity of behavior, which minimizes conflict in a stable environment, is a major source of conflict when adaptability is required.

Research on leadership and on role conflict also provides important insights into vertical conflict. Whereas bureaucratic developments have sought to minimize conflict by altering the *fact* of supervision (for example, the use of impersonal rules and emphasis on procedure), leadership developments have sought to alter the *style* of supervision (for example, Likert's "linking pin" proposal and the various techniques of participative management).[40] Instead of

[40]Rensis Likert, *New Patterns of Management* (New York: McGraw-Hill, 1961); See, for example, Chris Argyris, *Interpersonal Competence and Organizational Effectiveness* (Homewood, Ill.: Dorsey, 1962), or Douglas McGregor, *The Human Side of Enterprise* (New York: McGraw-Hill, 1960).

minimizing dependence and increasing autonomy, leadership theorists have proposed minimizing conflict by using personal persuasion and group pressures to bring subordinate goals more closely into line with the legitimate goals of the organization. They have prescribed solutions which decrease autonomy and increase dependence. By heightening the individual's involvement in the organization's activities, they have actually provided the basis for the intense personal conflict that characterizes intimate relations.[41]

Both the bureaucratic and the leadership approaches to vertical conflict, as discussed here, take the superior-subordinate dyad as the unit of analysis. The role-conflict approach opens up the possibility of examining the conflicts faced by a man-in-the-middle between the demands of his subordinates and the demands of his superiors. Blau and Scott have suggested that effective leadership can occur only on alternate levels of a hierarchy.[42] The "man-in-the-middle" must align himself with the interests of either his superior or his subordinate, and in so doing he alienates the other. Of the three conceptual models of conflict, the bureaucratic model has probably received the most attention from researchers from a wide variety of disciplines. Partly because of this diversity, and partly because of the ease with which researchers identify with values of efficiency or democracy, this model is the least straight-forward of the three.

Systems Model

The systems model, like Ephron's "administrative" model, derives largely from the March-Simon treatment of organizational conflict.[43] It is appropriate for the analysis of conflicts among the parties to a functional relationship. Or to use Walton's terminology, the systems model is concerned with "lateral" conflicts or conflicts among persons at the same hierarchical level.[44] Whereas the authority-structure model is about problems of control, and the interest-group model is about problems of competition, the systems model is about problems of coordination.

The dyad is taken as the basic building block of the conceptual system. Consider two individuals, each occupying some formal position in an organization and playing some formal role with respect to the other. For example, A is the production manager and B the marketing manager of the XYZ company. The production manager's position is defined by the responsibility to use resources at his disposal (for example, raw materials, workers, machines) to manufacture specified products within certain constraints of product mix, cost, profitability, customer satisfaction, and so on. The constraints under which each manager operates and the resources at his disposal may be set for him by

[41]Coser, *op. cit.*, pp. 67–72.
[42]Peter Blau and Richard Scott, *Formal Organizations* (San Francisco: Chandler, 1962), pp. 162–163.
[43]March and Simon, *op. cit.*, pp. 112–135.
[44]R. E. Walton, "Theory of Conflict in Lateral Organizational Relationships," (Institute Paper No. 85; Lafayette, Ind.: Purdue University, November 1964).

himself, by the other manager, or by someone else either in or outside of the company. The role of each with respect to the other is specified by the set of directions, requests, information, and goods which he minimally must or maximally may give to or receive from the other manager. The roles may also specify instances of and procedures for joint selection of product mix, schedules, and so on. These *formal* specifications of position and role are frequently described in written job descriptions, but may also form part of a set of unwritten, stable, widely shared expectations legitimized by the appropriate hierarchical authorities. If certain responsibilities and activities are exercised without legitimization, that is, without the conscious, deliberate recognition and approval of the appropriate authorities, then they constitute *informal* positions and roles. Such expectations may still be widely shared, and are not necessarily illegitimate, i.e., specifically proscribed by the hierarchical authorities.

The fundamental source of conflict in such a system arises out of the pressures toward suboptimization. Assume first that the organization is goal-oriented rather than procedure-oriented. The subunits in a goal-oriented system will, for various reasons, have different sets of active goals,[45] or different preference orderings for the same set of goals. If in turn, two subunits having differentiated goals are functionally interdependent, then conditions exist for conflict. Important types of interdependence matter are: *(1)* common usage of some service or facility, *(2)* sequences of work or information flow prescribed by task or hierarchy, and *(3)* rules of unanimity or consensus about joint activity.

Two ways of reducing conflict in lateral relationships, if it be desirable to do so, therefore, are to reduce goal differentiation by modified incentive systems, or by proper selection, training, or assignment procedures; and to reduce functional interdependence. Functional interdependence is reduced by *(1)* reducing dependence on common resources; *(2)* loosening up schedules or introducing buffers, such as inventories or contingency funds; and *(3)* reducing pressures for consensus. These techniques of preventing conflict may be costly in both direct and indirect costs. Interpersonal friction is one of the costs of "running a tight ship."

If the parties to the conflict are flexible in their demands and desires,[46] the conflict is likely to be perceived only as a transient disturbance. Furthermore, the conflict may not be perceived, if alternative relationships for satisfying needs are available. This is one of the persuasive arguments for building in redundant channels of work and information flow.

Some relationships may be traditionally conflictful (e.g., administration-faculty, sales-production, and others). The parties to such a relationship have a set to expect conflict, and therefore may perceive conflict when none exists.

As to the forms of manifested conflict, it is extremely unlikely that any

[45]Following Simon, we treat a goal as any criterion of decision. Thus, both purposes and constraints are taken to be goals. See Herbert A. Simon, "On the Concept of Organizational Goal," *Administrative Science Quarterly*, 9 (June 1964), 1–22.

[46]Such flexibility is one of the characteristics of a problem-solving relationship. Conversely, a bargaining relationship is characterized by rigidity of demands and desires.

violent or aggressive actions will occur. First, strongly held norms proscribe such behavior. Secondly, the reaction of other parties to the relationship is likely to be that of withdrawing all cooperation. A much more common reaction to perceived conflict is the adoption of a joint decision process characterized by bargaining rather than problem solving. Walton, Dutton, and Fitch have described some of the characteristics of a bargaining style: careful rationing of information and its deliberate distortion; rigid, formal, and circumscribed relations; suspicion, hostility, and disassociation among the subunits.[47] These rigidities and negative attitudes, of course, provide the potential for conflict over other issues in future episodes of the relationship.

SUMMARY

It has been argued that conflict within an organization can be best understood as a dynamic process underlying a wide variety of organizational behaviors. The term conflict refers neither to its antecedent conditions, nor its overt manifestations, nor its residues of feeling, precedent, or structure, but to all of these taken together as the history of a conflict episode.

Conflict is not necessarily bad or good, but must be evaluated in terms of its individual and organizational functions and dysfunctions. In general, conflict generates pressures to reduce conflict, but chronic conflict persists and is endured under certain conditions, and consciously created and managed by the politically astute administrator.

Conflict resolution techniques may be applied at any of several pressure points. Their effectiveness and appropriateness depends on the nature of the conflict and on the administrator's philosophy of management. The tension model leads to creation of safety-valve institutions and the semantic model to the promotion of open communication. Although these may be perfectly appropriate for certain forms of imagined conflict, their application to real conflict may only exacerbate the conflict.

A general theory of conflict has been elaborated in the context of each of three conceptual models: *(1)* a bargaining model, which deals with interest groups in competition for resources; *(2)* a bureaucratic model, which deals with authority relations and the need to control; and *(3)* a systems model, which deals with functional relations and the need to coordinate.

REVIEW AND DISCUSSION QUESTIONS

1 Briefly summarize the three conceptual models designed to deal with the major classes of conflict phenomena in organizations.
2 Briefly summarize the five stages of a conflict episode.
3 Analyze the functions and dysfunctions of conflict.
4 Take one of the three conceptual models of conflict and argue that it is the best.

---

[47]Walton, Dutton, and Fitch, *op. cit.*

Part Five

Organizational Behavior Dynamics: Power, Politics, and Leadership

This part is an extension of the area of organizational behavior dynamics. Specifically, this part covers power, politics, and leadership. The dynamics of power and politics may be the least known and understood but, perhaps, one of the most important of areas when attempting to understand organizational power. Leadership, along with motivation, has been given more attention than anything else in the field of organizational behavior, but still little is really known about it and its impact. The readings in this part reflect the state of the art on these important organizational behavior dynamics.

The importance of understanding power in organizations has been written about for a number of years. The most noteworthy early treatise on organizational power is *The Prince,* written by Machiavelli in the sixteenth century. Through the years the concept of power has always been considered an important aspect of survival in organizational life. While the notion of power has been deemed very important, there have been very few systematic analyses of organizational power. Part of the problem stems from the difficulty in operationally defining power. Discussions of power use the term in many different ways. This confusion of the terminology makes it difficult to operationally define power and systematically research it. The end result is that while organizational behavior theorists consider power an important concept, there have been few in-depth studies made that have attempted to increase the knowledge of power. Despite these limitations, there are some concepts of power that do provide insight into what power is and how it affects organizational behavior.

First of all, power can be considered to be a transactional type of concept. In essence, power is accomplished, acquired, or used between individuals. An individual gains power through the acceptance of others. Power is not a concept that is within the purview of one individual. In order for power to be gained, other individuals must allow the individual to acquire power. Power, too, can only be used if it is used on someone. Hence, power is transactional. Second, power is probably a concept with two dimensions. These two dimensions of power involve power acquisition and/or power use. The acquisition of power involves the individual committing certain behaviors that will tend to put the individual into a situation where others bestow, through rewards, the control over situations, resources, and so forth, creating the means to secure greater power. The use of power is the use of these resources in order to influence an individual or group. Finally, power is dynamic. If an individual does not use power, his or her power base could erode. If the individual uses power unsuccessfully, there is a chance that the power base will also fail. This is what one might call the dilemma of power. The use of power successfully could lead to an increase in the power base and a further granting of power. Power is an exciting concept and one that will be researched and studied over the next decades.

Closely related to power, and in some ways an outgrowth of it, is politics and leadership. The readings in this part cover all these dynamics. The first article discusses power and politics in the context of several organizations. It describes various tactics and characteristics of power and politicking in modern organizations. The second article, by Professor Robert Rothman, takes a more empirical view of the nature of power in work organizations. Rothman maintains that the power relationships in organizations change over time and that these power relationships profoundly affect the organizational structure both in terms of areas of responsibility and scope of activities. He claims that this is a natural occurrence and not always the deliberate attempt at enhancing one's own power base. The third article provides a behavioral approach to leadership. The authors apply an operant paradigm to analyze and better understand leadership. The final article is also on leadership and applies some of the current theories to practice and indicates what implications these theories have to the practicing manager. The authors provide some specific conclusions that should be of benefit to the practitioner and the student of leadership.

Reading 22

Organizational Politics:
Tactics and Characteristics of Its Actors

Robert W. Allen
Dan L. Madison
Lyman W. Porter
Patricia A. Renwick
Bronston T. Mayes

Organizational politics is conspicuous by its relative absence in the management and organizational theory and research literature. The reason for this absence is somewhat unclear. It is not because politics occurs infrequently in organizational settings or because behavior commonly referred to as political goes unnoticed. Practicing managers are familiar with politics in organizational settings from experience, as targets or observers, rather than from systematic inquiry.

Organizational politics involve intentional acts of influence to enhance or protect the self-interest of individuals or groups. "The study of politics is the study of influence and the influential . . . the influential are those who get most of what there is to get."[1] How do the influential get what there is to get? What tactics are used by political actors "in working the system to get what [they] need?"[2] What are the personal characteristics of politically effective individuals? This article reports the results of an exploratory study of managerial perceptions concerning these aspects of politics in organizations.

THE STUDY

Eighty-seven managerial personnel (thirty chief executive officers, twenty-eight high-level staff managers, twenty-nine supervisors) were interviewed using questions developed by the authors. The managers represented thirty different organizations in the electronics industry in Southern California. Each interview was conducted confidentially and lasted one to two hours. Two of the questions asked the managers were:

- Organizational politics takes many forms. What are the tactics of organizational politics of which you are aware?
- What are the personal characteristics of those people you feel are most effective in the use of organizational politics?

A coding system was developed and the open-ended responses were categorized independently by an analyst and at least one of the authors. The few differences between the coders in assigning the responses to the various categories were discussed and reconciled.

Respondents were asked to describe organizational political tactics and personal characteristics of effective political actors based upon their accumulated experience in *all* organizations in which they had worked. They were told their statements need not apply to their own behavior, their current subunit, or their current organization. No definition of organizational politics was given to the respondents, nor did any of them ask what was meant by the term. They were asked to provide a definition and use it in their responses. The definitions they provided convinced the authors that they and the respondents were talking about the same thing.

ORGANIZATIONAL POLITICS—TACTICS

Many writers concerned with behavior in organizations focus on an individual's reaction to others or to events, with less attention to proactive or initiating behavior. Typically, reactive behavior is intended to protect self-interest while proactive promotes self-interest. Organizational politics involve both.

Table 1 shows the eight categories of political tactics mentioned most frequently by each of the three groups of respondents (chief executive officers, high-level staff managers, supervisors). The first four categories are examined individually below.

Blaming or Attacking Others   This tactic, identified by over half of each of the three groups of respondents, is reactive and proactive in nature. The reactive behavior centers around "scapegoating," used when a situation is negatively

Table 1   Managerial Perception of Organizational Politics Tactics
Percent of Respondents that Mentioned Tactic

Tactic	Combined groups	Chief executive officers	Staff managers	Supervisors
Attacking or blaming others	54.0	60.0	50.0	51.7
Use of information	54.0	56.7	57.1	48.3
Image building/impression management	52.9	43.3	46.4	69.0
Support buildings for ideas	36.8	46.7	39.3	24.1
Praising others, ingratiation	25.3	16.7	25.0	34.5
Power coalitions, strong allies	25.3	26.7	17.9	31.0
Associating with the influential	24.1	16.7	35.7	20.7
Creating obligations/reciprocity	12.6	3.3	14.3	30.7

evaluated or when the individual feels he may be associated with an outcome that is failing or has failed. Respondents indicated that the political actor minimizes or avoids his association with the undesirable situation or result. Scapegoating tends to be impersonal, the emphasis on "getting off the hook" as in the old cliche, "When something goes wrong the first thing to be fixed is the blame."

Proactive blaming or attacking tactics are far more personal and appear to be geared toward reducing the competition for scarce resources, with other individuals or subunits viewed as rivals for promotions, salary increases, status, budgets. Proactive behavior includes making the rival look bad in the eyes of influential organizational members—blaming competitors for failures or denigrating their accomplishments as unimportant, poorly timed, self-serving, or lucky. The organizational politician finds a negative situation that might be blamed on a rival.

Use of Information   Almost half the supervisors and over half the chief executive officers and staff managers identified information as a political tool. The tactics of information use can be proactive, reactive, or both depending upon the situation. Information is withheld, distorted, or used to overwhelm another.

Few managers believed outright lying or falsification is a widely used technique due, at least in part, to the dire consequences of such acts if discovered. A variety of information uses were described, including withholding information when it might be detrimental to self-interest, avoidance of individuals and situations that might require explanation reflecting unfavorably on an individual, and distortion of information to create an impression by selective disclosure, innuendo, or "objective" speculation about individuals or events. Overkill, the opposite of withholding information, overwhelms the target with data, not all of it pertinent. The purpose of this tactic may be to bury or obscure an important detail the political actor believes could harm him, when the risk of withholding information is too great. The more data, the less likely the detail will be noticed. That the target was notified can be claimed if it later comes to light. Inundating a target with "evidence" is effective in exploiting any feeling that volume of information is a measure of the importance of an issue or the validity of an argument. The political actor assumes competition between the parties whose arguments are of equal merit will be decided in favor of whoever can muster the greatest volume of alleged supporting information. The impression of rationality and logic is given by the use of quantitative data in the form of graphs, formulas, tables, summations. One manager indicated that one of his most effective techniques is to arrive at a wholly subjective decision and then have his staff collect "objective" data to support it.

Creating and Maintaining a Favorable Image   This tactic was the third kind of political behavior most mentioned by respondents. It is predominantly, if not exclusively, proactive—designed to promote self-interests. Image building includes general appearance, dress and hair style, sensitivity to organizational norms, drawing attention to successes, even those the individual is not responsible for, and creating the appearance of being on the inside of important activities. Other types of image building center on enhancement of personal characteristics, developing a reputation of being liked, enthusiastic (not too aggressive or ambitious), thoughtful, honest, and such attributes as the individual considers to be thought desirable by influential members of the organization.

A particularly heinous image-building tactic, in the view of supervisors, is the taking of credit for the accomplishments or good ideas of someone else. This may be done with misleading statements, but is more likely to involve passing on an idea without reference to the source (unless the idea is ridiculed or leads to failure). Accepting recognition without explanation or making reference to the help of others in such a way as to appear humble and eager to share the recognition with "the team" rather than in honest admission that one was not responsible for the achievement are forms of this tactic.

Developing a Base of Support   Higher-level managers are more sensitive than lower-level managers to the importance of the proactive behavior of idea support building as a political tactic. Does occupying a higher-level position make a manager more sensitive to this tactic or does the successful use of this tactic lead to promotion to higher levels? The latter would cause one to expect that of the 24 percent of the supervisors describing this tactic, those who successfully practice it might be the future members of higher-levels groups.

Idea support building as seen by respondents includes getting others to understand one's ideas before a decision is made, setting up the decision before the meeting is called, and getting others to contribute to the idea (possibly making them feel it is theirs) to assure their commitment.

Other Tactics   The fifth most frequently mentioned tactic was ingratiation. Lower-level managers mentioned the use of this technique much more frequently than the higher-level managers, twice as often as chief executive officers. The tone and context of the descriptions seemed to change with the level of the respondent. Higher-level managers tended to speak in terms of praising others and establishing good rapport. Supervisors used expressions such as "buttering up the boss," "apple polishing," and other more colorful, but less printable, remarks.

The sixth and seventh most frequently mentioned tactics were developing strong allies and forming power coalitions, and associating with influential persons in business and social situations. An interesting tactic mentioned most often by supervisors, least by chief executive officers—indicating a trend toward greater use of it at lower levels—concerned performing services or favors to create obligations. The norm of reciprocity is invoked when assitance is required,[3] "You scratch my back, I'll scratch yours."

Use of rewards, coercion and threats in influencing others, mentioned by less than 10 percent of the respondents, is not shown on Table 1. The wide variation between the mention of it by the chief executive officers (20 percent) and other managerial respondents (staff managers, 7 percent; supervisors, 3 percent) is worth noting. It appears that promises and threats may be more instrumental to individuals at higher levels than to those at lower levels. The latter may have little to promise and be quite sensitive to the personal dangers involved in making threats.

PERSONAL CHARACTERISTICS OF EFFECTIVE POLITICAL ACTORS

Table 2 shows those personal characteristics perceived as conducive to successful organizational politics mentioned by 10 percent or more of the respondents, and the percentage of each group that mentioned them. Three distinct profiles of effective political actors come from the responses from these three groups. Not all members of a group will match the stereotype, nor can the profiles be generalized to individuals in similar levels in other organizational groupings, but the following picture seems to reflect the stereotype held by each group.

Chief Executive Officers' Perspective   In the chief executive officers' view, a successful politician must, first, be sensitive to other individuals, situations, and opportunities. He is highly articulate, usually highly intelligent, ambitious, and success-oriented, but does not forget the well-being of the organization.

Staff Managers' Perspective   Staff managers agree with the chief executive officers that the successful political actor must be articulate: they see this as his most important attribute. The politician must be socially adept, must understand the social norms of the organization and behave so as to be perceived by

Table 2   Personal Characteristics of Effective Political Actors

Percent of Respondents that Mentioned Characteristic

Personal characteristics	Combined groups	Chief executive officers	Staff managers	Supervisors
Articulate	29.9	36.7	39.3	12.8
Sensitive	29.9	50.0	21.4	17.2
Socially adept	19.5	10.0	32.1	17.2
Competent	17.2	10.0	21.4	20.7
Popular	17.2	16.7	10.7	24.1
Extroverted	16.1	16.7	14.3	17.2
Self-confident	16.1	10.0	21.4	17.2
Aggressive	16.1	10.0	14.3	24.1
Ambitious	16.1	20.0	25.0	3.4
Devious	16.1	13.3	14.3	20.7
"Organization man"	12.6	20.0	3.6	13.8
Highly intelligent	11.5	20.0	10.7	3.4
Logical	10.3	3.3	21.4	6.9

influential others as "fitting in well," not as a "rebel" or "trouble maker." Staff managers, as contrasted to the other two groups, said it is important for the politician to be logical and inoffensively clever. Successful politics, they said, requires competence and, agreeing with the chief executive officers, sensitivity to others and varying situations.

Supervisors' Perspective   A somewhat different picture of the successful politican emerges from the supervisory group. They see him as being aggressive, popular, and competent, also devious. There was less agreement among the supervisors than at higher levels on what personal characteristics are important to successful politicking: sensitivity and articulateness were mentioned by 50 percent and 36.7 percent of the chief executive officers; articulateness and social adeptness by 39.3 and 32.1 percent of staff managers. The two characteristics, named most often by supervisors, being aggressive and being popular, were identified by only 24.1 percent of the supervisory respondents.

The Eyes of the Beholder   Chief executive officers see the effective political actor as sensitive to varying situations. He is articulate, commendably ambitious, and of sufficiently high intellect. The major difference between the characteristics named by staff managers and chief executive officers is the staff managers' emphasis on social adeptness and playing down of the importance of sensitivity. This is understandable when viewed from each perspective. Chief executive officers perceive the effective political actor as behaving in a way that will increase the chance of accomplishing what is desired, regardless of whether he is socially adept. Being perceived as socially adept might be more instrumental for a staff manager, particularly in interactions with influential individuals, than for the relatively more powerful chief executive officer.

The viewing lens of supervisors tended to focus on a political actor striving for popularity. They agreed with the higher levels on his aggressiveness but not on the commendability of this behavior. The supervisors also said that political actors are competent, but saw them as more devious than did the higher levels. The responses of chief executive and staff officers referred to and favored politically effective individuals at their levels in the organization, while the supervisors referred to these same, but less favorably.

ATTRIBUTION THEORY AND ORGANIZATIONAL POLITICS

Managers in this study identified readily the tactics and personal characteristics of political actors. Observing behavior and naming attributes is the concern of the social psychological theory of attribution. This theory can be used to further understand political actors.

Attribution theory focuses on explaining how individuals account for the behavior of people. Attributions refer to the dispositional nature of the individual being observed or the situational forces confronting the person. "That's just the way he is" would be a dispositional attribution, "That's not like her but she had little choice," a situational attribution. A dispositional attribution refers to something within the person causing the observed behavior (as honesty), while a situational attribution uses external factors to explain behavior. According to attribution theory, most people tend to use dispositional explanations to understand the behavior of others.[4]

The tactics of organizational politics can be examined with attribution theory. Dennis Moberg points out:

> The legitimacy norm requires that observers do not attribute such behavior to illegitimate (self-serving) motives. . . . In attribution terms, politicians must avoid having their behavior attributed by others to a particular intent (illegitimate or self-serving motives). They may do so first by "creating the impression" that they have legitimate motives.[5]

To the extent that individuals perceive behavior as self-serving rather than legitimate (as was often the case in the present study), it appears that many actors are unsuccessful in their attempts to "create the impression." It also raises the question of how often the attributions of legitimate motives are the result of successful manipulative tactics.

Attribution theory can explain why the chief executive officers and staff managers view personal characteristics of political actors in more favorable terms than do supervisors. Politicking is thought to occur more frequently at higher levels of an organization, so higher-level participants may be attributing favorable characteristics to themselves. Supervisors, who have less power in the organization, may be less able as a group to practice politics successfully and less generous in attributing favorable characteristics to the mostly high-level politicians.

CONCLUSIONS AND IMPLICATIONS

The managers in this study were able and willing to identify organizational political tactics. Politics is an important behavioral process in organizational settings. It was not the purpose of the article to praise political behavior as "good" for organizations or individuals nor to condemn it as "bad." Politics is an important social influence process with the potential of being functional or dysfunctional to organizations and individuals.

In a recent study, managerial respondents indicated a high degree of ambivalence when asked to consider the harmful or helpful effects of politics on individuals and the organization.[6] Advancement of career and increased power were cited as self-interests that could be furthered through politics. Loss of an individual's credibility was perceived as a risk. The managers mentioned that politics could improve communications and coordination in the organization, but pointed out that political behavior could threaten task accomplishment. These findings and those in this article imply practicing managers should learn more about political processes to enable them to play a larger role in its management.[7]

There was considerable consistency among the three levels of respondents concerning tactics most used in organizations. More proactive than reactive behavior was identified, indicating greater use of politics for promotion than for protection of self-interests—the best defense, a good offense.

From an organization's perspective, tactics of withholding and distorting information are probably most potentially dysfunctional. Information and control systems can be designed to minimize this. Each tactic named above could be studied by management and channelled by them so as not to jeopardize organizational goals—again, the best defense.

There were differences in the perceptions of the groups of respondents as to what makes a good politician, but the nine most cited personal characteristics could also be considered attributes of an effective leader. The similarities between the influence processes of leadership and politics may be greater than their differences, particularly when viewed by higher level members of management. Lower-level supervisors may discriminate between personal objectives and the organizational interests that concern their leaders. Higher-level managers may feel what is good for them is good for the organization and vice versa, blurring the distinction between politician and leader.

REFERENCES

1 Harold D. Lasswell, "Politics—Who Gets What, When, How," *The Political Writings of Harold D. Lasswell* (Glencoe, Illinois: The Free Press, 1951).
2 Ann Scott, "Management: A Political Process: Overt vs. Covert," *American Council on Education* (Fifty-Seventh Annual Meeting, 10 Oct. 1974).
3 Alvin W. Gouldner, "The Norm of Reciprocity: A Preliminary Statement," *American Sociological Review* (1960), pp. 161–178.
4 Philip G. Zimbardo, Ebbe B. Ebbesen, and Christina Maslach, *Influencing Attitudes and Changing Behavior* (Reading, Mass.: Addison-Wesley, 1977).
5 Dennis J. Moberg, "Organizational Politics: Perspective from Attribution Theory," Paper presented to meeting of American Institute for Decision Sciences, Chicago (1977), p. 1.
6 Unpublished study recently completed at the Graduate School of Administration, University of California, Irvine. Manuscript in preparation.
7 Bronston T. Mayes and Robert W. Allen, "Toward a Definition of Organizational Politics," *Academy of Management Review* (1977), pp. 672–678.

REVIEW AND DISCUSSION QUESTIONS

1 What are some of the tactics used to heighten an individual's power in an organization?
2 Relate attribution theory to organizational politics.
3 Critique the experimental design used in this study.
4 What are the implications of this study for the practicing manager?
5 What personal characteristics are important in the degree of success one has in the acquisition of power in an organization?

Reading 23

Occupational Roles: Power and Negotiation in the Division of Labor

Robert A. Rothman

During recent years, scholars have applied new theoretical perspectives (or paradigms) to the analysis of occupational and professional roles. This development appears to reflect the convergence of perspectives flourishing in the broader discipline. One is the "conflict" framework which focuses attention on questions of inequality and power, competing interest groups, and social change. This offers a view of the occupational division of labor as: "the temporary outcome in a past, present, and future struggle between groups who are interested in the acquisition of power, prestige and reward even at the expense of others" [Krause, 1971:82]. A second perspective might be called "interactionist," and complements the first by emphasizing the social and interpersonal processes involved in the definition, maintenance and restructuring of social roles [e.g., Blumer, 1969; P. Hall, 1972; Strauss, 1978]. Emerging from this is a view of the division of labor as a: "process of social interaction in the course of which the participants are continuously engaged in attempting to define, establish, maintain and renew the tasks they perform and the relationships with others which the tasks presuppose" [Friedson, 1976:311]. Strauss's [1978] term "negotiations" can be used to describe these processes.

These perspectives have challenged the tendency to conceptualize occupational roles as merely a configuration of technical or intellectual operations within an overall economic division of labor. Rueschemeyer recently argued that prevailing conceptions have "neglected the part played by organized interests, power, regulation, and planning and emphasized impersonal socio-economic mechanisms which respond to changes in the scope of markets, in technology, and in the environment" [Rueschemeyer, 1977:19]. This older view is being superceded by recognizing that modern occupations are embedded in complex social, political and economic networks of individuals and groups. The form and content of occupational roles is emergent and dynamic, reflecting the outcome of interaction among these units. Occupational groups and individuals self-consciously act to defend or enhance their own interests and rewards while external groups and individuals act to impose constraints as one means of achieving their own goals and objectives. Interaction may take the form of deliberate bargaining, negotiation, and accommodation or may involve more subtle manipulation or overt social control. The outcome of negotiation and social control is ultimately influenced by the distribution of power among the groups.

This is not to suggest that such issues have been totally ignored. On the contrary, the pioneering work of Freidson [1960] on the power of clients, and

From *The Sociological Quarterly*, Autumn 1979, pp. 495–515. Reprinted with permission.

the work of Goode [1960] on power struggles between professional groups stretches back for two decades and provides the foundation for current activity. Rather, what appears to be happening is the widespread adoption of these broad perspectives in textbooks [e.g., Ritzer, 1977; Montagna, 1977] and in research on occupations and professions. This in turn has focused attention on three substantive areas. One, which might be labeled occupational/professional expansionism, examines deliberate attempts to increase the prerogatives and rewards of members. A second area involves a consideration of those groups and aggregates which form the social context or environment, and are in a position to exert some influence on occupational roles. The final area deals with the internal dynamics among heterogeneous segments of occupations and professions. The purpose of this paper is to assess the state of the field in these areas, using the perspectives of power and negotiation.

RESOURCES, POWER, AND SOCIAL CONTROL

Common to both the "conflict" and the "interactionist" perspectives is a concern with the question of power. In sociology, power generally has been defined as the ability to exert influence on (i.e., control) the behavior of others by using valued resources [cf., Bierstedt, 1950; Emerson, 1962; Rogers, 1974]. The ability of groups to impose constraints upon occupations resides in the command of resources. Formally, resources may be characterized as "any attribute, circumstance, or profession" which can be used to influence an individual or group [Rogers, 1974:1425]. Occupations are the point of convergence of the activities and competing demands of a number of groups controlling resources. Groups with resources may be in a position to define the tasks, areas of expertise, enforce deference and subordination, control access and socialization, and in many other ways control the evolution of specific roles. For example, pharmacists, physicians, nurses, ophthalmologists, and others compete for the legal right to prescribe and dispense drugs. The outcome—the issue of which group or groups will be able to perform this task—will, in large part, be a question of power. Social control is also exercised internally. When the various segments of an occupation have unequal power there may be internal attempts to impose definitions of appropriate tasks or attitudes and to sanction deviants. For example, senior members of occupations and professions usually control the socialization process and can define tasks for members of the entering cohort.

Resources may be grouped into three broad categories. One is comprised of general group-based resources, which operate in a number of contexts. The other categories derive from a conceptualization of occupations as *both* a set of physical, technical, and intellectual operations and a career providing economic, social and psychic rewards. All modern occupations involve the production of some goods or services. Occupations are, in this sense, input-output systems, and any variable used in the process is a resource. There are resources which are inputs (e.g., raw materials), those involved in processing (e.g., tools, knowledge), and those which have to do with the disposal of outputs (e.g., fees, salaries). Occupations are also careers for individuals in the sense of providing income, prestige, and other kinds of rewards. Therefore, the capability to enhance or inhibit careers will be a resource. For purposes of analyses the career process can be divided into three segments: access to the occupation (e.g., licensing), career mobility (e.g., promotions), and termination (e.g., disbarment). Table 1 provides a representative list of resources which are salient in

Table 1   The Distribution of Resources in the Occupational Sphere

Resources	Examples	Representative studies
Group-based resources		
Social-cultural	Legitimacy	Tagliacozzo & Mauksch, 1972
	Expertise	Wilensky, 1964
Organizational	Associations	Stevens, 1971
	Strikes	Oppenheimer, 1975
	Membership	Akers & Quinney, 1968
Process-based resources		
Input resources		
Clients; customers	Professional referrals	Shortell, 1973
	Client referrals	Freidson, 1960
	Repeated visits	Goode, 1957
Raw materials	Control of supplies	Shaw, 1972
Operations resources		
Information	Data on new products	Coleman, et al., 1966
Tools; equipment	Manufacturing equipment	Stone, 1974
Cooperation	Teamwork	Stebbins, 1966
	Interdependence	Shover, 1972
	Controlling clients	Scheff, 1961
Funding	Research grants	Useem, 1976
Output resources		
Utilization of product or service	Publication of work	Caplow & McGee, 1958
	Peer review	Gustafson, 1975
	Malpractice suits	Hershey, 1973
Career-based resources		
Access resources		
Sponsorship	Apprenticeships	Haas, 1974
	Political appointments	Marro, 1977
Licensure	State licensing	Cohen, 1973
Employment	Job opportunities	Graves, 1970
Mobility resources		
Promotion; demotion	Hospital appointments	Hall, 1948
	Advancement in organization	Hall, 1968
	Academic promotions	Caplow & McGee, 1958
Exclusionary resources		
Termination	License revocation	Derbyshire, 1969
	Losing jobs	Sykes, 1960
	Firing	Marglin, 1974

defining occupational or professional roles, along with references to the literature.

OCCUPATIONAL EXPANSIONISM

Wilensky [1964], Goode [1960], Johnson [1972], Eliott [1972], Kronus [1976a] and Klegon [1978] are among the authors who have called for more attention to the "expansionist" efforts of occupational groups and individual members of occupations who tend to be mobilized in the pursuit of extending their prerogatives and rewards. All other things being equal, *individuals and occupational groups act to define their roles so as to protect or increase member autonomy, maximize intellectual challenge, and to enhance the level of social and economic reward.* With respect to autonomy, Freidson [1970a:368] has noted that "Autonomy is the prize sought after by virtually all occupational groups, for it represents freedom from direction from others, freedom to perform one's work the way one desires."

Freedom to decide how work is done is rated as "very important" by a majority of workers [Quinn et al., 1974:16]. Documentation of attempts to exercise control in this area is abundant. The restriction of output among industrial workers represents an attempt to gain some discretion [Freidson, 1970a:368]. Workers meticulously manage the time it takes to do a total job as a strategy to allow themselves autonomy in the performance of the individual tasks within the sequence [Johnson, 1974]. Informal specialization in the wiring of small electrical circuits by some construction workers originated with a belief that this particular task gave them greater independence and control of the work situation [Brewer, 1974]. In some special cases workers may bargain away autonomy in return for some other reward. Waitresses are willing to surrender some of their discretion in return for the active support of management in dealing with disorderly customers [Hearn and Stoll, 1975]. It appears that part of the reason why occupations aspire to professional status is because of the autonomy this position usually confers.

Individuals rate challenging tasks as one of the most strongly desired attributes of jobs [e.g., Blauner, 1964]. This seems to explain workers' attempts to redefine their roles in pursuit of more interesting tasks. Industrial workers trade jobs to alleviate monotony and to introduce some variations in their work. At the group level redefinition may involve sloughing unrewarding tasks or increasing responsibilities in more challenging areas of work. Organized medicine has recently begun to delegate some of the more routine and standard medical tasks to the newly introduced role of physician's assistant [Engel, 1973].

Attempts to maximize social and economic rewards present a fairly obvious tendency among occupational groups—even professionals [Badgley, 1975]—operating in market economies, although individual practitioners may violate the pattern. Attempts at the expansion of prerogatives and rewards are supported by the use of five broad categories of resources: expertise, legitimacy, membership, organizations, and job actions.

Expertise

The level of expert knowledge of an occupation can be a major resource. As a general rule, *the more esoteric and circumscribed the knowledge base of an occupation the more likely it will be able to resist external control and define its own work* [e.g., Freidson, 1961; Moore, 1970; Eliott, 1972]. For occupations which claim professional status, expert knowledge serves to legitimize both authority and autonomy. The authority to advise and proscribe for clients is grounded in superior knowledge. Likewise, freedom from lay evaluation and control derives from the discrepancy between the expertise of the professional and the ignorance of the client. The authority of expertise is problematic and must constantly be verified [Freidson, 1960, 1968; Wrong, 1976]. One not unexpected consequence is that occupations and professions devote internal resources into protecting their monopoly over a body of knowledge or skills. This may take the form of attempts to "mystify" the knowledge through the use of jargon and by maintaining control over who may practice (by dominating the licensing process or apprenticeship programs) and by prohibiting practitioners from public criticism of each other [Berlant, 1975].

Despite such efforts there appears to be a general decline of public confidence in the expert authority of groups such as medicine [Haug and Sussman, 1969; Lyons, 1977], possibly due to the disappearance of the conditions which generated this authority. One obvious cause is the improving level of education of the general population [Lopata, 1976], but there are also problems in the application of knowledge which have contributed to the erosion of confidence. Because expert knowledge is always somewhat imperfect, practitioners are sometimes wrong, or uncertain, or have divided opinions. This suggests that *the saliency of the power of expert knowledge increases with the perceived certainty of the knowledge base.*

Legitimacy

Occupational groups may be able to establish legitimacy to perform a particular set of activities. Once established, this legitimacy subsequently functions to protect the group from encroachment. For example, physicians have firmly codified their position (vis-à-vis patients) at the head of the health case hierarchy [Freidson, 1970b; Tagliacozzo and Mauksch, 1972]. This has effectively limited the ability of other occupations such as nursing to expand its diagnostic and therapeutic role. Driscoll [1972] reports that this problem even surfaces in dealing with legislators because they share the prevailing stereotype of the subordination of nurse to physician.

Membership and Scarcity

Several authors have explored the relationship between the size of the occupation and power [e.g., Akers and Quinney, 1968; Kronus, 1976a]. They contend that larger occupations tend to be more powerful. It would appear, however, that it is not size *per se*; it is rather a question of scarcity. Other things being equal, *power is enhanced when the number of qualified practitioners falls short of demand.* Occupations themselves verify this premise when they act to limit membership or increase demand. At an interpersonal level, practitioners within an occupation who are more difficult to replace should be in a more advantageous position than those who are easily replaced. Lengermann [1976] provides confirmation in his study of CPAs, which showed increases in autonomy associated with difficulty of replacement.

Trade and Professional Associations, Unions

These groups function to enhance group interests especially by lobbying and to protect the group from external control [Haug and Sussman, 1973]. In the role of occupational advocate, unions and associations play an active role pressing for special interest legislation [Strauss, 1963; Akers, 1968; Gilb, 1966]. The American Medical Association has a long record of success in promoting or preventing legislation which would have an impact on medical practitioners [e.g., Harris, 1966; Stevens, 1971; Rayak, 1967]. When union members are compared to non-union members, certain patterns emerge. In strictly economic terms, members of unions earn significantly more than comparable non-union workers—wage differentials range between 17 and 43 percent depending upon the specific occupation [Ryscavage, 1974]. In addition, union workers enjoy greater fringe benefits such as vacations, have better health and job upgrading benefits and more well-defined grievance procedures [Levinson, 1974:179].

Strikes and Job Actions

The strike represents a resource available to most organized occupations, although some public employees such as teachers, police, and fire fighters are legally prohibited from striking in many areas. In 1972, there were 5,010 work stoppages involving over 1,700,000 workers [U.S. Department of Labor, 1974:381].

An interesting pattern of accommodation occurring in recent years is the union contract which circumscribes the issues on which a group may officially strike. The most extreme case of a union surrendering the right to strike was found in a contract signed by the United Steelworkers which contained an absolute non-strike clause. This may be viewed as the culmination of a long-term trend in which some unions have negotiated away the strike in return for economic benefits. This clearly reflects dominant priorities on the part of the adversaries, labor unions are concerned with economic matters while management seeks to assure uninterrupted production schedules.

Increasingly, the strike is a tactic being used by white collar and professional occupations. College professors, lawyers, physicians, nurses, and social workers have all been involved in job actions within the last four or five years. Professional groups have brought client-care and professional matters as well as economic issues to the bargaining table. Legal Aid attorneys in New York City, for example, struck for salary, a case load limit, support services, and continuity of services so a client would see the same lawyer for the duration of a case [Oppenheimer, 1975:34]. This strategy, however, is not without its drawbacks.

Professional claims to prestige and autonomy are based in part on the assertion of the primacy of client welfare, and withholding service can undermine this professional image. It is not surprising that ambivalence toward unionization and strikes exists at both the individual and occupational level. This dilemma is exemplified by this query by the American Nursing Association: "If the ANA truly becomes a labor union, how far can it get with professional issues: Can collective bargaining solve the problems of professional nursing?" [Koncel, 1977:73].

THE OCCUPATIONAL ENVIRONMENT

It is evident that the analysis of occupational roles must examine relations with the competing interest groups that inhabit their environment. The list of groups which must be considered is lengthy, and includes allied occupations, clients or customers, consumer advocate groups, employers, government (executive, judicial, legislative), insurers, the media, political parties, publics, and vendors. Any of these groups (whether organized or not) can possess resources which enable it to affect the structure of occupational or professional roles. Obviously not all occupations interact with every one of these groups, but each influences occupational roles in specific situations.

Clients or Customers

Any occupation involving the direct provision of goods or services invests some resources in the hands of their clients or customers. The idea of *patronage* in the arts is an extreme case of consumer control. When the relationship is face-to-face and on a fee-for-services basis (e.g., dentists, prostitutes, barbers and auto mechanics) consumers will have three primary resources at their disposal: income, by withholding the decision to purchase; referrals; and, in special cases the threat of malpractice. When the relationship is face-to-face and members of the occupation are salaried (e.g., teachers, waiters, police, salespeople) the power of clients is altered and somewhat neutralized, for they must act through employers, who are then more likely to affect the career.

Direct fee-for-service practitioners must attract and maintain a clientele. Each customer is important both as a source of income and as a possible reference for other clients. People seeking services and help frequently depend upon what Freidson [1960]—in his discussion of medical specialties—labeled "lay referral systems," informal networks of friends, relatives and neighbors who provide information, leads, and evaluations of practitioners [Freidson, 1961; Langlie, 1977].

Therefore, customers (whether they realize it or not) influence the manner in which occupational tasks are performed. As Goode has noted, "they determine the survival of a profession or specialty, as well as the career success of particular professionals" [Goode, 1957:198]. Concessions to clients may involve no more than attempts to display a pleasing demeanor. Or it may be more consequential if client expectations are able to determine the form and content of tasks. Customers' wishes define some of the tasks of prostitutes [Bryan, 1965] and salespeople [Miller, 1964], masseurs [Velarde and Warlick, 1973], waitresses [Karen, 1962] and physicians. Freidson [1960:378] notes that the prescription of placebos to hypochondriacs is one possible index of the power of clients. The demands may extend to pressure toward illegal behavior. Stockbrokers may use illegal tactics or forbidden information to improve their client's profits [Evan and Levin, 1966].

Occupations may develop techniques to neutralize the potential power of the consumer. Members of occupations may deliberately withhold information from clients [Millman, 1977; Quint, 1965]. Dentists, during their socialization, learn a personal style of behavior which is intended to convey the image of calmness and self-control [Linn, 1967]. The traditional professional prohibition against advertising was a tactic in the control of information; to advertise implies that the potential client has enough information about the competence of the various practitioners to choose among them [Greenwood, 1957]. Johnson [1972] and Larson [1977] argue that the concept of professionalism itself can be viewed as a nineteenth century innovation to control the producer-consumer relationship to the advantage of the occupation.

A more direct response found among service occupations is the attempt to manage the client relationship to their own advantage. As Mennerick [1974] has argued, the goal of this behavior may be directly financial (increasing sales, tips, or commissions), or simply a struggle to be free from constraints imposed by clients. There is evidence of this among taxi drivers [Heslin, 1967, 1968; Davis, 1959]; attorneys [Reed, 1969]; milkmen [Bigus, 1972]; employment counselors [Martinez, 1968]; waiters and waitresses [Whyte, 1948; Butler and Snizek, 1976] and even fortune-tellers [Tatro, 1974]. This process involves attempts to direct the relationship by initiating the interaction, defining the role of the client, and setting the parameters of the services to be provided. Members of occupational groups may even cultivate "friendship" with clients for use as a resource, hoping that they will express their regard by purchasing extras or paying their bills on time [Bigus, 1972:153]. When successful it frees the service worker from subordination to the consumer. It would seem that *generally, attempts at the management and manipulation of customers tends to increase with dependence upon them for rewards, and that the potential for client manipulation is enhanced by heterogeneity and lack of organization among customers.*

Organizationally based service occupations are more insulated from client power, but are not immune because client dissatisfaction can be referred to the employer. People lodge complaints about treatment by the police [Hudson, 1970], or about buses being behind schedule [Slosar, 1973], or about the speed of table service [Whyte, 1948]. Workers obviously cannot ignore the client, but not all clients need to be treated the same. Postal clerks [Goodsell, 1976], medical personnel [Sudnow, 1967; Roth, 1972a, 1972b] and bus drivers [Toren, 1973] respond differently to different types of people. In most cases, *higher status clients tend to receive more care, better service, or more deferential treatment.* A power perspective suggests one possible interpretation; these are the categories of people perceived to be most likely to file complaints with employers, and hence are accorded special treatment in order to avoid sanctions.

Malpractice suits are another type of resource at the disposal of clients. The legal right to sue a professional is not new; what is new is the widespread use of this strategy. The American Bar Association reports that the number of malpractice suits filed against lawyers doubled between 1972 and 1977, and are expected to double again over the next five years [Scott, 1977:74]. Malpractice has had some direct consequences for the shape of professional practice. In medicine, it has taken the form of "defensive medicine" with an emphasis upon detailed record keeping, more comprehensive work-ups and tests, and a reluctance to innovate or to adopt new procedures [Hershey, 1972]. Among lawyers, it will probably mean certain common practices such as representing both parties in property transfers and uncontested divorces will be abandoned because it leaves the attorney vulnerable to "conflict of interest" suits. In most professions it is probably too soon to assess the full impact of the recent burgeoning of malpractice suits.

Employing Organizations

A major historical trend has been a contraction of the proportion of the labor force employed as independent entrepreneurs. Most occupations are comprised of people who are employees of organizations. In fact, large numbers of clerical, sales, medical and engineering occupations have been generated by the very growth of large-scale organizations. The nature of employment in a market economy places major resources in the hands of the employer; hiring, promotion, termination, income, and tools are all controlled to some extent by employers.

Any such concentration of resources in a single group creates the potential for rigid social control. In a large number of organizations this potential has been articulated by an administrative ideology which has placed a premium on the standardization of tasks, narrow specialization, and the centralization of authorty. This has resulted in the creation of a large number of blue collar and clerical occupations organized around a few routine, repetitive operations performed under close supervision. Telephone operators are called upon to repeat predetermined speeches while supervisors listen [Langer, 1970]; assembly-line welders repeat exactly the same task on 48 cars an hour, eight hours a day [Terkel, 1972:221].

Although it is common to assert that the organizational division of labor is rationally enacted to improve efficiency and reduce labor costs there are those who argue that the occupational structure may also reflect other motives and other goals [e.g., Doeringer and Piore, 1971; Marglin, 1974]. A major point is that technology does not necessarily create the labor system; it merely defines the range of possibilities. And the ultimate reason for adopting a technological or social innovation may be to enhance the potential for social control. This may be observed in a recent analysis of the evolution of job specialization, plant-specific job, job ladders and wage-incentive systems over the last century.

In the latter part of the nineteenth century, employers faced the problem of the homogenization and "proletarianization" of the work force which was reflected in militancy, industrial conflict, and a growing labor movement with the potential for worker organization and collective action on a large scale. Partly to counter this trend, employers fostered the proliferation of narrow, specialized occupations [Reich, Gordon and Edwards, 1963]. This had the consequence of creating divisions within the working class. Such divisions were further encouraged by piece-work wage incentive systems designed to increase output, and to create social distance between the "efficient" and "inefficient" workers [Stone, 1974:72]. Positions were arranged in "job ladders" of increasing prestige and pay which became a chain of possible promotions. Stone [1974:73–75] argues this did not reflect any true increases in complexity, but rather was a technique to create a sense of vertical mobility and to throw workers into competition with each other for advancement. Thus, the *organizational division of labor may represent an attempt to impose social control or to weaken the power of occupational groups,* in addition to being motivated by considerations of efficiency and effectiveness.

The employer's capability to exert control is modified by a number of factors. The relative power of the occupation is important. So too is the history and evolution of the occupation. As a general rule, *occupations with craft, entrepreneur or professional roots tend to enjoy greater autonomy than occupations originating within organizations.* There is a sizeable literature here, including work with scientists [Kornhauser, 1962; Miller, 1967], printers [Lipset, Trow and Coleman, 1956; Sykes, 1960], and physicians [Engel, 1970]. All, to some extent, share certain features: a specialized expert knowledge, a sense of occupational community, and a training period which inculcates an emphasis upon autonomy and individual internalized standards of performance and accountability. Practitioners bring such orientations to their employment where they tend to come into conflict with the organizational emphasis on hierarchy, coordination and standardized procedures [Benson, 1973; Hall, 1968].

The use of employer power is also reduced by the nature and specifiability of organizational goals. As a general rule, the *autonomy of occupations is greater in organizations serving multiple goals or ambiguous goals.* Single-purpose organizations with clearly defined goals tend to attempt to impose the most stringent controls upon its employees. Military organizations provide a good example of this; the specification of behavior is greater during periods of conflict when the organization is mobilized toward a single objective than it is during peace-time when goals are less tangible. Ambiguity exists in those cases where there is no consensus about goals, or where procedures cannot be specified in advance [Perrow, 1979; Van de Ven et al., 1976]. This occurs in schools. Educational objectives are not easily defined, and there is not much agreement on appropriate methods of instruction. Consequently, classroom teachers have been able to maintain independence [Lortie, 1969].

Allied Occupations

Most, if not all, modern occupations are linked socially, technically, or economically to other occupations. For example, a successful career in burglary depends upon contacts with "partners" and "tipsters" and "fences" and bail bondsmen [Shover, 1972]. Physicians depend on each other for information about new drugs [Coleman et al., 1966]. Relationships among occupations may be casual or highly formalized, but the presence of such ties invests power in these groups. Reliance upon members of some other occupation for customer referrals is found in its most extreme form among what Freidson [1960] has called "dependent practices," those which subsist on referrals [Shortell, 1973]. Radiologists, pathologists, and anesthesiologists are examples [Katz, 1968]. Referrals are not always sought after as is evident in the case of prepaid group medical practices where referrals become a punishment rather than a reward because they increase the workload without any compensatory increase in income [see Freidson, 1975: Ch. 5].

The relative power of allied occupations is a function of dependence upon them, and the availability of alternatives. Interdependence in actual operations is shown by Crozier's [1967] analysis of maintenance workers and the machine operators who must depend upon them to do repair work. Maintenance men are consequently very powerful in the shops by virtue of the control of expert knowledge. Subordinates in organizations are sometimes able to exercise unusual power because they perform some necessary service for superiors. Attendants in mental hospitals were once very powerful because professionals depended upon them for control of patients [Scheff, 1961].

Publics

In the present context, publics may be defined as aggregates of people who are affected by the activities of an occupation and who are able to take some action which registers their response. The response may be voting, writing a letter, buying (or not buying) a book or purchasing a ticket to a performance. Publics are the ultimate consumers, but it is usually a remote and impersonal relationship. And yet, the sum of these individual acts can influence the structure of such occupational roles as professional athlete, member of the performing arts, political officeholder, journalist and novelist.

Members of all these occupations, to some extent, must cater to the preferences of their publics, or attempt to influence them. Sports in America offers many instances of responses to perceptions of public demand. Currently, professional hockey is dominated by the belief that fans want aggressive play punctuated by fistfights, and the players have moved in that direction. Dramatic increases in attendance serve to verify the belief [e.g., Gammons, 1977]. Likewise, the commercial success of particular books, films, plays, newspapers, or performances influences the manner subsequently in which these artist and support occupations are performed. Martorella [1977:364], who has pointed out that the nature of roles in the opera are related to the shifting tastes and socio-economic composition of the audiences, argues that

All energy seems to go toward incorporating new developments in lighting and stagecraft and developing an experience for the audience. These innovations are not innovations in opera as a musical form; they are undertaken primarily with reference to the restaging and redesigning of nineteenth century composition. This has, undoubtedly, had an impact on the meaning of interpretation as well as the social position of the performer.

While members of such occupations must be somewhat sensitive to their publics, there is a tendency for them to believe that the public lacks an understanding of the finer points of their work or their performance [e.g., Becker, 1963; Charnofsky, 1974]. This reflects the fact that *practitioners often hold values and standards different from those* of the public because of their specialized and esoteric training [cf., Gans, 1966]. These practitioners frequently attempt to impose their standards. It is usually accomplished with the assistance of certain allied occupations (viz., the occupational roles of critic, and of teacher). All three usually share the same standards and attempt to impose their standards on the public through their domination of the media and the classrooms.

Some occupational groups are also sensitive to a more generalized public. School teachers have always had to be concerned with public response to their demeanor in both the classroom and in private. The same is true of politicians. *Occupations typically respond to general publics by attempting to obscure physically their behavior from view.* Classroom doors are closed physically or symbolically, as are the doors of massage parlors. Legislators' decisions are made in the privacy of the caucus room or the cloakroom. The idea of "executive sessions" shields public administrators from the public.

Government

Many agencies of government at the state, local, and federal level may define certain aspects of occupational roles. Control is accomplished both by direct, deliberate intervention (via statutes, licensing, judicial rulings, etc.), and more indirectly by the manner in which government functions to protect the public welfare. In other cases special interest groups attempt to use the powers of the state to their own advantage. Then governmental involvement in occupational affairs merely represents an indirect form of social control by some third party.

Legislatures set criteria for work, mandate minimum performance standards, and establish procedures for the handling and processing of products, all of which impact on occupational roles. For example, food-handling regulations define the tasks of cooks, butchers, restaurant workers, while safety regulations define the schedules and tasks of truck drivers, airline pilots and coal miners. Law enforcement is always problematic for statutes designed to protect workers for the public may be circumvented when other groups have sufficient resources. For example, Sherrill [1977] argues that truckers drive unsafe vehicles and work unsafe hours because the power of the trucking industry in Washington blocks effective enforcement.

A large number of occupations are licensed by the states. In this category are such diverse groups as pharmacists and plumbers, masseurs and morticians, cab drivers and CPAs. One motivation is to establish standards where the public safety is at risk. Hence, licensing boards control access to the occupation, establish and enforce educational requirements, fee-splitting, confidentiality and eliminating unqualified practitioners. The history of licensing reveals that it is common for the regulated group to control these boards [Cohen, 1973; 1975; Shimberg et al., 1973; Akers, 1968]. Then those regulated have the potential to be able to use licensing to enhance their own interests. Control of licensing boards limits external involvement in internal matters. Control of access can be used to limit the number of practitioners and hence increase income [Berlant, 1975]. Licensing is thus sometimes a mechanism for enhancing the prerogatives and rewards of an occupation or profession.

The courts increasingly are playing a decisive role in defining the parameters of occupations. Accounting, for example, has seen its tasks and obligations expanded over the last decade by a series of court decisions dealing with the interrelationship between corporate clients and the investing public [Montagna, 1971]. Rulings now in effect hold that CPAs must go beyond their traditional, narrowly circumscribed jobs of examining financial statements to determine if they have been prepared following generally accepted accounting practices; they must concern themselves with the fairness of such disclosures, and accountants have a right and obligation to delve into corporate matters not included in these annual audits [Business Week, 1976]. It is clear that the courts are asserting that the primary responsibility of the accounting professions is to the investor, not the client.

One of the single most profound and far-reaching court actions occurred in 1975 when the U.S. Supreme Court decided that lawyers were not automatically exempt from the Sherman Anti-Trust Act by virtue of being a self-regulating "learned profession." It ruled that the standard fee schedules which had been in use in the legal profession since 1795 constituted a "classic illustration of price-fixing" [Kohlmeier, 1976]. Although the Court stopped short of eliminating all distinctions between professions and other business activities, it is clear that many traditional patterns in law, medicine, architecture, and engineering will be open to judicial review. Whatever the outcomes, it is apparent that the courts will be determining a number of important aspects of professional roles.

Government funds in the form of grants, subsidies, contracts and fellowships are a significant source of income in the sciences, medicine, and the arts. The scope of this funding can be quite dramatic. The National Institute of Health supports 75 percent of all bio-medical research in medical schools and 40 percent of all university research [Gustafson, 1975:1060]. The implications of this are neatly put by Krohn [1972:65–66] in his analysis of science, but may apply generally to any occupation which depends upon government money:

> The dangers in a unique dependence on government support seem more obvious; how can a science retain a critical measure of autonomy, self-discipline, and a sense

of direction? It is probably safe to say no government has yet supported science on a modern scale and allowed it broad and intellectually autonomous development. The United States certainly does not seem to be immune to a narrow and direct use of science on government's terms.

At a subtle level the competition for government funds may influence scientists (consciously or not) to modify their work or their methods to bring them in line with perceptions of governmental objectives. In a recent study of academic social scientists, a majority admitted altering their research topics and techniques in response to shifts in government priorities [Useem, 1976:154].

A more clearly defined form of governmental control is exercised when eligibility for public funds is made contingent upon the adoption of certain tasks. This is nowhere more evident than in the health related occupations. In New York the State Board of Health made participation in continuing education a requirement for dentists if they wished to treat Medicare patients. In 1971 the Public Health Service Act required that the curriculum in colleges of pharmacy place greater emphasis upon clinical work in order to qualify for federal assistance [Ruane, 1975]. It appears that these cases are symptomatic of expanding governmental involvement in defining and circumscribing occupational roles. Some instances signify a growing concern for the protection of the public welfare, while other activity is best seen as a response to the pressures of special interests.

Other Control Agents

A number of other groups have the power to define the parameters of occupational roles, but the relationships have generally been ignored by sociologists. Political parties and manufacturers are illustrative. Political parties have a direct impact on some specific occupations. The resource is nomination for elective and appointive office. The role of political parties is readily evident in the competition for access to the standard political careers (legislators, governors, mayors, sheriffs, etc.), as well as in quasi-political positions in the diplomatic corps or in various regulatory bodies or in cabinet appointments [Mitchell, 1958].

Politics may also intervene in "non-political" occupations such as police administration, or in the selection and advancement of judges. Judicial appointments, for example, are political in many states. At the national level, senators by tradition have the right to nominate or veto appointments to the federal bench [Marro, 1977; see also Goulden, 1974].

Often overlooked is the fact that the manufacturers and distributors of raw materials, parts, or products may exert control over occupational roles. The pricing policies of auto manufacturers put pressure on dealers and sales people for high sales volume and do not encourage quality servicing of cars [Farberman, 1975]. In contrast, suppliers may make more impersonal decisions based on criteria such as efficiency or profit which also serve to define occupational roles.

Retail pharmacists, for example, are strongly affected by the actions of drug firms. Developments such as pre-packaging, standardized dosages and a system of direct promotion of drugs to physicians have degraded the retail pharmacist from a compounder of prescriptions to a dispenser of pre-packaged items [Shaw, 1972].

INTRA-OCCUPATIONAL RELATIONS

Occupations and professions are not necessarily homogeneous groups. Bucher and Strauss [1961:326] made this point when they stated that professions are "loose amalgamations of segments pursuing different objectives in different manners and more or less delicately held together under a common name at a particular period in history."

This description may apply to some extent to all occupations. There are many sources of internal differentiation. Background factors such as religion [Rothman et al., 1972], different work settings [Kronus, 1976b; Kendall, 1965; Wilensky, 1964] and educational experiences [Corwin, 1961] have all been shown to contribute to the internal heterogeneity of occupations and professions.

When the various segments of an occupation/profession have unequal power, there may be internal struggles over tasks or codes of ethics or training or other aspects of the role. Reichstein [1965] has argued that the ethical prohibition against the solicitation of clients is imposed on the legal profession by those who enjoy the luxury of having a stable clientele. In blue collar occupations, "rank and file" concerns with working conditions and local grievances may not find expression in union leadership, and in turn generate "unauthorized" wildcat strikes such as the well-publicized one at Lordstown [Aronowitz, 1973].

The various segments of an occupation individually and collectively control resources which are salient because of the interdependence of members of occupations [Garnier, 1973]. O. Hall's [1946, 1948, 1949] classic examination of careers in medicine serves to document the power of colleagues: establishing a practice, getting known in the community, developing a clientele through referrals, hospital privileges, and appointments in the local medical society all depend to some extent upon the support of fellow practitioners. In academic positions people depend upon colleagues for employment, information, references, the solicitation of papers, appointments in professional associations, and invitations to meetings and conferences [Caplow and McGee, 1958]. There is a great deal of internal exchange of information about job opportunities in the construction industry [Graves, 1970]. This is a condition which has the potential to produce a counter-tendency toward homogeneity within occupations because of the constant selection process going on within the occupations; those whose values, beliefs, behavior, or social characteristics differ from those of the majority of the occupation may find themselves at a disadvantage.

The idea of interdependence influences the kind of social control which is exercised informally. The importance of informal social control by colleagues and co-workers was established by the Hawthorne studies, and has been reaffirmed in a number of more recent works. A consistent pattern emerging from this work is that *the intensity of informal social control varies directly with the degree of interdependence among members of the occupation.* It is not always easy to conceptualize interdependence, but it does appear to be evident in occupations which involve *personal risk, collective rewards,* or *gate-keepers.*

Stringent internal social control is a common characteristic of occupations which combine physical danger and reliance upon co-workers. These are typical: police work [Westley, 1956; Stoddard, 1968], high steel ironworkers [Haas, 1972, 1974, 1977], the military [Weiss, 1967; Stouffer et al., 1949; Shils, 1950] and mine workers [Gouldner, 1954; Lucas, 1969]. In each, senior co-workers assume responsibility for socialization and social control of recruits. A common feature of this process is to subject the newcomer to harassment, or even personal humiliation and degradation, designed to assess the apprentice's mettle and reliability under pressure. The rationale is that this is the best technique of anticipating behavior in a future crisis where their actions could endanger the lives of co-workers.

A somewhat different form of interdependence exists where individual rewards are based upon group performance or teamwork. This situation prevails in team sports such as hockey [Faulkner, 1974] and where there are collaborative performances such as musicians [Becker, 1963; Stebbins, 1966]. Individual performances can never be separated completely from the actions of others and these occupations tend to manifest a good deal of co-worker control.

An unusual power relationship prevails in some artistic, athletic and scientific occupations where colleagues are expected to judge performance or a product. Scientists must publish their research findings; athletes covet recognition in the form of "all-star" designations; awards for performance such as the Oscar for film actors and the Tony for theater actors are based on peer judgments. These colleagues are often referred to as "gate-keepers." It appears that the process of colleague evaluation is a mixture of universalistic and particularistic criteria but the potential for subtle pressure toward ideological or paradigmatic conformity does exist. A number of more formal, organized colleague review bodies are designed to monitor performance. Examples include internal review boards in police departments, grievance committees of state bar associations, and professional standards review organizations (PSROs) and utilization review committees in hospitals. At the individual level these groups attempt to assess the quality of performance, but only the most gross and visible deviance is sanctioned by internal review bodies. For example, in medicine the highly visible narcotics violations account for nearly one half the disciplinary actions [Derbyshire, 1969]. One interpretation suggested by the control and negotiation perspective is that a primary function of internal review bodies is to act as a buffer against the imposition of control by external agents [cf., Goode, 1957]. In general, however, it appears that *the greater the dependence upon colleagues for access or advancement the greater the behavioral and attitudinal homogeneity.*

The importance of homogeneity seems to increase with the degree of interdependence because it contributes to the predictability and reliability of the membership. Behavioral and attitudinal homogeneity is also a source of power [cf., Berlant, 1976; Akers and Quinney, 1968]. Internal competition is reduced; the mobilization of resources (money, letter-writing) is facilitated; and external encroachment is inhibited. Thus, internal control of individual members may be exercised as a means of achieving collective power.

CONCLUSION

The evidence of these patterns confirms the analytic potential of a power and negotiational framework. Deriving from this is a recognition that occupational and professional members collectively and individually act to enhance their prerogatives (autonomy and challenge) and rewards. The physical and intellectual tasks which define an occupation may thus have symbolic and economic value in the realization of these goals. The physician's exclusive legal right to prescribe drugs is much more than an activity related to the alleviation of suffering; it is a jealously guarded key to prestige and income and power and the position of the M.D. at the apex of the health care delivery system.

This perspective also locates work in a complex social, economic and political network of individuals and groups also pursuing prerogatives and rewards. They are attempting (deliberately or not) to protect their own interests or seeking to constrain the roles of others as a means of achieving their own goals. The division of labor at any point in time reflects, in part, the outcome of negotiations among these units. Negotiations may take the form of deliberate bargaining and accommodation or may involve more subtle manipulation and social control. The success of negotiation and social control ultimately is influenced by the distribution of power (in the form of resources) which affects either careers in the occupation or the physical/intellectual operations of the work.

Power is also exercised internally. Subgroups have unequal power and power is used to generate pressure toward homogeneity which contributes to predictability and reliability. Homogeneity may also be seen as a means of increasing the power of a group vis-à-vis external groups.

The patterns which have emerged may not qualify as empirically verified generalizations but do point the way to certain areas of research. Consequently, the analysis of the occupational division of labor at the structural level and role behavior at the individual level promises to be enriched by the inclusion of an examination of the dynamics of negotiation and social control. This perspective promises to contribute to a more comprehensive analysis of occupational role which will also continue to consider processes such as technological evolution, shifting socio-cultural values, the accumulation of knowledge, and demographic change.

REFERENCES

Akers, Ronald L. 1968. "The professional associations and the legal regulation of practice." *Law and Society Review* 11 (May):463–82.

Akers, Ronald L. and R. Quinney. 1968. "Differential organization of health professions: a comparative analysis." *American Sociological Review* 33 (February):104–21.

Aronowitz, Stanley. 1973. *False Promises*. New York: McGraw-Hill.

Badgley, Robin F. 1975. "Health worker strikes: social and economic bases of conflict." *International Journal of Health Services* 5 (November):9–17.

Becker, Howard S. 1963. *Outsiders*. New York: Free Press.

Benson, J. Kenneth. 1973. "The analysis of bureaucratic-professional conflict: functional versus dialectical approaches." *The Sociological Quarterly* 14 (Summer):376–94.

Berlant, Jeffrey L. 1976. *Profession and Monopoly*. Berkeley: University of California Press.

Bierstedt, Robert. 1950. "An analysis of social power." *American Sociological Review* 15 (December):730–38.

Bigus, Odia. 1972. "The milkman and his customer." *Urban Life and Culture* 1 (July):131–65.

Blauner, Robert. 1964. *Alienation and Freedom*. Chicago: University of Chicago Press.

Blumer, Herbert. 1969. *Symbolic Interactionism: Perspective and Method*. Englewood Cliffs, N.J.: Prentice-Hall.

Brewer, John D. 1974. "Informal occupational specialization: the case of the wireman." Pp. 215–23 in Phyllis L. Stewart and Muriel G. Cantor (eds.), *Varieties of Work Experience*. Cambridge, Mass.: Schenkman.

Bryan, James H. 1965. "Apprenticeships in prostitution." *Social Problems* 12 (Winter):287–97.

Bucher, Rue and Anselm Strauss, 1961. "Professions in process." *American Journal of Sociology* 66 (January):325–34.

Business Week. 1976. "The troubled professions." *Business Week* (August 16):126–38.

Butler, Suellen R. and William E. Snizek. 1976. "The waitress-diner relationship: a multimethod approach to the study of subordinate influence." *Sociology of Work Occupations* 3 (May):209–22.

Caplow, Theodore and Reese J. McGee. 1958. *The Academic Marketplace*. New York: Science Editions.

Charnofsky, Harold. 1974. "Ballplayers, occupational image, and the maximization of profit." Pp. 262–73 in Phyllis L. Stewart and Muriel G. Cantor (eds.), *Varieties of Work Experience*. Cambridge, Mass.: Schenkman.

Cohen, Harris S. 1973. "Professional licensure, organization behavior, and the public interest." *Milbank Memorial Fund Quarterly* 51 (Winter):73–88.

———. 1975. "Regulatory politics and American medicine." *American Behavioral Scientist* 19 (September/October):122–36.

Coleman, James S., Elihu Katz, and Herbert Menzel. 1966. *Medical Innovation: A Diffusion Study*. Indianapolis: Bobbs-Merrill.

Corwin, Ronald G. 1961. "Role conception and career aspiration: a study of identity in nursing." *The Sociological Quarterly* 2 (April):69–86.

Crozier, Michel. 1967. *The Bureaucratic Phenomenon*. Chicago: University of Chicago Press.

Davis, Fred. 1959. "The cabdriver and his fare: facets of a fleeting relationship." *American Journal of Sociology* 65 (September):158–65.

Derbyshire, Robert C. 1969. *Medical Licensure and Discipline in the United States.* Baltimore: Johns Hopkins Press.

Doeringer, Peter B. and Michael J. Piore. 1971. *Internal Labor Markets and Manpower Analysis.* Lexington, Mass.: D. C. Heath.

Driscoll, V. 1972. "Liberating nursing practice." *Nursing Outlook* 20 (January):24–28.

Elliott, Philip. 1972. *The Sociology of the Professions.* New York: Herder and Herder.

Emerson, Richard M. 1962. "Power-dependence relations." *American Sociological Review* 27 (February):31–41.

Engel, Gloria V. 1970. "Professional autonomy and bureaucratic organization." *Administrative Science Quarterly* 15 (March):12–21.

———. 1973. "Social factors affecting work satisfaction of the physician's assistant." *Sociological Review Monograph* 20 (December):245–61.

Evan, William M. and Ezra G. Levin. 1966. "Status-set and role-set conflicts of the stockbroker." *Social Forces* 45 (September):73–83.

Farberman, Harvey A. 1975. "A criminogenic market structure: the automobile industry." *The Sociological Quarterly* 16 (Autumn):438–57.

Faulkner, Robert R. 1974. "Making violence by doing work: selves, situations, and the world of professional hockey." *Sociology of Work and Occupations* 1 (August):288–312.

Freidson, Eliot. 1960. "Client control and medical practice." *American Journal of Sociology* 65 (January):374–82.

———. 1961. *Patients Views of Medical Care.* New York: Russell Sage.

———. 1968. "The impurity of professional authority." In Howard A. Becker et al. (eds.), *Institutions and the Person.* Chicago: Aldine.

———. 1970a. *Profession of Medicine.* New York: Dodd-Mead.

———. 1970b. *Professional Dominance: The Social Structure of Medical Care.* Chicago: Aldine.

———. 1975. *Doctoring Together: A Study of Professional Social Control.* New York: Elsevier.

———. 1976. "The division of labor as social interaction." *Social Problems* 23 (February):304–13.

Gammons, Peter. 1977. "Wild Willie gets a new lease on life." *Sports Illustrated* 47 (November 28):28–33.

Gans, Herbert J. 1966. "Popular culture in America: social problem in a mass society or social asset in a pluralist society?" Pp. 582–98 in Howard Becker (ed.), *Social Problems.* New York: Wiley.

Garnier, Maurice A. 1973. "Power and ideological conformity: a case study." *American Journal of Sociology* 79 (September):343–63.

Gilb, Corrine L. 1966. *Hidden Hierarchies: The Professions and Government.* New York: Harper and Row.

Goode, William J. 1957. "Community within a community: the professions." *American Sociological Review* 22 (April):194–200.

———. 1960. "Encroachment, charlatanism, and the emerging profession: psychology, medicine and sociology." *American Sociological Review* 25 (December):902–14.

Goodsell, Charles T. 1976. "Cross-cultural comparison of behavior of postal clerks towards clients." *Administrative Science Quarterly* 21 (March):140–50.

Goulden, Joseph C. 1974. *The Benchwarmers: the Private World of the Powerful Federal Judges.* New York: Weybright and Talley.

Gouldner, Alvin W. 1954. *Patterns of Industrial Bureaucracy.* New York: Free Press.

Graves, Bennie. 1970. "Particularism, exchange and organizational efficiency: a case study of construction industry." *Social Forces* 49 (September):72–81.

Greenwood, Ernest. 1957. "Attributes of a profession." *Social Work* 2 (July):45–55.

Gustafson, Thane. 1975. "The controversy over peer review." *Science* 190 (December 12):1060–66.

Haas, Jack. 1972. "Binging: education control among high steel ironworkers." *American Behavioral Scientist* 16 (September/October):27–34.

———. 1974. "The stages of the high-steel ironworker apprentice career." *The Sociological Quarterly* 15 (Winter):93–108.

———. 1977. "Learning real feelings: a study of high steel ironworkers reactions to fear and danger." *Sociology of Work and Occupations* 4 (May):147–70.

Hall, Oswald. 1946. "Informal organization of the medical profession." *Canadian Journal of Economics and Political Science* 12 (February):30–41.

———. 1948. "The stages of a medical career." *American Journal of Sociology* 53 (March):327–36.

———. 1949. "Types of medical careers." *American Journal of Sociology* 55 (November):243–53.

Hall, Peter M. 1972. "A symbolic interactionist analysis of politics." *Sociological Inquiry* 42 (3–4):35–75.

Hall, Richard H. 1968. "Professionalization and Bureaucratization." *American Sociological Review* 33 (February):92–104.

Harris, Richard A. 1966. *A Sacred Trust.* New York: New American Library.

Haug, Marie and Marvin Sussman. 1969. "Professional autonomy and the revolt of the client." *Social Problems* 17 (Fall):153–61.

Haug, Marie and Marvin Sussman. 1973. "Professionalism and unionism: a jurisdictional dispute?" Pp. 89–104 in E. Freidson (ed.), *The Professions and Their Prospects.* Beverly Hills: Sage.

Hearn, H. L. and Patricia Stoll. 1975. "Continuance commitment in low-status occupations: the cocktail waitress." *The Sociological Quarterly* 16 (Winter):105–14.

Henslin, James M. 1967. "Dispatched orders and the cab driver: a study in locating activities." *Social Problems* 14:424–43.

———. 1968. "Trust and the cab driver." Pp. 138–58 in M. Truzzi (ed.), *Sociology and Everyday Life.* Englewood Cliffs, N.J.: Prentice-Hall.

Hershey, Nathan. 1973. "The defensive practice of medicine: myth or reality." *Milbank Memorial Fund* 50 (January):69–97.

Hudson, James. R. 1970. "Police-citizen encounters that lead to citizen complaints." *Social Problems* 18 (Fall):179–93.

Johnson, Doyle P. 1974. "Social organization of an industrial work group: emergence and adaptation to environmental change." *The Sociological Quarterly* 15 (Winter):109–26.

Johnson, T. J. 1972. *Professions and Power.* London: Macmillan.

Karen, Robert L. 1962. "Some factors affecting tipping behavior." *Sociology and Social Research* 47 (October):68–74.

Katz, Fred E. 1968. *Autonomy and Organization: The Limits of Social Control.* New York: Random House.

Kendall, Patricia. 1965. "The relationship between medical educators and medical practitioners." *Journal of Medical Educators* 40 (January):137–215.

Klegon, Douglas. 1978. "The sociology of professions: an emerging perspective." *Sociology of Work and Occupations* 5 (August):259–83.

Kohlmeier, Louis M. 1976. "Price-fixing in the professions." *New York Times* (April 18):3F.

Koncel, Jerome A. 1977. "Hospital labor relations struggles through its own revolution." *Hospitals* 51 (April 1):69–74.

Kornhauser, William. 1962. *Scientists in Industry.* Berkeley: University of California Press.

Krause, Eliot A. 1971. *The Sociology of Occupations.* Boston: Little, Brown.

Krohn, Robert G. 1972. "Patterns of institutionalization of research." Pp. 29–66 in S. Z. Nagi and R. G. Corwin (eds.), *The Social Context of Research.* New York: Wiley.

Kronus, Carol L. 1976a. "The evolution of occupational power: an historical study of task boundaries between physicians and pharmacists." *Sociology of Work and Occupations* 3 (February):3–37.

———. 1976b. "Occupational versus organizational influences on reference group identification." *Sociology of Work and Occupations* 3 (August):303–30.

Langer, Elinor. 1970. "Inside the New York Telephone Company." *New York Review of Books* 14 (March 12):16–24.

Langlie, Jean K. 1977. "Social networks, health beliefs, and preventative health behavior." *Journal of Health and Social Behavior* 18 (September):244–59.

Larson, Magali S. 1977. *The Rise of Professionalism.* Berkeley: University of California Press.

Lengermann, Joseph J. 1976. "Exchange strengths and professional autonomy in organizations." Pp. 340–53 in M. Patricia Golden (ed.), *The Research Experience.* Itasca, Illinois: F. E. Peacock.

Levinson, Andrew. 1974. *The Working-Class Majority.* New York: Penguin.

Linn, Edwin L. 1967. "Role behaviors in two dental clinics." *Human Organization* 26 (Fall):141–48.

Lipset, Seymour M., Martin Trow, and James Coleman. 1956. *Union Democracy.* New York: Free Press.

Lopata, Helena Z. 1976. "Expertization of everyone and the revolt of the client." *The Sociological Quarterly* 17 (Autumn):435–47.

Lortie, Dan C. 1969. "The balance of control and autonomy in elementary school teaching." Pp. 1–53 in Amitai Etzioni (ed.), *The Semi-Professions and Their Organization.* New York: Free Press.

Lucas, Rex. 1969. *Men in Crisis: A Study of Mine Disaster.* New York: Basic Books.

Lyons, Richard D. 1977. "Refusal of many to heed government health advice is linked to growing distrust of authority." *New York Times* (June 12):55.

Marglin, Stephen A. 1974. "What do bosses do? The origins and functions of hierarchy in capitalist production." *Review of Radical Political Economics* 6 *(Summer): 33–60.*

Marro, Anthony. 1977. "Federal bench qualifications: merit and political connections." *New York Times* (August 14):5E.

Martinez, Thomas M. 1968. "Why employment-agency counselors lower their client's self-esteem." *Transaction* 5 (March):20–25.

Martorella, Rosanne. 1977. "The relationship between box office and repertoire: a case study of opera." *The Sociological Quarterly* 18 (Summer):354–66.

Mennerick, Lewis A. 1974. "Client typologies: a method of coping with conflict in the service worker-client relationship." *Sociology of Work and Occupations* 1 (November):396–418.

Miller, George A. 1967. "Professionals in bureaucracy: alienation among industrial scientists and engineers." *American Sociological Review* 32 (October):755–67.

Miller, Stephen J. 1964. "The social bases of sales behavior." *Social Problems* 12 (Summer):15–24.

Millman, Marcia. 1977. *The Unkindest Cut.* New York: Morrow.

Mitchell, William C. 1958. "Occupational role strains: the American elective public official." *Administrative Science Quarterly* 3 (September):211–28.

Montagna, Paul D. 1971. "The public accounting profession: organization, ideology, and social power." *American Behavioral Scientist* 14 (March–April):475–91.

———. 1977. Occupations and Society. New York: Wiley.

Moore, Wilbert E. 1970. *The Professions: Rules and Roles.* New York: Russell Sage.

Oppenheimer, Martin. 1975. "The unionization of the professional." *Social Policy* 5 (January/February):34–40.

Perrow, Charles. 1979. *Organizational Analysis: A Sociological View.* (2d Ed.) Belmont, CA: Wadsworth.

Quinn, Robert P. et al. 1974. Job Satisfaction. Is there a Trend? *Manpower Research Monograph* No. 30. Washington: U.S. Department of Labor.

Quint, Jeanne C. 1965. "Institutionalized practices of information control." *Psychiatry* 28 (May):119–32.

Rayak, Elton. 1967. *Professional Power and American Medicine: The Economics of the American Medical Association.* New York: World.

Reed, John P. 1969. "The lawyer-client: a managed relationship?" *Academy of Management Journal* 12 (March):67–80.

Reich, Michael, David Gordon, and Richard Edwards. 1963. "A theory of labor market segmentation." *American Economic Review* 53 (May):359–65.

Reichstein, Kenneth. 1965. "Ambulance chasing and the legal profession." *Social Problems* (Summer):3–17.

Ritzer, George. 1977. *Working: Conflict and Change.* 2d. Englewood Cliffs, N.J.: Prentice-Hall.

Rogers, Mary F. 1974. "Instrumental and infra-resources: the bases of power." *American Journal of Sociology* 79 (May):1418–33.

Roth, Julius A. 1972a. "Staff and client control strategies in urban hospital emergency services." *Urban Life and Culture* 1 (April):39–60.

———. 1972b. "Social contingencies of the moral evaluation and control of clientele: the case of the hospital emergency service." *American Journal of Sociology* 77 (March):839–56.

Rothman, Robert A., John H. McGrath, and Alan Schwartzbaum. 1972. "The religious factor in occupational behavior." Paper presented at annual meetings of the Eastern Sociological Society, Boston.

Ruane, Joseph W. 1975. "Controlling the pharmacist." *American Journal of Pharmacy* 147 (November-December):174–79.

Rueschemeyer, Dietrich. 1977. "Structural differentiation, efficiency, and power." *American Journal of Sociology* 83 (July):1–25.

Ryscavage, Paul M. 1974. "Measuring union-nonunion earnings differences." *Monthly Labor Review* 97 (December):3–10.

Scheff, Thomas J. 1961. "Control over policy by attendants in a mental hospital." *Journal of Health and Human Behavior* 2 (Summer):93–105.

Scott, Lael. 1977. "Lawyers who sue lawyers." *New York Times Magazine* (June 26):74–78.

Shaw, Clayton T. 1972. "Societal sanctioning—the pharmacist's tarnished image." *Social Science and Medicine* 6 (February):109–15.

Sherrill, Robert. 1977. "Raising hell on the highways." *New York Times Magazine* (November 27):38–40, 88–102.

Shils, Edward A. 1950. "Primary groups in the American Army." Pp. 16–39 in R. K. Merton and P. F. Lazarsfeld (eds.), *Continuities in Social Research*. New York: Free Press.

Shimberg, Benjamin, Barbara F. Esser, and Daniel H. Kruger. 1973. *Occupational Licensing: Practices and Policies*. Washington, D.C.: Public Affairs Press.

Shortell, Stephen M. 1973. "Patterns of referral among internists in private practice: a social exchange model." *Journal of Health and Social Behavior* 14 (December):335–47.

Shover, Neal. 1972. "Structures and careers in burglary." *Journal of Criminal Law, Criminology and Police Science* 63 (4):540–49.

Slosar, John A., Jr. 1973. "Ogre, bandit, and operating employee: the problems and adaptations of the metropolitan bus driver." *Urban Life and Culture* 1 (January):339–62.

Stebbins, Robert A. 1966. "Class, status and power among jazz and commercial musicians." *The Sociological Quarterly* 7 (Spring):197–213.

Stevens, Rosemary. 1971. *American Medicine and the Public Interest*. New Haven: Yale University Press.

Stoddard, Ellwyn. 1968. "The informal 'code' of police deviancy: a group approach to 'blue-coat' crime." *Journal of Criminal Law, Criminology and Police Science* 59 (June):201–13.

Stone, Katherine. 1974. "The origins of job structures in the steel industry." *Review of Radical Political Economics* 6 (Summer):61–97.

Stouffer, Samuel A. et al., 1949. *The American Solider*. Princeton: Princeton University Press.

Strauss, Anselm. 1978. *Negotiations: Varieties, Contexts, Processes, and Social Order*. San Francisco: Jossey-Bass.

Strauss, George. 1963. "Professionalism and occupational associations." *Industrial Relations* 2 (May):7–31.

Sudnow, David. 1967. *Passing On: The Social Organization of Dying*. Englewood Cliffs, N.J.: Prentice-Hall.

Sykes, A. J. M. 1960. "Unity and restrictive practices in the British printing industry." *Sociological Review* 8 (December):239–54.

Tagliacozzo, Daisy L. and Hans O. Mauksch. 1972. "The patient's view of the patient's role." Pp. 172–85 in E. Gartly Jaco (ed.), *Patients, Physicians and Illness*. New York: Free Press.

Tatro, Charlotte R. 1974. "Cross my palm with silver: fortunetelling as an occupational way of life." Pp. 289–99 in Clifton D. Bryant (ed.), *Deviant Behavior: Occupational and Organizational Bases*. Chicago: Rand McNally.

Terkel, Studs. 1972. *Working*. New York: Pantheon.

Toren, Nina, 1973. "The bus driver: a study in role analysis." *Human Relations* 26 (February):101–12.

U.S. Department of Labor. 1974. *Handbook of Labor Statistics*. Washington, D.C.: Government Printing Office.

Useem, Michael. 1976. "Government influence on the social science paradigm." *The Sociological Quarterly* 17 (Spring):146–61.

Van de Ven, Andrew H., Andre L. Delbeco and Richard Koenig, Jr. 1976. "Determinants of coordination modes within organizations." *American Sociological Review* 41 (April):322–38.

Velarde, Albert J. and Mark Warlick. 1973. "Massage parlors: the sensuality business." *Society* 11 (November):63–74.

Weiss, Melford S. 1967. "Rebirth in the Airborn." *Transaction* 4 (May):23–26.

Westley, William A. 1956. "Secrecy and the police." *Social Forces* 34 (March):254–57.

Whyte, William F. 1948. *Human Relations in the Restaurant Industry*. New York: McGraw-Hill.

Wilensky, Harold L. 1964. "The professionalization of everyone?" *American Journal of Sociology* 70 (September):137–58.

Wrong, Dennis H. 1976. "Competent authority: reality and legitimating model." Pp. 262–272 in Lewis A. Coser and Otto N. Larson (eds.), *The Uses of Controversy in Sociology*. New York: Free Press.

REVIEW AND DISCUSSION QUESTIONS

1   According to the author, what is the relationship between power and the division of labor?
2   Are occupational roles static or dynamic? Provide examples of your position.
3   What is meant by occupational expansionism?
4   What type of resources can one use to gain power?
5   What is the role of negotiation in power building?

Reading 24

Leadership Reexamined: A Behavioral Approach

Tim R. V. Davis
Fred Luthans

Over the years three generally accepted assumptions concerning leadership theory and research have emerged. They are: (a) that readily identifiable leadership events exist in empirical reality; (b) that leadership is a major variable impacting on human and organizational effectiveness; and (c) that theory and research are needed to explain and predict its role. Acceptance of the importance of leadership dates back to ancient times. Organization and management theorists embraced the term and, although certain value assumptions and normative assertions have been questioned [4, 50, 51], leadership remains a popular construct. However, no consistent, direct correlation has

From the *Academy of Management Review*, 1979, vol. 2, pp. 237–248. Reprinted with permission from the authors and the *Academy of Management Review*.

been demonstrated between leadership and improved organizational effectiveness [21, 30]. Still, leadership continues to be one of the most extensively researched social influence variables [8, p. 231].

Traditional theorists generally treated the leadership function as a relatively simple matter of downward dominance and headship [62]. More current theorists generally view leadership as having much more to do with interpersonal influence [26] and a broad set of contingent, situational factors [8]. Far from the simple idea of merely assessing whether the subordinate did what was instructed, the notion of leadership has undergone radical revision and expansion. This is due to changing views of acceptable interpersonal practices in organizations and an ever expanding research base that has probed its wider implications.

A large assortment of different theoretical frameworks have been developed to identify component elements of leadership. Trait [41], style [32, 33], behavioral description [60], and situational-contingency views [20] represent some of the main theoretical approaches. In addition, decision making [60], participation [17], and path-goal [27] models comprise major attempts to explain the key leadership processes. Despite the level of interest and the proliferation of leadership theories and research, the fundamental problem of operationalizing leadership still is not being solved.

This paper outlines some of the reasons for this failure. It argues the need, as Argyris [2], Dubin [19] have done, to focus leadership research on observable behavior rather than on questionnaire responses reflecting perceptions of behavior and vague inner states. A behavioral model is proposed that allows the examination of the contingencies that affect leader-subordinate performance behaviors. An expanded cognitive-behavioral approach to the functional analysis of leadership behaviors is taken.

PROBLEMS OF DEFINITION

Pondy [51, p. 88] asks of leadership: "Have we been misled by the existence of a single term in our language to think that it reflects some uniform reality?" Calder [14] also points out that in the progression from the trait approach to complex transactional-contingency views, leadership has taken on such expanded meaning that it cannot be differentiated from any other general model of behavior. An increasing number of behavioral scientists agree that leadership, in some way, involves the exercise of influence [25, 26]; but what this influence is, and how it is to be achieved, is subject to wide-ranging interpretation. A major problem is that leadership is seldom directly observed but is merely perceived and conferred. Generally, a person is considered to have exercised leadership and to have exerted influence on the basis of the effects achieved. As used in this sense, the terms leadership and influence are adjectives reflective of behavior after the fact. However, both terms have commonly been construed as nouns in the theoretical and research literature and given a separate analytic existence. It is assumed that a specifiable category of leadership, or influence, behaviors exist. The search for these behaviors has been futile. It turns out that an unlimited array of behaviors may be "influential" in nature.

Both Pondy [51] and Calder [14] emphasize the role that language and attribution play in what has heretofore been considered leadership behavior. The language that enables humans to distill meaning and purpose out of observable events and provide a remarkably accurate representation of empirical reality is also capable of providing an inaccurate portrayal [28]. The use of constructs that label behavior in terms of its assumed effects often ascribes meaning and inference beyond the empirical referents.

A Need for Accurate Definitions

Concepts in the behavioral sciences must largely depend on accurate definitions in terms of observable behaviors [59]. However, as Calder notes, it is not uncommon for organizational behavior and management scholars to accept vague lay terms and use them as if they were precise descriptors of behavior [14, pp. 179–190]. Many discussions in the literature speak of terms such as leadership or delegation as if they were observable, treating the metaphor as empirical reality. With these descriptors so accepted, the student of leadership attempts to categorize behavior in terms of the metaphor, instead of attempting to account for the reality of the metaphor in terms of the observable behavior. Some may argue that the extent of leader influence cannot be observed; it can only be a perceptual measure derived from questionnaires. In practice, this means a pooled estimate of supervisor and/or subordinate perceptions that may not have any relationship to actual behavior or observable outcomes. As Argyris [4] contends, not only are many of the items used on leadership questionnaires unobservable; but they also rely on inferences: For example, no cues are given regarding the actual behavior involved in "expresses appreciation," "is easy to understand," "makes those under him feel at ease." The variance of behavior that could be perceived to accomplish these may be very great. In one study, "friendly and easily approachable foremen" (upon observation) turned out to be foremen "who left the men alone and rarely pressured them" [2]. In another study "friendly foremen" were men who took the initiative to discuss "difficult issues" with the men.

Unfortunately, much of what passes as descriptive research merely investigates normal or ascribed attributions for behavior. When the current norm or accepted explanation for behavior changes, then the validity of the attitudinal data can be questioned [43]. No matter how high the correlations obtained, or the extent of variance accounted for, these data are representative of perceptions or attitudes on a selected number of phrases or adjectives contained on a questionnaire. This questionnaire data should not automatically be treated as being equivalent to the actual behavior. For example, Fishbein has emphasized that the attitudes of an individual may be completely unrelated to that person's behavior:

Here, I think is where our major problem lies: we psychologists have never really studied behavior per se. By this I mean that we have usually taken behavior as a given; to the best of my knowledge, we—at least in the attitude area—have seldom, if ever, subjected our behavioral criteria to the same rigorous analysis to which we subject our paper-and-pencil tests. Yet this is what we must do if we are to thoroughly understand the relations between attitudes and behavior (i.e., if we are ever going to predict the conditions under which, and the extent to which, behavior is determined by, or related to, attitudes—or to any other variable, for that matter) [23, p. 484].

Fishbein stresses the need to study the "stimulus situation" and notes the importance of the "consequences" for the individual actor in predicting behavior. These two issues will be considered in our behavioral model. As Schriesheim and Kerr conclude after their extensive examination of the validity of the major instruments that purport to measure aspects of leadership: "the leadership area is today without any instruments of demonstrated validity and reliability" [54, p. 33] and add: "data from numerous studies collectively demonstrate that in many situations leader behaviors (as operationalized) *are* irrelevant." At best we may have what Campbell suggests as a science of questionnaire behavior rather than leader behavior [15].

The Study of Leadership

At this point, we might ask if it makes any sense at all to study the concept of leadership. Miner [43] contends that the concept of leadership itself has outlived its usefulness while Kerr [29] has proposed a substitute taxonomy that encompasses other influence and control processes than those simply deriving from the formal hierarchy. However, the fundamental issue, whether distinguishing hierarchical control or any other systems of control, is: can what is referred to as leadership (or any other substitute metaphor) also refer to behavior?

We contend that the influence processes in organizations can be studied. The key for both leadership theory and research is in identifying and analyzing the relational effect between the *observable* behavior, its antecedents (both overt and covert), and contingent consequences (both overt and covert) instead of studying behavior independently. We contend that leadership can be meaningfully studied. To do so, the decision as to whether leadership has taken place must be founded less on subjective opinion, recall, and perception (via questionnaire responses) and more on *observable behavioral events* and overt and covert antecedents and consequences. What is called for is a functional analysis of leadership behaviors.

OPERATIONALIZING A BEHAVIORAL VIEW OF LEADERSHIP

Based on the principles of operant psychology [58, 59, 6], leadership can be viewed as a series of behavioral contingency relationships of varying stability.

Contingency relationships comprise the behavioral patterns that link leaders and followers to specified goals and task functions. Such a behavioral leadership model can be constructed in order to examine the relational effects between behavior and its antecedents and consequences—more specifically, in an organization, the effect of supervisor behavior on subordinate task accomplishment. Supervisor-subordinate behavior is only one example of leader relations that impinge on an organization member's task accomplishment. Horizontal relations with co-workers could be substituted for vertical supervisor-subordinate ones. Also using the terms supervisor and leader as interchangeable could be questioned but they are used here for illustrative purposes. The contingencies linking supervisor behavior and subordinate task accomplishment are broken down into their basic components in Figure 1.

As shown, the leader's behavior serves as a discriminative stimulus (S^D) or cue (part A in Figure 1) to evoke the subordinate's task behavior. The subordinate's task behavior in turn can act as a consequence (part B in Figure 1) for the leader which, in turn, reinforces, punishes, or extinguishes the leader's subsequent behavior. Similarly, the subordinate's behavior has its own consequences (part C in Figure 1) which serve to reinforce, punish, or extinguish this behavior. The consequences for the subordinate's behavior may be related to the leader's subsequent behavior, the work itself and its outcomes, or other organization members. The supervisor does not directly cause the subordinate's behavior, she merely sets the occasion (or provides a discriminative stimulus) for the behavior to be emitted; the behavior depends on its consequences. Environmental cues/discriminative stimuli, behaviors, and consequences form a behavioral contingency that can be functionally analyzed.

A more dynamic view is portrayed in Figure 2 which shows how consequences and behavior are in a continuous state of interaction. Both the leader and the subordinate are unavoidably providing S^Ds and consequences in an exchange relationship jointly reinforcing or modifying one another's behavior. However, modification need not necessarily take place through direct interaction between superior and subordinate. Figure 3 shows how the independent behaviors of the leader and the subordinate toward the task or with other

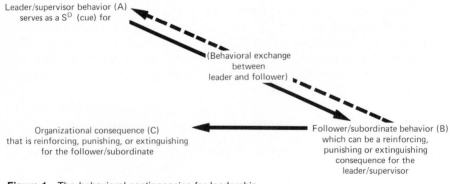

Leader/supervisor behavior (A) serves as a S^D (cue) for

(Behavioral exchange between leader and follower)

Organizational consequence (C) that is reinforcing, punishing, or extinguishing for the follower/subordinate

Follower/subordinate behavior (B) which can be a reinforcing, punishing or extinguishing consequence for the leader/supervisor

Figure 1   The behavioral contingencies for leadership.

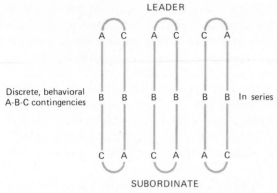

Figure 2   The micro behavioral exchange relationship.

organizational members can produce modified behavioral consequences for either the leader or the subordinate which, in turn, can affect their relationship.

Dynamic Leadership Model

The contingencies are conceptualized as being in series in Figures 2 and 3 because each group of behaviors is controlled by separate S^Ds and consequences. Leadership is conceived as a set of behavioral contingency relationships that constantly need to be reassessed rather than a uniform, developmental Gestalt. This behavioral model emphasizes that the influence process is best understood as a set of behavioral contingencies evolving over time between a leader and subordinate. The process can only be understood in terms of the reinforcing consequences of each distinct contingency situation. The separate behavior-consequence relationships produce a series of discrete behavioral events that cannot be analyzed as one uniform process. They must be examined independently for their particular effects (i.e., positive/negative reinforcement, extinction, or punishment) on the leader and the subordinate.

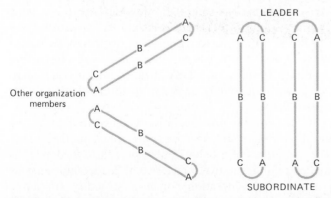

Figure 3   The impact of the macro environment on leader-subordinate behavior.

A major criticism of the operant approach has been the reluctance to acknowledge this role of cognitive processes. Recent behavioral research has convincingly demonstrated that covert processes play an instrumental role in regulating behavior [7, 59]. The methods of cognitive-behaviorism are virtually identical to those of the acognitive, operant approach except that covert processes (e.g., self-instructions) are manipulated for their effects on observable behavior in a particular stimulus setting [38, 7]. The same is true of covert consequences such as congratulating oneself for a job well done. Cognitive behavioral research has been conducted in a variety of field settings examining the controlling influence of the stimulus situation, cognitive processes and behavioral consequences [38, 39].

To be useful, the behavioral model of leadership must recognize the dynamic, emergent state of the organizational situation [63]. It should also take into consideration the macro- and micro-environmental variables that jointly affect superior-subordinate performance. Olmstead [46] and Pfeffer [50] have pointed out that the leader's behavior may be in full, or in part, determined by macro, situational events. Osborn and Hunt [47] provide an "adaptive-reactive" model of leadership that gives explicit recognition to this suggestion. Their mid-range theory of leadership "attempts to incorporate macro variables as antecedents of leader behavior" [47, p. 28]. The behavioral model proposed here suggests that functional analysis of behavioral events cannot be limited to the relations between leader and subordinate. It must take into consideration the broader environmental, macro [11] constraints that exert control over their behavior.

The macro variables surrounding the leader-subordinate relationship have not been extensively researched. Organizational size, the type of technology, and the level in the formal structure can be expected to affect leader behavior and subordinate outcomes [7]. In addition, the type of task worked on by the leader and subordinate, the relationship of the task to main processes in the organizational system, and the level of dependency on other work units can be expected to influence leader-subordinate interaction. For example, the work of Burns and Stalker [12] suggests that in mechanistic organizations, where tasks are more programmed, the constraints on leader-subordinate behavior are likely to be greater than in organic organizations where tasks are less structured and more discretionary behavior is required. Regardless of origin, these macro sources of influence must be reduced to localized, observable events impacting on leader-subordinate relations. In this way, all organizational activities (macro or micro) are capable of being functionally analyzed in terms of identifiable behavioral contingency relationships.

Observational studies [46, 49, 52] provide little evidence that managers actually spend much time on what could be commonly called motivating or leading subordinates. The usefulness of a behavioral approach to leadership is that it does not assume certain normative functions of leadership such as providing relationship support (consideration) or task structure (initiating structure). The approach suggested here focuses on the leader-subordinate relationship without attempting to categorize certain responses as "leadership" behaviors.

With the possible exception of those that work closely with machines and equipment with clearly defined output standards and the technology dictating the way the task is performed, the majority of people in organizations are required to operate in a relatively ambiguous task situation. In this situation the full repertoire of performance behaviors is not known or formally stated in advance. Under these circumstances, leaders and subordinates neither have a precise understanding of the many situations that will arise nor a clear understanding of how they will behave when they do occur. In this empirical reality, the behavior of the leader and subordinate is not the result of rational foresight; instead, it is "interactively" determined in the particular situation. Given the large number of events that are not thought through in advance but merely involve the leader and subordinate acting and reacting to one another (as in Figure 1), a large number of behaviors are exhibited in organizations that have virtually no rational basis other than the underlying rewards and punishments associated with that particular situation. For example, a subordinate is not told precisely how to behave in meetings or conferences with the boss but rapidly adapts behavior by observing the superior's reactions. The leader has no clear understanding of the degree to which a subordinate can be trusted with a particular assignment except through positive or negative results in the performance of the subordinate. It is through reacting and adapting in an exchange, *interactive* relationship that leaders and subordinates gradually establish stable patterns of behavior in different situations. The resulting patterns of leader-subordinate *behavior* in *each discrete contingency situation* represents the domain of a *behavioral* approach to leadership.

THE USE OF AN EXPANDED FUNCTIONAL ANALYSIS

It has been stressed that leaders and subordinates will engage in wide ranging activities and relations that create a complex array of behavioral contingencies between themselves and other members of the system. However, some of these behavioral contingencies will be more critical than others in their impact on key effectiveness and performance areas. It is in these critical areas that careful functional analysis becomes important to performance effectiveness. Previous operant views of leadership, for example, Scott [55], Sims [57], and Mawhinney and Ford [42], suggest the use of a basic analysis technique first proposed by Skinner [58] called functional analysis. This technique allows the leader (or researcher) to translate important task related activities into functional [A (antecedent cue), B (behavior), C (consequence)] behavioral contingencies. As traditionally used, this A-B-C approach to functional analysis concentrates only on the observable environmental contingencies but does not necessarily give specific recognition to the role of unobservable cognitive processes. This omission is the major criticism that the cognitvely-based theorists [45, 34] have of the behavioral approach.

The Mediational Role of Cognitive Processes

Increasingly, behavior theorists and researchers are recognizing the importance of the mediational role that cognitive symbolic processes play in understanding human behavior in general and learning in particular [6, 38, 59]. For example, Dawson and Furedy [18] and Grings [24] have shown that people do not learn much from repeated paired experiences unless they cognitively recognize that the events are associated. As Chatterjee and Eriksen [16] have demonstrated, cognitive awareness is a determinant responsible for learning, not merely a byproduct or outcome. Unobservable cognitive processes such as thoughts, images, self-evaluations, and expectations can play an important mediational role in regulating the person's relationship to the observable environment. These cognitive processes are recognized with the insertion of an "O" in an expanded version of functional analysis. This expanded functional analysis can be depicted as an S-O-B-C model [36] where "S" is the antecedent stimulus, "O" is the organism's covert processes, "B" is the behavior, and "C" is the consequence. This expanded version of functional analysis gives recognition to overt (S and C) and covert (O) contingencies of behavior (B).

Recognizing cognitive processes in functional analysis, a more comprehensive representation of the leadership process is provided. The operant approaches of Scott [55], Sims [57], and Mawhinney and Ford [42] do not directly address the issue of cognitive processes. Humans use cognitive symbolic processes to assign concepts to behavior and to infer relationships between events. When functional analysis is applied to leadership, it first requires that the leaders themselves must cognitively assign concepts such as "antecedent," "reinforcement" or "punishment" to behavioral events and then necessitates that leaders are able to perceive a relationship between these conceptually labelled events. Previous operant approaches to leadership give little recognition to such cognitive processes and therefore provide no explanation of how leaders may functionally analyze behavioral contingencies and communicate this knowledge to subordinates.

The expanded S-O-B-C functional analysis of leadership also accounts for mediational cognitive processes such as thoughts, images, self-evaluations, and expectancies [7, 38, 46, 59]. As Bandura points out:

> If human behavior could be fully explained in terms of antecedent inducements and response consequences, there would be no need to postulate any additional regulatory mechanisms. A great deal of human behavior, however, is initiated and sustained over long periods in the absence of compelling immediate external stimulation. In these instances, the inducements to action are rooted in cognitive activities [7, pp. 160–161].

A major criticism of the operant approach has been the reluctance to acknowledge this role of cognitive processes. Recent behavioral research has convincingly demonstrated that covert processes play an instrumental role in regulating behavior [7, 59]. The methods of cognitive-behaviorism are virtually identical to those of the acognitive, operant approach except that covert processes (e.g., self-instructions) are manipulated for their effects on observable behavior in a particular stimulus setting [38, 7]. The same is true of covert consequences such as congratulating oneself for a job well done. Cognitive behavioral research has been conducted in a variety of field settings examining the controlling influence of the stimulus situation, cognitive processes and behavioral consequences [38, 39].

The Importance of Observable Behavior

The suggested S-O-B-C functional analysis takes into consideration the role of cognitive processes. However, it should be pointed out that this recognition of cognitive processes does not mean that *observable* behavior is neglected. The majority of the classic models of leadership (e.g., Ohio State, Michigan, or Fiedler's Contingency model) are largely cognitively based models. These models all depend heavily upon perceptual and attitudinal questionnaire measures as the main means of analyzing leadership behavior. These measures have been found to have virtually no demonstrated construct validity [54]. Exclusive reliance on questionnaires with no attempt to examine the contingencies that regulate the observable behavior may merely provide a very misleading, metaphorical interpretation for the understanding, prediction, and control of leadership behaviors. By recognizing the cognitive processes in an S-O-B-C functional analysis, it does not deny that the antecedents and consequences should always be grounded in terms of observable components. The strength of a behavioral approach to leadership lies in its operational terms (e.g., reinforcement, extinction, punishment) which provide an unambiguous definition of behavioral events.

RESEARCH ISSUES AND PRACTICAL APPLICATIONS

One of the chief advantages of functional analysis is that it is both a research method and a practical tool that the leader and subordinate can use to understand one another's behavior. The research of Adam [1], Ottemann and Luthans [48] and Luthans and Bond [37] has demonstrated how the concepts of behaviorism in general and functional analysis in particular can be applied by the researcher in ongoing organizational situations. These experimental studies have shown how the analysis of antecedent stimuli and contingent consequences can be used in the prediction and control of organizational behavior.

The behavioral approach we suggest is an alternative to what Sayles has observed as the tendency to regard field work as rushing in and out of an organization with a questionnaire [53]. The risks of data distortion and contamination and the reliability and validity question would seem more severe in questionnaire studies of behavior than in systematic observational research [9, 44, 49, 13]. The recording of archival and observable behavioral frequency data and employing multiple baseline and reversal designs [5] can provide strong support for positing causal relations. It may be more sound than the interpretation of questionnaire responses and applying statistical techniques such as path analysis [10] or cross-lagged correlational analysis [64]. Behavioral research deals with real time events rather than historical reconstructions from perceptions and attitude data. The prospects of discovering, for example, whether leaders really do structure subordinates' paths to goals (e.g., the path-goal approach) or whether such procedures can actually be effective is more likely to be answered through real-time, in situation observational studies, than through questionnaire investigations which are many times removed from the actual behavior.

The application of functional analysis by the practitioner depends upon the leader's ability to bring into awareness the overt or covert antecedent cues and contingent consequences that regulate the leader's and subordinate's performance behavior. The leader must decide whether to bring these contingencies into public awareness and manage them more systematically or to ignore them and thereby sacrifice the opportunity for more effective performance.

The Behavioral Approach

Under a behavioral approach, if a leader determines that the subordinate's behavior does not result in acceptable outcomes there are two choices. The leader can facilitate desired behavior through a negative reinforcement strategy (avoidance learning on the part of the subordinate) or suppress the undesired behavior through the use of punishment. Neither form of negative control is very effective [35]. Research, using organizational performance as the criterion measure, confirms that positive reinforcement [1, 48] is the most effective organizational behavior modification strategy. However, fuller consideration of the range of forces affecting leader-subordinate relations confirms *the need for a bilateral* (leader-subordinate) rather than unilateral (leader-initiated) design of behavior modification programs.

The previous operant approaches, although designed to fulfill different purposes, portray a one-sided analysis of the leader-subordinate relationship. A paper by Sims [57] was devoted to the leader's behavior in dispensing rewards, or the role of leaders as focal points around which contingencies of reinforcement are structured. Scott's paper [55] accounted for the behavior of the leader; the subordinate's behavior was examined only insofar as it affects the leader's behavior. Mawhinney and Ford mainly [42] focused on the leader's role in structuring S^Ds and reinforcement contingencies in subordinate path-goal chains.

Our behavioral approach makes the individual behavior of both the leader and the subordinate with other members of the system, as well as their interactive behavior with one another, the subject of an expanded S-O-B-C functional analysis. We argue that the separate relationship of the leader and subordinate with other points of contact in the system must also be considered for their effects on the leader-subordinate relationship.

There are several reasons it is limiting to describe the role of the leader as the manager of a subordinate's S^Ds and reinforcement contingencies. *First*, the leader is unlikely to be aware of many of the covert-overt influences affecting the subordinate's behavior. *Second,* even if the leader is familiar with the environmental stimuli impacting on the subordinate's behavior, the leader is not likely to respond to these influences in the same way as the subordinate. By virtue of their roles, both leader and subordinate are likely to view the same set of circumstances very differently. In virtually every case, it would seem important to enlist the *subordinate's* aid in identifying the covert and overt sources of influence that regulate the *subordinate's* behavior.

To overcome these limitations, it is argued that functional analysis cannot be simply considered to be the role of the leader; the subordinate must also be equally involved in the process. More realistically, the leader's role in the behavioral approach might be considered as the following:

a The leader becomes acquainted with the macro and micro variables that control his/her own behavior.
b The leader works with the subordinate to discover the personalized set of behavioral contingencies that regulate the subordinate's behavior.
c The leader and the subordinate jointly attempt to discover ways in which they can manage their individual behavior to produce more mutually reinforcing and organizationally productive outcomes.

In our behavioral approach to leadership, both the leader and subordinate enter into a negotiable, *exchange relationship* in which both parties are conscious of how they can modify behavior by dispensing or withholding desired rewards.

SUMMARY AND CONCLUSIONS

Leadership remains one of the most heavily researched and written about areas in the field of management and organizational behavior. Over the last 50 years, leadership has been examined in terms of enduring traits, sets of behaviors or styles, situational properties, and presumed cognitive processes. Despite the number of theories and volumes of research, little cumulative knowledge has been gained. Much of the research has not been helpful precisely because it has neglected the observation of real events and focused instead on questionnaire responses. Many of the items contained on leadership questionnaires may describe commonly held *feelings* of leaders and subordinates but not necessarily describe the behavioral contingencies that control desired performance outcomes.

Our behavioral approach to leadership is based on the tested principles of operant research and focuses on observable behavioral events utilizing an operationally defined set of concepts. In this expanded behavioral approach to leadership, the influence of the macro-environment is treated as an important determinant of leader-subordinate behavior on the micro level. The previous strictly micro views of leader-follower operant behavior do not give adequate recognition to the relationships that the leader and subordinate share with other members of the system and each other. The expanded behavioral approach stresses the need to reduce all major forms of organizational influence impacting on the leader and subordinate to manageable behavioral contingencies. These contingencies can be identified through a proposed S-O-B-C functional analysis which gives recognition to both covert and overt events. The recognition of the role of covert processes is an important advance in the development of a "cognitive-behavioral" approach to leadership but does not diminish the important role of observable behaviors and tying back the contingencies to empirical reality.

Contrary to other operant approaches that focus primarily on the leader as a manager of the subordinate's reinforcement contingencies, our approach stresses the vital part played by the subordinate in the selection, design, and implementation of behavioral change programs. Functional analysis is conceived and carried out by both the leader and the subordinate so that both may become more aware of the contingencies that regulate one another's performance behavior. We hope the behavioral approach presented in this paper is a step in the direction of better understanding and practice of the complex but very important area of leadership.

REFERENCES

1 Adam, E. E., Jr. "Behavior Modification in Quality Control," *Academy of Management Journal,* Vol. 18 (1975), 662–679.
2 Argyris, C. *Understanding Organizational Behavior* (Homewood, Ill.: Dorsey, 1960).
3 Argyris, C. *Organization and Innovation* (Homewood, Ill.: Irwin, 1965).
4 Argyris, C. "Problems and New Directions for Industrial Psychology," in M. D. Dunnette (Ed.), *Handbook of Industrial and Organizational Psychology* (Chicago: Rand McNally, 1976), 151–184.
5 Baer, D. M., M. M. Wolf, and T. R. Risley, "Some Current Dimensions of Applied Behavior Analysis," *Journal of Applied Behavior Analysis,* Vol. 1 (1968), 91–97.
6 Bandura, A. *Principles of Behavior Modification* (New York: Holt, Rinehart & Winston, 1969).
7 Bandura, A. *Social Learning Theory* (Englewood Cliffs, N.J.: Prentice-Hall, 1977).
8 Barrow, J. C. "The Variables of Leadership: A Review and Conceptual Framework," *Academy of Management Journal,* Vol. 2 (1977), 231–251.
9 Bijou, S. W., R. F. Peterson, and M. H. Ault, "A Method to Integrate Descriptive and Experimental Field Studies at the Conceptual Level of Data and Empirical Concepts," *Journal of Applied Behavior Analysis,* Vol. 1 (1968), 175–191.
10 Blalock, H. M. (Ed.), *Causal Models in the Social Sciences* (Chicago: Aldine-Atherton, 1971).
11 Buck, V. E. "A Model for Viewing an Organization as a System of Constraints," in J. D. Thompson (Ed.), *Approaches to Organizational Design* (Pittsburgh: University of Pittsburgh Press, 1966), 103–172.
12 Burns, T., and G. M. Stalker. *The Management of Innovation* (London: Tavistock, 1961).
13 Burns, T. "The Comparative Study of Organizations," in V. H. Vroom (Ed.), *Methods of Organizational Research* (Pittsburgh: University of Pittsburgh Press, 1967), 113–170.

14 Calder, B. J. "An Attribution Theory of Leadership," in B. M. Staw and G. R. Salancik (Eds.), *New Directions in Organizational Behavior* (Chicago: St. Clair, 1977), 179–204.

15 Campbell, J. P. "Summary Comments," in J. G. Hunt and L. L. Larson (Eds.), *Leadership: The Cutting Edge* (Carbondale, Ill.: Southern Illinois University Press, 1977).

16 Chatterjee, B. B., and C. W. Eriksen, "Cognitive Factors in Heart Rate Conditioning," *Journal of Experimental Psychology,* Vol. 64 (1962), 272–279.

17 Coch, L., and J. P. R. French, "Overcoming Resistance to Change," *Human Relations,* Vol. 1 (1948), 512–532.

18 Dawson, M. E., and J. J. Furedy, "The Role of Awareness in Human Differential Autonomic Conditioning: The Necessary-Gate Hypothesis," *Psychophysiology,* Vol. 13 (1976), 50–53.

19 Dubin, R. "Theory Building in Applied Areas," in M. D. Dunnete (Ed.), *Handbook of Industrial and Organizational Psychology* (Chicago: Rand McNally, 1976), 17–39.

20 Fiedler, F. E. *A Theory of Leadership Effectiveness* (New York: McGraw-Hill, 1967).

21 Fiedler, F. E. "The Trouble with Leadership Training Is that It Doesn't Train Leaders," *Psychology Today,* Vol. 6, No. 9 (1973), 23–26, 29–30, 92, 106.

22 Fiedler, F. E., and M. M. Chemers, *Leadership and Effective Management* (Glenview, Ill.: Scott, Foresman, 1974).

23 Fishbein, M. "Attitudes and the Prediction of Behavior," in M. Fishbein (Ed.) *Readings in Attitude Theory and Measurement* (New York: Wiley, 1967), 477–492.

24 Grings, W. W. "The Role of Consciousness and Cognition in Autonomic Behavior Change," in F. J. McGuigan and R. Schoonover (Eds.), *The Psychophysiology of Thinking* (New York: Academic Press, 1973).

25 Hall, R. H. *Organizations: Structure and Process* (Englewood Cliffs, N.J.: Prentice-Hall, 1972).

26 Hollander, E. P., and J. W. Julian, "Contemporary Trends in the Analysis of Leadership Processes," *Psychological Bulletin,* Vol. 71 (1969), 387–397.

27 House, R. J., and T. R. Mitchell, "Path-Goal Theory of Leadership," *Journal of Contemporary Business,* Vol. 3, No. 4 (1974), 81–97.

28 Huxley, A. "Words and Their Meanings," in *The Importance of Language* (Englewood Cliffs, N.J.: Prentice-Hall, 1962).

29 Kerr, S. "Substitutes for Leadership: Their Meaning and Measurements," *Proceedings,* Annual Meeting of the American Institute for Decision Sciences (San Francisco, 1976), 150–152.

30 Korman, A. K. "Consideration, Initiating Structure, and Organizational Criteria— A Review," *Personnel Psychology,* Vol. 19 (1966), 349–362.

31 Leavitt, H. J. *Managerial Psychology* (Chicago: Rand McNally, 1958).

32 Lewin, K., R. Lippitt, and R. K. White, "Patterns of Aggressive Behavior in Experimentally Created 'Social Climates,'" *Journal of Social Psychology,* Vol. 10 (1939), 271–299.

33 Likert, R. *The Human Organization* (New York: McGraw-Hill, 1967).

34 Locke, E. A. "The Myths of Behavior Mod in Organizations," *Academy of Management Review,* Vol. 2 (1977), 543–553.

35 Luthans, F., and R. Kreitner, *Organizational Behavior Modification* (Glenview, Ill.: Scott, Foresman, 1975).

36 Luthans, F. *Organizational Behavior,* 2d ed., (New York: McGraw-Hill, 1977).

37 Luthans, F., and K. M. Bond, "The Use of Reversal Designs in Organizational Behavior Research," in R. L. Taylor, M. J. O'Connell, R. A. Zawacki, and D. D. Warrick (Eds.), *Academy of Management Proceedings,* 1977, pp. 86–90.

38 Mahoney, M. J. *Cognition and Behavior Modification* (Cambridge, Mass.: Ballinger, 1974).

39 Meichenbaum, D. H. *Cognitive Behavior Modification* (Morristown, N.J.: General Learning Press, 1974).

40 Meichenbaum, D. H. "Self-Instructional Methods," in F. H. Kanfer and A. P. Goldstein (Eds.), *Helping People Change* (New York: Pergamon, 1975).

41 Mann, R. D. "A Review of the Relationship between Personality and Performance in Small Groups," *Psychological Bulletin,* Vol. 56 (1959), 241–270.

42 Mawhinney, T. C., and J. C. Ford, "The Path-Goal Theory of Leader Effectiveness: An Operant Interpretation," *Academy of Management Review,* Vol. 2 (1977), 398–411.

43 Miner, J. B. "The Uncertain Future of the Leadership Concept: An Overview," in J. G. Hunt and L. L. Larson (Eds.) *Leadership Frontiers* (Kent, Ohio: The Comparative Administration Research Institute, Kent State University, 1975), 197–208.

44 Mintzberg, H. *The Nature of Managerial Work* (New York, Harper & Row, 1973).

45 Mitchell, T. R. "Cognitions and Skinner: Some Questions about Behavioral Determinism," *Organization and Administrative Sciences* (Spring, 1976), 41–72.

46 Olmstead, J. A. "Leader Performance as Organizational Process: A Study of Organizational Competence," in J. G. Hunt and L. L. Larson (Eds.), *Contingency Approaches to Leadership,* (Carbondale, Ill.: Southern Illinois University Press, 1974).

47 Osborn, R. N., and J. G. Hunt, "An Adaptive-Reactive Theory of Leadership: The Role of Macro Variables in Leadership Research," in J. G. Hunt and L. L. Larson (Eds.), *Leadership Frontiers* (Kent, Ohio: The Comparative Administration Research Institute, Kent State University, 1975), 27–44.

48 Ottemann, R., and F. Luthans, "An Experimental Analysis of the Effectiveness of an Organizational Behavior Modification Program in Industry," in A. G. Bedeian, A. A. Armenakis, W. H. Holley, and H. S. Field (Eds.), *Academy of Management Proceedings,* 1975, pp. 140–142.

49 Pettigrew, A. M. *The Politics of Organizational Decision-Making* (London: Tavistock, 1973).

50 Pfeffer, J. "The Ambiguity of Leadership," *Academy of Management Review,* Vol. 2 (1977), 104–112.

51 Pondy, L. R. "Leadership is a Language Game," in M. McCall and M. Lombardo (Eds.), *Leadership: Where Else Can We Go?* (Durham, M.C.: Duke University Press, 1976).

52 Sayles, L. *Managerial Behavior* (New York: McGraw-Hill, 1964).

53 Sayles, L. "Whatever Happened to Management?—or Why the Dull Stepchild?" *Business Horizons,* Vol. 13 (1970), 25–34.

54 Schriesheim, C. A., and S. Kerr. "Theories and Measures of Leadership: A Critical Appraisal," in J. G. Hunt and L. L. Larson (Eds.), *Leadership: The Cutting Edge* (Carbondale, Ill.: Southern Illinois University Press, 1977), 9–45.

55 Scott, W. E. "Leadership: A Functional Analysis," in J. G. Hunt and L. L. Larson (Eds.), *Leadership:The Cutting Edge* (Carbondale, Ill.: Southern Illinois University Press, 1977), 84–93.

56 Sherif, M. "On the Relevance of Social Psychology," *American Psychologist,* Vol. 25 (1970), 144–156.

57 Sims, H. P. Jr. "The Leader as a Manager of Reinforcement Contingencies: An Empirical Example and a Model," in J. G. Hunt and L. L. Larson (Eds.), *Leadership: The Cutting Edge* (Carbondale, Ill.: Southern Illinois University Press, 1977), 121–137.

58 Skinner, B. F. *Science and Human Behavior* (New York: Free Press, 1953).

59 Staats, A. W. *Social Behaviorism* (Homewood, Ill.: Dorsey, 1975).

60 Stogdill, R. M., and A. E. Coons *Leader Behavior: Its Description and Measurement* (Columbus, Ohio: Bureau of Business Research, Ohio State University, 1957).

61 Vroom, V. H., and P. W. Yetton. *Leadership and Decision-Making* (Pittsburgh, Pa.: University of Pittsburgh Press, 1973).

62 Weber, M. *The Theory of Social and Economic Organization,* Parsons Trans. (New York: Oxford University Press, 1947).

63 Weick, K. E. *The Social Psychology of Organizing* (Reading, Mass.: Addison-Wesley, 1969).

64 Yee, A. H., and N. L. Gage, "Techniques of Estimating Source and Direction of Influence in Panel Data," *Psychological Bulletin,* Vol. 70 (1968), 115–126.

REVIEW AND DISCUSSION QUESTIONS

1 Relate the operant paradigm to leadership transactions. Cite examples.
2 How can a behavioral approach to leadership aid in the prediction and control of organizational behaviors?
3 Give examples of overt and covert contingencies that a leader may employ.
4 How can a leader use the behavioral approach to enhance his or her own effectiveness?

Reading 25

Leadership Theory: Some Implications for Managers

Chester A. Schriesheim
James M. Tolliver
Orlando C. Behling

In the past seventy years more than 3,000 leadership studies have been conducted and dozens of leadership models and theories have been proposed.[1] Yet, a practicing manager who reads this literature seeking an effective solution to supervisory problems will rapidly become disenchanted. Although we have access to an overwhelming volume of leadership theory and research, few guidelines exist which are of use to a practitioner. Nevertheless, interest in leadership—and in those qualities which separate a successful leader from an unsuccessful one—remains unabated. In almost any book dealing with management one will find some discussion of leadership. In any company library there

From *MSU Business Topics,* Summer 1978, pp. 34–40. Reprinted by permission of the publisher, Division of Research, Graduate School of Business Administration, Michigan State University.

are numerous volumes entitled "Increasing Leadership Effectiveness," "Successful Leadership," or "How to Lead." Typical management development programs conducted within work organizations and universities usually deal with some aspect of leadership. This intensity and duration of writing on the subject and the sums spent annually on leadership training indicate that practicing managers and academicians consider good leadership essential to organizational success.

What is meant by leadership, let alone *good* leadership? Many definitions have been proposed, and it seems that most are careful to separate management from leadership. This distinction sometimes becomes blurred in everyday conversations. The first term, *management,* includes those processes, both mental and physical, which result in other people executing prescribed formal duties for organizational goal attainment. It deals mainly with planning, organizing, and controlling the work of other people to achieve organizational goals.[2] This definition usually includes those aspects of managers' jobs, such as monitoring and controlling resources, which are sometimes ignored in current conceptualizations of leadership. *Leadership,* on the other hand, is a more restricted type of managerial activity, focusing on the interpersonal interactions between a leader and one or more subordinates, with the purpose of increasing organizational effectiveness.[3] In this view, leadership is a social influence process in which the leader seeks the voluntary participation of subordinates in an effort to reach organizational objectives. The key idea highlighted by a number of authors is that the subordinate's participation is voluntary.[4] This implies that the leader has brought about some change in the way subordinates want to behave. Leadership, consequently, is not only a specific process (more so than management), but also is undoubtedly political in nature. The political aspect of leadership has been discussed elsewhere, so at this point it suffices to note that a major implication of leadership's political nature is that such attempts at wielding influence will not necessarily succeed.[5] In fact, other types of managerial tasks may have a stronger influence on organizational effectiveness than those interpersonal tasks usually labeled leadership.[6]

Despite this shortcoming, the examination of leadership as it relates to interpersonal interactions is still worthwhile simply because managers may, in many cases, have more control over how they and their subordinates behave than over nonhuman aspects of their jobs (such as the amount and types of resources they are given). In addition, some information does exist concerning which leadership tactics are of use under various conditions. For this information to be of greatest use, however, practicing managers should have some concept of the direction leadership research has taken. Thus, before attempting to provide guidelines for practitioners, we shall briefly review major approaches to the subject of leadership and point out their weaknesses and limitations.

BASIC APPROACHES TO LEADERSHIP

Thinking concerning leadership has moved through three distinct periods or phases.

The Trait Phase Early approaches to leadership, from the pre-Christian era to the late 1940s, emphasized the examination of leader characteristics (such as age and degree of gregariousness) in an attempt to identify a set of universal characteristics which would allow a leader to be effective in all situations. At first a few traits seemed to be universally important for successful leaders, but subsequent research yielded inconsistent results concerning these traits; in addition, research investigating a larger number of other traits (about one hundred) was generally discouraging. As a result of this accumulation of negative findings and of reviews of this evidence, such as that conducted by R. M. Stogdill, the tide of opinion about the importance of traits for leadership effectiveness began to change.[7] In the late 1940s, leadership researchers began to move away from trait research. Contemporary opinion holds the trait approach in considerable disrepute and views the likelihood of uncovering a set of universal leadership effectiveness traits as essentially impossible.

The Behavioral Phase With the fall of the trait approach, researchers considered alternative concepts, eventually settling on the examination of relationships between leader behaviors and subordinate satisfaction and performance.[8] During the height of the behavioral phase, dating roughly from the late 1940s to the early 1960s, several large research programs were conducted, including the Ohio State University leadership studies, a program of research which has received considerable publicity over the years.

The Ohio State studies started shortly after World War II and initially concentrated on leadership in military organizations. In one of these studies, a lengthly questionnaire was administered to B-52 bomber crews, and their answers were statistically analyzed to identify the common dimensions underlying the answers.[9] This analysis discovered two dimensions which seemed most important in summarizing the nature of the crews' perceptions about their airplane commanders' behavior toward them.

Consideration was the stronger of the two factors, and it involved leader behaviors indicative of friendship, mutual trust, respect, and warmth.

The second factor was Initiation of Structure, a concept involving leader behaviors indicating that the leader organizes and defines the relationship between self and subordinates.[10]

In subsequent studies using modified versions of the original questionnaire, Consideration and Structure were found to be prime dimensions of leader behavior in situations ranging from combat flights over Korea to assembly line work.[11] In addition, studies were undertaken at Ohio State and elsewhere to compare the effects of these leader behaviors on subordinate performance and satisfaction. A high Consideration-high Structure leadership style was, in many cases, found to lead to high performance and satisfaction. However, in a number of studies dysfunctional consequences, such as high turnover and absenteeism, accompanied these positive outcomes. In yet other situations, different combinations of Consideration and Structure (for example, low Consideration-high Structure) were found to be more effective.[12]

Similar behaviors were identified and similar results obtained in a large number of studies, such as those conducted at the University of Michigan.[13] Although the display of highly Considerate–highly Structuring behavior was sometimes found to result in positive organizational outcomes, this was not true in all of the cases or even in most of them.[14] The research, therefore, clearly indicated that no single leadership style was universally effective, as the relationship of supervisory behavior to organizational performance and employee satisfaction changed from situation to situation. By the early 1960s this had become apparent to even the most ardent supporters of the behavioral approach, and the orientation of leadership researchers began to change toward a situational treatment.

The Situational Phase Current leadership research is almost entirely situational. This approach examines the interrelationships among leader and subordinate behaviors or characteristics and the situations in which the parties find themselves. This can clearly be seen in the work of researchers such as F. E. Fiedler, who outlined one of the first situational models.[15]

Fiedler claims that leaders are motivated primarily by satisfactions derived from interpersonal relations and task-goal accomplishment. Relationship-motivated leaders display task-oriented behaviors (such as Initiating Structure) in situations which are favorable for them to exert influence over their work group, and they display relationship-oriented behaviors (such as Consideration) in situations which are either moderately favorable or unfavorable. Task-motivated leaders display relationship-oriented behaviors in favorable situations and task-oriented behaviors in both moderately favorable and unfavorable situations. Fiedler's model specifies that relationship-motivated leaders will be more effective in situations which are moderately favorable for the leader to exert influence, and that they will be less effective in favorable or unfavorable situations; the exact opposite is the case for task-motivated leaders. (They are most effective in favorable or unfavorable situations and least effective in moderately favorable ones.) According to Fiedler, the favorableness of the situation for the leader to exert influence over the work group is determined by (1) the quality of leader-group member relations (the warmer and friendlier, the more favorable the situation); (2) the structure of the tasks performed by the leader's subordinates (the more structured, the more favorable); and (3) the power of the leader (the more power, the more favorable the situation).[16]

A number of other authors propose similar types of interactions among the leader, the led, and the situation. We will not review all these other models, but the situational model of Victor Vroom and Phillip Yetton deserves mention.[17] Their model suggests the conditions under which the leader should share decision-making power. Five basic leadership styles are recommended. These range from unilateral decisions by the leader to situations in which the leader gives a great deal of decision power to subordinates and serves as a discussion coordinator who does not attempt to influence the group. Which style is recommended depends upon the leader's "yes" or "no" response to seven quality and acceptability questions which are asked sequentially. In those cases where more than a single style is suggested, the leader is expected to choose between recommendations on the basis of the amount of time to be invested. While this model, as is the case with most of the situational models, has not been fully tested, the literature supports the basic notion that a situational view is necessary to portray accurately the complexities of leadership processes.

ORGANIZATIONAL IMPLICATIONS

What does this discussion of leadership theory and research have to do with the practice of management?

Selection does not seem to be the primary answer to the organization's need to increase the pool of effective leaders. The results of the numerous trait studies summarized by Stogdill and others indicate that the search for universal personality characteristics of effective leaders is doomed.[18] This statement requires qualification, however. It should be recognized that the assertion concerns leadership effectiveness, which is only one aspect of managerial effectiveness. A manager may contribute to organizational effectiveness in many ways other than by being an effective leader. The role of selection in picking effective managers, as distinguished from effective leaders, consequently may be much greater. Furthermore, present disappointment with attempts at leader selection is derived from research which has sought to identify universal characteristics of effective leaders in all situations. Summaries such as Stogdill's demonstrate that leadership effectiveness is highly dependent upon the relationship between leader characteristics and the demands of particular situations, and thus universal approaches will not work. Exploration of leader traits as they relate to performance in particular situations may reveal that careful selection has some potential. Unfortunately, given the many situational factors which appear to influence leadership effectiveness, it seems unlikely that selection procedures will be able to follow typical actuarial (statistical) selection procedures.[19] (It appears almost impossible to gather enough individuals in identical jobs to do this.) However, this does not preclude the use of clinical (judgmental) techniques for selection of leaders.

A further limitation on selection procedures as ways of increasing the pool of effective managers and/or leaders within organizations is the dynamic nature of managerial jobs and managers' careers. If, as research seems to indicate, leadership success is situation-specific, then the continual and inevitable shifts in the nature of a manager's assignment and his or her movement from one assignment to another may make the initial selection invalid.

Another implication is that existing forms of leadership training appear to be inappropriate, based on the evidence outlined here. There are two reasons for this. First, the majority of such training programs are based upon the assumption that there exists one best way to manage. Great emphasis usually is placed on an employee-centered (Considerate) approach or one which combines a concern for employees with a concern for high output (Initiating Structure). For example, the Managerial Grid and its associated Grid Organizational

Development Program are popular approaches to management and organizational development.[20] Both are based on the premise that a managerial style which shows high concern for people and high concern for production is the soundest way to achieve excellence, and both attempt to develop this style of behavior on the part of all managers.[21] Rensis Likert's "System-Four" approach to managerial and organizational development, although different from the Grid approach, also assumes that one best way to manage exists (employee-centered leadership).[22] Clearly, these ideas are in conflict with the evidence and with contemporary opinion.

The other limitation of leadership training is that it seems ineffective in changing the behavior of participants. Leadership training aimed not directly at leadership behavior itself, but at providing diagnostic skills for the identification of the nature of the situation and the behaviors appropriate to it, appears to offer considerable potential for the improvement of leadership effectiveness. Obviously, however, additional research is needed to identify the dimensions of situations crucial to leadership performance and the styles effective under various circumstances.

Fiedler's suggestion that organizations engineer the job to fit the manager also has potential.[23] However, the idea is impractical, if not utopian. Application of this approach is limited because we have not identified the crucial dimensions of situations which affect leadership performance. Also, while the overall approach may offer theoretical advantages when leadership is treated in isolation, it ignores dysfunctional effects on other aspects of the organization's operations. Leadership effectiveness cannot be the only concern of administrators as they make decisions about job assignments. They must consider other aspects of the organization's operations which may conflict with their attempts to make good use of leadership talent. Some characteristics of the job, task, or organization simply may not be subject to change, at least in the short run. Thus, engineering the job to fit the manager may increase leadership effectiveness, but this approach seems risky, at least for the forseeable future.

It should also be noted that it is not unusual for work organizations to use traits and trait descriptions in their evaluations of both leadership and managerial performance. A quick glance at a typical performance rating form usually reveals the presence of terms such as *personality* and *attitude* as factors for individual evaluation. Clearly, these terms represent a modern-day version of the traits investigated thirty years ago, and they may or may not be related to actual job performance, depending upon the specifics of the situation involved. Thus, some explicit rationale and, it is hoped, evidence that such traits do affect managerial performance should be provided before they are included in performance evaluations. Just feeling that they are important is not sufficient justification.

INDIVIDUAL IMPLICATIONS

The implications of our discussion of leadership theory and research for individual managers are intertwined with those for the total organization. The fact that leadership effectiveness does not depend on a single set of personal characteristics with which an individual is born or which the individual acquires at an early age should provide a sense of relief to many managers and potential managers. Success in leadership is not limited to an elite, but can be attained by almost any individual, assuming that the situation is proper and that the manager can adjust his or her behavior to fit the situation. The process leading to effective leadership, in other words, is not so much one of changing the characteristics of the individual as it is one of assuring that he or she is placed in an appropriate situation or of teaching the individual how to act to fit the situation.

Thus, a manager's effectiveness can be improved through the development of skills in analyzing the nature of organizational situations—both task and political demands. Although it is difficult to provide guidelines, some recent research points to tentative prescriptions.[24]

Generally speaking, a high Consideration—high Structure style often works best. However, this approach cannot be used in all instances because dysfunctional consequences can result from such behaviors. For example, upper management sometimes gives highly considerate managers poor performance ratings, while in other instances high Structure has been related to employee dissatisfaction, grievances, and turnover. It sometimes will be necessary for a manager to choose between high Consideration and high Structure, and in these cases an individual's diagnostic ability becomes important.

If the diagnostician (manager) has little information, it is probably safe to exhibit high Consideration. Although it does not guarantee subordinate performance, its positive effects on frustration-instigated behavior—such as aggression—are probably enough to warrant its recommendation as a general style. However, in some situations Structure probably should be emphasized, although it may mean a decrease in subordinate perceptions of Consideration. Although the following is not an exhaustive list of these exceptions, it does include those which are known and appear important. The individual manager, from a careful analysis of the situation, must add any additional factors that can be identified.

Emergencies or High-Pressure Situations   When the work involves physical danger, when time is limited, or when little tolerance for error exists, emphasis on Initiating Structure seems desirable. Research has demonstrated that subordinates often expect and prefer high Structure in such instances.

Situations in Which the Manager Is the Only Source of Information   When the leader is the only person knowledgeable about the task, subordinates often expect him or her to make specific job assignments, set deadlines, and generally engage in structuring their behavior. This does not mean that the leader cannot be considerate if this is appropriate.

Subordinate Preferences   There is limited evidence that some subordinates prefer high Structure and expect it, while others expect low Consideration and are suspicious of leaders who display high Consideration. Other preference patterns undoubtedly exist, and managers should attempt to tailor their behavior to each individual employee, as the situation dictates.

Preferences of Higher Management   In some instances, higher management has definite preferences for certain leadership styles. Higher management sometimes prefers and expects high Structure and low Consideration, and rewards managers for displaying this behavioral style. The manager should be sensitive to the desires of superiors, in addition to those of subordinates. While it is not possible to specify how these expectations may be reconciled if they diverge, compromise or direct persuasion might be useful.[25] Once again, the success of these methods probably will depend both upon the situation and the manager's skill. This leads to the last point—adaptability.

Leader Ability to Adjust   Some managers will be able to adjust their behavior to fit the situation. For others, attempts to modify behavior may look false and manipulative to subordinates. In these instances, the manager probably would be better off keeping the style with which he or she is most comfortable.

LIMITATIONS AND CONCLUSION

The situational approach avoids the major shortcomings of both the trait and behavioral approaches to leadership. However, the implicit assumption that hierarchical leadership is always important has recently come into question. Steven Kerr, for example, points out that many factors may limit the ability of a hierarchical superior to act as a leader for subordinates.[26] Factors such as technology (for example, the assembly line), training, clear job descriptions, and the like, may provide subordinates with enough guidance so that supervisor Structure may be unnecessary to ensure task performance. Also, jobs which are intrinsically satisfying may negate the need for supervisor Consideration, since Consideration is not needed to offset job dullness.

Another problem with the situational approach, and with leadership as a major emphasis in general, is that effective leadership may account for only 10 to 15 percent of the variability in unit performance.[27] While this percentage is certainly not trivial, it is clear that much of what affects performance in organizations is not accounted for by leadership. While studying and emphasizing leadership certainly has its merits, it could be argued that there is much to be gained by treating leadership effectiveness as but one component of managerial effectiveness. As an earlier publication emphasized:

> It is necessary to note that leadership is only one way in which the manager contributes to organizational effectiveness. The manager also performs duties which are *externally oriented* so far as his unit is concerned. For example, he may spend part of his time coordinating the work of his unit with other units. Similarly, not all of the manager's *internally oriented* activities can be labeled leadership acts. Some of

them concern the physical and organizational conditions under which the work unit operates. For example, the manager spends part of his time obtaining resources (materials, equipment, manpower, and so on) necessary for unit operations. This is an essential internally oriented activity but hardly constitutes leadership. Clearly, the manager must perform a mix of internal and external activities if his unit is to perform well. Leadership is only one of the internal activities performed by managers.[28]

Thus, the manager should not overemphasize the importance of leadership activities, especially if this causes other functions to be neglected.

For managers to be effective as leaders, they must attempt to be politically astute and to tailor their behaviors, taking into account differences in subordinates, superiors, and situations. Leadership should be kept in perspective. Clearly, it is important, but it cannot be treated in isolation; the importance of leadership depends upon the situation, and the practicing manager must take this into account.

REFERENCES

1 R. M. Stogdill, *Handbook of Leadership* (New York: The Free Press, 1974).

2 A. C. Filley, R. J. House, and Steven Kerr, *Managerial Process and Organizational Behavior,* 2nd ed. (Glenview, Ill.: Scott, Foresman, 1976). See also R. C. Davis, *Industrial Organization and Management* (New York: Harper, 1957).

3 C. A. Gibb, "Leadership," in Gardner Lindzey and Elliot Aronson, eds., *The Handbook of Social Psychology* (Reading, Mass.: Addison-Wesley, 1969), vol. 4.

4 See, for example, R. H. Hall, *Organizations: Structure and Process* (Englewood Cliffs, N.J.: Prentice-Hall, 1972).

5 C. A. Schriesheim, J. M. Tolliver, and L. D. Dodge, "The Political Nature of the Leadership Process," unpublished paper, 1978.

6 For examples of other types of managerial tasks which may have more of an impact on organizations, see J. P. Campbell, M. D. Dunnette, E. E. Lawler, and K. E. Weick, *Managerial Behavior, Performance, and Effectiveness* (New York: McGraw-Hill, 1970).

7 R. M. Stogdill, "Personal Factors Associated with Leadership: A Survey of the Literature," *Journal of Psychology* 25 (January 1948): 35–71.

8 T. O. Jacobs, *Leadership and Exchange in Formal Organizations* (Alexandria, Va.: Human Resources Research Organization, 1970).

9 A. W. Halpin and B. J. Winer, "A Factorial Study of the Leader Behavior Descriptions," in R. M. Stogdill and A. E. Coons, eds., *Leader Behavior: Its Description and Measurement* (Columbus: Bureau of Business Research, The Ohio State University, 1957).

10 Ibid., p. 42.

11 Stogdill and Coons, *Leader Behavior.*

12 Steven Kerr, C. A. Schriesheim, C. J. Murphy, and R. M. Stogdill, "Toward a Contingency Theory of Leadership Based upon the Consideration and Initiating Structure Literature," *Organizational Behavior and Human Performance* 12 (August 1974): 62–82.

13 See, for example, Daniel Katz, Nathan Maccoby, and Nancy Morse, *Productivity,*

Supervision and Morale in an Office Situation (Ann Arbor: Survey Research Center, University of Michigan, 1951).

14 Kerr et al., "Contingency Theory."

15 See F. E. Fiedler, "Engineer the Job to Fit the Manager," *Harvard Business Review* 43 (September–October 1965): 115–22.

16 F. E. Fiedler, *A Theory of Leadership Effectiveness* (New York: McGraw-Hill, 1967).

17 V. H. Vroom and P. W. Yetton, *Leadership and Decision-Making* (Pittsburgh, Pa.: University of Pittsburgh Press, 1973).

18 R. M. Stogdill, "Personal Factors."

19 Kerr et al., "Contingency Theory."

20 R. R. Blake and J. S. Mouton, *The Managerial Grid* (Houston, Texas: Gulf, 1964), and *Building a Dynamic Corporation Through Grid Organizational Development* (Reading, Mass.: Addison-Wesley, 1969).

21 Ibid., p. 63.

22 Rensis Likert, *New Patterns of Management* (New York: McGraw-Hill, 1961), and *The Human Organization: Its Management and Value* (New York: McGraw-Hill, 1967).

23 Fiedler, "Engineer the Job."

24 Kerr et al., "Contingency Theory."

25 See Filley, House, and Kerr, *Managerial Process,* especially pp. 162–80; and George Strauss, "Tactics of Lateral Relations," in H. J. Leavitt and L. R. Pondy, eds., *Readings in Managerial Psychology,* 1st ed. (Chicago: University of Chicago Press, 1964), pp. 226–48.

26 Steven Kerr, "Substitutes for Leadership: Their Definition and Measurement," unpublished paper, 1978.

27 O. C. Behling and C. A. Schriesheim, *Organizational Behavior: Theory, Research and Application* (Boston: Allyn and Bacon, 1976).

28 Ibid., p. 294.

REVIEW AND DISCUSSION QUESTIONS

1 How are consideration and structure related to a leader's effectiveness?
2 What are some of the main limitations of current leadership theories?
3 Explain the trait theory of leadership.
4 Explain the situational theory of leadership.
5 How can the analysis of leadership theories as in this article make you a more effective leader?

Part Six

Macro Issues: The Management Processes and Organization Theory

The management processes and the organization structure serve as the macro framework for organizational behavior. Too often in the discussion of organizational behavior, there is a lack of awareness and the resultant analysis of this macro framework within which employee behaviors occur. Many of the processes that are generally discussed in a management or an organizational theory test are often ignored in an organizational behavior text. But to understand organizational behavior, there should be awareness of the macro environment. Often the management processes and organizational structure serve as antecedent cues for particular behaviors to be emitted. The macro environment can also provide reinforcers for the organizational behaviors. For example, one company was having a great deal of difficulty in obtaining cooperation between two important departments. The usual procedure was to fire each team of managers every year or two and start out with a new batch, hoping that they might be able to work together. The chief executive officer (CEO) couldn't understand why these department heads could not get along. A highly paid consultant finally "uncovered the situation." It seemed that each department was paid on an incentive basis for reducing the rate of scrap loss. Each department received the bonus based on their own scrap-rate reduction. In the production process, one of the departments was shipping their goods to the other department for assembly. The first department was being reinforced for shipping marginally acceptable parts to the other department by keeping their scrap rate down. The submarginal parts in turn caused the second department's scrap rate to increase thereby reducing their bonus. While the CEO felt that it was an employee problem, the real problem could be traced to the policies of the firm. A simple change in the scrap-rate incentive system from a departmental bonus base to a combination base between the two departments led to effective interdepartmental cooperation.

The above type of example points to the needs of processes and organizational theory in analyzing organizational behavior. The actions by management in the areas of decision making, control procedures, and organizational structure and design definitely have an impact on organizational behavior. Organizations must be designed to balance the technological and human systems. In like manner, the decision-making process must occur at the points in the organization and by the people in the organization that have the necessary information to make effective decisions. Control systems must be designed so that they are sensitive to the efforts of the organizational participants. When change is introduced into an organization, careful attention must be given to weighing the impact that this change will have on the organization as a whole and upon the participants in the organization. The direction for the future clearly points to greater importance being placed on improving the delivery systems of organizations. These delivery systems include the traditional quantity standards, of course, but new and vital emphasis is being placed upon the quality of products or service that is being provided. The key to quality lies more in terms of the individual employees rather than the technological system. Up to very recently, most organizations have simply not been sensitive to the quality aspects of an employee's performance. Clearly the emphasis of the 1980s will be on building an organizational system that will be more responsive to the quality behaviors of its participants.

This part provides four readings on the management processes and organizational theory. The first article provides an overall perspective on management theory and practice. A couple of decades ago Professor Harold Koontz wrote a new classic article in which he described a literal jungle of management theories and schools that were causing considerable confusion in the study and practice of management. In this article Koontz revisits the management theory jungle and gives his view of what has happened since the publication of his initial article. The second article provides an overall framework for the contingency approach to management. The third article examines the management process of control in depth. The author maintains that control mechanisms in organizations do not only evolve through management edict but also through the norms that the organizational participants share. Finally, Professor Perrow gives a comprehensive analysis of the evolution of organizational theory and the impact this theory has had on management practice.

Reading 26
The Management Theory Jungle Revisited
Harold Koontz

Nearly two decades ago, I became impressed by the confusion among intelligent managers arising from the wide differences in findings and opinions among academic experts writing and doing research in the field of management. The summary of these findings I identified as "the management theory jungle" [Koontz, 1961]. Originally written to clarify for myself why obviously intelligent academic colleagues were coming up with such widely diverse conclusions and advice concerning management, my summary was published and widely referred to under this title. What I found was that the thinking of these scholars fell into six schools or approaches in their analysis of management. In some cases, it appeared that, like the proverbial blind men from Hindustan, some specialists were describing management only through the perceptions of their specialties.

Judging by its reception over the years, the article and the concept of the "jungle" must have filled a need. In fact, so many inquiries have been made over the intervening years as to whether we still have a "management theory jungle" that I now believe the "jungle" should be revisited and reexamined. What I now find is that, in place of the six specific schools identified in 1961, there are at least eleven approaches. Thus, the jungle appears to have become even more dense and impenetrable. But various developments are occurring that might in the future bring a coalescence of the various approaches and result in a more unified and useful theory of management.

THE ORIGINAL MANAGEMENT THEORY JUNGLE

What I found nearly two decades ago was that well-meaning researchers and writers, mostly from academic halls, were attempting to explain the nature and knowledge of managing from six different points of view then referred to as "schools." These were: (1) the management process school, (2) the empirical or "case" approach, (3) the human behavior school, (4) the social system school, (5) the decision theory school, and (6) the mathematics school.

These varying schools, or approaches (as they are better called), led to a jungle of confusing thought, theory, and advice to practicing managers. The major sources of entanglement in the jungle were often due to varying meanings given common words like "organization," to differences in defining management as a body of knowledge, to widespread casting aside of the findings of early practicing managers as being "armchair" rather than what they were—the distilled experience and thought of perceptive men and women, to misunder-

From the *Academy of Management Review*, vol. 2, 1980, pp. 175–187. Reprinted with permission from the author and the *Academy of Management Review*.

standing the nature and role of principles and theory, and to an inability or unwillingness of many "experts" to understand each other.

Although managing has been an important human task since the dawn of group effort, with few exceptions the serious attempt to develop a body of organized knowledge—science—underpinning practice has been a product of the present century. Moreover, until the past quarter century almost all of the meaningful writing was the product of alert and perceptive practitioners—for example, French industrialist Henry Fayol, General Motors executive James Mooney, Johns-Manville vice-president Alvin Brown, British chocolate executive Oliver Sheldon, New Jersey Bell Telephone president Chester Barnard, and British management consultant Lyndall Urwick.

But the early absence of the academics from the field of management has been more than atoned for by the deluge of writing on management from our colleges and universities in the past 25 years. For example, there are now more than 100 (I can find 97 in my own library) different textbooks purporting to tell the reader—student or manager—what management is all about. And in related fields like psychology, sociology, system sciences, and mathematical modelling, the number of textbooks that can be used to teach some aspect—usually narrow—of management is at least as large.

The jungle has perhaps been made more impenetrable by the infiltration in our colleges and universities of many highly, but narrowly, trained instructors who are intelligent but know too little about the actual task of managing and the realities practicing managers face. In looking around the faculties of our business, management, and public administration schools, both undergraduate and graduate, practicing executives are impressed with the number of bright but inexperienced faculty members who are teaching management or some aspect of it. It seems to some like having professors in medical schools teaching surgery without ever having operated on a patient. As a result, many practicing managers are losing confidence in our colleges and universities and the kind of management taught.

It is certainly true that those who teach and write about basic operational management theory can use the findings and assistance of colleagues who are especially trained in psychology, sociology, mathematics, and operations research. But what dismays many is that some professors believe they are teaching management when they are only teaching these specialties.

What caused this? Basically two things. In the first place, the famous Ford Foundation (Gordon and Howell) and Carnegie Foundation (Pearson) reports in 1959 on our business school programs in American colleges and universities, authored and researched by scholars who were not trained in management, indicted the quality of business education in the United States and urged schools, including those that were already doing everything the researchers recommended, to adopt a broader and more social science approach to their curricula and faculty. As a result, many deans and other administrators went with great speed and vigor to recruit specialists in such fields as economics, mathematics, psychology, sociology, social psychology, and anthropology.

A second reason for the large number of faculty members trained in special fields, rather than in basic management theory and policy, is the fact that the rapid expansion of business and management schools occurred since 1960, during a period when there was an acute shortage of faculty candidates trained in management and with some managerial experience. This shortage was consequently filled by an increasing number of PhD's in the specialized field noted above.

THE CONTINUING JUNGLE

That the theory and science of management are far from being mature is apparent in the continuation of the management theory jungle. What has happened in the intervening years since 1961? The jungle still exists, and, in fact, there are nearly double the approaches to management that were identified nearly two decades ago. At the present time, a total of eleven approaches to the study of management science and theory may be identified. These are: (1) the empirical or case approach, (2) the interpersonal behavior approach, (3) the group behavior approach, (4) the cooperative social system approach, (5) the sociotechnical systems approach, (6) the decision theory approach, (7) the systems approach, (8) the mathematical or "management science" approach, (9) the contingency or situational approach, (10) the managerial roles approach, and (11) the operational theory approach.

Differences between the Original and Present Jungle

What has caused this almost doubling of approaches to management theory and science? In the first place, one of the approaches found nearly two decades ago has been split into two. The original "human behavior school" has, in my judgment, divided itself into the interpersonal behavior approach (psychology) and the group behavior approach (sociology and cultural anthropology). The original social systems approach is essentially the same, but because its proponents seem to rest more heavily on the theories of Chester Barnard, it now seems more accurate to refer to it as the cooperative social systems approach.

Remaining essentially the same since my original article are (1) the empirical or case approach, (2) the decision theory approach, and (3) the mathematical or "management science" approach. Likewise, what was originally termed the "management process school" is now referred to more accurately as the operational theory approach.

New approaches that have become popular in the past two decades include the sociotechnical systems approach. This was first given birth by the research and writings of Eric Trist and his associates in the Tavistock Institute in 1951, but did not get many followers to form a clear-cut approach until the late 1960s. Also, even though the systems approach to any science or practice is not new (it was recognized in the original jungle as the "social systems" approach), its scholarly and widespread approach to management theory really occurred in the 1960s, particularly with the work of Johnson, Kast, and Rosenzweig [1963].

The managerial roles approach has gained its identification and adherents as the result of the research and writing of Henry Mintzberg [1973, 1975], who prefers to call this approach the "work activity school."

The contingency or situational approach to management theory and science is really an outgrowth of early classical, or operational, theory. Believing that most theory before the 1970s too often advocated the "one best way", and often overlooking the fact that intelligent practicing managers have always tailored their practice to the actual situation, a fairly significant number of management scholars have begun building management theory and research around what should be done in various situations, or contingencies.

Many writers who have apparently not read the so-called classicists in management carefully have come up with the inaccurate shibboleth that classical writers were prescribing the "one best way." It is true that Gilbreth in his study of bricklaying was searching for the one best way, but that was bricklaying and not managing. Fayol recognized this clearly when he said "principles are flexible and capable of adaptation to every need; it is a matter of knowing how to make use of them, which is a difficult art requiring intelligence, experience, decision, and proportion" [1949, p. 19].

The Current Approaches to Management Theory and Science

I hope the reader will realize that, in outlining the eleven approaches, I must necessarily be terse. Such conciseness may upset some adherents to the various approaches and some may even consider the treatment superficial, but space limitations make it necessary that most approaches be identified and commented on briefly.

The Empirical or Case Approach The members of this school study management by analyzing experience, usually through cases. It is based on the premise that students and practitioners will understand the field of management and somehow come to know how to manage effectively by studying managerial successes and failures in various individual cases.

However, unless a study of experience is aimed at determining *fundamentally* why something happened or did not happen, it is likely to be a questionable and even dangerous approach to understanding management, because what happened or did not happen in the past is not likely to help in solving problems in a most certainly different future. If distillation of experience takes place with a view to finding basic generalizations, this approach can be a useful one to develop or support some principles and theory of management.

The Interpersonal Behavior Approach This approach is apparently based on the thesis that managing involves getting things done through people, and that therefore the study of management should be centered on interpersonal relations. The writers and scholars in this school are heavily oriented to individual psychology and, indeed, most are trained as psychologists. Their focus is on the individual, and his or her motivations as a sociopsychological being. In this school are those who appear to emphasize human relations as an art that managers, even when foolishly trying to be amateur psychiatrists, can understand and practice. There are those who see the manager as a leader and may even equate managership and leadership—thus, in effect, treating all "led" activities as "managed." Others have concentrated on motivation or leadership and have cast important light on these subjects, which has been useful to managers.

That the study of human interactions, whether in the context of managing or elsewhere, is useful and important cannot be denied. But it can hardly be said that the field of interpersonal behavior encompasses all there is to management. It is entirely possible for all the managers of a company to understand psychology and its nuances and yet not be effective in managing. One major division of a large American company put their managers from top to bottom through sensitivity training (called by its critics "psychological striptease") only to find that the managers had learned much about feelings but little about how to manage. Both research and practice are finding that we must go far beyond interpersonal relations to develop a useful science of management.

The Group Behavior Approach   This approach is closely related to the interpersonal behavior approach and may be confused with it. But it is concerned primarily with behavior of people in groups rather than with interpersonal behavior. It thus tends to rely on sociology, anthropology, and social psychology rather than on individual psychology. Its emphasis is on group behavior patterns. This approach varies all the way from the study of small groups, with their cultural and behavioral patterns, to the behavioral characteristics of large groups. It is often called a study of "organization behavior" and the term "organization" may be taken to mean the system, or pattern, of any set of group relationships in a company, a government agency, a hospital, or any other kind of undertaking. Sometimes the term is used as Chester Barnard employed it, meaning "the cooperation of two or more persons," and "formal organization" as an organization with conscious, deliberate, joint purpose [1938, p. 65]. Chris Argyris has even used the term "organization" to include "*all* the behavior of *all* the participants" in a group undertaking [1957, p. 239].

It is not difficult to see that a practicing manager would not likely recognize that "organizations" cover such a broad area of group behavior patterns. At the same time, many of the problems of managers do arise from group behavior patterns, attitudes, desires, and prejudices, some of which come from the groups within an enterprise, but many come from the cultural environment of people outside of a given company, department, or agency. What is perhaps most disturbing about this school of thought is the tendency of its members to draw an artificial and inaccurate line between "organization behavior" and "managing." Group behavior is an important aspect of management. But it is not all there is to management.

The Cooperative Social System Approach   A modification of the interpersonal and group behavior approaches has been the focus of some behavioral scientists on the study of human relationships as cooperative social systems. The idea of human relationships as social systems was early perceived by the Italian sociologist Vilfredo Pareto. His work apparently affected modern adherents to this school through his influence on Chester Barnard. In seeking to explain the work of executives, Barnard saw them operating in, and maintaining, cooperative social systems, which he referred to as "organizations" [1938, pp. 72–73]. He perceived social systems as the cooperative interaction of ideas, forces, desires, and thinking of two or more persons. An increasing number of writers have expanded this concept to apply to any system of cooperative and purposeful group interrelationships or behavior and have given it the rather general title of "organization theory."

The cooperative social systems approach does have pertinence to the study and analysis of management. All managers do operate in a cooperative social system. But we do not find what is generally referred to as managers in *all* kinds of cooperative social systems. We would hardly think of a cooperative group of shoppers in a department store or an unorganized mob as being managed. Nor would we think of a family group gathering to celebrate a birthday as being managed. Therefore, we can conclude that this approach is broader than management while still overlooking many concepts, principles, and techniques that are important to managers.

The Sociotechnical Systems Approach   One of the newer schools of management identifies itself as the sociotechnical systems approach. This development is generally credited to E. L. Trist and his associates at the Tavistock Institute of England. In studies made of production problems in long-wall coal mining, this group found that it was not enough merely to analyze social problems. Instead, in dealing with problems of mining productivity, they found that the technical system (machines and methods) had a strong influence on the social system. In other words, they discovered that personal attitudes and group behavior are strongly influenced by the technical system in which people work. It is therefore the position of this school of thought that social and technical systems must be considered together and that a major task of a manager is to make sure that these two systems are made harmonious.

Most of the work of this school has consequently concentrated on production, office operations, and other areas where the technical systems have a very close connection to people and their work. It therefore tends to be heavily oriented to industrial engineering. As an approach to management, this school has made some interesting contributions to managerial practice, even though it does not, as some of its proponents seem to believe, encompass all there is to management. Moreover, it is doubtful that any experienced manager would be surprised that the technology of the assembly line or the technology in railroad transportation or in oil companies affect individuals, groups, and their behavior patterns, the way operations are organized, and the techniques of managing required. Furthermore, as promising and helpful as this approach is in certain aspects of enterprise operations, it is safe to observe that there is much more to pertinent management knowledge that can be found in it.

The Decision Theory Approach   This approach to management theory and science has apparently been based on the belief that, because it is a major task of managers to make decisions, we should concentrate on decision making. It is not surprising that there are many scholars and theorists who believe that, because managing is characterized by decision making, the central focus of management theory should be decision making and that all of management thought can be built around it. This has a degree of reasonableness. However, it overlooks the fact that there is much more to managing than making decisions and that, for most managers, the actual making of a decision is a fairly easy thing—if goals are clear, if the environment in which the decision will operate can be fairly accurately anticipated, if adequate information is available, if the organization structure provides a clear understanding of responsibility for decisions, if competent people are available to make decisions, and if many of the other prerequisites of effective managing are present.

The Systems Approach   During recent years, many scholars and writers in management have emphasized the systems approach to the study and analysis of management thought. They feel that this is the most effective means by which such thought can be organized, presented, and understood.

A system is essentially a set or assemblage of things interconnected, or interdependent, so as to form a complex unity. These things may be physical, as with the parts of an automobile engine; or they may be biological, as with components of the human body; or they may be theoretical, as with a well-integrated assemblage of concepts, principles, theory, and techniques in an area such as managing. All systems, except perhaps the universe, interact with and are influenced by their environments, although we define boundaries for them so that we can see and analyze them more clearly.

The long use of systems theory and analyses in physical and biological sciences has given rise to a considerable body of systems knowledge. It comes as no surprise that systems theory has been found helpfully applicable to management theory and science. Some of us have long emphasized an arbitrary boundary of management knowledge—the theory underlying the managerial job in terms of what managers do. This boundary is set for the field of managment theory and science in order to make the subject "manageable," but this does not imply a closed systems approach to the subject. On the contrary, there are always many interactions with the system environment. Thus, when managers plan, they have no choice but to take into account such external variables as markets, technology, social forces, laws, and regulations. When managers design an organizational structure to provide an environment for performance, they cannot help but be influenced by the behavior patterns people bring to their jobs from the environment that is external to an enterprise.

Systems also play an important part within the area of managing itself. There are planning systems, organizational systems, and control systems. And, within these, we can perceive many subsystems, such as systems of delegation, network planning, and budgeting.

Intelligent and experienced practicing managers and many management writers with practical experience, accustomed as they are to seeing their problems and operations as a network of interrelated elements with daily interaction between environments inside or outside their companies or other enterprises, are often surprised to find that many writers regard the systems approach as something new. To be sure, conscious study of, and emphasis on, systems have forced many managers and scholars to consider more perceptively the various interacting elements affecting management theory and practice. But it can hardly be regarded as a new approach to scientific thought.

The Mathematical or "Management Science" Approach   There are some theorists who see managing as primarily an exercise in mathematical processes, concepts, symbols, and models. Perhaps the most widely known of these are the operations researchers who have often given themselves the self-annointing title of "management scientists." The primary focus of this approach is the mathematical model, since, through this device, problems—whether managerial or other—can be expressed in basic relationships and, where a given goal is sought, the model can be expressed in terms which optimize that goal. Because so much of the mathematical approach is applied to problems of optimization, it could be argued that it has a strong relationship to decision theory. But, of course, mathematical modelling sometimes goes beyond decision problems.

To be sure, the journal *Management Science,* published by the Institute of Management Sciences, carries on its cover the statement that the Institute has as its purpose to "identify, extend, and unify scientific knowledge pertaining to management." But as judged by the articles published in this journal and the hundreds of papers presented by members of the Institute at its many meetings all over the world, the school seems to be almost completely preoccupied with mathematical models and elegance in simulating situations and in developing solutions to certain kinds of problems. Consequently, as many critics both inside and outside the ranks of the "management scientists" have observed, the narrow mathematical focus can hardly be called a complete approach to a true management science.

No one interested in any scientific field can overlook the great usefulness of mathematical models and analyses. But it is difficult to see mathematics as a school of management any more than it is a separate school of chemistry, physics, or biology. Mathematics and mathematical models are, of course, tools of analysis, not a school of thought.

The Contingency or Situational Approach   One of the approaches to management thought and practice that has tended to take management academicians by storm is the contingency approach to management. Essentially, this approach emphasizes the fact that what managers do in practice depends on a given set of circumstances—the situation. Contingency management is akin to situational management and the two terms are often used synonymously. Some scholars distinguish between the two on the basis that, while situational management merely implies that what managers do depends on a given situation, contingency management implies an active interrelationship between the variables in a situation and the managerial solution devised. Thus, under a contingency approach, managers might look at an assembly-line situation and conclude that a highly structured organization pattern would best fit and interact with it.

According to some scholars, contingency theory takes into account not only given situations but also the influence of given solutions on behavior patterns of an enterprise. For example, an organization structured along the lines of operating functions (such as finance, engineering, production, and marketing) might be most suitable for a given situation, but managers in such a structure should take into account the behavioral patterns that often arise because of group loyalties to the function rather than to a company.

By its very nature, managerial practice requires that managers take into account the realities of a given situation when they apply theory or techniques. It has never been and never will be the task of science and theory to prescribe what should be done in a given situation. Science and theory in management have not and do not advocate the "best way" to do things in every situation, any more than the sciences of astrophysics or mechanics tell an engineer how to design a single best instrument for all kinds of applications. How theory and science are applied in practice naturally depends on the situation.

This is saying that there is science and there is art, that there is knowledge and there is practice. These are matters that any experienced manager has long known. One does not need much experience to understand that a corner grocery store could hardly be organized like General Motors, or that the technical realities of petroleum exploration, production, and refining make impracticable autonomously organized product divisions for gasoline, jet fuel, or lubricating oils.

The Managerial Roles Approach   Perhaps the newest approach to management theory to catch the attention of academics and practitioners alike is the managerial roles approach, popularized by Henry Mintzberg [1973, 1975]. Essentially this approach is to observe what managers actually do and from such observations come to conclusions as to what managerial activities (or roles) are. Although there have been researchers who have studied the actual work of managers, from chief executives to foremen, Mintzberg has given this approach sharp visibility.

By systematically studying the activities of five chief executives in a variety of organizations, Mintzberg came to the conclusion that executives do not act out the traditional classification of managerial functions—planning, organizing, coordinating, and controlling. Instead they do a variety of other activities.

From his research and the research of others who have studied what managers actually do, Mintzberg has come to the conclusion that managers act out a set of ten roles. These are:

A   Interpersonal roles
   1   Figurehead (performing ceremonial and social duties as the organization's representative)

      2 Leader
      3 Liaison (particularly with outsiders)
B Informational roles
      1 Monitor (receiving information about the operation of an enterprise)
      2 Disseminator (passing information to subordinates)
      3 Spokesperson (transmitting information outside the organization)
C Decision roles
      1 Entrepreneur
      2 Disturbance handler
      3 Resource allocator
      4 Negotiator (dealing with various persons and groups of persons)

Mintzberg refers to the usual way of classifying managerial functions as "folklore." As we will see in the following discussion on the operational theory approach, operational theorists have used such managerial functions as planning, organizing, staffing, leading, and controlling. For example, what is resource allocation but planning? Likewise, the entrepreneurial role is certainly an element of the whole area of planning. And the interpersonal roles are mainly aspects of leading. In addition, the informational roles can be fitted into a number of the functional areas.

Nevertheless, looking at what managers actually do can have considerable value. In analyzing activities, an effective manager might wish to compare these to the basic functions of managers and use the latter as a kind of pilot's checklist to ascertain what actions are being overlooked. But the roles Mintzberg identifies appear to be inadequate. Where in them does one find such unquestionably important managerial activities as structuring organization, selecting and appraising managers, and determining major strategies? Omissions such as these can make one wonder whether the executives in his sample were effective managers. It certainly opens a serious question as to whether the managerial roles approach is an adequate one on which to base a practical theory of management.

The Operational Approach The operational approach to management theory and science, a term borrowed from the work of P. W. Bridgman [1938, pp. 2–32], attempts to draw together the pertinent knowledge of management by relating it to the functions of managers. Like other operational sciences, it endeavors to put together for the field of management the concepts, principles, theory, and techniques that underpin the actual practice of managing.

The operational approach to management recognizes that there is a central core of knowledge about managing that exists only in management: such matters as line and staff, departmentation, the limitations of the span of management, managerial appraisal, and various managerial control techniques involve concepts and theory found only where managing is involved. But, in addition, this approach is eclectic in that it draws on pertinent knowledge derived from other fields. These include the clinical study of managerial activities, problems, and solutions; applications of systems theory; decision theory; motivation and leadership findings and theory; individual and group behavior theory; and the application of mathematical modeling and techniques. All these subjects are applicable to some extent to other fields of science, such as certain of the physical and geological sciences. But our interest in them must necessarily be limited to managerial aspects and applications.

The nature of the operational approach can perhaps best be appreciated by reference to Figure 1. As this diagram shows, the operational management school of thought includes a central core of science and theory unique to management plus knowledge eclectically drawn from various other schools and approaches. As the circle is intended to show, the operational approach is not interested in all the important knowledge in the various fields, but only that which is deemed to be most useful and relevant to managing.

The question of what managers do day by day and how they do it is secondary to what makes an acceptable and useful classification of knowledge. Organizing knowledge pertinent to managing is an indispensible first step in

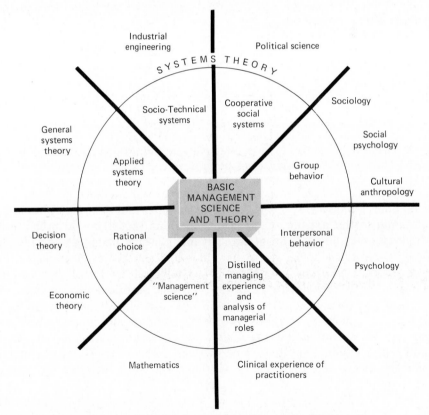

Operational management science and theory is that part of the diagram enclosed in the circle. It shows how operational management science and theory has a core of basic science and theory and draws from other fields of knowledge pertaining to management. It is thus, in part, an eclectic science and theory.

Figure 1 The scope of operational science and theory.

developing a useful theory and science of management. It makes possible the separation of science and techniques used in managing and those used in such nonmanagerial activities as marketing, accounting, manufacturing, and engineering. It permits us to look at the basic aspects of management that have a high degree of universality among different enterprises and different cultures. By using the functions of managers as a first step, a logical and useful start can be made in setting up pigeonholes for classifying management knowledge.

The functions some theorists (including me) have found to be useful and meaningful as this first step in classifying knowledge are:

1   Planning: selecting objectives and means of accomplishing them.
2   Organizing: designing an intentional structure of roles for people to fill
3   Staffing: selecting, appraising, and developing people to effectively fill organizational roles
4   Leading: taking actions to motivate people and help them see that contributing to group objectives is in their own interest
5   Controlling: measuring and correcting activities of people to ensure that plans are being accomplished

As a second step in organizing management knowledge, some of us have found it useful to ask basic questions in each functional area, such as:

1   What is the nature and purpose of each functional area?
2   What structural elements exist in each functional area?
3   What processes, techniques, and approaches are there in each functional area and what are the advantages and disadvantages of each?
4   What obstructions exist in effectively accomplishing each function?
5   How can these obstructions be removed?

Those who, like me, subscribe to the operational approach do so with the hope of developing and identifying a field of science and theory that has useful application to the practice of managing, and one that is not so broad as to encompass everything that might have any relationships, no matter how remote, to the managerial job. We realize that any field as complex as managing can never be isolated from its physical, technological, biological, or cultural environment. We also realize, however, that some partitioning of knowledge is necessary and some boundaries to this knowledge must be set if meaningful progress in summarizing and classifying pertinent knowledge is ever to be made. Yet, as in the case of all systems analyses where system boundaries are set, it must be kept in mind that there is no such thing as a totally closed system and that many environmental variables will intrude on and influence any system proposed.

THE MANAGEMENT THEORY JUNGLE: PROMISING TENDENCIES TOWARD CONVERGENCE OF THEORIES

As can be seen from the brief discussions above of the schools and approaches to management theory and science, there is evidence that the management theory jungle continues to flourish and perhaps gets more dense, with nearly twice as many schools or approaches as were found nearly two decades ago. It is no wonder that a useful management theory and science has been so tardy in arriving. It is no wonder that we still do not have a clear notion of the scientific underpinnings of managing nor have we been able clearly to identify what we mean by competent managers.

The varying approaches, each with its own gurus, each with its own semantics, and each with a fierce pride to protect the concepts and techniques of the approach from attack or change, make the theory and science of management extremely difficult for the intelligent practitioner to understand and utilize. If the continuing jungle were only evidence of competing academic thought and research, it would not much matter. But when it retards the development of a useful theory and science and confuses practicing managers, the problem becomes serious. Effective managing at all levels and in all kinds of enterprises is too important to any society to allow it to fail through lack of available and understandable knowledge.

At the same time, there appears to be some reason to be optimistic, in that signs exist indicating tendencies for the various schools of thought to coalesce. Although the convergence is by no means yet complete, there is reason to hope that, as scholars and writers become more familiar with what managers do and the situations in which they act, more and more of these schools or approaches will adopt, and even expand, the basic thinking and concepts of the operational school of management.

While acknowledging that these are only indications and signs along the road to a more unified and practical operational theory of management, and that there is much more of this road to travel, let us briefly examine some of these tendencies toward convergence.

Greater Emphasis on Distillation of Basics within the Empirical Approach

Within the many programs utilizing cases as a means of educating managers, there are indications that there now exists a much greater emphasis on distilling fundamentals than there was two decades ago. Likewise, in the field of business policy, by which term most of these case approaches have tended to be known, there has been increased emphasis in teaching and research toward going beyond recounting what happened in a given situation to analyzing the underlying causes and reasons for what happened. One major result of all this has been a new emphasis on strategy and strategic planning. This has been nowhere more noteworthy than at the Harvard Business School, which is regarded as the cradle of the case approach. This has led many empiricists to come up with distilled knowledge that fits neatly into the operational theorist's classification of planning.

Recognizing that Systems Theory Is Not a Separate Approach

When systems theory was introduced into the management field some two decades ago, it was hailed by many as being a new way of analyzing and classifying management knowledge. But in recent years, as people have come to understand systems theory *and* the job of managing better, it has become increasingly clear that, in its essentials, there is little new about systems theory and that practicing managers as well as operational theorists had been using its basics (although not always the jargon) for a number of years. Nonetheless, as those in the field of operational management theory have more consciously and clearly employed the concepts and theory of systems, their attempts at developing a scientific field have been improved.

Recognizing that the Contingency Approach Is Not a New or Separate Approach

Although perceptive and intelligent managers and many management theorists have not been surprised by the realization, it is now clear that the contingency view is merely a way of distinguishing between science and art—knowledge and practice. As I pointed out earlier, these are two different things, albeit mutually complementary. Those writers and scholars who have emphasized contingency approaches have, to be sure, done the field of management theory and practice a great service by stressing that what the intelligent manager actually does depends on the realities of a situation. But this has long been true of the application of *any* science.

That contingency theory is really application in the light of a situation has been increasingly recognized, as is evidenced by a recent statement by one of its founders. Jay Lorsch recently admitted that the use of the term "contingency" was "misleading" [1977, pp. 2–14]. He appeared to recognize that an operational management theorist would necessarily become a situationalist when it came to applying management concepts, principles, and techniques.

Finding that Organization Theory Is Too Broad an Approach

Largely because of the influence of Chester Barnard and his broad concept of "organization" as almost any kind of interpersonal relationships, it has become customary, particularly in some academic circles, to use the term "organization theory" to refer to almost any kind of interpersonal relationships. Many scholars attempted to make this field equal to management theory, but it is now fairly well agreed that managing is a narrower activity and that management theory pertains only to theory related to managing. Management theory is often thought of as being a subset of organization theory and it is now fairly well agreed that the general concept of organization theory is too broad.

This sign offers hope of clearing away some of the underbush of the jungle.

The New Understanding of Motivation

The more recent research into motivation of people in organizational settings has tended to emphasize the importance of the organizational climate in curbing or arousing motives. The oversimplified explanations of motives by Maslow and Herzberg may identify human needs fairly well, but much more emphasis must be given to rewards and expectations of rewards. These, along with a climate that arouses and supports motivation, will depend to a very great extent on the nature of managing in an organization.

Litwin and Stringer [1968] found that the strength of such basic motives as needs for achievement, power, and affiliation, were definitely affected by the organizational climate. In a sample of 460 managers, they found a strong relationship between highly structured organizations and arousal of the need for power, and a negative relationship with the needs for achievement and affiliation. Likewise, in a climate with high responsibility and clear standards, they observed a strong positive relationship between this climate and achievement motivation, a moderate correlation to power motivation, and an unrelated to negatively related relationship with affiliation motivation.

The interaction between motivation and organizational climate not only underscores the systems aspects of motivation but also emphasizes how motivation depends on what managers do in setting and maintaining an environment for performance. These researchers move the problem of motivation from a purely behavioral matter to one closely related to and dependent on what managers do. The theory of motivation, then, fits nicely into the operational approach to management theory and science.

The Melding of Motivation and Leadership Theory Another interesting sign that we may be moving toward a unified operational theory of management is the way that research and analysis have tended to meld motivation and leadership theory. Especially in recent years, leadership research and theory have tended to emphasize the rather elementary propositions that the job of leaders is to know and appeal to things that motivate people and to recognize the simple truth that people tend to follow those in whom they see a means of satisfying their own desires. Thus, explanations of leadership have been increasingly related to motivation.

This melding of motivation and leadership theories has also emphasized the importance of organization climate and styles of leaders. Most recent studies and theories tend to underscore the importance of effective managing in making managers effective leaders. Implied by most recent research and theory is the clear message that effective leaders design a system that takes into account the expectancies of subordinates, the variability of motives between individuals and from time to time, situational factors, the need for clarity of role definition, interpersonal relations, and types of rewards.

As can be readily seen, knowledgeable and effective managers do these things when they design a climate for performance, when goals and means of achieving them are planned, when organizational roles are defined and well structured, when roles are intelligently staffed, and when control techniques and information are designed to make self-control possible. In other words, leadership theory and research are, like motivation, fitting into the scheme of operational management theory, rather than going off as a separate branch of theory.

The New Managerially Oriented "Organization Development"

Both "organization development" and the field ordinarily referred to as "organization behavior" have grown out of the interpersonal and group behavior approaches to management. For a while, it seemed that these fields were far away and separate from operational management theory. Now many of these scientists are seeing that basic management theory and techniques, such as managing by objectives and clarifying organization structure, fit well into their programs of behavioral intervention.

A review of the latest organization behavior books indicates that some authors in this field are beginning to understand that behavioral elements in group operations must be more closely integrated with organizational structure design, staffing, planning, and control. This is a promising sign. It is a recognition that analysis of individual and group behavior, at least in managed situations, easily and logically falls into place in the scheme of operational management theory.

The Impact of Technology: Researching an Old Problem

That technology has an important impact on organizational structure, behavior patterns, and other aspects of managing has been recognized by intelligent practitioners for many years. However, primarily among academic researchers, there has seemed to be in recent years a "discovery" that the impact of technology is important and real. To be sure, some of this research has been helpful to managers, especially that developed by the sociotechnical school of management. Also, while perceptive managers have known for many years that technology has important impacts, some of this research has tended to clarify and give special meaning to this impact.

The impact of technology is easily embraced by operational management theory and practice. And it should be. It is to be hoped that scholars and writers in the area of technological impacts will soon become familiar with operational management theory and incorporate their findings and ideas into that operational framework. At the very least, however, those who subscribe to the operational approach can incorporate the useful findings of those who emphasize the impact of technology.

Defections among "Management Scientists"

It will be recalled that in the discussion of schools or approaches to management, one of them is identified as the mathematical or "management science" approach. The reader has also undoubtedly noted that "management science" was put in quotation marks; the reason for so doing is that this group does not really deal with a total science of management but rather largely with mathematical models, symbols, and elegance.

There are clear signs among the so-called management scientists that there are defectors who realize that their interests must go far beyond the use of mathematics, models, and the computer. These especially exist in the ranks of operations researchers in industry and government, where they are faced daily with practical management problems. A small but increasing number of academics are also coming to this realization. In fact, one of the leading and most respected academics, one widely regarded as a pioneer in operations research, C. West Churchman, has (in conversations with me) been highly critical of the excessive absorption with models and mathematics and, for this reason, has even resigned from the Operations Research Society.

There is no doubt that operations research and similar mathematical and modeling techniques fit nicely in the planning and controlling areas of operational management theory and science. Most operational management theorists recognize this. All that is really needed is for the trickle of "management science" defectors to become a torrent, moving their expertise and research more closely to a practical and useful management science.

Clarifying Semantics: Some Signs of Hope

One of the greatest obstacles to disentangling the jungle has long been, and still is, the problem of semantics. Those writing and lecturing on management and related fields have tended to use common terms in different ways. This is exemplified by the variety of meanings given to such terms as "organization," "line and staff," "authority," "responsibility," and "policies," to mention a few. Although this semantics swamp still exists and we are a long way from general acceptance of meanings of key terms and concepts, there are some signs of hope on the horizon.

It has become common for the leading management texts to include a glossary of key terms and concepts and an increasing number of them are beginning to show some commonality of meaning. Of interest also is the fact that the Fellows of the International Academy of Management, composed of some 180 management scholars and leaders from 32 countries of the world, have responded to the demands of its members and have undertaken to develop a glossary of management concepts and terms, to be published in a number of languages and given wide circulation among many countries.

Although it is too early to be sure, it does appear that we may be moving in the direction necessary for the development of science—the acceptance of clear definitions for key terms and concepts.

THE NEED FOR MORE EFFORT IN DISENTANGLING THE JUNGLE

Despite some signs of hope, the fact is that the management theory jungle is still with us. Although some slight progress appears to be occurring, in the interest of a far better society through improved managerial practice it is to be hoped that some means can be found to accelerate this progress.

Perhaps the most effective way would be for leading managers to take a more active role in narrowing the widening gap that seems to exist between professional practice and our college and university business, management, and public administration schools. They could be far more vocal and helpful in making certain that our colleges and universities do more than they have been in developing and teaching a theory and science of management useful to practicing managers. This is not to advocate making these schools vocational schools, especially since basic operational management theory and research are among the most demanding areas of knowledge in our society. Moreover, these schools are *professional* schools and their task must be to serve the professions for which they exist.

Most of our professional schools have advisory councils or boards composed of influential and intelligent top managers and other leading citizens. Instead of these boards spending their time, as most do, in passively receiving reports from deans and faculty members of the "new" things being done, these boards should find out more of what is going on in managerially related teaching and research and insist that some of these be moved toward a more useful operational science of management.

REFERENCES

Argyris, C. *Personality and organization.* New York: Harper & Brothers, 1957.

Barnard, C. I. *The functions of the executive.* Cambridge, Mass.: Harvard University Press, 1938.

Bridgman, P. W. *The logic of modern physics.* New York: Macmillan, 1938.

Fayol, H. *General and industrial management.* New York: Pitman, 1949.

Gordon, R. A.; & Howell, J. E. *Higher education for business.* New York: Columbia University Press, 1959.

Johnson, R. A; Kast, F. E.; & Rosenzweig, J. E. *The theory and management of systems.* New York: McGraw-Hill, 1963.

Koontz, H. The management theory jungle. *Academy of Management Journal,* 1961, *4* (3), 174–188.

Litwin, G. H.; & Stinger, R. A., Jr. *Motivation and organization climate.* Boston: Harvard Graduate School of Business Administration, 1968.

Lorsch, J. W. Organization design: A situational perspective. *Organizational Dynamics,* 1977, *6* (2), 12–14.

Mintzberg, H. *The nature of managerial work.* New York: Harper & Row, 1973.

Mintzberg, H. The manager's job: Folklore and fact. *Harvard Business Review,* 1975, *53* (4), 49–61.

Pierson, F. C. *The education of American businessmen: A study of university-college programs in business administration.* New York: McGraw-Hill, 1959.

REVIEW AND DISCUSSION QUESTIONS

1 What are the major differences between the original and present management theory jungle?
2 Identify and very briefly summarize the current approaches to management theory and science suggested by Koontz.
3 Do you agree with Koontz that both systems theory and the contingency approach are not separate approaches?
4 What is your overall reaction to this article?

Reading 27

A General Contingency Theory of Management

Fred Luthans
Todd I. Stewart

A major goal of any academic pursuit is the development of an overall theory which can serve as a conceptual framework for understanding, research, and application [8]. The search for such a theory in management has resulted in a myriad of complementary, but more often conflicting assumptions and constructs. About 15 years ago Koontz [22] identified six major theoretical approaches to management: process, decision theory, empirical, human behavior, social system and mathematical. He appropriately labelled the existing situation as the "management theory jungle." Today there are at least four widely recognized theoretical approaches to management: process, quantitative, behavioral and systems.

There has been a proselytic tendency on the part of theorists identified with the various approaches. Prominent theorists promote their ascribed frameworks as conceptually valid and pragmatically applicable to all organizations in all situations, criticizing alternative approaches as conceptually weak, myopic in perspective and inapplicable to practice.

During the formative years of the theoretical development of management, the process approach dominated [11, 31, 41]. But with the accelerating theoretical development, research and application of the behavioral and quantitative approaches, the process approach proved to be an inadequate theoretical framework.

In recent years, the systems approach has emerged as an important conceptual framework which attempts to integrate and redirect some divergent theoretical management constructs. Systems concepts such as the environmental suprasystem, the interrelated nature of constitutent organizational subsystems, and system boundary permeability which lead to the concepts of "closed" and "open" systems have been particularly useful in integrating process, quantitative and behavioral constructs [21, 40].

The systems approach will undoubtedly continue to have a significant integrating effect, but it is not pragmatic enough to serve as a theoretical framework for the understanding, research, and practice of management [20]. At the same time there is a growing awareness that the process, quantitative and behavioral advocates have been unable to substantiate their respective claims for universality. Although each construct from the various approaches to management has been effective in particular situations [12, 24, 36, 38,], quantitative advocates have had considerable difficulty accommodating behavioral factors,

From the *Academy of Management Review*, vol. 2, 1977, pp. 181–195. Reprinted with permission from the authors and the *Academy of Management Review*.

and behavioral theorists have been only marginally successful in solving management problems more adaptable to quantative approaches.

There is need for a new theoretical framework for management—not just another approach but one that can achieve the following goals:

1 Integrate and synthesize diverse process, quantitative and behavioral concepts into an interrelated theoretical system [26].

2 Functionally incorporate the systems perspective to organization and management, particularly in developing and defining specific functional relationships between situational factors, management concepts and applications, and organizational performance.

3 Provide a pragmatic basis for analyzing and interpreting the existing body of management knowledge and empirical research, thereby facilitating understanding, prediction and control [8].

4 Provide a framework for systematic and coordinated direction of new research on the complex functional relationships between management and situational variables.

5 Establish a mechanism for effectively translating theoretical constructs and the results of empirical research into management information and application techniques that are relevant and useful to the practitioner.

This article proposes that a General Contingency Theory (GCT) can best meet these important goals for the field of management.

TOWARD A GENERAL CONTINGENCY THEORY

The Situational Approach

A situational perspective has been receiving increased attention. Partly the result of open systems thinking and probably more a direct result of the growing skepticism surrounding the univesality assumption of other management approaches, the situational approach argues that the most effective management concept or technique depends on the set of circumstances at a particular point in time [3, 7, 26, 30].

Child [5] relates the situational approach to open systems thinking and the universalist approach to closed system thinking. There is a conceptual dichotomy between situational and universalist approaches. Although the universalist/closed-system constructs ignore potentially significant, but complicating, situational variables, they are easier to apply in practice. The situational approach takes a more conceptually realistic, but complex, open systems perspective, making practical application much more difficult. In other words, the situational approach achieves greater conceptual validity at the expense of practical applicability.

One way of resolving the dichotomy suggested by Child is to propose a synthesis of the two extremes. The goal would be to modify the situational approach in such a way as to maintain theoretical (open systems) validity, but, at the same time, improve its potential as a framework for practical application. A contingency approach seems best able to accomplish this goal.

The Contingency Approach

The contingency approach is generally situational in orientation, but much more exacting and rigorous. As used in this discussion, the contingency approach is defined as identifying and developing *functional relationships between environmental, management and performance variables*. There have been diverse contingency applications. Some of the more widely recognized include the following:

1 *Organization Design.* Woodward's [42] classic study of British companies demonstrated contingent relationships between environmental variables (technology), management variables (organization structure), and performance. Probably the most widely recognized work has come from Lawrence and Lorsch [24]. Chandler [4] found a contingent relationship between environment, structure/strategy, and performance. There is also more recent work on contingency approaches to organization design [17, 38, 40].

2 *Leadership and Behavioral Applications.* Fiedler's [12] model demonstrated a contingent relationship between environmental variables, leadership style, and effectiveness. Other recent behaviorally oriented applications include models of job design [15] and behavioral change [27].

3 *Quantitative Applications.* Although specific applications are not yet developed, increasing attention is given to situational considerations. Groff and Muth note that:

> . . . the capabilities developed within the operations area should match the requirements of the firm. These requirements are determined primarily by the characteristics of the environment in which the firm operates [13, p. 4].

Miller and Starr [29] developed specific contingency relationships between various situations and quantitative decision-making techniques that lead to effective performance.

The contingency approach has also played an important part in classification taxonomies for organizational systems. With the recent emphasis on open-systems models, many of these classification frameworks are based directly or indirectly on the nature of the organization's environmental suprasystem. Particular attention is devoted to the manner in which the organization interacts with its environment. Katz and Kahn [21], Burns and Stalker [2], Thompson [40], Terryberry [39], Perrow [34] and Etzioni [10] offer organization typologies that are environmentally based. In general, these taxonomies were developed through a deductive methodology. In contrast, Haas, et al. [14], Pugh, et al. [35], McKelvey [28] and others have taken an inductive approach. They propose taxonomies developed empirically through multivariate analysis. McKelvey concludes:

> The recent flourishing of contingency approaches . . . is in fact a grassroots response to the absence of useful classifications . . . Organization and management researchers need contingency theories because there is no taxonomy to make it clear

that one does not, for example, and only for example, apply findings from small British candy manufacturers to large French universities [28, p. 523].

A CONTINGENCY MODEL OF THE ORGANIZATION

The formulation of a General Contingency Theory of Management must start with a sound construct of the organization system. Drawing on the work of Katz and Kahn [21], Thompson [40], Churchman [6], Shetty and Carlisle [38], Lorsch and Morse [25], and Kast and Rosenzweig [20], an organization can be defined as *a social system consisting of subsystems of resource variables interrelated by various management policies, practices and techniques which interact with variables in the environmental suprasystem to achieve a set of goals or objectives.* The goals and objectives are defined by constituents of the social system in terms of relevant environmental and resource constraints. This definition emphasizes several important constructs relevant to development of a comprehensive contingency theory of management.

First, the systems paradigm is viewed as conceptually viable. A systems perspective is needed to emphasize the organization's inherent interaction with its external environment and, internally, the organization is comprised of interrelated subsystems. Second is identification of relevant system variables, which can be placed into a taxonomical hierarchy of primary, secondary and tertiary levels.

The Primary System Variables

The primary variables are the elemental "building blocks" of the organization. Specifically, the primary system includes environmental, resource and management variables.

Environmental Variables These factors affect the organization, but are beyond the direct or positive control of the organization's resource managers [6]. Thompson [40] and others have emphasized that an organization can affect the environment in which it operates. In the context of this discussion, such influences are indirect results of the manager operating more directly on organizational resources to produce some desired change in the system. As the organization and its management gain more direct control over a segment of its environment, this segment is effectively annexed into the organizational system as its boundaries are expanded. As environmental variables are not subject to the direct control of management, they must be considered as "givens" or independent variables in the contingency framework.

A distinction is made between external and internal environmental factors. External environmental variables, such as federal legislation, are considered to be outside the organizational system. Internal environmental variables are also beyond the direct control of the manager in question, but are within the control of the formal organizational system. For example, the environment for a middle manager is not only affected by those factors external to the organization but, probably more important, by the internal environment (e.g., top management policy) over which he or she has no control.

Another important refinement is to distinguish between specific and general variables. Specific environmental variables affect the organization directly and significantly, while general environmental variables have only an indirect influence on the organization and provide a context for the more directly relevant specific factors. A synthesis of the classification schemes offered by Duncan [9], Hall [16], Kast and Rosenzweig [20] and Negandhi [32] suggests the following representative general environmental variables: cultural, social, technological, educational, legal, political, economic, ecological and demographic. Representative specific environmental variables would include customers/clients, suppliers (including labor), competitors, technology and socio-political factors.

Resource Variables These are tangible and intangible factors over which management has more direct control and on which it operates to produce desired changes in the organizational system or its environmental suprasystem [6]. Clearly particular variables may transfer between environmental and resource states (with reference to a specific manager or group of managers), as management gains or loses direct control over such factors. For example, if an organization depends on the independent commercial trucking industry for delivery of supplies and distribution of products, its means of transportation is effectively an environmental variable. Should this same organization acquire its own trucks and drivers to gain control of this transportation variable (i.e., expansion of the organization's system boundaries), the transportation factor is now a resource variable.

Many system variables simultaneously exhibit both environmental and resource characteristics. Extending the transportation example, even though an organization may own its own trucks and employ its own drivers, these drivers, while employees of the organization (and therefore resource variables), are also likely to be members of the Teamsters Union and not subject to the total control of management. The extent to which management's influence over these operators is limited is a measure of the environmental quality of this system variable. A particular system variable can be a resource variable to one manager and an environmental variable to another manager in the same organization. In the final analysis, the manager is also (at least partially) a resource to superiors and a critical factor in the environment of subordinates.

Resource variables can be classified as human and non-human. *Human resource variables* include both demographic characteristics such as number, skills, knowledge, size, race and age, and behavioral characteristics including individual and social behavior and such attendent concepts as needs, attitudes, values, perceptions, expectations, goals, group dynamics and conflict. *Non-human resource variables* include such elements as raw materials, plant, equipment, capital and product or service. Since the set of resource variables on which the manager operates is a "given" at any particular point in time, they too, like environmental variables, are treated as independent variables in the contingency function.

Management Variables   A manager is defined as any individual within the organization system having formal authority to make decisions affecting the allocation or utilization of available resources. Management variables are those concepts and techniques expressed in policies, practices and procedures used by the manager to operate on available resource variables in defining and accomplishing system objectives. Recognizing the eclectic nature of the contingency construct, process, quantitative and behavioral concepts are all represented as management variables. On a more micro perspective, process variables include planning/goal-setting, organizing, communicating and controlling. Behavioral variables can be further classified into individual (motivational techniques, reward systems, etc.) and group/inter-group (organization development techniques, leadership styles, etc.). Quantitative variables can be classified into areas such as decision-making models and information/data management.

Relationship between the Primary Variables   Relationships between the primary system variables are illustrated in the Venn diagram of Figure 1. This figure illustrates the role that management plays in coordinating interaction of the resource subsystem and environmental suprasystem. Specifically, it illustrates the concept proposed by Thompson [40] in which the management subsystem serves as a "buffer" between the uncertain environment (i.e., the set of stochastic environmental variables) and what he called the organization's "core technology."

The Secondary System Variables

Figure 1 also illustrates the secondary system variables, which result from interaction of subsets of the primary variables. As shown, there are three important secondary system variables: situation, organization and performance criteria.

Situation Variables   The set of variables defined by the interaction of environmental *(E)* and resource *(R)* variables are called situational variables in

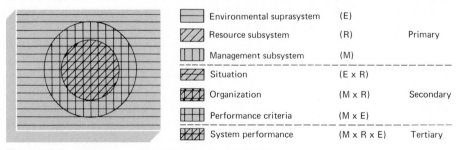

Environmental suprasystem	(E)	
Resource subsystem	(R)	Primary
Management subsystem	(M)	
Situation	(E x R)	
Organization	(M x R)	Secondary
Performance criteria	(M x E)	
System performance	(M x R x E)	Tertiary

Figure 1   A contingency model of the organization system.

the secondary subsystem. This set describes the given state of the organization system with which the manager must interact and operate.

Organization Variables   The intersection of managerial *(M)* and resource *(R)* variable sets results in a secondary subsystem variable set defined as operational organizational variables. This set presents a relatively closed-system description of a particular state of "the organization" at a given point in time, without reference to the environmental suprasystem in which the organization operates.

An example of the organizational variable set is the familiar construct of organizational structure. Structure is, in and of itself, a theoretical concept commonly used to describe the set of formalized or sanctioned social relationships existing between members (primary/resource variables) of the organization system. With regard to the formal organization, these social relationships have been developed by management to facilitate the accomplishment of organization goals. This characterization should not imply that structure, as an organizational variable, is completely independent of environmental variables. The research of Lawrence and Lorsch [24], Woodward [42] and others has clearly demonstrated the correlation between structure and environment. However, the concept of closed-system organizational variables emphasizes that the structure is not *determined directly* or *caused* by the environment. Management develops structure in consideration of (among other factors) environmental variables. The degree to which management is successful in developing a structure compatible with its perception of the environmental suprasystem is reflected in organizational performance.

Performance Criteria Variables   The third set of secondary subsystem variables is determined by the intersection of the environmental *(E)* and management *(M)* variable sets. The critical product of this intersection is a set of performance criteria variables relevant to a particular organizational system. Of direct significance to the manager are organizational goals which are conceived to be desired or acceptable levels of performance. These levels are measured by the respective performance criteria variables. A major goal for the manager, particularly the top level manager with strategic decision making concerns, is to effectively analyze the relevant set of environmental variables to determine the continuing viability of the organization's performance criteria and associated goals. The object of this analysis is to determine what changes must be made in the allocation of available resources to achieve and/or sustain acceptable performance as measured against specific performance criteria.

The Tertiary System Variables

The third level of hierarchical system variables is generated by the interaction of secondary system variables (and, therefore, constituent primary system variables). The product of this interaction is defined as the set of *system performance variables*, which represent the actual performance output of the organization as measured by relevant performance criteria variables. As previously suggested, goals or objectives are defined as a specific subset of these organizational performance variables. This set of performance variables is perhaps the single most distinctive feature of the contingency model, setting this model apart from theoretical constructs that do not emphasize this important link between theory and practice [e.g., 2, 20, 32, 36].

Figure 2 illustrates the relationships between primary, secondary and tertiary variables. It is an illustrative compendium of the conceptual contingency model as a theoretical foundation for developing a GCT framework for management.

GENERAL CONTINGENCY THEORY

As Dubin [8] notes in his thorough discussion of theory construction, a theory must include both conceptual units (variables) and lawful relationships between these variables. The contingency model illustrated in Figures 1 and 2 depicts relevant constituent variables and suggests the general form of the functional relationships between these variables. To facilitate discussion of these GCT functions, the following notation is introduced:

E = the primary set of environmental variables
R = the primary set of resource variables
M = the primary set of management variables
S = the secondary set of situational variables $(E \times R)$
O = the secondary set of organizational variables $(M \times R)$
PC = the secondary set of performance criteria variables $(M \times E)$
P = the tertiary set of performance variables as measured against PC
P^* = the subset of P which meets or exceeds desired or objective levels of performance
f = function of
X = the interaction/intersection of
$s.t.$ = subject to/such that
$.GE.$ = greater than or equal to

From the contingency model of the organization, it is apparent that system

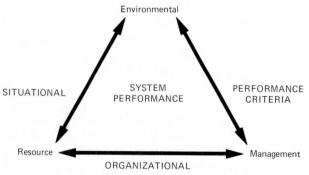

Figure 2   A summary of the variables and relationships in a contingency model of the organization.

performance is a function of the interaction of subsystem variable sets. This suggests that a GCT function will be of the following general form:

$$P = f(E \times R \times M) \qquad (1)$$

Here, system performance *(P)* is cast as the dependent variable, while environment, resource and management variable sets are independent. Further, the situational variable set can be expressed as:

$$S = f(E \times R) \qquad (2)$$

Consequently, substitution of expression (2) into expression (1) yields:

$$P = f(S \times M) \qquad (3)$$

Expression (3) is particularly revealing as it emphasizes the inherent situational nature of the contingency approach (i.e., system performance is a function of the interaction of situational and management variable sets). From a more pragmatic perspective, the practicing manager is primarily interested in that subset of functions in which performance exceeds the desired minimums.

$$P = f(S \times M) \text{ s.t. } P \text{ .GE. } P^* \qquad (4)$$

Theoretically, it can be argued that in any organizational system, all primary, secondary and tertiary variables are continuous in nature, i.e., there exists an infinite number of variable states [8]. But from a more realistic perspective, these system variables can be reasonably approximated by a finite number of discrete and independent variable states. Under this assumption, each of the constituent variable sets can be indexed to represent these discrete states. For example:

$$S_j \text{ i} = 1,2, \ldots ,l \qquad (5)$$

$$M_j \text{ j} = 1,2, \ldots ,m \qquad (6)$$

Using this indexed notation, expression (6) can be written as:

$$P_{ij} = f(S_i \times M_j) \text{ s.t. } P_{ij} \text{ .GE. } P^*_{ij} \qquad (7)$$

Further, by similarily indexing specific performance criteria as:

$$PC_k \text{ k} = 1,2, \ldots ,n \qquad (8)$$

Expression 7 can be extended and refined as:

$$P_{ijk} = f(S_i \times M_j \times PC_k) \text{ s.t. } P_{ijk} \text{ .GE. } P^*_{ijk} \qquad (9)$$

The general functional relationship of expression (9) indicates that a particular level or state of system performance (P_{ijk}) is a dependent variable which is functionally determined by the interaction of independent situational, management and performance criteria variables in states S_i, M_j and PC_k.

The GCT Matrix

The general form of the contingency function of expression (9) suggests the possibility of organizing these system variables and relationships as a three dimensional conceptual matrix (see Figure 3). The respective axes represent nominal scales along which are aligned the various independent and discrete states of S_i, M_j and PC_k. The matrix cell *(i, j, k,)* determined by the intersection of these variable states holds the associated dependent value of system performance *(P_{ijk})*. This conceptual contingency matrix provides the integrating framework necessary for the development of a GCT of Management. As Dubin [8] observes, a simple collection of propositions or, in this case, contingency functions, does not constitute a theory. A theory depends on a lawful relationship between these functions. The GCT matrix provides the theoretical framework necessary to organize and relate these contingency functions and to facilitate the continuing development of a true general theory of management.

The effectiveness of the matrix as a framework for a GCT of management is postulated from comparison of its characteristics with those definitive objectives required for such a general theoretical approach to management. First, the M_j axis includes management concepts and application techniques from the process, quantitative and behavioral schools. These concepts are systematically integrat-

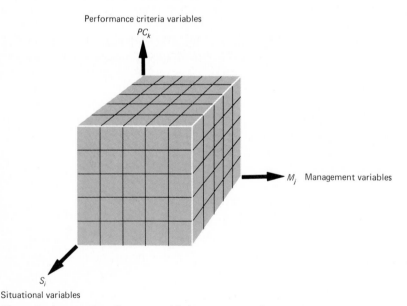

Figure 3   A general contingency matrix for management.

ed by their functional interaction with specific situational and performance criteria variables, as well as to the resultant level of system performance or output. Secondly, the GCT matrix, derived directly from a systems-based model of the organization, incorporates both environmental and resource factors as constituent elements of these situational variables. The matrix framework functionally relates these independent situational variables to management concepts, performance criteria and system performance. Thus the matrix also satisfies the third definitive objective, providing a pragmatic basis for organizing, analyzing and interpreting the existing body of management knowledge.

Implications for Research   The GCT matrix can also provide an integrating framework for existing research findings and serve as a guide for future research. Churchman notes that:

> . . . so much social research is conducted in a fragmented way in which enormous amounts of data are collected, correlated and filed away in reports that at best have a mild interest to the reader, and at worst are totally irrelevant for decision-making purposes [6, p. 102].

The empty cells of the matrix indicate specific combinations of situational, management and performance criteria variables for which a functional relationship to system performance has yet to be defined. The framework can also be used to identify contingency functions that require validation by rigorous, empirically-based research methodologies. For example, functions that have been derived deductively from case studies are candidates for validation through replication in controlled laboratory or field experiments.

Finally, the framework can serve as an important vehicle for inductively or deductively generating hypotheses for testing and validation. The framework itself provides a data base upon which secondary or indirect research can be conducted. For example, by holding M_j and PC_k variables constant and varying S_i, functional relationships could be developed relating a given management concept or technique at a given performance level across a range of situations. Only after a particular management variable M_j has been systematically and empirically validated across a wide range of situations S_i could a practical claim for universality be justified. In this way, research progress could be made in an orderly, systematic manner, thereby building an integrated, valid general theory of management.

Implications for Management Practice   Perhaps the acid test of the GCT matrix is its potential for translating theoretical constructs and associated empirical research data into management information and application techniques that are relevant to the practitioner. The key to facilitating this application is development of an operational matrix, i.e. a data base of contingency functions organized in the format of the GCT matrix framework. Development of an operational GCT data base in turn depends on availability of the data reduction instruments necessary to translate the existing body of management research into functional contingency relationships. To be of value to the practitioner, these data reduction instruments, or a complementary set of diagnostic instruments, must also be effective in analyzing, measuring and defining the current state of system variables in operational organizations. In addition, storing and manipulating the vast amount and wide variety of data implied in an operational GCT data base matrix requires efficient and effective automated data processing hardware and software. For example, a GCT matrix dimensioned at only 100 discrete states on each axis generates an array of one million cells or system state combinations. Consequently, the development of a realistic GCT data base depends in part on availability of adequate computer support.

These problems represent formidable barriers to application of the GCT approach to management. Their resolution would provide the manager with a powerful tool for diagnosis of organizational systems and implementation of planned change designed to improve performance.

With such an automated GCT data base matrix and the associated diagnostic instruments, a manager could periodically conduct a "contingency audit" to identify and measure the current states of relevant system variables and highlight specific performance criteria for which system performance is less than the corresponding objective value. By programmatically comparing results of the contingency audit with the GCT data base, the information system could provide the manager with alternate management applications that have resulted (or are likely to result) in an acceptable level of system performance in a similar situation.

With development of an automated GCT data base, selection of the intervention strategy can be made more effectively. Using simulation and sensitivity analysis techniques, potential intervention strategies can be tested and evaluated without incurring the associated investment and opportunity costs. This process for applying the GCT approach to management practice is summarized more formally in the following algorithm:

Step 1: The Contingency Audit
A   Identify through diagnostic techniques the current state of system variables:
   1   The situation (S_i), as defined by the interaction of environmental and resource variables.
   2   The existing set of management variables (M_j).
   3   Relevant performance criteria (PC_k) and associated goals $(P^*_{ijk}$ or, if constant over $S_i \times M_j$, $P^*_k)$.
   4   System performance states (P_{ijk}).
B   Identify those system performance criteria (PC_k) for which P_{ijk} is less than P^*_{ijk}.

Step 2: Develop the Strategy for Planned Change
A   For those criteria (PC_k) for which P_{ijk} is currently less than P^*_{ijk}, identify

those states in the conceptual matrix (the existing data base) for which P_{ijk} .GE. P^*_{ijk} for all values of k.

B Using a specific criterion (e.g., performance/cost ratio), determine from acceptable alternates the most effective change strategy, considering changes in management and resource variables, thereby changing the situational state.

Step 3: Implement the Change Strategy

Step 4: Evaluate the Results of the Change Intervention
A Determine if management and/or situational variables have been changed to the target state as intended.
B Determine if P_{ijk}. GE. P^*_{ijk} for all values of k.
C Determine if the results of the intervention are consistent with the results predicted by the data base.
D Update the data base to reflect the results of the intervention (to insure the continuing accuracy and validity of the data base).

The steps of this algorithm are illustrated in the schematic of Figure 4.

A specific example is described in the finite conceptual matrix of Figure 5. Assume that the Step 1 diagnosis reveals that the organization is currently in the state represented by $(S_4 \times M_1)$. Step 1 would also identify unsatisfactory performance against, for example, criteria C_3 (i.e., $P_{4, 1, 3}$ is less than $P^*_{4, 1, 3}$). In a systematic search of the matrix, $(S_4 \times M_2)$ and (at least) $(S_2 \times M_4)$ result in performance levels that exceed the associated P^*_{ijk}. However, adopting a change strategy that results in system state $(S_4 \times M_2)$ suggests that performance will become unsatisfactory as measured against criteria PC_1 and PC_4. In contrast, system states $(S_4 \times M_3)$ and $(S_2 \times M_4)$ both satisfy all performance objectives. Based on this determination, the system manager selects the most potentially effective intervention stragegy, i.e., to change the management variable from M_1 to M_3 in situation state S_4, or to change both management and situational (resource) variables from $(S_4 \times M_1)$ to $(S_2 \times M_4)$. The actual choice of intervention would depend on the decision criteria employed by the manager.

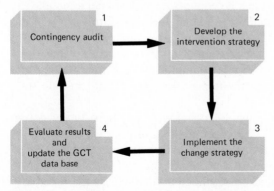

Figure 4 A contingency approach to managing planned change.

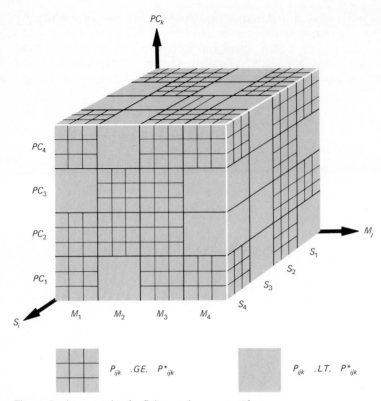

Figure 5   An example of a finite contingency matrix.

Operationalizing the GCT Framework

A number of complex developmental problems must be resolved if the GCT matrix construct is to be effectively operationalized and extended beyond the state of intellectual exercise. First, an operational taxonomy must be developed that effectively defines and measures the state of each primary and secondary system variable. Such a taxonomy must be comprehensive enough to handle the highest order of operational measures (nominal, ordinal, interval and ratio scales) that can be validly applied to a particular system variable state. Ideally, these variable taxonomies must describe both a system variable value in its steady-state mode, and also such critical parameters as state stability/state dynamics and the relative deterministic/stochastic nature of the variable state value.

Instruments and techniques must be developed to apply these system variable state taxonomies to source data. Essentially, this problem breaks down into two specific applications. First, data reduction instruments must be devised to translate the research data currently reported in the management literature into appropriate taxonomical dimensions included in the GCT matrix data base. Secondly, a similar set of instruments and techniques is required to support the contingency audit of an operational organization. Such diagnostic tools provide the necessary operational link between the data base of empirically-expressed management contingency functions and the complex problematic realities confronting the practicing manager.

A second fundamental problem attendant to development of an operational GCT matrix is expression of the contingency functions themselves, i.e., the lawful relationships between the various system variable state values. Like the state variables which constitute the other necessary component element of a true theory, these relationships must be operationally defined. Any scheme for expressing these functions must effectively accommodate the range in types of interactions reported in the management research literature.

Dubin [8] recognizes a relative hierarchy of three general forms of interaction expressions. *Categoric laws* of interaction indicate that the value of one system variable is *associated* with the value of another. *Sequential laws* of interaction express *time ordered* relationships between the values of two or more system variables. *Sequential laws* are commonly used to suggest *causal* relationships between various system variable states. A *deterministic law* of interaction is one that associates *specific deterministic values* of one system variable with deterministic values of another. GCT contingency functions may be categoric, sequential or deterministic.

The third major problem is development of a computer software code capable of effectively and efficiently processing the tremendous amounts of data involved with operationalizing a GCT data base matrix of meaningful capacity. Developing this code requires consideration of such factors as input/output modes, input/output formats, storage requirements, data analysis options, advantages/disadvantages of various programming languages and system hardware compatibility.

The problems confronting development of an operational automated GCT matrix data base are complex. Just as research is a continuing process, the development, expansion and refinement of the data base to include an increasing number of system variable states and functional contingency relationships is an unbounded effort, commensurate with development of management knowledge. This process of operationalizing the GCT matrix has been initiated by the authors in the form of descriptive research designed to identify and discuss specific problems, assumptions and decision processes attendant to development of operational system variable taxonomies, data reduction and contingency audit instruments, operational measures of contingency functions, and a computer code for feasibility testing.

CONCLUSIONS AND IMPLICATIONS FOR THE FUTURE

In spite of the significant practical problems to be resolved, GCT offers the theorist, researcher and practitioner a real and potential framework for integrating existing contingency approaches and for orchestrating future management research and development. As the rate of change and the associated degree of complexity continues to accelerate, the influence of environmental variables will be increasingly significant to effective management. This increasing environmental impact should make a contingency approach to management more important in the future. However, if the contingency approach is to realize its potential as an effective construct for maintaining and improving managerial effectiveness in a hyperdynamic environment, its development must proceed in a systematic, unified and directed manner. The General Contingency Theory of Management is offered as a conceptually-pragmatic, research-based framework with considerable potential for impact on the future course of management.

REFERENCES

1 Bass, B. M., and E. R. Valenzi. "Contingent Aspects of Effective Management Styles," *Technical Report No. 67,* National Technical Information Service, May 1973.
2 Burns, T., and G. M. Stalker. "Mechanistic and Organic Systems," in *The Management of Innovation* (Tavistock Publications, 1961).
3 Carlisle, H. M. *Situational Management* (New York: AMACOM, 1973).
4 Chandler, A. D. *Strategy and Structure: Chapters in the History of the American Industrial Enterprise* (Cambridge, Mass.: MIT, 1962).
5 Child, J. "What Determines Organization Performance?—The Universals vs. The It-All-Depends," *Organizational Dynamics* (Summer 1974), 2–18.
6 Churchman, C. W. *The Systems Approach* (New York: Delta, 1968).
7 Dessler, G. *Organization and Management: A Contingency Approach* (Englewood Cliffs, N.J.: Prentice-Hall, 1976).
8 Dubin, R. *Theory Building* (New York: The Free Press, 1969).
9 Duncan, R. B. "Characteristics of Organizational Environment and Perceived Environmental Uncertainty," *Administrative Science Quarterly* (September 1972), 313–327.
10 Etzioni, A. *A Comparative Analysis of Complex Organizations* (New York: The Free Press, 1961).
11 Fayol, H. *General and Industrial Management* (London: Sir Isaac Pitman & Sons, Ltd., 1949).
12 Fiedler, F. *A Theory of Leadership Effectiveness* (New York: McGraw-Hill, 1967).
13 Groff, G. K., and J. F. Muth. *Operations Management: Analysis for Decisions* (Homewood, Ill.: Richard D. Irwin, 1972).
14 Haas, J. E., et al. "Toward an Empirically Derived Taxonomy of Organizations," in R. V. Bowers (Ed.), *Studies on Behavior in Organizations* (University of Georgia Press, 1966).
15 Hackman, J. R., et al. "A New Strategy for Job Enrichment," *California Management Review* (Summer 1975), 57–71.
16 Hall, R. H. *Organizations: Structure and Process* (Englewood Cliffs, N.J.: Prentice-Hall, 1972).
17 Hellriegel, D., and J. W. Slocum, Jr. "Organization Design: A Contingency Approach," *Business Horizons* (April 1973), 59–68.
18 Hofer, C. W. "Toward a Contingency Theory of Business Strategy," *Academy of Management Journal,* Vol. 18 (December 1975), 784–810.
19 Hunt, J. G., et al. "Upper Level Technical Orientation and First Level Leadership

within a Noncontingency and Contingency Framework," *Academy of Management Journal* (September 1975), 476–488.

20 Kast, F. E., and J. E. Rosenzweig. *Organization and Management: A Systems Approach* (New York: McGraw-Hill, 1974).

21 Katz, D., and R. L. Kahn. *The Social Psychology of Organizations* (New York: Wiley, 1966).

22 Koontz, H. "The Management Theory Jungle," *Academy of Management Journal* (December 1961), 174–188.

23 Korman, A. K., and R. Tanofsky. "Statistical Problems of Contingent Models in Organization Behavior," *Academy of Management Journal,* Vol. 18 (June 1975), 393–397.

24 Lawrence, P. R., and J. W. Lorsch. *Organization and Environment: Managing Differentiation and Integration* (Boston: Harvard, 1967).

25 Lorsch, J. W., and J. J. Morse. *Organizations and Their Members: A Contingency Approach* (New York: Harper & Row, 1974).

26 Luthans, F. *Introduction to Management: A Contingency Approach* (New York: McGraw-Hill, 1976).

27 Luthans, F., and R. Kreitner. *Organizational Behavior Modification* (Glenview, Ill.: Scott, Foresman, 1975).

28 McKelvey, B. "Guidelines for Empirical Classification of Organizations," *Administrative Science Quarterly* (December 1975), 509–525.

29 Miller, W. M., and M. K. Starr. *Executive Decisions and Operations Research* (Englewood Cliffs, N.J.: Prentice-Hall, 1970).

30 Mockler, R. J. "Situational Theory of Management," *Harvard Business Review* (May–June 1971), 146–154.

31 Mooney, J. D., and A. C. Reiley. *Onward Industry!* (New York: Harper & Brothers, 1931).

32 Negandhi, A. R. "Comparative Management and Organization Theory: A Marriage Needed," *Academy of Management Journal* (June 1975), 334–344.

33 Pennings, J. M. "The Relevance of the Structural Contingency Model of Organizational Effectiveness," *Administrative Science Quarterly,* Vol. 20 (September 1975), 393–410.

34 Perrow, C. "The Short and Glorious History of Organizational Theory," *Organizational Dynamics* (Summer 1973), 3–14.

35 Pugh, D. S., et al. "An Empirical Taxonomy of Structures of Work Organizations," *Administrative Science Quarterly* (March 1969), 115–126.

36 Reif, W. E., and F. Luthans. "Does Job Enrichment Really Pay Off?" *California Management Review* (Fall 1972), 30–37.

37 Shetty, Y. K. "Is There a Best Way to Organize a Business Enterprise?" *S. A. M. Advanced Management Journal* (April 1973), 47–52.

38 Shetty, Y. K., and H. M. Carlisle. "A Contingency Model of Organizational Design," *California Management Review,* Vol. 15 (Fall 1972), 38–45.

39 Terryberry, S. "The Evolution of Organizational Environments," *Administrative Science Quarterly* (March 1968), 590–613.

40 Thompson, J. D. *Organizations in Action* (New York: McGraw-Hill, 1967).

41 Urwick, L. *The Elements of Administration* (New York: Harper & Brothers, 1943).

42 Woodward, J. *Industrial Organization: Theory and Practice* (Oxford University Press, 1965).

REVIEW AND DISCUSSION QUESTIONS

1   Briefly explain the general contingency theory of management. How does it differ from the situational approach?
2   How can the GCT framework be used to analyze and classify management research?
3   Explain the three dimensional contingency matrix. Cite an example of how this matrix could be used by a practicing manager.
4   What is a contingency audit? Explain the steps and give a hypothetical example.

Reading 28

A Conceptual Framework for the Design of Organizational Control Mechanisms

William G. Ouchi

1   INTRODUCTION

Organizational control has many meanings and has been interpreted in many ways, Tannenbaum [42], whose view has dominated organizational theory, interprets control as the sum of interpersonal influence relations in an organization. In a similar vein, Etzioni [13] finds it useful to treat control in organizations as equivalent to power. Other than the power-influence approach to control, organization theorists have also treated control as a problem in information flows (Galbraith [15], Ouchi and Maguire [30]), as a problem in creating and monitoring rules through a hierarchical authority system as specified by Weber [46] and interpreted by Perrow [33], Blau and Scott [7], and many organizational sociologists, and as a cybernetic process of testing, measuring, and providing feedback (Thompson [43], Reeves and Woodward [35]).

This paper considers a more simple-minded view of organizational control stated in the following two questions: What are the mechanisms through which an organization can be managed so that it moves towards its objectives? How can the design of these mechanisms be improved, and what are the limits of each basic design?

2   AN EXAMPLE: THE PARTS SUPPLY DIVISION

For the last two years, the author has worked with the parts distribution division of a major company. From the outset, I was struck with this problem: the purchasing department buys approximately 100,000 different items each year

Reprinted from *Management Science,* September 1979, pp. 833–848, with permission of the publisher and the author.

from about 3,000 different manufacturers, and it accomplishes this huge volume of work with only 22 employees, of whom 3 are managerial-level. On the other hand, the warehousing operation, which stores these items until they are ordered by a customer and then fills the customer orders, has about 1,400 employees, of whom about 150 are managers. Why is it that it takes relatively so few people to accomplish the very complex task of evaluating the quality and price of so many items, compared to the number of people required to store and then to distribute them?

Out in a warehouse, the "pickers" must pick out the proper items to fill an order from a customer, the "packers" must check the items to be sure that the order is as specified and then must pack them properly for shipping, and the foreman must see to it that the work is going along properly. What we are interested in is the control process which the foreman uses to get the work out. The foreman is engaged in an elaborate task: he gathers information concerning the flow of work by watching the actions of the workers, knowing from their behavior which workers are doing their jobs well or poorly; he confirms his observations by checking a record of output for each worker at the end of each day. As he observes the pickers and packers at work, the foreman also, from time to time, will stop to inquire of a worker why he or she is doing a job in a particular manner. He may also ask someone to stop what they are doing and to do a different job instead; in some cases, he will angrily confront a "trouble maker" and demand that they behave as he directs. In all of these actions, the supervisor is working within a well-defined set of rules which prescribe both his behavior and that of the pickers and packers; he does so within both the formal limits of authority which are given him by virtue of his rank and within the informal limits of authority granted to him by the workers as a result of their trust in and respect for him as an individual. These formal limits of authority and of power are not implicit, they are written down in black and white, and each employee, both picker and foreman, knows them by memory. The informal agreements, while equally effective, remain implicit.

In the purchasing department, each purchasing officer does his or her work by sending out a description of the item desired to three or four different manufacturers, asking each one to quote a price for it. After the prices are in, the purchaser adds in any information that he may have concerning the honesty and reliability of the supplier and the past performance that he has demonstrated, and then decides to order from one of them. The supervisor occasionally consults with each purchasing agent to see if they need help, and the supervisor strictly reminds each and every person that under no conditions are they ever to accept gifts of any sort from any supplier. Now what is the control mechanism here?

Analysis of the Example

Three mechanisms have been identified: a market mechanism, which primarily characterized the purchasing function; a bureaucratic mechanism, which primarily characterized the warehousing function; and an informal social mechanism, which was mentioned in passing. This example illustrates that the mechanisms themselves overlap in organizations; although it may be helpful to treat them as conceptually distinct from one another, they in fact occur in various combinations.

Market Mechanisms

The work of the purchasing agent is, largely, subject to market mechanisms. At least two important effects are evident. First, the work of each agent is greatly simplified because he is relieved of the necessity of determining, for each part purchased, whether the supplier's intended manufacturing and delivery process is the most efficient possible. Instead, he simply puts each part out for competitive bids and permits the competitive process to define a fair price. In the second place, the work of the manager who supervises these agents is also greatly simplified, because he needs only to check their decisions against the simple criterion of cost minimization rather than observing the steps through which they work and forming an assessment of their unique skills and effort (however, this is a bureaucratic mechanism). Clearly, a parts division which chose to ignore market information and relied instead upon its own internal evaluation of the particulars of each bid would be at a significant cost disadvantage due to the much greater administrative overhead that it would incur.

As a pure model, a market is a very efficient mechanism of control (cf. Arrow [4, pp. 1–29]). In a market, prices convey all of the information necessary for efficient decision-making. In a frictionless market, where prices exactly represent the value of a good or service, decision-makers need no other information. Arbitrary rules such as those found in the warehouse are unnecessary. In addition to information, prices provide a mechanism for solving the problem of goal incongruity. Given a frictionless price mechanism, the firm can simply reward each employee in direct proportion to his contribution, so that an employee who produces little is paid little, and all payments, being exactly in proportion to contribution, are fair.

Of course, in this perfect example of a frictionless market, there is little reason for a formal organization to exist at all (Coase [9]). The fact that purchasing takes place within the corporate framework in our example suggests that some major market defects must exist. At least some of the parts purchased are sufficiently unique that only one or two potential manufacturers exist, so that a more detailed evaluation of those contracts is necessary, and a more thorough bureaucratic surveillance of the purchasing agents in such cases is also called for (see Williamson, [48] for a more complete discussion). More importantly, the work of the purchasing agents themselves is controlled through a process of bureaucratic surveillance rather than through a price mechanism. That is, the director of purchasing does not simply determine a market price for purchasing agents and then occasionally audit performance. Rather, he agrees upon an employment contract with each purchasing agent at some price (cf. Simon [37, pp. 183–195]) and then resorts to hierarchical order-giving and performance evaluation to control them. It is important to distinguish between the market mechanism employed by purchasing agents and the bureaucratic mechanism to which they are subject. Thus, in reality, there is a mixture of market and bureaucratic mechanisms which provide control in the case of purchasing, although it is the market mechanisms which are most clearly evident in this example.

Bureaucratic Mechanisms

In marked contrast to purchasing, warehousing in our example is subject to a variety of explicit routines of monitoring and directing which conform quite closely to the bureaucratic model described by Weber [46]. The fundamental mechanism of control involves close personal surveillance and direction of subordinates by superiors. The information necessary for task completion is contained in rules; these may be rules concerning processes to be completed or rules which specify standards of output or quality. In any case, rules differ from prices in the important sense that they are partial rather than complete bundles of information. A price implies that a comparison has taken place; a comparison between alternative buyers or sellers of the value of the object in question. A rule, however, is essentially an arbitrary standard against which a comparison is yet to be made. In order to use a rule (e.g., a budget, or cost standard), a manager must observe some actual performance, assign some value to it, and then compare that assigned value to the rule in order to determine whether the actual performance was satisfactory or not. All of this consumes a good deal of administrative overhead. If the rule is expressed qualitatively rather than quantitatively, the cost of administration can be expected to be even higher.

Given these inadequacies of bureaucracy, one might reasonably ask why the warehouse does not emulate the purchasing office and rely instead upon a price mechanism. The answer to that question has been the subject of a good deal of recent work by institutional economists, but an organization theorist might focus on one or two dimensions of the problem. Let us approach the question by beginning with the scenario of a warehouse manager who indeed decides to manage through an internal price mechanism. His first task is to set a price for each task, a job that may be impossible since many of the tasks are at least in part unique and thus not subject to market comparisons. Supposing that he can establish reasonable prices for a number of tasks, he must then have a mode of determining when an assigned task has been completed. Unlike the purchasing manager, who can sample delivered products for the purposes of determining contractual satisfaction, the warehouse manager has no correspondingly inexpensive way to determine performance and will have to establish a set of performance standards. In order to see that these standards are applied, he will have to create a system of hierarchical superiors who will closely monitor the performance of individual workers. Furthermore, he will have to create an atmosphere in which the workers willingly permit this close surveillance, or else morale and productivity will suffer. In some cases, tasks will inherently require teamwork, and then superiors will have to apply judgment to attribute value added among the team members. In order to simplify these problems of surveillance, the manager will attempt to create sub-specialities within the warehouse to more readily permit comparison of performance between like workers. Finally, when one task becomes particularly critical, the manager will want to increase the price that he will pay for it in order to increase the supply of workers who are willing to perform it. If he is unable to exactly price the critical task, he will have either an oversupply or an undersupply of workers performing it, to the detriment of the warehouse. Given the difficulty of correctly pricing any task, he will instead invest hierarchical superiors with the right to direct the efforts of subordinates on an *ad hoc* basis; and again he will need to create an atmosphere in which such directives will be willingly followed.

Having done all of these things, our warehouse manager who set out to create an internal market will have exactly instituted a bureaucratic hierarchy instead. Both bureaucratic and market mechanisms are directed towards the same objectives. Which form is more efficient depends upon the particulars of the transactions in question. Indeed, at this point we have an answer to the original dilemma: how can the purchasing department carry out its task with so few people compared to the number in warehousing? Purchasing in this example participates in a market mechanism, which is a far more efficient mechanism of control in terms of the administrative overhead consumed. Prices are a far more efficient means of controlling transactions than are rules. However, the conditions necessary for frictionless prices can rarely be met, and in such conditions the bureaucratic form, despite its inadequacies, is preferred.

Clan Mechanisms

The example also mentioned briefly the informal social structure which, in addition to market and bureaucratic mechanisms, also contributes to control in the warehouse. In order to illustrate the operation of these clan mechanisms, let us return briefly to the example.

Consider the foreman in the warehouse. His task is to oversee the work of pickers and packers. How is the warehouse manager to evaluate the work of the foreman? To some extent, he can rely on bureaucratic mechanisms such as output schedules, budgets, and inventory rules, but these in turn require surveillance. Given that the task of the foreman is significantly more subtle than that of the picker, the manager's task of bureaucratically supervising the foreman becomes very complex. However, if the manager is capable of selecting for promotion to foreman only that subset of workers who display a high internal commitment to the firm's objectives, and if he can maintain in them a deep commitment to these objectives, then his need for explicit surveillance and evaluation is reduced. In short, once the manager knows that they are trying to achieve the "right" objectives, he can eliminate many costly forms of auditing and surveillance.

Consider a different example—the general hospital. In the case of many health care employees, even the most dedicated attempts at systematic performance auditing would be frustrated. Task performance is inherently ambiguous, and teamwork is common, so that precise evaluation of individual contribution is all but impossible. In such cases, we observe a highly formalized and lengthy period of socialization during which would-be doctors and nurses are subjected not only to skill training but also to value training or indoctrination. When they are certified, they are certified with respect not only to their technical skills but also with respect to their integrity or purity of values.

When these socialization processes characterize groups such as physicians or nurses who occupy different organizations but with similar values, we refer to them as professions. When the socialization process refers to all of the citizens of a political unit, we refer to it as a culture. When it refers to the properties of a unique organization, we may refer to it as a clan. The functions of socialization are similar in professions, cultures, and clans, but our present interest centers on the clan.

The discovery that an informal social system characterizes most work organizations was noted first in the Hawthorne Studies (Roethlisberger and Dickson [36]). The subtle and widespread impact of local values on behavior has been thoroughly documented (Selznick [38], Gouldner [16]) as well as theoretically treated (Blau [6], Blau and Scott [7, pp. 89–99]). In organizational studies, the socialization mechanisms have been found to be unique to a particular organization (Trist and Bamforth [44]), to an industry (Lipset, Trow, and Coleman [24], Kaufmann [19]), or they may characterize most of the firms in an economy, as in the case of Japan (Nakane [29], Dore [12], Rohlen [37]).

Until recently, however, organization theorists have regarded this informal social system as either an anomaly or an epiphenomenon, not as the subject of analysis central to the problem of organization. However, a clan may serve as the basis of control in some organizations, just as the market was the basic form in the purchasing function and bureaucracy the basic form in the warehouse.

3   THE SOCIAL AND INFORMATIONAL PREREQUISITES OF CONTROL

It is possible to arrange the three modes of control along each of two dimensions: the informational requirements necessary to operate each control type, and the social underpinnings necessary to operate each control type. These are summarized in Table 1.

Let us consider first the social requirements, and then we will consider the informational issues. What we mean by social requirements is that set of agreements between people which, as a bare minimum, is necessary for a form of control to be employed. Any real organization, of course, will have developed a highly elaborated set of understandings which goes far beyond this. At the moment, however, our task is to understand the bare minimum without which a control mechanism cannot function.

A market cannot exist without a norm of reciprocity, but it requires no social agreements beyond that. A norm of reciprocity assures that, should one party in a market transaction attempt to cheat another, that the cheater, if

Table 1   Social and Informational Prerequisites of Control

Type of control	Social requirements	Informational requirements
Market	Norm of reciprocity	Prices
Bureaucracy	Norm of reciprocity Legitimate authority	Rules
Clan	Norm of reciprocity Legitimate authority Shared values, beliefs	Traditions

discovered, will be punished by all members of the social system, not only by the victim and his or her partners. The severity of the punishment will typically far exceed the crime, thus effectively deterring potential future opportunists (Gouldner [17]). The norm of reciprocity is critical in a market if we think, for a moment, about the costs of running a market mechanism as opposed to the costs of any mechanism of control. In a market mechanism, the costs of carrying out transactions between parties have mostly to do with assuring oneself that the other party is dealing honestly, since all information relevant to the substance of the decision is contained in prices and is therefore not problematic. If honesty cannot be taken for granted, however, then each party must take on the cripplingly high costs of surveillance, complete contracting, and enforcement in order not to be cheated (Williamson [48]). These costs can quickly become so high that they will cause a market to fail.

When a market fails as the mechanism of control, it is most often replaced by a bureaucratic form. A bureaucracy contains not only a norm of reciprocity, but also agreement on legitimate authority, ordinarily of the rational/legal form (see Blau and Scott [7, pp. 27–36] for a discussion). In a bureaucratic control system, the norm of reciprocity is reflected in the notion of "an honest day's work for an honest day's pay," and it particularly contains the idea that, in exchange for pay, an employee gives up autonomy in certain areas to his organizational superiors, thus permitting them to direct his work activities and to monitor his performance. These steps are possible only if organization members accept the idea that higher office holders have the legitimate right to command and to audit or monitor lower persons, within some range (also known as the "zone of indifference," see Barnard [5]). Given social support for a norm of reciprocity and for the idea of legitimate authority, a bureaucratic control mechanism can operate successfully.

A Clan requires not only a norm of reciprocity and the idea of legitimate authority (often of the "traditional" rather than the "rational/legal" form), but also social agreement on a broad range of values and beliefs. Because the clan lacks the explicit price mechanism of the market and the explicit rules of the bureaucracy, it relies for its control upon a deep level of common agreement between members on what constitutes proper behavior, and it requires a high level of commitment on the part of each individual to those socially prescribed behaviors. Clearly, a clan is more demanding than either a market or a bureaucracy in terms of the social agreements which are prerequisite to its successful operation.

The Informational Prerequisites of Control

While a Clan is the most demanding and the Market the least demanding with respect to social underpinnings, the opposite is true when it comes to information. It has been observed (see Galbraith [15], Lawrence and Lorsch [21]) that, within large corporations, each department tends to develop its own peculiar jargon; it does so because the jargon, being suited to the particular task needs of the department, provides it with a very efficient set of symbols with which to communicate complex ideas, thus conserving on the very limited information-carrying capacity of an organization. We can also think of the accounting system in an organization as the smallest set of symbols which conveys information that is relevant to all organizational subunits. An accounting system is a relatively explicit information system compared, say, to the traditions of the U.S. Senate (see Matthews [27]). Each of these mechanisms carries information about how to behave, but the accounting system, being explicit, is easily accessed by a newcomer while the traditions of the Senate, being implicit, can be discovered by a freshman senator only over a period of years. On the other hand, the explicit system is far less complete in its ability to convey information and it has often been noted (see, for example, Vancil [45]) that there is no accounting measurement which fully captures the underlying performance of a department or corporation, since many of the dimensions of performance defy measurement (see Ouchi and Maguire [30]). Typically, an explicit information system must be created and maintained intentionally and at some cost, while an implicit information system often "grows up" as a natural by-product of social interaction.

In a true market, prices are arrived at through a process of competitive bidding, and no administrative apparatus is necessary to produce this information. However, many economists have argued that the conditions necessary for such perfect prices are rarely if ever met in reality, with the result that inefficiencies are borne by the parties to the market. Although some would contend that markets are explicitly not organizations (Arrow [4]), we can consider as a limit case the profit—or investment—center in a business as an attempt to control an organization through a price mechanism. In some large organizations, it is possible, with great effort and a huge accounting staff, to create internal numbers which will serve the function of prices. That is, if division general managers and department heads attempt simply to maximize their profit by taking the best prices available within the firm, then the firm as a whole will benefit. These "transfer prices" should not be confused with output, cost, or performance standards which are common in all organizations: those measures are effectively bureaucratic rules. The critical difference is that an internal price does not need a hierarchy of authority to accompany it. If the price mechanism is at work, all that is needed in addition to prices is a norm of reciprocity, accompanied by self-interest.

Only rarely is it possible for an organization to arrive at perfect transfer prices, however, because technological interdependence and uncertainty tremendously complicate the problem for most organizations, to the point where arriving at prices is simply not feasible. Under that condition, the organization can create an explicit set of rules, both rules about behavior and rules about levels of production or output. Although an organization can never create an explicit set of rules that will cover every situation that could possibly confront any of its employees, it can cut the information problem down to size by writing a relatively small set of rules that will cover 90% of all events and depending upon hierarchical authority to settle the remaining 10% of events. Thus, we see again that acceptance of legitimate authority is critical to a bureaucracy, since it is that property which enables the organization to incompletely specify the duties of an employee, instead having the employee agree that, within bounds, a superior may specify his or her duties as the need arises (Williamson [48, pp. 57–81]). In this manner, the organization deals with the future one step at a time, rather than having to anticipate it completely in advance in a set of explicit rules.

In a Clan, the information is contained in the rituals, stories, and ceremonies which convey the values and beliefs of the organization (Clark [8]). An outsider cannot quickly gain access to information concerning the decision rules used in the organization, but the information system does not require an army of accountants, computer experts, and managers: it is just there. Ivan Light [22] has described the Chinese-American *Hui* and the Japanese-American *Tanomoshi,* revolving-credit lending societies which provide venture capital for starting new businesses. They carry out all of the functions of any Wall Street investment bank, but, within their ethnic group, they are able to make loans which would be far too risky for any bank because they enjoy considerable advantages in obtaining, interpreting, and evaluating information about potential borrowers or members. None of their practices are explicit—even the rate of interest paid by borrowers is left unspecified and implicit. Entry into a *Hui* or *Tanomoshi* is strictly limited by birthright, a practice which guarantees that each member is a part of a social and kinship network which will support the values and beliefs upon which the control mechanism is founded. Clearly, the Clan information system cannot cope with heterogeneity nor with turnover, disadvantages which make it all but infeasible as a central mechanism of control in modern organizations, but the Clan, like the market, can operate with great efficiency if the basic conditions necessary to its operation can be met.

If the price requirements of a Market cannot be met and if the social conditions of the Clan are impossible to achieve, then the Bureaucratic mechanism becomes the preferred method of control. In a sense, the Market is like the trout and the Clan like the salmon, each a beautiful, highly-specialized species which requires uncommon conditions for its survival. In comparison, the bureaucratic method of control is the catfish—clumsy, ugly, but able to live in the widest possible range of environments and, ultimately, the dominant species. The bureaucratic mode of control can withstand high rates of turnover, a high degree of heterogeneity, and it does not have very demanding informational needs.

In reality, of course, we will never observe a pure market, a pure bureaucracy, or a pure clan. Real organizations will each contain some features of each of the modes of control. The design problem thus becomes one of assessing the social and informational characteristics of each division, department, or task and determining which of the forms of control ought to be emphasized in each case. Present organization theory, however, concentrates on the bureaucratic form to the exclusion of all else. The work of March and Simon [25] deals with decision-making in bureaucratic organizations, Parsons [32] describes problems of vertical control in bureaucracies, Perrow [33] concentrates on rules as a control mechanism in bureaucracies, and Argyris [3], Likert [23], and Tannenbaum [42] prescribe techniques for reducing some of the undesirable by-products of what remains an essentially bureaucratic mode of control.

Let us next consider some of the cost implications of each form of control. We will approach this task by looking at each of the stages at which an organization can exercise discretion over people. By doing so, we may discover some additional design variables which can influence the form of organizational control.

4 DESIGNING CONTROL MECHANISMS: COSTS AND BENEFITS

Basically, there are two ways in which an organization can achieve effective people control: either it can go to the expense of searching for and selecting people who fit its needs exactly, or else it can take people who do not exactly fit its needs and go to the expense of putting in place a managerial system to instruct, monitor, and evaluate them.

Which of these approaches is best depends on the cost to the organization of each. On the one hand, there is a cost of search and of acquisition: some skills are rare in the labor force and the organization wanting to hire people with those skills will have to search widely and pay higher wages. Once hired, however, such people will be able to perform their tasks without instruction and, if they have also been selected for values (motivation), they will be inclined to work hard without close supervision, both of which will save the organization money. On the other hand, there is the cost of training the unskilled and the indifferent to learn the organization's skills and values, and there is the cost of developing and running a supervisory system to monitor, evaluate, and correct their behavior. Once in place, however, such a system can typically take in a heterogeneous assortment of people and effectively control them; in addition, its explicit training and monitoring routines enable it to withstand high rates of turnover. High turnover is costly if search and acquisition costs are high, but turnover is relatively harmless to the organization if it hires all comers.

It has also been observed, by sociologists (Etzioni [13]), social psychologists, (Kelman [20]), and economists, (Williamson [48]), that various forms of evaluation and control will result in differing individual levels of commitment to or alienation from the organization and its objectives. In general, a control mode which relies heavily on selecting the appropriate people can expect high commitment as a result of internalized values.

At the other extreme, a control mode which depends heavily upon monitoring, evaluating, and correcting in an explicit manner is likely to offend people's sense of autonomy and of self-control and, as a result, will probably result in an unenthusiastic, purely compliant response. In this state, people require even more close supervision, having been alienated from the organization as a result of its control mechanism. Indeed, as is always true of any form of measurement, it is not possible for an organization to measure or otherwise control its employees without somehow affecting them through the very process that it uses to measure them: there is no completely unobtrusive measurement in most organizations. In general, the more obvious and explict the measurement, the more noxious it is to employees and thus, the greater the cost to the organization of employing such methods. However, other conditions may demand the use of these more explicit yet offensive techniques of control. We can summarize these in Table 2.

At one extreme, an organization could be completely unselective about its members, taking anyone (although we assume that everyone is to some extent self-interested, hedonistic, or profit-maximizing). At the other extreme, an organization could be highly selective, choosing only those individuals who already have both the skills and the values which the organization needs; this practice is most common in the "professional bureaucracies" such as hospitals,

Table 2   Organizational Control: People Treatment

People treatment	Form of commitment*	Corresponding control type
Totally unselective; take anyone, no further treatment	Internalization	Market
Selection/screening		Clan
Training —skill training —value training	Identification	Bureaucracy
Monitoring —monitor behavior —monitor output	Compliance	

*Taken from Kelman (20).

public accounting firms, and universities. In an apparent paradox, these most and least selective kinds of organizations will both have high levels of commitment; that is, members will have internalized the underlying objectives of the organization. Of course, the paradox is resolved by noting that the completely unselective organization relies on commitment of each individual to self, since it employs a market mechanism of control in which what is desired is that each person simply maximize his or her personal well-being (profit). Since the organization's objective is thus identical to the individual's objective, we can say that internalization of objectives exists and thus no close supervision will be necessary, and enthusiasm for pursuing the organization's goals will be high (since they are also the individual's selfish goals).

Most organizations, however, cannot take on all comers (they do not have a price mechanism) and they can rely upon selection and screening only to a limited extent, that is, they can select partially for the skills and values desired but will not be able to find people who fit exactly their needs. In this case, the organization may rely on training, both in the form of formalized training programs and in the form of on-the-job or apprenticeship training, to impart the desired skills and values. Typically, training will result in the trainee identifying with either the trainer (who may also be a respected superior) or with the work group or department. In this case, the employee will possess the necessary skills and will pursue the organization's objective, but only because he or she identifies with and wants to emulate the respected person or group, not because the underlying objectives have been internalized to the point where the employee believes them to be good and desirable objectives in their own right.

The link between forms of commitment and types of control is quite direct. Internalized commitment is necessary for a market, since a market possesses no hierarchical monitoring or policing capabilities. Internalization is also necessary to a clan, which has weak monitoring abilities, that is, evaluation is subtle and slow under this form of control, and thus, without high commitment, the mechanism is capable of drifting quite far off course before being corrected. A clan can also be supported with identification, however, and over time, the identification may be converted into internalization of the values of the clan.

Identification is also compatible with bureaucratic control, although it exceeds the minimum commitment that is necessary in a bureaucracy. Compliance is the minimum level of commitment necessary for bureaucratic control, but it is beneath the threshold of commitment necessary for the clan and market forms. The social agreement to suspend judgment about orders from superiors and to simply follow orders (see Blau and Scott [7, pp. 29–30]) is fundamental to bureaucratic control.

The issue of commitment and control may also pose a moral question of some significance. If organizations achieve internalized control purely through selection, then, it would seem, both the individual and the organization are unambiguously satisfied. If internalization is achieved through training of employees into the values and beliefs of the organization, however, then it is possible that some individuals may be subject to economic coercion to modify their values. Indeed, this kind of forced socialization is common in certain of our institutions (what Etzioni refers to as "coercive" organizations) such as the U.S. Marine Corps and many mental hospitals. In some such cases, we accept the abrogation of individual rights as being secondary to a more pressing need. In the case of a company town or a middle-aged employee with few job options, however, we are less likely to approve of this kind of pressure. As long as organizations maintain an essentially democratic power structure, this danger remains remote. If the hierarchy of authority becomes relatively autocratic, however, the possiblity of loss of individual freedom becomes real.

5 LOOSE COUPLING AND THE CLAN AS A FORM OF CONTROL

In the present literature on organizations, a new and somewhat revolutionary view of "organizational rationality" is developing which has direct implications for our view of designing control mechanisms. This new view, which is coming to be known as "loose coupling" (see Weick [47]), implies that bureaucratic forms of control are unsuitable for many contemporary organizations. Let us briefly consider the underlying "organizational rationality" which dominates the current view of control, and then we will consider the loose coupling perspective.

The essential element which underlies any bureaucratic or market form of control is the assumption that it is feasible to measure, with reasonable precision, the performance that is desired. In order to set a production standard which effectively controls, it is essential that the industrial engineers or accountants be able to measure the desired output with some precision. In order to effectively control through the use of rules, it is essential that the personnel department know which rules to specify in order to achieve the desired performance. Indeed, the ability to measure either output or behavior which is relevant to the desired performance is critical to the "rational" application of market and bureaucratic forms of control. Table 3 specifies the contingencies which determine whether or not measurement is possible.

In order to understand Table 3, let us agree, for the moment, that if we

Table 3 Conditions Determining the Measurement of Behavior and of Output

		Knowledge of the transformation process	
		Perfect	Imperfect
Ability to measure outputs	High	Behavior or output measurement (Apollo program)	Output measurement (women's boutique)
	Low	Behavior measurement (tin-can plant)	Ritual and ceremony, "clan" control (research laboratory)

wanted to control an organization, we would have to monitor or measure something and that, essentially, the things which we can measure are limited to the behavior of employees or the results, the outputs of those behaviors. If we understand the technology (that is, the means-ends relationships involved in the basic production or service activities) perfectly, as is the case in a tin-can plant, then we can achieve effective control simply by having someone watch the behavior of the employees and the workings of the machines: if all behaviors and processes conform to our desired transformation steps, then we know with certainty that proper tin cans are coming out the other end, even without looking. By specifying the rules of behavior and of process, we could create an effective bureaucratic control mechanism in this case.

On the other hand, suppose that we are designing a control system for a high-fashion women's boutique. What it takes to be a successful buyer or merchandiser is beyond our understanding, so we could not possibly hope to create a set of rules which, if followed by our buyers, would assure success. We can measure with precision, however, the average markdowns which each buyer's leftover dresses must take, the average inventory turnover for each buyer, and the sales volume and profit margin of each buyer, thus giving us the alternative of an output control mechanism. If our output control mechanism consists of this multiple set of objectives, then it is effectively a bureaucratic mechanism which will be managed by having a superior in the hierarchy who will monitor the various indicators for each buyer and, using the legitimate authority of office, will enforce not only close monitoring but also will order the necessary corrections in the buyer's decisions.

In the third case, we could be designing a control mechanism for the Apollo moon-shot program. We can completely specify each step of the transformation process which must occur in order for a manned capsule to get to the surface of the moon and back to earth, thus giving us the possibility of behavior control. However, we also have an unambiguous measure of output: either the capsule gets there and back, or it doesn't. Thus we have a choice of either behavior control or of output control. In such a case, the lower cost alternative will be preferred; clearly, since the cost of one failure is prohibitive, we will choose an elaborate behavior control mechanism, with literally hundreds of ground controllers monitoring every step of the process.

Finally, suppose that we are running a research laboratory at a multibillion dollar corporation. We have no ability to define the rules of behavior which, if followed, will lead to the desired scientific breakthroughs which will, in turn, lead to marketable new products for the company. We can measure the ultimate success of a scientific discovery, but it may take ten, twenty, or even fifty years for an apparently arcane discovery to be fully appreciated. Certainly, we would be wary of using a strong form of output control to encourage certain scientists in our lab while discouraging others. Effectively, we are unable to use either behavior or output measurement, thus leaving us with no "rational" form of control. What happens in such circumstances is that the organization relies heavily on ritualized, ceremonial forms of control. These include the recruit-

404   THE MANAGEMENT PROCESSES AND ORGANIZATION THEORY

ment of only a selected few individuals, each of whom has been through a schooling and professionalization process which has taught him or her to internalize the desired values and to revere the appropriate ceremonies. The most important of those ceremonies, such as "hazing" of new members in seminars, going to professional society meetings, and writing scientific articles for publication in learned journals, will continue to be encouraged within the laboratory.

Now, it is commonly supposed that such rituals, which characterize not only research laboratories but also hospitals, schools, government agencies and investment banks, constitute quaint but essentially useless and perhaps even harmful practice. But if it is not possible to measure either behavior or outputs and it is therefore not possible to "rationally" evaluate the work of the organization, what alternative is there but to carefully select workers so that you can be assured of having an able and committed set of people, and then engaging in rituals and ceremonies which serve the purpose of rewarding those who display the underlying attitudes and values which are likely to lead to organizational success, thus reminding everyone of what they are supposed to be trying to achieve, even if they can't tell whether or not they are achieving it?

Whereas output and behavior control (see also Ouchi and Maguire [30], Ouchi [31]) can be implemented through a market or a bureaucracy, ceremonial forms of control (see Meyer and Rowan [28]) can be implemented through a clan. Because ceremonial forms of control explicitly are unable to exercise monitoring and evaluation of anything but attitudes, values, and beliefs, and because attitudes, values and beliefs are typically acquired more slowly than are manual or cognitive abilities, ceremonial forms of control require the stability of membership which characterizes the clan.

It has recently become fashionable among organization theorists to argue that relatively few real organizations possess the underlying "rationality" which is assumed in market and bureaucratic forms of control. Parsons [32], Williamson [48], and Ouchi [31] have argued that most hierarchies fail to transmit control with any accuracy from top to bottom. Simon has made a convincing case that most organizations do not have a single or an integrated set of goals or objectives [41] and that the subunits of organizations are, as a matter of necessity, only loosely joined to each other [40]. Evan [14], Pfeffer [34], and Aldrich [2] have argued that the structure of most organizations is determined more by their environment than by any purposive, technologically-motivated managerial strategy. Hannan and Freeman [18] have argued even more strongly that organizational form is isomorphic with ecological conditions, thus implying that organizations can be designed only by nature, through a process of selection; and Cohen, March, and Olsen [10] have argued that organizational decision processes are far from our view of "rationality" and have chosen instead the metaphor of the "garbage can" to describe them.

If there is any truth in this very considerable attack on our notions of the orderliness and rationality with which organizations function, then we must guess that the forms of control which are dominant today may be inappropriate in future organizations.

Under conditions of ambiguity, of loose coupling, and of uncertainty, measurement with reliability and with precision is not possible. A control system based on such measurements is likely to systematically reward a narrow range of maladaptive behavior, leading ultimately to organizational decline. It may be that, under such conditions, the clan form of control, which operates by stressing values and objectives as much as behavior, is preferable. An organization which evaluates people on their values, their motivation, can tolerate wide differences in styles of performance; that is exactly what is desirable under conditions of ambiguity, when means-ends relationships are only poorly understood; it encourages experimentation and variety.

6 A FEW CLOSING OBSERVATIONS

Organizations vary in the degree to which they are loosely or tightly coupled. Many organizations, particularly those in relatively stable manufacturing industries, fit the requirements for behavior control or for output control. Control mechanisms of the market or bureaucratic variety can be designed into such organizations. Organizations in the public sector, in service industries, and in fast-growing technologies may not fit these specifications and perhaps should have cultural or clan forms of control instead.

The student of organizational control should take care to understand that clans, which operate on ceremony and on ritual, have forms of control which by their nature are subtle and are ordinarily not visible to the inexperienced eye. Many is the eager young manager who has taken a quick look around, observed that no control mechanisms exist, and then begun a campaign to install a bureaucratic or market mechanism of some sort, only to trip over the elaborate ceremonial forms of control which are in place and working quite effectively.

This paper has presented the argument that the design of organizational control mechanisms must focus on the problems of achieving cooperation among individuals who hold partially divergent objectives. Basically, such a collection of people can be moved towards cooperative action through one of three devices: a market mechanism which precisely evaluates each person's contribution and permits each to pursue non-organizational goals, but at a personal loss of reward; a clan mechanism which attains cooperation by selecting and socializing individuals such that their individual objectives substantially overlap with the organization's objectives; and a bureaucratic mechanism which does a little of each: it partly evaluates performance as closely as possible, and it partly engenders feelings of commitment to the idea of legitimate authority in hierarchies.

There are two underlying issues which are of central importance in determining which form of control will be more efficient. First is the question of the clarity with which performance can be assessed. Second is the degree of goal incongruence. These two dimensions are intimately related in determining the forms of control that will emerge, but each of these dimensions is shaped by an independent set of forces.

The intimate relationship between the two dimensions is evidenced in the observation that high levels of goal incongruity can be tolerated only so long as performance can be evaluated with precision. Conversely, high ambiguity concerning performance can be tolerated only if goal incongruity is trivial. In everyday language, people must either be able to trust each other or to closely monitor each other if they are to engage in cooperative enterprises.

However, the possibility of goal compatibility is shaped by forces independent of those which determine the level of performance evaluation. It has long been argued by sociologists and organization theorists that geographical mobility, urbanization, and industrialization, which tend to occur together, all undermine the basic forms of goal compatibility on which communal trust is founded. While these arguments have been advanced to explain the increasing bureaucratization of whole societies, they apply equally to work organizations. Growth, turnover, and specialization all undermine the possiblity of developing goal congruence in work organizations and thus imply the dominance of bureaucratic and market forms.

On the other hand, it has equally been argued by organization theorists that technological interdependence is inimical to clear performance assessment, and that such interdependence will increase over time among organizations generally. This argument forecloses the development of market and bureaucratic forms, which require clarity of assessment.

In the immediate sense, the problem of organization design is to discover that balance of socialization and measurement which most efficiently permits a particular organization to achieve cooperation among its members. In the longer run, the problem is to understand how, in a society that is increasingly pluralistic and thus goal-incongruent, in which interest groups become more distinct and in which a sense of community seems remote, the control of organizations can be achieved without recourse to an unthinking bureaucratization which is at odds with the increasing interdependence and ambiguity which characterize economic organizations.[1]

REFERENCES

1 Alchian, Armen A. and Demesetz, Harold, "Production, Information Costs, and Economic Organization," *Amer. Econom. Rev.*, Vol 62 (1972), pp. 777–795.
2 Aldrich, Howard, "An Organization-Environment Perspective on Cooperation and Conflict Between Organizations in the Manpower Training System," in Anant Negandhi, ed., *Conflict and Power in Complex Organizations,* Kent State Univ., Kent, Ohio, 1972.
3 Argyris, Chris, *Integrating the Individual and the Organization,* Wiley, New York, 1964.
4 Arrow, Kenneth J., *The Limits of Organization,* Norton, New York, 1974, pp. 1–29.

[1]I am indebted to Thomas R. Hofstedt, with whom I first taught a course on Organizational Control, to Thomas L. Whistler, who introduced me to this topic, and to John W. Meyer and Oliver E. Williamson, whose creative insights to the problem of control have opened up my mind. I am also indebted to Arie Lewin, Patrick Connor, Kathleen Eisenhardt, and Charles T. Horngren for their constructive criticisms.

5   Barnard, Chester I., *The Functions of the Executive,* Harvard Univ. Press, Cambridge, Mass., 1938.

6   Blau, Peter M., *The Dynamics of Bureaucracy,* Univ. of Chicago Press, Chicago, Ill., 1955.

7   —— and Scott, W. Richard, *Formal Organizations,* Scott, Foresman, San Francisco, Calif., 1962.

8   Clark, Burton R., *The Distinctive College: Antioch, Reed, and Swarthmore,* Aldine, Chicago, Ill., 1970.

9   Coase, R. H., "The Nature of the Firm," *Economica,* New Series, Vol. 4 (1937), pp. 386–405.

10 Cohen, Michael D., March, James G. and Olsen, Johan P., "A garbage Can Model of Organizational Choice," *Admin. Sci. Quart.,* Vol. 17 (1972), March, pp. 1–25.

11 Davis, Stanley M. and Lawrence, Paul R., *Matrix,* Addison-Wesley, Reading, Mass., 1977.

12 Dore, Ronald, *British Factory—Japanese Factory,* Univ. of California Press, Berkeley, Calif., 1973.

13 Etzioni, Amitai, "Organizational Control Structure," in J. G. March, ed., *Handbook of Organizations,* Rand McNally, Chicago, Ill., 1965, pp. 650–677.

14 Evan, William M., "The Organization-Set," in James D. Thompson, ed., *Approaches to Organizational Design,* Univ. of Pittsburgh Press, Pittsburg, Pa., 1966.

15 Galbraith, Jay, *Designing Complex Organizations,* Organization Development Series, Addison-Wesley, Reading, Mass., 1973.

16 Gouldner, Alvin W., *Patterns of Industrial Bureaucracy,* Free Press, New York, 1954.

17 ——, "The Norm of Reciprocity," *Amer. Sociological Rev.,* Vol. 25 (1961), pp. 161–179.

18 Hanna, Michael T. and Freeman, John H., "The Population Ecology of Organizations," *Amer. J. Sociology,* Vol. 82 (1977), pp. 929–964.

19 Kaufman, Herbert, *The Forest Ranger: A Study in Administrative Behavior,* The Johns Hopkins Univ. Press, Baltimore, Md., 1967.

20 Kelman, H. C., "Compliance, Identification, and Internalization: Three Processes of Attitude Change," *J. Conflict Resolution,* Vol. 2 (1958), pp. 51–60.

21 Lawrence, Paul R. and Lorsch, Jay W., *Organization and Environment: Managing Differentiation and Integration,* Harvard University, Graduate School of Business Administration, Boston, Mass., 1967.

22 Light, Ivan H., *Ethnic Enterprise in America,* Univ. of California Press, Berkeley, Calif., 1972.

23 Likert, Rensis, *The Human Organization: Its Management and Value,* McGraw-Hill, New York, 1967.

24 Lipset, Seymour M., Trow, Martin A. and Coleman, James S., *Union Democracy,* Free Press, Glencoe, Ill., 1956.

25 March, James G. and Simon, Herbert A., *Organizations,* Wiley, New York, 1958.

26 Marschak, Thomas A., "Economic Theories of Organization," in J. G. March (ed.), *Handbook of Organizations,* Rand McNally, Chicago, Ill., 1965, pp. 423–450.

27 Matthews, Donald R., *U.S. Senators and Their World,* Univ. of North Carolina Press, Chapel Hill, N.C., 1960.

28 Meyer, John W. and Rowan, Brian, "Institutionalized Organizations: Formal Structure as Myth and Ceremony," *Amer. J. Sociology,* Vol. 83, No. 2 (September 1977), pp. 340–363.

29 Nakane, Chie, *Japanese Society,* Penguin Books, Middlesex, 1973.
30 Ouchi, W. G., and Maguire, M. A., "Organizational Control; Two Functions," *Admin. Sci. Quart.,* Vol. 20 (December 1975), pp. 559–569.
31 ——, "The Transmission of Control Through Organizational Hierarchy," *Acad. Management J.,* Vol. 21, No. 2 (1978).
32 Parson, Talcott, *Structure and Process in Modern Society,* Free Press, New York, 1960.
33 Perrow, Charles, *Complex Organizations: A Critical Essay,* Scott, Foresman, Glenview, Ill., 1972.
34 Pfeffer, Jeffrey, "Beyond Management and the Worker: The Institutional Function of Management," *Acad. Management Rev.,* Vol. 1 (1976), pp. 36–46.
35 Reeves, T. Kynaston and Woodward, Joan, "The Study of Managerial Control," in J. Woodward, ed., *Industrial Organization: Behaviour and Control,* Oxford Univ. Press., London, 1970.
36 Roethlisberger, Fritz J. and Dickson, William J., *Management and the Worker,* Harvard Univ. Press, Cambridge, Mass., 1939.
37 Rohlen, Thomas P., *For Harmony and Strength: Japanese White-Collar Organization in Anthropological Perspective,* Univ. of California Press, Berkeley, Calif., 1974.
38 Selznick, Philip, *TVA and the Grass Roots,* Univ. of California Press, Berkeley, Calif., 1949.
39 Simon, H. A., "A Formal Theory of the Employment Relation," in H. A. Simon, *Models of War,* Wiley, New York, 1957, pp. 183–195.
40 ——, "The Architecture of Complexity," *Proc. Amer. Philos. Soc.,* Vol. 106 (December 1962), pp. 467–482.
41 ——, "On the Concept of Organizational Goal," *Admin. Sci. Quart.,* Vol. 9, No. 1 (June 1964), pp. 1–22.
42 Tannenbaum, Arnold, *Control in Organizations,* McGraw-Hill, New York, 1969.
43 Thompson, James D., *Organizations In Action,* McGraw-Hill, New York, 1969.
44 Trist, Eric L. and Bamforth, K. W., "Some Social and Psychological Consequences of the Longwall Method of Coal-Getting," *Human Relations,* Vol. 4 (February 1951), pp. 3–38.
45 Vancil, Richard F., "What Kind of Management Control Do You Need?," in *Harvard Business Review—On Management,* Harper and Row, New York, 1975, pp. 464–481.
46 Weber, Max, *The Theory of Social and Economic Organization,* translated by A. M. Henderson and T. Parsons, Free Press, New York, 1947.
47 Weick, Karl E., "Educational Organizations As Loosely Coupled Systems," *Admin. Sci. Quart.,* Vol. 21 (March 1976), pp. 1–19.
48 Williamson, Oliver A., *Markets and Hierarchies: Analysis and Antitrust Implications,* Free Press, New York, 1975.

REVIEW AND DISCUSSION QUESTIONS

1 How is goal setting related to organizational controls?
2 What is meant by markets, bureaucracies, and clans?
3 How is control related to decision making?
4 Are control mechanisms related solely to formal organizational policies?
5 How can an organization effectively manage all three forms of control mechanisms?

Reading 29

The Short and Glorious History of Organizational Theory

Charles Perrow

From the beginning, the forces of light and the forces of darkness have polarized the field of organizational analysis, and the struggle has been protracted and inconclusive. The forces of darkness have been represented by the mechanical school of organizational theory—those who treat the organization as a machine. This school characterizes organizations in terms of such things as:

- centralized authority
- clear lines of authority
- specialization and expertise
- marked division of labor
- rules and regulations
- clear separation of staff and line

The forces of light, which by mid-twentieth century came to be characterized as the human relations school, emphasize people rather than machines, accommodations rather than machine-like precision, and draws its inspiration from biological systems rather than engineering systems. It has emphasized such things as:

- delegation of authority
- employee autonomy
- trust and openness
- concerns with the "whole person"
- interpersonal dynamics

THE RISE AND FALL OF SCIENTIFIC MANAGEMENT

The forces of darkness formulated their position first, starting in the early part of this century. They have been characterized as the scientific management or classical management school. This school started by parading simple-minded injunctions to plan ahead, keep records, write down policies, specialize, be decisive, and keep your span of control to about six people. These injunctions were needed as firms grew in size and complexity, since there were few models around beyond the railroads, the military, and the Catholic Church to guide organizations. And their injunctions worked. Executives began to delegate, reduce their span of control, keep records, and specialize. Planning ahead still is difficult, it seems, and the modern equivalent is Management by Objectives.

Reprinted by permission of the publisher from *Organizational Dynamics,* Summer 1973, pp. 3–14. ©1973 by AMACOM, a division of American Management Association.

But many things intruded to make these simple-minded injunctions less relevant:

1 Labor became a more critical factor in the firm. As the technology increased in sophistication it took longer to train people, and more varied and specialized skills were needed. Thus, labor turnover cost more and recruitment became more selective. As a consequence, labor's power increased. Unions and strikes appeared. Management adjusted by beginning to speak of a cooperative system of capital, management, and labor. The machine model began to lose its relevancy.

2 The increasing complexity of markets, variability of products, increasing number of branch plants, and changes in technology all required more adaptive organization. The scientific management school was ill-equipped to deal with rapid change. It had presumed that once the proper structure was achieved the firm could run forever without much tampering. By the late 1930s, people began writing about adaptation and change in industry from an organizational point of view and had to abandon some of the principles of scientific management.

3 Political, social, and cultural changes meant new expectations regarding the proper way to treat people. The dark, satanic mills needed at the least a white-washing. Child labor and the brutality of supervision in many enterprises became no longer permissible. Even managers could not be expected to accept the authoritarian patterns of leadership that prevailed in the small firm run by the founding father.

4 As mergers and growth proceeded apace and the firm could no longer be viewed as the shadow of one man (the founding entrepreneur), a search for methods of selecting good leadership became a preoccupation. A good, clear, mechanical structure would no longer suffice. Instead, firms had to search for the qualities of leadership that could fill the large footsteps of the entrepreneur. They tacitly had to admit that something other than either "sound principles" or "dynamic leadership" was needed. The search for leadership traits implied that leaders were made, not just born, that the matter was complex, and that several skills were involved.

ENTER HUMAN RELATIONS

From the beginning, individual voices were raised against the implications of the scientific management school. "Bureaucracy" had always been a dirty word, and the job design efforts of Frederick Taylor were even the subject of a congressional investigation. But no effective counterforce developed until 1938, when a business executive with academic talents named Chester Barnard proposed the first new theory of organizations: Organizations are cooperative systems, not the products of mechanical engineering. He stressed natural groups within the organization, upward communication, authority from below rather than from above, and leaders who functioned as a cohesive force. With the spectre of labor unrest and the Great Depression upon him, Barnard's emphasis on the cooperative nature of organizations was well-timed. The year following the publication of his *Functions of the Executive* (1938) saw the publication of F. J. Roethlisberger and William Dickson's *Management and the*

Worker, reporting on the first large-scale empirical investigation of productivity and social relations. The research, most of it conducted in the Hawthorne plant of the Western Electric Company during a period in which the workforce was reduced, highlighted the role of informal groups, work restriction norms, the value of decent, humane leadership, and the role of psychological manipulation of employees through the counseling system. World War II intervened, but after the war the human relations movement, building on the insights of Barnard and the Hawthorne studies, came into its own.

The first step was a search for the traits of good leadership. It went on furiously at university centers but at first failed to produce more than a list of Boy Scout maxims: A good leader was kind, courteous, loyal, courageous, etc. We suspected as much. However, the studies did turn up a distinction between "consideration," or employee-centered aspects of leadership, and job-centered, technical aspects labeled "initiating structure." Both were important, but the former received most of the attention and the latter went undeveloped. The former led directly to an examination of group processes, an investigation that has culminated in T-group programs and is moving forward still with encounter groups. Meanwhile, in England, the Tavistock Institute sensed the importance of the influence of the kind of task a group had to perform on the social relations within the group. The first important study, conducted among coal miners, showed that job simplification and specialization did not work under conditions of uncertainty and nonroutine tasks.

As this work flourished and spread, more adventurous theorists began to extend it beyond work groups to organizations as a whole. We now knew that there were a number of things that were bad for the morale and loyalty of groups—routine tasks, submission to authority, specialization of task, segregation of task sequence, ignorance of the goals of the firm, centralized decision making, and so on. If these were bad for groups, they were likely to be bad for groups of groups—i.e., for organizations. So people like Warren Bennis began talking about innovative, rapidly changing organizations that were made up of temporary groups, temporary authority systems, temporary leadership and role assignments, and democratic access to the goals of the firm. If rapidly changing technologies and unstable, turbulent environments were to characterize industry, then the structure of firms should be temporary and decentralized. The forces of light, of freedom, autonomy, change, humanity, creativity, and democracy were winning. Scientific management survived only in outdated text books. If the evangelizing of some of the human relations school theorists was excessive, and if Likert's System 4 or McGregor's Theory Y or Blake's 9 × 9 evaded us, at least there was a rationale for confusion, disorganization, scrambling, and stress: Systems should be temporary.

BUREAUCRACY'S COMEBACK

Meanwhile, in another part of the management forest, the mechanistic school was gathering its forces and preparing to outflank the forces of light. First came the numbers men—the linear programmers, the budget experts, and the financial analysts—with their PERT systems and cost-benefit analyses. From another world, unburdened by most of the scientific management ideology and untouched by the human relations school, they began to parcel things out and give some meaning to those truisms, "plan ahead" and "keep records." Armed with emerging systems concepts, they carried the "mechanistic" analogy to its fullest—and it was very productive. Their work still goes on, largely untroubled by organizational theory; the theory, it seems clear, will have to adjust to them, rather than the other way around.

Then the works of Max Weber, first translated from the German in the 1940s—he wrote around 1910, incredibly—began to find their way into social science thought. At first, with his celebration of the efficiency of bureaucracy, he was received with only reluctant respect, and even with hostility. All writers were against bureaucracy. But it turned out, surprisingly, that managers were not. When asked, they acknowledged that they preferred clear lines of communication, clear specifications of authority and responsibility, and clear knowledge of whom they were responsible to. They were as wont to say "there ought to be a rule about this," as to say "there are too many rules around here," as wont to say "next week we've got to get organized," as to say "there is too much red tape." Gradually, studies began to show that bureaucratic organizations could change faster than nonbureaucratic ones, and that morale could be higher where there was clear evidence of bureaucracy.

What was this thing, then? Weber had showed us, for example, that bureaucracy was the most effective way of ridding organizations of favoritism, arbitrary authority, discrimination, payola and kick-backs, and yes, even incompetence. His model stressed expertise, and the favorite or the boss' nephew or the guy who burned up resources to make his performance look good was *not* the one with expertise. Rules could be changed; they could be dropped in exceptional circumstances; job security promoted more innovation. The sins of bureaucracy began to look like the sins of failing to follow its principles.

ENTER POWER, CONFLICT, AND DECISIONS

But another discipline began to intrude upon the confident work and increasingly elaborate models of the human relations theorists (largely social psychologists) and the uneasy toying with bureaucracy of the "structionalists" (largely sociologists). Both tended to study economic organizations. A few, like Philip Selznick, were noting conflict and differences in goals (perhaps because he was studying a public agency, the Tennessee Valley Authority), but most ignored conflict or treated it as a pathological manifestation of breakdowns in communication or the ego trips of unreconstructed managers.

But in the world of political parties, pressure groups, and legislative bodies, conflict was not only rampant, but to be expected—it was even functional. This was the domain of the political scientists. They kept talking about power, making it a legitimate concern for analysis. There was an open acknowledgement of "manipulation." These were political scientists who were "behaviorally" inclined—studying and recording behavior rather than constitutions and formal systems of government—and they came to a much more complex view of organized activity. It spilled over into the area of economic organizations, with the help of some economicsts like R. A. Gordon and some sociologists who were studying conflicting goals of treatment and custody in prisons and mental hospitals.

The presence of legitmately conflicting goals and techniques of preserving and using power did not, of course, sit well with a cooperative systems view of organizations. But it also puzzled the bureaucratic school (and what was left of the old scientific management school), for the impressive Weberian principles were designed to settle questions of power through organizational design and to keep conflict out through reliance on rational-legal authority and systems of careers, expertise, and hierarchy. But power was being overtly contested and exercised in covert ways, and conflict was bursting out all over, and even being creative.

Gradually, in the second half of the 1950s and in the next decade, the political science view infiltrated both schools. Conflict could be healthy, even in a cooperative system, said the human relationists; it was the mode of resolution that counted, rather than prevention. Power became reconceptualized as "influence," and the distribution was less important, said Arnold Tannenbaum, than the total amount. For the bureaucratic school—never a clearly defined group of people, and largely without any clear ideology—it was easier to just absorb the new data and theories as something else to be thrown into the pot. That is to say, they floundered, writing books that went from topic to topic, without a clear view of organizations, or better yet, producing "readers" and leaving students to sort it all out.

Buried in the political science viewpoint was a sleeper that only gradually began to undermine the dominant views. This was the idea, largely found in the work of Herbert Simon and James March, that because man was so limited—in intelligence, reasoning powers, information at his disposal, time available, and means of ordering his preferences clearly—he generally seized on the first acceptable alternative when deciding, rather than looking for the best; that he rarely changed things unless they really got bad, and even then he continued to try what had worked before; that he limited his search for solutions to well-worn paths and traditional sources of information and established ideas; that he was wont to remain preoccupied with routine, thus preventing innovation. They called these characteristics "cognitive limits on rationality" and spoke of "satisficing" rather than maximizing or optimizing. It is now called the "decision making" school, and is concerned with the basic question of how people make decisions.

This view had some rather unusual implications. It suggested that if managers were so limited, then they could be easily controlled. What was necessary was not to give direct orders (on the assumption that subordinates were idiots without expertise) or to leave them to their own devices (on the assumption that they were supermen who would somehow know what was the best for the organization, how to coordinate with all the other supermen, how to anticipate market changes, etc.). It was necessary to control only the *premises* of their decisions. Left to themselves, with those premises set, they could be predicted to rely on precedent, keep things stable and smooth, and respond to signals that reinforce the behavior desired of them.

To control the premises of decision making, March and Simon outline a variety of devices, all of which are familiar to you, but some of which you may not have seen before in quite this light. For example, organizations develop vocabularies, and this means that certain kinds of information are highlighted, and others are screened out—just as Eskimos (and skiers) distinguish many varieties of snow, while Londoners see only one. There is a form of attention directing. Another is the reward system. Change the bonus for salesmen and you can shift them from volume selling to steady-account selling, or to selling quality products or new products. If you want to channel good people into a different function (because, for example, sales should no longer be the critical function as the market changes, but engineering applications should), you may have to promote mediocre people in the unrewarded function in order to signal to the good people in the rewarded one that the game has changed. You cannot expect most people to make such a decision on their own because of the cognitive limits on their rationality, nor will you succeed by giving direct orders, because you yourself probably do not know whom to order where. You presume that once the signals are clear and the new sets of alternatives are manifest, they have enough ability to make the decision but you have had to change the premises for their decisions about their career lines.

It would take too long to go through the dozen or so devices, covering a range of decision areas (March and Simon are not that clear or systematic about them, themselves, so I have summarized them in my own book), but I think the message is clear.

It was becoming clear to the human relations school, and to the bureaucratic school. The human relationists had begun to speak of changing stimuli rather than changing personality. They had begun to see that the rewards that can change behavior can well be prestige, money, comfort, etc., rather than trust, openness, self-insight, and so on. The alternative to supportive relations need not be punishment, since behavior can best be changed by rewarding approved behavior rather than by punishing disapproved behavior. They were finding that although leadership may be centralized, it can function best through indirect and unobtrusive means such as changing the premises on which decisions are made, thus giving the impression that the subordinate is actually making a decision when he has only been switched to a different set of alternatives. The implications of this work were also beginning to filter into the human relations school through an emphasis on behavioral psychology (the modern version of the much maligned stimulus-response school) that was supplanting personality theory (Freudian in its roots, and drawing heavily, in the human relations school, on Maslow).

For the bureaucratic school, this new line of thought reduced the heavy weight placed upon the bony structure of bureaucracy by highlighting the muscle and flesh that make these bones move. A single chain of command, precise division of labor, and clear lines of communication are simply not enough in themselves. Control can be achieved by using alternative communication channels, depending on the situation; by increasing or decreasing the static or "noise" in the system; by creating organizational myths and organizational vocabularies that allow only selective bits of information to enter the system; and through monitoring performance through indirect means rather than direct surveillance. Weber was all right for a starter, but organizations had changed vastly, and the leaders needed many more means of control and more subtle means of manipulation than they did at the turn of the century.

THE TECHNOLOGICAL QUALIFICATION

By now the forces of darkness and forces of light had moved respectively from midnight and noon to about 4 A.M. and 8 A.M. But any convergence or resolution would have to be on yet new terms, for soon after the political science tradition had begun to infiltrate the established schools, another blow struck both of the major positions. Working quite independently of the Tavistock Group, with its emphasis on sociotechnical systems, and before the work of Burns and Stalker on mechanistic and organic firms, Joan Woodward was trying to see whether the classical scientific principles of organization made any sense in her survey of 100 firms in South Essex. She tripped and stumbled over a piece of gold in the process. She picked up the gold, labeled it "technology," and made sense out of her otherwise hopeless data. Job-shop firms, mass-production firms, and continuous-process firms all had quite different structures because the type of tasks, or the "technology," was different. Somewhat later, researchers in America were coming to very similar conclusions based on studies of hospitals, juvenile correctional institutions, and industrial firms. Bureaucracy appeared to be the best form of organization for routine operations; temporary work groups, decentralization, and emphasis on interpersonal processes appeared to work best for nonroutine operations. A raft of studies appeared and are still appearing, all trying to show how the nature of the task affects the structure of the organization.

This severely complicated things for the human relations school, since it suggested that openness and trust, while good things in themselves, did not have much impact, or perhaps were not even possible in some kinds of work situations. The prescriptions that were being handed out would have to be drastically qualified. What might work for nonroutine, high-status, interesting, and challenging jobs performed by highly educated people might not be relevant or even beneficial for the vast majority of jobs and people.

It also forced the upholders of the revised bureaucratic theory to qualify their recommendations, since research and development units should obviously be run differently from mass-production units, and the difference between both of these and highly programmed and highly sophisticated continuous-process firms was obscure in terms of bureaucratic theory. But the bureaucratic school perhaps came out on top, because the forces of evil—authority, structure, division of labor, etc.—no longer looked evil, even if they were not applicable to a minority of industrial units.

The emphasis on technology raised other questions, however. A can company might be quite routine, and a plastics division nonroutine, but there were both routine and nonroutine units within each. How should they be integrated if the prescription were followed that, say, production should be bureaucratized and R&D not? James Thompson began spelling out different forms of interdependence among units in organizations, and Paul Lawrence and Jay Lorsch looked closely at the nature of integrating mechanisms. Lawrence and Lorsch found that firms performed best when the differences between units were *maximized* (in contrast to both the human relations and the bureaucratic school), as long as the integrating mechanisms stood half-way between the two—being neither strongly bureaucratic nor nonroutine. They also noted that attempts at participative management in routine situations were counterproductive, that the environments of some kinds of organizations were far from turbulent and customers did not want innovations and changes, that cost reduction, price, and efficiency were trivial considerations in some firms, and so on. The technological insight was demolishing our comfortable truths right and left. They were also being questioned from another quarter.

ENTER GOALS, ENVIRONMENTS, AND SYSTEMS

The final seam was being mined by the sociologists while all this went on. This was the concern with organizational goals and the environment. Borrowing from the political scientists to some extent, but pushing ahead on their own, this "institutional school" came to see that goals were not fixed; conflicting goals could be pursued simultaneously, if there were enough slack resources, or sequentially (growth for the next four years, then cost-cutting and profit-taking for the next four); that goals were up for grabs in organizations, and units fought over them. Goals were, of course, not what they seemed to be, the important ones were quite unofficial; history played a big role; and assuming profit as the pre-eminent goal explained almost nothing about a firm's behavior.

They also did case studies that linked the organization to the web of influence of the environment; that showed how unique organizations were in many respects (so that, once again, there was no one best way to do things for all organizations); how organizations were embedded in their own history, making change difficult. Most striking of all, perhaps, the case studies revealed that the stated goals usually were not the real ones; the official leaders usually were not the powerful ones; claims of effectiveness and efficiency were deceptive or even untrue; the public interest was not being served; political influences were pervasive; favoritism, discrimination, and sheer corruption were commonplace. The accumulation of these studies presented quite a pill for either the forces of light or darkness to swallow, since it was hard to see how training sessions or interpersonal skills were relevant to these problems, and it was also clear that the vaunted efficiency of bureaucracy was hardly in evidence. What could they make of this wad of case studies?

We are still sorting it out. In one sense, the Weberian model is upheld because organizations are not, *by nature,* cooperative systems; top managers must exercise a great deal of effort to control them. But if organizations are tools in the hands of leaders, they may be very recalcitrant ones. Like the broom in the story of the sorcerer's apprentice, they occasionally get out of hand. If conflicting goals, bargaining, and unofficial leadership exists, where is the structure of Weberian bones and Simonian muscle? To what extent are organizations tools, and to what extent are they products of the varied interests and group strivings of their members? Does it vary by organization, in terms of some typological alchemy we have not discovered? We don't know. But at any rate, the bureaucratic model suffers again; it simply has not reckoned on the role of the environment. There are enormous sources of variations that the neat, though by now quite complex, neo-Weberian model could not account for.

The human relations model has also been badly shaken by the findings of the institutional school, for it was wont to assume that goals were given and unproblematical, and that anything that promoted harmony and efficiency for an organization also was good for society. Human relationists assumed that the problems created by organizations were largely limited to the psychological consequences of poor interpersonal relations within them, rather than their impact on the environment. Could the organization really promote the psychological health of its members when by necessity it had to define psychological health in terms of the goals of the organization itself? The neo-Weberian model at least called manipulation "manipulation" and was skeptical of claims about autonomy and self-realization.

But on one thing all the varied schools of organizational analysis now seemed to be agreed: organizations are systems—indeed, they are open systems. As the growth of the field has forced ever more variables into our consciousness, flat claims of predictive power are beginning to decrease and research has become bewilderingly complex. Even consulting groups need more than one or two tools in their kit-bag as the software multiplies.

The systems view is intuitively simple. Everything is related to everything else, though in uneven degrees of tension and reciprocity. Every unit, organization, department, or work group takes in resources, transforms them, and sends them out, and thus interacts with the larger system. The psychological, sociological, and cultural aspects of units interact. The systems view was explicit in the institutional work, since they tried to study whole organizations; it became explicit in the human relations school, because they were so concerned with the interactions of people. The political science and technology viewpoints also had to come to this realization, since they dealt with parts affecting each other (sales affecting production; technology affecting structure).

But as intuitively simple as it is, the systems view has been difficult to put into practical use. We still find ourselves ignoring the tenets of the open systems view, possibly because of the cognitive limits on our rationality. General systems theory itself has not lived up to its heady predictions; it remains rather nebulous. But at least there is a model for calling us to account and for stretching our minds, our research tools, and our troubled nostrums.

SOME CONCLUSIONS

Where does all this leave us? We might summarize the prescriptions and proscriptions for management very roughly as follows:

1 A great deal of the "variance" in a firm's behavior depends on the environment. We have become more realistic about the limited range of change that can be induced through internal efforts. The goals of organizations, including those of profit and efficiency, vary greatly among industries and vary systematically by industries. This suggests that the impact of better management by itself will be limited, since so much will depend on market forces, competition, legislation, nature of the work force, available technologies and innovations, and so on. Another source of variation is, obviously, the history of the firm and its industry and its traditions.

2 A fair amount of variation in both firms and industries is due to the type of work done in the organization—the technology. We are now fairly confident in recommending that if work is predictable and routine, the necessary arrangement for getting the work done can be highly structured, and one can use a good deal of bureaucratic theory in accomplishing this. If it is not predictable, if it is nonroutine and there is a good deal of uncertainty as to how to do a job, then one had better utilize the theories that emphasize autonomy, temporary groups, multiple lines of authority and communications, and so on. We also know that this distinction is important when organizing different parts of an organization.

We are also getting a grasp on the question of what is the most critical function in different types of organizations. For some organizations it is production; for others, marketing; for still others, development. Furthermore, firms go through phases whereby the initial development of a market or a product or manufacturing process or accounting scheme may require a non-bureaucratic structure, but once it comes on stream, the structure should change to reflect the changed character of the work.

3 In keeping with this, management should be advised that the attempt to produce change in an organization through managerial grids, sensitivity training, and even job enrichment and job enlargement is likely to be fairly ineffective for all but a few organizations. The critical reviews of research in all these fields show that there is no scientific evidence to support the claims of the proponents of these various methods; that research has told us a great deal about social psychology, but little about how to apply the highly complex findings to actual situations. The key word is *selectivity:* We have no broad-spectrum antibiotics for interpersonal relations. Of course, managers should be sensitive, decent, kind, courteous, and courageous, but we have known that for some time now, and beyond a minimal threshold level, the payoff is hard to measure. The various attempts to make work and interpersonal relations more humane and stimulating should be applauded, but we should not confuse this with solving problems of structure, or as the equivalent of decentralization or participatory democracy.

4 The burning cry in all organizations is for "good leadership," but we have learned that beyond a threshold level of adequacy it is extremely difficult to know what good leadership is. The hundreds of scientific studies of this phenomenon come to one general conclusion: Leadership is highly variable or "contingent" upon a large variety of important variables such as nature of task, size of the group, length of time the group has existed, type of personnel within the group and their relationships with each other, and amount of pressure the group is under. It does not seem likely that we'll be able to devise a way to select the best leader for a particular situation. Even if we could, that situation would probably change in a short time and thus would require a somewhat different type of leader.

Furthermore, we are beginning to realize that leadership involves more than smoothing the paths of human interaction. What has rarely been studied in this area is the wisdom or even the technical adequacy of a leader's decision. A leader does more than lead people; he also makes decisions about the allocation of resources, type of technology to be used, the nature of the market, and so on. This aspect of leadership remains very obscure, but it is obviously crucial.

5 If we cannot solve our problems through good human relations or through good leadership, what are we then left with? The literature suggests that changing the structures of organizations might be the most effective and certainly the quickest and cheapest method. However, we are now sophisticated enough to know that changing the formal structure by itself is not likely to produce the desired changes. In addition, one must be aware of a large range of subtle, unobtrusive, and even covert processes and change devices that exist. If inspection procedures are not working, we are now unlikely to rush in with sensitivity training, nor would we send down authoriative communications telling people to do a better job. We are more likely to find out where the authority really lies, whether the degree of specialization is adequate, what the rules and regulations are, and so on, but even this very likely will not be enough.

According to the neo-Weberian bureaucratic model, as it has been influenced by work on decision making and behavioral psychology, we should find out how to manipulate the reward structure, change the premises of the decision-makers through finer controls on the information received and the expectations generated, search for interdepartmental conflicts that prevent better inspection procedures from being followed, and after manipulating these variables, sit back and wait for two or three months for them to take hold. This is complicated and hardly as dramatic as many of the solutions currently being peddled, but I think the weight of organizational theory is in its favor.

We have probably learned more, over several decades of research and theory, about the things that do *not* work (even though some of them obviously *should* have worked), than we have about things that do work. On balance, this is an important gain and should not discourage us. As you know, organizations are extremely complicated. To have as much knowledge as we do have in a fledgling discipline that has had to borrow from the diverse tools and concepts of psychology, sociology, economics, engineering, biology, history, and even anthropology is not really so bad.

SELECTED BIBLIOGRAPHY

This paper is an adaptation of the discussion to be found in Charles Perrow, *Complex Organizations: A Critical Essay,* Scott, Foresman & Co., Glenville, Illinois, 1972. All the points made in this paper are discussed thoroughly in that volume.

The best overview and discussion of classical management theory, and its changes over time is by Joseph Massie—"Management Theory" is the *Handbook of Organizations* edited by James March, Rand McNally & Co., Chicago, 1965, pp. 387–422.

The best discussion of the changing justifications for managerial rule and worker obedience as they are related to changes in technology, etc., can be found in Reinhard Bendix's *Work and Authority in Industry,* John Wiley & Sons, Inc., New York, 1956. See especially the chapter on the American experience.

Some of the leading lights of the classical view—F. W. Taylor, Col. Urwick, and Henry Fayol—are briefly discussed in *Writers on Organizations* by D. S. Pugh, D. J. Hickson and C. R. Hinings, Penguin, 1971. This brief, readable, and useful book also contains selections from many other schools that I discuss, including Weber, Woodward, Cyert and March, Simon, and Hawthorne Investigations, and the Human Relations Movement as represented by Argyris, Herzberg, Likert, McGregor, and Blake and Mouton.

As good a place as any to start examining the human relations tradition is Rensis Likert, *The Human Organization,* McGraw-Hill, New York, 1967. See also his *New Patterns of Management,* McGraw-Hill Book Company, New York, 1961.

The Buck Rogers school of organizational theory is best represented by Warren Bennis. See his *Changing Organizations,* McGraw-Hill Book Company, New York, 1966, and his book with Philip Slater, *The Temporary Society,* Harper & Row, Inc., New York, 1968. Much of this work is linked into more general studies, e.g., Alvin Toffler's very popular paperback *Future Shock,* Random House, 1970, and Bantam Paperbacks, or Zibigniew Brzezinsky's *Between Two Ages: America's Role in the Technitronic Era,* the Viking Press, New York, 1970. One of the first intimations of the new type of environment and firm and still perhaps the most perceptive is to be found in the volume by Tom Burns and G. Stalker, *The Management of Innovation,* Tavistock, London, 1961, where they distinguished between "organic" and "mechanistic" systems. The introduction, which is not very long, is an excellent and very tight summary of the book.

The political science tradition came in through three important works. First, Herbert Simon's *Administrative Behavior,* The MacMillan Co., New York, 1948, followed by the second half of James March and Herbert Simon's *Organizations,* John Wiley & Sons, Inc., New York, 1958, then Richard M. Cyert and James March's *A Behavioral Theory of the Firm,* Prentice-Hall, Inc. Englewood Cliffs, N.J., 1963. All three of these books are fairly rough going, though chapters 1, 2, 3, and 6 of the last volume are fairly short and accessible. A quite interesting book in this tradition, though somewhat heavy-going, is Michael Crozier's *The Bureaucratic Phenomenon,* University of Chicago, and Tavistock Publications, 1964. This is a striking description of power in organizations, though there is a somewhat dubious attempt to link organization processes in France to the cultural traits of the French people.

The book by Joan Woodward *Industrial Organisation: Theory and Practice,* Oxford University Press, London, 1965, is still very much worth reading. A fairly popular attempt to discuss the implications for this for management can be found in my own book, *Organizational Analysis: A Sociological View,* Tavistock, 1970, Chapters 2 and 3. The impact of technology on structure is still fairly controversial. A number of technical studies have found both support and nonsupport, largely because the concept is defined so differently, but there is general agreement that different structures and leadership techniques are needed for different situations. For studies that support and document this viewpoint see James Thompson, *Organizations in Action,* McGraw-Hill Book Company, New York, 1967, and Paul Lawrence and Jay Lorsch, *Organizations and Environments,* Harvard University Press, Cambridge, Mass., 1967.

The best single work on the relation between the organization and the environment and one of the most readable books in the field is Philip Selznick's short volume *Leadership in Administration,* Row, Peterson, Evanston, Illinois, 1957. But the large number of these studies are scattered about. I have summarized several in my *Complex Organizations: A Critical Essay.*

Lastly, the most elaborate and persuasive argument for a systems view of organizations is found in the first 100 pages of the book by Daniel Katz and Robert Kahn, *The Social Psychology of Organizations,* John Wiley and Co., 1966. It is not easy reading, however.

REVIEW AND DISCUSSION QUESTIONS

1 What are some of the characteristics of organizations labeled "machinelike" and some of those labeled "people-oriented"?

2 What impact did scientific management and human relations have on organization structures?

3 Comment on the statement, "the technological insight was demolishing our comfortable truths" about organizations?

4 According to Perrow, what are some major organizational prescriptions and proscriptions for management?

Part Seven

Human Resource Management Applications

The management of human resources represents the application of the academic field of organizational behavior. The importance of human resources is being increasingly recognized, not only through government regulations but also through the escalating cost of employees and declining productivity. As with other resources, the practicing managers want to ensure that their human resources are cost-benefit.

The effective management of human resources starts even before the individual is hired. There is a need to determine with greater clarity the specific skills and attributes that are needed for a particular position in an organization. Once these needs are determined great care must be taken in order to match the job with the individual. Second, there is a need to be able to clarify performance expectations. Employees need to be held accountable for their performance. For the most part, organizations tend to use a form of post hoc analysis, where an employee is cited for performance deficiencies that the employee may not have even known were part of job duties. The direction for the future will be toward a greater clarity of performance objectives for the employee and a greater consensus between employees and supervisors as to the levels of proficiency that the employees should be attaining.

Besides selection and appraisal, organizational development (OD) is discussed in this section. This is an area that offers much promise in the future. Currently, the OD field is highly fragmented with a plethora of approaches with little rigorous evaluation of the concepts. There needs to be a recentralization of OD as a discipline and some building of a theoretical base before OD can progress as a field. As Koontz talks of a "management theory jungle" in the last section, one might also speak of an "organizational development jungle." In the future these problems need to be addressed.

A couple of areas of personal development that have recently come to the fore are behavioral self-management and career development. While the emphasis has been and remains directed toward how managers can more effectively manage subordinates, groups, and organizations, there are increasing concerns and techniques for managing oneself more effectively. Programs such as career development and behavioral self-management are entirely directed at what individuals can do to improve their own effectiveness.

The six readings in this final section are directed toward the application of human resource management. The first article presents a comprehensive program to develop employees. This development program starts with the initial selection process and follows the individual through the full career path. The second article, by Professors Schneier and Beatty, is directed at building a comprehensive system of performance appraisals for individuals. The program attempts to combine the behavioral aspects with overall effectiveness measures of individual performance. The third and fourth articles discuss organizational development (OD). The first OD article discusses some of the current problems in the field and offers some direction for the future of OD. The second OD article addresses some of the methodological and evaluation problems and offers some direction for the future of OD research, specifically by the use of multiple-measurement techniques. The fifth article spells out the meaning and analysis of behavioral self-management. The thrust of this article is that one must first manage his or her own behavior before one can expect to manage other people more effectively. The final article in this book provides an overall framework for the development of a career-planning program. This is a fitting conclusion because the readers can use the suggested approaches as a point of departure for planning and developing their own careers.

Reading 30

Total Development: Selection, Assessment, Growth

Jac Fitz-enz
Kathryn E. Hards
G. E. Savage

A great deal has been written about assessment techniques and centers over the past decade. The methodology has become somewhat standardized, the problems have been explored and the results reviewed. The only remaining question seems to be, "What's left to talk about." The answer to that is, "Assessment must be integrated with other employee growth activities to create an efficient, effective and holistic development program."

Assessment is generally treated in isolation. In our view assessment is, or should be, part of a development system. (See Figure 1.) The objective of development is to identify individuals with advancement potential, assess their strengths and weaknesses and assist their long-term growth. Following that premise, it is then obvious that assessment is only one of several tasks and that it

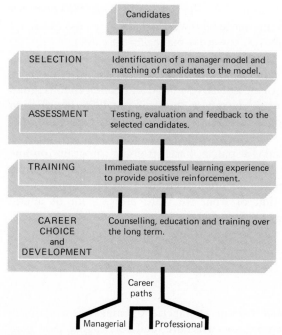

Figure 1 A career development system.

is interdependent with selection and training. (The word training is used here to mean management development courses.) The systems approach requires that relationships among the parts be acknowledged. By accounting for interdependencies, the subsets or modules of each component are designed to build on and mesh with each other. The end result is a very efficient delivery system and a very powerful development methodology. This article will present a case history of how the three components were designed as parts of a total development system.

GETTING STARTED

The first question we addressed at the onset of this project dealt with how we could identify those individuals with the greatest potential for success as managers. The objective at that point was merely efficiency. We wanted to invest a limited training budget where we could obtain the best return. It was purely a business decision. The humanitarian considerations would follow closely behind.

Assuming that we could legally and ethically differentiate levels of potential with a high degree of accuracy, the second question facing us was to determine how we could enhance the skills and prepare the majority of the population who have a wide range of potential. Our job is to develop *all* employees to their level of aspiration and capability. The selection and timing of each training experience is critical if our goal is to optimize efficiency and effectiveness for both the individual and the organization.

Finally, but not least important, we had to anticipate the plan for counselling, redirecting and training those who were satisfactory employees but who showed little aptitude or interest toward a management career.

We were fortunate in this project that we had a divisional vice president who placed a very high value on management development and who backed it up with money. He could also provide a relatively large and homogeneous group to work with. At the time this work started, in the spring of 1976, the division had approximately 300 professional and managerial employees. Three-and-one-half years later, there are over 800. The system's development did not proceed sequentially. That is, the need to put a basic training program on-line superseded all other considerations. Thereafter, we often found ourselves designing parts of the three components simultaneously. The whole project was held together by a shared notion of what we were after, a lot of lateral communications and some filing and fitting when the pieces did not quite mesh. There is still work to be done with some portions of the group. However, the largely complete system has been in operation almost two years.

PHASE ONE: IDENTIFICATION

Identification of likely candidates for future managerial openings has never been an easy job. Experience and technical expertise are relatively easy to ascertain, but managerial abilities are much more difficult to identify. The classic case of the excellent technician who becomes an ineffective manager is all too true. The ability to design or sell does not always coexist with the ability to manage people.

While it is granted that managerial talent is a generic capability applicable in many settings, the authors nevertheless maintain that managing accountants, for example, requires somewhat different approaches than managing salesmen, assembly workers or engineers. Therefore, off-the-shelf packages rarely can be applied with equal value to all settings. Some degree of customization is necessary. In the case at hand, a selection modelling methodology was developed which met the scientific and legal tests and still was simple enough to satisfy the practical needs of a fast moving organization.

MODELLING

The basic question which the modelling had to answer was, "Out of hundreds of potential candidates, how do we select the ones who have the best chance of becoming successful managers?" The most obvious and simplest answer would be to pick out the best managers currently available and select from the candidate pool those that look most like the "good guys." Consciously or unconsciously, this is what many organizations have always done. The reason that the hit rate is inconsistent is that management often has not been able to identify what it is in the multifaceted personality of the effective manager that differentiates him from others. Clearly, some form of scientific rigor had to be introduced in place of our past intuitive system.

The task of developing a manager model started with an agreement between the development staff and division management as to the job skills, behaviors and, most important, results that probably constituted "good management." This became our hypothetical model. We began the data gathering step by designing and purchasing survey instruments. We wanted to develop information which would range from personal data through attitudes, interests and values to education and work history. These instruments were mailed to the 20 plus branch managers then operating in the United States.

While we waited for the data to be returned, we met with the division's senior management team. Referencing the hypothetical model mentioned above, we asked each executive to rank order the branch managers in terms of performance. (If the number of subjects is relatively few, the paired comparison method is also a very effective ranking tool.) No discussion of individuals was allowed before the ranking and each person performed the task independently. It turned out that a very high correlation occurred among the rankings. There was almost perfect agreement on the ranking of the top seven and the bottom seven.

When all the data was returned by the branch managers it was analyzed for value and significance. Some instruments were discarded because they did not yield anything worthwhile. Given then a data base common throughout the subject group, correlational studies were run on the top seven and the bottom seven. The results showed a clear separation between groups on a number of factors. In short, we had created a profile of an effective manager and found that it was very much different from the one at the other end of the continuum. The model was so distinct that in no case did a variable appear with the same value in both groups. That is, we had total exclusivity.

Now that we had our model, the next step was to apply it to the pool of employees which would provide the next generation of managers.

It must be kept in mind that the object of modelling was not to eliminate all but a few from a chance to grow in the organization. The idea was simply to identify the group which we should bring in first for further assessment and development. Obviously, all those who shared some characteristics with the model would also have their turn. We knew that we would need a large number of managers over the next several years and we wanted to improve everyone's odds of being successful.

At this point, we proceeded to administer the proven instruments to the total pool of over 200. We did this by mail and promised to provide them with a personal report of their data. This apparently had an impact because our return rate exceeded 98 percent. We kept our promise by sending each participant his profile with an explanation of the results. The data was analyzed for the whole group and participants were identified according to their similarity to the model.

The plan was to construct the first group of trainees from those who were most similar to the model. The second class would be those next most like the model. Classes would continue to be developed until we ran out of interested persons.

PHASE TWO: ASSESSMENT/TRAINING

From the beginning we were sensitive to the term assessment. We never used the word publicly and we titled the process, "Career Development Program." Assessment has overtones of Orwell's *1984* for many people. We wanted to do more than test and evaluate. The key factors which were to make our program rather unique were that it would provide an immediate opportunity to work on some skills which appeared weak and it would involve supervisors very directly. Previous experience with other assessment programs had given us a feeling of incompleteness. Participants left such programs with the assessor's report and an action plan, but often nothing ensued.

The classic weakness of any off-site training experience is the transfer problem. For a variety of reasons, even the best program often does not get carried back and implemented on the job. This well-known problem is accentuated when dealing with assessment data. Quite often people leave the experience in a confused and anxious state of mind. As a result, they are not very effective even if they try to do something with what they have learned.

In an attempt to overcome that syndrome, we took several very deliberate steps. First, we designed-in some personalized training which would immediately follow the feedback report. This provided a little short term confidence building. Second, we contacted the subjects' supervisors and filled them in on the key points of the process (but not the data) and the topics they should be ready to discuss with the returning trainee. While it was to be the trainee's responsibility to initiate a meeting with the supervisor, we wanted to be certain that the supervisor was comfortable with the process and prepared through knowledge of the objectives so that he or she would be helpful and supportive during the discussion.

The supervisor was to be an integral part of the process in three ways:

1   Serve as a reality checkpoint to correlate the assessment data with the trainee's part observed behavior.
2   Help the trainee work out a career plan by matching his needs with the organization's objectives.
3   Choose and initiate some specific near-term development project with the trainee.

If we could return the trainee to the job in a confident frame of mind and help the supervisor become a supportive resource, this would greatly reduce the need for the development staff to follow-up and prod the process.

THE PROGRAM

The first two days were spent preparing the line managers who had to act as assessors and carrying out the assessment exercises with the participants. Day 2 was composed of four assessment/learning experiences. They were not especially unique processes. We used an in-basket, a stand-up presentation, an individual fact-finding/decision-making interview and a group problem-solving exercise. All processes were designed for this group with examples and data from their division. On the evening of Day 2 and the following morning, assessors spent their time discussing the trainees and writing feedback reports.

Day 3 started for the trainees with a training session dealing with feedback. Using the Johari window as a sample, we tried to prepare the people for coping in a positive way with the feedback they would receive. We also gave them some time to complete work on a personal career planning kit. The kit guided them through development of information on skills, values and work perferences; perceived career options and required skills; and a career planning scheme. In the afternoon, assessors and trainees got together, one-on-one, and went over feedback reports. By the end of the third day, each participant had received his personal feedback session, had set objectives and had been given an overnight assignment to prepare.

The next day assessees were divided into groups according to preassessed needs and given training in those areas. The training exercises were structured to give the participants an opportunity to experience a sense of achievement and positive reinforcement. Self-esteem and learning theories support the notion that success prompts further effort on a given subject. It was hypothesized that this approach offered the best chance of stimulating future developmental efforts back home. Our experience was that participants left the program in a very positive state of mind. This was not always the case we had observed in other assessment centers. Our people did not feel that they had been under a microscope, but, rather that they had had an opportunity to develop some information and skills which they could use to achieve their career goals. We never encountered anyone leaving with that uncertain, slightly sick and fearful feeling which sometimes comes from these programs.

It was very important that the trainees left in a positive, confident frame of mind. The program had been set up as a self-development exercise. The assessment tools were used as a vehicle for providing information to the person, not as an opportunity for the company to play Big Brother.

PHASE THREE: CAREER CHOICES AND DEVELOPMENT

We can safely predict that some candidates will choose not to pursue management careers as a result of their assessment experience. That is perfectly acceptable. The company has created a dual career path system which offers exactly the same potential for salary growth for an individual contributor as for a manager. This does away with the old problem of good technicians choosing unappealing management jobs simply to earn more money. Opportunities for continued professional growth are available both in-house and outside. Hence, the development needs of the career technician were addressed. We will focus the remainder of the study on those who chose the managerial ladder.

The last link in the process which began with identification and selection ties together assessment and development. The initial agreement reached between the development staff and line management covered the skills, behavior and results inherent in effective management. This agreement now provided the context within which courses would be created.

It has always been our approach to design management development programs around skills rather than concepts. Our objective was to train, not to educate. We broke down the function of management into observable, measurable tasks. The course content was created to help trainees learn how to perform specific administrative and behavioral tasks. This gave us an opportunity to test each module for skill acquisition. Since the trainees invariably did better on the post test than on the pretest, they felt good about themselves and the training and were anxious to move to the next module.

After teaching interviewing, performance appraisal, salary administration, discipline, coaching and counselling and other basic skills in Development I, we devoted Development II entirely to communications skills. Because the managers we worked with had to do a lot of internal and external communicating, this was obviously a key ability to strengthen. Again, little time was spent on theory and concepts. The majority of the effort was dedicated to practicing effective presentation methods, interpersonal communications and negotiating. Development III assumed that a manager had been in the job two years or more. At that point, we wanted him or her to start to focus on managing in the larger arena. The program was built around Oncken's Management Molecule and the leadership model of Hersey and Blanchard. Development IV is being designed for use in 1980.

In addition to this preplanned series, we have created special workshops to handle unforeseen needs. By designing a system of sequential courses, each of which builds on the last, by supplementing it with workshops to satisfy special requests and by advising management on appropriate education and OJT experiences, we have been able to speed the development of inexperienced managers to meet the needs of a fast growing organization.

CAUTIONS

We all know that nothing ever goes as well as an author makes it sound. This project was no exception. We had our share of frustrations and mistakes. Here are some of the key lessons we learned.

1 Care should be taken in selecting the data gathering instruments. Several surveys, tests, etc., should be tried because some will not yield discriminating data. *Do not buy an off-the-shelf total package.*

2 A trained professional, i.e., industrial psychologist or equivalent, should direct the instrument selection, validation, data gathering and analysis steps.

3 The managerial functions should be thoroughly analyzed to select out the traits and tasks which are currently critical to job effectiveness. Senior management sometimes has misperceptions of what the job is really like, even if at one time they have held the position.

4 Assessment exercises should directly relate to the job. If you are working with computer salesmen for example, do not choose a pre-packaged product that is built around samples from other industries. We believe that your findings will be limited if not invalid.

5 Design training and later, management development sessions initially around skills. A new manager needs to know how to handle a variety of situations more than the theory behind the behavior. There are tasks he must perform daily in order to survive. Later he can be taught management and human relations concepts.

6 Put each design decision to the test. Ask, "How does this serve our objective of optimizing our investment in employee growth?" If the answer is not readily apparent you must have slipped off the track somewhere.

CONCLUSION

A training and development professional has a unique opportunity. Very few occupations in industry have as their charter the creation of experiences dedicated to helping fellow employees fulfill their career aspirations. Most jobs have as the end product of their labor the generation and manipulation of financial, electro/mechanical or administrative processes. In human resource management, we have a hand in the lives of hundreds of human beings. This is an exciting and awesome responsibility. It demands that we extend ourselves to the full reaches of our knowledge and skill. We can never be satisfied with what has gone before. We are obliged to continually provide the best resources available. In order to do this, we must add the uniqueness of the individual to the demands of the job and then find ways to optimally fit them one to the other.

REVIEW AND DISCUSSION QUESTIONS

1   Describe the total development program for human resource management.
2   Currently, do you think organizations are practicing this total development approach? If not, why aren't they?
3   How would you convince the top management of an organization to use the type of development program suggested by this article.
4   Should an employee manage his or her own career? How can he or she do this? Cite specific actions that can be taken.

Reading 31

Integrating Behaviorally-Based and Effectiveness-Based Appraisal Methods

Craig Eric Schneier
Richard W. Beatty

Most organizations are dissatisfied with their performance appraisal (PA) process, particularly for administrative/managerial positions. They have concerns about its objectivity, its relevance and its validity. In many cases the complaint is that the appraisal system simply does not work! In a three-part series on this topic which begins with this article, we take a good, hard look at appraisal. First the objectives and legal requirements for appraisal systems are discussed and potential problem sources are identified. Appraisal is seen as a process involving key decisions and having important consequences. PA is not simply a form or a rating scale, but an integral managerial tool which can improve performance of individuals and units.

In the second article, the advantages of behaviorally-based and effectiveness-based systems are noted. A detailed procedure is given for developing Behaviorally-Anchored Rating Scales (BARS), a job-related practical and valid system. In the third article BARS are combined with Management by Objectives (MBO) to form a behaviorally-based/effectiveness-based system which is truly integrated. A large organization's success with such a system is described and a diagnostic procedure for identifying performance problems is detailed.

. . . you could always tell how you were doing by the way the (pitching) coach said good morning. If he said, 'Well, now, good morning Jimsie boy,' that meant you'd won your last two or three games and were in the starting rotation. If he nodded his head to you and said, 'Jimbo, how are you doin', how are you doin'?' you were still in the starting rotation, but your record probably wasn't much over .500. If he just said, 'Mornin', that meant you were on your way down, that you'd probably lost four out of five and it was doubtful if you would be getting any more starts. If he simply looked at you and gave a solemn nod, that meant you might get some mop-up relief work, or you might not, but you definitely weren't starting anymore and would never get into a close game again. And if he looked past you, over your shoulder as if you didn't exist, it was all over and you might as well pack your bag because you could be traded or sent down at any moment.[1]

The appraisal of human performance in organizations is vital, yet problematic. Herbert Meyer was recently led to remark, "of all the uncertainties that have kept executives from sleeping peacefully at night, probably none are quite so unsettling as those related to the difficulty of figuring out their boss's real opinion of them."[2]

Performance appraisal (PA) is required for it forms the rationale for key decisions regarding promotion, wage and salary administration and selection for training programs. However, despite noteworthy advances in scaling techniques to reduce such psychometric errors as leniency, many organizations still feel their appraisal systems are ineffective[3] and still have problems removing subjectivity and bias of raters. They have given up the search for perfect form, hoping to develop any acceptable one.

WHAT IS JOB PERFORMANCE?

Much of the activity observed on a job results in an evaluation of the *performance* of a person, team, unit, or an entire organization. In order to understand how such evaluations are made, the distinction between the following three terms is essential: behavior, performance and effectiveness (see also Figure 1).[4]

Behavior is simply what people do on a job—their activity. Writing reports, holding meetings, analyzing documents and conversing with others are possible behaviors exhibited on the job. Effective behavior is a function of the interaction between ability *and* effort—the behavior initiated to put one's ability to use. *Performance* is the term used for the evaluation of these behaviors as to their desirability or efficacy on the job. For example, writing reports in a specific style is evaluated as desirable performance. The report writing is evaluated according to a set of standards, or *criteria,* used by the evaluator. Certain behaviors or groups of behaviors are evaluated as good performance, others as fair performance and still others as unacceptable performance. Performance is the evaluated behavior and is what is measured in appraisal systems.

Effectiveness refers to the outcomes or results of various degrees of performance at the individual, unit, or organizational level. Did the behaviors

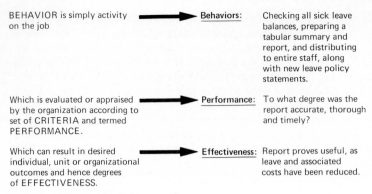

BEHAVIOR is simply activity on the job ➤ **Behaviors:** Checking all sick leave balances, preparing a tabular summary and report, and distributing to entire staff, along with new leave policy statements.

Which is evaluated or appraised by the organization according to set of CRITERIA and termed PERFORMANCE. ➤ **Performance:** To what degree was the report accurate, thorough and timely?

Which can result in desired individual, unit or organizational outcomes and hence degrees of EFFECTIVENESS. ➤ **Effectiveness:** Report proves useful, as leave and associated costs have been reduced.

Figure 1   What is job performance?

which produced an excellent report actually result in a desired organizational outcome, such as more efficient spending or the development of more relevant programs? Did holding a meeting with appropriate persons actually result in a more effective plan?

A key aspect of judgment in the appraisal setting thus involves drawing cause and effect inferences between behaviors and effectiveness. For example, if a rater observes that profit in a unit has gone down (i.e., the unit has become less effective), he or she must draw a conclusion concerning whether behaviors exhibited by management or others responsible were inappropriate or whether other factors may have caused the decline, such as a drop in demand for the product. As will be discussed in subsequent sections, Management by Objectives (MBO) appraisal systems, designed to measure outcomes or effectiveness, are deficient if they are unable to identify and measure the effectiveness of the behaviors which produced (or failed to produce) the outcomes.

WHAT IS PERFORMANCE APPRAISAL?

Performance appraisal or evaluation is the *process of identifying, measuring and developing human performance* in organizations. An effective appraisal system must not only *accurately measure current performance levels,* but also contain mechanisms for *reinforcing strengths, identifying deficiencies* and feeding such information back to ratees in order that they may *improve future performance.* This second, developmental aspect of appraisal is as important as the measurement aspect.

As noted in the preceding section, the term performance itself denotes judgment—behavior which has been evaluated. Performance appraisal is thus the process of *observing* and *identifying, measuring* and *developing* human behavior in the organization. These activities are described as follows:

• *Observation* and *identification* refers to the process of viewing or scrutinizing job behaviors. It consists of choosing what job behaviors to look at among all that are emitted by a ratee, as well as how often to observe them. The choices inherent in this process add subjectivity to appraisal.

- *Measurement* refers to ascertaining the extent, degree, level, etc., of a behavior. After raters choose what information to examine, they compare this information about ratee behavior against a set of organizational or personal expectations for each job. The degree to which observed behavior meets or exceeds the expectations determines its desirability, or the level of performance it reflects, such as excellent or satisfactory.

- *Development* refers to performance improvement over time. An appraisal system must contain mechanisms to communicate the expectations and measurement process to persons being appraised, motivate them to remove any deficiencies uncovered and reinforce them to build on strengths in order to improve future performance.

When PA is considered in terms of its utility to an organization, several operational PA objectives seem critical. These include (1) the ability to provide adequate feedback to employees to improve subsequent performance, (2) the identification of employee training needs, (3) the identification of criteria used to allocate organizational rewards, (4) the validation of selection techniques to meet Equal Employment Opportunity (EEO) requirements and (5) the identification of promotable employees from internal labor supplies (see Figure 2). In order to accomplish these objectives, the PA system must, of course, be an accurate measure of performance.

A PA's adequacy to *provide feedback and improve performance* requires that it possess the following characteristics: be unambiguous and clearly specify the job-related performance expected, use behavioral terminology, set behavioral targets for ratees to work toward and use a problem-solving focus which culminates in a specific plan for performance improvement. If PAs are to identify training needs, the format must specify ratee deficiencies in behavioral terms, include all relevant job dimensions, and identify environmental deterrents to desired performance levels.

PAs are also used in the *allocation of organizational rewards* such as merit pay and punishments, such as disciplinary actions. Effective reward allocation may require a valid PA which ranks employees according to a quantifiable scoring system. Sufficient variance in scores is essential to differentiate across performers. In allocating rewards, PAs must have credibility with employees. The same PA format must also be used for disciplinary action, which may range from warnings to termination. Thus, the documentation required for such decisions must also be facilitated by the PA format. With the recent passage of Civil Service Reform Act and its provisions tying performance to merit pay and bonuses, the importance of PAs in the public sector has been greatly heightened.

PAs must be designed to facilitate the *validation of selection* techniques. This process requires, in general terms and at a minimum, measures of employee output or job-related dimensions that tap the behavioral domain of the job obtained through systematic job analysis, the facilitation of inter-rater reliability

1 Feedback/ development requires:	2 Assessing training needs requires:	3 Identifying promotion potential requires:	4 Rewards allocation requires:	5 Validation of selection techniques requires:	6 Measurement accuracy requires:
Specifying behavioral terminology on the format.	Specifying deficiencies in behavioral terms.	Job-related criteria	Ability to rank order ratees or results in quantifiable, performance scores.	Job relatedness and a comprehensive list of dimensions tapping the behavioral domain of the job.	Reducing rater responses set errors (e.g., leniency, restriction of range, halo).
Setting behavioral targets for ratees to work toward.	Rating on all relevant job dimensions.	Job dimensions dealing with ability to assume increasingly difficult assignments, built into the form.	Facilitating a variance or spread of scores to discriminate between good, bad, fair, etc. ratees.	Systematic job analysis to derive criteria.	Agreeing with other performance measures not on the format (e.g., direct indices such as salary, number of promotions.)
Job-related, problem-solving performance review which ends with a plan for performance improvement.	Identifying motivation/ attitude and environmental conditions as causes of inadequate performance.	Ability to rank ratees comparatively. Measuring of contribution to organization/ department objectives.	Measuring contributions to organization/ department objectives.	Assessing interrater reliability.	Reliability across multiple raters.
Reducing ambiguity/ anxiety of ratees regarding job performance required and expected by raters/organization.		Assessing of ratee's career aspirations and long-range goals.	Accuracy and credibility with employees.	Professional, objective administration of format. Continual observation of ratee performance by raters.	Flexibility to reflect changes in job or environment.
					Job-related criteria.
					Commitment of raters to observe ratee performance frequently and complete format seriously.

Figure 2 Objectives of performance appraisal systems.

measures, professional and objective administration of the PA and continual rater observation of ratee performance.[5]

The *identification of promotion potential* requires that job-related PAs have several dimensions in the incumbent's job, the same, or similar to, the job to which the incumbent may be promoted. This indicates the incumbent's ability to assume increasingly difficult assignments. The PA must also rank ratees comparatively, measure the contribution to departmental objectives and perhaps capture a ratee's career aspirations and long-term goals.

The final but perhaps most important PA objective is its accuracy in measuring performance. In some ways, it could be conceived as essential for meeting the PA objectives mentioned above. The issues of concern here would include PA formats which minimize rater response set errors (e.g., leniency, restriction of range, halo), those which agree with other measures of performance using alternative formats (e.g., direct indices such as salary or number of promotions), those which obtain reliability across raters, those which have the flexibility to reflect changes in the job environment and those possessing credibility with raters such that they complete the format seriously.

Thus, there are several criteria which PAs should meet to be fully operational. But which types of formats—those which measure worker behavior or those which measure the outcomes of that behavior—are more effective? No simple answer is available, but the utility of various types of behavior-based and effective-based formats can best be ascertained by comparing them against the PA objectives identified above.

COMPARISON OF FORMATS

Global Ratings   The first PA format alternative is a uni-dimensional, global rating which uses a rater's overall estimate of performance without distinguishing between critical job elements or dimensions. There are numerous problems in the use of uni-dimensional formats and when compared to the six PA objectives described above, they generally fall far short (see Figure 3). Uni-dimensional PA formats are also questionable as measures of performance (i.e. criteria) from a legal standpoint because they are not based on job analysis and thus are not job-related.

Trait-Based Scales   There are numerous multi-dimensional (or graphic) approaches to measuring performance. They are more useful than global scales because they recognize that job performance consists of separate dimensions, or job elements. The first of these is the familiar trait-based scale using dimensions such as loyalty, dependability, etc. Other dimensions traditionally found on these formats are cooperation, initiative and self-confidence. There are problems in the use of trait-based scales centering around potential ambiguity and subjectivity. That is, specifically what is meant by "lack of cooperation"? Thus, many trait-based scales are generally evaluated as only poor to fair relative to PA objectives. Further, and perhaps most important, trait-based scales are typically

Format \ Objective	Feedback/ Development	Assessing training needs	Identification of promotion potential	Reward allocation	Selection system validation	Measurement accuracy
Global	Poor	Poor	Poor to fair	Poor	Poor	Poor
Trait-Based	Poor	Poor	Poor to fair	Poor to fair	Poor to fair	Poor to fair
Behavior-Based (if behaviorally anchored)	Very good to excellent	Very good	Very good	Very good	Very good to excellent	Good
Effectiveness-Based	Fair to good	Fair to good	Fair to good	Very good to excellent	Fair to good	Very good to excellent

Figure 3 Generalized evaluation of PA formats compared to PA objectives.

not sufficiently job-related or based on a thorough job analysis. Thus an organization's vulnerability to Equal Employment Opportunity (EEO) litigation is not alleviated.

Behavior-Based Scales   A significant step beyond global and trait-based formats are behaviorally based scales. These are based upon a job analysis and attempt to determine what an employee actually *does* at work. A behavior-based scale provides specific feedback to employees because it is based on the activities required of the job. It captures specific information across employees for reward allocation and about each employee specifically in the assessment of training needs because it identifies the activities (dimensions) in which an employee may be deficient. For promotion potential, a dimension-based scale can certainly be useful because it may specify the kinds of behaviors incumbents are to demonstrate in their present jobs. Performance on these dimensions can then be compared to the dimensions required in the next job level (for which the employee is a promotion candidate). Behavior-based scales are often seen as more accurate than the previous two PA formats because of their job-relatedness and specificity. Thus we can expect less rater error and higher interrater agreement (and/or reliability). Finally, because dimension-based scales can meet the legal requirements for criterion measures, these certainly can be an improvement for the validation of selection procedures.

The major drawback with dimension-based scales is that although they provide specification of the particular activities of an employee, the scale points are of limited use if they are only numerically and/or adjective-anchored. They provide little specific feedback on what behaviors led to the particular rating given, even though the area of performance deficiency has been identified. Thus, a dimension-based PA may be deficient in assessing an employee's specific behaviors within job dimensions since only adjective or numerical anchors are used.

Behavioral expectation scales or *behaviorally-anchored rating scales*

(BARS) are also dimensional scales.[6] The scale points are behavioral statements illustrating various degrees of performance, not merely adjectives or numbers. Thus, BARS are far more specific in terms of identifying employee behavior relative to performance on a specific job dimension. These are also more sophisticated than dimensions-based formats and require more time to develop.

Behavior-based scales seem to provide excellent feedback to employees in specifying not only what activities employees are to engage in, but also the behaviors a rater perceives that a ratee has demonstrated during the performance period. In fact, performance improvement has been demonstrated through the use of behavior-based systems.[7]

Effectiveness-Based Systems   Another multi-dimensional system is results, or effectiveness, based scaling. Effectiveness-based scales attempt to provide "objective" indicators for levels of performance and are, of course, typically called Management by Objectives (MBO) systems.[8] Although it is a multi-dimensional approach in that there are often many objectives which are to be accomplished, effectiveness-based scaling is unique in that what it provides is a measure of an employee's *contribution,* not an employee's *activities or behaviors.*

Ratees evaluated with effectiveness-based scaling are being evaluated not on what they *do* but what they *produce;* not on how they spend their time, but what they contribute. This is an important difference and a major shortcoming of the previously discussed PA approaches. Obviously, it is difficult to develop specific indicators of employee contribution, but it can be done for many jobs. It is accomplished with more ease in lower level jobs and entry-level jobs within an organization than in higher level jobs.

Thus, effectiveness-based scales offer something that is critical and often overlooked in the assessment of performance appraisals. MBO systems are often used to measure unit productivity to which a manager presumably makes a contribution.

WHAT ARE THE CAUSES OF PROBLEMS?

Regardless of what format is used, problems can deter PA system effectiveness. The cause of the ineffectiveness of any particular PA system is a function of many variables, acting singly or in groups, which characterize the job, organizational setting and users. However, most often specific causes are located within the following broad problem categories: human judgment, raters, criteria and formats, organization policy, legal requirements and Equal Employment Opportunity (EEO) legislation and inflexibility. Each of these six broad categories contains several possible sources of PA problems (see Figure 4), discussed briefly below.

Problems in a PA system ultimately can only be judged as to their degree of severity and dysfunctional consequences in light of the original objectives developed for each system. For example, a PA system may sacrifice some degree

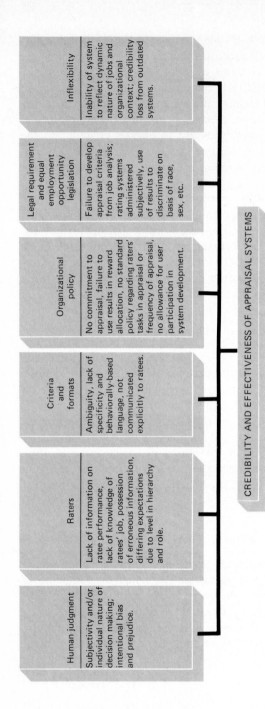

Human judgment	Raters	Criteria and formats	Organizational policy	Legal requirement and equal employment opportunity legislation	Inflexibility
Subjectivity and/or individual nature of decision making; intentional bias and prejudice.	Lack of information on ratee performance, lack of knowledge of ratees' job, possession of erroneous information, differing expectations due to level in hierarchy and role.	Ambiguity, lack of specificity and behaviorally-based language, not communicated explicitly to ratees.	No commitment to appraisal, failure to use results in reward allocation, no standard policy regarding raters' tasks in appraisal or frequency of appraisal, no allowance for user participation in system development.	Failure to develop appraisal criteria from job analysis; rating systems administered subjectively, use of results to discriminate on basis of race, sex, etc.	Inability of system to reflect dynamic nature of jobs and organizational context; credibility loss from outdated systems.

CREDIBILITY AND EFFECTIVENESS OF APPRAISAL SYSTEMS

Figure 4   Sources of problems in appraisal systems.

of applicability across job-type (and would, possibly have higher developmental costs) in order to have a greater amount and specificity of information about performance available to a certain group of ratees. Hence, it may have greater ability to pinpoint performance deficiencies and thus reduce costs of unnecessary training programs. If the objectives of a PA system are predetermined and prioritized, the system can be designed to make such trade-offs rationally and at minimal cost. Further, after PA design and implementation, problems diagnosed can be judged as to seriousness and corrective action planned in light of objectives. This relationship between PA objectives and both the design and revision of PA systems, while considering various PA problems, is emphasized in the discussion to follow.

Problem No. 1: Human Judgment A fundamental source of problems in PA is the *subjectivity and individuality* which accompanies the human judgment process. Individual differences among people influence their attitudes, values, perceptions, behavior and judgment, a fact as true in the PA setting as it is in all others. Intelligence, cognitive style, amount of education, age, sex and self-esteem are but a few of the individual level characteristics which have been found to influence the making of judgments of others. The expectations raters' supervisors hold for them, as well as a rater's own level of job performance and competence, have also been found to effect ratings.[9]

All of these factors, however, act in an implicit manner. They reflect "honest" or legitimate differences in personality, background or ability between participants in PA which influence their perception—their view of reality—and thus perceptions of the behavior of ratees. While these individual differences typically do not result in deliberate attempts to bias or prejudice ratings, their result on PA (e.g., inaccuracies) is similar.

Besides these *un*intentional PA errors resulting from individual differences, are those overt, deliberate attempts to distort PAs based upon personal prejudices and biases against others of a certain religion, national origin, race, sex, age, political ideology, etc. The result can be the setting of different performance standards for two people performing the same job or the distorting of PA results upward or downward to correspond to one's prejudices. Even when performance criteria are quantifiable and visible, figures can be distorted or interpreted erroneously by such judgmental factors as perceived amount of effort or initiative and hence intentional bias can still enter the process.

Problem No. 2: Raters PA problems stem from conscientious raters who possess *inadequate and/or erroneous information* about ratee performance. Many supervisors, due to their own job duties which may physically separate them from their subordinate ratees, are able to observe ratee performance too infrequently to accurately judge typical performance. Many must thus "sample" performance over a long period. But non-representative sampling or allowing a typical positive or negative performance occurring during their infrequent observation periods to bias their judgments of performance over the entire period can lead to inaccurate appraisals.

In addition, members of each hierarchical level within an organization may view a ratee's performance from a different vantage point or hold differing expectations for desired performance based upon their roles.[10] Thus a ratee's supervisor may be in an excellent position to judge the ratee's technical competence, but not his or her ability to effectively interact with others. Peer raters may possess the best information regarding a ratee's interpersonal effectiveness. Supervisors of ratees, as critics and evaluators of their subordinates, typically judge performance more harshly than do job incumbents themselves.

Problem No. 3: Criteria and PA Formats   The identification of specific, consistent, performance criteria are the first objective of a PA system, as discussed earlier. The easiest way to assure that a ratee's performance can be evaluated based upon only the whim of a rater is of course to keep the criteria ambiguous and/or secret, to change them capriciously, or never to develop them at all! As discussed above, each type of appraisal format has advantages and disadvantages relative to this issue of defining the criteria against which to base evaluations. The overall objective, of course, is to develop a format which identifies and defines the criteria in explicit, concrete terms.

Problem No. 4: Organizational Policy   Problems in PA systems arise from the relationship between organizational policies regarding performance, promotion, merit raises and other decisions and the uses for which PA results are intended. If these types of decisions are actually to be made on the basis of performance, rather than on the basis of seniority or other criteria, results of a PA obviously assume a great deal of importance. Here problems arise when PA formats are ambiguous, criteria are not communicated to raters and ratees and/or if each of several degrees of performance (e.g., good, fair, etc.) do not have observable, behavioral referents.

For example, if a supervisor (rater) is given the authority to set merit raises for a group of subordinates (ratees) and the PA format which is used to measure performance is of the global type involving overall ranking, the supervisor can easily feel trapped. Of course, the supervisor might have a definite and accurate overall impression as to the relative performance of his or her ratees and can easily discriminate between the excellent and average performers. But if the top performers are given merit raises and the others are not, the supervisor needs a rationale for this action to give to those who were denied the merit raise. The global PA format provides little help since it does not specify and define the exact criteria used in PA or the different levels of performance within each criteria. To develop a formal, written rationale for each rating may not only be seen as too bothersome for many raters but they may find it difficult to articulate the exact criteria to ratees. The result is often that either extreme leniency is used on many ratings or that all ratees are rated about the same and hence each receives a smaller merit raise. Thus, expediency rather than discriminability between good and poor performers characterizes the PA system and its credibility is destroyed.

Problem No. 5: Legal Requirements and Equal Employment Opportunity (EEO) Legislation   The risk of precipitating charges of discrimination as a result of policy decisions based upon PA results is now itself a serious cause of problems in PA systems. The ramifications of subjective, unsubstantiated PAs can be devastating to an organization. Recently, through several pieces of legislation, court decisions and guidelines of various Federal agencies, the issue of discrimination in employment as a result of PAs has become more visible and spelled out in more detail than ever before.[11]

Organizations must present PA forms and any instructions given to raters as part of the evidence for the validity of such selection techniques as employment tests. Thus, the use of, for example, an application blank, would be judged acceptable in certain situations only if answers to particular items on the blank were found to correlate highly with the probability of future job "success" of workers in the job. Job "success" is demonstrated typically by results of a PA system. The PA system is thus open to scrutiny by the courts and must therefore be thorough and as bias-free as possible.

Violation of civil rights legislation can also come from the use of PAs *directly* in promotion decisions. The following excerpts from discussions of recent court cases involving PAs illustrate the potential consequences of an inadequate system:

> *The court found the following as a basis for discrimination: recommendations by foremen were based on standards which were vague and subjective and were made without written instructions concerning qualifications necessary for promotion . . . one company was required to offer training programs to upgrade personnel, to provide foremen with written instructions delineating objective criteria. . . . The other company was ordered to post announcements of pre-foremen training classes, to post notices of qualifications required for salaried positions. . . .*
>
> *Using performance ratings for determining personnel layoffs was found to be in violation of Title VII of the Civil Rights Act when an employer failed to validate the appraisal methods according to EEOC guidelines. The evaluations were judged invalid because they were based on subjective observations (two of three evaluators did not observe the employee on a daily basis), evaluations were not administered and scored under controlled and standardized conditions. . . . The courts ordered the company to reinstate the employees with nominal back pay and required the company not to use performance ratings until they had been validated.*[12]

Problem No. 6: Inflexibility The final cause of problems in PA systems is the dynamic nature of jobs and job performance and the static nature of any written PA document typically developed several months before it is to be used. As job responsibilities, duties, requirements and job environments change over time, a PA format may become obsolete before it is even used! Further, as worker's performance levels change over time, perhaps due to training and experience, the standards set in PA formats may be too low, geared only for newer workers. Even the same jobs within classes are not identical.

One solution is, of course, to continually develop new PA formats as all of the above factors change and to develop separate PA formats for each and every position. But this solution is an economic impossibility. A solution often used by organizations is to develop a few broad categories of formats—perhaps one format for operating-level workers, one for clerical workers, one for technical workers, and one for managers. A reasonable solution? Yes, provided raters are knowledgeable, competent, use identical standards, observe performance equally, are generally bias-free and are provided with specific, detailed criteria. But in the all too often instances when the "ideal" rater is unavailable, PA formats applicable across job types may lead to subjectivity and possibly to litigation for discrimination.

The view of PA systems presented above is, admittedly, problematic. Yet it is a realistic one as many organizations find their appraisal system to be the source of continual problems. As discussed, no system is capable of alleviating all appraisal problems completely. Yet there are a few things which can be done to enhance a system's effectiveness.

The first way to improve appraisal systems is to recognize that the appraisal process entails far more than measurement and the use of a form. It also includes observation and identification of performance, as well as development of performance. As discussed, PA systems have several objectives. They must be developed in light of both the trade-offs between these objectives and the potential problem sources in appraisal.

The second mechanism for improved appraisal is to integrate the best aspects of the various formats. Behavior-based systems, such as Behaviorally-Anchored Rating Scales (BARS), specify criteria in very concrete terms to improve accuracy, provide detailed feedback to ratees and help comply with legal requirements due to the job-relatedness of criteria. Effectiveness-based systems, such as Management by Objectives (MBO) are very popular due to their ability to measure and quantify results, redirect effort to important tasks and allow for ratee participation in goal-setting. The next article in this series demonstrates how and why BARS and MBO can be integrated to derive the benefits from both systems. The developmental procedure for BARS is explained and the samples of all required forms are included. The last article in the series describes the final, integrated system and explains its operation through an actual case study.

REFERENCES

1   Bill Bouton, cited in M. W. McCall and D. L. DeVries, *Appraisal in Context* (Greensboro, N.C.: Center for Creative Leadership, 1977).
2   H. E. Meyer, "The Science of Telling Executives How They're Doing," *Fortune,* Vol. 89, No. 1 (Jan., 1974), 102.
3   Bureau of National Affairs, *Management of Performance Appraisal Systems* (Washington, D.C.: BNA, 1974).
4   See also J. P. Campbell, et al., *Managerial Behavior, Performance, and Effectiveness* (NY: McGraw-Hill, 1970).
5   See "Uniform Guidelines on Employee Selection Procedures," *Federal Register,* Dec. 30, 1977; D. B. Schneier, "The Impact of EEO Legislation on Performance APPRAISAL," *Personnel,* 1978, 55 (4), 24–34.
6   The development and utility of BARS is the subject of Part II of this series of three

articles. See also C. E. Schneier and R. W. Beatty, *Personnel Administration Today* (Reading, MA: Addison-Wesley, 1978) and S. J. Carroll and C. E. Schneier, *Performance Appraisal* (Goodyear Pub. Co., forthcoming).

7 R. W. Beatty, C. E. Schneier and J. R. Beatty, "An Empirical Investigation of Perceptions of Ratee Behavior Frequency and Ratee Behavior Change Using Behavioral Expectation Scales (BES)," *Personnel Psychology,* 1977, *30,* 647–658.

8 See S. J. Carroll and H. Tosi, *Management by Objective* (New York: Macmillan, 1973).

9 See e. g., C. E. Schneier, "The Psychometric Characteristics and Operational Utility of Behavioral Expectation Scales (BES): A Cognitive Reinterpretation," *Journal of Applied Psychology,* 1977, *62,* 541–548.

10 See C. E. Schneier and R. W. Beatty, "The Influence of Role Prescriptions on the Performance Appraisal Process," *Academy of Management Journal,* 1978, *21,* 129–134.

11 See W. H. Holley and H. S. Feild, "Performance Appraisal and the Law," *Labor Law Journal,* July, 1975, 423–429; "Uniform Guidelines on Employee Selection Procedures," op. cit; D. B. Schneier, op. cit.

12 Holley and Feild, op. cit., pp. 427–428.

REVIEW AND DISCUSSION QUESTIONS

1 What are the differences between behaviorally based and effectiveness-based performance appraisal systems?
2 Why is the trait appraisal form rated so poorly? Why, then, is it still used so much by today's organizations?
3 Quantify five quality standards for a job of your choice.

Reading 32

Organizational Development: Some Problems and Proposals

Robert L. Kahn

INTRODUCTION

Advising people in power about how they can better attain their goals is a very old occupation. Organizational Development (OD), on the other hand, is a new label for a conglomerate of things an increasing number of consultants do and write about. What that label refers to depends to a considerable extent upon the doer or writer. Among the critics and practitioners of organizational develop-

Reprinted from *The Journal of Applied Behavioral Science,* October–November–December 1974, pp. 485–502, with permission of the publisher.

The author is pleased to acknowledge the very helpful comments and materials provided by Jerome Franklin, Marshall Sashkin, George Strauss, and Arnold Tannenbaum.

ment, who are often the same people, there is a continuing argument over the state of the art, its proper definition, and the requisite skills for practicing it.

For example, Harry Levinson [1972], a clinical psychologist writing in the journal *Professional Psychology,* criticized OD practice for its neglect of diagnostic procedures, along with other theoretical and methodological short-comings. He was answered in the same journal by Marshall Sashkin [1973a] and by Warner Burke [1973b], both of whom undertook a specific rebuttal of Levinson's criticisms and a general defense of organizational development as practiced. Levinson [1973a] responded; Sashkin [1973b] replied; Burke [1973a] commented further; and Levinson [1973b] offered summary comments, which included the inarguable observation that the discussion had reached the point of diminishing returns.

Such exchanges reveal a good deal about current practice and preference, and several recent review articles provide more comprehensive statements. One of the most instructive is Friedlander and Brown's chapter in the current *Annual Review of Psychology* [1974], which is built around the familiar dichotomy between people-oriented ("human processual") and technology-oriented ("technostructural") approaches to organization change. Comprehensive reviews have also been written by Alderfer [1974], Sashkin *et al.* [1973], Strauss (in press), and Hornstein *et al.* [1971]. Leavitt's earlier chapter [1965] speaks in terms of applied organizational change rather than development, but the difference is more terminological than substantive and the review remains a useful commentary on what is now called OD.

More numerous than such reviews are books and articles that describe a preferred approach to organizational development, sometimes in very general terms, sometimes with a good deal of theoretical elaboration, occasionally with some substantiating empirical data. Examples are provided by Argyris [1970, 1971] on intervention theory, Blake and Mouton [1968, 1969] on grid organization development, Schein [1969] on process consultation, Schmuck and Miles [1971] on the OD Cube, and others.

My present purpose is neither to rehearse the OD arguments nor to review the reviews. Much less do I wish to dispute whether the practice of organizational development has been nearly completed, is well en route, or has barely begun the long transition from being a miscellany of uncertain devices to becoming a mature, usable set of principles and procedures for organizational change. I want instead to cite some problems, the resolution of which will facilitate that transition and thus make organizational development better than it is, in theory and practice.

OMISSIONS AND REDUNDANCIES

No reasonable person can complain that written material on organizational change and development is meager. In 1962 Everett Rogers [Rogers & Shoemaker, 1962, 1971], working in an admittedly broader area, the communication of innovations, generated a bibliography of some 1,500 items. In 1968

Ronald Havelock [Havelock *et al.*, 1968, 1972] found almost 4,000 titles in the area of planned innovation, and offered the terrifying bibliographic projection that the number was increasing at the rate of 1,000 per year. Such volume invites specialization; in the more circumscribed area of organizational development, Jerome Franklin [1973] lists about 200 books, chapters, and articles. That is the body of material most relevant for our present purposes; what does it tell us?

About 15 years ago, March and Simon [1958] observed that rather little had been said about organizations, but that little had been said repeatedly and in many different ways. In the years since then, I believe that caustic judgment has become less accurate for organizational research in general, but it remains unhappily true of writings on organizational development. A few theoretical propositions are repeated without additional data or development; a few bits of homey advice are reiterated without proof or disproof, and a few sturdy empirical generalizations are quoted with reverence but without refinement or explication.

For example, Kurt Lewin's [1947 a, b] suggestion that the process of planned change be conceptualized in terms of three successive phases—unfreezing, moving, and freezing—is often quoted or paraphrased as a preamble to research, but seldom with any clear indication of how that formulation determined the design of the research that follows its invocation. The Lewinian concept of quasi-stationary equilibrium [1947c] is also frequently mentioned, but without any systematic conceptualization or measurement of the alleged opposing forces. Gordon Lippitt [1969] presents this model as "force-field analysis," and 40 driving and restraining forces are represented by opposing arrows in a diagram [p. 156]. The forces, however, are unidentified; their identification and measurement is left to the reader. Such presentations are common. The Lewinian schema thus remains not only unelaborated and untested, but really unused. It deserves more serious attention.

The OD literature contains other slogans, less theoretical but recited no less often. Consider, for example, the advice that the "change agent" should "start at the top" of the organization he intends to change. Beckhard [1969] makes "management from the top" one of five defining characteristics of organizational development; Blake and Mouton [1969] assert that "to change a company, it is necessary for those who head the company to lead the change of it." Argyris' recent cases [1971] begin with discussions between the author and chief executives of the companies described.

I have neither experience nor data to challenge the advice that one should start at the top, and certainly it has a pleasant ring. Nevertheless, it would benefit from specification and test. Does it mean that the top of the organization must change before any other part can do so? Does it mean that the people at the top of the organization must actively support the proposed program of change without necessarily becoming "trainees" themselves? Or does it mean merely that some degree of top-echelon sanction for the new enterprise of organizational development must be visible in order for others to accept the proposed changes? One can readily imagine research to answer these questions, but it has yet to be done. Nor can it be, until the homily about starting at the top is stated with enough specificity to be tested.

As an example of a third sort of redundancy without development, empirical generalization, let us take the proposition that organizational changes are more likely to be accepted by people who have had a voice in determining their content. This is the principle of participation, perhaps the best established and most widely accepted empirical generalization in the literature of organizational change. The research pedigree for this principle dates back at least to 1948, when Coch and French published their classic article on overcoming resistance to change. Their experiment demonstrated that varying degrees of employees' participation in changes of work methods were related to their expressed acceptance of the new methods, to the rapidity with which they learned those methods, and to their decision to remain as employees of the company.

As good research should, the Coch and French experiment not only answered old questions; it raised new ones. Some of them—the interaction of participation with individual personality differences, for example—have been the subject of subsequent investigations [Tannenbaum & Allport, 1956; Vroom 1960]. Others remain unstudied; for example, the important question of distinguishing the motivational effects of participation from substantive effects of participative decisions.

It would be exciting to see an organizational development program that included research designed to obtain separate estimates of the effects of identical substantive changes generated under participative and non-participative conditions. Such data could be provided, I think, by means of a design using "master" and "slave" groups. (I use the terms only in their figurative, mechanical sense.) Workgroups would be chosen in sets of three, one in each set randomly designated master, one slave, and one control. If one of the master groups decided in the course of an OD program that the group should have the authority to set its own standards or choose its own methods of work or have access to current cost data, these same changes would be initiated in the slave group, but by conventional managerial instruction. An increase in productivity or satisfaction in the master groups, as compared to control groups, would be interpreted as the effect of the substance of the decisions without the motivational effect of participation. The difference in criterion changes in a master group as compared to the matched slave group would be interpreted as reflecting the effect of participation alone, the effects of decision content having been held constant experimentally within each such pair of groups.

Whether or not readers share my enthusiasm for this particular case of unexplored research is not important. The foregoing examples of omission and redundancy in the literature of organizational development and change are not intended to urge some particular research project. Rather, they are intended to rouse in the reader a thirst for movement—for elaboration and strengthening of old theoretical formulations, for systematic test of old injunctions, for the refinement and extension of old empirical generalizations. Argument by example, however, is always judgmental; let us state the criticism of redundancy in more objective terms. Of the 200 items in the Franklin [1973] bibliography of organizational development, only 25 per cent include original quantitative data; the remaining 75 per cent consist for the most part of opinions, narrative material, and theoretical fragments. No branch of science can long afford such a ratio. Ideas and personal impressions need desperately to be tested by collision with facts. The mill of science grinds only when hypotheses and data are in continuous and abrasive contact.

PACKAGES AND CONCEPTS

Organizational development is not a concept, at least not in the scientific sense of the word: it is not precisely defined; it is not reducible to specific, uniform, observable behaviors; it does not have a prescribed and verifiable place in a network of logically related concepts, a theory. These statements hold, I believe, in spite of some serious efforts to provide a workable definition and a meaningful theoretical context.

Lawrence and Lorsch [1969] provided one such example, building on their earlier work on differentiation and integration [1967] and describing organizational development in terms of activities at three interfaces—organization and environment, group to group, and individual in relation to organization. Argyris [1970] provides another example, in his sustained effort to conceptualize and describe his own experience in organizational change. His emphasis is on the autonomy and "health" of the client organization, and on OD as a means of increasing those valued characteristics by increasing the capacity of the organization to generate and utilize valid information about itself.

Argyris, like Lawrence and Lorsch, is stating his own definition and theoretical position; he is not attempting a formulation that accommodates everything that goes by the name of organizational development. Attempts at such broader and more eclectic statements sacrifice a good deal in precision and theoretical connectedness. For example, Bennis [1969] says that "organization development is a response to change, a complex educational strategy intended to change the beliefs, attitudes, values, and structure of organizations so that they can better adapt to new technologies, markets, and challenges, and the dizzying rate of change itself." His co-editor, Richard Beckhard [1969] says that "organizational development is the name that is being attached to *total-system,* planned-change efforts for coping with the above-mentioned conditions." (These conditions include four assertions about "today's changing world," five about "today's business environment," and six about "today's changing values.") I find those definitions too inclusive to be helpful, and others go still farther. Margulies and Raia [1972] offer a definition broad enough to include everything from market research to industrial espionage. They define organizational development as consisting of "data gathering, organizational diagnosis, and action interventions."

Other authors give us other descriptions, and their variety serves to underline my assertion that *organizational development* is not a concept. This assertion is in itself neither praise nor damnation; it merely reminds us that the term is a convenient label for a variety of activities. When we remember that fact about the term *OD*, we benefit from its convenience, as we do from the convenience of other colloquial terms—*mental health* and *illness*, for example. Scientific research and explanation, however, require concepts that get beneath convenient labels and represent explicitly defined and observable events and behaviors. The literature of organizational development is disappointing in this respect; it is tied too closely to the labels in terms of which the varied services of organizational development are packaged and marketed.

Moreover, this criticism holds even when we consider more specific terms. *Sensitivity training,* for example (also known as *laboratory method* or *T-Group training,* and partially inclusive of such variants as *encounter groups* and *personal development groups*), is itself a convenience term for a number of activities that probably vary as much with the preferences of the trainer as with anything else [Back, 1972]. *Grid organization development* is another such term; it refers to those consulting and training activities marketed by Blake and Mouton and their colleagues [1964, 1968, 1969]. Indeed, their firm has registered the term as a trademark or brand name—the antithesis of scientific conceptualization.

One of the persisting problems with research on organizational development is that it has incorporated such colloquial and commercial terms as independent variables. I have noted that of the more than 200 bibliographic entries on organizational development, about 25 per cent (53) present quantitative data. Within that subset, more than 65 per cent (35) utilized independent variables that must be considered packages rather than concepts. In most of those, the package was "the T Group," variously employed and mingled with lectures, skill-practice, and other training activities. In about 10 per cent of the data-reporting articles, the "independent variable" was "Managerial Grid Training."

In a few cases the experimental treatment was simply—or rather, complicatedly—"Organizational Development." And a few others offer as the independent variable a sort of omnibus treatment in which the social scientist and management seem to have done a variety of things—T Groups, consultation, lectures, surveys, explicit changes in formal policies, and the like, which they hoped might produce wanted changes in employee attitudes and behavior. Evidence of such changes is presented, but we are left in doubt as to the potent ingredient or synergistic combination of ingredients that produced the effect.

Such aggregate treatments need not be bad, but they can be made scientifically good only when the package treatment is sufficiently described to permit replication and "dissection" of its ingredients. I have found no examples of sustained refinement of independent variables in the articles that make up the bibliography of organizational development, although some beginnings have been made from time to time. In 1965, Bunker, for example, showed that conventional T Group experience produced changed interpersonal behavior in the back-home work situation, as measured in terms of the perceptions of co-workers, not merely the perceptions of the trainees themselves. Shortly thereafter, Bunker and Knowles [1967] replicated those findings, with variations in the duration of the experimental treatment. They compared the effects of two-week with three-week T Groups, and found that the latter generated the greater perceived changes in behavior. We could wish for more work along these lines, especially in view of the tendency toward shorter and more intensive use of T Groups and encounter groups—a tendency that appears to be based on administrative convenience rather than evaluative research.

There is another encouraging sign in the research that uses packages as independent variables: a few experiments or quasi experiments have compared packages. Perhaps the best example of such comparative work is Bowers' [1973] article "OD Techniques and Their Results in 23 Organizations." This research is based on data from 14,000 respondents in 23 industrial organizations and reports gain scores (before and after treatment) for four patterns of developmental activity—Survey Feedback, Interpersonal Process Consultation, Task Process Consultation, Laboratory (T Group) Training—and two "control" treatments, "data handback" and "no treatment." Bowers found that "Survey Feedback was associated with statistically significant improvements on a majority of measures, that Interpersonal Process Consultation was associated with improvement on a majority of measures, that Task Process Consultation was associated with little or no change, and that Laboratory Training and No Treatment were associated with declines."

These findings are not definitive, nor are they presented as such. There are the now-familiar problems with raw gain scores [Cronbach, Gleser, *et al.*, 1972], although Bowers has done supplementary analyses to control for initial differences in the several treatment groups and to test for the plausibility of the alternative hypothesis that his results merely reflect the regression of extreme scores toward the mean. There are other explicit limitations: the treatments are defined only approximately; there is confounding of change agents with treatment differences (since each change agent conducted the treatment of his choice); there is some self-selection of treatments by populations as well as change agents; and there is the absence of hard criteria of organizational change (productivity, profit, turnover, and the like). Finally, a sociologist of knowledge might express some lurking skepticism that Survey Feedback had been discovered by its proponents to be the most effective form of organizational development. Nevertheless, the comparison of treatments is most welcome; I applaud it and only wish that it were more frequent.

Friedlander and Brown [1974], in a careful review article of some 18 pages, require only three paragraphs to summarize comparative studies of OD interventions. Moreover, of the three studies summarized, two [Greiner, 1967; Buchanan, 1971] do not evaluate alternative interventions; the third study cited is that of Bowers.

Even such comparative studies, however, leave us with needs for explanation that can be satisfied only by research that clarifies the nature of the independent variable, the experimental treatment itself. Such conceptualization and explicit definition of the experimental treatment is well illustrated in three field experiments that are widely regarded as classics in organizational change—Coch and French's [1948] work on the effects of participation. Morse and Reimer's [1956] on hierarchical locus of decision-making power, and Trist and Bamforth's [1951] on changes in sociotechnical structure. There are other and more recent examples, of course, but the list remains short. Let us hope that it will lengthen.

AUTOBIOGRAPHY AND ORGANIZATION

My third criticism of research on organizational development may seem to include a contradiction in terms: the research on organizational development is not sufficiently organizational. It is too autobiographical a literature, too concentrated on the experience of the trainees and change agents. It is a literature of training episodes, and those episodes are often nonorganizational or extra-organizational.

Research that carries the term *organizational* in its title often consists of the group experience of a few people, far from the organizations that are allegedly being developed. More often than not, the criteria by which the success of the developmental process is judged are the reactions of these participants to the temporary group experience. Let us be specific: of the projects [in the Franklin (1973) bibliography] reporting empirical data interpreted in terms of organizational development, about 60 per cent are based on data from the training episode only; 40 per cent include some measure of the persistence of the training effect to some later time. A much smaller proportion, 15 per cent, trace the training effect in terms of behavior in the organization itself. Forty per cent measure the effect of the experimental treatment only in terms of self-report, and an equal proportion include no control or comparison group, either as part of an experimental design or in the statistical analysis of a large population.

Friedlander and Brown [1974] report similar conclusions in the three kinds of process-oriented intervention that have been most researched—survey feedback, group development, and intergroup development. They find "little evidence that survey feedback alone leads to changes in individual behavior or organizational performance," but considerable evidence for reported attitudinal change, at least in the short run. They speak of research on group development intervention in comparable terms: "There remains a dearth of evidence for the effects of team building external to the group developed." As for intergroup relations development—

> . . . there is very little systematic research on the effectiveness of such interventions in the field. Case studies abound [e.g., Blake, Mouton, and Sloma (1965)], but they leave many questions about the efficacy of the intervention unresolved.

Most OD activities seem to emphasize process rather than structure as the primary target of change, and most research describing the effects of structural changes in organizations seems to exemplify a different tradition from organizational development. However, definitional distinctions are difficult to make when definitions are unclear. If one includes in the realm of organizational development those studies that Friedlander and Brown call "technostructural," the evidence for persisting organizational effects increases. Certainly such effects were attained in the coal-mine experiments of Trist and his colleagues [1951, 1963] and in the textile-mill experiments of Rice [1958, 1969]. Thorsrud [1969], working in the same theoretical tradition, reported still broader and more ramifying changes in a series of Norwegian field experiments. In all these cases, the primary aim was to improve the goodness of fit between the social and the technical aspects of the work organizations. The improvement involved changes in both organizational aspects.

Significant increases in performance, attendance, and satisfaction have also been accomplished by organizational changes that begin with the division of labor, the definition of individual jobs. Such approaches include job design, job enlargement, and job enrichment, the distinctions among which are not always clear. All three share the assumption that many industrial jobs have been fragmented beyond the point of maximum efficiency, and that gains in performance and satisfaction are obtainable by reducing the fragmentation and increasing the variety of content. Results of such work are described by Davis and Taylor [1972] and Ford [1969], and are summarized by Stewart [1967] and Friedlander and Brown [1974]. The findings are not uniform, nor are the changes in job content that serve as independent variables or the organizational circumstances in which the experiments were attempted. One must conclude, nevertheless, that the content of the job makes a difference, and that intervention in terms of job content is likely to have effects.

Our present point, however, is not where OD intervention should begin but rather where it should end. As the term *organizational development* reminds us, the organization is the major target of change. Persisting change in the organization must therefore be the criterion of OD success or failure.

STRUCTURE AND PROCESS

The penultimate problem that I wish to raise about organizational development is the separation of structure and process. It is a familiar enough distinction in organizational theory and in writings on organizational change. Friedlander and Brown [1974] classify all efforts at organizational development as either "technostructural" or "human processual." Leavitt [1965] had earlier proposed a trichotomy: a similar distinction between structure and process, and an additional distinction between technological structure and social structure. As classifications that remind us of the different emphases or starting points of various approaches to change, I find these schemes useful. As classifications that imply the separation of organizational process and structure, however, I find them misleading.

We have argued elsewhere [Katz & Kahn, 1966] that human organizations be viewed as a class of open systems which lack the usual properties of physical boundedness and therefore lack structure in the physical or "anatomical" sense of the term. The structure of an organization can thus be said to consist in the pattern of interdependent events or activities, cyclical and repetitive in nature, that in combination create the organizational product or service. Organizational structures can therefore be well described in terms of roles, those activities expected of persons occupying certain positions in a network of such expectations and behaviors.

The structure of the living organization is not the charts and job descriptions and work-flow diagrams usually employed to describe those roles and the relationships among them. The structure of an organization is the pattern of actual behaviors as that pattern is created and re-created by the human beings we call members of the organization.

It may be useful for some purposes to distinguish this actual organization from some idealized or preferred structure, to distinguish the paper organization from the living organization, for example. There are many ways of making such distinctions—formal versus informal organizational behavior, role prescriptions versus role elaborations, and the like. But the central point remains: the structure of the organization *is* the pattern of actual recurring behaviors.

If we are agreed on that point, the issue of structural versus processual approaches to organizational development takes on a new and clearer form. To change an organization means changing the pattern of recurring behavior, and that is by definition a change in organizational structure. For example, suppose that an OD practitioner somehow gets all the supervisors in an organization to tell employees in advance about any developments that may affect their jobs. Suppose that the giving of such advance information becomes a continuing supervisory practice, a norm among supervisors, and an expectation on the part of subordinates. It will then be part of the role structure of the organization.

Providing such information may or may not be written into the job descriptions of supervisory duties, may or may not be included among criteria for promotion of supervisors. Likelihood of providing such information may or may not be built into the selection procedures for supervisors. To the extent that these things are also done, the giving of advance information becomes more a part of the "formal" structure of the organization, by which I mean management's representation of the organization. The incorporation of some change into the formal structure of the organization—that is, into the management-prescribed roles—has its own significance. But the main issue is change in the enactment of roles; if there is change in those recurring behavior patterns, then the structure of the living organization has changed. Organizational development, if it implies change at all, must change those behaviors, regardless of whether it calls itself structural or processual.

I believe that these issues become clearer if we discuss separately the target and the means of organizational change, and if we do so in terms of role concepts. There is by now some consensus about these concepts and their definition. A role consists simply of the expected behaviors associated with a particular position or office. The people who occupy positions somehow interdependent with that office typically hold and communicate expectations about the behaviors they want enacted by its occupant. The job description thus becomes a special case of such role expectations, probably sent to the occupant by someone in the personnel department acting as a surrogate for upper management. The actual behavior of a person in a role is likely to be a complex combination of responses to the expectations of relevant others and spontaneous activities that are neither prescribed nor proscribed by others. These latter activities are referred to as role elaborations, in contrast to role prescriptions.

Now let us use these terms to discuss first the target of change and then the means of change. I assume that when people speak of the target as structural change, they mean changing the roles and the official or formal expectations associated with them. The number of jobs, their formally prescribed activities, and their prescribed relationships to other positions are examples of such changes.

When people speak of changes in process rather than structure, I assume that they are referring to aspects of role behavior that are not usually prescribed but left to the discretion of the occupant—role elaborations rather than role prescriptions. For example, in most organizations, the extent to which supervisors express consideration and interest toward workers is a matter of role elaboration—unspecified in the formal description of the supervisory job and not included in the role expecations expressed by the workers themselves. If an OD program increases supervisory consideration, the changes might ordinarily be referred to as processual. It might be argued, of course, that what the OD program has done is to move certain consideration-expressing behaviors from role elaborations (options) to role prescriptions (managerial expectations, in this case), and that the target is therefore the formal structure of the organization, after all. I would not disagree, except to point out that the observation illustrates my point about the special meaning of structure in human organizations, and the ultimate fusion of structure and process.

A similar distinction and unity with respect to structure and process is involved in the means of organizational change. One can, for example, attempt to bring about change by altering the formal role prescriptions, introducing new technology, new written policies, new division of labor, and the like. Or one can attempt to bring about change by means of process interventions—counseling, consultation, encounter groups and the like.

But in the means of change, as in the target, we see some blurring of the usual dichotomy between structure and process. Even Frederick W. Taylor [1923], that classic exemplar of the structural approach to organizational change, began with process-like persuasion and interaction, first at the top of the company and then with the immortal Schmidt. Morse and Reimer [1956] used counseling, role playing, T Groups, and other process-emphasizing activities to bring about and anchor the systematic organizational change they sought.

On the other hand, the most process-oriented OD practitioner necessarily enters the organizational structure in which he hopes to encourage change. He creates a role for himself in that structure, and probably changes the role expectations and prescriptions of the people with whom he meets—if only because they are expected to speak with him, attend the group sessions he arranges, and the like. Moreover, his processual interventions, to the extent they are successful, are likely to lead to changes in formal policies, role prescriptions, and other representations of organizational structure.

The process-oriented OD specialist is likely to avoid specifying what structural changes he prefers; he expects those decisions to emerge from the heightened sensitivity and problem-solving abilities of the individuals and groups with which he has worked. He thus illustrates a certain complementarity with his structure-emphasizing counterpart. One OD specialist speaks in terms of process and says little about the structural end-state that he hopes to see the organization attain. The other concentrates on advocated changes in formal structure (job size, division of labor, and the like) and tells us little about the process by which changes are to be attained.

If there is a lesson for us as researchers and as observers of organizational development, it is to avoid being too absorbed with terminological distinctions and to concentrate instead on what is actually done by the change agent, what subsequent behavioral changes in the organization can be identified, their duration, and their ramifying or receding effects.

CHANGING THE UNWRITTEN CONTRACT

I believe that the body of material on organizational development, with its distinctive strengths and weaknesses, is itself the product of special conditions—the concentration of developmental experience in business and industry, and the nature of the role relationship between managements and researcher-consultants. A management, typically concerned with the productivity and profitability of its enterprise, with secondary interests in job satisfaction and the meaningfulness of work, pays a specialist in organizational development to do certain agreed-upon things in expectation of improved productivity and profit. If these results can be brought about with concomitant gains in satisfaction and worker identification with task and mission, all the better; hence the special appeal of approaches that promise some explicit linkage of satisfaction and productivity. Management also assumes in most cases that the process of organizational development will not alter or infringe traditional managerial prerogatives in matters of personnel, resource allocation, and the like.

The change agent, in his writings about organizational development, gives more emphasis to humanistic values in organizational life. He accepts his role in relation to management in the hope of contributing to the realization of those values, in the hope of increasing the satisfaction and meaningfulness of work. He also wishes to add to the store of things known about human organizations and to learn how they can be influenced. He usually enters into the relationship with management as a paid consultant, and with implied agreement about areas of activity and reservation. Too often, in my view, that implies agreement to induce some change in satisfaction, motivation, and productivity without becoming involved in resource allocation, availability of equipment, choice of supervisors, content of jobs, allocation of rewards, and the like. In the extreme case, the organizational developer agrees to leave the role structure alone and to induce changes in role elaboration—those activities and stylistic characteristics that are left to the discretion of individuals.

Progress in organizational change and the knowledge about change has been made sometimes in spite of those limitations, and sometimes because of welcome exceptions to them. Now there are numerous signs that the contract between management and behavioral science is being redrawn. Managements are less insistent on tangible results from intangible manipulations, and behavioral scientists are less willing to attempt such legerdemain. As one visible sign of this tendency, I welcome the work on job design [Davis & Taylor, 1972], which approaches organizational improvement through change in one of the major aspects of organizational structure—the division of labor. I hope that more research is done on job design, and that comparable lines of research develop on other aspects of formal organizational structure. Not only will this strengthen the practice of organizational development; it will also bring the language of organizational development into the larger realm of organizational theory and research. It is a long awaited convergence.

REFERENCES

Alderfer, C. P. Change processes in organizations. In M. D. Dunnette (Ed.). *Handbook of industrial and organizational psychology.* Chicago: Rand McNally, 1974.

Argyris, C. *Intervention theory and methods.* Reading, Mass.: Addison-Wesley, 1970.

Argyris, C. *Management and organizational development: The path from Xa to Yb.* New York: McGraw-Hill, 1971.

Back, K. W. *Beyond words.* New York: Russell Sage, 1972.

Beckhard, R. *Organizational development—Strategies and models.* Reading, Mass.: Addison-Wesley, 1969.

Bennis, W. G. *Organization development: Its nature, origins, and perspectives.* Reading, Mass.: Addison-Wesley, 1969.

Blake, R. R., & Mouton, J. S. *Corporate excellence through grid organizational development.* Houston: Gulf Publishing Co., 1968.

Blake, R. R., & Mouton, J. S. *Building a dynamic organization through grid organization development.* Reading, Mass.: Addison-Wesley, 1969.

Blake, R. R., Mouton, J. S., & Sloma, R. The union-management intergroup laboratory: Strategy for resolving intergroup conflict. *Journal of Applied Behavioral Science,* 1965, 1, 25–57.

Blake, R. R., Mouton, J. S., Barnes, L., & Greiner, I. Breakthrough in organizational development. *Harvard Business Review,* 1964, 42, 37–59.

Bowers, D. OD techniques and their results in 23 organizations: The Michigan ICL study. *Journal of Applied Behavioral Science,* 1973, 9, 21–43.

Buchanan, P. C. Crucial issues in OD. In *Social Intervention: A behavioral science approach.* New York: Free Press, 1971. Pp. 386–400.

Bunker, D. R. Individual application of laboratory training. *Journal of Applied Behavioral Science,* 1965, 1, 131–147.

Bunker, D. R., & Knowles, E. S. Comparison of behavioral changes resulting from human relations training laboratories of different lengths. *Journal of Applied Behavioral Science,* 1967, 3, 505–523.

Burke, W. W. Further comments by Burke. *Professional Psychology,* May 1973, pp. 207–208.(a)

Burke, W. W. Organization development. *Professional Psychology,* May 1973, pp. 194–199.(b)

Coch, L., & French, J. R. P., Jr. Overcoming resistance to change. *Human Relations,* 1948, 1 (4), 513–533.

Cronbach, J., Gleser, G., Nanda, H., & Rajartnam, N. *The dependability of behavioral generalizability for scopes and profiles.* New York: John Wiley, 1972.

Davis, L. E., & Taylor, J. C. (Eds.) *Design of jobs.* New York: Penguin Books, 1972.

Ford, R. N. *Motivation through work itself.* New York: American Management Association, 1969.

Franklin, J. I., Organizational development: An annotated bibliography. Ann Arbor, Mich.: Center for Research on the Utilization of Scientific Knowledge, Institute for Social Research, University of Michigan, 1973.

Friedlander, F., & Brown, L. D. Organization Development. *Annual Review of Psychology,* Vol. 25, Palo Alto, Calif.: Annual Reviews, 1974.

Greiner, L. E. Patterns of organizational change. *Harvard Business Review,* 1967, 45, 119–128.

Havelock, R., *et al. Bibliography on knowledge utilization and dissemination.* Ann Arbor, Mich.: Institute for Social Research, 1968, Rev. 1972.

Hornstein, H. A., *et al.* Some conceptual issues in individual and group oriented strategies of intervention into organizations. *Journal of Applied Behavioral Science,* 1971, 7, 557–567.

Katz, D., & Kahn, R. L. *The social psychology of organizations.* New York: John Wiley, 1966.

Lawrence, P. R., & Lorsch, J. W. *Organization and environment.* Boston: Division of Research, Harvard Business School, 1967.

Lawrence, P. R., & Lorsch, J. W. *Developing organizations: Diagnosis and action.* Reading, Mass.: Addison-Wesley, 1969.

Leavitt, H. J. Applied organizational change in industry: Structural, technological, and humanistic approaches. In J. G. March (Ed.). *Handbook of organizations.* Chicago: Rand McNally, 1965.

Levinson, H. The clinical psychologist as organizational diagnostician. *Professional Psychology,* 1972, 3, 34–40.

Levinson, H. Levinson's response to Sashkin and Burke. *Professional Psychology,* May 1973, pp. 200–204.(a)

Levinson, H. Summary comments. *Professional Psychology,* May 1973, p. 208.(b)

Lewin, K. Frontiers in group dynamics I. *Human Relations,* 1947, 1, 5–41.(a)

Lewin, K. Frontiers in group dynamics II. *Human Relations,* 1947, 1, 143–153.(b)

Lewin, K. Group decision and social change. In T. M. Newcomb and E. L. Hartley (Eds.). *Readings in social psychology.* New York: Holt, 1947.(c)

Lippitt, G. L. *Organization renewal.* New York: Appleton-Century-Crofts, 1969.

March, J., & Simon, H. *Organizations.* New York: John Wiley, 1958.

Margulies, N., & Raia, A. P. *Organization development: Values, process, and technology.* New York: McGraw-Hill, 1972.

Morse, N., & Reimer, E. The experimental change of a major organizational variable *Journal of Abnormal and Social Psychology,* 1956, 52, 120–129.

Rice, A. K. *Productivity and social organization: The Ahmedabad experiment.* London: Tavistock, 1958.

Rice, A. K. Individual group and intergroup processes. *Human Relations,* 1969, 22, 565–584.

Rogers, E., & Shoemaker, F. *Communication of innovations.* New York: The Free Press, 1962. Rev. 1971.

Sashkin, M. Organization development practices. *Professional Psychology,* May 1973, pp. 187–192.(a)

Sashkin, M. Sashkin's reply to Levinson. *Professional Psychology,* May 1973, pp. 204–207.(b)

Sashkin, M., *et al.* A comparison of social and organizational change models: Information flow and data use processes. *Psychological Review,* 1973, 80 (6), 510–526.

Schein, E. H. *Process consultation: Its role in organization development.* Reading, Mass.: Addison-Wesley, 1969.

Schmuck, R. A., & Miles, M. B. (Eds.) *Organization development in schools.* Palo Alto: National Press. 1971.

Stewart, P. A. *Job enlargement.* Iowa City: College of Business Administration, University of Iowa. 1967.

Strauss, G. Organization development. In R. Dubin (Ed.) *Handbook of work organization in society.* Chicago: Rand McNally. In press.

Tannenbaum, A., & Allport, F. H. Personality, structure and group structure: An interpretative study of their relationship through an event structure hypothesis. *Journal of Abnormal and Social Psychology,* November 1956, 53 (3), 272–280.

Taylor, F. W. *The principles of scientific management.* New York: Harper, 1923.

Thorsrud, E. A strategy for research and social change in industry: A report on the industrial democracy project in Norway. *Social Science Inform,* 1969, 9 (5), 65–90.

Trist, E. L., & Bamforth, R. Some social and psychological consequences of the long wall method of coal-getting. *Human Relations,* 1951, 4 (1), 3–38.

Trist, E. L., Higgin, G. W., Murray, H., & Pollack, A. B. *Organizational choice.* London: Tavistock, 1963.

Vroom, V. *Some personality determinants of the effects of participation.* Englewood Cliffs, N.J.: Prentice-Hall, 1960.

REVIEW AND DISCUSSION QUESTIONS

1 What are some examples of omission and redundancy in organization development?
2 The author states that organizational development is not a concept. What does he mean by this? Do you agree?
3 What is the relationship between structure and process in organizational development?
4 Summarize the major strengths and weaknesses of OD as presented in this reading.

Reading 33

Multiple Measures to Assess the Impact of Organization Development Interventions

Diane L. Lockwood
Fred Luthans

Inevitably, at some time during the career of every organization development (OD) change agent, he or she confronts the enigmatic question "How is it possible to know if what is being done in this organization is really effective?" Obviously, the answer is to *measure* the impact of interventions. Not so obvious, however, are the criteria used to assess so-called "effectiveness" and the particular methods or tools employed to collect data. All change agents have their "pet" assessment tools such as pre- and post-intervention surveys, formal interviews, informal discussions with managers and others, "hard" data from company records, or systematic observations of organizational behavior. Relying unduly on any one particular assessment tool, however, is behaving somewhat like the child who, given a hammer, proceeds to pound everything with it. In other words, it is no more plausible to rely on one method or only a few methods of assessment than it is to use the same type of OD intervention strategy regardless of the particular needs and constraints of the client organization. Sechrest [1971] suggests that any single data-collection method, to a greater or lesser extent, is fallible in its validity and that proper recognition of the effects of the method on assessment techniques is lacking. Webb, Campbell, Schwartz, and Sechrest [1966] have, therefore, maintained that "it is convergence in the consistency and direction of findings yielded by a combined series of different measures, each with its idiosyncratic weaknesses, which leads to the most fertile search for validity" [p. 174].

Taking the lead of Webb et al. [1966], we are suggesting that OD practitioners and researchers should employ a multiple approach to measuring the nature and extent of organizational change. Specifically, the purposes of this paper are (1) to survey the different methods and techniques currently used to assess the impact of OD interventions; (2) to discuss the strengths and weaknesses that characterize these methods; and, finally, (3) to suggest some alternative but heretofore seldom-used methods of data collection and measurement that could be used in future assessment research.

Measurement of the impact of planned-change programs is greatly dependent on *what* criterion variables are selected to be analyzed and *how* data relevant to these variables are collected. For example, criterion variables used to assess organizational change may include overall performance, productivity,

Reprinted from *The 1980 Annual Handbook for Group Facilitators*, University Associates, Inc., 8517 Production Ave., San Diego, Calif.; used with permission.
[1]An earlier version of this paper was presented at the Midwest Academy of Management meeting, Milwaukee, Wis., 1977.

employee satisfaction, and/or profit. These variables, in turn, may be operationalized and measured by utilizing employee and supervisory performance ratings, unit productivity data, self-report satisfaction questionnaires, and/or financial records. Obviously, these examples of criterion variables are not the only ones that may be used to assess change. Furthermore, the above variables may be operationalized and measured in ways different from those previously mentioned. However, it is usually recognized [e.g., Cantalanello & Kirkpatrick, 1968] that four levels of evaluation can best be used to assess the impact of OD interventions:

a *Affective Reactions:* participants' attitudinal responses to the intervention program *per se* (e.g., Did participants *like* the program? Did they find it interesting, useful, or beneficial?)
b *Learning:* participants' understanding and retention of material covered in the program (e.g., Did participants *learn* anything as evidenced by, for example, pre-post difference scores on multiple-choice tests, follow-up interviews, or open-ended survey responses?)
c *Behavioral Changes:* participants' actual behavioral changes on the job, as evidenced by, for example, observational response frequency charts
d *Performance Changes:* "hard" organizational measures (e.g., productivity and quality rates, sales volume, profit, absenteeism, and turnover), as well as more subjective performance appraisal ratings

All too often we are tempted to stop at the first level of analysis (affective reactions), or, conversely, we jump to the fourth level (performance changes) without an adequate assessment of learning and behavioral-change correlates of organizational performance changes. Obviously, various assessment techniques are more or less appropriate to these different levels of evaluation.

ASSESSMENT TECHNIQUES FOR OD

Five assessment methods (the questionnaire, the interview, observation, archives, and self-generated measures) are reviewed here with special emphasis given to the strengths and limitations of each (see Table 1). This list of methods is not intended to be exhaustive, but it does include the most common and potentially useful techniques.

The Questionnaire

In the behavioral sciences as a whole, research and resulting field applications are based largely on questionnaire data. In a recent literature review of organization development research, Pate, Nielsen, and Bacon [1976] found that over half the studies did not employ any data-collection methods other than attitude and perception questionnaires. A quick examination of any journal in the field of organization change gives evidence of the reliance on questionnaire instruments.

Table 1 Methods Used to Assess the Impact of OD Interventions

Method	Examples	Type(s) of data generated	Strengths	Limitations
Questionnaire/ Survey	• Michigan Organizational Assessment Package (Nadler, 1975) • Quality of work life or climate surveys • Job Diagnostic Survey (Hackman & Oldham, 1974) • Job Orientation Inventory (Blood, 1969) • Study of Values (Allport, Vernon, & Lindzey, 1960) • Managerial Grid (Blake & Mouton, 1964) • Various instruments contained in Pfeiffer & Jones (1972-1980) • Sociometric choice questionnaires • Tests/exams	• Affective reactions: attitudes, satisfaction, personality, preferences, perceptions, motivations, values • Demographic details: age, sex, job position, salary, length of service, education location • Structural variables: hierarchy, span of control, decentralization, ownership, departmentation, environment • Subjective performance ratings (e.g., employee or supervisory performance appraisal forms) • Learning and understanding of concepts	• Ease of administration, especially for longitudinal purposes • Relatively low cost of processing results • Ease of generalizing results in comparison to more situationally bound methods • Assurances of anonymity of responses • Known reliability with standardized instruments • Few restrictions on content	• Obtrusiveness (e.g., "social desirability" response biases) • Individual differences in interpretation of items and scales • Reactive effects of testing in which a pretest becomes an intervention in itself • Questionable validity • Need to exercise caution when making inferences from attitudinal to behavioral or performance data
Interview	• Individual: one-on-one interchange with internal or external change agent in which questions vary on a continuum from unstruc-	• Affective reactions (e.g., attitudes, perceptions, likes/dislikes, desired changes) • Descriptive (e.g., organizational policies and	• Virtually unrestricted content, depending on the nature of the questions asked • Usefulness in hypotheses-generation	• Cost and time necessary to conduct and process • Reactive effects: interviewee self-selection of information and interviewer perceptual

462

Interview (cont.)	• tured (open-ended) to structured • Work groups: interviews with intact work units using group-on-group techniques, tape recordings, etc.	• procedures, organizational history, job descriptions long-and-short-range goals) • Processes (e.g., decision making communication, planning, control, coordination, conflict management)	phase to identify critical variables • Flexibility to probe ambiguous questions and responses • Ability to give change agent some indication of clients' willingness to confront issues (i.e., climate of trust) • Increase in the probability that individuals will be involved in subsequent action and follow-up because of specific attention paid them	biases • Less amenability to quantitative analysis • Difficulty of generalizing results
Observation	• Unstructured naturalistic observation of ongoing phenomena to develop categorical schemes (Mintzberg, 1973; Bales, 1950) • Content analysis of journal, client log, or calendar entries • Deposit studies (famous content of the "trash can" studies, Webb et al., 1966) • Structured participant observation or "confederate" studies of ongoing phenomena	• Virtually unlimited (e.g., affective reactions; descriptive structural learning; behavioral, performance, process data)	• Provision of insight into previously unexplored phenomena, thus facilitating development of new categorical schemes • Minimal respondent reactivity, depending on the degree to which observers and methods constitute a natural part of the original environment • Reliable results, provided high intercoder agreement achieved • Provision of construct validation for instruments,	• Cost and (especially) time needed to record and process • Need for internal "confederates" or access to the client organization over an extended period of time • Requirement of a high level of expertise in the initial stages of development • Ethical issues surrounding unobtrusive data collection • Observer biases, although minimized when

Table 1 *(Continued)*

Method	Examples	Type(s) of data generated	Strengths	Limitations
Observation (cont.)			using comparison of "known groups" methods, enhancing meaningfulness and relevancy of data generated	intercoder agreement is achieved • Changes in standards of observation when different observers are used at different times
Archives	• Organizational history documents	• Corporate by-laws, stock issuance and transfers, minutes from board of directors' meetings, policies of all types	• Relative inexpensiveness and minimal time necessary to collect, particularly if ongoing in-house MIS records are used	• "Selective editing" of records or "doctored" reports • Susceptibility to changes in record-keeping procedures over time, thus making comparisons across time difficult
	• Productivity records	• Quantity, quality, ratio, or percentage data (e.g., productivity, quality, maintenance, scrap, sales, inventory control rates)	• Top management's preference of quantifiable performance data to other more qualitative data	• "Mushy measurements" problem, which contributes to the difficulty of data interpretation
	• Financial records	• Fiscal data (e.g., profit/loss, return on investment, labor cost, support system cost, forecasting errors, taxes, reserves, bank notices, stockholders' dividends)	• Particular suitability to longitudinal, forecasting, and quantitative decision-making techniques	
	• Personnel records	• Job descriptions, promotion-demotion, transfers, recruitment, exit or debriefing data,		

	Examples	Type	Advantages	Cautions
• Time records	attendance, absenteeism, turnover rates, grievances • In/out time, overtime, turn-around time, shipping or delivery time, claim processing time			• Reactive effects: possible recorder biases in self-assessment strategies • Need to exercise caution when making inferences from behavioral data to affective or psychological states • Possibility of overloading employees with paperwork
• Government regulatory reports	• OSHA safety records, EPA, EEOC/affirmative action, Labor Department, SEC, FDA, Treasury Department, ICC, FAA, FCC, etc.			
Self-Generated	• Action plans • MBO • Behavioral frequency charts • Behaviorally Anchored Rating Scales (BARS) • Performance check-off systems (e.g., number of units completed, customer service calls, pickup and delivery logs) • Employee-completed performance appraisals and career development self-assessments	• Learning and development • Behavioral • Performance	• Relative inexpensiveness when collected as part of ongoing organizational activities • Particular usefulness for follow-up studies that assess progress toward goals and objectives • Ability to determine coder reliability and accuracy of recording through cross-checking of reports • Likelihood of generating meaningful and valid data because of employees' active participation in assessment • A potentially valuable mechanism for immediate and ongoing feedback	

Advantages Reasons for the extensive use of questionnaires are obvious. First, there are numerous standard questionnaires that are easily accessible to evaluators. This availability eliminates the tedious rigor and time involved in developing new instruments for each assessment effort. Second, questionnaires are relatively easy to administer. This becomes an especially important consideration when data are collected at multiple points in time for purposes of longitudinal analyses. Third, questionnaires do have certain advantages over other assessment techniques. In general, the positive aspects of questionnaires include the following:

a Ability to generalize is greater in comparison to other more situationally bound methods (e.g., "critical incident" methods).

b Restrictions on content are minimal.

c High reliability can be obtained by using standardized procedures that are generally known and successfully tested.

d Clarification and depth of responses are possible when open-ended items are included on the instrument.

Disadvantages On the other hand, questionnaires also have some severe limitations. Webb et al. [1966] have emphasized that questionnaires tend to be highly reactive and obtrusive. In other words, when respondents are aware that their behavior is under scrutiny, their behavior changes on this basis alone. Questionnaires also may lack validity. Even though a questionnaire may have reliability (consistency and accuracy), this is not a guarantee of its validity (measurement of what it is supposed to measure). Possible threats to the validity of questionnaires include "social desirability biases" [Golembiewski & Munzenrider, 1975], questionable anonymity, language difficulties, and extreme-response sets. In addition, the concept of individual differences [Guion, 1973] can be particularly problematic. For example, it is difficult to determine whether questionnaire measures of attitudes are more reflective of individual differences in perceptions of different work roles or of the intended properties of the organizational environment. Most importantly, perhaps, questionnaire results should not be regarded as an end in themselves; rather, they should be considered only as a springboard or means to stimulate further discussion and analysis of the issues surfaced.

Questionnaires are obviously needed for a variety of reasons, but they should clearly not be the only measure used and should always be used in combination with other measures. A multiple-measure approach enables the evaluator to examine the extent of convergence among many different findings. Simply, consistency or inconsistency of findings across different measures is very important to the validity of any assessment effort.

The Interview

Interviews rank with questionnaires as a popular way of gathering data for organizational-change research. White and Mitchell [1976], for example, found that twenty-six out of the forty-four studies reviewed relied on subjective reports by participants as their method of measurement. Despite its popularity, there is a tendency to disparage the interview method on the ground that it yields qualitative "anecdotal" or "testimonial" evidence. The advantages are seldom recognized. [See Jones, 1973, for a full consideration.]

Advantages According to Crano and Brewer [1973], the interview represents one of the most useful methods of data collection in the hypothesis-generation phase of a study or a systematic assessment. Rather than arbitrarily choosing a specific set of hypotheses from the multitude of possibilities, the evaluator can more clearly focus efforts through the use of questioning techniques in an interview. Such interviewing can lead to a concrete, manageable series of propositions. Lofland [1971] provides a useful guide for conducting such interviews.

Interviews also have the advantage of flexibility. There is the possibility of exploiting an unexpected lead or of probing ambiguous responses [Sechrest, 1971]. Finally, the interview can be legitimately employed in a field setting to cross-validate obtained relationships. For example, one study of organizational change [Benedict, Calder, Callahan, Hornstein, & Miles, 1967] found that qualitative data and the interviewees' impressions prior to seeing the data agreed that the OD intervention was not successful.

One comparison of questionnaire and interview data that was collected by one of the authors in a consulting project is shown in Figure 1. Using the interview transcripts, frequency counts of specific responses were made by two highly trained interviewers working independently. Items on which the coders agreed were retained for the content analytic summary report. Comparison of the data yielded by the two methods, summarized in Figure 1, illustrates that there is substantial agreement between the two results, although the interview data are relatively more explanatory. Such convergence of results yielded by two different methods increases the validity of the assessment.

Disadvantages Serious weaknesses to the method of interviewing, however, are that it can be extremely costly and time consuming. In addition, similar reactive threats to validity discussed under questionnaires also apply to interviews.

Observation

Ideally, the evaluation of organizational change should follow three major stages:

1 First, there should be *systematic observation* of the change that occurs in the actual setting. This observation in the naturalistic setting allows the assessor to suggest functional or causal relationships between the change technique and its intended effect.

2 Second, the suggested *relationships should be isolated* and verified under more highly controlled experimental (field or laboratory) settings.

QUESTIONNAIRE ITEM

Which of the following best describes how problems are resolved *between* departments in this organization?

1975 (pre) %	1976 (post) %		
11.7	7.8	(1)	Little is done about these problems—they continue to exist.
15.6	8.6	(2)	Little is done about these problems—they work themselves out in time.
7.8	11.7	(3)	The problems are appealed to a higher level—but are still not resolved.
39.8	40.6	(4)	The problems are appealed to a higher level—and are usually resolved.
25.0	31.3	(5)	The problems are worked out at the level where they appear through mutual effort and understanding.

CONTENT ANALYTIC SUMMARY OF INTERVIEW RESPONSES

Q. 13 "How are conflicts *between* departments resolved?"

Time 1. Summary for January 1975

The most frequent response was "by discussion between the department heads involved." In descending order of frequency, other responses included: (1) president has the final say; (2) they are turned over to a higher authority; (3) not sure they ever got resolved, or we work around them; (4) by edict, or people pull rank; (5) arbitration by insurance committee; and (6) "don't know" or "no response."

Time 2. Summary for October 1976

"Personal contact between the department heads involved" was by far the most frequent response. The second most frequent response was "if the conflict is not resolved at the first level, it is sometimes necessary to go up a level." "By using OD process" was also a frequent response. Finally, five respondents mentioned that they "didn't know of any conflict."

Changes from Time 1 to Time 2

Responses in period 2 were more consistent than in period 1. That is, a variety of methods were stated in period 1 as opposed to "resolution primarily at the level where the conflict occurred" in period 2. The application of OD principles was evident in period 2. Finally, comments pertaining to "they never get resolved" appeared less frequently in period 2 than in period 1.

Figure 1   Sample comparison of questionnaire and interview data.

3   Finally, there should be a *re-evaluation* and *verification* of the findings in the second stage through systematic observation in the naturalistic setting.

Traditionally academic researchers have ignored the first and third phase and concentrated on experimental studies; OD practitioners have done a peripheral, nonsystematic job of the first and third steps and ignored the second experimental step. What is called for is *systematic* observational techniques that precede and follow the more scientifically rigorous experimental methods (e.g., control-group designs) of evaluation of organizational-change efforts.

Advantages   Observational techniques have very distinct advantages as a basic data-collection method for the assessment of organizational change. Even relatively unstructured observations can provide initial descriptive information useful in the construction of a category system for investigating previously unexplored phenomena. Bales' [1950] early work with interaction analysis, for example, was originally developed by utilizing a series of relatively unstructured observations of group processes. Later Mintzberg [1973] developed an effective observational method to describe characteristics that typified the nature of managerial work. Another example is the use of observational techniques by Benedict et al. [1967] to provide a detailed content-and-process summary of group meetings within an educational system. Written or tape-recorded "process observations" by participants in OD team skill-training sessions are an example of the way observational analyses can be conducted. Also, Nadler, Jenkin, Miruis, and Macy [1975] have urged the use of structured observations of task characteristics for validating the assessment of job-enrichment interventions. To help the practitioner better understand and use the mechanics of systematic observation and analysis, the work by Lofland [1971] is suggested.

Probably the greatest single advantage of the measurement technique of observation is that it can minimize respondent reactions. The key to this advantage is to use natural participant or "confederate" methods and to conduct the observation unobtrusively. It may not be as difficult as it sounds. Margulies and Wallace [1973] point out that with a little practice managers and secretaries alike can become skillful in the use of structured observations. Furthermore, these employees are a natural part of the organizational environment. An example of an unobtrusive observational approach is the measurement of physical distance between interacting persons [Hall, 1963, 1966]. A relatively large physical distance may be indicative of stress in supervisor-subordinate relationships.

Methods for observing and recording nonverbal behaviors are reviewed by Knapp [1972]. As previously discussed, instruments are subject to biases about social desirability, particularly with "leadership style" questionnaires. That is, respondents assume that some styles are more socially acceptable than others and thus create an evaluation bias. Every internal psychological dimension, according to Webb et al. [1966], can be expected to manifest itself in a variety of ways, some more or less accessible to observation. The point is that the gathering of observational data appears to be limited only by the creativity and imagination of the evaluator.

Disadvantages The disadvantages inherent in observational techniques are fairly apparent. First, when the behavior being observed is obtrusively recorded, these techniques are subject to the same response biases as questionnaires and interviews. Although the highest ethical standards must always be maintained, observational methods should be as unobtrusive as possible: hidden, secretive recording is not called for; common sense is.

Second, a primary consideration in any method of assessment is its reliability: "Do the ratings of two or more observers who have witnessed the same event(s) coincide?" Agreement between raters is the major goal, since, without it, little use can be made of the unreliable data. Unless the data are *reliable,* they cannot be *valid.* Paul, Robertson, and Herzberg [1969] were able to obtain reliable data (i.e., data with high rater agreement) from unobtrusive observational techniques in a research and development department of a major chemical firm.

Other potential methodological problems with observational techniques are observer bias, changes in standards of observation over time, and high dross (useless data) rates [Webb et al., 1966]. However, used appropriately, observational methods can be a valuable *supplement* to almost any other kind of measurement in OD assessment.

Archives (Organizational Records)

Public and private organizations continuously keep numerous records that relfect various dimensions of organizational performance. Productivity, quality rates, profit, cost, grievances, absenteeism, and turnover are common examples. Nadler et al. [1975] developed some useful behavioral economic measures that include standardized methods of data retrieval from archival records. Longitudinal data on hard measures of organizational performance, however, are notably absent in the OD assessment literature [Nielsen & Kimberly, 1974].

Perhaps a major reason for the under-utilization of hard measures is that the dominant way of thinking about organizational behavior purports that attitudinal changes precede behavioral or performance changes. It follows, then, that change agents will concentrate their assessment efforts on attitudinal rather than on performance changes. However, if a behavioristic instead of a cognitive perspective is taken, the behavioral, not the attitudinal, link to performance is emphasized more. There is as much evidence that behavioral changes lead to attitudinal changes as there is for the reverse. For example, Porter and Lawler [1968] have demonstrated that performance *led to* satisfaction. Furthermore, quantifiable performance data are, from a pragmatic viewpoint, generally preferred by top management to other "soft" attitudinal measures.

Once again, the suggestion is not that assessment of attitudes should be abandoned when determining the impact of OD interventions; rather attitudinal data should always be used in combination with other quantifiable, archival measures of performance. Such emphasis would enhance the overall credibility of OD as a viable change strategy.

Advantages   Archival data have certain clear advantages when compared to other assessment measures. For example, archival data generally do not prompt reactions since the records constitute a natural part of the organizational environment; they have been compiled for other than current purposes. In addition, archival data are "just lying there" and thus cost little to obtain and are usually readily accessible. Another big advantage of archival data is that they allow evaluation over changing conditions and times and thus are particularly suitable for longitudinal analyses of organizational change.

Disadvantages   Just as with other techniques, caution must be exercised in the interpretation of archival data. First, information contained in organizational records may be selectively edited in order to make the figures "look good." In other words, "the statistical lie" syndrome is often present. Consequently, organizational records should be checked against other reports for validity. Second, archival data are subject to intra-instrument processes [Campbell & Stanley, 1966] in which record-keeping procedures may change over time. This problem is especially acute if a large personnel turnover or absenteeism rate is evident. Therefore, if possible, basic record-keeping procedures for performance assessment should be held constant throughout the period of evaluation. Record-keeping procedures should also be the same across comparison groups.

A third problem encountered in the use of archival data concerns what Meyer [1971] calls "the mushy measurements problem." Clearly, many contaminating variables affect performance measures, and, consequently, the interpretation of organizational change data is difficult. Normal fluctuations in business cycles, large wage settlements, and new competitors are only a few examples of contaminating variables that may be beyond the control of the evaluator but that nevertheless affect performance measures. If care is taken to recognize and account for record-keeping errors, however, they need not preclude the use of archives as an effective method for assessing the impact of OD interventions.

Self-Generated Measures

There are some occasions on which dimensions of organizational change can be measured by those directly involved. For instance, organizational participants are often the only ones who can realistically determine which specific behaviors will have the greatest impact on performance. Data relevant to such performance-related behaviors can then be used to assess organizational change. Examples of self-generated measures include action plans, objectives used in management by objectives (MBO), behavioral-frequency charts, self-recorded performance check-off systems, and behaviorally anchored rating scales (BARS).

Action planning is commonly used in OD survey feedback and team-building techniques to identify: (1) *what* has to be done (goals); (2) *how* it is going to be done (processes and procedures); (3) *who* is going to be involved and who is responsible; and (4) *when* it is going to take place (start/finish dates). Once organizational goals or objectives are identified by participants in the planned-change process, means for attaining those goals must be specified in ways that are quantifiable, i.e., measurable. For example, if one objective of an employment agency is to increase job placements by 10 percent by the end of the following year, then the *number* of job placements is quantifiable. Similarly, if one supporting aim of the employment firm is to increase the number of phone calls made by personnel agents to client organizations, then the number of phone calls made in a given time period is quantifiable. In this manner, progress data generated from follow-up studies of action plans could be measured and analyzed to assess changes in organizational performance. Similar data are generated using MBO techniques.

Another method of collecting quantifiable performance-related data is by the use of response-frequency charts generated during organizational behavior-modification interventions [Luthans & Kreitner, 1975]. In this approach, performance-related behaviors are first identified and then their occurrences are charted over a specified time period. Data collected from the tally sheets can be analyzed to assess quantifiable performance changes tracked over time.

Specific employee behaviors related to organizational performance can also be measured by the appraisal technique of behaviorally anchored rating scales (BARS). In essence, the BARS instrument is developed by asking supervisors to identify behaviors directly relevant to job performance. Supervisors then rate employee performance on the basis of these behaviors, and items with low interrater reliability are discarded. According to Cummings and Schwab [1973], the BARS technique is still subject to most of the limitations inherent in questionnaires (e.g., reactive effects), but it does appear to have at least two major advantages. First, items are tested on supervisors within the organization to determine the extent of intercoder reliability. Second, the supervisors' participation aids in the development of scales with a high degree of relevant meaning to the users of the instrument.

Advantages and Disadvantages The fact that self-generated measures represent the respondents' own criteria for effectiveness and that these measures are usually flexible enough to be tailored to the relevant situation are two of their advantages. In addition, because these measures are collected in most organization development interventions and some appraisal programs, they are easily obtained for analysis. However, there is the possiblity that the data in self-generated measures will be distorted because the respondent is obviously aware that he or she is being measured. Therefore, the researcher should always check the accuracy of self-reports by cross-validating them with other measures. On the other hand, there is some evidence [Emery Air Freight, 1973] to indicate that valuable data may be obtained by positively reinforcing accurate, not necessarily good, self-recorded behavior. Finally, and perhaps most importantly, self-generated measures are an invaluable mechanism for immediate and ongoing performance feedback to employees.

SUMMARY AND IMPLICATIONS FOR THE FUTURE

The use of multiple assessment measures that compensate one another in strengths and weaknesses adds an important degree of validity to the conclusions concerning the impact of OD interventions. It must be recognized that no single measure is satisfactory by itself; all measures are subject to the effects of the particular method. Recognition of the factors that jeopardize the reliability and validity of measures as well as their consistency of findings is critical to the meaningful assessment of organizational change.

Professional respectability should not be based on the particular methods by which data are collected. Rather, the key should be the validity and appropriateness of the measuring techniques as applied to the specific organizational setting. Recent critical self-appraisals by many organizational practitioners and researchers have resulted in a renewed appreciation for data-collection methods other than questionnaires and interviews. Following the lead of Webb et al. [1966], it is suggested that increased attention be given to the availability of organizational-change assessment methods such as (1) naturalistic observations, (2) participant observations, (3) archival data retrieval, and (4) self-generated measures.

Clearly, a major task confronting future OD change agents is the determination of specific "if-then" contingency relationships [Luthans, 1976] between various types of OD interventions and the most effective assessment methods appropriate to a given client organization. Ideally, a contingent relationship of this nature would take the following form: "*Given* X intervention(s), *then* a combination of A, B, and C methods would be most appropriate to assess organizational impact along specified criteria."

Unfortunately, OD assessment research appears to be lagging far behind the practice of OD. Thus, specification of such verifiable contingency relationships is not yet possible. Moreover, the particular combination of measures that would be most appropriate depends on the idiosyncratic characteristics of a given client organization. Renewed attention is, however, being paid to assessment by both practitioners and academicians. It is hoped that this discussion has made the reader more aware of the methodological options available, as well as of the necessity for using multiple measures, in assessing organization development change efforts.

REFERENCES

Allport, G. W., Vernon, P. E., & Lindzey, G. *Study of values test booklet.* Boston: Houghton Mifflin, 1960.

Bales, R. F. *Interaction process analysis.* Reading, MA: Addison-Wesley, 1950.

Benedict, B. A., Calder, P. H., Callahan, D. M., Hornstein, H. A., & Miles, M. A. The clinical-experimental approach to assessing change efforts. *Journal of Applied Behavioral Science,* 1967, *2,* 347–380.

Blake, R. R., & Mouton, J. S. *The managerial grid.* Houston, TX: Gulf Publishing, 1964.

Blood, M. R. Work values and job satisfaction. *Journal of Applied Psychology,* 1969, *53,* 456–459.

Campbell, D. T., & Stanley, J. C. *Experimental and quasi-experimental designs for research.* Chicago: Rand McNally, 1966.

Cantalanello, R. F., & Kirkpatrick, D. L. Evaluating training programs. *Training and Development Journal,* May 1968, *22,* 2–9.

Crano, W. D., & Brewer, M. B. *Principles of research in social psychology.* New York: McGraw-Hill, 1973.

Cummings, L. L., & Schwab, D. P. *Performance in organizations.* Glenview, IL: Scott, Foresman, 1973.

Emery Air Freight. Positive reinforcement boosts performance. *Organizational Dynamics,* Winter 1973, pp. 41–50.

Golembiewski, R. T., & Munzenrider, R. Social desirability as a intervening variable in interpreting organization development effects. *Journal of Applied Behavioral Science,* 1975, *11,* 317–332.

Guion, R. M. A note on organization climate. *Organizational Behavior and Human Performance,* 1973, *9,* 120–125.

Hackman, J. R., & Oldham, G. R. The job diagnostic survey and an instrument for diagnosing the motivational potential of jobs. *Technical Report No. 4* (Department of Administrative Sciences), Yale University, 1974.

Hall, E. T. A system for the notation of proxemic behavior. *American Anthropologist,* 1963, *65,* 1003–26.

Hall, E. T. *The hidden dimension.* New York: Doubleday, 1966.

Jones, J. E. The sensing interview. In J. E. Jones & J. W. Pfeiffer (Eds.), *The 1973 annual handbook for group facilitators.* San Diego, CA: University Associates, 1973.

Knapp, M. L. *Nonverbal communication in human interaction.* New York: Holt, Rinehart and Winston, 1972.

Lofland, J. *Analyzing social settings.* Belmont, CA: Wadsworth, 1971.

Luthans, F. *Introduction to management.* New York: McGraw-Hill, 1976.

Luthans, F., & Kreitner, R. *Organizational behavior modification.* Glenview, IL: Scott, Foresman, 1975.

Margulies, N., & Wallace, J. *Organizational change: Techniques and applications.* Glenview, IL: Scott, Foresman, 1973.

Meyer, H. H. Practical problems in implementing field research studies. *Academy of Management Proceedings,* 1971, *31,* 72–80.

Mintzberg, H. *The nature of managerial work.* New York: Harper & Row, 1973.

Nadler, D. A. (Ed.). *Michigan organizational assessment package: Progress report II.* Ann Arbor, MI: Institute for Social Research, University of Michigan, 1975.

Nadler, D. A., Jenkin, G. D., Miruis, P. H., & Macy, B. A. A research design and measurement package for the assessment of quality of work interventions. *Academy of Management Proceedings,* 1975, *35,* 360–362.

Nielsen, W. R., & Kimberly, J. R. The impact of organization development on the quality of organizational output. *Academy of Management Proceedings,* 1974, *34,* 528–529.

Pate, L. E., Nielsen, W. R., & Bacon, P. C. Advances in research on organization development: Toward a beginning. *Academy of Management Proceedings,* 1976, *36,* 389–394.

Paul, W. J., Robertson, K. B., & Herzberg, F. Job enrichment pays off. *Harvard Business Review,* 1969, *47,* 61–78.

Pfeiffer, J. W., & Jones, J. E. (Eds.). *The annual handbook for group facilitators* (1972–1980). San Diego, CA: University Associates, 1972–1980.

Porter, L. W., & Lawler, E. E. *Managerial attitudes and performance.* Homewood, IL: Irwin, 1968.

Sechrest, L. Unobtrusive measures in data collection. *Academy of Management Proceedings,* 1971, *31,* 58–66.

Webb, E. J., Campbell, D. T., Schwartz, R. D., & Sechrest, L. *Unobtrusive measures: Nonreactive research in the social sciences.* Chicago: Rand McNally, 1966.

White, S. E., & Mitchell, T. R. Organization development: A review of research content and research design. *Academy of Management Review,* 1976, *1,* 57–73.

REVIEW AND DISCUSSION QUESTIONS

1 What are some of the major problems with many of the OD experiments?
2 What are some of the strengths and weaknesses of using questionnaires in assessing OD interventions?
3 What are some of the strengths and weaknesses of using archival data in assessing OD interventions?
4 What is meant by using multiple measures to assess OD interventions?
5 Why are multiple measures more effective than single measures in assessing the effects of an OD intervention?

Reading 34

Behavioral Self-Management—The Missing Link in Managerial Effectiveness

Fred Luthans
Tim R. V. Davis

Hank Emery had been in his management position for several years, and he was becoming increasingly frustrated. His management courses back in college had stressed the need to plan, organize, staff, lead, motivate, and control. The numerous short courses and executive development seminars he had attended over the years emphasized the use of techniques—strategic planning, management by objectives, decentralization, adult-to-adult transactions, job enrichment, and Theory Y/System 4 styles. Yet, his day-to-day activities—the constant interruptions, telephone conversations, meetings, firefighting, paper shuffling, and constant hassles—didn't seem to coincide with all he had been taught and had come to believe in. A good manager got the most out of his people and ran his department efficiently, according to these principles and techniques. Yet, Hank didn't seem to be able to do this. Whenever his wife asked him, after a hard day at the office, how things had gone that day, it seemed he always replied, "I didn't get a thing done." He was beginning to feel guilty. He was constantly asking himself: "What's missing? Why can't I apply those management principles and techniques to make *myself* more effective?"

The answer to Hank's questions may be found in behavioral self-management. Research and writing in the management field have given a great deal of attention to managing societies, organizations, groups, and individuals. Strangely, almost no one has paid any attention to managing oneself more effectively. Yet, isn't this really Hank's problem? Self-management seems to be a basic prerequisite for effective management of other people, groups, organizations, and societies. It is our contention that behavioral self-management may be the important missing link—the first step in the inductive chain—for increased managerial effectiveness.

Recent studies that get away from the metaphorical principles and techniques and really *observe* what managers such as Hank Emery do indicate that self-management skills should not be taken for granted. It turns out that most scholars and managers have very little knowledge or understanding of what managers *do* and even less a grasp on ways to improve their effectiveness. This reduces not only the effectiveness of the individual manager, but the effectiveness of those who have to work with him or her as well, and eventually the organization suffers. The purpose of this article is to examine exactly what is meant by behavioral self-management, to cite specific examples of how it has been successfully applied, and to provide guidelines for more effective management in the future.

Reprinted with permission of the publisher from *Organizational Dynamics,* Summer 1979, pp. 42–60. Copyright © 1979 by AMACOM, a division of the American Management Association.

WHAT IS MEANT BY BEHAVIORAL SELF-CONTROL?

When managers think of self-control, the word willpower usually comes to mind. A behavioral interpretation, however, is based on the manager's ability to manipulate the surrounding environment—both the antecedent stimuli and the response consequences. Behavior and its environment—not elusive concepts such as willpower—should be the focus of analysis of self-control. At the same time, however, we take a social learning theory approach, rather than an operant approach. We recognize the critical mediating role of thoughts, feelings, and self-evaluative behavior, but we do not minimize the controlling role of the environment.

In particular, our formal definition of behavioral self-management, or what we shall simply call BSM, is *the manager's deliberate regulation of stimulus cues, covert processes, and response consequences to achieve personally identified behavioral outcomes.* Three conditions that satisfy the BSM approach to managerial effectiveness are:

- The individual manager is the proactive agent of change.
- Relevant stimulus cues, cognitive processes, and response consequences must be brought under control by the manager.
- The manager must be consciously aware of how a personally identified target outcome is being achieved.

THE USE OF FUNCTIONAL ANALYSIS IN BEHAVIORAL SELF-MANAGEMENT

B. F. Skinner suggested the use of functional analysis to predict and control human behavior through antecedent cues (A), behaviors (B), and consequences (C). However, on the basis of social learning theory, a three-term A-B-C contingency is too limiting—it fails to recognize cognitive mediating processes. To account for human cognitions, we propose a four-term contingency analysis depicted as:

Stimulus $\longleftrightarrow$	Organism $\longleftrightarrow$	Behavior $\longleftrightarrow$	Consequence
S	O	B	C

Each of these variables has an implicit feedback loop.

Unlike Skinner's A-B-C analysis, which concentrates on the need to identify observable environmental contingencies (A, C) in order to predict and control behavior (B), our expanded S-O-B-C functional analysis includes the mediating role of cognitive processes (O). When the four-term functional analysis is applied to self-management, the antecedent cues, or discriminative stimuli (S) and the behavior itself (B), and/or the contingent consequences (C) can be either overt (observable events) or covert (inner, private events).

The few but very important observational studies of managerial work suggest that managers spend a great deal of time reacting to immediate stimuli in the environment. The typical manager's day appears to be unstructured, filled with constant disruptions and distractions arising from a continual round of personal visits, telephone calls, meetings, and incoming paperwork (letters, memos, reports, reference data, and so on). These constantly recurring activities appear to fill most of the manager's time. The S-O-B-C functional analysis is an ideal framework for explicating these interactional events. It serves as a model for the researcher and as a practical, analytic tool for the manager who wants to apply BSM for increased effectiveness.

INTERVENTIONS FOR BEHAVIORAL SELF-MANAGEMENT

BSM has the twofold purpose of making the manager aware of behavioral contingencies that regulate his or her behavior and of extending control over these contingencies. The methods most frequently used to increase individual self-control are known as stimulus management and consequence management.

Stimulus management constitutes the introduction of cuing stimuli not already present in the environment or the removal of—or selective exposure to—stimuli already present in the environment. The cuing stimuli that are introduced or taken away may be overt or covert.

Consequence management involves the introduction of self-monitoring or overt/covert rewards or punishments to regulate behavior. The S-O-B-C framework can be used to show how these two BSM interventions can be used by managers to gain greater control over their behavior.

The Managerial Telephone Hangup

A simple, but relevant, example of a problem most managers would like to handle more effectively is the persistently ringing office phone. Invariably, the manager simply keeps answering the phone without thinking about the consequences of this act. When the phone rings, then, it possesses almost total stimulus control over the manager's behavior. The behavioral response can be regularly predicted from the antecedent stimulus. The immediate consequence may be an enjoyable conversation. However, if there are a number of long telephone conversations on a given day, ultimately, a great deal of important work may get interrupted. Over the long term, this makes for time mismanagement. Translated into S-O-B-C:

Antecedent stimulus	Covert 0	Behavior	Consequence(s)
Telephone rings	Zero	Long conversation	An enjoyable discussion Incompleted work leads to ineffective performance

To exercise better control over this behavior, managers in this situation have several options—ask the switchboard operator to take all calls during certain periods of the day (stimulus removal) or simply decide to put a two-minute time limit on all calls (selective stimulus exposure). In either case, you have an instance of a stimulus approach to BSM. The antecedent stimulus that created problems for the manager has now been brought under control.

Having a secretary take the call is a relatively simple way of coping through stimulus removal, but it still has one problem—the strategy would also require the manager to remember the resolution to limit calls to two minutes. Thus, another stimulus might have to be introduced to cue the event—either a new overt stimulus, such as a note attached to the phone, or a covert stimulus, such as prerehearsed self-instruction. In terms of S-O-B-C:

Antecedent stimulus	Covert 0	Behavior	Consequence
Switchboard operator takes call	———— Eliminated ————		Work is completed
Telephone rings— note on phone (Two minutes maximum!)	Two minutes maximum! (subvocal instructions)	Conversation kept within two minutes	Work is completed

Another selective stimulus exposure strategy would be to tell the switchboard operator to interrupt any conversation that exceeds a given time period with: "You have a long distance call on another line." This is another way of regulating the stimulus contingencies to support the desired behavior.

The targeted behavior will be maintained and strengthened if the manager obtains a reinforcing consequence for engaging in the desired behavior. Consequence management, which takes place after the desired behavior, concentrates on providing this reinforcement. The manager using a consequence management approach to BSM may record the instance of a self-controlling behavior (self-monitoring) and feel pleased (covert reward) about being able to keep telephone conversations within certain self-imposed time limits. The targeted behavior might be further reinforced by self-administering an overt reward, such as taking a ten-minute time out to read a trade journal or newspaper or taking a coffee break. Concentration on stimulus management or consequence management helps the manager learn to regulate behavior-environment interactions purposefully through a specific BSM strategy.

SELF-REINFORCEMENT TECHNIQUES FOR BSM

Self-reinforcement in consequence management consists of either contingently presenting oneself with a positive stimulus (known as positive self-reinforcement) or contingently removing a negative stimulus (negative self-reinforcement). Positive self-reinforcement is generally recognized as the more effective technique.

A proven method of applying positive self-reinforcement is through the

Premack Principle (developed by psychologist David Premack). This principle states that any behaviors that a person engages in frequently (high-probability behaviors) can serve as a reward to increase infrequently occurring behaviors (low-probability behaviors). For instance, a manager of a retail store who enjoys working with customers on the sales floor (a high-probability behavior) may not permit himself or herself to do this until all incoming paperwork is processed for the day (something that is constantly put off). Studies of self-control have clearly demonstrated the effectiveness of this technique. For example, one study used a Premack-type reward to increase the telephone sales of new service contracts (low-probability behavior) by making them contingent on the chance to sell renewal contracts (a high-probability behavior). The Premack approach is adaptable to many different situations. It requires the rearrangement of existing, frequently occurring, reinforcing responses to support less frequently occurring behaviors.

The rearrangement of reinforcing consequences, such as in the Premack approach, produces more effective managerial behaviors and is a vital component of a self-reward strategy in BSM. A manager who is frequently interrupted is probably providing reinforcing consequences for this to occur. Behavioral self-management makes managers aware of the consequences they provide for others in particular situations and indicates how these consequences may, in turn, control their own behavior. Managers may not be able to exercise direct control over other people's undesirable behaviors, but by altering their own behaviors in particular situations, managers can alter the consequences that tend to maintain dysfunctional behaviors.

HOW BSM DIFFERS FROM TIME MANAGEMENT

The strategies and techniques discussed so far point out how the BSM approach differs from time management and other programs of self-discipline. For instance, the time-management approach recognizes that deadlines can serve as important consequences for managerial action. However, this provides virtually no explanation about *how* a manager can stick to deadlines. In practice, a manager's day consists of a trail of broken deadlines. The manager's behavior may be controlled by other-imposed consequences (rewards/punishments) or self-imposed consequences (rewards/punishments). From a BSM perspective, managers can create a buffer from discomforts of other-imposed pressures by creating a system of self-rewards and/or self-punishments to ensure that deadlines are, in fact, met. A self-imposed and self-maintained system of behavioral control is likely to be more satisfactory for the individual and the organization than continuously reacting to random demands.

When a program of BSM is undertaken, a self-contract is entered into with resulting commitment. By using the S-O-B-C technique, the precise specification of the stimulus setting, behaviors, and consequences reduces any potential ambiguity and fosters a commitmnet to the BSM program to increase managerial effectiveness.

THE CASE FOR AND AGAINST BEHAVIORAL
SELF-MANAGEMENT

It is the premise of this article that BSM is the missing link for improved
managerial effectiveness. At this point we would like to pinpoint and weigh the
pros and cons of BSM.

BSM—Pro Arguments

*1   The Need for Self-Management Skills As Well As Organizational Manage-
ment Skills*   A body of theory and a set of techniques dealing with self-
management has received virtually no attention in management literature or in
management practice. Generally, the term management applies to the management of others or organizations. Self-management has been either taken for
granted or totally ignored. Yet, observational studies of managerial work
suggest that individual managers in highly "reactive" jobs need some techniques
and skills that will allow them to exercise more control over their own behavior.
The ability of managers to manage other individuals or organizational units
effectively when their own behavior is continually in turmoil is highly suspect.
Observational studies indicate that managers do not spend their time in
"other-centered" activities, such as planning, organizing, controlling, motivating, or leading. Instead, they spend their time worrying about their own
situation and taking care of their own immediate demands. BSM is closely
related to what managers actually do when effective managerial action is
absolutely necessary.

*2   Measurable Changes in the Situation-Cognition-Behavior Dynamic Rather
Than Measurable Changes in Attitudes*   Traditionally, research on managerial
work and organizational change has depended almost exclusively on the use of
attitude surveys. Behavior descriptions on questionnaires are assumed to
provide an accurate portrayal of empirical reality. Most of the literature on
"organizational behavior" is based on a body of knowledge derived almost
exclusively from questionnaire responses rather than from observations of actual
behaviors. There is growing evidence that the assumption of a close correspondence between attitudes and behavior may not be correct. Behavior-description
items on questionnaires are an inadequate representation of the complexity of
empirical reality. Questionnaire responses do not necessarily describe either the
stimulus conditions that prompt a behavior or the reinforcing circumstances that
maintain a behavior. The social learning theory view taken by BSM switches
from situation-free people, using broad trait adjectives to describe what they are
doing, to an analysis of the specific interactions between environmental stimuli
and the cognitions and behaviors of people. The BSM approach proposed here
systematically evaluates changes in individual behavior and cognitions in the
stimulus setting in which they occur. A major weakness of traditional human
resources management techniques has been the reliance on postintervention
attitude measures as the proof of substantive changes in behavior. A BSM
approach is specifically designed to evaluate the dynamics of the situation-
cognition-behavior paradigm and, as such, offers an advance over present
approaches.

   3   An Interactional Rather Than Goal-Oriented Approach to Managerial Behavior   Behavior processes in organizations are depicted in rational, linear, goal-oriented terms by most modern motivation and leadership models. For example, the expectancy models of motivation, the path-goal approach to leadership, and the contingency, decision-making model of leadership all view the manager as working through an objective set of expectancies to accomplish predefined goals. These models are noninteractional and generally ignore the reactive state of the stimulus situation in organizations. Observational studies provide evidence that managers spend most of their time responding to recurring, disruptive activities—dealing with visitors, answering phones, and handling budgetary crises. The view of the manager as a contemplative, goal-oriented planner, decision maker, and leader/motivator of subordinates can be highly misleading.

   The BSM approach takes into consideration the interactive nature of organizational behavior. By focusing on behavior in the dynamic stimulus environment in which it occurs, rather than on linear goal-oriented processes abstracted from the organizational setting, the BSM approach seems to be a more accurate and realistic view of managerial work.

   4   An Individual Rather Than Group-Centered Approach to Organizational Change and Development   The traditional strategies of OD have focused primarily on group-centered processes—sensitivity training, Grid® training, survey feedback, and team building—and, to a lesser extent, on third-party consultation and dyadic negotiation. The individual has received little attention as the unit of analysis for OD efforts. In general, individual change has been viewed as being most effectively accomplished through group interaction. A major difference between BSM and group-centered approaches is that individuals can use BSM techniques independent of the group setting. Most group-centered approaches provide neither a specific framework for analyzing individual behavior nor a set of specific guidelines for modifying behavior. Group-centered approaches create group interaction removed from the ongoing work situation. Many produce an initial high level of enthusiasm followed by a rapid decline in interest. There is little evidence to show that new behavior learned under these conditions is necessarily transferred to the workplace.

   5   A Closer Relationship between Theory and Practice   A growing number of critics—both academics and practitioners—contend that management theory and education are out of step with reality. It neither represents the real world of the practicing manager nor offers much useful insight into coping with everyday or challenging managerial problems. Again, observational studies of managerial work tend to support this view by disproving the relevance of behavioral science models of leadership and motivation and management science models of planning, programming, and decision making.

   Real-time field studies that deal with managerial behavior in the natural environment reduce the likelihood of developing models or simulations that are not grounded in the organizational situation in which the manager operates. The S-O-B-C framework used in BSM is expressly designed to ground behavior in the organizational situation. It also examines the reciprocal interaction between stimulus setting and managerial action. BSM techniques, applied to work behaviors that the manager engages in every day, develop more effective management practice.

6 A More Ethically Defensible Approach to Behavior Change   Behavior modification techniques have been criticized as being mechanistic, dehumanizing, and manipulative. These criticisms arise because human awareness and cognition are treated as unimportant in the operant conditioning approach. Also, behavior-modification (B. Mod.) techniques are seen as being imposed on others, thereby controlling their behavior unethically. The social learning approach used by BSM is person centered and acknowledges the important place of human awareness and cognitive processes. The individual chooses the behavior to be changed, monitors his or her own progress, and judges the effectiveness of the change effort. This is more ethically defensible than B. Mod. approaches or even externally imposed job enrichment, MBO, and OD programs.

BSM—Con Arguments

1 Some Managers neither Want to nor Can Control Their Behavior   BSM involves thinking about one's behavior and deciding what behaviors are in need of change. Some managers may neither wish to exercise more control over their behavior nor want to improve what they are doing. Evidence of resistance to improvement is found in studies of job enrichment where some employees prefer to remain in semidependent jobs. They do not wish their work improved with greater responsibility, autonomy, and choice. In addition, the work itself may preclude the opportunity for increased self-control. For example, in highly routine jobs, managers may be able to change their covert responses (thoughts and feelings) to the job, but they may be unable to change the immediate overt stimulus conditions and response consequences. BSM may be of limited use in those situations where people do not wish to exercise more control over their behavior or in jobs that are so rigidly structured that the potential for discretionary behavior is minimal. Most managers and their jobs do not fit into either of these categories. Data from job enrichment studies plus recent quality of work life surveys support the view that most people—especially managers— want to exercise more personal control over what they do at work. A BSM approach is compatible with this view of worklife.

2 BSM Deals with the Minutiae of Behaviors and Is Slow and Tedious   Behavior modification techniques deal with specific behaviors in particular situations. If there are many changes to be made, it may take a long time before all behaviors have been systematically modified. Similarly, most BSM applications involve such mundane behavior as learning to stay seated in the office, getting reports done on time, reading correspondence only at specific times, or learning to end meetings on time, none of which are very exciting or earthshaking to the casual observer. Indeed, one of the major problems of management education is that the practice of management has become associated with glamorous metaphorical concepts, such as strategic planning and matrix management. But the fact is that a great deal of important managerial behavior may involve seemingly minor or even mundane behavioral events. Until management scholars and practitioners can grasp the reality that management involves concrete behaviors in concrete situations, they will continue to dismiss the seemingly tedious flood of discrete responses as unimportant and not worth examining.

3 BSM Involves a Strong Personal Commitment to Change The BSM approach requires the individual to be committed at the outset and to remain committed throughout. A BSM approach may involve a stronger individual commitment than is asked for in more traditional change programs supported by the work group or the organization. Commitment is not an easily measured, stable attribute. The targeted behavior must be important to the person, and reinforcing conditions either support or do not support the effort. Relatively little research has been done on commitment in behavior-change programs. However, there is some evidence that self-contracts that spell out situational cues, behavioral requirements, and reinforcing consequences do tend to increase the likelihood of followthrough. Most change efforts have no clear definition of the results to be achieved or the steps in between, which makes it difficult to evaluate progress toward reaching a desirable goal. Thus, although a strong personal commitment may be an important factor in BSM, it should be easier to assess because of a clearer, operational definition of the behavioral requirements and the results to be achieved.

4 BSM Requires Behavioral Self-Recording and Careful Display of the Data Many individuals may either refuse to record their behavior or forget to do so. The need for a strong personal commitment to BSM may be accurately thought of as a strong commitment to self-recording. Data display may serve a stimulus function (feedforward) that cues the desired response as well as an evaluative, consequence function (feedback) after the behavior and recording have taken place. If the data display set the occasion for the behavior as well as provide a consequence for it, the display must be prominent and located in close physical proximity to where the event occurs. This creates difficulties when the behavior occurs while the manager is moving around a lot or is in a situation where the environment cannot be prearranged to cue the appropriate behavior. Many people will be unprepared or flat-out reject wearing devices such as wrist counters or carrying special cuing devices with them. Since people are often concerned about what others in the environment will think, this is a major reason to co-opt others into the BSM approach, either as stimulus modifiers or as reinforcement providers. If the management is not prepared to rearrange the stimulus environment to support the target behavior, BSM is not likely to succeed.

5 Self-Control Techniques Are As Yet Untested As a "General" Strategy of Increasing Managerial Effectiveness Thus far research has examined the potential usefulness of self-management strategy in naturally occurring complex organizational settings. The research evidence supporting the use of BSM is just beginning. However, our own research has been very encouraging.

THE RESULTS OF USING BSM IN ACTUAL PRACTICE

A wide variety of managers—in advertising, retailing, manufacturing, and public service in both line and staff positions—have targeted a wide range of behaviors to improve their effectiveness as managers. Representative examples include leaving the office without informing anyone, time spent on the phone, leaving one's own work to assist others, or filling out a daily expense form. Other examples are visiting salespersons without appointments; daily events, such as getting to work on time, writing a plan, following the plan, and deviations from the plan by subordinates; processing paperwork and decreasing the dependence of subordinates on the manager communicating with subordinates, visiting with them, and scheduling their work. Another goal for managers is to relax and not become tense when interacting with others.

A systematic analysis employing experimental and/or reversal/multiple-baseline research designs was done in several cases, with impressive results. Systematic application of BSM *caused* managers to improve their identified target behaviors and become more effective in their jobs. A few examples of these applications will help clarify how BSM actually works in practice.

An Assistant Store Manager:
Decreasing Dependence on the Boss

The assistant manager of a retail store had major responsibilities consisting of supervising sales clerks, pricing and displaying merchandise, managing the stockroom, checking in goods from suppliers, and reordering goods. She determined that one of the major problems affecting her effectiveness was overdependence on her boss, and her boss agreed. Most of the assistant manager's visits to her boss were unnecessary—she was able to answer most of her own questions.

The boss was enlisted to keep a record of the number of times the assistant asked for information over a period of one month. After the boss kept data for one week (the baseline period), the assistant was given a short orientation to the S-O-B-C model used in BSM and was asked to analyze her behavior accordingly. This analysis is shown below:

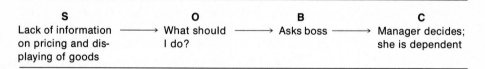

S	O	B	C
Lack of information on pricing and displaying of goods	What should I do?	Asks boss	Manager decides; she is dependent

The assistant manager pinpointed her main problem as a lack of information concerning the pricing and displaying of goods. If she was placed in charge of ordering from suppliers, she would not need to ask her boss about price markdowns, special purchases, special displays, and dates of shipments, which made her unnecessarily dependent on him. After considering the possibility of changes that would improve the situation, the assistant stated that she was very doubtful that her boss would give her any additional responsibility. With this limited potential for effecting changes, the assistant was faced with the choice of either altering what she did or accepting the situation as it was. She decided that her dependence on her boss was partly caused by her own behavior. She therefore decided to try to reduce the number of times she asked him for information.

In order to cue the targeted behavior and maintain a record of the number of times she resisted going to see her boss, she agreed to carry an index card to note her visits. She also agreed to keep a record in a diary of the type of information that prompted her to see her boss and to write down what happened as a consequence of not going to see her boss. In S-O-B-C terms:

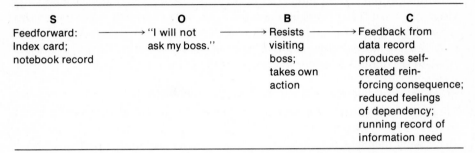

S	O	B	C
Feedforward: Index card; notebook record	"I will not ask my boss."	Resists visiting boss; takes own action	Feedback from data record produces self- created rein- forcing consequence; reduced feelings of dependency; running record of information need

The effects of this BSM intervention are shown in Figure 1. The graph indicates that the self-monitoring intervention tended to decrease the frequency of problem behavior. For example, the behavior occurred 22 times during the baseline period and only four times during the two-week BSM intervention period. The behavior did not return to the same level after self-monitoring intervention was withdrawn. But the data clearly indicate that the frequency was appreciably higher than during the intervention phase. This base-

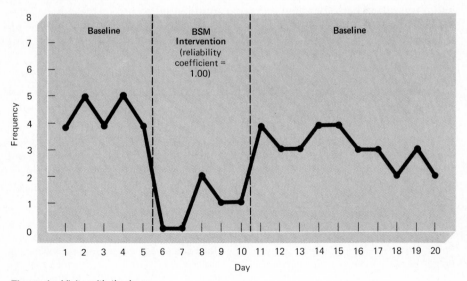

Figure 1 Visits with the boss.

line/intervention/return-to-baseline design (called a reversal) gives considerable support to the claim that the BSM intervention did indeed cause the change in the problem behavior. As for the reliability coefficient for recording the frequency during intervention, the manager's and the assistant's frequency records were identical. Since the manager did not know when the intervention period began or ended, it seems reasonable to assume that he was not just making a special effort to keep an accurate record during the intervention phase. Thus, frequency data were undoubtedly accurate throughout the analysis. The BSM intervention worked for the assistant manager in decreasing her dependence on the boss. The boss was pleased with the assistant manager's performance during the intervention period and with her reduced number of visits. Now that the study is finished, the assistant manager has gone back to her self-managing with the intent of reducing the number of her visits with the boss as during the intervention period. The experimental results reinforced her use of BSM to decreased dependence on the boss.

An Advertising Manager: Changing Dysfunctional Behaviors

Managers have successfully applied BSM to seemingly mundane, but important, behaviors for managerial effectiveness. Representative would be the case of the advertising manager of a newspaper. Upon observation, it was clear that this manager's job was very busy—requests and interruptions from staff within his department, queries from people in the plant, and calls from outside customers—followed by temporary lulls in activity in which the manager could get his work done. After discussions with both the manager and his staff, the manager identified behaviors that could be improved. The following were singled out for analysis and change: processing paperwork, leaving the office without informing anyone, and failure to fill out a daily expense form.

In-house observers (secretary and clerk) recruited during the interviewing and observation period agreed to keep a confidential record of these behaviors. Use was also made of actual measures where the manager left "traces" of his behavior, for example, how much paperwork was on the desk at the end of the day.

Processing Paperwork   After the observers gathered baseline data, the manager received a brief orientation. He was asked to analyze his paperwork-processing behavior according to the S-O-B-C model. The manager tried to handle the great amount of paperwork as it arrived. Much incoming mail was delivered by messenger or collected by his secretary at various times throughout the day. Each item of paperwork was handled randomly. Usually, it was picked up and acted upon immediately, or put down on one of the several steadily growing piles on his desk. Thus:

S	O	B	C
Paperwork enters office	Zero	Read and acted on or placed on pile	Growing pile of paper on desk

Since the manager continually responded to the influx of paperwork, he was frequently interrupted from what he was doing. Putting the paperwork to one side helped get rid of it temporarily. The long-term consequences were negative, however. Creating piles of paper that were only disturbed when a crisis situation occurred made it necessary to rummage through the heaps to find a particular item of information.

After considering his behavior in S-O-B-C terms, the manager decided that both the stimulus and his own behavior needed to be carefully considered. On the stimulus side, he determined that it was not necessary to receive all the paperwork when it arrived. His secretary opened the mail and stamped the date on the correspondence. She held the mail and presented it to him at one or two convenient times throughout the day. Then, clarifying his own behavior, he identified what the incoming paperwork consisted of—breaking it down by category—and decided what his possible response options were—acting or noting for future reference, filing, or discarding—in relation to this material, a more systematic approach than he had been using.

After analyzing the paperwork in detail with his secretary, the manager developed an information-processing flowchart that broke out the material by categories of information, action steps, and maximum retention times. The stimulus inflows were now differentiated into categories and the behaviors to be performed by the manager and his secretary were clarified. For the manager, much of the material was either held outside the office or presented in a consolidated form. Instead of vacillating over each item of incoming paperwork and eventually putting it on a pile, he now either acted immediately or noted a future action step on his desk diary or in his box file. The material was then filed or discarded with a minimum of delay.

The ongoing maintenance of his new behaviors was facilitated through a BSM strategy of self-monitoring and the use of a wall-chart display. The manager recorded each piece of paperwork by category and noted the action step taken. The approach capitalized on the feedforward-feedback effects of the data display (environmental) plus a clarified understanding (cognitive) of the response repertoire as the means of supporting the behavior change.

This is how it looks in S-O-B-C terms:

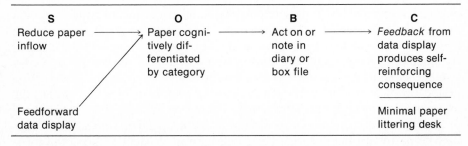

S	O	B	C
Reduce paper inflow	Paper cogni-tively dif-ferentiated by category	Act on or note in diary or box file	*Feedback* from data display produces self-reinforcing consequence
Feedforward data display			Minimal paper littering desk

The effects of this BSM intervention on the manager's paperwork processing behavior are shown in Figure 2. The frequency data represent numbers of unprocessed items piled on the desk each day. Numbers along the

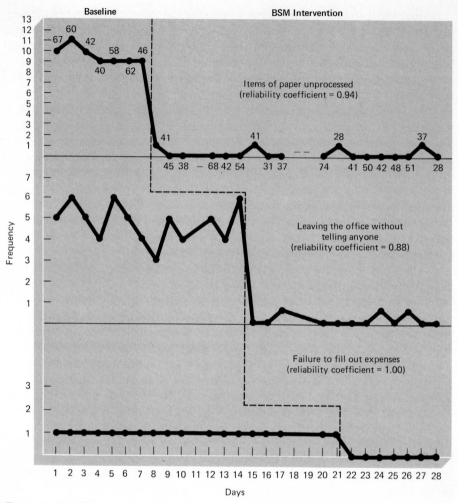

Figure 2 A multiple baseline design to analyze the effects of BSM on a manager's dysfunctional behaviors.

behavior frequency line represent the total number of units of paperwork that entered the office each day. (Note on days 11, 18, and 19 no mail was processed by the manager due to out-of-town trips.) As can clearly be seen from the graph, the number of items remaining unprocessed on the desk during the seven-day baseline period (average of 9.4) was greatly reduced during the intervention period (average of only 0.22). The reliability coefficient of 0.94 between the manager's self-recording and the actual evidence on the desk shows a high level of agreement between the self-recording and an independent source. The results may be partly attributed to the decreased inflows of paper entering the office (baseline averaged 52, while intervention was 38.) However, the extent of the change during the intervention phase is far greater than any improvements that could be explained by the reduced inflows. The BSM strategy of feedforward and feedback self-monitoring plus clarified cognitive understanding of what was to be done with the paperwork provides the best explanation for the changes in the manager's paperwork behavior.

Walking Out of the Office without Telling Anyone   Another behavior the manager considered dysfunctional was his habit of leaving the office without telling anyone. Frequently, members of the staff did not know where he was or when he would return. The manager would continually forget to let people know his whereabouts. Sometimes this sort of behavior is intentional. However, in this case, the manager wanted to change. This behavior problem could either be attributed to a deficient stimulus environment or to the manager's inability to produce his own subvocal cues. In either case, the solution to this problem would consist of building cuing stimuli into the office environment that would set the occasion for the necessary response. Hence, in S-O-B-C terms the problem can be represented as:

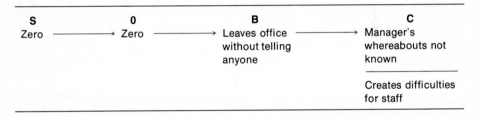

The crucial point in the environment where communication had to take place was at the office door. An "in-out" board was placed at the door. The manager indicated whether he was in or out of the office building; whether he would or would not return; and, if applicable, the time of his return. The manager merely had to move a magnetic disk to indicate an answere to each of these questions. Thus, the use of the in-out board became incorporated into a feedforward-feedback self-monitoring BSM strategy. The manager also kept a record of his behavior on a display chart in his office. He maintained a running-frequency tally of his behavior on an index card that was transferred to the office display chart when he returned from a visit. In S-O-B-C terms:

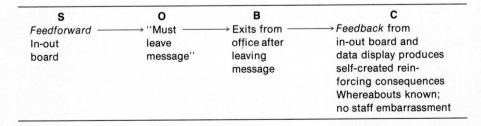

Figure 2 shows the effects of this BSM intervention on the manager's tendency to leave the office without telling anyone. The secretary's record of the manager's behavior was checked against the data collected by a clerk who had a desk by the office door. A reliability coefficient of 0.88 was found between these two sets of data. Again, these figures do not include a record of days 11, 18, and 19 when the manager did not come into the office. The baseline period shows that the manager had a tendency to leave the office nearly five times each day without telling anyone. The results during the BSM intervention phase show that the frequency of this behavior almost disappeared. The manager left the office only three times during the entire intervention period without marking the in-out board or telling his secretary.

Incompleted Expense Claims   Still another important dysfunctional behavior identified by the manager was failure to fill out expense claims forms. He would frequently fail to fill out a form for several months, even though he incurred daily expenses. With a gap in time, he usually underestimated the amount he spent. Since he was only required to furnish receipts for airfare and motel expenses, he had no formal record of other incidentals—drinks, lunches, cabfares, and parking—that were quite expensive. This meant that he was losing money on expenses and had an inaccurate picture of costs for his department. The situation may be depicted as follows:

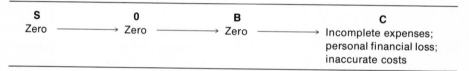

S	0	B	C
Zero	Zero	Zero	Incomplete expenses; personal financial loss; inaccurate costs

Again, this difficulty was partly the result of a lack of natural stimuli in the environment to cue the necessary behavior. The solution required a stimulus management approach that would introduce a cue, setting the stage for the appropriate response to occur.

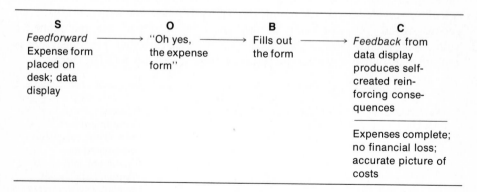

S	O	B	C
Feedforward Expense form placed on desk; data display	"Oh yes, the expense form"	Fills out the form	*Feedback* from data display produces self-created reinforcing consequences
			Expenses complete; no financial loss; accurate picture of costs

The best time for the manager to fill out his expense claim form was in the evening, just before he went home. When he had business off the premises, he tried to get back into the office during the late afternoon or early evening to deal with any problems that may have come up during his absence. Usually, nothing major needed his attention at this time so this was a good time for filling out his expense form.

After discussing the matter with his secretary, the secretary agreed to place an expense form on his desk at 4:30 P.M. each evening. The manager then would fill out the form regardless of whether any expenses had been incurred. If there was nothing to be charged, he would simply write no expense; otherwise, he would fill out the form in full. The secretary agreed to pick up the form just before going home. Again, the ongoing maintenance of the behavior was integrated with the BSM strategy of self-monitoring and the use of a wall-chart display. The data display and self-monitoring could be expected to support the cuing (feedforward) of the response. This would reduce the likelihood of missing a day and provided the manager with a record of the continuity of his behavior (feedback).

The data in Figure 2 are an actual record of the number of days the manager completed an expense form. No expense forms were filled out during the baseline period. The graph shows that the manager completed his expense form every day during the intervention period. The manager's self-recording and the actual check were in perfect agreement throughout this intervention period.

Overall, the multiple baseline—a staggered intervention research design in applied behavioral analysis experiments—used to analyze this advertising manager's use of BSM provides powerful evidence for asserting cause and effect. The BSM intervention was responsible for the improvement in the manager's dysfunctional behaviors. The advertising manager demonstrated increased self-control over behaviors that were creating problems for himself and his staff. Improving these behaviors made him more effective as a supervisor and manager.

A FINAL WORD

After weighing the pros and cons and considering the research evidence of the impact in actual practice, we feel there is a strong case for behavioral self-management being an important missing link to increased managerial effectiveness. Obviously, BSM is not the only answer to managerial effectiveness, but it certainly deserves more attention than it has received in the past. It is hoped that by applying the perspective and specific techniques of BSM, managers will be able to manage themselves as capably as they manage others and their organizations.

REFERENCES

Behavioral self-management is grounded in social learning theory. The most comprehensive readable book on this subject is Albert Bandura's *Social Learning Theory* (Prentice-Hall, 1977). Behavioral self-control has been an important clinical technique in psychological practice for a number of years; two of the best sources on this kind of application are Carl E. Thoresen and Michael J. Mahoney's *Behavioral Self-Control* (Holt, Rinehart and Winston, 1974) and David L. Watson and Rowland G. Tharp's *Self-Directed Behavior* (Brooks/Cole, 1977). Behavioral self-management has not, however, been directly applied to management and organizational behavior. Two books that stimulated our thinking about what managers really do and the potential of BSM for increasing managerial effectiveness are Henry Mintzberg's *The Nature of Managerial Work* (Harper & Row, 1973) and Leonard Sayles's *Leadership* (McGraw-Hill, 1979). Last, this article represents an extension of our previous work, in particular, Fred Luthans and Robert Kreitner's *Organizational Behavior Modification* (Scott, Foresman, 1975) and Tim Davis and Fred Luthan's recent article "Leadership Reexamined: A Behavioral Approach" (*Academy of Management Review*, April 1979, pp. 237–248).

REVIEW AND DISCUSSION QUESTIONS

1 Define behavioral self-management. Summarize the pros and cons of BSM.
2 Why is managing your own behaviors important for overall managerial effectiveness?
3 Give an example of how you can use BSM to manage your own behavior.
4 Compare BSM with a more group-centered approach to organizational change. What are the strengths and limitations of each approach?

Reading 35
Toward a More Comprehensive Career Planning Program
Stephen L. Cohen
Herbert H. Meyer

It is very true, though seemingly trite, to say that the continuity and success of any organization depend to a great extent on its ability to attract, evaluate, develop, utilize and retain well-qualified people at professional and managerial levels. Translated into fewer words, this merely means that a successful organization must have well-organized and well-administered human resource and career planning programs. What follows here is an integrated series of suggested procedures, techniques and programs that are designed to serve this need, featuring the use of the assessment center approach as a fundamental component of the overall program.

In establishing a comprehensive career planning program, we are often inclined to focus primary attention on the direct value of such a program to the organization as a whole: i.e., if the best-qualified people are identified, and development efforts for those individuals are targeted directly on organizational needs, then it follows that the functions that are critical to the success of the organization are likely to be performed more effectively.

On the other hand, a well-organized and administered career planning program also has equally important benefits for the individuals who make up the organization. Such a program enables individuals to learn to carry out their own self-development efforts more effectively. Consequently, they will be less likely to get placed in positions which do not fit their talents than would be the case if career planning and development were handled in a less individualized way. More important, they will be able to obtain a clearer picture of what the future might hold for them in the organization. Indeed, research has shown that employees' satisfaction with an organization (and decisions to leave the organization) is more often dependent on their estimates of what the future holds for them there than on their present lot.[1]

THE OVERALL PROGRAM

In an overall program, job analysis information and human resource planning projections provide essential background information for career planning. A career planning program, for example, might focus on two levels:

1 Nonmanagement personnel, with special emphasis placed on the identification of people who have the potential to move into first-line supervisory positions
2 Management-level personnel, with special emphasis on identifying the development needs of individuals now in the lower-level management ranks.

The latter program can also be designed to identify high-potential personnel for whom special career development efforts should be made. Such efforts will provide these individuals with the type of job experience needed to handle higher-level management positions effectively.

In general, such a program can aid in systematizing human resource and career planning activities for an organization. It also places joint responsibility for initiative in implementing most of the career planning and development activities on both management and the individual employee.

Human Resource Planning   Career planning can be carried out intelligently only in the context of a thorough and accurate human resource planning program which projects the future needs of the organization. This information provides the basis for realistic career planning and development from both the company's and the individual's point of view.

The basic information needed for accurate human resource planning is best known to top management. However, managers throughout the organization must have detailed and accurate information about the future human resource needs of the organization if they are to provide meaningful counsel to their subordinates with regard to career plans. Needless to say, individual managers also need such information if they are to make realistic career plans for themselves. They need answers to such questions as:

- How is the business changing?
- What products or services will be affected by projected changes?
- What are the basic problems facing the business?
- What are the potential expansion areas of the business?
- How is the business organized?
- How might the organization change in the future?
- In what specific functions or jobs is turnover anticipated?
- What top management philosophies and policies will influence the development of the business?

While these questions must be answered by line management, it is desirable that a central staff personnel or human resources planning committee of some kind coordinates and integrates human resource planning activities. This kind of staff effort can help to ensure that companywide human resource needs are being projected in a consistent and up-to-date manner. The use of qualified consultants to assist such staff personnel in establishing a systematic, company-wide human resource program may also help to ensure that these needs are met.

The Human Resource Inventory An inventory is almost always an important component of an overall human resource planning program. That is, some kind of centralized inventory of managerial talent is usually maintained by the staff group responsible for administering the program. Such an inventory may include not only data regarding the skills and experiences of individuals, but also demographic data and salary information. Thus, a centrally maintained inventory of talent can serve many important purposes:

- To provide up-to-date personnel transition data, e.g., turnover, promotions, lateral moves, demotions, etc.
- To ensure the optimum use of in-house talent
- To determine the training and experience needs of employees to fill anticipated vacancies in the organization
- To reduce turnover of highly valued employees
- To compile reports of various types that are needed for intelligent business planning
- To provide trend data on salaries that are needed to monitor the salary program effectively
- To provide immediately accessible and up-to-date information needed to administer an effective EEO program.

Career Planning While human resource planning focuses primarily on organizational needs, a career planning program will usually emphasize managers in the organization as individuals. The objectives of a career planning program might include the following:

- To define for each individual manager the career opportunities that might be available in the organization.
- To enable individual managers to formulate realistic career plans. More specifically, the program would be expected to provide for managers at all levels an accurate picture of alternative career paths for people in different areas of the organization. They should also know about the knowledge and skill requirements of various positions to which individuals might aspire or toward which their development might be targeted.
- To identify the development needs of individuals and groups of persons in the management ranks.

Specific Components

In order to achieve the objectives listed above, an overall career planning program should include several component procedures and programs.

The figure presents a model of an overall career planning program. As the figure indicates, there are two primary target groups on which intensive career planning efforts would be focused: 1) nonmanagement personnel who are judged to have potential for moving into the management ranks and 2) management personnel in the lower-level positions who seem to have the potential to move up to higher positions in the management ranks. However, many of the specific forms and procedures used in a program of this kind are applicable to all employees at all levels in the organization.

It can be seen in the diagram that the component parts or steps in the career planning programs for both groups are almost identical. Therefore, the specific programs, approaches or procedures to be used for each stage or component part of the two subprograms will be described together.

Self-Nomination A career development program should require some initiative on the part of the individual to start the career planning and development process. Therefore, a formalized procedure can be designed to accommodate this voluntary action on the part of each interested employee. The self-nomination process, however, will not preclude action on the part of a supervisor or manager to encourage a reluctant employee (who the manager feels may not fully appreciate his or her own potential) to volunteer.

Career Planning Self-Analysis Forms and guideline materials, in a workbook format, can aid the individual employee in analyzing his or her own strengths, interests, desires and goals. The guideline materials should also include information about various functions in the company and the kinds of abilities, training and experience needed to carry out these functions at different position levels. This kind of job information, along with a systematic and thorough self-analysis, can help individuals to formulate more realistic aspirations for themselves. Needless to say, information developed in the human resource planning process about numbers and types of future opportunities will also help individuals to formulate realistic career plans.

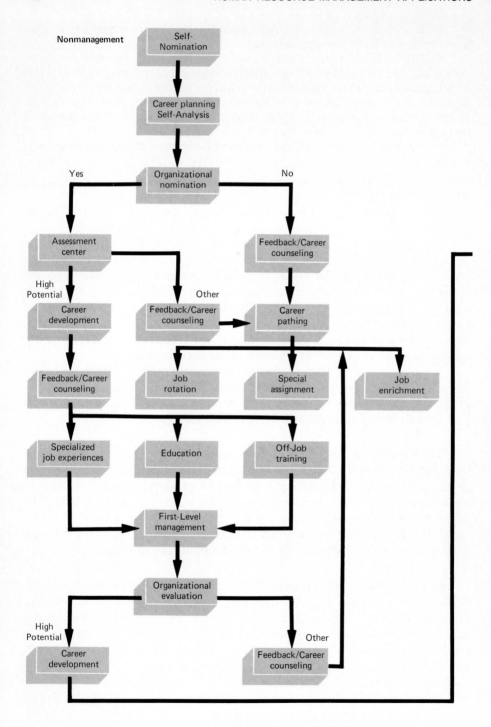

Figure 1 A proposed career planning model for nonmanagement and lower-management personnel.

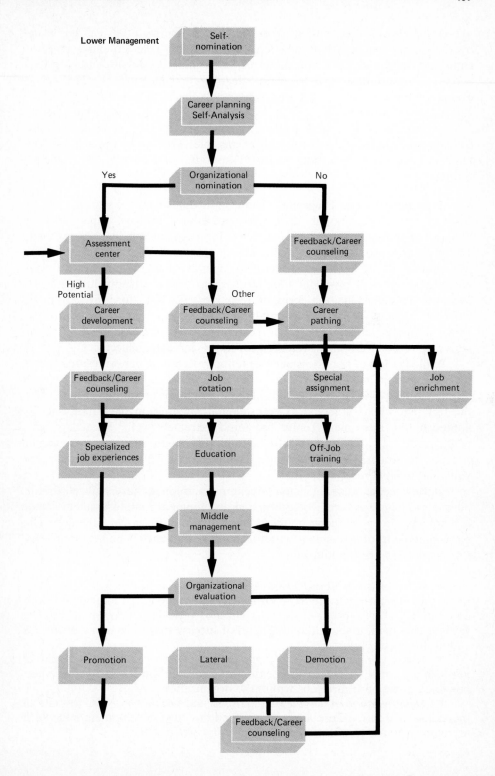

Organizational Nomination   Forms and guideline materials can be developed to assist management personnel in evaluating the potential of each employee for whom career planning has been initiated. Some kind of group appraisal procedure is usually most effective for this purpose. The group evaluation process helps to ensure objectivity because the observations of various people who may have seen the candidate from different vantage points are considered. Forms and guideline materials can aid in making these evaluations as objective and relevant as possible. The evaluators at this stage might also consider each individual's self-appraisal of strengths, interests and aspirations.

Assessment Center Programs   Those individuals who are judged, on the basis of the organizational nomination procedure, to have supervisory or managerial potential should be scheduled for participation in an assessment center program appropriate to their present job level. The assessment center provides for a very intensive appraisal of supervisory and administrative skills and can serve as a powerful tool for helping both the individual and the organization determine the level of resources available for upward career mobility. Because of its demonstrated success as a predictive measure of a person's future job success, it is recommended as the cornerstone of the individual skill development required for future job/career success.

While the use of the assessment center approach has been widespread since the first program at Michigan Bell over twenty years ago, its growth during the last five to ten years has been astonishing. Much of this growth has been due to the fact that when subjected to experimental research on the validity of the approach, the assessment center has fared extremely well.[2] Because of this considerable research, it can now be said that when an assessment center program is properly developed and administered, it will provide significantly valid and reliable results.

During recent years, assessment center practitioners have realized that in addition to its use as a valid selection and development tool, assessment center technology has encouraging applications in the area of career planning. The basic ingredients of assessment center technology that have been responsible for this application are the following:

- *Reliance on exhibited behavior in observing an individual*—This technique provides for relatively more objective evaluation of that individual's skills and abilities. This type of evaluation will also provide employees with more realistic information about the likelihood of success at various upper-level jobs within the organization.
- *Use of simulation exercises that represent the work activities of the actual job*—This permits for evaluation of the more job-relevant behaviors and their possible impact on future jobs within the organization.
- *Determination of relative skill strengths and weaknesses*—This permits an individual to identify those areas which need the most development and which are more relevant to effective performance in certain jobs.

• *Relatively objective feedback to an individual regarding his or her strengths and weaknesses*—Such feedback, based on exhibited behaviors recorded by several trained evaluators, confronts the employee with more factual (and therefore more palatable) evaluations. This type of objective, job-relevant feedback encourages employees to initiate developmental activities, since they can now readily see the link between improved skills and success in higher-level jobs.

The above aspects of assessment center technology facilitate the career planning process by:

• Matching an individual's current skills with those identified (through job analyses) as critical to success in a number of jobs in the organization
• Determining a developmental action plan tailored to individual needs that will train employees in the skills necessary to perform effectively in certain targeted positions
• Identifying realistic career paths for individuals, based on the following: (1) their current determined skill level and their potential for skill improvement (from assessment center data), (2) their past job performance, (3) their technical competence and (4) their interest in and motivation for career programs.

Feedback/Career Counseling As the model shows, some feedback and career counseling is involved at various stages of the career planning process. Much of this counseling might be carried out by line managers. In addition, it is highly desirable that company staff be available to individual employees for career counseling in those cases where an employee desires to discuss his or her career plans with someone other than the immediate manager.

Career Pathing Some kind of career plan can be developed for every employee, whether or not he or she is judged to have special talents to rise to higher-level positions in the organization. For some, a career path might involve horizontal job rotation to keep interest and motivation at a high level. For others, there may be opportunities to carry out special assignments or to have their present jobs enriched. Progress up the ladder will undoubtedly be slower for those people who are judged not to have high levels of managerial potential. However, they may still progress, but in a shoelace (or lateral) pattern, rather than in the traditional stairway (horizontal) format. That is, one or more horizontal moves might be made between each upward step.

Career Development Those employees who are identified through assessment center performance as having considerable supervisory and managerial ability should be scheduled for "fast-track" development. At nonmanagement levels, these high potential employees might be encouraged to get more formal education, or they might be given special assignments to develop certain skills, or scheduled for supervisor or manager training programs. They should also be placed in supervisory positions as soon as possible.

The participant who demonstrates high levels of administrative skills in the middle-management level assessment center should be scheduled for similar experience at higher levels. Here, job function matrices and similar job requirement information can serve as valuable aids in the process of formulating path/goal models for the career development of individuals.

Organizational Evaluation　A procedure should also be formulated for conducting an annual review of talent in the organization. This review should focus primarily on the career potential and development needs of individuals, rather than on their present job performance. The kinds of decisions made about employees' development needs and future plans will be similar to those described under the career pathing and career development steps. First-line supervisors who are performing very well should be scheduled for participation in the middle-level management assessment center. Most of these people will probably have started their careers in the organization in the nonmanagement ranks. Thus, entry into higher levels of management is possible for employees, whether or not they started their careers in the management ranks.

BENEFITS TO AN ORGANIZATION

In a very general sense, the value of career planning will result from the improved use of key human resources, since it provides for better matching of individual strengths with organizational needs. Furthermore, the motivation of employees should be enhanced because of the objective and supportive climate the system will help to create.

The potential cost savings to an organization that implements a systematic career planning program could be great. Savings may result from:

- More efficient use of human resources
- Improved performance of incumbents in key jobs
- Decreased turnover because of increased opportunities for development within the organization
- More efficient achievement of affirmative action goals.

By-product benefits might include the establishment of a trained staff—i.e., the development of internal expertise—to provide continuity in the administration of the program over the years. In addition, many managers could develop performance appraisal and counseling skills through their participation as assessors in the assessment center programs. These skills are likely to be invaluable in facilitating improved management of their own work groups.

To be fully effective, a career planning program requires the strong endorsement and continued support of top management personnel in the organization. This support may have to take the form of establishing company policies to ensure that the program is implemented properly. With this kind of backing from top management, it seems logical to expect that a comprehensive and integrated human resource and career planning program could contribute substantially to the long-range success of any organization.

REFERENCES

1 A. I. Kraut, "Predicting Turnover of Employees from Measured Job Attitudes," *Organizational Behavior and Human Performance,* 13 (1975): 233–243; T. Lyons, "Role Clarity, Need for Clarity, Satisfaction and Withdrawal," *Organizational Behavior and Human Performance,* 6 (1971): 99–110; J. Weitz, "Job Expectancy and Survival," *Journal of Applied Psychology,* 40 (1956): 245–247.

2 C. L. Jaffee and S. L. Cohen, "Manpower Planning and Career Developing Utilizing Assessment Center Technology," in E. Burack and E. Miller, eds., *Human Resource Management* (Englewood Cliffs, New Jersey: Prentice-Hall, in press); D. W. Bray, "The Assessment Center Method," in R. L. Craig, ed., *Training and Development Handbook,* 2nd ed. (New York: McGraw-Hill, 1976), Ch. 16; R. B. Finkle, "Managerial Assessment Centers," in M. Dunnette, ed., *Handbook of Industrial and Organizational Psychology* (Chicago: Rand-McNally, 1976), pp. 861–888.

REVIEW AND DISCUSSION QUESTIONS

1 Why should an organization become more active in career planning?
2 What is the role of assessment centers in career planning?
3 Can an organization meet EEOC guidelines with a comprehensive career-planning system? How?
4 Briefly sketch a career plan for yourself.